Readings and Cases in Auditing
Fifth Edition

THOMAS D. HUBBARD, Ph.D., CPA
Nebraska CPAs Distinguished Professor of
Accountancy and Director,
School of Accountancy
University of Nebraska, Lincoln

DAVID J. ELLISON, Ph.D.
Associate Professor of Accounting
Creighton University

ROBERT H. STRAWSER, DBA, CPA
Professor of Accounting
Texas A&M University

I3364I-II
5/86

1985

Dame Publications, Inc.
P.O. Box 35556
Houston, Texas 77235-5556

Typographer: Jan Tiefel
Designer: Stephen Emry
Artist: Sandra Kay Foster

• DAME PUBLICATIONS, INC. 1985

ISBN 0-931920-94-9
Library of Congress Catalog Card No. 83-70549

Printed in the United States of America

Preface

Readings and Cases in Auditing was developed to fill a gap in both the undergraduate and graduate courses in auditing. *Statements on Auditing Standards* (SASs), issued by the American Institute of Certified Public Accountants' Auditing Standards Board, and its predecessor, the Auditing Standards Executive Committee, establish the promulgated generally accepted auditing standards and procedures that provide general and specific guidelines that an auditor must follow in examining financial statements. Auditing courses offered at both the undergraduate and graduate levels have traditionally incorporated many of the SASs in the course material. However, due to the time constraints of the typical single semester (or quarter) course in auditing, many auditing texts and instructors are often forced to give only superficial treatment to auditing pronouncements. This text attempts to fill this gap in auditing education by providing a means whereby SASs can be introduced through both readings and cases illustrating the content of the SASs and their application in practical auditing situations. Statements on Standards for Accounting and Review Services (SSARSs), issued by the Accounting and Review Services Committee of the AICPA, are also included in the text to provide coverage of the standards applicable to the preparation of "unaudited" financial statements of nonpublic companies.

The materials included in this text were developed and tested in professional education courses conducted for Associated Regional Accounting Firms, local CPA firms, and in developing course material for the AICPA. In addition, certain of the cases evolved from the authors' experience in teaching auditing courses at both the undergraduate and graduate level. The case materials included in the text have been thoroughly classroom tested and, in many instances, the cases have been used by the authors in professional training courses involving CPA firms. The text is revised annually to provide an up-to-date review of the SAS material.

The text facilitates a classroom discussion approach to gaining an understanding of both the meaning and the application of SASs and SSARSs. Since SASs form the basic foundation for auditing theory and practice, a thorough understanding of these pronouncements by accounting students is essential in preparing them for a career in either public accounting or any other accounting field. Many auditing educators feel that an important objective of the undergraduate auditing course is to assist in preparing the accounting student for the Uniform CPA Examination. A second exposure to the SASs and the SSARSs is crucial in preparing for the CPA examination and this text provides that approach with a minimum allocation of class time. Many of the cases and related reading materials are short and may be covered with the regular auditing course material without sacrificing an inordinate amount of time. The text can be used with any basic auditing text by assigning readings and cases that relate to the subject material being covered. The cases may be discussed in class or written solutions can be requested. In either case, the student will have the opportunity to study the SASs and the SSARSs in a practical environment and thereby gain an improved understanding of the statements and how they are intended to be applied in actual practice.

The instructor's manual includes detailed outlines of the SASs and SSARSs and solutions to the case discussion questions. The outline provides a tool which is most useful in developing classroom lectures and in leading discussion of the standards.

Selected liability cases are also included in the text. This material supplements the SASs and provides an understanding of the promulgation of auditing standards and their relevance in the real world of accounting practice and auditing. Many of the SASs, of course, resulted from accountants' liability cases.

The authors have attempted to avoid using generic pronouns; when they are used, it is simply for convenience in writing and is intended to refer to both females and males.

Acknowledgments

The authors wish to express their appreciation to those groups and individuals who played a role in the origination of the idea for this text and in encouraging its completion. We are especially grateful to Dr. Austin Smith and the member firms of Associated Regional Accounting Firms; Dr. Robert E. Schlosser of Coopers & Lybrand (now dean of Rutgers University); the Partners and Staff of Anderson & Reed and Berry, Dail & Company; the accounting students (who participated in classroom testing much of the material in this text) at Virginia Polytechnic Institute and State University, especially the Master of Accountancy students of the Class of 1976 who wrote certain cases included in the test; and the accounting students at the University of Nebraska, Lincoln, Kansas State University, and the University of Houston. The authors appreciate the financial support provided by the Lincoln, Nebraska office of Peat, Marwick, Mitchell & Co., which aided in the development of the first edition of this text. A special thanks is due to Dr. Mattie C. Porter of the University of Houston for her review and insightful comments and to Anna and Sandi, who typed and proofed the manuscript; Jan Tiefel, who typeset the manuscript; and Stephen Emry, who did all the artwork and cover design.

October 1984

Thomas D. Hubbard
David J. Ellison
Robert H. Strawser

Contents

1

Introduction

Statements on Auditing Standards are issued by the Auditing Standards Board (AudSEC 1977-1978), the senior technical committee of the American Institute of Certified Public Accountants (AICPA) designated to issue authoritative pronouncements on auditing matters. Rule 202 of the AICPA *Code of Professional Ethics* requires adherence to the applicable generally accepted auditing standards (GAAS). It recognizes Statements on Auditing Standards (SAS) as interpretations of GAAS, and requires that AICPA members be prepared to justify departures from such Statements. Likewise, the SSARSs, which are issued by the AICPA's Accounting and Review Services Committee, are covered by Rule 204 (Other Technical Standards) of the Code of Ethics and accountants are required to justify departures from those standards in compilation and review engagements involving the unaudited financial statements of non-public clients.

The SASs outline the ten GAAS. They relate to the qualifications of the auditor (the general standards), determine the quality and quantity of work performed by the auditor (the field work standards), and require the CPA to state whether the financial statements examined were prepared in accordance with GAAP or another comprehensive basis of accounting. They require the auditor to indicate whether such principles were consistently followed, whether adequate disclosure of pertinent information was made in the financial statements, and to express an opinion on the financial statements or state why an opinion cannot be expressed (the reporting standards). In addition, the SASs present generally accepted auditing procedures which require the auditor to perform selected compliance and substantive tests and gather specific evidence in the course of the audit examination.

The general standards require that audits be performed by persons with adequate technical training and proficiency as auditors, that independence in mental attitude be maintained, and that due professional care be exercised in the performance of the examination and the preparation of the audit report.

The three standards of field work require the auditor to undertake adequate planning and proper supervision, make a proper study and evaluation of internal control, and gather sufficient competent evidential matter as a basis for evaluating the assertions made in the financial statements examined.

The four standards of reporting require the auditor to express an opinion when he or she is associated with the financial statements of a client or to disclaim an opinion and disclose all of the substantive reasons for the disclaimer. The auditor must state in the opinion whether or not the statements are presented fairly in conformity with GAAP or another comprehensive basis of accounting, applied on a basis consistent with that of the preceding period. The reporting standards also require that informative disclosures in the financial statements are to be regarded as reasonably adequate or an exception must be taken in the auditor's report.

GAAS constitute the principles of auditing for the practicing CPA. They form the foundation for promulgating auditing procedures and support auditing procedures that eventually become accepted because of their general usage. An understanding of the ten GAAS and the related promulgated auditing procedures provides the necessary foundation for an understanding of basic auditing principles and procedures. Such knowledge, in turn, provides a basic foundation for a career in both public and private accounting.

2

Responsibilities and Functions of the Auditor

(Sections 110 and 150, SAS No. 1, Section 327, SAS No. 16, and Section 328, SAS No. 17)

The objective of the ordinary examination of financial statements by a CPA is the expression of an opinion on the fairness with which they present financial position, results of operations, and changes in financial position in conformity with GAAP. The CPA performs an examination in accordance with GAAS and at its conclusion, expresses either an unqualified opinion or if circumstances require a qualified or adverse opinion or if sufficient evidential matter is lacking, a disclaimer of opinion.

RESPONSIBILITY OF MANAGEMENT

The management of a company has the basic responsibility for the fairness of its financial statements. Management is responsible for adopting sound accounting policies, for maintaining an adequate and effective system of accounts, for the safeguarding of assets, and for devising a system of internal control that will, among other things, help assure the production of meaningful and useful financial statements. A CPA may make suggestions as to the form or content of financial statements or in some circumstances may draft them in whole or in part, based on management's accounts and records. However, the auditor's responsibility for the statements is confined to the expression (or denial) of opinion on them.

PROFESSIONAL QUALIFICATIONS OF THE CPA

The professional qualifications of the CPA are those of a person with both the education and experience to practice as an independent auditor. They do not include those of a person trained for or qualified to engage in other professions or occupations. For example, the CPA, in observing the taking of a physical inventory does not purport to act as either appraiser, a valuer, or an expert in materials. Similarly, although the CPA is informed in a general manner about matters of commercial law, he or she is not a lawyer and may appropriately rely upon the advice of attorneys in all matters regarding the law.

GENERALLY ACCEPTED AUDITING STANDARDS

Auditing standards differ from auditing procedures. Procedures relate to the acts to be performed during the course of the examination while standards measure the quality and objective to be obtained by the use of auditing procedures. The CPA must exercise the informed judgment of a professional in determining which GAAS (and procedures) are applicable in the particular circumstances to afford a reasonable basis for the opinion. There are ten GAAS, as follows:

The General Standards

1. Training and Proficiency
    The examination is to be performed by a person or persons having adequate technical training and proficiency as an auditor.

2. Independence
    In all matters relating to the assignment, an independence in mental attitude is to be maintained by the auditor or auditors.

3. Due Professional Care
    Due professional care is to be exercised in the performance of the examination and the preparation of the report.

Field Work Standards

1. Planning and Supervision
    The work is to be adequately planned and assistants, if any, are to be properly supervised.

2. Internal Control
    There is to be a proper study and evaluation of the existing internal control as a basis for reliance thereon and for the determination of the resultant extent of the tests to which auditing procedures are to be restricted.

3. Evidential Matter
    Sufficient competent evidential matter is to be obtained through inspection, observation, inquiries and confirmations to afford a reasonable basis for an opinion regarding the financial statements under examination.

Reporting Standards

1. Adherence to Generally Accepted Accounting Principles (GAAP)
    The report shall state whether the financial statements are presented in accordance with generally accepted principles of accounting.

2. Consistency
    The report shall state whether such principles have been consistently observed in the current period in relation to the preceding period.

3. Informative Disclosure
    Informative disclosures in the financial statements are to be regarded as reasonably adequate unless otherwise stated in the report.

4. Expression of Opinion
    The report shall either contain an expression of opinion regarding the financial statements, taken as a whole, or an assertion to the effect that an opinion cannot be expressed. When an overall opinion cannot be expressed, the reasons therefore should be stated. In all cases where an auditor's name is associated with financial statements the report should contain a clearcut indication of the character of the auditor's examination, if any, and the degree of responsibility he is taking.

SASs are issued by the Auditing Standards Board (AudSEC 1977-1978), the senior technical committee of the American Institute of CPAs designated to issue pronouncements on auditing matters. Rule 202 of the AICPA *Code of Professional Ethics* requires adherence to the applicable GAAS promulgated by AudSec. SASs are recognized as interpretations of the ten GAAS, and CPAs must be prepared to justify any departures from such authoritative statements.

Materiality and relative risk are two concepts basic to auditing that underly the GAAS, especially the standards of field work and reporting. There should be stronger grounds to sustain the CPA's opinion with respect to those items which are relatively more important and for those items in which the possibilities of material error are greater than with respect to those of lesser importance or those in which the possibility of material error is remote. The degree of risk involved in the circumstances at hand also has an important bearing on the nature of the examination. Cash transactions, for example, are more susceptible to irregularities than plant and equipment and the work undertaken by the auditor on cash may therefore have to be carried out in a more conclusive manner.

SAS No. 43 (Section 1010.01) amends SAS No. 1, stating that the ten generally accepted auditing standards apply to all services covered by the SASs to the extent that they are relevant. For instance, independence, the second general standard, is applicable to engagements covered by Section 642, *Reporting on Internal Accounting Control*. But, the requirement to state whether financial statements are presented in compliance with GAAP, the first standard of reporting, does not apply because it is not relevant to internal control engagements.

ILLEGAL ACTS BY CLIENTS

(SAS No. 17)

In performing an examination of financial statements, the auditor must be concerned with the fact that the client may have committed an illegal act which may require either disclosure in the financial statements or other possible action on the part of the client and/or the auditor. Illegal acts include an illegal political contribution to a candidate in an election for a federal office, bribes to obtain business, and other violations of laws and regulations that control business.

An examination of financial statements made in accordance with GAAS cannot be expected to provide assurance that illegal acts will be detected by the auditor. Determining whether an act is illegal is usually beyond the professional capabilities of the auditor (a CPA is not a lawyer). However, the auditor's training and experience should provide a reasonable basis for determining that certain acts may be illegal. When the CPA believes that illegal acts may have occurred, additional procedures should be employed to investigate those matters, including consultation with legal counsel to obtain an understanding of the nature of the acts and their possible effects on the statements. Procedures the auditor ordinarily performs that may uncover illegal acts include evaluation of internal control and related tests of transactions and balances and inquiries of management personnel and others, including the client's legal counsel.

In the course of performing an examination the auditor should consider the following types of transactions carefully as they may raise questions concerning the possible existence of an illegal act:

Transactions that appear to be unauthorized

Transactions improperly recorded as to amount, accounting period, or classification

Transactions not recorded in a complete or timely manner to maintain accountability for assets

Transactions that appear to have a very unusual or questionable purpose (the auditor should inquire as to the business purpose of the transaction)

Since income tax laws and certain government regulations are within the expertise of the auditor, the effect these requirements may have on amounts recognized as expenses or revenue accrued should be considered as they may involve an illegal act. An auditor also should inquire about the client's compliance with laws and regulations and the procedures used which are relevant to the prevention or detection of illegal acts such as policy directives and periodic representations obtained from management at appropriate levels concerning compliance with laws and regulations.

When evaluating the materiality of a possible illegal act the auditor should consider the monetary effects of the act, if any, including the related contingent monetary effects. Contingent monetary effects include fines, penalties, and damages that may result from the act. Loss contingencies that should be disclosed and other matters requiring disclosure should also be considered. Loss contingencies that may require disclosure (see FASB Statement No. 5) include threat of expropriation of assets, enforced discontinuance of operations in a foreign country and possible litigation. Also, if a significant amount of revenue is derived from transactions involving illegal acts, this fact may require disclosure. For certain illegal acts not having a material effect on the statements, there may exist a material loss contingency requiring disclosure because of management's failure to make a required non-financial statement disclosure.

An auditor should consider the circumstances of illegal acts promptly and consider seeking legal counsel or consultation with other specialists. After the auditor has determined that an illegal act has occurred, the circumstances should be reported to client personnel at a sufficiently high level so that appropriate action may be taken regarding adjustments or disclosures in the statements, disclosures in other documents issued on a more timely basis (such as interim statements and reports to regulatory agencies), and consideration of appropriate remedial action.

When the CPA concludes that illegal acts are material and require disclosure in the statements and disclosure is not made ordinarily, the opinion would have to be qualified or an adverse opinion be expressed because of a departure from GAAP (the disclosure standard). When the auditor is unable to obtain sufficient competent evidence as to a possible illegal act, disclaiming an opinion or qualifying the opinion as to a scope restriction should be considered.

When there are illegal acts that *are not considered material* and when the auditor cannot persuade management to take appropriate remedial action, the auditor should consider withdrawing from the current engagement and possibly dissociating themselves from a future relationship with the client. This decision ordinarily will be affected by the effects on the auditor's ability to rely on management's representations and the possible effects of continuing the association with the client, including the appearance of a loss of independence.

The auditor is ordinarily under no obligation to notify outside parties concerning illegal acts committed by the client. Deciding whether there is a need to notify outside parties of an illegal act is the responsibility of management.

THE CPA'S RESPONSIBILITY FOR THE DETECTION OF ERRORS OR IRREGULARITIES (SAS NO. 16)

A CPA's objective in performing an examination is to form an opinion on the overall fairness of the presentation in the financial statements. GAAS require the auditor to plan the examination to search for errors or irregularities that would have a material effect on the financial statements. Auditing standards do not require the CPA to plan the examination to search for either errors or irregularities that would not have a material effect on the statements.

The term errors refers to unintentional mistakes in financial statements and includes mathematical or clerical mistakes, misinterpretations or mistakes in the application of accounting principles, and oversight or misinterpretation of facts that existed at the time the statements were prepared. Irregularities, on the other hand, refer to intentional distortions of financial statements such as deliberate misrepresentation by management (management fraud) and misappropriations of assets (defalcation). The auditor should be aware that irregularities may result from a number of situations including, but not limited to the following:

Misrepresentation or omission of the effects of events or transactions

Manipulation, falsification, or alteration of records or documents

Omission of significant information from records or documents

Recording of transactions without substance

Intentional misapplication of accounting principles

Misappropriation of assets for the benefit of management, employees, or third parties

The independent audit is only one vehicle for controlling errors and irregularities in accounting records. Businesses generally operate under a variety of controls including, for example, legal requirements, monitoring of management activities by boards of directors and audit committees, internal audit functions, and internal control procedures. These controls, along with the independent audit, should provide assurance that errors will be prevented or detected on a timely basis. The independent audit provides reasonable, but not absolute, assurance that statements are not materially affected by errors and irregularities. An auditor's examination is influenced by the possibility of errors or irregularities and his or her judgment concerning the integrity of management and the quality of internal control. The auditor performs an examination with the attitude of professional skepticism and recognizes that the application of customary auditing procedures may produce evidence of errors or possible irregularities. For example, the following circumstances, if not reasonably explained may lead a CPA to question whether errors or possible irregularities exist:

Discrepancies within the accounting records, such as difference between a control account and its subsidiary records

Differences disclosed by confirmations

Significantly fewer responses to confirmation requests than expected

Transactions not supported by proper documentation

Transactions not recorded in accordance with management's general or specific authorizations

The completion of large, unusual, or complex transactions at or near year-end

The auditor, in conducting the examination, as a practical matter must rely on a number of management assertions and accept at face value many documents presented by management. The auditor should recognize, however, that collusion between client personnel and third parties or among management or employees may result in falsified records or documents being presented. Examples of records that could be so falsified and are normally accepted by the auditor include:

Representations by management concerning the completeness of the accounting records or the minutes of the board of directors meetings

Documents containing representations from third parties, such as confirmations of accounts receivable and accounts payable and confirmations of other documents received from banks or other depositories

An auditor cannot confirm or corroborate the truthfulness of all documents or statements made by the client during the course of an examination of financial statements. Consequently, in the absence of evidence raising questions as to the truthfulness of a representation of the validity of a record or document, the auditor's reliance on it is reasonable. Furthermore, an auditor cannot be expected to detect transactions unless evidence of their existence is noted in the course of applying GAAS. The CPA should always recognize, however, that management can perpetrate irregularities by overriding controls that would prevent similar irregularities by other employees. Management integrity is, therefore, important to the effective operation of internal control procedures. The extent to which an auditor goes in corroborating information received from management is a matter of judgment. The auditor, in the course of an examination should, however, consider whether there are matters that might predispose management to misstate financial statements. Such circumstances might include:

A company in an industry experiencing a large number of business failures

Lack of sufficient working capital or credit to continue operations

A company that is preoccupied with maintaining a favorable earnings trend

An auditor should evaluate the risk that management may have misstated the financial statements. Circumstances that may cause the CPA to be concerned about the possibility of a material misrepresentation include:

Operating management appears to have little regard for the need to establish and follow internal control procedures

The company needs, but lacks, an internal audit staff

Key financial positions, such as controller, have a high turnover rate

The accounting and financial functions appear to be understaffed, resulting in a constant crisis condition and related loss of controls

Providing reasonable assurance that errors and irregularities in statements will be prevented or detected within a timely period is a function of internal control. Management is responsible for developing and maintaining a sound system of internal control. The CPA's responsibility is to study and evaluate internal control as a basis for determining the extent of evidence to be obtained in the examination of the financial statements. A conceptually logical approach to the auditor's evaluation of accounting control includes:

Consider the types of errors and irregularities that could occur

Determine the accounting control procedures that should prevent or detect errors and irregularities

Determine whether the necessary procedures are prescribed and are being followed satisfactorily

Evaluate any weaknesses to determine their effect on the nature, timing, and extent of procedures to be applied and suggestions to be made to management

Effective internal control reduces the probability that errors or irregularities will occur, but does not eliminate the possibility that they can occur. Achieving the objectives of internal control depends in large part on the competence and integrity of company personnel. The auditor, therefore, does not place complete reliance on internal control to prevent or detect errors and irregularities. The audit examination normally includes procedures designed to test for the existence of errors or irregularities that could occur and that might have a material effect on the statements even in the absence of material weaknesses in internal control.

When the auditor suspects that material errors or irregularities exist, their implications should be considered and the matter should be discussed with the appropriate level of management. If the auditor believes that material errors or irregularities may exist, an attempt should be made to obtain sufficient evidential matter to determine their existence and their effect. In this regard the auditor may want to consult legal counsel on those matters concerning questions of law. If practicable, the auditor should extend the scope of the examination to obtain such evidential matter. If it is not practicable to extend scope or if the client limits scope or for any other reason the auditor remains uncertain as to whether there are errors or irregularities that may materially affect the statements, consideration should be given to qualifying or disclaiming an opinion or, depending on the circumstances, withdrawing from the engagement, indicating the reasons for so doing and reporting any findings to the board of directors in writing.

When the CPA detects errors or irregularities that could not be so material as to affect the statements (such as petty cash misappropriations), the matter should be referred to an appropriate level of management for consideration. The auditor should recommend that the matter be pursued to a conclusion and consider the effect the irregularity and the personnel involved may have on other aspects of the examination.

An opinion that the financial statements are presented fairly implicitly indicates that, in the judgment of the auditor, the statements taken as a whole are not materially misstated as a result of errors or irregularities. In reaching this opinion the auditor's responsibility is to exercise due skill and care in planning and conducting the examination. However, identifying irregularities resulting from collusion, forgery, or certain unrecorded transactions ordinarily is not practicable for the auditor. Reasonable reliance on the client's accounting records ordinarily is warranted and unavoidable. Accordingly, an audit examination as normally conducted cannot be expected to provide absolute assurance that the statements are not materially affected by errors or irregularities.

An Auditing Interpretation of Section 328, *Illegal Acts by Clients*, considers the question of whether the auditor of an entity subject to the SEC Act of 1934 is now required, because of the enactment of the *Foreign Corrupt Practices Act of 1977* and the provisions of SAS No. 17, to expand the scope of his or her study and evaluation of internal accounting control beyond that which is required by the second standard of field work to identify illegal acts that may result from weaknesses in internal control.

The Interpretation states that the provisions of the FCPA do not require the CPA to expand his or her consideration of internal accounting control. Section 328 (SAS No. 17) indicates that the auditor should be aware that some client acts coming to his or her attention in the performance of the examination might be illegal. It does not require the auditor to plan his or her examination specifically to search for illegal acts. Furthermore, there is nothing in the FCPA or the related legislative history that purports to alter the auditor's study and evaluation of internal accounting control. The FCPA creates express new duties only for companies subject to the SEC Act of 1934, not for auditors.

Another Interpretation of Section 328, in consideration of the FCPA, does indicate that a material weakness identified by the auditor in his or her evaluation of internal accounting control may, because of the provisions of the FCPA, be considered an illegal act. In such circumstances, the auditor should inquire of the client's management and consult with the client's legal counsel as to whether the material weakness is a violation of the FCPA.

UNCOVERING CORPORATE IRREGULARITIES: ARE WE CLOSING THE EXPECTATION GAP?

To what extent do new auditing standards satisfy the need for increased auditor responsibility?

by C. David Baron, Douglas A. Johnson, D. Gerald Searfoss and Charles H. Smith

Corporate fraud, bribes and illegal political contributions pose a particular problem to the financial community at a time when public confidence in business is already low. Many individuals, including the Securities and Exchange Commission and certain members of Congress seem to believe that it is the role of the auditing profession to do something to prevent such irregularities and to restore public confidence. Auditors, on the other hand, are much less certain about their proper role and how they can best serve society in this regard.

The American Institute of Certified Public Accountants' traditional position has been that the normal audit engagement is not designed to detect fraud and cannot be relied upon to do so. However, the profession has been reassessing its detection and disclosure responsibilities in this area. Noteworthy examples of these efforts may be found in the work of the AICPA auditing standards executive committee (AudSEC), which recently issued two new audit standards: Statement on Auditing Standards nos. 16 and 17[1] and the Commission on Auditors' Responsibilities which recently issued its preliminary report.[2]

The impetus for these efforts by the profession lies primarily in a recognition of the importance of consensus within the financial community on the duties and responsibilities of the auditor. This was expressed by the commission in the following words: "It is vital to the economy that users of information have confidence in auditors. Such confidence is dependent on mutual understanding as to the appropriate responsibilities of auditors and a belief by users that such responsibilities are being fulfilled."[3]

This concern for public confidence in the auditor was expressed in more practical terms: "The expectation gap is at the heart of the criticism of the profession. Only when this gap is narrowed and reasonable levels of expectation are established as guidelines for professional conduct will the litigious environment in which we exist be sharply narrowed."[4]

One of the central issues faced by the profession is the extent to which expectations

---

[1] Statement on Auditing Standards no. 16, *The Independent Auditor's Responsibility for the Detection of Errors or Irregularities*, and Statement on Auditing Standards no. 17, *Illegal Acts by Clients* (New York: AICPA, 1977).

[2] *Commission on Auditors' Responsibilities: Report of Tentative Conclusions* (New York: AICPA, 1977).

[3] Commission on Auditors' Responsibilities, *Statement of Issues: Scope and Organization of the Study of Auditors' Responsibilities* (New York: AICPA, 1975), p.39.

[4] Carl D. Liggio, "Expectation Gap: The Accountants' Legal Waterloo." *Journal of Contemporary Business*, Summer 1974.

of auditors and other members of the financial community are compatible as they relate to the former's obligation to detect and disclose corporate irregularities and illegal acts.

Does such an expectation gap exist? Are there significant differences between the views of auditors and the financial community on this important issue? In order to address these questions, the authors conducted a survey of the opinions of auditors and other major segments of the financial community. This article will report the results of that survey. The data will then be compared with the main provisions of the new audit standards (SAS nos. 16 and 17) and the recommendations of the commission in order to determine the extent to which these recent pronouncements are responsive to the views expressed in the survey data.

The Survey Plan

In order to learn the extent of any expectation gap, a survey was conducted by the authors in May 1975. Several instances of corporate irregularities and questionable acts had recently been made public. Thus, the survey data was obtained after the financial community had become aware of the issues, but well before the revisions of generally accepted auditing standards had been published.

The survey questionnaire was designed to elicit the views of individuals within the financial community on two major issues: (1) the auditor's responsibility for *detecting* corporate irregularities and illegal acts and (2) the auditor's responsibility for *disclosing* irregularities and illegal acts.

The sample was randomly selected from five groups within the financial community, who were assumed to be well informed about and concerned with auditing standards. In general, these five groups represent the pre-

C. DAVID BARON, *CPA, Ph.D., is associate professor of accounting at Arizona State University in Tempe. He is a member of the Arizona Society of CPAs and the AICPA.* DOUGLAS A. JOHNSON, *CPA, Ph.D., is assistant professor of accounting at Arizona State University and is also a member of the American Accounting Association.* D. GERALD SEARFOSS, *DBA, is associate professor of accounting at the University of Utah in Salt Lake City. He is a member of the AAA and the American Institute for Decision Sciences.* CHARLES H. SMITH, *CPA, Ph.D., is professor of accountancy at the University of Illinois at Urbana. A member of the* Journal's *editorial advisory committee, Dr. Smith is also a member of the AAA and the National Association of Accountants.*

parers (corporate financial managers), the auditors (small-firm CPAs and large-firm audit partners) and the users (bank loan officers and financial analysts) of financial statements. Individuals receiving the questionnaire were selected randomly from the following sources:

☐ Large-firm audit partners were selected from rosters supplied by 10 of the largest national accounting firms.

☐ Small-firm CPAs were selected from the membership directory of the AICPA.

☐ Bank loan officers, financial analysts and corporate financial managers were selected from membership lists of their respective national organizations.

Just under 25 percent of the questionnaires were returned in usable form.

The number of responses received from each group was as follows:

Large-firm audit partners	105
Small-firm CPAs	35
Bank loan officers	83
Financial analysts	52
Corporate financial managers	79

The Auditor's Detection Responsibility

Three types of events may require different degrees of auditor responsibility: (1) deliberate material falsifications, (2) other material misstatements and (3) illegal acts not material in amount.

Deliberate material falsifications are distortions of the financial statements by corporate management in order to deceive the investing public, such as attempts to overstate earnings so as to enhance share values. These distortions and their effects are material in amount in relation to the financial statements.

Other material misstatements represent distortions of the financial statements resulting from various forms of improper or illegal behavior on the part of corporate officers or employees. This broad category includes illegal acts by which the company might benefit immediately, such as bribes, payoffs and illegal political contributions. This category also includes acts undertaken for the personal enrichment of individual officers or employees, such as embezzlement, theft and other misappropriations of assets. The distortions and their effects are material in relation to the statements taken as a whole.

Illegal acts not material in amount represent illegalities and other forms of unacceptable corporate behavior, such as bribes and illegal political contributions, that are immaterial in the customary economic sense. These acts do not involve large dollar amounts in relation to the financial statements, nor will their contingent monetary effects have serious financial consequences.

This article will summarize the results of the survey, examine the relevant provisions of SAS nos. 16 and 17 to determine the extent to which these standards are responsive to the needs expressed by the survey respondents, and review selected recommendations of the commission as they relate to the survey results. The overall objective of this analysis is to learn if an expectation gap exists, and if so, to determine the nature of that gap and to consider whether recent pronouncements will narrow the gap.

Survey Results

Those selected from the five segments of the financial community were asked to rate the extent of auditors' detection responsibility assuming the engagement was conducted under (1) existing standards as of May 1975 and (2) a new set of audit standards which they believed should be established. This task required separate ratings for deliberate material falsifications, other material misstatements and illegal acts not material in amount. The resulting data permits comparisons of the preferences of the groups surveyed by type of irregularity. A Kolmogorov-Smirnov test was used to determine if the group ratings were significantly different from the ratings of large-firm audit partners. In addition, a comparison between pre-SAS nos. 16 and 17 ratings and the preferred responsibility ratings provides an indirect indication of the desire for a change in professional standards. The statistical significance of this desire was tested by a sign test on the number of respondents changing their ratings from existing standards to preferred standards. Finally, respondents' preferences for auditor responsibility under new audit standards provide a basis for evaluating the adequacy of the audit standards that have recently been issued.

Deliberate Material Falsifications

Table 1, page 59, summarizes the ratings of auditor responsibility for detection of deliberate material falsifications. It can be seen that prior to SAS no. 16, most respondents

in each of the five groups thought that auditors already had a high or very high responsibility for detecting deliberate material falsifications. However, differences in the responses among the groups were significant. More specifically, the nonauditors indicated higher levels of responsibility than did auditors, and large firm partners in particular believed there was less responsibility than did any other group.

In considering the preferences for new auditor responsibility expressed by those surveyed (in table 1), it is clear that the auditor groups felt that responsibility should be lessened somewhat as evidenced by the slightly higher mean ratings. The other groups, and particularly the bankers and corporate financial managers, thought the auditors' responsibility should be extended further. Thus, the survey data demonstrates an expectation gap between auditors and other segments of the financial community about the duty to discover deliberate material falsifications of the financial statements.

Other Material Misstatements

Table 2, page 60, summarizes the survey data related to the auditors' responsibility for the detection of other material misstatements. It can be seen that all five groups thought the auditor had a substantial responsibility for discovering these items under pre-SAS no. 16 standards. They thought, however, this duty was lower than that for detecting deliberate material falsifications shown in table 1. The auditors in particular felt a considerably lower responsibility. Differences among the views expressed by the groups were noticeable. For example, the financial analysts perceived pre-SAS no. 16 standards as requiring a significantly greater degree of auditor responsibility than did the large-firm audit partners. Thus, an expectation gap between the surveyed auditor and nonauditor groups is again apparent.

Table 2 also shows that those surveyed thought the auditor's duties should be expanded beyond the standards they perceived to be in effect at the time of the survey. Small-firm CPAs and corporate financial managers in particular expressed a desire for an extension of auditor responsibilities. Financial analysts who had previously reported that a very high responsibility existed (pre-SAS no. 16) indicated there should be some

Table 1

Responsibility for detection of deliberate material falsifications

		Small-firm CPAs	Large-firm audit partners	Corporate financial managers	Bankers	Financial analysts
Pre-SAS no. 16 (percentage of respondents)						
Very high	1,2	66	61	74	82	86
High	3	31	21	20	12	4
Neutral	4	3	8	3	2	2
Low	5	0	3	1	0	2
Very low	6,7	0	7	2	4	6
Mean rating		2.0	2.5	1.8*	1.7*	1.8*
Preferred (percentage of respondents)						
Very high	1,2	68	59	85	95	79
High	3	23	24	13	5	13
Neutral	4	6	6	1	0	4
Low	5	0	4	1	0	0
Very low	6,7	3	7	0	0	4
Mean rating**		2.1	2.6	1.4*	1.4*	1.8*
Number of respondents changing ratings (Pre-SAS no. 16 to preferred)						
Increases		6	17	19	17	9
Decreases		6	18	4	7	12
Sign test significance				.001	.10	

* Group ratings were statistically lower than ratings by large-firm audit partners per Kolmogorov-Smirnov test (Prob. = .01).
** For purposes of the mean rating computation, responses of those participants who did not respond to both the pre-SAS no. 16 and preferred sections were omitted. This resulted in use of a sample slightly smaller than that described on page 57.

slight decrease in this responsibility although this difference was not statistically significant.

Illegal Acts
Not Material in Amount

Table 3, page 61, summarizes the respondents' attitudes toward auditor responsibility for the detection of illegal acts not material in amount. As would be expected, all five groups surveyed felt the auditor had less responsibility to discover immaterial items, even though illegal, than he does for the material types of fraud presented in the two previous tables. Here again, however, significant differences appear among the perceptions of the groups as to what constituted auditor responsibility under pre-SAS no. 17 guidelines. For example, bankers and financial analysts thought the auditor had a moderately high duty for discovery, as contrasted with the moderately low rating expressed by

the large-firm audit partners. Thus the expectation gap prevails, even with the requirement to discover immaterial occurrences of illegal acts.

When the preferences for revised auditor standards are considered, table 3 clearly shows that large-firm audit partners desire a slight lowering of their responsibility with respect to these immaterial items. The other groups, particularly the corporate financial managers, would like to see the auditor extend his responsibility for discovering illegal acts, even if they involve small amounts. Thus, there appear to be forces operating to widen the expectation gap.

The New Audit Standards

In January 1977, AudSEC issued two new audit standards dealing with corporate irregularities and illegal acts. These new stan-

Table 2

Responsibility for detection of other material misstatements

		Small-firm CPAs	Large-firm audit partners	Corporate financial managers	Bankers	Financial analysts
Pre-SAS nos. 16 and 17						
(percentage of respondents)						
Very high	1,2	28	37	62	70	77
High	3	46	30	23	19	15
Neutral	4	11	12	0	5	2
Low	5	9	8	6	2	0
Very low	6,7	6	13	9	4	6
Mean rating		3.1	3.3	2.4*	2.1*	1.9*
Preferred						
(percentage of respondents)						
Very high	1,2	49	36	68	77	81
High	3	31	33	22	17	13
Neutral	4	14	12	6	5	2
Low	5	6	5	3	0	0
Very low	6,7	0	14	1	1	4
Mean rating**		2.6	3.2	1.9*	1.8*	1.9*
Number of respondents changing ratings						
(Pre-SAS nos. 16 and 17 to preferred)						
Increases		14	25	25	19	11
Decreases		7	27	12	15	12
Sign test significance		.10		.02		

* Group ratings were statistically lower than ratings by large-firm audit partners per Kolmogorov-Smirnov test (Prob. = .01).
** For purposes of the mean rating computation, responses of those participants who did not respond to both the pre-SAS nos. 16 and 17 and preferred sections were omitted. This resulted in use of a sample slightly smaller than that described on page 57.

dards are designed to provide guidance on the independent auditor's responsibilities for detecting irregularities (SAS no. 16) and illegal acts (SAS no. 17). They are evidence that the AICPA is striving to respond to calls for a clarification of the auditor's role in this difficult area.

SAS no. 16

SAS no. 16 addresses the auditor's responsibility for the detection of errors[5] and irregularities. It acknowledges that the auditor has a substantial responsibility for detecting irregularities that would materially distort the financial statements. Specifically the statement says that the auditor must "plan his examination . . . to search for errors or ir-

regularities that would have a material effect on the financial statements, and to exercise due skill and care in the conduct of that examination."[6]

This strong statement of auditor responsibility is qualified to some extent when the standard carefully points out the inherent limitations of the audit process: "The subsequent discovery that errors or irregularities existed during the period covered by the independent auditor's examination does not, in itself, indicate inadequate performance on his part."[7]

Although it is not possible to make a direct statistical comparison between the level of responsibility prescribed in SAS no. 16 and the preferences for increased auditor responsibility contained in the survey data, it does

[5] Reference is made in the standard to errors, defined as unintentional mistakes, but these are not controversial and will not be considered herein.

[6] SAS no. 16, par.5.
[7] SAS no. 16, par.13.

seem clear that SAS no. 16 requires the auditor to assume a high level of responsibility for detecting both deliberate material falsifications and other material misstatements of the financials that result from irregularities. Thus, SAS no. 16 is an important step toward narrowing the gap between the expectations of auditors and the financial community.

SAS no. 17

SAS no. 17 is concerned with the auditor's role in the detection of illegal acts. This troublesome issue has not been specifically dealt with in previous audit standards and a conclusive interpretation of the meaning and implication of this new standard is difficult. The authors' interpretation of the substance of SAS no. 17 is that the auditor

now has a moderate responsibility for the discovery of illegal transactions that are material in and of themselves (not considering their contingent monetary effects). On the other hand, the auditor has a minimal responsibility for detecting immaterial illegal acts under SAS no. 17. This position does not satisfy the preferences expressed by nonauditors in the survey data, nonetheless it does represent a carefully measured response to these desires in an area of audit scope that is yet evolving. An explanation of this conclusion is in order.

SAS no. 17 includes what appears to be a very constricted delineation of the auditor's detection responsibilities: "An examination made in accordance with generally accepted auditing standards cannot be expected to pro-

Table 3

Responsibility for detection of illegal acts not material in amount

		Small-firm CPAs	Large-firm audit partners	Corporate financial managers	Bankers	Financial analysts
Pre-SAS no. 17						
(percentage of respondents)						
Very high	1,2	3	3	21	30	42
High	3	40	11	19	33	21
Neutral	4	17	20	21	19	21
Low	5	23	24	18	9	8
Very low	6,7	17	42	21	7	10
Mean rating		4.2*	5.1	3.9*	3.2*	3.2*
Preferred						
(percentage of respondents)						
Very high	1,2	23	7	25	35	48
High	3	31	11	30	33	19
Neutral	4	14	12	16	20	12
Low	5	9	19	16	6	10
Very low	6,7	23	51	13	6	11
Mean rating**		3.9*	5.2	3.4*	3.0*	3.0*
Number of respondents changing ratings						
(Pre-SAS no. 17 to preferred)						
Increases		14	25	35	32	19
Decreases		8	25	16	20	12
Sign test significance				.01	.10	.05

*Group ratings were statistically lower than ratings by large-firm audit partners per Kolmogorov-Smirnov test (Prob. = .01).
** For purposes of the mean rating computation, responses of those participants who did not respond to both the pre-SAS no. 17 and preferred sections were omitted. This resulted in use of a sample slightly smaller than that described on page 57.

vide assurance that illegal acts will be detected."[8] The primary argument given in support of this position is that an auditor is not professionally competent to determine the legality or illegality of an event.[9]

However, a careful reading of the standard indicates that the auditor is not absolved from all responsibilities. The new standard also says, "the auditor's training and experience . . . should provide a reasonable basis for an awareness that some client acts coming to an auditor's attention in the performance of his examination might be illegal."[10]

The difficulty with this is that illegal acts would seldom be material in and of themselves. The dollar payments associated with a bribe, for example, would normally be small in relation to the financial statements. The materiality of these illegal payments lies in the consequences of their discovery and disclosure, that is, in the contingent monetary effects of fines, penalties and damages. Thus, for most illegal acts, they would need to be discovered before the auditor could assess their relative materiality.

What, then, is the position of SAS no. 17 on the discovery of immaterial illegal acts? The new standard implies that the auditor has a minimal responsibility for illegal acts that are not material. That is, the act must be material in and of itself in order for the discovery responsibility provisions of SAS no. 17 to be operative.

In summary, SAS no. 17 represents a cautious response on the part of AudSEC to the demands for an expanded auditor responsibility for the detection of illegal acts. The auditor has a moderately high duty to discover illegal acts involving large dollar amounts. However, he has a relatively low responsibility for discovering illegal acts that involve small amounts in relation to the financial statements. While direct comparisons are difficult, the new standard does not go as far as the nonauditor groups surveyed would like. It clearly does not satisfy their preferences with respect to illegal acts that are not material in amount. In general, the new standard more nearly reflects the views expressed by the large-firm audit partners surveyed.

The Commission on Auditors' Responsibilities

The work of the Commission on Auditors' Responsibilities represents an in-depth study of the auditor's role, including his duties for the detection of corporate fraud and illegal acts. For this reason, a number of the more pertinent recommendations contained in the commission's report of March 1977 will be mentioned here.

First of all, one of the charges to the commission when it was established in 1974 was to determine if an expectation gap exists. The commission concluded that a significant gap does exist between the performance of auditors and the expectations of users of financial statements, and auditors should work toward a narrowing of this gap."[11]

On the whole, the commission's report calls for an expansion of auditor responsibilities for the detection of irregularities and illegal acts that goes beyond SAS nos. 16 and 17. Its recommendations are more reflective of the preferences expressed by financial analysts and bankers in the survey data. For example, the commission's recommendations are stronger and more specific than SAS no. 16 with respect to irregularities. The commission recommends that the auditor should actively search for fraud and the "audit should be designed to provide reasonable assurance that the financial statements are not affected by material fraud. . . ."[12]

As for illegal acts, the commission concluded that the "independent auditor should be expected to detect those illegal or questionable acts that the exercise of professional skill and care would normally uncover."[13] On immaterial illegal acts, the commission recommended that the auditor be required to search with skill and care, but recognizes that it may not be reasonable to expect the auditor to discover all instances of relatively small amounts.

One of the more innovative suggestions of the commission related to illegal acts was

---

[8] SAS no. 17, par.3.

[9] An additional factor that constrains the auditor's ability to become aware of or recognize a possible illegal act is the fact that many illegalities are removed from the events and transactions specifically reflected in the financial statements. For example, violations of the Occupational Health and Safety or Truth in Lending Acts.

[10] SAS no. 17, par.3.

---

[11] *Report of Tentative Conclusions*, p.xi.

[12] Ibid., p.36.

[13] Ibid., p.46.

that management, assisted by legal counsel, should develop and disseminate a clear statement of acceptable and unacceptable corporate behavior and the auditor might then be able to provide a service by reviewing the statement, and the extent to which procedures have been complied with.[14]

The commission's greatest contribution toward ultimately narrowing the expectation gap was in their explanation to auditors and nonauditors of the concept of due professional skill and care in the detection of fraud and illegal acts.[15] Overall, judging auditor detection performance by a well-defined concept of due professional care should result in improved service to the financial community. Adoption of the commission's recommendations would greatly reduce the expectation gap.

The Auditor's Disclosure Responsibility

When a corporate irregularity or illegal act is discovered by an auditor during the course of his normal engagement, action is necessary, usually including some form of disclosure. The exact nature of this disclosure—the form it would take, its content and the recipient of the communication—may vary, depending on the circumstances and on managements' judgments, as well as the auditor's.

Survey Results

Table 4, page 64, summarizes the percentage of respondents in each group who selected the reporting strategy indicated. This was in response to the question, "Which reporting strategy should an auditor adopt if he discovers an irregularity or illegal act which would result in a material misstatement of the financial statements?"[16] Two separate situations were presented in the survey questionnaire:

[ ] Respondents were to assume that the auditor is guided by standards in effect at the time the survey was conducted, i.e., pre-SAS nos. 16 and 17 standards.

□ Respondents were to assume that the auditor is guided by a new set of reporting requirements they would like to see established.

Statistical tests were performed on the survey responses to highlight intergroup differences in views (expectation gap), as well as differences between respondents' perceptions of pre-SAS no. 16 requirements and preferred auditor reporting requirements (desire for change in current audit standards).

Several useful insights can be drawn from table 4. In general, statistically significant differences occurred among the responses of the respective groups, particularly between the auditors and the financial analysts. In addition, significant differences were found between respondents' perceptions of auditor duties under pre-SAS nos. 16 and 17 standards and those responsibilities they would prefer the auditor to have. In almost every case, the preference was for an increase in auditor disclosure responsibilities.

As expected, the first two forms of auditor action, namely, notification of the board of directors, and adjustment of amounts in the financial statements, received high support from all groups. Respondents felt these actions were currently being performed by the auditor and should continue. Neither group differences nor pressure for increased disclosure action were found to be significant on these two items.

However, when the other forms of auditor action were considered, substantial differences emerged among the views expressed by those surveyed. First of all, in comparing the responses for each group in table 4, it can be seen they differ in their perceptions of the auditor's pre-SAS nos. 16 and 17 reporting duties, and in what they would like those responsibilities to be under a new standard. An expectation gap is clearly visible from this data. If one considers the more significant differences, the five groups can be reduced to two major groups: the preparer-auditor group composed of the small- and large-firm CPAs along with the corporate financial managers and the user group made up of the bankers and financial analysts. Although some variation exists among all of the five original groups, there are sharp differences in the views of the two major groupings. On the whole, under pre-SAS nos. 16 and 17 standards, the banker-financial analyst group holds the auditor to a more extensive reporting responsibility than that felt to be the case by auditors and corporate financial managers.

---

[14] The commission suggested that the annual report should include a report by management as to the existing code of conduct and procedures to ensure compliance. The auditor's report would then describe his review and conclusions. Ibid., p.48.

[15] Ibid., p.37-40.

[16] Materiality, in this context, is used in its customary sense, namely, the dollar magnitude of an irregularity or illegal act, including its monetary effects, in relation to the financial statements taken as a whole.

Table 4

The disclosure of material irregularities and illegal acts

		Percentage of respondents selecting reporting strategy***				
Auditor reporting strategies for material irregularities		*Small-firm CPAs*	*Large-firm audit partners*	*Corporate financial managers*	*Bankers*	*Financial analysts*
The auditor should notify the board of directors and/or an appropriate level of management.	Pre-SAS nos. 16 and 17	89	91	88	96	98
	Preferred	94	95	95	100	96
The auditor should insist on adjustments in order that the financial statement amounts be fairly presented.	Pre-SAS nos. 16 and 17	100	98	90	95	96
	Preferred	97	96	91	100	96
The auditor should notify other auditors of affiliated companies within the corporate group.	Pre-SAS nos. 16 and 17	31	46	57	57	50
	Preferred	77**	70**	79**	79**	79**
* The auditor should insist on a detailed disclosure of the incident in the annual report.	Pre-SAS nos. 16 and 17	36	32	35	57	60
	Preferred	58**	49**	56**	75**	81**
* The auditor should notify the appropriate agency (e.g., SEC) if a violation of regulations occurs.	Pre-SAS nos. 16 and 17	29	34	33	45	57
	Preferred	50**	47**	49**	71**	78**
The auditor should notify the appropriate law enforcement agency if an illegal act occurs.	Pre-SAS nos. 16 and 17	20	9	21	33	54
	Preferred	31**	18**	37**	51**	77**

* Intergroup differences for both pre-SAS nos. 16 and 17 and preferred are statistically significant at the .05 level per a Chi Square test.
** The change for pre-SAS nos. 16 and 17 standards to preferred is statistically significant at the .05 level per a McNemar test.
*** Responses of those participants who did not respond to *both* the pre-SAS nos. 16 and 17 *and* preferred sections were omitted. This resulted in use of a sample slightly smaller than that described on page 57.

One of the more striking insights apparent from an examination of table 4 is the fact that all the groups surveyed felt that pre-SAS nos. 16 and 17 guidelines for reporting on irregularities and illegal acts were inadequate. Even the large- and small-firm CPAs held this view. In almost all instances, respondents preferred an expansion of the auditor's disclosure responsibilities, although the levels of support for each type of reporting strategy were not uniform. For example, an expansion beyond the current standards to require the auditor to notify other auditors of affiliated companies within the same corporate group

received substantial favor from all respondents. The reporting strategies drawing the least support were those that require the auditor to take a more direct and active role in disclosing irregularities, such as requiring the auditor to notify an appropriate regulatory or law enforcement agency. Even on this point, however, a large proportion of the financial analysts (77 percent) felt such actions should be required of the auditor.

In summary, the survey data contained in table 4 shows an expectation gap between auditors and the bankers and financial analysts with respect to a number of possible auditor disclosure actions. Individuals within these two groups do not share a common understanding of the auditor's present responsibilities, nor do they agree on what those duties should be. However, all groups expressed a desire for an extension of the auditor's reporting duties for material irregularities and illegal acts. Considerable support was expressed for having the auditor notify the other auditors of affiliated companies when an irregularity is discovered and requiring the client to provide detailed disclosure of the circumstances and effects of the incident in the annual report. There was also considerable support for having the auditor notify a regulatory agency such as the SEC, when a violation of regulations has occurred.

SAS nos. 16 and 17 on the Auditor's Disclosure Duties

We have seen how AudSEC's new audit standards have extended the auditor's responsibilities for the discovery of irregularities and illegal acts. Have similar changes occurred with respect to his reporting responsibilities? An examination of SAS nos. 16 and 17, and comparison of their main points with the preferences for an expansion of the auditor's disclosure duties that were expressed in the survey data may answer this question.

SAS nos. 16 and 17 provide that, upon discovery of an irregularity or illegal act that is judged to be material, the auditor should notify an appropriate level of management.[17] In many cases this would be the board of directors or its audit committee since the primary responsibility for remedial action and possible public disclosure of the incident usually rests with the officers and directors of the company. At a minimum, the auditor would require that the financial statement amounts be adjusted to ensure fair presentation of financial condition and results of operations. It is not entirely clear from the new standards, however, what degree of detailed disclosure of the circumstances and effects of an irregularity or illegal act is necessary.

For example, in SAS no. 16 there is little direct discussion of how an auditor should report or what kind of financial statement disclosure is required when a material irregularity has been discovered whose monetary effects are known and reasonably certain. One might deduce that some special disclo-

sure is necessary from the following passage contained in SAS no. 16: "An independent auditor's standard report implicitly indicates his belief that the financial statements taken as a whole are not materially misstated as a result of errors or irregularities."[18] Apparently, a nonstandard (modified) audit report would result when a material irregularity has occurred; however, it is not clear from the new standard what form this modified report should take.

Similarly, in SAS no. 17 the auditor is advised to qualify his opinion or express an adverse opinion if a material illegal act "has not been properly accounted for or disclosed in the financial statements. . . ."[19] However, the new standard contains insufficient guidance on what constitutes, in the authors' view, proper accounting and disclosure.[20]

The general problem is that in the absence of clear-cut guidance on how the auditor should require disclosure of a material item, it becomes a matter of professional judgment on the part of the individual auditor. Considerable variation can be expected in the manner in which auditors will choose to report on discovered irregularities and illegal acts, given the lack of specific guidance in SAS nos. 16 and 17. For example, the amount of detailed explanation of circumstances and effects may vary, the location of the disclosure within the financial statements or the auditor's report may vary, as may the degree of emphasis given the matter by the auditor. For this reason, it is difficult to assess the extent to which the new audit standards will satisfy the preference for detailed disclosure of irregularities and illegal acts as expressed by bankers and financial analysts in the survey.

As for the more specialized reporting strategies considered in table 4, there are no guidelines contained in the new standards recommending their use. In fact, even though it enjoyed considerable support among all of the groups, including small- and large-firm CPAs, professional ethics requirements and legal concerns might make it difficult to implement the reporting strategy which calls for notification of other auditors of affiliated companies within the same corporate group.

---

[17] SAS no. 16, par.14 and SAS no. 17, par.13.

[18] SAS no. 16, par.5.

[19] SAS no. 17, par.15.

[20] SAS no. 17 does include some guidance on the amount of detailed explanation that should be required in the financial statements. If the effects of an illegal act involve unusual risks of losing significant amounts of revenue or earnings, these facts should be considered for disclosure. SAS no. 17, par.12.

The auditor is not required by SAS no. 17 to notify law enforcement agencies, the SEC or other parties outside of the client's organization; that is considered management's responsibility. However, if the auditor withdraws from the engagement, he is advised to consult with his legal counsel. The new standards, then, suggest a more active, but nonetheless indirect, role for the auditor in encouraging corporate compliance with legal and ethical codes of behavior. In SAS no. 17, for example, the auditor is advised to consult with and counsel the client "so that appropriate action can be taken by the client with respect to disclosures that may be required in . . . documents [other than the financial statements]."[21]

In summary, the new audit standards are responsive to some of the preferences for increased auditor disclosure duties expressed in the survey data. However, these reporting responsibilities will continue to be linked closely with the annual financial statements, contrary to the desires of the bankers and financial analysts who would like to see use of more specialized reporting strategies.

Summary

The results of a survey conducted in 1975 indicate that auditors and nonauditors have significantly different beliefs and preferences on the extent of the auditor's responsibility for detecting and disclosing irregularities and illegal acts. Since that time, however, AudSEC has made substantial progress in clarifying the auditor's duties that can be expected to reduce this expectation gap to more manageable proportions. Generally, SAS no. 16 has redefined professional standards related to the detection of material irregularities so that they are now in closer agreement with the preferences of the bankers, financial analysts and corporate financial managers included in the survey. There is less compatibility on the auditor's disclosure duties, however. SAS no. 17 also represents an important clarification of the auditor's duties with respect to illegal acts, although it is somewhat less responsive than SAS no. 16 to the user preferences expressed in the survey data. The Commission on Auditors' Responsibilities has recommended further changes in professional standards and made several innovative suggestions designed to narrow the expectation gap.

There is little question that the efforts of AudSEC and the commission will bring about a greater understanding of the auditor's duties, even though disagreements on specific points may remain. It is believed that the expectation gap is being narrowed by movement on the part of both auditors and the financial community. ∎

---

[21] SAS no. 17, par. 13.

ACCOUNTANTS' LIABILITY AND THE LITIGATION EXPLOSION

CPAs' liability— no further than fair.

by Newton N. Minow

Since the early days of the Republic, most people believed that the American legal system worked reasonably well. Today, however, there is widespread concern that the system is breaking down. The concern reflects in part the dramatic rise in litigation in recent years, seemingly unaccompanied by a corresponding extension of justice.

The increased number of American law cases is by now familiar. In 1982 there were 206,193 civil lawsuits filed in federal court—double the number filed in 1974 and three and a half times the number filed in 1960. Federal appeals jumped sevenfold between 1960 and 1982. The number of state suits increased by 22 percent between 1977 and 1982, and state appeals increased by 32 percent in the same period.

Although the vast majority of these suits are settled and not fully litigated, the burden on the legal system of these many thousands of cases weighs heavily nonetheless. Moreover, a recent analysis indicates that many civil cases which do go to trial—with or without a jury—can easily cost the taxpayers more money than is at stake for any of the litigants.[1]

The figures on the legions of American lawyers are also familiar; the number has doubled since 1960. With 612,000 lawyers, there is now one attorney for every 390 Americans—3 times as many per capita as in West Germany and England, 10 times as many as in Sweden and more than 20 times as many as in Japan. (One American writer has suggested that the United States should trade one American lawyer to Japan for every Japanese car exported to California.)

To the extent that this proliferation of litigation and lawyers represents an extension of justice and the realization of rights, it should be welcomed. Unlike in some societies, U.S. law exists to protect rights as well as to preserve order. Unfortunately, it seems instead that the litigation explosion is in fact hindering the quest for fair, efficient administration of justice.

Derek C. Bok, president of Harvard University and former dean of Harvard Law School, recently charged that the current legal system has become "grossly inequitable and inefficient. . . . The blunt, inexcusable fact is that this nation, which prides itself on efficiency and justice, has developed a legal system that is the most expensive in the world, yet cannot manage to protect the rights of most of its citizens."[2] In a speech to the American Bar Association on February 12, 1984, Chief Justice Warren E. Burger observed, "Our system is too costly, too painful, too destructive, too inefficient for a truly civilized people."

---

[2]Derek C. Bok, *President's Report to the Overseers* (Cambridge, Mass.: Harvard University, 1983); reprinted in *Harvard* magazine, May-June 1983, p.41.

NEWTON N. MINOW, L.L.D., is a partner in the law firm of Sidley & Austin, Chicago, Illinois. A member of the American Bar Association, Dr. Minow is a former chairman of the Federal Communications Commission and the Arthur Andersen & Co. public review board. This article is an adaptation of one first published by Arthur Andersen.

Author's note: I wish to acknowledge and thank Cliff Sloan, a Harvard law student at the time, for his valuable help in preparing this article. I also thank my colleagues at Sidley & Austin—R. Eden Martin, Robert McLean and David Hiller—for their contributions and suggestions.
[1]J. Kabalik and R. Ross, *A Price Tag for Civil Justice: An Estimate of the Public Costs of All Civil Cases* (Santa Monica, Calif.: Rand Corporation, The Institute for Civil Justice, 1983).

The origins of the current predicament are varied. They may be found partly in the individualistic, competitive traits of Americans—a spirit that has been adapted to the courtroom as well as to the marketplace. These traits have found their political expression in a highly volatile style of pluralist, interest-group politics in which litigation has become an accustomed means of advancing political and social ends.

Burgeoning regulatory and social welfare legislation, moreover, often drafted vaguely—through inadvertence or the calculated ambiguity of legislative compromise—invites recourse to the courtroom as the place to solve every problem. Statutory rights are created, other rights are inferred by judges, still others are imagined by litigants—and soon it is believed that the courts will be hospitable to any contention on any issue.

Justice Richard Neely, of the West Virginia Court of Appeals, has compared the plight of the current judicial system to the "tragedy of the common"—the phenomenon in which traditional agricultural communities that permitted each farmer to raise livestock on pasturage held in common broke down because each farmer began to graze as many cattle as possible.[3] A system that holds out magnificent promise and offers easy access cannot realize that promise if its users lack a sense of self-restraint, shared responsibility and mutual cooperation.

American legal procedures offer little resistance to this avalanche of new claims. Access to the system is easy, if not equal in practical terms. Unlike litigants in other nations, the American litigant may bring a lawsuit with a

---

[3]Richard Neely, "Loser Pays Nothing," *Washington Monthly*, June 1983, p.42.

minimal burden of having to show injury. Filing a suit entitles one to invoke our uniquely broad discovery system—permitting access to files and documents and allowing one to compel depositions. Unlike the system in many other countries, the American system rarely forces the losing party to pay the other side's legal costs. Also unlike the system in many other nations, the U.S. system permits lawyers to operate on a contingent fee arrangement, the result of which is that it costs a plaintiff nothing to sue unless he wins the case.

The immense number of plaintiffs in search of compensation for losses, allegedly at the hands of the persons they sue, has put enormous pressure on elastic legal doctrines, such as negligence and fault, which in earlier times limited recoveries to cases in which the defen-

"Lawsuits against professionals of all types are proceeding at an unprecedented pace. . . . "

dant's conduct was truly culpable. As applied by sympathetic judges and more so by juries, these doctrines of personal responsibility and fault have given way to the notion that the highest good of a legal system is its capacity to shift losses to those with deep pockets or insurance, for which it is often assumed no one pays.

It All Began with Product Liability . . .

The movement away from rigorous conceptions of fault and toward a notion of "strict liability" affects many areas of the law. This movement began in the field of product liability. In this context, "strict liability means that whenever a particular product emerges from an assembly line in a defective condition, the manufacturer will be liable for any injury that the defect causes,"[4] regardless of whether there is a showing of specific fault in the manufacturing of the defective product. The intellectual underpinnings of this theory are that risks should be borne by society rather than by

[4]Jethro Lieberman, *The Litigious Society* (New York: Basic Books, 1981), p.42.

the individual, and that large, prosperous economic actors are effective risk bearers because they can plan for and insure against the claimed damages.

The theory of strict product liability has been expanded by some courts to the area of professional liability. Lawsuits against professionals of all types are proceeding at an unprecedented pace and based on legal theories that would have been unthinkable only a decade or two ago. Architects, doctors, lawyers, accountants—all face a steady stream of lawsuits. The suits seem premised on the view that the professionals' responsibilities extend to every possible occurrence. The cases appear to reflect a rejection of the notion that a professional may be living up to his or her best professional ability and yet still be unable to prevent risk or the misfortunes of patients or clients. Examples of this view abound.

James Brady, the former presidental press secretary wounded by John Hinckley, is suing the psychiatrist who treated Hinckley before he attempted to assassinate President Reagan. A recent Supreme Court decision involved a suit against a client's attorney for the latter's selection of issues and arguments in his appellate presentation.[5] Doctors are held liable for prescribing drugs believed safe at the time but that led to complications a generation later. Students sue teachers for failing to teach them adequately. Children sue parents for improper rearing. Sailing clubs have been sued for sponsoring races on windy days. Sports fans have even sued losing teams.

The motivation behind such suits seems to be the belief that no risk is to be borne as simply bad luck or fate but that all loss should be compensable by someone. Just as the automobile manufacturer should be held responsible for an automobile that doesn't function properly, the thinking seems to be, so too a psychiatrist should be held responsible for a patient who doesn't function properly.

. . . and Expanded to Accountants' Liability

It is in this context of unprecedented litigation and broadened liability that sweeping new assertions of accountants' liability should be understood. The new theory seems to be that the accountant should be held responsible for a business that doesn't function properly.

Until the last decade, accountants were

[5]*Jones* v. *Barnes*, 51 USLW 5151 (1983).

(Continued on page 76)

largely unaffected by these systematic legal changes, but the proliferation of lawsuits against them since the 1970s has drawn accountants into the midst of the legal thicket. Indeed, accountants' relatively recent exposure to assertions of greater liability appears symptomatic of the system's larger predicament. The number of lawsuits against accountants has soared, the damages awarded have skyrocketed and novel theories of liability are imposed by courts. More lawsuits have been filed against accountants in the last decade and a half than in the entire previous history of the profession.

The first English lawsuit against an auditor was in 1887.[6] Such suits were a relative rarity through much of the 20th century in Britain and the United States. A few celebrated cases

"The great expansion of accountants' liability has proceeded through an erosion of rules of fault and causation. . . . "

had a profound impact—Judge (later Justice) Benjamin N. Cardozo's opinion in *Ultramares Corp.* v. *Touche* in 1931[7] and the McKesson & Robbins business fraud and ensuing settlement with accountants in 1938.[8] These cases received a great deal of attention and reflection precisely because they were so rare.

Recent decisions have imposed vast new liability on accountants. The concept of accountants' liability that has emerged in these cases is broad and expansive, almost limitless, as are the number and classes of people to whom the accountant is held responsible. Some investors and creditors automatically sue accountants and their firms when businesses fail without regard to what caused the failure or whether the accountants were negligent in the performance of their audit responsibilities.

There is an obvious lure in suing the accounting firms, for they are frequently the only solvent party left standing in the wake of corporate bankruptcy. Not coincidentally, the two great surges in litigation against accoun-

tants have occurred during times of enormous business failures—the recessions of the early 1970s and 1980s.

The great expansion of accountants' liability has proceeded through an erosion of rules of fault and causation now typical of many areas of the law. First, there has been a broad expansion of the classes of people to whom accountants are liable.

The classic opinion on the subject had long been Judge Cardozo's in *Ultramares*. Judge Cardozo held that accountants could not be held liable to third parties for negligence because it might "expose accountants to a liability in an indeterminate amount for an indeterminate time to an indeterminate class. The hazards of business conducted on these terms are so extreme as to enkindle doubt whether a flaw may not exist in the implication of a duty that exposes to these consequences."[9]

In recent decisions, however, courts have held that accountants' liability extends to any investor or creditor who convinces a court or jury that the accountant, in hindsight, could have done something more than he did that would have revealed a business failure or fraud by a corporate insider. The effect of these rulings is precisely to expose the accountants to the indeterminate liability that Judge Cardozo feared. More important, the accountants can be held liable for the entire amount of the claimed loss even if their alleged negligence contributed to only a small portion of the total losses; the accountants, meanwhile, are given nothing more than a hollow right to try to recover some of the losses from the usually bankrupt corporation.

Second, in cases alleging fraud under the federal securities laws, courts have relaxed the requirement that plaintiffs actually have relied on alleged misrepresentations by defendants, including accountants' reports on financial statements. Adopting the so-called fraud-on-the-market theory, a number of courts have ruled that investors may recover from defendants for alleged misrepresentations of which the investors were completely

---

[9]*Ultramares Corp.* v. *Touche*, 225 N.Y. 170, 179-80, 174 N.E. 441, 444 (1931).

---

[6]*Leeds Estate, Building & Investment Co.* v. *Shepherd*, 36 Ch.D. 787 (1887).
[7]*Ultramares Corp.* v. *Touche*, 225 N.Y. 170, 174 N.E. 441 (1931).
[8]See Denzil Y. Causey, Jr., *Duties and Liabilities of Public Accountants* (Homewood, Ill.: Dow Jones-Irwin, 1982), pp.16-17.

unaware as long as reliance on the statements by other investors affected the price at which the plaintiff bought or sold the security.[10]

In imposing this expansion of liability, courts have extended the reasoning and analytical framework developed for product liability to accountants' liability. For instance, in rejecting the *Ultramares* concerns, the New Hampshire Supreme Court compared accountants and manufacturers to justify the broad, new liability: "[A]n accountant, like the manufacturer under products liability law, is in the best position to regulate the effects of his conduct by controlling the degree of care exercised during the performance of his professional duty. The accountant, through the fee structure, can pass along to his clients the cost of insuring against financial loss sustained by them through reliance upon his negligent misstatement of fact."[11]

The New Jersey Supreme Court recently came to a similar conclusion and applied similar reasoning: "If recovery for defective products may include economic loss, why should such loss not be compensable if caused by negligent misrepresentation? The maker of the product and the person making the written representation with intent that it be relied upon are, respectively, impliedly holding out that the product is reasonably fit, suitable, and safe, and that the representation is reasonably sufficient, suitable, and accurate."[12]

The New Jersey court further emphasized its view that accountants are effective and appropriate risk bearers because they are able to plan and to insure: "Independent auditors have apparently been able to obtain liability insurance covering these risks or otherwise to satisfy their financial obligation. We have no reason to believe they may not purchase malpractice insurance policies that cover their negligent acts leading to misstatements relied upon by persons who received the audit from the company pursuant to a proper business purpose. . . . Much of the additional costs incurred either because of more thorough auditing review or increased insurance premiums would be borne by the business entity and its stockholders or its customers."[13]

The principles and conclusions derived from product liability are thus playing a major role in inspiring the current expansion of accountants' liability.

A third factor in this expansion is the extreme broadening of the concept of accountants' negligence—a widening of the practices found negligent and legally actionable. Much of this expansion is rooted in a misperception of the accounting profession and its work product.

Victor Earle, general counsel of Peat, Marwick, Mitchell & Co., precisely described this misperception with prescience 12 years ago: "The misconceptions in the public mind are at least fivefold: first, as to *scope*—that auditors make a 100% examination of the company's records, which can be depended upon to uncover all errors or misconduct; second, as to *evaluation*—that auditors pass on the wisdom and legality of a company's multitudinous business decisions; third, as to *precision*—that the numbers set forth in a company's audited financial statements are immutable absolutes; fourth, as to *reducibility*—that the audited results of a company's operations for a year can be synthesized into a

> "Perhaps the most startling imposition of new liability on accountants has been the application to them of a sweeping antiracketeering statute."

single number; and fifth, as to *approval*—that by expressing an opinion on a company's financial statement, the auditors 'certify' its health and attractiveness for investment purposes."[14]

In practical terms, the effect of these misconceptions is the failure of courts and juries to distinguish between an audit failure and a business failure. As a comprehensive treatise on the law governing accountants recently put it, "From [the public misperception of the auditor's duties] flows an erroneous legal supposition that [the auditor's] responsibility

---

[10]See, for example, *Blackie* v. *Barrack,* 524 F.2d 891 (9th Cir. 1975), cert. denied, 429 U.S. 816 (1976); *In re LTV Securities Litigation,* 88 F.R.D. 134 (N.D. Tex. 1980).
[11]*Spherex, Inc.* v. *Alexander Grant and Co.,* 451 A.2d 1308, 1312 (N.H. 1982).
[12]*Rosenblum* v. *Adler,* Slip Op. A-39/85 (N.J. June 9, 1983), p.21.
[13]Ibid., pp.34-36.

[14]Victor Earle, "Accountants on Trial in a Theater of the Absurd," *Fortune,* May 1972, p.227.

should be coextensive with that of the client."[15]

Nor is the misperception of the accounting profession and the resulting expansion of accountants' liability confined to audits. The same phenomenon is true of compilation and review services. A recent *Journal of Accountancy* article by three CPAs observed, "An accountant's exposure to the risk of legal liability results in part from an 'expectation gap' between the perceived and the actual responsibilities assumed by an accountant in performing compilation and review services."[16] The article reviewed several decisions revealing judicial perspectives on the accounting profession and found that "user and court confusion has [occurred] and can occur regarding the responsibilities of the accountant in his varying roles."[17] The authors concluded that this confusion has resulted in the imposition of liability on unsuspecting accountants.

The problem of public misperception of the accounting profession is not unique to the United States. A statute recently passed in the

" . . . there is no justification for shifting the normal risks of investment from the investor to the accountant. . . . "

United Kingdom requires far greater uniformity in the forms of financial statements.

An analysis in the *Journal of the Law Society of Scotland* sharply criticized these new rules: "Accountants like to describe the profession as 'an art, not a science.' Outsiders may see this claim as pretentious, or as an attempt to cloak accountancy in a veil of mystique, but the essence of the sentiment is that presenting financial information well requires exercise of professional judgement which cannot readily be replaced by generalized rules. The Companies Act 1981 is rather full of these rules. . . . [T]he detailed headings

which will now appear in company accounts might lead the user to expect a greater degree of reliability and relevance than the figures which appear against these headings can deliver."[18]

Congress As Part of the Problem

Perhaps the most startling imposition of new liability on accountants has been the application to them of a sweeping antiracketeering statute. In 1970 Congress sought to create a powerful legal weapon against organized crime. It considered outlawing membership in the Cosa Nostra but was advised that such legislation would be unconstitutional. Ultimately, Congress passed the Racketeer Influenced and Corrupt Organizations Act (RICO). This broad statute defined *racketeering* as any two instances over a 10-year period of a variety of offenses, including securities fraud and mail fraud. As one of many deterrents and penalties, it included a private civil action with treble damages.

Congressman Abner Mikva, now a judge on the U.S. Court of Appeals for the District of Columbia, was among the few at the time who sensed the potential problems with the statute's breadth: "This bill is for the purpose of controlling organized crime in the United States. . . . [W]here in the bill does one find the definition of organized crime? . . . My objection to this bill in toto is that whatever its motives to begin with, we will end up with cases involving all kinds of things not intended to be covered, and a potpourri of language by which you can parade all kinds of horrible examples of overreach."[19]

But such thoughts were not in the minds of many legislators as they acted on their zeal to wield a powerful new weapon against organized crime.

Fourteen years later, the statute is being applied to businesses, including accounting firms, that have nothing to do with the organized crime—controlled entities the statute sought to attack. A recent Seventh Circuit decision specifically upheld the application of RICO to three accounting firms. The court concluded, "Congress chose to provide civil remedies for an enormous variety of conduct, balancing the needs to redress a broad social ill against the virtues of tight, but possibly

[15]R. James Gormley, *The Law of Accountants and Auditors* (Boston: Warren, Gorham & Lamont, 1981), pp.1-23.
[16]Kenneth Ira Solomon, Charles Chazen and Richard L. Miller, Jr., "Compilation and Review: The Safety Factor," JofA, July83, p.51.
[17]Ibid., p.52.

[18]R. M. Patterson, "Unaccountable Rules," *Journal of the Law Society of Scotland*, October 1982, pp.428-30.
[19]*Congressional Record*, October 6, 1970, p.35204.

overly astringent, legislative draftsmanship.''[20]

In addition to greatly expanded concepts of the extent and nature of their liability, therefore, accountants also find themselves subject to the draconian penalties intended to drive racketeers out of legitimate businesses.

The application of the RICO statute to accountants may be seen as another example of the tendency, recently described by Derek Bok, of our fractured legal system to lead to

"The audit may be entirely competent even though the business later fails."

surprising and undesirable results: a statute is passed, it produces unanticipated consequences as it is interpreted in the courts, and inadequate consideration is given to the relationship between original goals and eventual results.[21]

Downside of the Legal Burden

Taken together, these developments have the potential to create a crushing burden of limitless liability in which accountants become the insurers for all business failures—sometimes at treble damages. But there is no justification for shifting the normal risks of investment from the investor to the accountant or, through accountants' liability insurance, to all investors or the public generally.

The function of accounting is to provide information to those in the market who place capital at risk—not to guarantee all such risks. Business risks are properly borne by those who make the business and investment decisions, for they are the ones who reap the rewards of business successes and who can respond most efficiently to profit and loss and other market information. A no-fault, riskless capital market would deaden economic incentives and sap entrepreneurialism because, in a market or world with no losers, there can be no winners.

Even assuming that some kind of investor insurance arrangement is desirable, it would be irrational to provide it through the cumbersome, costly and time-consuming process of the courts. A straightforward scheme of investor insurance at least would have the advantages of candor and lower cost of administration. It should be obvious, moreover, that any such insurance or strict liability scheme would do little or nothing to deter those whose conduct caused the business failure, since they would have escaped liability, as they often do now.

Even if the expansion of accountants' liability stops short of insurance for all business risk, however, accountants are left in the dark about the nature and extent of their liability. They are left to the vagaries of each litigational outcome, to a situation of litigational roulette, and always subject to the proclivity of triers of fact to give plaintiffs relief at the expense of defendants.

There are many social costs to this situation, costs rarely considered in the decisions expanding accountants' liability. The general confusion about the extent of this liability encourages frivolous litigation and clouds meritorious claims. Amorphous, expansive liability could also discourage the accounting profession from serving riskier enterprises—in other words, the kinds of new, daring entrepreneurial ventures that the economy so desperately needs, including experimental high-technology companies. If accountants are asked to be the ultimate insurers for businesses, their natural response will be deep caution and reluctance about enterprises the prospects of which are less than certain.

Accountants might also undertake wasteful and redundant procedures as a defense against being second-guessed by judges and juries, much as physicians are encouraged to practice defensive medicine by the threat of malpractice liability. Finally, accountants would be discouraged from innovations within their own practice, such as review of earnings forecasts, which, though potentially highly useful to the investing public, are necessarily speculative and, in the current climate, pose obvious litigation risks to accountants.

For all these reasons, the problem of accountants' liability should be carefully and deliberately reconsidered. Looking closely at the question of accountants' liability requires, first, distinguishing audit failures from business failures, those elements for which an accountant can justly be held responsible and those for which he cannot. It also requires reexamining some of the assumptions that

---

[20]*Schact v. Brown*, nos. 82-2088, 82-2089, 82-2090 (7th Cir. April 8, 1983).
[21]Bok, *President's Report*, pp.42-43.

have guided the great expansion of accountants' liability.

Auditors' Reports and Autos: A Poor Analogy

Perhaps the principal assumption that needs to be reanalyzed is the appropriateness of the product liability analogy in the context of accountants' liability. The accountant differs from the auto manufacturer in many important respects. An auditor doesn't have absolute knowledge of or control over a company's finances and records in the same way that an auto manufacturer has knowledge of and control over its production process. The auditor does have control over his or her examination of a client's financial statement, but the relationship between the statement and a claimed loss is far more indirect than the relationship between a defective product and a claimed harm.

As noted, an audit adds credibility to information provided to the investment community concerning risks that inhere, to varying degrees, in all business enterprises. The audit may be entirely competent even though the business later fails. And even if the difficult judgment is made that the auditor was in fact negligent in his examination, the extent to which the auditor's report affected the judgment of investors and creditors is uncertain

> " . . . we must repair the legal doctrines governing liability that have become distorted by the quest for compensation for every loss."

and speculative. In product liability cases, in contrast, there ordinarily is no question that the flaw in the product was within the producer's control, nor is there a question that the flawed product is the reason for the resulting harm.

The equities are also different in the product liability and accountants' liability contexts. Product liability litigation pits a consumer, expecting an adequate product, against a company with a stake in each product sold. Accountants' liability litigation, in contrast, pits sophisticated investors and creditors, risk takers who hope to reap financial profit from their investments but who are aware of the ever-present possibility of loss as well, against accountants—professionals who perform the auditing service for a fee.

Imposing broad liability on accountants reaps windfalls for investors and creditors: they alone obtain the fruits of successful investments and at the same time become insured against losses from those that fail if they can pin liability on accountants.

A most difficult challenge facing society and the professions is how to restore some reason to the way the legal system responds to the risks of everyday life, including the vagaries of investment. The first step surely must be to abandon the tendency, spawned in the product liability area, to translate every risk into a legal liability. That instinct has proved to be decidedly unsound in defining accountants' responsibility.

Second, we must repair the legal doctrines governing liability that have become distorted by the quest for compensation for every loss. Liability doctrines affecting accountants must clearly distinguish business failures from audit failures, leaving the former to be borne by the investors who assumed such normal risks or, perhaps, in the appropriate circumstances, to be recovered from the directors or managers of the failed enterprise who in some cases can be fairly held to account. Accountants' liability should be preserved when an actual audit failure has in fact caused injury.[22]

Better Ways to Go

One change in legal doctrine that might maintain more sharply the distinction between compensable losses caused by audit failures and other business losses would be the adoption in accountants' liability cases of the doctrine of comparative negligence with limited, proportionate liability. Under comparative negligence, the extent to which a party is at fault is determined on a percentage basis by the judge or jury; under limited, proportionate

---

[22]One suggestion that has been advanced to prevent disproportionate accountants' liability is a system of fixed limits on liability, perhaps corresponding to the amount of fees the accountants received for their services. Such statutory limits on liability are currently in effect in West Germany, and the European Economic Community is now considering a proposal to impose similar limits. Although a fixed limit of this sort could reduce the anomalies and unfairness of exposing accountants to unlimited liability for business failures, it also would arbitrarily cap liability in cases in which the accountants' conduct was truly culpable. Clearly, reason and measure must be introduced into determinations of accountants' liability, but the various reforms discussed in this article would seem, on balance, preferable to a rule of fixed maximum liability.

liability, moreover, the amount that the party must pay cannot exceed the percentage of the damage reflecting that party's share of the fault.[23] The principle guiding these concepts is that each should pay according to his fault, and no further.

The operation of these doctrines can be demonstrated with an illustration. Assume that a company went bankrupt and the investors lost $50 million. The investors sued the management, the board of directors and the company's accountants, alleging fraud and negligence. Under the current law in most jurisdictions, if the plaintiffs proved their allegations against any of the defendants, they could recover the full $50 million from any who lost. But often, as noted, the accountant would be the most—sometimes the only—

"Perhaps a more basic problem . . . is the confusion regarding the standard of negligence itself. . . ."

solvent defendant and thus the only one pursued by the plaintiffs. The accountants would be liable for the full amount and be left with only the futile opportunity to seek contributions from the other defendants.

Under a standard of proportionate liability, however, the judge or jury would assess relative blameworthiness among the parties. If, for example, the company's board of directors had conspired with the management to defraud the company, but the accountants would have discovered the fraud through an audit procedure that ordinarily should be performed, a jury might conclude that the fault lay 40 percent with the board of directors, 40 percent with management and 20 percent with the accountants. In this case the accountants would be liable for 20 percent, or $10 million, of the investors' damages, but no more. The virtue of this comparative negligence with limited, proportionate liability is that it imposes liability for fault, as determined by a court or jury, without thereby conscripting accountants into service as general societal insurers against business failures.

Perhaps a more basic problem, but one not readily solved, is the confusion regarding the

standard of negligence itself—the wide gap between the expectations revealed by judges and juries and the reality of what it is that accountants do.

The accounting profession itself bears a good measure of responsibility for this confusion. Consensus within the profession on important points is often lacking. For instance, in considering the expectation gap in compilation and review services, the *Journal of Accountancy* noted gloomily, "All practitioners do not have the same conception of compilation and review responsibilities, and, to the extent that there are differences within the profession itself regarding actual responsibilities undertaken, the expectation gap may be unbridgeable."[24] To the extent that the expectation gap results from an inflated public perception of an accountant's statement, the profession may be the victim of its own inability to define clearly and precisely its responsibility.

There are no easy answers to the problems of this expectation gap. At a minimum, if there are areas of legitimate professional disagreement or latitude concerning either accounting principles or the standards for the performance of audits, the parameters of that latitude should be clarified. In addition, the American Institute of CPAs should undertake a wide-ranging project to educate the public about the profession, its work and its standards.

Beyond the efforts of the profession itself to clarify its standards and educate the public, consideration should be given to a range of other actions that may further narrow the expectation gap. One possibility is the modification of the accountant's report to reflect greater tentativeness about the conclusions. Unfortunately, with the product liability analogy in mind, courts might reject such qualifications as boilerplate language with no legal effect.

Other reforms could also assist in restoring rational limits on accountants' liability litigation. Consideration might be given to creating safe harbors from liability for activities that, though beneficial to the public, are known to be accompanied by high risk, such as reports on earnings forecasts and financial statements of highly speculative enterprises. Additionally, when legislation has spawned unintended and unwanted consequences, such as the application of the RICO law to the professions,

[23]See, for example, *Kennedy* v. *City of Sawyer*, 228 Kan. 439, 618 P.2d 788 (1980).

[24]Solomon, Chazen and Miller, "Compilation and Review," p.54.

those laws should be reformed or repealed. More generally, the legal procedures governing class actions and pretrial discovery of evidence should be reexamined with an eye to changes that would discourage frivolous or harassing suits without foreclosing legitimate claims.

Another intriguing suggestion for checking impulsive litigation is to adopt the British system (or a variation), in which the losing side picks up the other side's costs. And when claims do go to trial, reforms of the trial process itself could expedite the resolution of complicated issues. The expanded use of special masters in litigation is one possibility. In accountants' liability litigation, as in other complex, specialized fields, the need for expert judgments justifies the use of such masters to review evidence and report to the court. These suggestions, and others as well, should be part of a sustained national effort to refine and improve the legal system.

In a broader context, the problem of accountants' liability cannot be separated from the societal revolution of which it is a part. The nation is beginning a fruitful debate on the direction and character of the legal system. Thoughtful observers like Derek Bok and Justice Neely are contributing new insights into ways in which the vast increase in litigation and sweeping assertions of liability may be justly restrained without impeding meritorious claims and access to redress.

There can be no progress, however, unless and until the legislatures, the courts, the lawyers and the public recognize that the legal system is not a means of spreading and compensating for every risk that comes with living in a complicated world. There is no way to have a riskless society, and even the pursuit of such a chimera is extraordinarily costly. Not only are costs shifted to persons without fault, but enormous resources are consumed by the process itself, leaving delayed and unfulfilled the one purpose such a system seeks to serve.

Society properly should hold persons, including those in the professions, accountable for losses caused by their misconduct. Indeed, the concept of compensable wrongs is at the heart of the American legal system. But the delusion current in the law that all risks must be recompensed by someone else is eclipsing the principles of individual freedom and responsibility—the fundamental values the legal system is intended to preserve. ∎

CASE 1

THE AUDITOR'S RESPONSIBILITIES AND FUNCTIONS IN COMPLYING WITH GAAS

Block, Stock & Barrel, CPAs, have been requested to perform an examination of Johnson Company's financial statements. Johnson intends to issue a complete set of financial statements (balance sheet, income statement, and statement of changes in financial position). Johnson Company is a closely-held corporation and has never been required to have its financial statements audited by a CPA. Mr. Lyndon, president of Johnson and a stockholder in the Company, explains that Johnson Company wants audited financial statements for several reasons, including the following:

1.   Johnson has applied for a loan at the State Savings and Investment Co. to facilitate the expansion of its widget division. The loan officer at State Savings has requested audited financial statements.

2.   Johnson has experienced rapid growth in the last few years and management feels the need to have an independent review of the Company's financial statements to ascertain that sound accounting policies are being followed and the Company has an adequate and efficient system of accounts and internal controls.

3.   A major stockholder who does not participate in management decisions has requested an audit to determine whether management has made wise use of the firm's resources and to ascertain that no illegal or fraudulent acts have and/or are being perpetrated by Company personnel.

During discussions with Mr. Lyndon and other corporate officers prior to the engagement, several questions were raised concerning matters such as the following:

1.   Mr. Richard, Vice President in charge of marketing, asked a question concerning the responsibilities of both the auditor and management with respect to the accuracy of the Company's financial statements.

2.   Charles Sharp, the Company's accountant, in response to a question raised by the President explained the phrase "generally accepted auditing standards" as involving pronouncements of the SEC that the Company would not be concerned with.

3.   Both Mr. Lyndon and Mr. Richard raised a question concerning the auditor's professional qualifications and responsibility. They seemed especially concerned with the auditor's responsibility regarding disclosure of possible illegal acts and irregularities that may have been committed by Company personnel.

CASE DISCUSSION QUESTIONS

1.   What is the objective of the ordinary examination of financial statements by a CPA?

2.   Distinguish between the responsibilities of management and those of the auditors regarding the financial statements and the supporting records and documents.

3.   What are the professional qualifications for a CPA? Is the CPA expected to be an appraiser or a valuer of merchandise inventory? Is he or she expected to make legal decisions concerning aspects of business law?

4.   Outline the ten generally accepted auditing standards (GAAS). Explain the source of GAAS and how they differ from auditing procedures.

5.   Can the CPA, based on an examination made in accordance with GAAS, provide assurance that illegal acts will be detected? Explain.

6.   When a CPA who is conducting an examination of financial statements in accordance with GAAS determines that his or her client may have committed an illegal act, are additional auditing procedures required? Explain.

7. What auditing procedures do CPAs ordinarily perform that may indicate an illegal act? What types of transactions may alert the CPA to the possibility of illegal acts being committed by the client?

8. Explain the auditing concepts of "materiality" and "relative risk" and discuss the impact that each has on the application of auditing procedures. How does materiality relate to illegal acts a client may have committed? Explain.

9. When it has been determined that a client has committed an illegal act, what financial statement disclosures are required? What impact does materiality have on any disclosures regarding illegal acts that may be required in financial statements?

10. Assume that a CPA discovers an illegal act committed by the client and believes outside parties should be informed of the situation. With whom does responsibility rest in notifying outside parties of the illegal act? If the CPA decides to withdraw from an engagement because of an illegal act, what action should be taken by the CPA regarding the notification of outside parties of the existence of the illegal act? Explain.

11. Explain the auditing definitions of the terms "errors" and "irregularities."

12. In planning and performing an examination of financial statements, the CPA is expected to maintain an attitude of professional skepticism. The CPA should also recognize that the application of many customary auditing procedures may produce evidence indicating possible errors or irregularities in the financial statements. Explain. Indicate in your discussion, circumstances that may lead the CPA to question further whether errors or irregularities exist.

13. A basic auditing principle is that there is "no necessary conflict between the CPA and management regarding the fairness of presentation of the financial statements."

    a. Explain the meaning of this basic auditing principle, and include in your discussion examples of records or documents that could be falsified but that the auditor would normally accept from management at their face value.

    b. What circumstances might predispose management to misstate financial statements?

CASE 2

ULTRAMARES LIABILITY CASE *

A firm of public accountants, Touche, Niven & Co., were employed by Fred Stern & Co., Inc. to prepare and certify a balance sheet exhibiting the financial position of its business as of December 31, 1923. This CPA firm had been similarly employed at the end of the three preceding years by Fred Stern & Co., Inc. which was engaged in the importation and sale of rubber. Extensive credit was required to finance the Company's operations and the accounting firm knew that the Company borrowed large sums of money from banks and other lenders and that in the usual course of business the balance sheet when certified would be exhibited by the Stern Company to banks, creditors, stockholders, purchasers or sellers (among others) as the basis of financial dealings.

When the balance sheet was prepared, the accounting firm supplied the Stern Company with thirty-two copies certified with serial numbers as counterpart originals. Nothing was mentioned concerning the persons to whom these counterparts would be shown or the extent or number of transactions in which they would be used, and in particular, there was no mention of the plaintiff, Ultramares, which was a corporation doing business chiefly as a factor, but which had never made advances to the Stern Company in the past although it had sold merchandise to Stern in small amounts.

The audit was completed and the balance sheet dated as of February 26, 1924. The balance sheet indicated assets of $2,550,671, liabilities of $1,479,956, and net worth of $1,070,715. A certification by Touche, Niven and Co. was attached to the balance sheet stating:

> We have examined the accounts of Fred Stern & Co., Inc. for the year ending December 31, 1923, and hereby certify that the annexed balance sheet is in accordance therewith and with the information and explanations given us. We further certify that, subject to provision for federal taxes on income, the said statement, in our opinion, presents a true and correct view of the financial condition of Fred Stern & Co., Inc., as at December 31, 1924.

In reality, the balance sheet was inaccurate and the corporation was insolvent, with liabilities exceeding assets by $200,000. The audit had been negligently conducted.

Since at the start of the audit there had been no posting of the general ledger since April, 1923, a junior accountant of the firm, Siess, was assigned that task. He had completed the posting on Sunday, February 3, 1924, and was ready to assist with the preparation and audit of the balance sheet the following day. The total of the accounts receivable for December, 1923, as posted by Siess from the entries in the journal was $644,758.17. Sometime on February 3, Romberg, who was employed by the Stern Company in general charge of its accounts, placed below that total in his own handwriting an additional item of $706,843.07 representing additional accounts receivable arising from the month's transactions.

All sales represented by the new item were fictitious. Opposite the entry were placed other figures which were intended to indicate journal references. When Siess resumed his work, he included the new item in making up his footings, thus apparently increasing the assets of the business by over $700,000. Siess later stated that he assumed the entries to be correct, and that since his task at the moment was merely to post the books, he postponed the work of audit or verification thinking that it might come later. However, no verification was ever attempted by either Siess or his superiors. If attempted, such an examination would have disclosed that the entry added to the ledger was not supported by any entry in the journal. Further examination would have uncovered invoices which amounted in the aggregate to the interpolated item, but a mere glance at these invoices would have disclosed suspicious features in that they had no shipping number nor a customer's order number and varied in terms of credit and in other respects from those normal and usual in the business.

A careful and skillful auditor would have wished to investigate other items in addition to the December accounts receivable entry. There was cause for suspicion because of inflation of the inventory. The inventory given to the auditors totaled $347,219, but the auditors discovered errors in the amount of $303,863 and adjusted the balance sheet amount accordingly. Both the extent of the discrepancy and its causes should have cast discredit upon the business and its records. Additional grounds for suspicion were noted when inquiry of the creditors gave notice to the auditors that identical accounts had been simultaneously pledged to two, three and four banks. Although the pledges did not

* This case (255 N.Y. 170, 1931) was written by Mike Conley, Ronald Cardwell, Janet Caruso, and George Prillaman, Master of Accountancy students, Virginia Polytechnic Institute and State University.

diminish the value of the assets, in such circumstances they should have evoked a doubt as to the solvency of a business where such conduct was permitted.

The plaintiff, Ultramares, was approached by Stern in March of 1924 with a request for loans of monies to finance the sales of rubber. Since Ultramares insisted that it receive a balance sheet certified by public accountants as a condition of any loan, it was given one of the certificates previously signed by Touche. Ultramares made numerous loans to Stern on the faith of that certificate. On January 2, 1925, the house of cards collapsed and the Stern Company was declared bankrupt with Ultramares suffering a sizable loss. The plaintiff brought suit against the accountants on the grounds of negligence and later added a second cause of action asserting fraud.

Although a jury found for the plaintiff on the claims of both fraud and negligence, the trial judge dismissed the complaint and set aside the verdict. On appeal, the Lower New York Court of Appeals held the defendants liable to the plaintiff for negligence, basing its decision on *Glanzer vs. Shepard* (135 N.E. 275) and stating "that the particular person who was to be influenced by defendants' act was unknown to the defendants is not material to a right to recovery, for it is not 'necessary that there should be an intent to defraud any particular person.'" But the Lower Court of Appeals threw out the charge of fraud holding that "Misjudgment, however gross, or want of caution, however marked, is not fraud and the mere breach of duty, or the omission of due care, is not fraud."

In the final decision, however, the Upper New York Court of Appeals reversed the lower court on both the charges of negligence and fraud and granted a new trial on the charge of fraud. The Court upheld privity of contract by affirming that ordinary negligence is bound to contracting parties, but it ruled that auditors can be held liable for their own *fraud. Glanzer vs. Shepard* involved the seller of beans requesting public weighers to furnish the buyers of beans with a certificate of weight. The court held that this bond was so close as to approach that of privity since the service rendered was primarily for the benefit of a third party. But with respect to the *Ultramares* case, the Court held that the service was primarily for the benefit of the Stern Company.

Justice Cardozo, in writing the Court's opinion, expressed his fear that:

> If liability for negligence exists, a thoughtless slip or blunder, the failure to detect a theft or forgery beneath the cover of deceptive entries, may expose accountants to a liability in an indeterminate amount for an indeterminate time to an indeterminate class.

"A change so revolutionary," he wrote, "must be wrought by legislation."

As a result of this case, privity became an essential requirement of any suit brought against an accountant by third parties and based on negligence.

On the other hand, the Court held in this case that "constructive fraud" exists if "gross negligence" is proven. The Court believed that gross negligence existed in this case because "in certifying to the correspondence between balance sheet and accounts the defendants made a statement as true to their own knowledge, when they had . . . no knowledge on the subject."

The court also made it clear that the partners of the firm are responsible for the supervision of their staff: "having delegated the performance of the work to agents of their own selection, the defendants are responsible."

RUSCH FACTORS, INC. vs. LEVIN*
(Companion Case to Ultramares)

In late 1963 a Rhode Island corporation sought financing from Rusch Factors, a New York banker and factor. In order to assess the financial stability of the corporation, Rusch Factors requested certified financial statements. Leonard Levin, a CPA, prepared statements representing the corporation to be solvent by a substantial amount. However, the corporation was in fact insolvent. The corporation submitted the financial statements to Rusch Factors, and relying upon them, it loaned the corporation amounts in excess of $337,000. The corporation soon went into receivership and Rusch Factors was able to recover only a portion of the loan to the corporation. Rusch Factors brought suit, claiming that it had been injured as a result of its reliance upon the fraudulent or negligent misrepresentations included in the financial statements certified by the defendant accountant. The defendant moved to dismiss on the basis that the absence of privity of contract between the defendant accountant and the plaintiff reliant party is a complete defense.

* 284 F Supp. 85 (1968)

The Court dismissed this motion. It cited *Ultramares* as demonstrating that privity of contract is clearly no defense in a fraud action and that an intentionally misrepresenting accountant is liable to all those persons whom he should reasonably have foreseen would be injured by his misrepresentation. It is not necessary for the accountant to have actual knowledge of the third person's reliance nor that there be a quantitative limitation of the class of reliant persons in order to have recovery for fraud. This broad perimeter also applies if "the misrepresenter's conduct" is heedless enough to permit an inference of fraud.

However, is the doctrine of privity of contract a defense against mere negligence? The Court noted that no appellate court, whether English or American, had ever held an accountant liable for negligence to reliant parties not in privity. But the Court noted that the wisdom at the *Ultramares* decision has been doubted and stated that: "This Court shares the doubt." To support its belief, the Court asked:

> Why should an innocent reliant party be forced to carry the weighty burden of an accountant's professional malpractice? Isn't the risk of loss more easily distributed and fairly spread by imposing it on the accounting profession which can pass the cost of insuring the risk onto its customers, who can in turn pass the cost onto the entire consuming public? Finally, wouldn't a rule of foreseeability elevate the cautionary techniques of the accounting profession?

For all of these reasons, the Court believed that the *Ultramares* decision constituted "an unwarranted inroad upon the principle that 'the risk reasonably to be perceived defines the duty to be obeyed.'"

Further weakening the *Ultramares* decision, stated the Court, was a recent United States District Court decision [*Fischer* vs. *Kletz*, 266 F. Supp. 180 (1967)] which held that accountants may have a common-law duty to disclose to the *investing and lending public* the discovery of misrepresentations in their already issued and circulated financial statements.

However, with regard to the *Rusch Factors* case, the Rhode Island state court held that it was not necessary to show that the Court would overrule the *Ultramares* decision if it had the opportunity, because the *Rusch Factors* case was more akin to *Glanzer vs. Shepard* than to *Ultramares*. Rusch Factors, Inc. was a single party whose reliance was actually foreseen by the defendant. In *Ultramares*, the plaintiff, was a member of an "undefined, unlimited class of remote lenders and potential equity holders not actually foreseen but only foreseeable."

The *Glanzer* principle as reported in the Restatement (Second) of Torts (paragraph 552) provides the following rule of law:

> One who, in the course of his business, profession or employment, or in a transaction in which he has a pecuniary interest, supplies false information for the guidance of others in their business transactions, is subject to liability for pecuniary loss caused to them by their justifiable reliance upon the information, if he fails to exercise reasonable care or competence in obtaining or communicating the information.

However, this liability is limited to loss suffered "by the person or one of the persons for whose benefit and guidance he intends to supply the information, or knows that the recipient intends to supply it; and through reliance upon it in a transaction which he intends the information to influence, or knows that the recipient so intends, or in a substantially similar transaction."

But this limitation does not apply in the following circumstances:

> The liability of one who is under a public duty to give the information extends to loss suffered by any of the class of persons for whose benefits the duty is created, in any of the transactions in which it is intended to protect them.

The Restatement (Second) of Torts provides the following hypothetical illustration of the above-stated rule of law:

> A is negotiating with a bank for a credit of $50,000. The bank requires an audit by certified public accountants. A employs B & Company, a firm of accountants, to make the audit, telling them he is going to negotiate a bank loan. A does not get his loan from the first bank but does negotiate a loan with another bank, which relies upon B & Company's certified statements. The audit carelessly overstates the financial resources of A, and in consequence the second bank suffers pecuniary loss. B & Company is subject to liability to the second bank.

In *Rusch Factors, Inc. vs. Levin*, the Court held that "an accountant should be liable in negligence for careless financial misrepresentations relied upon by actually foreseen and limited classes of persons." Because the defendant knew that "his certification was to be used for, and had as its very aim and purpose, the reliance of potential financiers of the Rhode Island corporation," the accountant is liable. However, the Court refused to rule upon the question of whether "an accountant's liability for negligent misrepresentation ought to extend to the full limits of foreseeability."

CASE QUESTIONS FOR RESEARCH AND DISCUSSION

1. With respect to an audit examination, what do the terms "negligence," "gross negligence," and "fraud" encompass?

2. In *Ernst & Ernst vs. Hochfelder*, the U.S. Supreme Court distinguishes the words "manipulative," "device," "contrivance," and "fraud," from the type of conduct that is described as "negligence." How does this interpretation affect the idea that "gross negligence" constitutes "constructive fraud?"

3. How was the doctrine of "privity" affected by the Securities Act of 1933?

4. How was the decreasing importance of the doctrine of "privity" indicated in *Rusch Factors, Inc. vs. Levin* (284 F. Supp. 85)?

5. What did the Court mean when it found in *Rusch Factors, Inc.* that "an accountant should be liable in negligence for careless financial misrepresentations relied upon by actually foreseen and limited classes of persons?"

6. What types of discoveries should reasonably lead an auditor to be suspicious of the representations made by management?

7. Is an accountant liable to third party creditors such as Ultramares under the Securities Exchange Act of 1934?

Quality Control
and Omitted Procedures

(Section 161, SAS No. 25 and Section 390, SAS No. 46)

Rule 202 of the AICPA *Code of Professional Ethics* requires CPAs to follow GAAS when conducting an examination of financial statements. SASs are considered interpretations of the ten GAAS and are, therefore, also covered by Rule 202.

THE AICPA DIVISION OF CPA FIRMS

The AICPA at its annual meeting held on September 17, 1977 approved a resolution establishing a division of CPA firms into two segments. These two segments or divisions are the "SEC Practice Section" and the "Private Companies Practice Section." CPA firms are eligible for membership on a voluntary basis in either or both divisions. The SEC Practice Section provides a basis for self-regulation by the profession of member firms through mandatory peer review, sanctions of firms by the AICPA, required rotation of partners in charge of audit engagements, reporting certain firm information to the public, and monitoring of all Section activities by an oversight board composed of public members. The goal of the SEC Practice Section is to improve the quality of auditing services offered to those business enterprises that are required to file financial statements with the SEC and report to the public.

The Private Practice Section also provides for self-regulation of its member firms through mandatory peer reviews and quality controls as well as sanctions of those firms that fail to meet membership requirements. An objective of the Private Practice Section is to provide a means for greater recognition of the different needs of smaller businesses and to provide for increased participation by local and regional CPA firms in AICPA matters. The Private Section has the goal of improving the quality of auditing services and accounting services offered to those business enterprises that are not required to file financial statements with the SEC or report to the public.

Many small or regional CPA firms achieve a level of quality control through membership in an association. These associations provide smaller CPA firms with many of the services that the larger national CPA firms make available to their local offices. Services provided include quality control review by association members, practice reviews, educational courses to update member firms on new accounting and auditing pronouncements and other matters, and, in certain instances, a centralized data bank for member firm convenience in researching practical accounting and auditing problems.

QUALITY CONTROL CONSIDERATIONS

SAS No. 25, *The Relationship of GAAS to Quality Control Standards*, superseded SAS No. 4 (which originally established elements of quality control for a firm of CPAs) because of the establishment of a new technical committee by the AICPA to establish quality control standards for CPA firms. SAS No. 25 recognizes the AICPA Quality Control Standards Committee and the senior technical committee of the AICPA to issue pronouncements on quality control standards. SAS No. 25 also states that a firm of CPAs must comply with GAAS in conducting an audit practice.

Accordingly, a CPA firm should establish quality control policies and procedures to provide it with reasonable assurance of conforming with GAAS in its audit engagements. A CPA firm will, of course, look to the guidance provided by Statements on Quality Control in establishing such standards. *Statement on Quality Control Standards* No. 1 identifies the elements of quality control (as originally presented in SAS No. 4) that a CPA firm should consider.

ELEMENTS OF QUALITY CONTROL

Independence

Policies and procedures should be established to provide reasonable assurance that persons at all organizational levels maintain independence in fact and in appearance.

Assigning Personnel to Engagements

Policies and procedures for assigning personnel to engagements should be established to provide reasonable assurance that audit work will be performed by persons having the degree of technical training and proficiency required in the circumstances. In making assignments, the nature and extent of supervision to be provided should be considered. Generally, the more able and experienced the personnel assigned to a particular engagement, the less is the need for direct supervision.

Consultation

Policies and procedures for consultation should be established to provide reasonable assurance that auditors will seek assistance on accounting and auditing questions, to the extent required, from persons having appropriate levels of knowledge, competence, judgment, and authority. The nature of the arrangements for consultation will depend on a number of factors, including the size of the accounting firm and the levels of knowledge, competence, and judgment possessed by the persons performing the work.

Supervision

Policies and procedures for the conduct and supervision of work at all organizational levels should be established to provide reasonable assurance that the work performed meets the firm's standards of quality. The extent of supervision and review appropriate in a given instance depends on many factors, including the complexity of the subject matter, the qualifications of the persons performing the work, and the extent of consultation available and used.

Hiring

Policies and procedures for hiring should be established to provide reasonable assurance that those employed possess the appropriate characteristics to enable them to perform competently. The quality of a firm's work ultimately depends on the integrity, competence, and motivation of those who perform and supervise the work. Thus, a firm's recruiting programs are factors in maintaining audit quality.

Professional Development

Policies and procedures for professional development should be established to provide reasonable assurance that personnel will have the knowledge required to enable them to fulfill responsibilities assigned. Continuing professional education and training activities enable a firm to provide personnel with the knowledge required to fulfill responsibilities assigned to them and to progress within the firm.

Advancement

Policies and procedures for advancing professional personnel should be established to provide reasonable assurance that the people selected will have the qualifications necessary for fulfillment of the responsibilities they will be called on to assume. Practices in advancing personnel have important implications for the quality of audit work. Qualifications that people selected for advancement should possess include, but are not limited to, character, intelligence, judgment and motivation.

Acceptance and Continuance of Clients

Policies and procedures should be established for deciding whether to accept or continue a client in order to minimize the likelihood of association with a client whose management lacks integrity. Suggesting that there should be procedures for this purpose does not imply that an auditor vouches for the integrity or reliability of a client, nor does it imply that an auditor has a duty to anyone but himself with respect to the acceptance, rejection, or retention of clients. However, prudence suggests that an auditor be selective in determining professional relationships.

Inspection

Policies and procedures for inspection should be established to provide reasonable assurance that the other procedures designed to maintain the quality of the firm's auditing practice are being effectively applied. Procedures for inspection may be developed and performed by persons acting on behalf of the firm's management. The type of inspection procedures used will depend on the controls a firm establishes.

Omitted Procedures

SAS No. 46, "Consideration of Omitted Procedures After the Report Date," explains the course of action that the auditor should pursue when he or she discovers, after the completion of an examination of financial statements and the issuance of the audit report, that an auditing procedure(s) considered necessary in the circumstances of the engagement was omitted. Discovery of such circumstances in an audit engagement may result from a quality control review of audit work by audit staff or by an external quality control review team.

SAS No. 46 does not apply to situations in which the auditor's work is being questioned in a threatened or pending legal proceeding or regulatory investigation.

If information comes to the auditor's attention subsequent to the date of the audit report indicating that the statements he or she reported on may be false or misleading, the auditor should follow the guidance in Section 561, SAS No. 1, "Subsequent Discovery of Facts Existing at the Date of the Auditor's Report," as discussed in part 20 of this text.

Once an auditor has reported on financial statements, there is no responsibility to make further inquiry or to review the audit work. However, when an omitted procedure(s) is identified the auditor should assess the importance of the omitted procedure(s) in support of the previously expressed opinion. Because of legal implications, the auditor is advised to consult with an attorney to determine an appropriate course of action. If the auditor concludes that the evidence that would have been provided by the omitted procedure(s) is critical for support of his or her opinion on the financial statements, the auditor should undertake to perform the omitted procedure(s) or alternative procedures.

If omitted procedures are discovered during the performance of interim or year-end audit work for subsequent period-financial statements, the omitted procedures may be performed at that time.

Omitted Audit Procedures

Thomas R. Weirich, CPA, Ph.D. and Elizabeth J. Ringelberg, CPA

The likelihood of identifying omitted procedures after the auditor has issued the audit report has increased as a result of recent quality control policies, such as a firm's internal inspection progam or a peer review. It may be determined, after the audit report has been issued, that a situation may exist in which the audit has not been performed in accordance with Generally Accepted Auditing Standards (GAAS), but where there is no evidence that the financial statements have not been prepared in accordance with Generally Accepted Accounting Principles (GAAP). Such a situation has often caused a dilemma for the auditor.

Background

In 1981, at the request of the chairman of the Executive Committee of the SEC Practice Section of the AICPA's Division for CPA Firms, the Auditing Standards Board (ASB) assigned a task force to study the matter. The ASB's task force considered the appropriateness of various methods in addressing this issue, including: the issuance of an interpretation of existing auditing literature; the issuance of non-authoritative guidance through an article in the *Journal of Accountancy*; the referral of the issue to the Quality Control Standards Committee, the Peer Review Committee, or the Ethics Division; or providing no guidance at all.

During its deliberations, the ASB discussed the applicability of the procedures and considerations that were described in the proposed SAS, "Subsequent Discovery of Failure to Apply Procedures Ordinarily Considered Necessary in the Circumstances," to both omitted procedures and failure to apply GAAS in the broader sense. The ASB concluded that the scope of the proposed SAS should address only omitted procedures. Also, the Board agreed that the guidance in the proposed SAS would be referred to only when the auditor has determined that an omitted procedure would have influenced his/her report on the audited financial statements.

After much discussion of the appropriate method to implement in addressing the issue, the ASB in June, 1982 decided that issuing an SAS would be the most suitable means of handling this matter. Thus, in September, 1983 the ASB issued *Statement on Auditing Standards—No. 46—"Consideration of Omitted Procedures After the Report Date."*

The purpose of this article is to present a practical analysis and summary of this newly issued SAS and contrast the new SAS with SAS No. 1, Sec. 561, which applies to discovery of facts, subsequent to the date of the audit report, that might have affected the report had their existence been known.

HEADNOTE: Increasing attention to quality control on professional engagements gives rise to dealing with omissions of auditing procedures, discovered after a report has been issued. The authors present an analysis of SAS 46 and their suggestions for dealing with specific problems raised in that statement. Readers are referred to related articles in our Accounting and Auditing department columns of January and February 1984.

Thomas R. Weirich, CPA, Ph.D., is Professor of Accounting at Central Michigan University. He is a member of the AICPA, Missouri Society of CPAs, and AAA. He also serves on the editorial advisory board of the Journal of Accountancy. *He is the author of the text* Accounting and Auditing Research: A Practical Guide. *Elizabeth J. Ringelberg, CPA, is an Instructor of Accounting at Central Michigan University. She is a member of the AICPA and Michigan Association of CPAs. She was also a staff auditor with Coopers & Lybrand.*

SAS No. 46

Audit guidance is now provided to the auditor who discovers, after issuing the audit report, that certain procedures were omitted that would have been considered necessary in the examination of the financial statements. Figure 1 presents a flowchart of the guidance provided in SAS No. 46. On discovery of one or more omitted auditing procedures, the auditor is first advised to consult with legal counsel to determine an appropriate course of action in light of the potential legal implications.

. . . guidance . . . only when . . . an omitted procedure would have influenced his/her report . . .

After consulting legal counsel, the importance of the omitted procedure to the auditor's ability to support the audit opinion with sufficient, competent evidential matter under GAAS must be assessed. Procedures such as reviewing work papers, discussing the omitted procedures with engagement personnel and others knowlegeable of the client, and re-evaluating the overall scope of the examination as to the sufficiency and competence of evidence gathered may aid in this assessment. These steps may identify audit procedures that were applied that tend to compensate for, or make less significant, the one or more omitted procedures.

Example 1. During a firm's internal inspection review of an audit of client X in a depressed industry, the reviewers questioned the thoroughness of inventory obsolesence procedures. Specific procedures considered appropriate in the circumstances were not conducted by the auditors. Considering SAS No. 46, the firm re-evaluated the scope of the examination and reviewed in detail the completed audit workpapers. The conclusion reached was that compensating audit procedures were conducted and considered sufficient to support the valuation of the inventory and the previously expressed audit opinion. Therefore, the questioned omitted procedures were not performed.

If, after a thorough investigation of possible procedures that would compensate in some way for the omitted procedure(s), the auditor concludes that his present ability to support his previously expressed opinion is impaired, he should determine if there are persons relying or likely to be relying on the audit report. If it seems reasonable that there may be persons relying on the audit report, the auditor should promptly undertake to apply the omitted procedure(s), or to perform alternative procedures that would provide a satisfatory basis for his opinion.

Example 2. As required by SAS No. 19, the auditors of client Y obtained a client representation letter. However, during a peer review being conducted in the subsequent period, it was brought to the auditing firm's attention that the client representation letter was from a management company for client Y rather than directly from the client's own management.

Aware of the fact that third parties were still relying on the audited financial statements and the requirement of SAS No. 19, the auditors concluded that a new client representation letter should be obtained on client Y's letterhead signed by the client's management.

Application of the omitted procedure(s) or the alternative procedures may lead the auditor to become aware of facts related to the financial statements. If these facts existed at the report date, the auditor should refer to Sec. 561 of SAS 1 *Subsequent Discovery of Facts Existing at the Date of the Auditor's Report* for further guidance. At times, circumstances may preclude the performance of the omitted procedure or alternatives. In this situation, the auditor should consult with his attorney to plan a course of action with regard to the auditor's responsibilities to his client, regulatory authorities having jurisdiction over the client, and third party persons relying or likely to rely on the audit report. The auditor, in consultation with his legal counsel, may conclude that a revised report qualifying or disclaiming an opinion may be more appropriate than the previously released report. SAS No. 46, unlike Sec. 561 of SAS No. 1, does not provide guidance or directives on revised reports.

Example 3. In auditing client Z, the auditors were aware of the fact that the client maintained both computerized and manual checking accounts. When the auditors completed their search for unrecorded liabilities, only the computerized checking account was investigated. However, during subsequent interim work, the auditors discovered that, if the manual checking account had been analyzed, additional material unrecorded liabilities might have been disclosed.

. . . circumstances may preclude the performance of the omitted procedure or alternatives.

The auditors concluded that third parties could still be relying on the audited financial statements and audit report and, therefore, decided that the omitted procedures related to the manual checking account be conducted. After performing the omitted procedures, additional material unrecorded liabilities were disclosed; thus the auditors followed the guidelines stated in SAS No. 1, Sec. 561 concerning the subsequent discovery of facts.

Section 561: SAS No. 1

Sec. 561 of SAS No. 1 provides guidance to the auditor who discovers after issuing the audit report, facts that may have existed at the report date which relate to the audited financial statements. Figure 2 flowcharts Sec. 561. This section is to be distinguished from the "subsequent events"

FIGURE 1

STATEMENT ON AUDITING STANDARDS NO. 46

**"CONSIDERATION OF OMITTED PROCEDURES
AFTER THE REPORT DATE"**

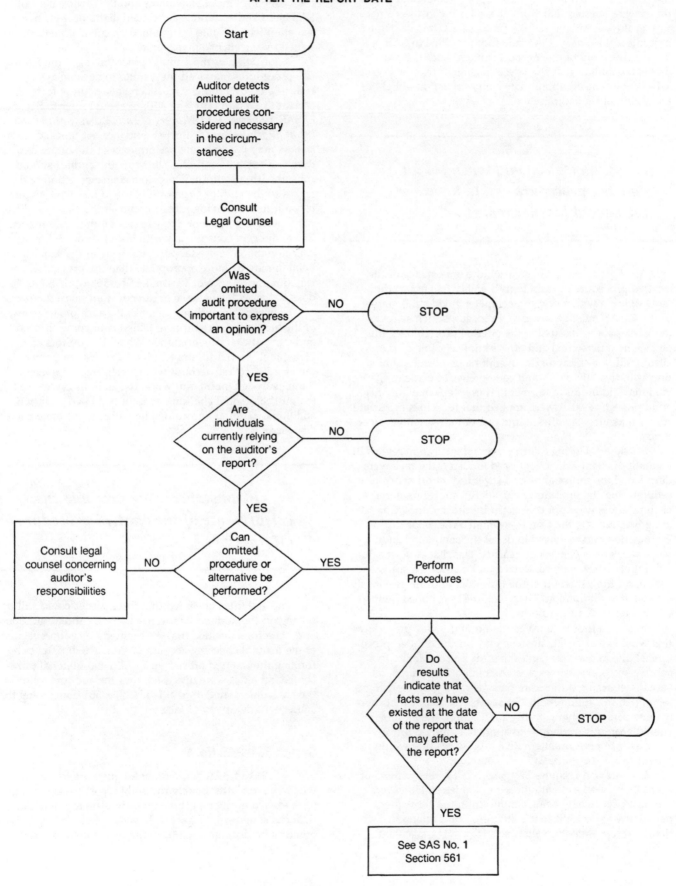

FIGURE 2

STATEMENT ON AUDITING STANDARDS NO. 1 SECTION 561

"SUBSEQUENT DISCOVERY OF FACTS EXISTING AT THE DATE OF THE AUDITOR'S REPORT"

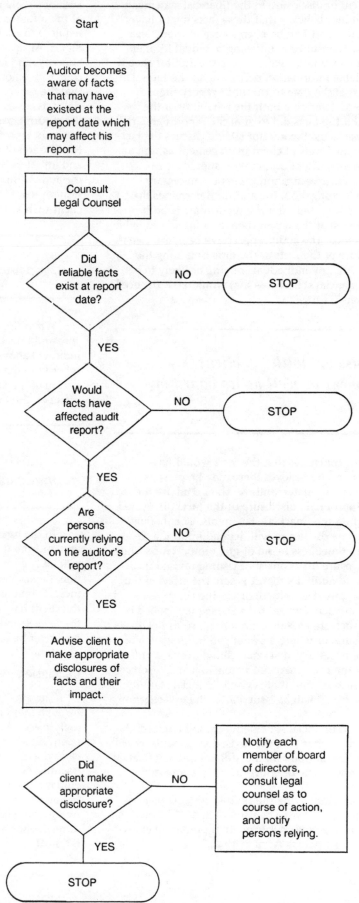

addressed in SAS No. 1, Sec. 560, in which events or transactions may occur subsequent to the balance sheet date, but prior to the issuance of the audit report. Such events may require adjustment or disclosure in the financial statements.

Once the auditor believes that these facts might have affected the audit report had he been aware of them, legal counsel should be consulted concerning potential legal implications. After consulting legal counsel, the auditor should investigate available information pertaining to the facts that may have existed at the date of the audit report. Steps should be taken to determine both the reliability of the information and if the facts did exist at the report date. In undertaking these steps, the auditor should discuss the matter with appropriate levels of client management as well as its board of directors. Client cooperation should be requested in whatever investigation is deemed necessary.

If, after the investigation, the auditor determines that the information discovered after the report date is both reliable and did exist at the report date, two facts need to be considered: (a) Would the audit report have been affected if he had been aware of the facts at the time of issuing the report?; and (b) Are any individuals relying or likely to be relying on the financial statements that would be influenced by these new facts?

. . . discuss . . . with . . . client management as well as its board of directors.

If the auditor concludes that the facts would have affected the report and he believes there may be persons relying on the financial statements, he should advise the client to make appropriate disclosure of the facts discovered and their impact on the financial statements. The method used for appropriate disclosure will depend upon the circumstances, with timeliness being of great importance. Thus appropriate disclosure may consist of issuing revised financial statements and auditor's report where the effect of the facts can be promptly determined; disclosing the revision with financial statements issued for a subsequent period if the issuance of such statements is imminent, so as not to delay the disclosure; or where a prolonged investigation of the facts may be necessary, disclosure should consist of notification that the prior financial statements and report should not be relied on and that revised financial statements and audit report will be issued after the investigation is completed.

Where revised financial statements are to be issued, the auditors' report accompanying the revised statements would read as follows: "In our opinion, the aforementioned financial statements, revised as described in Note X, present fairly . . ."

The report accompanying the revised statements may be redated or dual dating may be used such as: "February 4, 19__, except as to the revised information presented in Note X for which the date is April 2, 19__."

The auditor should take steps to determine whether the client has made adequate disclosure in the circumstances. If the client refuses to make the appropriate disclosure, the auditor should notify each member of the board of directors of the refusal and inform them that the auditor is now required to take steps to prevent future reliance on the audit report. At this time, the auditor should consult with his attorney, and unless the attorney suggests an alternative course of action, the auditor should: (a) notify the client that the report must no longer be associated with the financial statements; (b) notify regulating agencies not to rely on the report, and (c) notify persons relying or likely to rely on the audit report that the report should not be relied on. Notification of persons likely to rely, such as stockholders and investors at large, whose identities are not known to the auditor, may be appropriately carried out through notification to a regulatory agency having jurisdiction over the client such as the SEC.

. . . timeliness being of great importance.

When the client refuses to make the appropriate disclosure and thus the auditor is required to make disclosure as indicated above, the content of the disclosure to parties other than the client should include a description of the nature of the subsequently acquired information and of its effect on the financial statements.

. . . determine whether the client has made adequate disclosure . . .

In the case where the auditor, because of lack of cooperation from the client, has not been able to substantiate the reliability or lack of reliability of the subsequent information, details need not be specific. The auditor may simply indicate that information has come to his attention which the client has not cooperated in substantiating, and that if the facts so indicate, the auditor believes his report should no longer be relied on.

Conclusion

The attempts by the profession to enhance quality through internal inspection and peer review have increasingly placed auditors in the position of encountering "subsequent discovery" information. Such a position has often caused a dilemma as to what procedures to follow. With the issuance of SAS No. 46 and Sec. 561 of SAS No. 1 as guidance to the auditor, such anxiety may be reduced. It is important to note, however, the distinction between these two pronouncements. SAS No. 46 relates to "omitted procedures," whereas SAS No. 1, Sec. 561 relates to "omitted facts." Ω

CASE 3

QUALITY CONTROL CONSIDERATIONS

Smith & Jones, CPAs, have practiced public accounting in a medium-sized midwestern town since 1955. Since its inception, the firm has grown steadily both in terms of gross billings and by type of clients served. Due to the firm's growth, Smith & Jones have added new staff accountants and admitted new partners into the firm. By 1974 the firm had ten partners and thirty-five staff accountants. During the initial twenty years of practice, the partners were well acquainted with each other, their staff, and the clients served by their accounting practice. Because of the size of their practice and personal relationships, the firm's partners did not feel there was a need for formal (written) policies regarding quality control of their practice. However, in the last four years the firm's gross billings have more than doubled. In addition, the firm now has twenty partners and seventy-five staff accountants (the firm has remained a local—one office—firm). Because of the rapid growth experienced in the past five years, the partners have been unable to remain as knowledgeable as they would like to be in such matters as acceptance and continuance of clients, professional development, supervision at the various staff levels and advancement of professional staff. Furthermore, the firm has no formal policies and procedures for assigning personnel to engagements or in hiring new staff members.

J. Jones (affectionately known as J.J.), a partner, has been asked by his associates to develop a plan for adopting a formal quality control program within the firm. This request arose from several situations that have been embarrassing with respect to both old and new clients served by the firm. The following situations are indicative of some of the problems experienced by the firm:

A manager on an engagement accepted an expensive gift from an officer in the client company.

A partner was assigned to an engagement where a close relative was an officer in the company.

A staff member who had been with the firm for two years was found, by accident, to have served a prison sentence for embezzlement.

An engagement was accepted that required timely reporting by the client and the firm subsequently discovered that it did not have qualified staff available to complete the engagement on a timely basis.

As a result of a continuing education program conducted for the firm's personnel, it was revealed that performance of audit procedures and documentation of working papers was often grossly inadequate.

Training and professional development was found to be so lacking within the firm that most of the staff and several of the partners were having difficulty meeting the state's continuing education requirements.

The firm does not have any standards regarding acceptance and continuance of clients and as a result the firm has a few clients which they are not fully qualified to serve.

CASE DISCUSSION QUESTIONS

1. For each of the following identified elements of quality control, discuss the quality control policies and procedures that would be appropriate for a local (one office) CPA firm. Indicate which policies and procedures would best serve to prevent the recurrence of the kinds of problems identified in the case with respect to Smith & Jones:

   a. Independence.

   b. Assigning personnel to engagements.

   c. Consultation.

   d.   Supervision.

   e.   Hiring.

   f.   Professional development.

   g.   Advancement.

   h.   Acceptance and continuance of clients.

   i.   Inspection.

2. As indicated in the case, Smith & Jones are having problems in performing appropriate audit procedures and documenting work papers. In a particular engagement, for example, a subsequent review of working papers plainly showed that the sample size selected for confirmation of accounts receivable was not nearly as large as it should have been considering risk factors, materiality levels, and the degree of planned reliance on this audit test.

   How should Smith and Jones deal with this known audit deficiency?

4

The General Standards

(Sections 201, 210, 220, and 230, SAS No. 1)

The general standards are personal in nature and relate to the professional qualifications of the auditor and the quality of work performed. The first general standard is:

> The examination is to be performed by a person having adequate technical training and proficiency
> as an auditor

Proficiency in accounting practice and auditing procedures is attained by a combination of formal education and experience. As with any profession, the quality of judgment or proficiency demanded in public accounting varies with the level of experience of the auditor. A partner, for example, is expected to exercise a much higher level of judgment or proficiency than a relatively new staff person. Continuing professional education and training are necessary to maintain and improve the skills and knowledge of the auditor.

Independence is the second general standard. It requires that:

> In all matters relating to the assignment, an independence in mental attitude is to be maintained by
> the auditor or auditors

Independence requires that the auditor be free from any bias. The auditor must not have any obligation to or interest in the client and maintain independence in both fact and appearance. Independence, however, does not imply the attitude of a prosecutor but rather a judicial impartiality that recognizes an obligation for fairness not only to the management and owners of a business but also to its creditors and to those who may otherwise rely (in part, at least) upon the auditor's report. Maintaining the confidence of the general public in the independence of the CPA is of the utmost importance to the profession. The CPA's attestation to the fairness of financial statements, which is the foundation of the public accounting profession, would be meaningless without public confidence in the independence of the CPA. Public confidence would be impaired by evidence that independence was actually lacking, and it might also be impaired by the existence of circumstances which reasonable people might believe likely to influence independence.

The profession, being unable to measure independence in fact, establishes rules to guard against the presumption of an apparent loss of independence (AICPA *Code of Professional Ethics*, Rule 101). A CPA must be intellectually honest to be independent. To be recognized as independent, the CPA must be free from any obligation or interest in the client, its management, or its owners. For example, a CPA examining the financial statements of a client while simultaneously serving as a director of the company might be intellectually honest, but it is unlikely that third parties would accept the CPA as being independent since the CPA would be in effect auditing decisions which he or she had participated in making. Likewise, an auditor with a substantial financial interest in a client might be unbiased in expressing an opinion on the financial statements, but the public might not view the CPA as unbiased.

In emphasizing independence from management, the auditor should be appointed by the board of directors and this appointment should be ratified by the stockholders.

Due professional care is the third general standard. It requires that:

> Due professional care is to be exercised in the performance of the examination and the preparation of the report

Due care requires that each individual in a CPA firm observe the standards of field work and reporting. It requires critical review at each level of supervision (senior, manager, and partner). Due care encompasses the concept that the CPA holds himself out to the public as possessing the degree of skill commonly possessed by professional accountants and that the CPA undertakes to perform with good faith and integrity, but not infallibility. The CPA is liable for negligence in applying professional standards, bad faith, and dishonesty. The CPA is not, however, responsible for losses due to pure errors of judgment unless negligence can be demonstrated. The matter of due care concerns what the CPA does in the course of performing the examination and how well it is done. For example, due care in the matter of working papers requires that working paper content be sufficient to support the CPA's opinion and the representations as to compliance with GAAS.

ACCOUNTING & AUDITING PROBLEMS

EDITOR:

JOE R. FRITZEMEYER, CPA
Director, Auditing and Reporting
American Institute of CPAs

ASSOCIATE EDITOR:

DOUGLAS R. CARMICHAEL, CPA
Assistant Director,
Auditing and Reporting
American Institute of CPAs

Competence and Independence in Auditing

Independence and competence are standards central to the profession's performance of the auditing function. In the following discussion, A. R. WYATT, CPA, Arthur Andersen & Co., emphasizes the continual need to re-examine these standards in the light of the profession's responsibility to the public. Following this discussion are several Accounting Interpretations on the investment credit, the Ohio corporation franchise tax and accounting for leveraged leases.

THE standards of competency and independence established by the accounting profession are interrelated and of vital significance. Any professional group that merits the label of "profession" must espouse and enforce the highest possible standards of competency for its members. Minimum levels must be established for entry, with the professional group thereafter assuming responsibility for continual upgrading. The accounting profession has developed standards of competency, independence and professional development insofar as the auditing phase of accountants' services are concerned.

Many accounting firms have in recent years extended their services into areas, such as production, marketing, personnel evaluation and insurance, which are only indirectly related, if at all, to the real competency of the auditor. Efforts by the profession to establish boundaries for practices in nonauditing and nonaccounting areas have been largely ineffective. Likewise, the profession has no real standards of competency for many services rendered by public accountants outside of the traditional auditing area.

While controversy reigns as to the role the profession should play in establishing standards in those ex-

tended areas of service, the fact remains that the public users of the accountants' services have every right to expect a professional level of competency regardless of the particular service rendered. Certainly the third-party user cannot be expected to attribute professional competency to certain services and a lesser degree of competence to other services performed by a professional.

Competency

The users of the services of an auditing firm expect the auditor to have the level of competency in performing his services that has become associated over the years with professionals generally. The public deals directly with attorneys, doctors, teachers, the clergy, etc., and these professional groups help establish in the minds of the public a level of competency which can be reasonably expected from professionals. This level of competency stops short of perfection; not even the professional is viewed as infallible. The focus of competency may well center more on the manner in which the services are performed by the professional than on the absolute end result. Thus, if the attorney thoroughly researches a case, if he explores all reasonable avenues for presenting his client's position most favorably, the client may be satisfied with the competency demonstrated even if the arguments made do not prevail. Likewise, not all of a doctor's patients recover, but so long as the doctor makes every reasonable effort to diagnose the case thoroughly and follows a reasonable course of treatment and medication, his competency will be unquestioned even if the patient dies.

Similarly, the auditor should be expected to demonstrate a professional level of competency in the conduct of every audit. In addition, clearly articulated standards of performance may well be more necessary for the auditor than for other professionals because the auditor in performing his services does not deal directly with many who use such services. All that many of the third-party users see is the end result, the auditor's report. The user is not normally in a position to observe the manner in which the auditor carries out his examination.

Thus, while all professionals concentrate on the actual performance of their services in a manner which demonstrates their competency, auditors must go beyond mere performance of services in a competent manner; they must also develop and articulate in understandable terms positive standards of performance. The standards developed must be responsive to the needs and expectations of the public as best they can be perceived. In addition, auditors must not only perform their services in accordance with these standards, but also must maintain a record of having done so in order to support, if called upon, the basis for the opinion rendered.

Any policy adopted by a profession as to standards of competency can be effective only if those standards conform to the reasonable expectations of those who use the professional's services. Protestations that standards of competency pertain only to the auditing services, those leading to an expression of opinion on financial statements, are unsupportable. The public's reasonable expectations as to competency, recognizing the competency levels they have been conditioned to expect in the auditing area over many years, are paramount.

The accounting profession must move quickly to identify those services which accountants can be expected to render at the level of competency established by past services rendered. Likewise, the profession must urge its members to discontinue any services for which these competency standards cannot be attained. Failure to move in these directions can result in loss of confidence by users in the entire range of services, audit and otherwise, rendered by auditors. Or, such failure can result in establishment of standards, or restrictions on services, by agencies outside the profession which may be undesirable from either the profession's or the public's view.

Independence

Interwoven with this problem of competency standards in areas of service other than auditing is the relationship of the standard of independence to these additional areas of service. The concept of independence for the accounting profession is unique in relation to other professions. Likewise, the independence standard is considered to be of critical significance by the accounting profession.

Independence in Auditing Services. The independence standard of the accounting profession is stated: "In all matters relating to the assignment an independence in mental attitude is to be maintained by the auditor or auditors." Meeting this standard involves several dimensions, but as far as auditing services are concerned, independence in all its dimensions is essential. This necessity is a unique aspect of the accounting profession and arises from the role in society which the accounting profession has undertaken to assume and which society—to date at least—has been content to permit the public accountant to fill. This role involves a challenge which is significantly different from that facing practitioners in other professions, namely the rendering of satisfactory services to clients (who pay the fees) and at the same time meeting the needs of nonclient users of financial information for dependable and reliable data. Thus, the auditor must act somewhat in the role of both attorney and judge, i.e., he serves his client but at the same time provides the public assurance as to fairness, an assurance that the courts provide in legal matters. Client pressures can become severe, but even in the face of such pressures the public's interest must be primary.

The burden imposed on the auditor in this connection is substantial. As concerns his client, the auditor many times must present analyses of alternatives which are objective and thorough, yet which are responsive to the client's needs. Many requests are made of an auditor by his client for advice and counsel in financial, accounting and related matters. The advice so rendered must be that which the auditor considers most closely attuned to his client's goals and objectives. At the same time, the auditor must adopt an independent stature on matters which affect the fairness of financial presentation. At times the auditor and his client may violently disagree on a financial presentation matter. In such a circumstance the auditor must recognize the primacy of his role as public guardian of fair financial presentations. Under all circumstances, however, the auditor would emphasize that his role is one of developing and analyzing information and expressing opinions, whereas management has the ultimate responsibility for making decisions.

The independence posture of the auditor is unique as far as the public is concerned. Other professionals do adopt regularly a posture of objectivity, e.g., a surgeon not operating on a member of his family, but the thrust of the objectivity standard is mainly toward the professional's client. The independence standard for auditors is necessary, however, largely because of the use of auditors' services by third parties. Professionals generally may be viewed as bringing an objective and competent force to bear on a problem situation. For the auditor the impact of objectivity or independence may be relatively greater because so many third-party users are involved.

The public may equate reputation and independence to some degree so that if a given auditor or auditing firm has developed a good reputation his independence would not normally be called into question. The public is likely far less concerned with the particulars of independence which the accounting profession establishes than it is concerned with the de facto independence of the auditor. Therefore, if the auditor is in fact independent, if he in fact strives constantly to maintain his independence, and if his actions and relationships as viewed by the public reflect his professional and independent nature, he will continually re-establish such a reputation in the public's eye.

Independence in Other Services. Independence is a characteristic the public expects, possibly even demands, insofar as the auditors' reports on financial statements are concerned. Today, however, the existing standard of independence is being challenged on many sides as auditors' services extend into nontraditional areas. Some say that independence is necessary only in connection with opinions on financial statements and that independence is not significant for other services. Others reason that a lack of independence on any service for a client casts doubt on one's ability to be independent in connection with a different service.

Many of the special services which accountants offer to their clients today may appear to outsiders virtually to require an attitude of nonindependence, of advocacy. The question emerges, of course, as to how the public accountant can be an advocate of a client one day and independent when giving his opinions as to fairness of financial presentations the following day. The conflict between advocacy and independence remains unresolved. One suggestion is to limit auditors' services to that of giving opinions on financial statements. Further analysis, however, leads one to conclude that this suggestion is undoubtedly too restrictive and not necessarily in the best interests of any of the parties involved.

The real danger to loss of independence is that the auditor will move far beyond his traditional functions and become too involved in the area of the so-called special or management services. This danger is twofold: (1) that such services may be so remotely related to the basic practice of independent public accountants as to cast serious doubt on competency to perform at a level equal to the professional reputation associated with auditing and (2) that such services will become involved with client operations to such an extent that public accountants are in reality making management decisions. Serious impairment of the auditor's independence can certainly result if he is an active participant in his client's decision-making. Likewise, serious impairment of the auditor's reputation for competent professional service can result if he ventures into areas of service for which his competency is not clearly established.

The need for the accounting profession to meet aggressively the interwoven issues of independence, competency and special services is critical. A clear and forthright statement of policy is needed which would limit the services of auditors to participation in the collection, analysis and communication of economic information and to participation in the development and installation of systems to provide data to be appraised by management or other qualified users in making informed operating, financial or other decisions. Further, additional interpretation of the independence standard is necessary to make positive that the making of, or the appearance of making, decisions for management or the substituting of his judgment for that of management puts the auditor in the position of violating the independence standard. The range of services offered by public accountants has changed considerably over the past twenty years, and with such changes comes the need to reappraise the several dimensions of professional responsibility. In this broad area of independence the time for reappraisal may be growing critically short.

Other Aspects of Independence. As the accounting profession comes to recognize more fully the increasing impact of its services resulting from the needs of the widely expanded group of third-party users, independence may need to be viewed in a broader context than in the past. The concept of independence may need to embrace newer aspects of the auditor's responsibilities to the expanded body of third-party users as opposed to his direct client, the company under audit.

For example, the profession's literature is mostly silent on the extent of responsibility of the auditor to "ring the bell," so to speak, when he finds a management abrogating the trust placed in it. While the auditor may resign his engagement and may provide sufficiently vague explanations of his reasons for resigning as to cast doubt on the situation, no substantive position of the profession has been expressed for this type of situation.

One can doubt that the mass of third-party users who have become conditioned to place substantial reliance on the auditor and his independent status would conclude that the auditor had met fully his responsibilities, that he was in fact independent, if resignation was the only action taken. The profession needs to express a forthright position to interpret this aspect of its responsibilities so that all interested parties may understand fully the auditor's position in such circumstances.

One suggestion that appears to possess substantial merit in helping the auditing profession bridge the gap between its direct client, the board of directors (stockholders) of the company being audited, and the broad group of third-party users is the establishment of audit committees of boards of directors. It is desirable that audit committees should consist at least in part of "outside directors," i.e., directors not a part of the management group. One function of an audit committee would be to serve as a reporting unit to which the auditor could turn on a timely basis to report adverse developments or other matters of genuine interest to all who may have an interest in the financial affairs of the company. While many boards of directors have established such audit committees to assist them in meeting their responsibilities to their shareholders, the general concept of such committees and the role they could play in adding assurance to the timely dissemination of reliable financial information is as yet largely undeveloped.

To the extent the accounting profession has been slow to act on some of these matters, the inaction may reflect a somewhat natural fear of expanding its legal liability beyond that which appears predictable based on existing statutes and past cases. The problems will not go away, however, and the profession can hardly expect to come off more favorably in the eyes of the court if it has failed to give prompt attention to knotty problems having a public impact.

Likewise, unilateral actions which are self-serving in nature and attempt to limit responsibility or liability cannot be successful. Wider service and wider influence bring with them wider responsibilities and tougher problems. The public's interest will be served in some manner, but the accounting profession's chances for effective and positive action diminish as time passes.

Evolving Standards

The explosion in public ownership of American businesses has generated a broadened interest in financial data so that today in most audit engagements leading to the expression of an opinion on financial representations the auditor's most substantive user is the public. To the extent that the auditor's direct client appears to be the central interest in present-day standards, one can recognize that this bias represents an influence from earlier environments. To the extent that present standards fail to reflect the increased real interest of the public, one can recognize an "evolutionary lag" similar to that which prevails in many other areas of our society—a lag in adapting fully to changing environmental demands. Historical perspective also provides evidence that progress toward fulfillment of objectives is not always steady. Sometimes dramatic, or even tragic, events have been necessary to spur notable progress. Hopefully, the accounting profession can overcome evolutionary lag without having to experience any such dramatic or tragic events.

All parties interested in financial presentations need greater understanding that the accountant primarily reports on economic and financial data. Business managements make the decisions which culminate in the transactions that produce the economic facts. The accountant reports on these facts; he does not make them. At times the reporting accountants may obscure the facts or may mislead the reader. If so, the facts as they exist lose significance, and the reporting of them may be accepted as the facts themselves. Eventually, the inadequacies of the representations that have been made will be recognized. At this point accountants will find that the responsibility for fair assessment of the economic facts cannot be avoided.

Public expectations are high. The public likely does not understand the significance of the phrase "generally accepted accounting principles." Fairness means absence of bias. It means reflective of facts. It means representative of significant factual relationships. Fairness is a standard the public expects of any professional.

Standards of accounting that result in anything less than the fairest possible reflection of factual relationships fail to meet the public's justifiable expectations and needs. The accounting profession will achieve the real fulfillment of its role in our economic society only as the responsibilities it shoulders in its daily practice harmonize with the standards the public expects.

Concluding Remarks

In summary, the accounting profession must review on a continuing basis its standards and its performance. Certainly, some comfort can be gained from the existing level of acceptance and recognition which the public has for the services rendered by the accounting profession. But new challenges make such comfort transitory. Can the accounting profession continue to assert its own level of responsibilities, e.g., independence, auditing standards, etc.? It can only if these pronouncements remain responsive to the needs of clients in the broad sense, including interested third-party users of audited financial information. The investing public can be powerful, and failure or inability to meet its needs would produce consequences far more severe than those faced by public accountants in simpler times. Many areas exist for clarification of responsibilities and for development of new and positive philosophies. The primary responsibility of the accounting profession is to the public. Forthright recognition of this fact is essential. Positive positions accepting the responsibility expected by the public are a necessity; self-serving attempts to limit unilaterally responsibilities assumed must be eliminated. After all, if the accounting profession is truly a profession, no alternative philosophy is possible.

CASE 4

THE QUALIFICATIONS OF THE AUDITOR

Georgia Stevens was graduated from an accredited university, earning a Bachelor's degree in accounting. She passed the CPA examination in the final quarter of her senior year at the University. After two years' experience with Arthur Price & Co., CPAs, she was awarded her CPA certificate.

To date, Georgia's experience with Arthur Price & Co. has included work with a number of clients, both small and large, in a wide variety of fields. She performed audit field work, prepared income tax returns, and worked on a management services engagement. After two years, she progressed to the level of a semi-senior and was supervising the work on major portions of several large audits and had acted as a senior accountant on a smaller engagement.

During this period, Georgia attended several professional development courses covering a number of subjects including the preparation of working papers, audits of inventories, preparation of corporate tax returns, and review of recent pronouncements on accounting principles and auditing procedures. She also attended a course sponsored by her local chapter of CPAs on planning and supervising an audit.

Georgia's work was reviewed and evaluated throughout her employment with Arthur Price & Co. and she was frequently counseled as to her progress in the firm.

CASE DISCUSSION QUESTIONS

1. What is the nature of the general standards? Discuss.

2. The first general standard states:

   The examination is to be performed by a person or persons having adequate technical training and proficiency as an auditor.

   Consider this first general standard and discuss the implications of each of the following with respect to Georgia's training and proficiency to practice public accounting:

   a. Proper education and training.

   b. Seasoned judgment.

   c. Understanding and applying new pronouncements on accounting principles and auditing procedures.

3. Discuss the significance of the general standards of independence and due care with respect to each of the following:

   a. Bias toward the client.

   b. Public confidence in the work of the CPA.

   c. Appointment of the CPA by the board of directors or election by stockholders.

   d. Observing the standards of field work and reporting.

   e. Critical review of staff accountants.

4. What factors determine whether an auditor appears to be independent? What determines whether or not an auditor is independent in fact?

5

Relationship Between the Auditor's Appointment and Planning

[Section 310, SAS No. 1 (as amended by SAS No. 45, Section 313), Section 311, SAS No. 22, Section 312, SAS No. 47 and Section 315, SAS No. 7]

The first standard of field work requires that:

> The work is to be adequately planned and assistants, if any, are to be properly supervised

The first standard of field work recognizes that the early appointment of the auditor has many advantages to both the client and the auditor. Early appointment permits the work to be performed in a more efficient manner and allows the auditor to determine the extent to which audit work can be done before the balance sheet date.

A CPA may undertake an engagement to examine financial statements near or after the close of the client's fiscal year. In such circumstances, however, the CPA may be unable to satisfy himself concerning major portions of the audit (observation of inventory, for example) and may not be able to obtain sufficient competent evidential matter to warrant the expression of an opinion. Also, the timing of the application of auditing procedure is an important consideration in planning an audit engagement and the appointment of the CPA near or after year-end may complicate this process. When appointment of the CPA occurs either near or after year-end, the timing of the engagement and other circumstances may require the auditor to disclaim an opinion on the financial statements taken as a whole, or to issue a separate opinion on the balance sheet while disclaiming an opinion on the income statement and statement of changes in financial position because of an inability to obtain sufficient evidence regarding, for example, the beginning inventory balance. When the CPA is appointed near or after year-end and there are circumstances which may preclude the issuance of an unqualified opinion, the situation should be discussed with the client before accepting the engagement and the possibility that a disclaimer of opinion may be necessary should be explained.

SUBSTANTIVE TESTING PRIOR TO THE BALANCE SHEET DATE

SAS No. 45 provides guidance on performing substantive (balance) testing prior to the balance sheet date.

The third standard of field work requires the auditor to gather sufficient evidence to support the balances reported in the financial statements. The auditor's opinion must be based upon such evidence. Substantive evidence is obtained through two general classes of audit procedures: (a) tests of details of transactions and balances, and (b) analytical review procedures. These procedures are referred to as substantive tests.

Although the performance of interim audit procedures is usually desirable and provides for a more efficient audit, audit risk is increased by the performance of interim work. Audit risk is the risk that material errors may occur in the accounting process and may not be detected by the auditor—thus misstating the financial statements. If an auditor carefully plans the nature and timing of interim substantive tests (see SAS No. 39 on audit sampling) audit risk is reduced to a minimum level usually acceptable to the auditor.

Audit tests should be designed so that interim tests and year-end tests taken together provide a reasonable basis for the expression of an opinion on the financial statements. Substantive tests should be designed so that year-end work will roll-forward or validate the interim results. Year-end validation tests ordinarily should include:

> Comparison of information concerning the balance at the balance-sheet date with the comparable information at the interim date to identify amounts that appear unusual and investigation of any such amounts.

> Other analytical review procedures or substantive tests of details, or a combination of both.

If internal accounting controls or accounting records do not provide an adequate basis for updating interim substantive tests, such test should not be performed. Also, the auditor should consider the efficiency of interim testing. If it would be more economical to perform all tests regarding a particular account balance or class of transactions at year-end, then interim tests should not be performed.

Some substantive tests can be applied to transactions through any selected date prior to the balance-sheet date and completed as part of the auditor's year-end procedures. Such tests include:

> Tests of details of the additions to and reductions of accounts such as property, investments, and debt and equity capital.

> Tests of details of transactions affecting income and expense accounts and other accounts that are not to be audited by testing the details of items composing the balance.

> Analytical review procedures applied to income and expense accounts.

PLANNING AND SUPERVISION

SAS No. 22, *Planning and Supervision*, provides guidance to the CPA making an examination in accordance with GAAS regarding the considerations and procedures applicable to planning an engagement and supervising the work. Included are the preparation of audit programs, obtaining an understanding of the client's business operations, and dealing with differences of opinion among audit personnel that may arise in the course of the examination.

The flow chart and the related article, *Planning and Supervision Flowcharts*, from *The CPA Journal* summarizes the requirements of SAS No. 22 and presents a planning and supervision flowchart. In reading the article, it should be recognized that SAS No. 48, *The Effects of Computer Processing on the Examination of Financial Statements*, has amended SAS No. 22 to add to the list of required planning considerations the methods used by an entity to process accounting information—such as EDP.

MATERIALITY AND AUDIT RISK

SAS No. 47, *Audit Risk and Materiality in Conducting an Audit*, provides guidance as to the auditor's consideration of audit risk and materiality when planning and performing an examination of financial statements in accordance with GAAS.

The concepts of "materiality" and "audit risk" affect the application of GAAS, especially the standards of field work and reporting, and are implicit in the auditor's standard report.

Audit Risk is the risk that the auditor may unknowingly fail to appropriately modify his or her opinion on financial statements that are materially misstated.

In addition to audit risk, there is the risk that the auditor's evaluation of the evidential matter may lead him or her initially to erroneously conclude that the statements are materially misstated. However, it is expected that application of additional audit procedures would ordinarily lead to the correct conclusion. Also, the auditor is exposed to *business risk* which is the risk of loss or injury to the auditor's professional practice as a result of events unrelated to professional standards. For example, an auditor may appropriately examine and report on statements in accordance with GAAS and yet incur loss or injury from litigation or adverse publicity concerning those statements. However, even though an auditor may assess his or her business risk as low in certain engagements, the auditor should *not* perform less extensive procedures than are required by GAAS. When the auditor expresses an opinion that the statements "present fairly" in conformity with GAAP, it is implicit that the statements taken as a whole are not materially misstated.

An auditor's consideration of materiality is a matter of professional judgment and is influenced by his or her perception of the needs of a reasonable person who will rely on the statements.

An auditor should consider audit risk and materiality both in planning the audit and designing audit procedures and evaluating whether the statements taken as a whole present fairly. Audit risk may be assessed in quantitative or non-quantitative terms; and preliminary judgment about materiality may or may not be quantified.

In planning an audit, the auditor should use his or her judgment in establishing appropriately low levels of audit risk and materiality in a way that can be expected to provide sufficient evidential matter in support of the statements. Estimates of materiality levels include an overall level for each statement, but because of the interrelationship of the statements and for reasons of efficiency, the auditor ordinarily considers materiality for planning purposes in terms of the smallest aggregate level of errors that could be considered material to any one of the statements. For example, if the auditor believes that errors aggregating approximately $25,000 would have a material effect on income but that such errors would have to aggregate approximately $50,000 to materially affect financial position, it would not be appropriate to design audit procedures that would be expected to detect errors only if they aggregate approximately $50,000.

The auditor normally plans audit procedures to detect errors or irregularities that are quantitatively material; however, qualitative considerations should influence an auditor in reaching a final conclusion regarding the materiality of an error.

Preliminary estimates of materiality may change during the audit and if they are lowered, the auditor should consider the need for additional evidential matter in support of the statements.

In planning the audit the auditor should, of course, consider the nature, cause, if known, and amount of errors that he or she is aware of from prior-period audits.

The auditor recognizes that there is an inverse relationship between audit risk and materiality considerations. Holding other planning considerations equal, either a decrease in the level of audit risk or a decrease in the amount of error in the balance or class that the auditor believes could be material would require the auditor to do one or more of the following:

Select a more effective auditing procedure,

Perform auditing procedures closer to the balance sheet date, or

Increase the extent of a particular auditing procedure.

Audit risk as it relates to an account balance or class of transactions is a combination of three component risks—*inherent risk, control risk,* and *detection risk.*

Inherent risk is the susceptibility of an account balance or class of transactions to error that could be material, when aggregated with error in other balances or classes, assuming there were no related internal accounting controls.

Control risk is the risk that error that could occur in an account balance or class of transactions and that could be material, when aggregated with error in other balances or classes, will not be prevented or detected on a timely basis by the system of internal accounting control.

Detection risk is the risk that an auditor's procedures will lead him or her to conclude that error in an account balance or class of transactions that could be material, when aggregated with error in other balances or classes, does not exist when in fact such error does exist.

Detection risk arises partly from uncertainties that exist when the auditor does *not* examine 100 percent of an account balance or class of transactions and partly because of uncertainties that exist even if the auditor were to examine every item. These risks are referred to as *sampling and nonsampling risks*, respectively. For example, even if the auditor does examine all of the items in an account balance or class, he or she may arrive at inappropriate conclusions based on applied procedures or the auditor may misapply a procedure that is appropriate in the circumstances. These *nonsampling risks* are controlled through proper audit planning, supervision, and firm quality control review. *Sampling risk* is generally related to the auditor's application of inappropriate sampling techniques or judgment that results in selection of samples that ae not representative of the population from which they were drawn.

Detection risk should bear an inverse relationship to inherent and control risk.

If an auditor concludes that the effort required to evaluate inherent risk for a balance or class would exceed the potential reduction in the extent of his or her auditing procedures derived from reliance on the evaluation, the auditor should assess inherent risk as being at the maximum when designing auditing procedures.

The auditor should aggregate errors that the entity has not corrected in a way that enables him or her to consider whether in relation to individual amounts, subtotals, or totals in the statements, they materially misstate the statements taken as a whole.

The auditor's aggregation of errors should include his or her best estimate of error in the account balance or classes of transactions examined (*likely error*), not just the amount of errors the auditor specifically identifies (*known error*).

When an auditor uses *audit sampling* (see SAS No. 39) to test an account balance or class of transactions, the auditor projects the amount of *known errors* he or she identifies in the sample to the items in the balance or class from which the sample was selected; this projected error, along with the results of other substantive tests, contributes to the auditor's assessment of *likely error* in the balance or class.

The risk of material misstatement of the financial statement amounts is generally greater when account balances and classes of transactions include accounting estimates rather than essentially factual data. If the auditor believes the estimated amount of an account balance or a transaction is unreasonable, he or she should treat the difference between that estimate and the closest reasonable estimate as a likely error and aggregate it with other likely errors.

COMMUNICATIONS BETWEEN PREDECESSOR AND SUCCESSOR AUDITORS

SAS No. 7 provides guidance regarding communications between predecessor and successor auditors. The term "predecessor auditor" refers to an auditor who has resigned or who has been notified by the client that his or her services have been terminated. A "successor auditor" is an auditor who has accepted a new client or who has been invited to make a proposal for a new engagement. GAAS requires certain communications between successor and predecessor auditors prior to the acceptance of a new client by a successor auditor. The initiative in communication rests with the successor auditor who may communicate with the predecessor either orally or in writing. Both the predecessor and the successor auditor should, of course, hold in confidence all information relative to the client.

REQUIRED COMMUNICATIONS

All CPAs have quality control standards regarding the acceptance of new clients. Before accepting a new client, when there has been a predecessor auditor, a successor CPA is required to make certain inquiries of the predecessor. These inquiries are necessary because the predecessor may be able to provide the successor with information useful in determining whether a potential new client meets quality control standards adhered to by the successor auditor. The successor should explain to the prospective client the need to make an inquiry of the predecessor and request permission to do so. If a prospective client refuses to permit the inquiries or limits the response, the successor should inquire as to the reasons and consider the implications in deciding whether to accept the engagement.

The successor should make specific and reasonable inquiries of the predecessor auditor regarding matters that the successor believes will be of assistance in determining whether to accept the engagement. The inquiry should include specific questions regarding, among other issues, facts that might bear on the integrity of management; on any disagreements with management as to accounting principles, auditing procedures, or other similarly significant matters; and on the predecessor's understanding as to the reasons for the change of auditors. The predecessor auditor should respond promptly and fully, on the basis of known facts. Should the predecessor decide, due to unusual circumstances such as impending litigation, not to respond fully to the successor's inquiry, the fact that the response is limited should, of course, be indicated. If the successor auditor receives a limited response, its implications should be considered in deciding whether to accept or reject the new engagement.

OTHER COMMUNICATIONS

A successor auditor may wish to make other inquiries of a predecessor auditor because such communication may facilitate the performance of the examination. The successor's examination may be facilitated, for example, by inquiry and communication with the predecessor concerning areas of the predecessor's examination that have required an inordinate amount of time or audit problems that arose from the condition of the accounting system or records. Reviewing the working papers of the predecessor and consultation regarding possible problem areas and other matters will likely facilitate the successor's examination.

The successor should request the client to authorize the predecessor to allow a review of working papers and it is customary in such circumstances for the predecessor auditor to be available to the successor for consultation. The predecessor and successor auditors should, of course, agree on those working papers that are to be made available for review and those that may be duplicated. Ordinarily, the predecessor auditor should permit the successor to review working papers relating to matters of continuing accounting significance, such as the working paper analysis of balance sheet accounts, both current and noncurrent, and those relating to contingencies. Valid business reasons may, however, lead the predecessor to decide not to allow a review of the working papers. When more than one successor auditor is considering acceptancce of an engagement, the predecessor auditor should not be expected to make himself or herself or the prior-period's working papers available until a successor has accepted the engagement.

In issuing a report, the successor must gather sufficient competent evidential matter to support the opinion rendered and may not rely on work done by a predecessor.

FINANCIAL STATEMENTS REPORTED ON BY THE PREDECESSOR

When the successor auditor, during the course of the examination, becomes aware of information that might indicate that financial statements reported on by the predecessor may require revision, the successor must take certain action. The client should be requested to arrange a meeting among the three parties (client, successor, and predecessor) to discuss the information and attempt to resolve the matter. The predecessor auditor, for example, may be required to take action in accordance with Section 561, SAS No. 1, *Subsequent Discovery of Facts Existing at the Date of the Auditor's Report*.

THE CPA JOURNAL   OCTOBER 1978

AUDITING AND REPORTING

SAS No. 22 — Planning and Supervision

By James D. Blum, CPA, and Angelo E. Di Antonio, Ph.D., CPA. Department of Accounting, University of Delaware.

Issue date, March 1978. Effective date, September 30, 1978.

1. This Statement provides guidance to the independent auditor making an examination in accordance with generally accepted auditing standards on the considerations and procedures applicable to planning and supervision.

2. The auditor with final responsibility for the examination may delegate portions of planning and supervision of the examination to other firm personnel.

3. Audit planning involves developing an overall strategy for the expected conduct and scope of the examination. The nature, extent and timing of planning vary with the size and complexity of the entity, experience with the entity and knowledge of the entity's business.

4. Procedures that an auditor may consider in planning the examination usually involve review of his records relating to the entity and discussion with other firm personnel and personnel of the entity. The auditor may wish to prepare a memorandum setting forth the preliminary audit plan, particularly for large and complex entities.

5. In planning his examination, the auditor should consider the nature, extent, and timing of work to be performed and should prepare a written audit program (or a set of written audit programs). As the examination progresses, changed conditions may make it necessary to modify planned audit procedures.

PLANNING AND SUPERVISION*
Statement on Auditing Standards No. 22

PLANNING	DESCRIPTION
Engagement Objectives	Establish engagement (audit) objectives. Develop overall strategy for expected conduct and scope of exam. The nature, extent and timing of the engagement vary with the size and complexity of the entity, experience with the entity, and knowledge of the entity's business.
Consider entity's business and industry environment	Consider nature of entity's business, its organization, and its operating characteristics such as types of business, products and services, capital structure, related parties, locations, production, distribution, compensation methods and industry conditions such as economic conditions, government regulations, technology changes, common accounting practices. Competitive conditions and financial trends and ratios.
Consider entity's accounting policies and procedures	Determine their general acceptance and appropriateness in the circumstances.
Consider entity's internal accounting controls	Plan preliminary review and evaluation to determine extent of reliance.
Consider entity's materiality levels	Materiality levels should be established prior to audit program development.
Consider items likely to require adjustment	Determine items likely to require adjustment and plan collection of necessary adjusting journal documentation.
Consider items requiring extended audit procedures	Such as the possibility of material errors or irregularities or the existence of related party transactions.
Consider types of reports to be rendered	Such as reports on consolidated statements, statements filed with SEC, special reports, etc.
Perform review and discussion of auditor's records	Review prior year's work papers and correspondence, non-audit services performed by firm personnel, relevant current business developments, current year's interim financial statements, and prepare memo of preliminary audit plan.
Prepare written audit program(s)	Consider nature, extent, and timing of work to be performed. Set forth in reasonable detail necessary procedures to accomplish objectives of exam. Consider applicable accounting and auditing pronouncements, use of client personnel, consultants, specialists, and internal auditors.

6. The auditor should obtain a level of knowledge of the entity's business that will enable him to plan and perform his examination in accordance with generally accepted auditing standards. The level of knowledge customarily possessed by management relating to managing the entity's business is substantially greater than that which is obtained by the auditor in performing his examination.

7. The auditor should obtain a knowledge of matters that relate to the nature of the entity's business, its organization and its operating characteristics. The auditor should also consider matters affecting the industry in which the entity operates, such as economic conditions, government regulations, and changes in technology, as they relate to his examination. Other matters, such as accounting practices common to the industry, competitive conditions, and, if available, financial trends and ratios should also be considered by the auditor.

8. Knowledge of an entity's business is ordinarily obtained through experience with the entity or its industry and inquiry of personnel of the entity. Audit working papers from prior years may contain useful information about the nature of the business, organizational structure, operating characteristics, and transactions that may require special consideration. Other sources an auditor may consult include AICPA accounting and audit guides, industry publications, financial statements of other entities in the industry, textbooks, periodicals, and individuals knowledgeable about the industry.

9. Supervision involves directing the efforts of assistants who are involved in accomplishing the objectives of the examination and determining whether those objectives were accomplished. The extent of supervision appropriate in a given instance depends on many factors, including the complexity of the subject matter and the qualifications of persons performing the work.

10. Assistants should be informed of their responsibilities and the objectives of the procedures that they are to perform. The auditor with final responsibility for the examination should direct assistants to bring to his attention significant accounting and auditing questions raised during the examination so that he may assess their significance.

11. The work performed by each assistance should be reviewed to determine whether it was adequately performed and to evaluate whether the results are consistent with the conclusions to be presented in the auditor's report.

12. The auditor with final responsibility for the examination and assistants should be aware of the procedures to be followed when differences of opinion concerning accounting and auditing issues exist among firm personnel involved in the examination.

PLANNING AND SUPERVISION*
(Continued)

| Obtain level of knowledge of entity's business | Obtain level of knowledge necessary to perform exam in accordance with GAAS. Identify problem areas; assess data accumulation conditions; reasonableness of estimates and management representations; judgments concerning accounting principles and disclosure.

Sources of knowledge include past experience with the entity or industry, inquiry of client personnel, prior years' audit work papers, AICPA accounting and audit guides, industry publications, financial statements of other entities in industry, textbooks, periodicals, and individuals knowledgable about the industry. |

SUPERVISION	**DESCRIPTION**
Determining extent of supervision	Depends on complexity of subject matter and experience of personnel.
Directing and instructing assistants	Instructing assistants includes informing them of the responsibilities and objectives of their work; matters that may affect the nature, extent, and timing of procedures they are to perform.
Keeping informed of significant problems	Direct assistants to bring to the attention of the auditor in charge significant accounting and auditing questions.
Review of work performed	Determine if work is adequately performed and evaluate results to determine if they are consistent with conclusions to be presented in auditor's report.
Resolving differences of opinion among firm personnel	Provide documentation for resolution of differences of opinion including provisions for firm personnel to document disagreement with conclusions reached by firm.

* Prepared by Joyce C. Lambert, Ph.D., C.P.A., and Thomas D. Hubbard, Ph.D., C.P.A., both professors at the University of Nebraska, Lincoln.

Planning and Supervision Flowcharts*

By Thomas D. Hubbard, Ph.D., CPA, and Joyce C. Lambert, Ph.D., CPA, Department of Accounting, University of Nebraska, Lincoln.

Planning and supervision relates to the first standard of field work, which reads, "The work is to be adequately planned and assistants, if any, are to be properly supervised." The Statement provides guidance on considerations and procedures applicable to planning and supervision, including:

• Preparing audit programs; Obtaining knowledge of the client's business;
• Dealing with differences of opinion among firm personnel.

In planning his engagement, the Statement requires the CPA to consider a number of matters, including:

• Matters relating to the client's business and industry;
• Client's accounting policies and procedures;
• Anticipated reliance on internal accounting control;
• Preliminary estimates of materiality levels;
• Likely adjusting journal entries;
• Conditions that may require extension or modification of audit tests such as material errors or irregularities and related party transactions;
• Nature of reports the CPA is expected to render as, for example, reports to regulatory agencies.

Procedures performed by CPAs in planning engagements usually involve review of audit files and discussion with assistants and client personnel. Assistants are all members of the firm working on the engagement with the partner in charge. Examples of procedures usually performed in planning an audit engagement include the following:

• Review of files (correspondence, audit and permanent) including financial statemnts and audit reports;
• Discussing audit with firm personnel performing nonaudit services for the client;

* Paper is based on material developed by the authors for *Accounting and Auditing Updating Workshop*, Thomas D. Hubbard, Continuing Professional Education Division, AICPA, New York, New York, 1978.

• Inquiry concerning current business developments;
• Reading the current year's interim financial statements;
• Discussing the type, scope and timing of audit plan with client's management, board and audit committee;
• Considering the potential effects of applicable accounting and auditing pronouncements, especially recently issued pronouncements;
• Coordinating the assistance of client personnel;
• Determining the extent of involvement of consultants, specialists, and internal auditors;
• Establishing the timing of audit work;
• Establishing and coordinating staffing requirements.

The CPA may wish to prepare a memo setting forth the preliminary audit plan, especially for large engagements. The CPA should prepare a written audit program in reasonable detail and obtain a level of knowledge of the entity's business that will enable him to plan and perform his audit in accordance with generally accepted auditing standards.

Supervision involves directing the efforts of assistants and determining if objectives were accomplished. Elements of supervision include:

• Instructing assistants;
• Keeping informed of significant problems;
• Reviewing the work of assistants;
• Dealing with differences of opinion among firm personnel;

Assistants should be informed of their responsibilities and the objectives of the procedures that they are to perform. The work performed by each assistant should be reviewed to determine whether it was adequately performed and to evaluate whether the results are consistent with the conclusions to be presented in the auditor's report. Provisions should be established to enable assistants to document their disagreement with conclusions reached in the audit and to dissociate themselves from the audit opinion.

The flowcharts on pages 4–6 summarize the Statement's requirements regarding planning and supervision. The reader should recognize that both planning and supervision occur simultaneously and, accordingly, two separate flowcharts are presented for these functions. Also, it should be apparent that many of the functions indicated in the flowcharts may occur in a parallel pattern as well as in sequence. Ω

MAY 1979

The Initial Audit Engagement

These engagements may become more frequent because of a likely increase in rotation of auditors. The author discusses detailed considerations in initial audits and perceives an inconsistency in reporting requirements.

Arthur G. Hendricks, CPA

THE unique problems encountered during the initial audit of an entity previously examined by other accountants have not been extensively covered in the profession's official pronouncements. An auditor searching for guidance may conclude that an initial audit presents few problems not encountered in a repetitive engagement, even though that conclusion may not seem logical. Although a few of the SASs do mention the problem (notably SAS No. 7, "Communications Between Predecessor and Successor Auditors), they do so without significant elaboration.

The problem caused by this lack of attention is no longer academic, since several factors are encouraging the periodic change of independent auditors. For instance, the repeal of the ethical prohibition against advertising and the elimination of the prohibition against competitive bidding can be expected to accelerate changes.

Further, there seems to be a tendency for new management to replace auditors associated with the previous management, particularly where there is a question of fraud or improper financial statements and a potential for auditor culpability.

Existing Audit Standards

This article relates these standards and their interpretations (SASs) to the initial audit. The problem is divided into three sections, each of which involves a basic decision or an area of concern unique to the initial audit. They are: (1) the decision to accept or reject the engagement, (2) accumulation of sufficient competent evidential matter concerning the prior financial statements to support an opinion on the current statements, and (3) meet-

Arthur G. Hendricks, CPA, was for many years a partner of Alexander Grant & Company. After retirement he achieved a Ph.D. degree at the University of Houston. He is presently Assistant Professor at the University of Delaware. A member of the AICPA and the Texas Society of CPAs, his writings on professional subjects have been published in the Journal of Accountancy *and elsewhere.*

ing the reporting standards as they apply to the previous statements, and dealing with the problem of association with the prior statements.

The secondary purpose of this article is to suggest revision of SAS 15 (now AU Sec. 505.12, Codification of Statements on Auditing Standards) to resolve an apparent conflict between it and one of the reporting standards. The recommendation is made so that a report issued as a result of the initial examination will capture the essence of the actual auditing performed and the true relationship of the new auditor to the prior period's statements.

Accepting the Engagement

The decision to accept or reject a proffered audit engagement intended to result in an unqualified opinion is based on business and professional factors. These factors are sometimes inseparable. For instance, the professional decision must include consideration of whether the auditor can reasonably expect to comply with the first six auditing standards (i.e., the general and field work standards). At the same time, the business decision will include consideration of capital and manpower requirements. This article focuses on the professional considerations and will omit discussion of business considerations.

The General Standards—Training and Proficiency

Some specific professional considerations for complying with the first general standard (training and proficiency) were identified by the AICPA in SAS No. 4, "Quality Control Considerations for a Firm of Independent Auditors." This SAS discusses the ability of the auditor to render proper service to the client, mentioning specifically industry specialization requirements and the timing, quality and quantity of staffing needs.

Generally speaking, the auditor is required to have industry expertise, acquired by experience or education, as well as adequate hours available for the engagement. The SAS also mentions communications with the predecessor auditor, which was to become a required procedure and which is discussed later in this article.

Independence

The next or second general standard, concerning independence, was also mentioned in SAS No. 4. Compliance with this standard is as important and deserving of attention in a new engagement as in an existing one, and obviously must be considered in the client acceptance/ rejection decision. Since the relationship under consideration is new, the problems of rendering services which might impair independence can be explored without past problems impinging on the determination. The determination of probable future independence may logically include a consideration of the prospective client's ability and willingness to pay the fee. Certainly, the payment history and current status of billings with the predecessor will contribute to a decision.

'Generally speaking, the auditor is required to have industry expertise, acquired by experience or education, as well as adequate hours available for the engagement.'

Due Care and Field Work Standard I

Compliance with the third general standard, as well as with the first field work standard, which relates to planning and supervision, is prospective and thus not a consideration, per se, in the decision of whether to accept the engagement. All preliminary work should demonstrate the exercise of due professional care. Information gathered at this time may well affect planning since the ability to comply with the other field work and general standards is at the heart of the acceptance decision. Further, the provisions of SAS No. 22, "Planning and Supervision," are obviously as applicable to the initial audit as to any other.

Other Field Work Standards—Internal Control

The second field work standard imposes on an auditor the duty to study and evaluate internal control in order to establish a basis for reliance thereon. This standard appears, on its face, to be prospective in application like the third general and first field work standards, and thus not a factor in the decision to accept the engagement. However, SAS No. 16 points out the importance of management's integrity to the effective operation of internal accounting control procedures. Therefore, before accepting the engagement, the auditor should consider whether past history or current circumstances might dispose management to misstate financial statements.

Contact with Predecessor Auditor

Included in the investigation of past history is the requirement, imposed by SAS No. 7, to contact the predecessor auditor prior to the acceptance of the engagement. In this connection, the predecessor auditor might properly be questioned about the integrity of management, client-auditor differences of opinion, or other matters which may help the potential successor to decide whether to accept the engagement. In addition to these questions it is appropriate to ask if the predecessor has sent, or contemplated sending, a report to the client on material accounting control weaknesses as required under SAS No. 20. This inquiry is prompted by SAS No. 16, which deals with the subject of errors and irregularities, and which further suggests that one indication of possible irregularities occurs when the company does not correct material weaknesses in internal accounting control that are practicable to correct. Thus management's reaction to the predecessor auditor's identification of internal control weaknesses could affect the new auditor's estimation of his ability to comply with the second field work standard.

Similarly, current circumstances may alert the auditor to a potential misstatement of financial statements. SAS No. 16 suggests that a company which lacks adequate working capital or credit or is in an industry experiencing a large number of failures, runs a higher than normal risk of irregularities. Other circumstances such as economic dependence on one or a few customers or suppliers as suggested by SAS No. 6, may indicate special accounting or disclosure problems not evident from a reading of previous financial statements. It is appropriate to inquire into these possibilities by questioning management and the predecessor auditor, and by investigating other sources, such as credit reporting agencies.

' . . . it is appropriate to ask if the predecessor has sent . . . a report . . . on material accounting control weaknesses . . .'

Existence of Accounting Records and the Third Field Work Standard

Finally, the third standard of field work (the accumulation of sufficient competent evidential matter) requires reasonable assurance that the necessary accounting records exist, and that the company maintains a relationship with an attorney sufficient to permit the proper evaluation of claims, litigation and assessments. The first consideration here, i.e., the expectation that certain critical records exist, bears directly on the possible scope of the examination. A potential client is expected to maintain records supporting account balances and transactions for the most recent year. The auditor may not assume that support exists for older transactions. While it may be possible to reconstruct certain long-term accounts from recent information, such as the effective rate of interest on an outstanding debt issue, other information cannot be so reconstructed and must be available from the client. For instance, records supporting property acquisition costs must ordinarily exist. The lack of records or documentation for such acquisition costs may result in a scope limitation, which in turn may prevent the auditor from meeting the third field work standard or from rendering an unqualified opinion.

Attorney-Client Relationship

The other factor relating to possible compliance with the third field work standard is the existence of a bona fide attorney-client relationship. Such a relationship is now, because of SAS No. 12, normally required before an auditor can express an unqualified opinion on financial statements. A very limited survey of local accounting practitioners which I conducted in 1977 indicated, at best, uneven compliance with SAS 12. The reason most often given for noncompliance was the inability to obtain the information from attorneys, and the attorneys' ignorance of the requirements of FAS No. 5. In view of uncertain compliance by the previous auditor, the need not only for an accurate assessment of current contingent liabilities, but also for candor with the client, suggest strongly that the cost and implications of the required relationship be fully explored.

Auditor Compliance with the General and Field Work Standards

It has been shown thus far that the first problem area encountered in the decision of whether to accept a new audit engagement is the auditor's reasonable expectation of being able to comply with the first three generally accepted auditing standards. These three standards embrace the professional concepts of adequate training and technical proficiency as appropriate in the circumstances, independence and due professional care. In addition, the auditor estimates his ability to meet the field work standards, having to do with the adequacy of planning and supervision, the study and evaluation of internal control, and the accumulation of sufficient, competent evidential matter. This process includes the required communication with the predecessor auditor, the confirmation of the existence of an attorney-client relationship, and the search for the existence of related party transactions.

Satisfactory resolution of these issues permits the auditor to progress to the second stage and to evaluate

conformity of the client's prior year's records and financial statements with generally accepted accounting principles.

The Application of Generally Accepted Accounting Principles—Consistency

The potential new auditor needs to 'etermine the propriety of accounting principles used in previous years for three reasons: first, the regular short-form auditor's opinion includes an assertion of consistency in the application of generally accepted accounting principles (GAAP) in the current year and in the prior year; second, income for the current year is directly dependent on the fairness of presentation of the most recent year-end balance sheet; and third, if, as is common practice, comparative financial statements are presented, the new auditor may very well be associated with the old financial statements and must accept the responsibilities implicit with such association.

'A . . . survey of . . . practitioners . . . conducted in 1977 indicated . . . uneven compliance with SAS 12.'

The GAAP problem, in turn, is composed of three elements: (1) the Summary of Significant Accounting Policies (Summary); (2) the compliance of previously issued statements (for the preceding year) with generally accepted accounting principles; and (3) the amounts in the previous year's financial statements. Each of these is examined in the following paragraphs.

The requirement that financial statements include a separate Summary of Significant Accounting Policies, which is to precede the notes to financial statements or be the initial note, was adopted in 1972, as APB No. 22. The pronouncement suggests that the Summary include a description of the methods of revenue recognition and of the allocation of asset costs to present and future periods, particularly where alternative methods exist or where there is an unusual application of an accounting method. The fairness of the Summary is therefore important because it serves as the basis of comparison with the accounting principles applied during the current year. The comparison of principles, in turn, supports the new auditor's assertion that the accounting principles were applied on a consistent basis. Sufficient transactions in the previous year must be tested to give the auditor reasonable assurance that the assertion of consistency is correct.

The second of the three problems involves determining whether GAAP has been applied in the previous year's financial statements. If comparative statements are not to be issued at the end of the year, then the discussion in this paragraph is irrelevant. If comparative statements are to be presented, the new auditor must be satisfied with the *prima facie* compliance with GAAP of the previously issued statements, since the new auditor may be associated with those statements (as that term is defined in SAS 1, Sec. 516.03). While SAS 15, does, by implication, waive the application of the fourth reporting standard (relating to the expression of opinion when the auditor is associated with financial statements) insofar as the disclaimer of opinion is concerned, it does not waive the auditor's responsibility for the fair presentation of all statements included, to the extent of his (the auditor's) knowledge.

Prior Year's Financial Statements

The final problem to be addressed in this phase of the examination is the accuracy of the amounts in the prior year's financial statements, particularly the balance sheet, but including also the amounts used in the notes to financial statements. Since amounts from the operating statements do not enter directly into current year calculations, support of operating statement amounts is limited to the test of accounting policies suggested above. On the other hand, amounts in the balance sheet demand attention not only to assure fair presentation of financial position, but also because of the impact that any significant error may have on income for the current period. The emphasis in supporting the amounts in the prior year's statements will ordinarily be on the direct tests of balances, rather than any significant reliance on internal controls which may be appropriate for the current year. Therefore, it may be necessary to examine the detail supporting balance sheet amounts, and to reconcile the financial statements to the underlying ledgers. Specific instructions are given for the situation where inventories are involved in SAS No. 1, Sec. 331.13, as follows:

> . . . tests of prior transactions, reviews of records of prior counts, *and* the application of gross profit tests, provided that (the auditor) has been able to become satisfied as to the current inventory. [emphasis mine]

Extension of this rationale to all other current assets and to current liabilities seems appropriate. Francis X. Fee[1] has offered a number of specific audit procedures for this aspect of the examination. The remaining audit problems, then, are those of allocated asset costs (property and equipment), long-term liabilities, capital and the related disclosures.

Property, plant and equipment and other costs subject to depletion, depreciation or amortization (the long-term allocation processes), present problems somewhat different from those of monetary assets and inventory accounts. They are different because of the cumulative na-

ture of the cost and accumulated amortization amounts and the continuing use of the periodic amortization in the calculation of net income. The problem may simply be a lack of records needed to associate costs and specific identifiable assets or a lack of documentation concerning costs or ownership. Further, records supporting useful lives, the periodic calculation of depreciation, and the reconciliation of accumulated amounts with the general ledger may simply not exist. Difficulty in accumulating sufficient, competent evidential matter concerning the costs and the accumulated depreciation accounts must be overcome, or recognition given to the resulting scope limitation. Further difficulties may arise in the situation where the client has failed to provide adequate depreciation in the past. Such failure may serve to reduce the future deductibility of unamortized costs, through the "allowed or allowable" depreciation provisions of the Internal Revenue Code (see Gardiner, 76-1 USTC pp9454, 38AFTR 2d 76 5107 [CA-10, 1976]).

The final area of concern, long-term liabilities and capital, should present no unusual measurement or disclosure problems, provided that the attorney-client relationship discussed earlier exists and that the attorney responds adequately (for FAS 5 and SAS 12 purposes) for the previous year. Data and documentary support other than the attorney's letter may be developed when creating a permanent file for such items as leases and long-term debt documents, which may include the related amortization and lapsing schedules. Tests for compliance with contractual obligations may have to be performed, if satisfactory evidence of testing and evaluation of results is not gathered from the predecessor auditor or from the client's files. Relating this permanent file data and associated disclosures to similar data for previous years may be viewed as an extension of calculations and current year confirmations.

Historically, evaluating the results of this phase of the initial audit has involved judging whether sufficient, competent evidential matter has been gathered to support the assertion of consistency in application of accounting principles. Further, there is an implication that the amounts included in the previous year's ending balance sheet were materially correct as presented (or as corrected, as the case may be). This judgment is one no less demanding of professionalism than the judgment on the current statements. No criteria for making this judgment are suggested or are to be inferred in this paper.

The Financial Statements and the Auditor's Report

The preceding discussion of factors affecting the planning for the initial audit focused attention on existing auditing standards and technical aids. Nothing new was suggested. Obvious extensions resulting from the modern audit environment were explored to assist the auditor faced with an initial audit.

In the examination of the financial statements of the

---

[1] "How to Handle the First Audit of a New Client"—*The Practical Accountant* (March/April 1977), pp. 30-38.

current year the planning must be based on partial information and experienced judgment, rather than on recent history. Sufficient time must be allowed for gathering evidential matter normally in the auditor's files. Such evidential matter may include descriptions of the internal control systems, descriptions of EDP and other information gathering systems, and permanent-file type documents and contracts mentioned previously.

Following the path of existing literature to its conclusion in the auditor's report on the financial statements, however, leads to two incongruous results.

The fourth standard of reporting is straightforward concerning the responsibility of the auditor. That standard says, in part,

> In all cases where the auditor is associated with financial statements, the report should contain a clearcut indication of the character of the auditor's examination, if any, and the degree of responsibility he is taking.

It appears that if the auditor is associated with the prior year's statements, then this standard requires an appropriate comment in the scope paragraph of his report on the examination performed, and specific inclusion or exclusion of the statements in the opinion. The definition of association often quoted from SAS 1, Sec. 516.03, says,

> A certified public accountant is associated with unaudited financial statements when he has consented to the use of his name in a report, document, or other written communication setting forth or containing the statements.

Clearly, if any of the financial statements for the previous year are unaudited, then the new auditor is associated with them. Unaudited statements are defined in the paragraph immediately preceding the above quote, as,

> Financial statements are unaudited if the certified public accountant (a) has not applied any auditing procedures to them, or (b) has not applied auditing procedures which are sufficient to permit him to express an opinion concerning them as described in section 509.

In the cases under consideration here, the auditor has applied audit procedures to the statements, including, among others, the determination of which accounting principles were followed. The decision then, is whether the auditing procedures applied are sufficient to permit the auditor to express an opinion.

The sufficiency of the evidence in support of an opinion is a matter of professional judgment. Because evidence is required to support the amounts included in the balance sheet at the end of the previous year and the related notes, there will normally be no area in which

there is a lack of needed evidence. It would appear that there is no reason, therefore, why the new auditor cannot express an unqualified opinion on the beginning balance sheet when the auditor has, in the process of supporting the opinion on the current operating statements, collected sufficient, competent evidential matter. The previous year's operating statements do not offer the same opportunity for an unqualified opinion, since the balance sheet at the beginning of that year was not examined, and the internal controls were not tested for any purpose other than to identify the accounting principles used. Normally, this circumstance would indicate that a disclaimer of opinion is appropriate, because of the scope limitation.

The conclusion above, however, conflicts with SAS 15, "Reports on Comparative Financial Statements." That document, by implication in its para. 12, suggests that the new auditor maintain complete silence on his association with the previous year's financial statements, and on the extent of his examination and any conclusions reached. Instead, the new auditor is instructed to indicate in the scope paragraph the fact that the prior period statements were examined and reported on by other auditors, and to furnish the date of that report, as well as the type of opinion and certain other appropriate information. These instructions are, in my opinion, not consistent with the fourth reporting standard and in addition, may be misleading insofar as the predecessor's intended opinion coverage is concerned.

'. . .the most useful presentation is . . . to have the predecessor auditor re-express his opinion . . .'

The second problem area relating to the earlier year's financial statements results from the required reference to the predecessor auditor. The predecessor auditor expressed an opinion on the financial statements (including the notes) as they were presented at that time. If that presentation also included more than one year's statements, the auditor's opinion should have embraced both or all years presented. The number of years' financial statements presented and their manner of presentation, as well as such things as the form and arrangement of statements, their content, the items included, parenthetical and line item disclosures, and the report itself are part of the informative disclosures which must be reasonably adequate to comply with the third reporting standard.

Given the breadth of the disclosure concept, its integration into the auditing and accounting standards, and the inclusion of extensive required communication of any material data in notes to financial statements, there is no basis to conclude that excerpts or revisions of previously issued statements can be expected to fairly present financial position or results of operations. The profession feels so strongly about excerpts, for instance, that the AICPA now bluntly asserts that piecemeal opinions (i.e., opinions on partial or excerpted materials) are not appropriate. While special reports on less-than-complete information are allowed and often used, the financial data therein do not purport to fairly present financial position or the results of operations in accordance with GAAP.

Nonetheless, the instruction to the successor auditor in SAS No. 15 is clear. In those situations where the predecessor does not reissue or re-express an opinion (as is the practice with publicly owned companies filing with the SEC), the successor is to comment on the fact of the issuance of an opinion by another auditor which included the previous year's statements. The successor is not instructed or bound to reproduce the previous financial statements exactly as they were originally issued. In fact, it is reasonable to expect differences because not only will the previous statements be only partially presented, but the arrangement and wording suggested by different auditors normally tend to reflect individual auditing firm policies and therefore are apt to be different.

Summary

The professional objectives to be met by the auditor undertaking an initial audit engagement include meeting the general and field work auditing standards. These standards have been expanded and articulated by several interpretations, which impose requirements not necessarily evident from the standards themselves. Prudence and the due care standard dictate that a preliminary investigation be undertaken to determine whether the new auditor can reasonably expect to be able to comply with the auditing standards. The evidence requirements for the initial audit are not unique, except that the evidence must be gathered anew, assuming that it exists. The message conveyed is that the successor must do more work than simply rely to any significant extent on the predecessor auditor's opinion or his audit work.

The reporting standards are not so easily met by the new auditor. The apparent conflict between the standards and one of the interpretations (SAS No. 15) is currently unresolved. If SAS No. 15 is followed, I suggest that the reproduction of the prior statements be as faithful to the original as possible, to avoid any unfair inference about the opinion of the predecessor. There is no reason that the new auditor should be prevented from expressing an opinion on the prior year's balance sheet, consistent with the results of his current examination, if this would be useful. I recommend, consistent with the fourth reporting standard, that any part of SAS No. 15 suggesting otherwise, be withdrawn.

However, the most useful presentation is obviously to have the predecessor auditor re-express his opinion, as described in SAS 15.Ω

CASE 5

ATLANTIC CORPORATION

Alice Reynolds, president and major shareholder of Atlantic Corporation (a nonpublic company), visits your office on February 14, 19x2 and requests that your firm perform the audit of Atlantic Corporation for the year ended March 31, 19x2. Alice informs you that Atlantic was audited previously (19x1) by J. Bullington & Co., a local CPA firm that you are well acquainted with. Alice explains that Atlantic wishes to present to its approximately 40 shareholders and certain banking creditors comparative statements of financial position, results of operations, and changes in financial position. Alice gives you permission to communicate with the former auditors concerning the prior year's financial statements and other matters that may relate to your acceptance and performance of the engagements. However, Alice does not wish to be involved in any of the discussions or receive any communications from the former CPAs.

CASE DISCUSSION QUESTIONS

1. Why is early appointment of the auditor considered advantageous? Discuss. How may an audit engagement be complicated by appointment of the auditor near or after year-end? Explain.

2. In planning the audit of Atlantic Corporation, what are the significant matters that should be considered? When would it be appropriate to perform interim substantive audit procedures?

3. What is the purpose of an audit program? What types of procedures should be included in an audit program?

4. In planning an audit engagement, auditors should obtain a level of knowledge of the client's business that will enable them to plan and perform their examination in accordance with GAAS. How does knowledge of the client's business help the auditors in conducting an examination? Discuss.

5. During discussions with J. Bullington & Co., Jack Frost, the partner in charge, explains that there was a dispute concerning last year's audit report. The firm issued an unqualified opinion but a staff accountant working on the engagement felt that a qualified opinion was warranted based on evidence relating to an apparent material contingency that was not disclosed. Jack stated that after considerable argument he overruled the junior accountant and ordered the unqualified opinion. However, he warned Alice that in the future such information would have to be disclosed in the financial statements. Is there any procedure for a staff member of a CPA firm to disassociate himself or herself from the audit report issued by the firm? Discuss.

6. Why is inquiry of the predecessor auditor considered a necessary procedure before a successor auditor accepts an engagement?

7. In initiating communications with a predecessor auditor, what procedures should the successor auditor follow?

8. What specific inquiries would you direct to J. Bullington & Co. before accepting the Atlantic audit?

9. What obligation does a predecessor auditor have to respond to a successor auditor's proper inquiries?

10. Is J. Bullington & Co. required to make their working papers for the Atlantic audit available to you? Explain.

11. What working papers, regarding the Atlantic audit, would be of most interest to you as a successor auditor?

12. Assume that during the current examination of Atlantic's financial statements you discover information that leads you to believe that the prior year's financial statements may require revision. What actions should you take? Explain.

13. Discuss the problems that may be involved in an initial audit engagement. (Hint: see the article "The Initial Audit Engagement.")

14. The auditor's consideration of materiality is a matter of professional judgment. In planning audit procedures for the Atlantic Corporation audit, the auditor is generally influenced by the quantitative characteristics and susceptibility to risk of the account or class of transactions.

    To what extent should development of audit procedures be influenced by qualitative considerations related to errors or irregularities that may exist in the accounts?

15. In planning the nature, timing, and extent of audit procedures, the auditor must make certain decisions regarding audit risk and materiality.

    a.   Must the auditor make a preliminary estimate of audit risk and materiality levels?

    b.   How should an auditor apply a quantified preliminary estimate of materiality to the income statement and the balance sheet?

16. In continuing engagements, the auditor's procedures applied in the current period are generally influenced by the nature and cause of errors discovered in prior-period examinations.

    Specifically, to what extent would an error discovered in a prior-period affect consideration of audit procedures in the current period if a similar error is discovered during the current audit?

17. The concept of materiality is inherent in the work of the independent auditor. There should be stronger grounds to sustain the auditor's opinion with respect to those items which are relatively more important and with respect to those in which the possibilities of material error are greater.

    a.   What is audit risk?

    b.   What is business risk as it relates to the audit practice of a CPA?

18. Audit risk as it relates to an account balance or class of transactions is a combination of three component risks—inherent risk, control risk, and detection risk. Explain the meaning of each of these component risks:

    a.   Inherent risk:

    b.   Control risk:

    c.   Detection risk:

19. Detection risk arises partly from uncertainties that exist when the auditor does not examine 100 percent of an account balance or class of transactions and partly because of uncertainties that exist even if the auditor does examine every item in an account balance or class of transactions.

    a.   What is "nonsampling risk"?

    b.   What is "sampling risk"?

20. In the examination of the financial statements of Atlantic Corporation, you identify materiality thresholds of $10,000 for the income statement and $30,000 for the balance sheet.

    How is your establishment of materiality thresholds for the income statement and the balance sheet related to restricting audit risk for individual account balances or classes of transactions?

6

Analytical Review Procedures

(Section 318, SAS No. 23)

SAS No. 23 establishes a requirement that an auditor perform analytical review procedures which are considered substantive audit procedures, when conducting an examination of financial statements in accordance with GAAS. The statement does not require the performance of specific analytical review procedures but, rather, provides guidance for consideration by the auditor when he or she applies such procedures.

Analytical review procedures involve a study and comparison of relationships among data. A basic premise underlying analytical review procedures is that "relationships among data may reasonably be expected by the auditor to exist and continue in the absence of known conditions to the contrary." Accordingly, the results of applying analytical review procedures may indicate the need for additional evidence or indicate that subsequent substantive evidential procedures may be reduced regarding specific financial statement items.

Exceptions and unusual conditions indicated by the results of performing analytical review procedures should be investigated by the auditor if the auditor believes that they are indicative of matters that may have a significant effect on his or her examination.

Analytical review procedures may be performed early in the examination, during the conduct of the examination, or at or near the conclusion of the examination. The timing of the procedures depends on the auditor's objectives in applying the procedures. For example, some auditors apply the procedures early in the engagement as part of the planning of other audit tests. Others use analytical review procedures near the end of the examination as an overall review of the financial information.

Analytical review procedures may be performed using dollars, physical quantities, ratios, or percentages and they include the following procedures:

Comparison of the financial information with information for a comparable prior period(s)

Comparison of the financial information with anticipated results (for example, budgets and forecasts)

Study of the relationships of elements of financial information that would be expected to conform to a predictable pattern based on the entity's experience

Comparison of the financial information with similar information regarding the industry in which the entity operates

Study of relationships of the financial information with relevant nonfinancial information

Analytical review procedures may be applied to the overall financial information of an entity or to components of the financial statements. The following matters should be considered in planning and performing analytical review procedures:

The nature of the entity. For example, it may be more informative to apply the procedures to individual components of financial statements of entities rather than to statements taken as a whole.

The scope of the engagement. For example, an examination of a specified element, account, or item of a financial statement (in accordance with SAS No. 14, *Special Reports*) may result in fewer procedures than would an examination of financial statements taken as a whole.

The availability of financial information about the entity's financial position and results of operations. This may include such factors as budgets and forecasts as well as detailed financial information concerning interim periods, subsidiaries, and so forth.

The availability of relevant nonfinancial information. For example, this includes information such as units produced, sold, number of employees, etc., which may relate to financial information.

The reliability of financial and nonfinancial information. For example, if in previous examinations the auditor has determined that significant adjustments are required, he or she may decide not to conduct certain analytical review procedures until the adjusting journal entries have been made.

The comparability of available financial information regarding the industry in which the entity operates. For example, when comparing the results of analytical review procedures such as ratios or percentages with such information for the industry in which the client operates, the auditor must assure himself or herself that the industry data has been determined based on the same GAAP and procedures as those followed by the client. Also, the data must be representative of the client's operations. For example, it would be misleading to compare data of a client that sells specialty items with industry data relating to general merchandising type firms.

The increased availability of data prepared for management's use when computer processing is used. Computer systems have created an ability to store, retrieve, and analyze data for use in achieving broader management objectives. These data and analyses, although not necessarily part of the basic accounting records, may be valuable sources of information for the auditor to use in applying analytical review procedures, other substantive tests, or compliance testing (an amendment of SAS No. 23 from Section 1030, SAS No. 48, *The Effects of Computer Processing on the Examination of Financial Statements*).

The auditor should investigate exceptions indicated by the results of his or her analytical review procedures when he or she believes they may have a material effect on the examination. The auditor should investigate fluctuations that are not expected, the absence of fluctuations that are expected, and other items that appear to be unusual. Procedures would include inquiry of appropriate management personnel and additional procedures if considered necessary. For example, the auditor would make inquiry of management regarding an unusual matter or exception revealed by his or her analytical review procedures and evaluate management's response in light of his or her knowledge of the client's industry and business and information already developed during the audit engagement. If management's response is considered reasonable, no further action is required. Otherwise, the auditor would extend audit procedures to corroborate management's response. Such procedures may involve, for example, testing transactions or obtaining confirmations from other parties. If the auditor is unable to gather evidence to resolve the matter, the scope of the examination may be affected. Of course, the objective in performing analytical review procedures will affect the extent and nature of procedures performed regarding material exceptions or unusual items.

Analytical Review Procedures

By S. J. Lambert, CPA, Ph.D.
and Joyce C. Lambert, CPA, Ph.D.
at the University of Nebraska,
Lincoln.

One method of obtaining evidential matter required by the third standard of field work is by analytical review procedures. Analytical review procedures are defined in SAS No. 23 as "substantive tests of financial information made by a study and comparison of relationships among data."[1] SAS No. 23 was issued to provide guidance for an auditor applying analytical review procedures in an examination made in accordance with generally accepted auditing standards. No specific analytical review procedures are required by the statement since the particular procedures an auditor may employ in a given situation are a matter of judgment based on the circumstances of that situation.[2] The purpose of this article is to summarize some of the main points in SAS No. 23 entitled "Analytical Review Procedures" and to present a flowchart of that SAS.

Analytical review procedures provide evidential matter by demonstrating that expected relationships among data either exist or do not exist. Such analytical review procedures then indicate the nature and extent of other auditing procedures appropriate for the circumstances. They may be performed at various stages in the audit depending on the auditor's objectives. During the audit *planning stages* analytical review procedures assist the auditor in determining the auditing procedures to be employed. *During the actual audit examination* analytical review procedures may be applied to individual financial information elements in conjunction with other procedures. *At the conclusion of the audit* analytical review procedures can be used as an overall review of the financial information.[3]

Application of Analytical Review Procedures

As shown in Flowchart 2, using judgment the auditor selects various methods to apply selected analytical review procedures to financial information of the entity. A number of factors should be considered when planning and performing analytical review procedures. These include:

1. The nature of the entity;
2. The scope of the engagement;
3. The availability of financial information about the entity's financial position and results of operations;
4. The availability of relevant nonfinancial information;
5. The reliability of financial and nonfinancial information; and
6. The availability and comparability of financial information regarding the industry in which the entity operates.[4]

Significant Fluctuations

The auditor should investigate significant fluctuations that are not expected, the absence of expected fluctuations, and other items that appear to be unusual when they may have a significant effect on his examination. Ordinarily, management is able to explain these fluctuations. The auditor needs to evaluate management's replies and consider the need to corroborate these replies by using other auditing procedures. If management is not able satisfactorily to explain unexpected deviations, the auditor should perform additional procedures.[5]

In investigating fluctuations, the auditor should consider the following:

1. The purpose of the analytical review procedures;
2. The nature of the item;
3. His knowledge of the entity's business;
4. The results of other auditing procedures; and
5. His study and evaluation of internal control.[6]

The auditor also should be alert to relate his findings to other parts of his examination where additional procedures may be warranted.[7]

Conclusion

SAS No. 23 does not impose any required procedures in an audit. It is intended to provide guidance to the auditor in the area of analytical review procedures.

[1] *SAS No. 23, "Analytical Review Procedures,"* (New York, AICPA), 1978, paragraph 2.
[2] *Ibid.*, paragraphs 1 and 2.
[3] *Ibid.*, paragraph 5.
[4] *Ibid.* paragraph 7.
[5] *Ibid.*, paragraph 8.
[6] *Ibid.*, paragraph 9.
[7] *Ibid.*, paragraph 10.

FLOWCHART II
Statement on Auditing Standards 23 Analytical Review Procedures

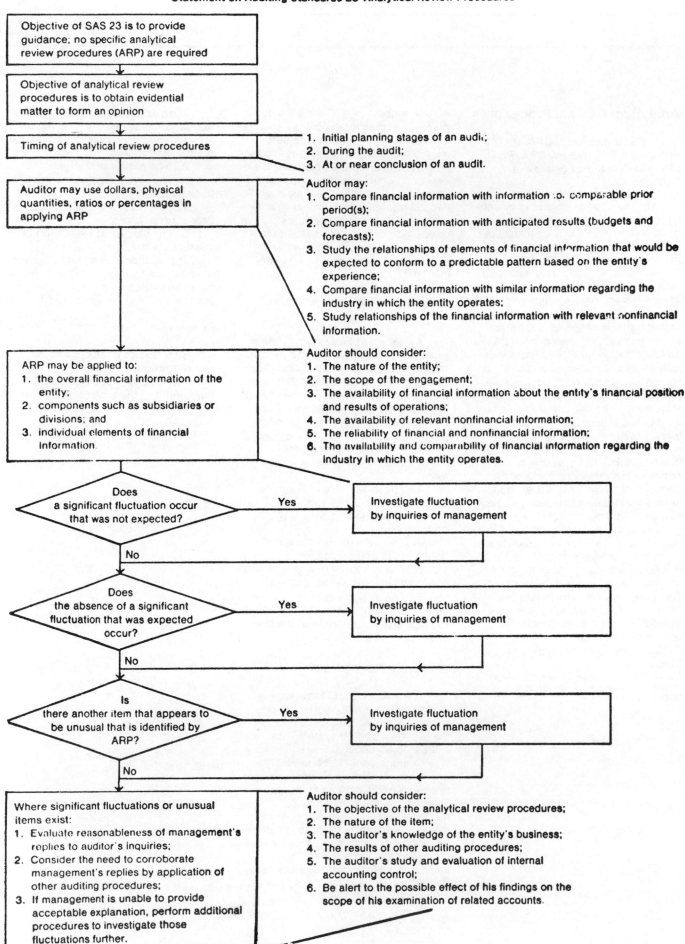

Objective of SAS 23 is to provide guidance; no specific analytical review procedures (ARP) are required

Objective of analytical review procedures is to obtain evidential matter to form an opinion

Timing of analytical review procedures

1. Initial planning stages of an audit;
2. During the audit;
3. At or near conclusion of an audit.

Auditor may use dollars, physical quantities, ratios or percentages in applying ARP

Auditor may:
1. Compare financial information with information of comparable prior period(s);
2. Compare financial information with anticipated results (budgets and forecasts);
3. Study the relationships of elements of financial information that would be expected to conform to a predictable pattern based on the entity's experience;
4. Compare financial information with similar information regarding the industry in which the entity operates;
5. Study relationships of the financial information with relevant nonfinancial information.

ARP may be applied to:
1. the overall financial information of the entity;
2. components such as subsidiaries or divisions; and
3. individual elements of financial information.

Auditor should consider:
1. The nature of the entity;
2. The scope of the engagement;
3. The availability of financial information about the entity's financial position and results of operations;
4. The availability of relevant nonfinancial information;
5. The reliability of financial and nonfinancial information;
6. The availability and comparability of financial information regarding the industry in which the entity operates.

Does a significant fluctuation occur that was not expected? — Yes → Investigate fluctuation by inquiries of management

No

Does the absence of a significant fluctuation that was expected occur? — Yes → Investigate fluctuation by inquiries of management

No

Is there another item that appears to be unusual that is identified by ARP? — Yes → Investigate fluctuation by inquiries of management

No

Where significant fluctuations or unusual items exist:
1. Evaluate reasonableness of management's replies to auditor's inquiries;
2. Consider the need to corroborate management's replies by application of other auditing procedures;
3. If management is unable to provide acceptable explanation, perform additional procedures to investigate those fluctuations further.

Auditor should consider:
1. The objective of the analytical review procedures;
2. The nature of the item;
3. The auditor's knowledge of the entity's business;
4. The results of other auditing procedures;
5. The auditor's study and evaluation of internal accounting control;
6. Be alert to the possible effect of his findings on the scope of his examination of related accounts.

JANUARY 1983

Analytical Review: Misconceptions, Applications and Experience—Part I

This is the first of a two-part article on analytical review developments in practice. The author describes six common misconceptions concerning analytical review techniques; these misconceptions should clear up as the fallacies underlying each are made clear. The author outlines the continuum of available analytical review procedures, as well as potential applications.

Wanda A. Wallace, CPA, CMA, CIA, Ph.D.

WHEN the term "analytical review techniques" is mentioned to the auditor, the first word association made is likely to be "reasonableness tests" and the second "planning tool." This latter part of the reaction is an unfortunate effect of traditional auditor training that stressed the role of reasonableness checks of account balances in allocating audit time. Yet, SAS 23, "Analytical Review Procedures," defines such procedures as "*substantive tests* of financial information made by a study and comparison of relationships among data" (emphasis added).

While accustomed to describing confirmation procedures, inventory observation and the examination of vouchers and related documents as substantive testing techniques, the auditor is unaccustomed to giving equal weight to analytical review procedures. Perceived apprehension is, in part, justifiable due to the specific techniques which come to mind when an analytical review approach is discussed:

• Percentage change in an account from the prior period or from the corresponding time in the prior fiscal year,

• The difference between recorded numbers and budgeted figures, and

Wanda A. Wallace, CPA, CMA, CIA, Ph.D., is the Marilyn R. and Leo F. Corrigan, Jr., Trustee Professor at Southern Methodist University and currently consults with Price Waterhouse. She is a member of the AICPA, AAA, IMA, and IIA, and a member of the IIA Board of Regents. Dr. Wallace has written articles for a number of professional and academic journals.

• The stability of such key ratios as gross profit, return and turnover statistics.

These are what might be termed "soft evidence" techniques which frequently consider only a few pieces of data, aggregated at the annual or entity level, and require a high degree of subjectivity in their implementation. For example:

• What is a reasonable percentage change? Ten percent?

• What if a 40 percent change were expected? Should it be investigated merely because it exceeds some ten percent benchmark? What of those five percent fluctuations that were expected to be 40 percent?

• How accurate should budgets be to justify their use in analytical review? If a budget is continually updated, can it serve as an effective benchmark for evaluating actual operations?

• When is a large change in some key ratio sufficiently "explained," and when is additional testing required?

The subjectivity that permeates currently used techniques is perhaps clearest on review of a set of working papers for a limited review engagement. The documentation tends to be lengthy, replete with explanatory memos about what supposedly caused the "unusual fluctuations" observed. Every environmental factor from the weather to inflation and every internal factor from employees' turnover to new product developments can be invoked, frequently "explaining" fluctuations in offsetting directions. Little objective support for the reasonableness of the explanations received, particularly about their relevance to the total dollars of the unusual fluctuations that have been detected, is available. In fact, a telling and popular anecdote in the field of the perceived value of verbal explanations of unusual fluctuations, involves the CPA who mistakenly asked why an expense item was down, when in fact it was up, relative to prior years. The client provided a list of explanations as to why that account might be low. Upon discovery of the error, the CPA returned to the client, explaining the prior mistake, and asked why that same expense item was, in fact, up. With little effort, the client developed a list of explanations of why the account that had been previously ''explained'' to be low, could similarly be ''explained'' to be high!

There can be little question that the prevalence of ''soft'' analytical review procedures has relegated the technique to one on which little reliance is placed throughout the audit process. However, this widespread ''mind-set'' by practitioners is analogous to the results one would expect if sampling procedures had been introduced into the auditing literature with no explanation of their theoretical foundations or of acceptable systematic sampling plan approaches, and with an emphasis on drawing samples that achieved a 50 percent confidence level. If practitioners thereby inferred that sampling conclusions were subjective and could provide no greater comfort than a 50 percent confidence level, CPAs' interest in such techniques might well have diminished.

'. . . the auditor is unaccustomed to giving equal weight to analytical review procedures.'

Analytical review techniques can be placed on a continuum from ''soft evidence'' to ''hard evidence,'' depending on the particular audit procedure used. Kinney and Felix (1980) present a summary table that classifies the analytical review methods, termed judgmental, rules of thumb, time trend and structural techniques, according to the objectivity of predictions and the determination of the reliability of predictions. Another dimension of these methods is the quantity, quality and type of data used in their application. The distinction made by Kinney and Felix stressed the use of ''any available information'' for judgmental methods, ''past audited values'' for each of the other methods, and ''quantifiable environmental information'' in structural models. Such a summary both overstates the capabilities of judgmental methods and understates the capabilities of structural models for analytical review. To claim that subjective methods are apparently able to incorporate any data available is similar to saying that because one is not deaf and hears someone speaking Japanese, he is able to understand and assimilate what is heard. The behavioral literature is replete with problems that decision makers have with analyzing large quantities of data (see Libby, 1981). Conversations with

practitioners similarly confirm that CPAs have a general feeling of frustration regarding how the effects of *numerous* environmental and company-specific attributes on reported accounting numbers can be appropriately evaluated as being either reasonable or unreasonable. In fact, if one wishes to include many types of statistics in an analytical review procedure, a more formalized approach to modeling relationships has clear and significant advantages due, in part, to its data management capabilities. The information to be integrated need not be quantifiable, since multivariate modeling techniques can reflect qualitative attributes such as geographical location or seasonality through the creation of so-called ''dummy variables.'' What's more, information used need not rely on stable operations over time, since cross-sectional applications, comparing substantive balances across similar units of operation at a single point in time as a check on reasonableness, can also be valuable analytical review tools.

Of course, how well a structured analytical review procedure will perform depends on how well structured the selected model is, but that problem relates to all alternative analytical review procedures. In other words, how well a rule of thumb works will, in large part, depend on whether the rule of thumb is well specified and captures the particular operating attributes of interest.

Misconceptions Concerning Analytical Review

Table 1 describes common misconceptions concerning analytical review techniques; I believe these represent obstacles or ''blotches'' on the profession's road to progress in gathering a sufficient evidential base for rendering an audit report in the most efficient manner. The first two points I have already stressed: analytical review need not depend on ''soft tools,'' and formal structural approaches can consider all the available relevant information, as defined by the auditor, more effectively than a purely judgmental model. Granted, the cost of formalizing and quantifying certain relevant factors may lead the CPA to select a combined structural/judgmental approach. In such an approach certain unusual but expected fluctuations are judgmentally analyzed, rather than being ''controlled'' through the structural model. However, the existence of numerous relevant operating and environmental factors affecting operations does not preclude the usefulness of parsimonious structural models in providing assurance that recorded financial figures are fairly stated. Many of the so-called relevant factors will have only an indirect (a third-or-fourth-order) effect that results in no more than an immaterial change in an account of audit interest. For example, the unemployment rate in a region may affect business sales, but while having a direct effect on car sales, it is likely to have only a minor effect on food sales. Hence, in modeling a grocery store's sales, the unemployment rate, while relevant, is likely to be an insignificant factor when formulating projections.

This leads to the third misconception raised in Table 1 of ''no news is better than bad news'' which could just

TABLE 1

Misconceptions Concerning Analytical Review Techniques
"Blotches" on the Profession's Road to Progress

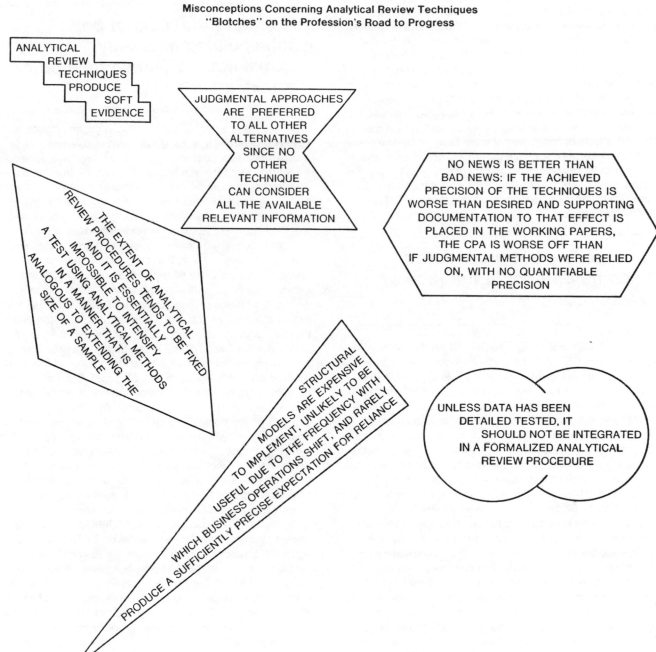

as easily be phrased "ignorance is bliss." The misconception reflects a misunderstanding of the audit process and the method by which the auditor assimilates evidence from a variety of sources to formulate the final opinion on the financial statements. At the risk of overdoing clichés, the misconception stresses the attitude "it's all or nothing" whereby a tool which helps the CPA to assess the

reasonableness of accounting figures is of no use if that tool must be complemented by any other audit procedure. Part of this misconception stems from some illogic that is prevalent in the literature's discussion of analytical review.

Holder and Collmer claim "the absence of unusual fluctuations may not represent adequate evidence to cause the auditor to limit other substantive tests; however, the presence of unexpected fluctuations should normally result in an expansion of other substantive tests.'' Similarly, Kinney and Felix state, ''In a sense, the lack of expected relationships should cause the auditor to extend planned tests. Whether the converse is true may be the subject of considerable debate.'' The example provided by Kinney and Felix involves the possibility of fraud whereby results are manipulated to match to expectations and, therefore, the capability of analytical review procedures to perform effectively is thwarted. First, it must be acknowledged that many audit procedures become defunct in the face of fraud, and that, in fact, analytical review procedures which utilize data that cannot be manipulated internally, despite poor controls, may prove more effective than other substantive tests in detecting irregularities. This point will be discussed in greater depth in Part II of this article.

'. . . many audit procedures become defunct in the face of fraud, . . .'

Second, an inconsistency exists when the claim is made that a tool can tell the auditor where some problem lies, yet, for some inexplicable reason, is incapable of simultaneously telling the auditor where the problem does not lie. An attention-director by definition also diminishes attention elsewhere; to suggest otherwise is asymmetric logic. What has happened, in the literature, is that instead of discussing the capabilities of analytical review or evaluating its actual performance, the loss function of the auditor has been emphasized, drawing a conclusion that is contrary to SAS No. 23. The auditor must assess the sufficiency of audit evidence and is likely to stress Type II errors, i.e. errors in assuming account balances are right when they are wrong. In attempting to minimize such errors, the auditor will combine a variety of compliance and substantive tests, not because any particular test is deemed to be ineffective, but because the professional responsibilities of the auditor to detect material errors, with the concurrent liability exposure to Type II errors, lead to a rigorous standard in judging audit evidence to be sufficient. The analytical review tool itself provides evidence concerning whether balances are reasonable, with a stated precision if structural models are used, just as it provides evidence concerning whether balances are unreasonable. The fact that additional precision may be required before determining that evidence is sufficient to judge the financial figures to be fairly presented reflects the asymmetrical loss function of the CPA, not an inherent asymmetrical power of analytical review procedures. When SAS No. 23 suggests the possibility of substituting analytical review procedures for other substantive tests, no asymmetry in the type of evidence provided is implied,

as the issue of procedures' performance is kept distinct from the issue of what is sufficient evidence.

'. . . data that cannot be manipulated internally, . . . may prove more effective than other substantive tests. . .'

This leads to the question of whether an analytical review procedure that supports ''reasonableness'' at a ten percent level is of any use to an auditor who assesses materiality to be three percent. The answer from an experienced auditor will be ''yes,'' but that procedure will have to be augmented by additional audit evidence to reduce the ten percent uncertainty to three percent. Those who respond ''no'' are likely to misunderstand the ten percent statistic. That figure does not mean that an account is ''wrong'' by ten percent; it merely means that the technology in use only has the power to support recorded balances as being within ten percent of expected balances. That piece of evidence is a quantifiable, objective reasonableness check which can be used to determine that the extent of additional tests will be less than would have been the case had no such reasonableness tests been performed. If a structural model only provided a 50 percent precision measure, the CPA may find that the audit team's knowledge of client operations is inadequate or the modeled operations are illogical. Auditing problems can be uncovered which may not have been identified, had the analytical review procedure not been applied. For example, if payroll expenses are not well described by the number of employees and the average pay rate, the CPA receives a signal to investigate for misclassified or bogus charges to that account. If something is in error or if some key aspect of operations or the environment affects recorded accounting numbers differently than expected, such information is of value to the CPA. Similarly, when the balances appear reasonable at some level of precision, a contribution is made to assessing the overall reasonableness of the financial statements. Precedence exists for the merger of audit test findings, none of which alone would provide the overall required precision for the audit engagement. For example, when compliance tests indicate a maximum error rate of five to seven percent, the auditor combines this finding with other audit evidence to judge the system's performance. However, if the five to seven percent limit were the actual error, such figures would very likely exceed the overall desired precision. What is recognized is that the five to seven percent rate: (1) relates to compliance errors which may or may not cause financial statement errors; and (2) represents an upper limit that may substantially exceed the actual error rate. This sampling result contributes to the evidential base that, when combined with other tests, is used to formulate an audit opinion.

TABLE 2

Varying the Extent of Analytical Review Procedures

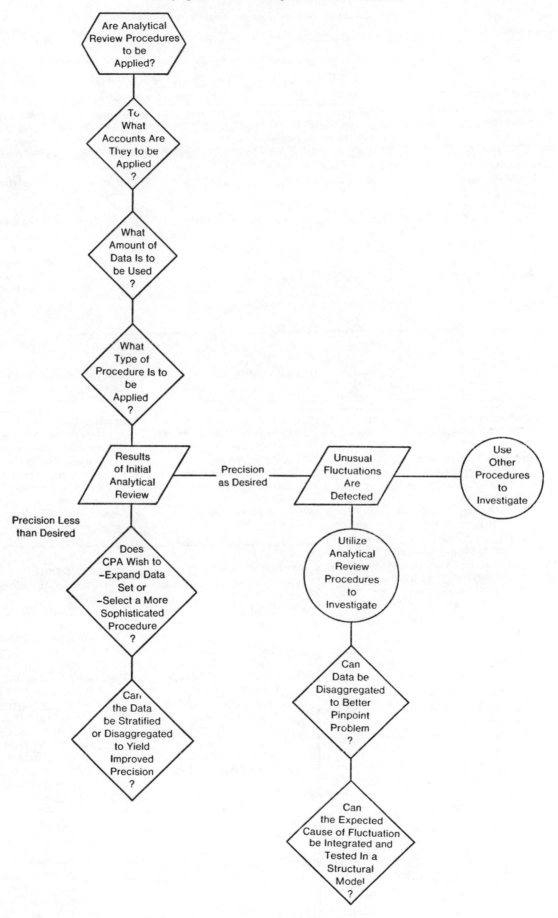

TABLE 3

The Continuum of Available Analytical Review Procedures

A COMPARISON OF 2 POINTS IN TIME	USE OF A SINGLE BENCHMARK	USE OF HISTORICAL DATA FOR A SINGLE ACCOUNT	USE OF A SMALL SET OF INTERNAL DATA
%Change from Prior Period %Change from Similar Period in Prior Year What Were the Risk Areas Last Period? In Which Accounts Were Adjustments Booked Last Period?	Budgeted Amount Industry Rate of Return Chief Competitor's Performance A Turnover Ratio or Similar Operating Statistic	Time Trend Extrapolations –graphical –regressions –other ARIMA techniques Useful Rules of Thumb from Past Experience, Such as Known Cyclical Patterns	Ratio Analysis on Three to Five Years of Annual Data Variance Analysis Over the Recent Past Extrapolations from a Short Historical Base Period, Such as the Gross Profit Rate for Three Years Implying a Rate for Next Year Comparison of One Unit of Operation to Other Similar Units of Operation

USE OF A SMALL SET OF INTERNAL/EXTERNAL DATA	USE OF A LARGE NUMBER OF DATA POINTS GENERATED INTERNALLY	USE OF A LARGE NUMBER OF DATA POINTS GENERATED INTERNALLY AND EXTERNALLY
Comparison of Recent Experience to the Industry, Including Ratio Analysis Market Share Performance Economic Benchmarks –for the industry –for the company –for particular regions Operating Statistics' Comparison to the Environment, e.g. A Utility's Comparison to Weather Statistics Extrapolations from a Short Historical Base Period, Such as the Relationship of Degree Days to Gas Production Statistics for Three Years Implying a Relationship for Next Year	Structural Regression Models –time series comparisons of accounts and internal operating statistics –cross-sectional comparisons of units of operation Judgmental Comparisons	Structural Regression Models –time series comparisons of accounts, internal operating statistics, industry statistics, environmental attributes, and economic barometers Judgmental Comparisons

ATTRIBUTES THAT DIFFER ACROSS AVAILABLE PROCEDURES
- EASE OF USE
- NUMBER OF DATA POINTS UTILIZED
- SOURCE OF DATA INTEGRATED
- BUSINESS APPROACH FACILITATED
- HISTORICAL PERSPECTIVE PROVIDED
- OBJECTIVITY OF INFERENCES DRAWN
- RELIABILITY OF PROJECTIONS FORMULATED

SOURCES OF DATA FOR USE IN ANALYTICAL REVIEW PROCEDURES
- ACCOUNTING DEPARTMENT
- CLIENT'S LONG-RANGE FORECASTING DEPARTMENT
- MARKETING, PRODUCTION, AND OTHER OPERATING DEPARTMENTS
- GOVERNMENT
- TRADE JOURNALS, MOODY'S, STANDARD & POOR'S, VALUE LINE, AND SIMILAR SERVICES
- ON-LINE DATA BASES, INCLUDING
  * NAARS
  * DISCLO
  * NEXIS
  * DIALOG & ORBIT
  * THE NEW YORK TIME INFORMATION BANK
  * THE DOW JONES NEWS/RETRIEVAL SYSTEM
  * CITIBANK

A fourth and related misconception concerns the ability of the CPA to extend analytical review procedures. The claim has been made that the extent of analytical review procedures tends to be fixed (Kinney and Felix). This claim reflects existing practice more than it reflects possibilities. Consider Table 2. Means of varying the extent of analytical review in terms of number of accounts audited, quantity of data used in such analyses, and sophistication of audit procedures used are perhaps obvious. Less obvious is the ability to take a particular month of operations that is out-of-line and to extend analytical review procedures by performing an analysis across subunits of operations, to investigate which appears to be out-of-line, in relation to all other units, in that month. Similarly, by stratifying data as frequently done in sampling, the CPA may be able to achieve desired precision and to better pinpoint trouble-spots, than through some alternative approach. If the CPA has an idea that, for example, the unusual fluctuations were due to the periodic closing of a nuclear plant, such an operating characteristic could be formally integrated into a structural model to see if, in fact, the fluctuations were thereby "explained." In this manner a CPA can objectively assess the "reasonableness" of client explanations by extending analytical review procedures.

'. . . whether it is appropriate to use nonaccounting data which has not been tested by the auditor. . .'

Returning to Table 1, the fifth prevalent misconception concerns the expense of sophisticated analytical review procedures and the plausibility of applying them to clients, most of whose business operations are in a continual state of flux. The use of structural models requires improved planning, additional training of personnel, computer software and the collection of more than merely the prior year's data or a small subset of operating units' data. However, the ongoing cost of using such structural models, once familiarity with the technique is obtained, is likely to be nominal (see Akresh and Wallace, 1982). The benefits of the modeling approach relate to audit efficiency and effectiveness. The audit coverage can include an historical perspective from three to any number of years' monthly data, taking all of the monthly figures for those periods to formulate predictions of monthly balances for the current period. Similarly, the coverage can compare all 100 or more operating units to one another in a systematic manner, which produces a quantifiable precision. While by no means synonymous with a 100 percent sample for a particular account, the technique does review the reasonableness of numbers that is intended to reflect 100 percent of the transactions in that account.

The concern for instability of operations is likely to be overstated relative to the robustness of modeling techniques and the frequent ability to capture variability in operations through the structuring of the models themselves. If the period of interest includes a major strike or some similar source of instability, a dummy variable can be used for that strike period, in addition to relevant volume statistics, and the precision obtained—while not as tight as would be possible had no strike occurred—might well be sufficient to meet the CPA's objectives for a particular substantive test. In addition, cross-sectional analysis techniques can often be of use in auditing multi-unit operations that are not stable across time but tend, nevertheless, to be comparable across units. The units need not be separate operating units, as departments and similar subunits can be effectively analyzed by cross-sectional regression models.

Experience reported to date suggests that structural models are useful in auditing a wide variety of companies and that the effects of normal business fluctuations do not significantly limit the models' usefulness. Prime rate, inflation and similar contributors to instability can be explicitly incorporated in models to generate useful predictions.

'. . . using judgmental analytical review procedures, the CPA has implicitly relied on nonaccounting data. . .'

An important benefit to a structural modeling approach is the ability to integrate external data that can be effective in exposing the manipulation of internal data, which might otherwise be overlooked. This brings us to the final misconception noted in Table 1. The question is raised whether it is appropriate to use nonaccounting data which has not been tested by the auditor and which may not be subject to the internal accounting control system that has been reviewed. At least two considerations are relevant. The first is the source of that data. If the question is posed—should the auditor concentrate on accounting generated data to test the reasonableness of accounting data or should data generated by other departments, such as marketing, production and long-range forecasting, be used in spite of the risk of error in such data. The layman is likely to prefer an "independent" check on the accounting department. Economical means of checking the reasonableness of the nonaccounting internal data to be used are frequently available through comparisons to industry statistics, demographic data and other externally available information. For example, the number of customers serviced can be compared to population statistics and reported market share; kilowatt hours can be compared to production capacity and degree days as maintained by the weather bureau; and the correlation

TABLE 4

Potential Applications of Analytical Review Techniques

AUDIT SAMPLING SAS #39

AUDITING CLIENTS' JUDGMENT PROCESS

COMPLYING WITH STATEMENTS ON AUDITING STANDARDS*

"The auditor often is aware of account balances and transactions that may be more likely to contain errors. He considers this knowledge in planning his procedures, including audit sampling" (AICPA, 1981, p. 1)

Audit risk tends to increase as the issue involved is
- nonroutine,
- subjective,
- uncontrollable, and
- subject to manipulation

Past cases involving such issues include:

CASE	ISSUE
Mill Factors	Collectibility of Receivables
Talley Industries, Inc.	Estimates of future contracts to be awarded and future cost reductions
National Telephone, Inc.	Estimate of provisions for future maintenance costs
Fisco, Inc.	Estimates of insurance loss reserves

SOURCE: "Auditing the Client's Judgments" by Cohen and Pearson, *Journal of Accountancy* (May 1981)

GOING CONCERNS
SAS No. 34 "The Auditor's Considerations When a Question Arises About an Entity's Continual Existence"

SUPPLEMENTARY DISCLOSURES
SAS No. 33 and 40 "Supplementary Oil and Gas Reserve Information"; "Supplementary Mineral Reserve Information"

INTERIM REVIEWS
SAS No. 36 "Review of Interim Financial Information"
* [see also, Statement on Standards for Accounting and Review Services No. 1 (December, 1978) and *The AICPA Guide for a Review of a Financial Forecast* (1980) for the techniques used in providing review services and in reviewing forecasts.]

ANALYTICAL REVIEW CAN BE A USEFUL DIRECTING TECHNIQUE, OR PRESAMPLING METHODOLOGY; MORE MILEAGE IS OBTAINABLE FROM SAMPLING "UNREASONABLE" ACCOUNTS

JUDGMENTS CANNOT EASILY BE SUBJECTED TO DETAILED TESTING; RIGOROUS ANALYTICAL REVIEW TECHNIQUES ARE PARTICULARLY APPROPRIATE. STRUCTURAL MODELS CAN BE USED TO TEST THE REASONABLENESS OF ASSUMPTIONS, AND SENSITIVITY ANALYSIS CAN BE PERFORMED TO INVESTIGATE THE EFFECT OF ASSUMPTIONS. IN ADDITION, WHENEVER CLIENTS PROVIDE EXPLANATIONS OF UNUSUAL ACCOUNT BALANCES, SUCH EXPLANATIONS OFTEN CAN BE TESTED THROUGH INCLUSION OF ANOTHER EXPLANATORY VARIABLE IN THE MODEL BEING APPLIED.

ANALYTICAL REVIEW PROCEDURES ARE DISCUSSED THROUGHOUT THE AUDITING AND REVIEW LITERATURE, OFTEN WITH REFERENCES TO PARTICULAR RATIOS OR RELATIONSHIPS TO BE EVALUATED. IF "SOFTER, MORE FUTURE-ORIENTED DISCLOSURES" CONTINUE TO GROW IN NUMBER, ANALYTICAL REVIEW PROCEDURES MAY VERY WELL BE THE ONLY AVAILABLE AUDIT PROCEDURE TO EFFICIENTLY ASSESS THE REASONABLENESS OF SUCH INFORMATION

TABLE 4 (cont'd)

Potential Applications of Analytical Review Techniques

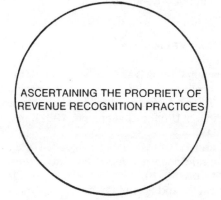

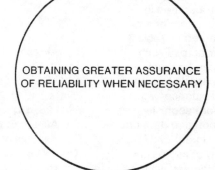

ASCERTAINING THE PROPRIETY OF REVENUE RECOGNITION PRACTICES	OBTAINING GREATER ASSURANCE OF RELIABILITY WHEN NECESSARY	AUDIT RISK DETECTION

Bill and Hold Sales
Layaway Sales
Sales/repurchase agreements
Publication and record subscriptions
Servicing fees included in the price of the product
Admission fees relating to the subscription to a number of special events like artistic performances

"When evidential matter can be obtained from independent sources outside an entity, it provides greater assurance of reliability for the purposes of an independent audit than that secured solely within the entity."
(SAS No. 31, pp 5 and 6)

– Bankruptcy Models, if the Type I error rate could be reduced
– Market reaction tests of news announcements, particularly to support rate case requests
– Perusal of media stories on prospective clients to evaluate their image, business associates, performance, and liabilities from existing claims and litigation, as well as to formulate expectations as to recorded financial figures and predictable patterns.

REVENUE RECOGNITION PRACTICES ARE OFTEN BASED ON PAST TRENDS AND EXPERIENCES, IMPLYING THAT ANALYTICAL REVIEW PROCEDURES CAN CHECK THE REASONABLENESS OF RECORDED FIGURES. FOR EXAMPLE, THE QUESTION CAN BE ADDRESSED AS TO WHAT AMOUNT OF A DEPOSIT HAD TYPICALLY BEEN PAID AND HOW MANY DAYS HAD NORMALLY PASSED BEFORE A CUSTOMER COULD BE DEEMED TO BE UNLIKELY TO LEAVE LAYAWAY MERCHANDISE, WITHOUT COMPLETING THE PURCHASE TRANSACTION?

ANALYTICAL REVIEW FACILITATES THE USE OF A BROADER SCOPE OF DATA IN RATIO ANALYSIS, THE REVIEW OF INDUSTRY LEVEL TRENDS, AND THE FORMULATION OF STRUCTURAL MODELS, THEREBY YIELDING MORE ASSURANCE THAN PROVIDED FROM TESTING ONLY INTERNAL DATA.

THE POTENTIAL OF ANALYTICAL REVIEW TECHNIQUES IN SELECTING AUDIT CLIENTS, EVALUATING RISK PROFILES OF CLIENT PORTFOLIOS, AND USING MARKET MEASURES TO EVALUATE THE EFFECT OF VARIOUS EVENTS ON PRESENT CLIENTS IS VIRTUALLY UNTAPPED BY CURRENT PRACTICE.

of company-specific pricing data with industry pricing statistics may establish the acceptability of such information for integration in structural models. Traditionally, using judgmental analytical review procedures, the CPA has implicitly relied on nonaccounting data as useful benchmarks for assessing the reasonableness of accounting information; the formalization of analytical review in no way alters the propriety of such reliance.

Continuum of Available Analytical Review Procedures and Potential Applications

As the misconceptions outlined in Table 1 begin to erode, the potential of analytical review procedures in practice can begin to be realized. The continuum of available analytical review procedures is presented in Table 3, with summaries of the attributes that differ across such procedures and the sources of data that can be used in the various approaches. The continuum extends from the left end, representing fairly simple, "soft evidence" approaches, to the far right, representing more sophisticated, "hard evidence" approaches. As practice develops toward the right end of the continuum, the intent of SAS No. 23 will begin to be fulfilled. Current practice has emphasized the first two points along the continuum with only occasional attention to the remaining available procedures. Yet despite the use of only a small subset of available analytical review procedures, the potential applications of analytical review techniques are an integral part of auditing standards and are suggested throughout the literature, as useful approaches in auditing clients' judgments, revenue recognition practices and audit risk exposure (Kida, 1980). Mathematical models to predict client failure (Altman and McGough) are being used by Touche Ross (1975) and Arthur Andersen. Table 4 provides excerpts from the literature, references to auditing standards that suggest the application of analytical review procedures and examples of specific issues which could be addressed with analytical review techniques to provide more reliable evidential matter than would be provided from testing only internally generated data. Ω

References

Akresh, Abraham D. and Wanda A. Wallace, "The Application of Regression Analysis for Limited Review and Audit Planning," *Fourth Symposium on Auditing Research* (University of Illinois at Urbana-Champaign, 1982), pp. 67–128; 147–161.

Altman E. I. and T. P. McGough, "Evaluation of a Company as a Going Concern," *Journal of Accountancy* (December, 1974), pp. 50–57.

Holder, William W. and Sheryl Collmer, "Analytical Review Procedures: New Relevance," *The CPA Journal* (November, 1980), pp. 29–35.

Kida, Thomas, "An Investigation into Auditors' Continuity and Related Qualification Judgments," *Journal of Accounting Research* (Autumn, 1980), pp. 506–523.

Kinney, William R., Jr. and William Felix, Jr., "Analytical Review Procedures," *Journal of Accountancy* (October, 1980), pp. 98–103.

Libby, Robert, *Accounting and Human Information Processing: Theory and Applications* (Prentice-Hall, 1981).

Touche Ross & Company, *Financial Analysis as an Audit Tool* (New York: Touche Ross & Co., 1975).

Thought for the Month

Experience is a wonderful thing. It enables you to recognize a mistake when you make it again.

FEBRUARY 1983

Analytical Review: Misconceptions, Applications and Experience* —Part II

This is the second of a two-part article on analytical review developments in practice. In this part, the author covers the effectiveness of analytical review procedures, focusing on companies that have reported erroneous accounting results and have received media coverage that has cited auditors' apparent inability to uncover the problem. The shortcomings of traditional auditing techniques and the capability of analytical review procedures to signal such problems are described. The advantages to developing more sophisticated analytical review techniques are enumerated.

Wanda A. Wallace, CPA, CMA, CIA, Ph.D.

IN this Part II of the article, the potential uses of analytical review techniques are elaborated by providing some "what if" descriptions of how such techniques might have uncovered accounting problems that have been reported by the press. In addition, actual field experience with the structural modeling approach of regression analysis is shared with the profession, including how the evidence collected could be effectively integrated with evidence gathered from applying other auditing techniques.

Relative Effectiveness of Analytical Review Procedures

Even as the misconceptions concerning analytical review procedures are resolved, another obstacle to any change from traditional auditing techniques will remain. That important obstacle to effectively addressing key auditing issues with "strong evidence" analytical review approaches is the bias that exists in the field to do what was done last year and not to place one's self in the position of justifying why a past audit procedure was no longer necessary. The latter position assumes risk; what if that omitted procedure would have uncovered a defalcation which subsequently comes to light? The CPA is typically not concerned that liability responsibility will arise from not using a more effective and efficient approach, as long as that approach has never been used in prior years' audits. Yet, history has suggested otherwise. In the "Salad Oil King" discovery, an important question arose of why wasn't the client's inventory compared with the reported world's supply of salad oil? Similarly, in Equity Funding, the public questioned why someone did not notice that the implied growth rate in reinsurance would have shortly led to 100 percent of the market being controlled by a single company? Surely such techniques would have been preferable to many of the detailed tests which were performed on bogus documentation to evaluate the fairness of financial statements. The CPA must evaluate the quality of evidence currently being collected and the effectiveness of alternative procedures, particularly analytical review procedures, in providing assurance of the reasonableness of account balances.

Wanda A. Wallace, CPA, CMA, CIA, Ph.D., is the Marilyn R. and Leo F. Corrigan, Jr. Trustee Professor at Southern Methodist University and currently consults with Price Waterhouse. She is a member of the AICPA, AAA, IMA and IIA, and a member of the IIA Board of Regents. Dr. Wallace has written articles for a number of professional and academic journals.

* The author thanks Price Waterhouse for permitting her to report on some of the firm's field experience with regression analysis.

The Equity Funding type of case is an obvious example of where mere reasonableness tests using external data would have presumably signalled the irregularity. However, let's consider a less obvious case, that of *Heinz* (Table 1). This case involved misstatements that were immaterial on an annual basis and "just material" on a quarterly basis. Many would immediately acknowledge the low probability of any CPA identifying the irregularity.

'. . . the bias . . . exists . . . to do what was done last year . . .'

However, the purpose of Table 1 is to suggest the obvious limitations of commonly applied substantive testing techniques in uncovering this type of irregularity, in which collusion with third parties provided detailed documentation of transactions that appeared, on face value, to be totally legitimate. In such cases, the presumed "hard evidence" techniques, like confirmation procedures and the sampling and inspection of detailed documentation, are likely to be entirely ineffective in providing any clue of an audit problem. In contrast, various analytical review procedures do have the capability of providing signals of a problem.

'Modeling tends to formalize a thought process already familiar to auditors.'

Consider other recent litigation, involving issues which may have been uncovered had an analytical review approach to the audit been emphasized. Geon Industries involved an overstatement of earnings from five percent to 24 percent from 1971 to 1974, created through the failure to eliminate some intracompany profits from financial statements ("Arthur Andersen," 1981). Had the expected mix of intercompany and external sales been checked, based on long-term historical patterns, and had the reasonableness of total sales been assessed relative to market data, the inadequate elimination entries might have been detected. American Reserve Unit concealed its insolvency by understating its reserves for claims and claim administration expenses and by delaying its payments of claims and administrative expenses ("American Reserve," 1981). Reserves are a particularly difficult account area to audit because they tend to reflect management judgments. However, if the CPA understands the basis for such estimates and accepts the basis as reasonable, then a structural model can be formulated that measures the criteria for the estimation process and forms an objective estimate to which management's judgment can be compared. Additionally, historical trends reflecting the rela-

tionship of reserves to various aspects of operations may have proven helpful in evaluating the balance in reserves. Similarly, the erroneous amounts and manipulated payment patterns for claims and administrative expenses might well have been signalled by examining historical structural models and their implications. Mercantile Bank & Trust involved the creation of shell companies to "buy" bad loans (Drinkhall, 1981). The question arises as to how Mercantile Bank & Trust compared in its "bad loan" performance to similar operations. If the company were performing exceptionally well in that regard, apparently due to the selling of loans, further work on the buyer of these loans would have been recommended in an analytical review testing approach. In Data Access Systems, Inc., collateralized borrowings (lease financings) were recorded as sales, and "certain irregular transactions and payments" involving related parties were incorrectly classified as cost of sales, assets or charges to paid-in capital ("Data Access," 1982). Again, an historical trend analysis of each of the misstated accounts, as well as a comparison to market data, may have identified the unusual charges and classifications. Even Fund of Funds Ltd., although the critical issue is confidentiality, concerns an area of dispute that could effectively use analytical review. The gross overvaluation of natural resource assets purchased (Gigot, 1982) might have been detected through market comparisons, including comparisons to industry competitors.

'As more sophisticated . . . techniques are applied . . . a more objective means of forming expectations . . . will become prevalent.'

Analytical review procedures provide a new perspective to the auditor not effectively captured by other auditing techniques; this relative advantage of analytical review procedures should be explicitly considered in judging how to allocate audit time. Should the overall reasonableness of reported numbers be established, particularly through the use of "hard" analytical review techniques that integrate externally-generated data, a basis exists for decreasing other substantive tests and for having greater assurance that the accounting numbers produced internally are not bogus numbers.

The Precision of Evidence Provided: Field Experience

When the phrase is used, "should the overall reasonableness of reported numbers be established," the common question raised is whether analytical review proce-

TABLE 1

The H.J. Heinz Case . . . With the Advantage of Hindsight . . .

SYNOPSIS

By colluding with at least 6 suppliers, legal fees, advertising, and market research expenses were manipulated from 1971 to 1979. Bogus invoices were prepared upon request. If services were not subsequently rendered, prior cash payments were returned to Heinz. Sales cutoff was also manipulated by adjusting internal documentation. Over 325 employees were aware of the impropriety, perpetrated in large part for the purpose of maximizing managers' bonus-incentive awards.

THE DILEMMA

The Wall Street Journal reported
">. . . it is unclear how the improper accounting practices escaped the notice of . . . Heinz's auditors for the entire period of the improprieties"
(November 23, 1979)

WHICH SUBSTANTIVE TESTS COULD NOT DISCOVER THESE IMPROPRIETIES?

—Confirmations to vendors
—Normal cutoff tests
—Tests directed at overstatement of revenues and income and understatement of expenses

—Inquiry and observation procedures
—Those tests emphasizing large account balances, such as inventory
—Year to year comparisons from 1972 through 1979

WHAT ANALYTICAL REVIEW PROCEDURES, OUTLINED IN SAS#23, MIGHT HAVE DETECTED THE IMPROPRIETIES?

—Ratio analysis, comparing the percentage relationship of marketing, advertising, and legal expenses to sales across divisions, as well as comparing such divisional ratios to industry statistics
—In 1971 and possibly 1972, a comparison of multi-year historical patterns, pre-1971
—In the course of formulating structural models, the five-year business plans have been reviewed by the CPA, offering the chance of detecting one strong clue of the problem: the account "Pre-billed Advertising Invoice" for services it paid for but did not receive, on Ore-Ida's 1974, 1975, and 1976 reports

—Comparison to budget at the end of the first two months of each quarter could indicate much more variance on a monthly basis than a quarterly basis
—A comparison of the division's pattern of payment practices across vendors
—The business background required for analytical review procedures would increase the CPA's awareness of the smoothing incentives and division's autonomy in reporting, thereby encouraging two-sided check of balances in miscellaneous accounts which have a weaker audit trail, i.e. purchase of services, which typically lack shipping and receiving documentation, and the use of data external to a single division when performing analytical review

dures can possibly "establish" anything worthy of reliance, i.e., isn't within 25 percent about as well as such techniques can perform? Table 2 reports on some field experience with regression analysis as an auditing tool. The standard error ranges from two percent to seven percent of the balance being predicted. At a 95 percent confidence level this provides a precision measure ranging from four percent to 14 percent. The models reported are not large, as they contain only one to seven explanatory variables. Yet, the models manage to explain most of the variability in the account being analyzed, e.g., 99.6 percent of the variability in sales across the 40 stores of a retailing client is explained by the regression model. Frequently the models integrate nonaccounting data, thereby improving the ability of the regression analysis to identify unusual fluctuations in accounting data. From 36 to 80 observations (data points) are used in the estimation process. Such experience supports the ability of analytical review procedures that use a structural model approach—often with only a small number of variables—to provide reasonably tight precision and, most assuredly, to thereby provide a basis for decreasing the extent of other substantive test procedures. The ability of the audit teams who conducted this work to specify relationships with high explanatory power and tight precision suggests that the structural modeling approach is workable in the field and presents few problems in implementation. Modeling tends to formalize a thought process already familiar to auditors. Of relevance is that the models reported in Table 2 were verified as complying with all the underlying

TABLE 2

Field Experience With Regression Analysis

Type of Client	Nature of Explanatory Variables	Audit Objective	Average Value of Variable Being Explained (Number of Observations in Model)	Average Difference between the Regression Estimate and the Client's Book Value (Absolute Value)	Model Precision at a 95% Level of Confidence	Percent of Fluctuation in the Variable of Audit Interest that Is Explained by the Regression Model*
Retailer	6 Accounting 1 Verifiable Physical Characteristic of stores	To select stores to visit during an audit	$9,960 (40 stores)	$401 4% of $9,960	$1,051 10% of $9,960	99.6% of sales
Credit Union	1 Accounting (Detailed testing of explanatory variable was performed)	Substantive test of reported share balances	$12,409 (72 months)	$334 2.7% of $12,409	$531 4% of $12,409	43.9%** of share balances
Manufacturer	4 Operating Statistics 1 Forecast 2 Economic Indicators	Substantive test of revenue [Note: No control over price fluctuations was in the model]	$336,999 (48 months)	$33,119 9.8% of $336,999	$36,959 11% of $336,999	95.2% of revenue
Ski Lodge	2 Operating Statistics 1 Marketing Statistic	Substantive test of revenue	$198,955 (80 weeks)	$31,540 15.9% of $198,955	$28,103 14% of $198,955	98.6% of revenue
Utility	2 Accounting 1 Production Statistic 1 Environmental Statistic 2 Economic Indicators	Substantive test of revenue	$22,317 (36 months)	$1,078 4.8% of $22,317	$1,002 4.5% of $22,317	99.8% of revenue

* This value is known statistically as the adjusted R^2 ($\bar{R}^2$). The term "adjusted" means that the value reflects the number of explanatory variables that were used in modeling.

** The lower value is largely due to the use of first-differences in this model. The approach is analogous to the use of differencing and ratios in statistical sampling, rather than mean per unit. The standard error is reduced by differencing the data used in the regression estimation process. Therefore, the extent of fluctuation in share balances is reduced, making it more difficult to explain 90% of the movement, or better. In fact, 43% $\bar{R}^2$ for first-differencing compares well to 90% or better $\bar{R}^2$ for a "levels" regression model (recall what happens to the standard deviation in a ratios or differencing sampling approach, relative to mean per unit and what the implications are for achieved precision).

statistical assumptions of the estimation process and that some outliers which were identified led to material adjustments which had not been located by detailed testing procedures.

Integrating Evidence Gathered Through Structural Modeling Approaches

As was suggested in Part I of this article, the analytical review procedure is one aspect of the audit process, the reliance on which will depend on its precision. However, the absence of full reliance on a single procedure in

no way negates the contribution of that procedure. Table 3 provides a general description of the decision process by which analytical review evidence, obtained by applying regression analysis as an audit tool, can be integrated with other sources of evidence.

Advantages to Further Developments in Practice

As more sophisticated "hard-evidence" analytical review techniques are applied in practice, a more objective means of forming expectations concerning a client's au-

TABLE 3

**Illustration: Integrating Regression Analysis
With Other Sources of Evidence**

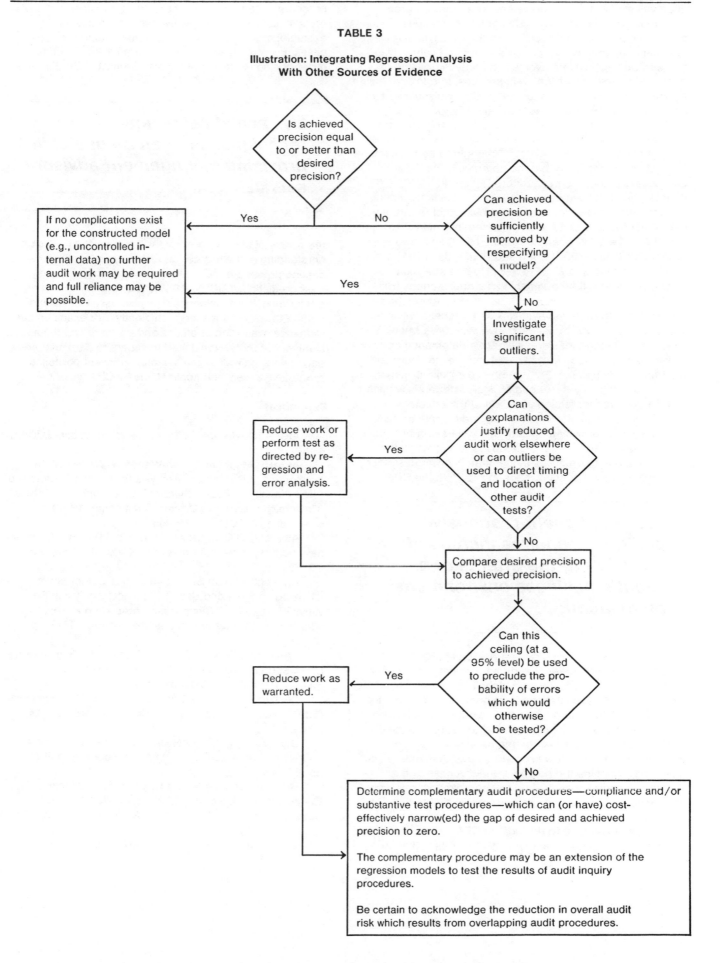

dited values will become prevalent. The reported problems that can arise in more judgmental approaches, such as the effects of auditors anchoring their analytical review judgments on the current period's unaudited values (Kinney and Uecker), will be avoided, thereby increasing the overall effectiveness of the audit process. In addition, the potential of the regression tool (as recently discussed by Barnes, 1981; Graham, 1981; Leininger and Conley, 1980; and Akresh and Wallace, 1982), as well as possible extensions of that tool (for example, Clark, 1981 and Albrecht and McKeown, 1977), can begin to be realized. It should be recognized that the potential is available to both external and internal auditors (Albrecht, 1980). Of course, the increased use of structural models by external and internal auditors is expected to coincide with the more effective use of alternative limited information (Kinney, 1979; Lev, 1979; and Stringer, 1979) and ratio approaches (Casey, 1980; Chen and Shimerda, 1981; and Kinney, 1981) to analytical review. No one analytical review procedure will be optimal in all circumstances (Hillison, 1981 for related research); however, a more structured approach to the analytical review process will make it easier for the CPA to use objective measures when possible, isolating those areas where a judgmental approach is required, so that the CPA can devote increased attention to such areas. For example, the "client-responsive" audit, recently described by McAllister and Dirsmith (1982), requires increased attention to the effects of a client's business environment on an audit; some of these effects can be formally modeled, and others can be judgmentally analyzed in a more effective manner when the decision aid of a structured model that incorporates other known business aspects is made available to the CPA.

> '. . . the "client-responsive"
> audit, . . . requires increased
> attention to the effects of a
> client's business environment
> on an audit; . . .'

A recent study by Hylas and Ashton (1982) reported that 20 percent of material audit adjustments booked for 152 clients of Peat, Marwick, Mitchell were found by comparisons to expectations from prior years and related inquiry procedures and 27 percent were found by other analytical review techniques. This study supports the effective audit role assumed by the relatively "weak evidence" analytical review procedures that dominate practice today. Imagine the potential effectiveness of the "hard evidence" analytical review approaches, relatively untapped audit tools that are currently available to practitioners.

A final advantage to developing CPAs' understanding of sophisticated analytical review techniques is that such procedures can be useful in providing management advisory services, as well as review services to clients. For example, regression analysis has been applied in rate cases, particularly in the form of reliance on the capital asset pricing model (Brigham and Crum, 1978). Similarly,

> '. . . analytical review
> techniques . . . can be useful in
> providing management advisory
> services, . . .'

the review of clients' forecasts will require the CPA's understanding of the regression technique or similar forecasting procedure, as applied by clients in generating their predictions (AICPA, 1980). The regression tool and similar modeling techniques may also assist CPAs in operating their own firms more efficiently. For example, performance evaluation of offices and partners and the assignment of professional staff members to particular engagements, as well as the selection of client portfolios, are potential modeling applications by CPA firms.

References

AICPA, *Guide, Review of Financial Forecasts* (AICPA, 1980).

Akresh, Abraham D. and Wanda A. Wallace, "The Application of Regression Analysis for Limited Review and Audit Planning," *Fourth Symposium on Auditing Research* (University of Illinois at Urbana-Champaign, 1982), pp. 67–128; 147–161.

Albrecht, William Steve, "Analytical Reviews for Internal Auditors," *The Internal Auditor* (August, 1980), pp. 20–25.

Albrecht, William Steve and James C. McKeown, "Toward an Extended Use of Statistical Analytical Reviews in the Audit," *Symposium on Auditing Research II* (University of Illinois at Urbana-Champaign, 1977), pp. 53–69.

"American Reserve Unit Hid Insolvency; Suit Seeking Up to $500 Million Alleges," *The Wall Street Journal* (March 19, 1981), p. 10, column 1.

"Arthur Andersen Is Censured by SEC Over Financial Data," *The Wall Street Journal* (June 23, 1981), p. 14, column 2.

Barnes, Paul, "Regression Analysis—A Tool for Accountants," *Journal of Accountancy* (February, 1981), pp. 80, 82.

Brigham, Eugene F. and Roy L. Crum, "Reply to Comments on 'Use of the CAPM in Public Utility Rate Cases,'" *Financial Management* (Autumn, 1978), pp. 72–76.

Casey, Cornelius J., Jr., "The Usefulness of Accounting Ratios for Subjects' Predictions of Corporate Failure: Replication and Extensions," *Journal of Accounting Research* (Autumn, 1980), pp. 603–613.

Chen, Kung H. and Thomas A. Shimerda, "An Empirical Analysis of Useful Financial Ratios," *Financial Management* (Spring, 1981), pp. 51–60.

Clark, Myrtle, "A Decision Theoretic Approach to Analytical Review: Bayes' Theorem Applied to Audit Regression Analysis," *The Woman CPA* (October, 1981), pp. 8–13.

"Data Access Had Loss, Not Profit, In 4-Year Period," *The Wall Street Journal* (March 17, 1982), p. 14, column 2.

Drinkhall, Jim, "Suit Prompted by Failure of Bahamas Bank Puts Accounting Industry Practice on Trial," *The Wall Street Journal* (February 17, 1981), p. 33, column 4 and p. 39, column 1.

Gigot, Paul A., "Big Fraud Verdict Against Andersen Shakes Up Accounting Profession," *The Wall Street Journal* (February 3, 1982), p. 27, column 4.

Graham, Lynford E., "Analytical Review Techniques: Some Neglected Tools," *The CPA Journal* (October, 1981), pp. 18–24.

Hillison, William, "Analytical Review Evaluation Report," Unpublished Research Project Summary Statement (The Florida State University, 1981).

Hylas, R. E. and R. H. Ashton, "Audit Detection of Financial Statement Errors," *The Accounting Review* (October, 1982), pp. 751–765.

Kinney, William R., Jr. and Wilfred C. Uecker, "Mitigating the Consequences of Anchoring in Auditor Judgments," *The Accounting Review* (January, 1982), pp. 55–69.

Kinney, William R., Jr., "Predicting Auditor-Initiated Adjustments Using Paired Balance Methods," *Journal of Accounting, Auditing & Finance* (Fall, 1981), pp. 5–17.

Kinney, William R., Jr., "The Predictive Power of Limited Information in Preliminary Analytical Review: An Empirical Study," *Journal of Accounting Research* (Supplement, 1979), pp. 148–165.

Leininger, Wayne E. and Michael J. Conley, "Regression Analysis in Auditing," *The CPA Journal* (October, 1980), pp. 43–47.

Lev, Baruch, "Discussion of the Predictive Power of Limited Information in Preliminary Analytical Review: An Empirical Study," *Journal of Accounting Research* (Supplement, 1979), pp. 166–168.

McAllister, John P. and Mark W. Dirsmith, "How the Client's Business Environment Affects the Audit," *Journal of Accountancy* (February, 1982), pp. 68–74.

Stringer, Kenneth W., "Discussion of the Predictive Power of Limited Information in Preliminary Analytical Review: An Empirical Study," *Journal of Accounting Research* (Supplement, 1979), pp. 169–171. Ω

CASE 6

ANALYTICAL REVIEW PROCEDURES

You are an audit partner in the CPA firm of Miller and Kuhn and are responsible for your firm's continuing education activities. You are also active in the Houston Chapter of the Texas Society of CPAs, currently serving on the Society's Continuing Professional Education Committee. In addition to these activities, you also teach an undergraduate course in auditing at a local university. Because of these interests, you were asked to participate in a panel discussion held at the monthly meeting of the University's Student Accounting Society. The other panelists were a full-time faculty member and a recent graduate of the University who is employed as a staff accountant by a "big eight" accounting firm. The general topic for the panel discussion was listed as "the Auditor's Approach" and each panelist made a short presentation which was well received by the audience of students, faculty and practitioners. After a short intermission, the panel has reconvened to take questions from the audience. A general comment concerned with analytical review procedures seemed to spark considerable interest and was quickly followed by a series of specific inquiries on this topic, which have been directed to you for your response.

CASE DISCUSSION QUESTIONS

1. What are analytical review procedures? Which specific analytical review procedures are required of the auditor by GAAS?

2. At what point during the examination should the auditor perform analytical review procedures? What factors should be considered in making this decision?

3. Several approaches may be used in applying analytical review procedures. For example, dollars, physical quantities, ratios or percentages may be used. Give an example of a situation in which each of these bases (i.e.—dollars, physical quantities, ratios, percentages) might be useful to the auditor in an examination of a retail clothing store.

4. What matters should be considered by the auditor in planning and performing analytical review procedures? Discuss.

5. Under what circumstances should the auditor investigate exceptions noted during the application of analytical review procedures? What follow-up procedures should the auditor employ?

6. In performing analytical review procedures the auditor would normally investigate fluctuations that are unexpected. Would the auditor ever be concerned by the absence of any fluctuations? Explain.

Internal Control

(Section 320, SAS No. 1, Section 322, SAS No. 9, Section 323, SAS No. 20, Section 324, SAS No. 44 and Section 1030, SAS No. 48)

The second standard of field work requires that:

> There is to be a proper study and evaluation of the existing internal control as a basis for reliance thereon and for the determination of the resultant extent of the tests to which auditing procedures are to be restricted

The basic purpose of the auditor's study and evaluation of internal control is to establish a basis for reliance in determining the nature, extent, and timing of audit tests to be applied in the examination of financial statements. Secondarily, this review may provide a basis for constructive suggestions that may be made to the client as to how the system may be modified and improved.

DEFINITIONS AND BASIC CONCEPTS

Internal control is defined as comprising the plan of organization and all of the coordinate methods and measures adopted within a business to safeguard its assets, check the accuracy and reliability of its accounting data, promote operational efficiency, and encourage adherence to prescribed managerial policies. In the broad sense, internal control includes controls which may be characterized as either accounting controls or administrative controls.

Administrative controls include, but are not limited to, the plan of organization and the procedures and records that are concerned with the decision processes leading to management's authorization of transactions.

Internal accounting controls consist of the plan of organization and the procedures and records that are concerned with the safeguarding of assets and reliability of financial records. Consequently, accounting controls are designed to afford reasonable assurance that transactions are effected in accordance with management's general or specific authorization; that transactions are recorded as necessary to allow preparation of financial statements in compliance with GAAP or another comprehensive basis of accounting; and that transactions are recorded in a manner that maintains accountability for assets. Accounting control also assures that access to assets is permitted only in accordance with management's authorization and that the recorded accountability for assets is compared with the existing assets at reasonable intervals and appropriate action is taken with respect to any differences noted.

Implicit in the definition of accounting controls are basic concepts that apply to the definition generally and to its essential characteristics. These basis concepts are discussed below.

Management Responsibility

Management is responsible for establishing and maintaining a system of internal accounting control. Management must also assume responsibility for continuing supervision of the control system to ascertain that it is functioning as prescribed and is modified as appropriate for any changes in conditions.

Reasonable Assurance

The definition of accounting control comprehends reasonable, but not absolute, assurance that the objectives expressed therein will be accomplished by the system. The cost of the system must, of course, be related to benefit received. Because of this cost-benefit relationship, accounting control procedures may appropriately be applied on a test basis in certain circumstances.

Methods of Data Processing

The definition and related basic concepts and principles of accounting control are independent of the method of data processing used. Consequently, they apply equally to manual, mechanical, and electronic data processing systems. However, the organization and procedures required to accomplish the objectives of internal accounting control are sometimes influenced by the data processing methods used in particular circumstances.

Effects of Computer Processing on the Examination of Financial Statements

Section 320 is amended by Section 1030, *The Effects of Computer Processing on the Examination of Financial Statements*, to describe the characteristics of computer processing that may have an effect on the system of internal accounting control.

The method an entity uses to process significant accounting applications may influence the control procedures designed to achieve the objectives of internal accounting control.

Those characteristics that distinguish computer processing from manual processing include:

Transaction trails. Some computer systems are designed so that a complete transaction trail that is useful for audit purposes might exist for only a short period of time or only in computer-readable form.

Uniform processing of transactions. Computer processing uniformly subjects like transactions to the same processing instructions.

Segregation of functions. Individuals who have access to the computer may be in a position to perform incompatible functions. As a result, other control procedures may be necessary in computer systems to achieve the control objectives ordinarily accomplished by segregation of functions in manual systems—other controls may include, for example, adequate segregation of incompatible functions within the computer processing activities (such as programming and operations) or establishing a control group to prevent or detect processing errors or irregularities.

Potential for errors and irregularities. Potential to gain unauthorized access to assets may be greater in computerized accounting systems.

Potential for increased management supervision. Computer systems offer management a wide variety of analytical tools that may be used to review and supervise the operations of the company. The availability of these additional controls may serve to enhance the entire system of internal accounting control.

Initiation or subsequent execution of transactions by computer. Certain transactions may be automatically initiated or certain procedures required to execute a transaction may be automatically performed by a computer system. The authorization of these transactions or procedures may not be documented in the same way as those initiated in a manual system, and management's authorization of those transactions may be implicit in its acceptance of the design of the computer system.

Whether the control procedures are classified by the auditor into general and application controls, the objective of the system of internal accounting control remains the same—to provide reasonable, but not absolute, assurance that assets are safeguarded from unauthorized use or disposition and that financial records are reliable to permit the preparation of financial statements.

General controls are those controls that relate to all or many computerized accounting activities, for example, controls over access to computer programs and data files. *Application controls* relate to individual computerized accounting applications, for example, programmed edit controls for verifying customers' account numbers and credit limits.

Limitations

There are inherent limitations within a system of internal accounting control that may weaken the system. For example, misunderstanding of instructions, errors in judgment, and personal carelessness, distraction, or fatigue all may result in temporary breakdowns in a system. Also, collusion by employees and outsiders and errors or irregularities perpetrated by management may deter the effectiveness of an internal accounting control system.

Personnel

An internal accounting control system in a large organization cannot operate efficiently and effectively without competent personnel who have been adequately trained to perform their functions. Personal integrity and competency are essential ingredients. In a smaller organization control procedures may be performed effectively by the owner-manager. In these circumstances certain of the limitations discussed above may be particularly applicable.

Segregation of Functions

Incompatible functions for accounting control purposes are those that place any one person in a position both to perpetrate and to conceal errors (refers to unintentional mistakes) or irregularities (refers to intentional distortions of financial statements and to defalcations) in the normal course of his or her duties. Anyone who records the entity's transactions or has access to its assets usually is in a position to affect errors or irregularities. Therefore, elimination of opportunity for concealment is an important part of accounting control. Accordingly, personnel operating within a business structure should not be placed in a position where they perform conflicting duties. The basic functions of production, custodianship, financing, and accounting should be separated at all levels in the organization.

Execution of Transactions

Transactions should be executed according to the general or specific authorizations of management. Accounting control should provide reasonable assurance that authorized transactions are properly executed and that unauthorized transactions do not occur. Obtaining reasonable assurance that transactions are executed only as authorized requires independent evidence that authorizations are issued by individuals acting within the scope of their authority and that all transactions conform with the terms of the authorizations. Accounting control should provide sufficient supervision, observation, and documentation to provide reasonable assurance that transactions are exercised as authorized.

Recording of Transactions

With regard to the recording of transactions, the objective of accounting control requires that transactions be recorded at their proper amounts and in their related accounting periods as well as being properly classified in the appropriate accounts. Accounting periods refer to periods for which financial statements are prepared. Thus, accounting control is expressed in terms of allowing the preparation of financial statements in conformity with GAAP or other applicable criteria. In addition to recording transactions it is essential that management use judgment in making estimates and the other decisions necessary in preparation of the statements.

The likelihood for acquiring assurance that events have been properly recorded relies, to a great extent, on the availability of an independent source of information indicating that the transactions were made. Independent sources of information vary widely with the nature of the transactions as well as the nature of the business and its environment.

Transactions with parties external to the entity should be recorded individually and as soon as possible when such recording is necessary to provide accountability for resources such as cash, securities, and other assets which may be susceptible to loss from errors or irregularities. The term *recording*, as used here, refers to the initial record, document, or copy supporting the transaction and not to subsequent summarization. Timeliness also applies to the recording of the internal use of assets, services or transfers. However, it is not necessary to record on an individual basis certain transfers and cost allocations when the total amounts may be ascertained satisfactorily.

Access to Assets

Only authorized personnel should have access to assets. The term *access* refers to both direct physical access and indirect access obtained in the preparation or processing documents authorizing the use or disposition of assets. Normal business operations require personnel to have access to the entity's assets. Therefore, limiting access to authorized personnel is the maximum constraint that is feasible for purposes of accounting control. The number and caliber of personnel to whom access is authorized should be influenced by the nature of the assets and the related susceptibility to loss through either errors or irregularities. Limitation of direct access to assets requires appropriate physical segregation and protective equipment or devices. Limitation of indirect access requires procedures such as segregation of functions and appropriate documentation and authorization.

Comparison of Recorded Accountability With Assets

The purpose of comparing recorded accountability with assets is to determine whether the actual assets on hand and in use agree with the recorded accountability or records. Typical examples of this comparison include counts of cash and securities, bank reconciliations, and physical inventories. If the comparison reveals that assets are not in agreement with the recorded accountability, it provides evidence of unrecorded or improperly recorded transactions and a breach of internal control. The converse, however, is not necessarily true. For example, comparison of a cash count with the balance per the accounting records does not provide conclusive evidence that all cash receipts have been properly recorded. This fact demonstrates an unavoidable distinction between fiduciary and recorded accountability. For example, the former arises immediately upon receipt of the cash while the latter occurs when the initial cash transaction is recorded. With respect to assets that are susceptible to loss through errors or irregularities, a comparison with recorded accountability should be made by an individual who is independent of those employees who account for and have physical responsibility for the assets. The frequency of such comparisons should be based on the nature and amount of the assets involved as well as the cost of making such comparisons.

STUDY OF THE SYSTEM OF INTERNAL CONTROL

The scope of the study of the system of internal control normally includes accounting controls but not administrative controls. In other words, the second standard of field work requires that the auditor study the system of internal accounting controls but does not require a review of the system of internal administrative controls. The auditor may, however, review administrative controls when it is possible that these controls will influence the scope of the examination.

The study of accounting control includes two phases. The initial phase involves obtaining a knowledge and understanding of the procedures and methods prescribed and is termed "review of the system." During the second phase, "tests of compliance," the auditor attempts to obtain reasonable assurance that the procedures described in the review of the system (initial phase) are in use and are operating as planned and intended.

REVIEW OF THE SYSTEM OF INTERNAL CONTROL

Reviewing the system of internal accounting control involves a process of obtaining information concerning the organization and the procedures prescribed. This review is intended to serve as the basis for tests of compliance and also for evaluating the system. Information is obtained through discussion with appropriate client personnel and reference to documentation. Review procedures may involve the use of questionnaires, narrative memoranda, flowcharts, decision tables, or any other form or combination of review techniques that meets the auditor's needs or preferences. After reviewing the system of internal accounting control, the auditor should make a preliminary evaluation of the quality of the system in specific areas.

SAS No. 43 (Section 1010.02) amends SAS No. 1, Section 320 to clarify that the independent CPA's review of internal accounting control may be restricted to acquiring only an understanding of the control environment and the flow of transactions. This is the case if the CPA determines that additional study and evaluation will not allow him or her to restrict substantive tests. Under these circumstances, the minimum documentation required by this amendment (Section 1010.02) may be limited to a record of the CPA's reasons for making only a limited review of the internal accounting control. Therefore, it is not necessary for the CPA to complete an internal control questionnaire or provide other documentation of his or her review.

If the CPA plans to rely on the internal accounting control, he or she should document the review of the system and conduct tests of compliance.

Tests of Compliance

Tests of compliance are made to provide reasonable assurance that accounting control procedures are being applied as prescribed. These tests are essential if the prescribed procedures are to be relied upon in determining the nature, timing or extent of substantive tests of particular classes of transactions or balances, but are not necessary if the procedures are not to be relied upon for that purpose. An auditor must always *review* the system of internal control. However, the auditor may decide not to rely on the prescribed procedures in restricting or limiting the amount of substantive testing of particular classes of transactions or balances for either of two reasons. First, the internal control procedures in particular areas may not be satisfactory for the purpose of reliance. Second, the audit effort required to test compliance with the procedures to justify reliance on them in making substantive tests would exceed the reduction in effort that could be achieved by such reliance. In other words, the cost may exceed the benefit.

Nature of Tests

Accounting control requires that certain procedures be performed properly and independently. Therefore, tests of compliance are concerned primarily with whether the necessary procedures were performed, how were they performed, and by whom were they performed. Certain factors of accounting control necessitate procedures that are not necessarily required for the execution of transactions. Procedures of this type would include the approval or checking of documents evidencing transactions. To test these procedures, the auditor would need to inspect the related documents to obtain evidence in the form of signatures, initials, audit stamps, and the like in order to determine whether and by whom they were performed as well as to permit an evaluation of the propriety of their performance. Other aspects of accounting control necessitate a separation of duties so that certain procedures are performed independently. Performance of these procedures is generally self-evident from the operation of the business or the existence of its essential records. Therefore, tests of compliance for these procedures are primarily intended to ascertain whether these duties were performed by persons having no incompatible functions. Normally such procedures provide no audit trail of documentary evidence as to the identity of those who performed them. Hence, tests of compliance in these circumstances are made through inquiries of personnel and observation.

TIMING AND EXTENT OF TESTS

The degree of assurance that a system of internal accounting control is functioning necessarily depends on the nature, timing, and extent of the tests of transactions and on the results obtained. As to accounting control procedures that leave an audit trail, tests of compliance should be applied to transactions executed throughout the period under audit because of the general sampling concept that the items to be examined should be selected from the entire set of data (universe) to which the resulting conclusions are to be applied. Such tests are usually made during the interim period and are not repeated at year-end. Tests of compliance may be applied on either a subjective or a statistical sampling basis. As to accounting control procedures that depend primarily on segregation of duties and leave no audit trail, the inquiries should relate to the entire period under audit, but the observations may be confined to the periods during which the auditor is present at the client's premises in conducting other phases of the audit.

EVALUATION OF THE SYSTEM OF INTERNAL CONTROL

Internal accounting control must be reviewed, tested, and evaluated order for the auditor to place reliance on the system in restricting the amount of substantive testing to be performed in a given area of the audit. In evaluating accounting control it is important to remember that controls and weaknesses affecting different classes of transactions (i.e.,cash receipts and cash disbursements) are not off-setting in their effect and overall evaluations of the control system are useful. For example, a statement that a client has a good system of internal control is meaningless. The system may be strong in certain areas and weak in others. Internal control within each specific area, such as cash receipts, must be reviewed, tested, and evaluated. For example, a strong system of control in cash receipts would not in any way offset weaknesses in cash disbursements—the two areas are independent with respect to accountability and control.

A conceptually logical approach to the auditor's evaluation of accounting control, which focuses directly on the purpose of preventing or detecting material errors and irregularities in financial statements, is to apply steps such as the following in considering each significant class of transactions and related assets involved in the audit:

1.   Consider the types of errors and irregularities that could occur.

2.   Determine the accounting control procedures that should prevent or detect such errors and/or irregularities.

3.   Determine whether the necessary procedures have been prescribed and are being followed satisfactorily.

4.   Evaluate any weaknesses—i.e., types of potential errors and irregularities not covered by existing control procedures—to determine their effect on:

     a.   The nature, timing, or extent of auditing procedures to be applied, and

     b.   Suggestions to be made to the client.

The first two steps outlined above are performed primarily through the development of questionnaires, checklists, instructions, or similar generalized material used by the auditor. The third step is accomplished through the review of the system and by tests of compliance. The final step is accomplished through the exercise of professional judgment by the auditor in evaluating the information obtained in the preceding steps.

The auditors' evaluation of accounting controls with reference to each significant class of transactions and related assets should enable them to arrive at a conclusion as to whether the prescribed procedures and compliance therewith are satisfactory for purposes of the examination.

Procedures and compliance should be considered satisfactory if the review and tests fail to disclose a condition the auditor believes to be a material weakness. A material weakness is defined as a condition in which the auditor believes the prescribed procedures or the degree of compliance with them does not provide reasonable assurance that material errors or irregularities would be prevented or detected within a timely period by client employees in the normal course of performing their assigned duties.

CORRELATION WITH OTHER AUDITING PROCEDURES

Since the purpose of the evaluation required by the second standard of field work is to provide a basis "for the determination of the resultant extent of the tests to which auditing procedures are to be restricted," it is clear that its ultimate purpose is to contribute to the "reasonable basis for an opinion" comprehended in the third standard of field work (obtaining sufficient competent evidential matter).

The evidential matter required by the third standard of field work is obtained through two general classes of auditing procedures:

Tests of details of transactions and balances, and

Analytical review procedures.

These procedures are referred to as *substantive tests*. Their purpose is to obtain evidence as to the validity and the propriety of the accounting treatment of transactions and balances as well as errors or irregularities therein. Although this objective differs from that of compliance tests (compliance with internal control) both purposes often are accomplished concurrently through tests of transactions or details.

The second standard of field work recognizes that the extent of tests required to constitute sufficient evidential matter under the third standard should vary inversely with the auditor's reliance on internal control. The second and third standards taken together imply that the combination of the auditor's reliance on internal control and on the auditing procedures employed should provide a reasonable basis for an opinion in all cases, although the portion of reliance derived from the respective sources may properly vary between and among cases.

The relationship of the extent of reliance on internal accounting controls and the amount of substantive evidence under the third standard of field work is illustrated by the following graph:

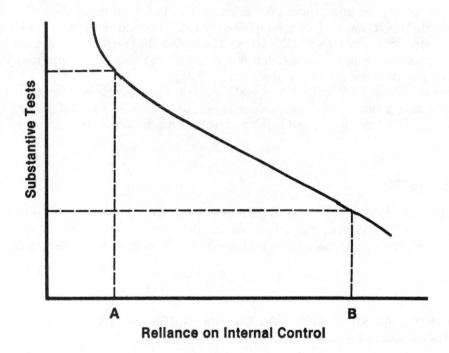

As can be seen in the above graph, in situation A where there is minimal or nonreliance on internal accounting control a significant amount of substantive testing is required to produce evidence to support financial statement assertions. In the case of situation B, where there is significant reliance on internal accounting control, a minimal amount of substantive testing is required. Thus is the correlation of the second and third standards of field work.

TESTS OF COMPLIANCE

The purpose of tests of compliance is to provide reasonable assurance that control procedures are being applied as prescribed. Tests of compliance are concerned primarily with the following questions:

> Were the necessary procedures performed?
>
> How were they performed?
>
> By whom were they performed?

Certain control procedures within the EDP activity leave visible evidence indicating that they were performed. Other procedures, however, leave no visible evidence as to performance. For those procedures that leave no visible evidence, the auditor should test for their performance by reviewing transactions submitted for processing to determine that no transactions tested have unacceptable conditions or that unacceptable conditions present were reported and appropriately resolved. This review may be accomplished manually if conditions permit or it may be necessary to use EDP equipment to detect unacceptable conditions. An alternative approach to testing compliance with control procedures in computer programs is to review and test the programs and then to perform tests in order to provide assurance that the tested programs were actually used for processing.

Certain control procedures within EDP leave neither visible nor machine-readable evidence that they were performed (i.e., segregation of functions). Evidence that such accounting control procedures are functioning is usually obtained by the auditor by observing client personnel and making corroborative inquiries.

EVALUATION OF THE SYSTEM

Evaluation of the EDP aspects of a system of internal accounting control does not differ conceptually from the evaluation of other aspects of the system of internal control and should be an integral part of the auditor's evaluation of the system. A conceptually logical approach to the evaluation of internal control was discussed in a previous section of this reading.

THE EFFECT OF AN INTERNAL AUDIT FUNCTION ON THE SCOPE OF THE INDEPENDENT AUDITOR'S EXAMINATION

The work of internal auditors cannot be directly substituted for the work of the independent auditor. The independent auditors should, however, consider the procedures, if any, performed by internal auditors in determining the nature, timing, and extent of their auditing procedures. SAS No. 9 provides guidance on the factors that affect an independent auditor's consideration of the work of internal auditors in an examination in accordance with GAAS. This statement is applicable to the independent auditor's consideration, in making the study and evaluation of internal accounting control, of the work performed by internal auditors. The statement applies whether the work performed by internal auditors is part of their normal duties or is performed at the request of the independent auditor. It also applies to situations in which internal auditors perform work directly for the independent auditor. The statement is not applicable to personnel with the title "internal auditor" who do not perform such a function.

The independent auditor should acquire an understanding of the internal audit function as it relates to the study and evaluation of internal accounting control as work to be performed by internal auditors may be a factor in determining the nature, timing, and extent of the independent auditor's procedures. If the independent auditors decide that the work performed by internal auditors may have a bearing on their procedures, they should consider the competence and objectivity of internal auditors in evaluating their work.

Reviewing the Competence and Objectivity of Internal Auditors

In the process of reviewing the competence of internal auditors, the independent auditor should make inquiries into the qualifications of the internal audit staff. In this regard, the independent auditor should give consideration to client practices used in hiring, training and supervising the internal audit staff.

In assessing the objectivity of internal auditors, the independent auditor should evaluate the organization level to which internal auditors report the results of their audit work. Also, the independent auditor should consider the organization level of the internal auditors' administrative reporting in ascertaining their ability to act independently of the individuals being audited.

Evaluating the Work of Internal Auditors

In order to evaluate the work of internal auditors, the independent auditor should examine, on a test basis, evidence supporting work done by internal auditors. Consideration should be given to the scope of their work, adequacy of audit programs and working papers, appropriateness of conclusions reached, and the consistency of work performed with reports prepared. The independent auditor should also conduct tests of selected work done by the internal auditors and compare the results of these tests with the results of the internal auditors' work. The independent auditor's tests do not necessarily have to be over transactions or balances examined by internal auditors.

Arrangements with Internal Auditors

When the work of internal auditors is significant to the independent auditor's study and evaluation of internal accounting control, they should be informed, prior to the engagement, of the reports and working papers which will be required by the independent auditor. Also, the independent auditors should remain in communication with the internal auditors concerning work not yet completed since it may have a bearing on their examination.

Using Internal Auditors to Provide Direct Assistance to the Independent Auditor

The independent auditor may make use of internal auditors to provide assistance in performing an examination in accordance with GAAS. Under these circumstances the independent auditor must evaluate the competence and objectivity of internal auditors as well as supervise and test their work.

Judgments on Audit Matters

When internal auditors are used by the independent auditor in determining the nature, timing, and extent of audit procedures, judgments as to the effectiveness of internal accounting control rests with the independent auditor.

COMMUNICATION OF MATERIAL WEAKNESSES IN INTERNAL ACCOUNTING CONTROL

SAS No. 20 requires that an independent auditor communicate to the senior management of the client and to its board of directors (or its audit committee) material weaknesses in internal accounting control that were noted during an audit of financial statements made in accordance with GAAS. A material weakness in accounting control was defined in a previous section as:

> A condition in which the auditor believes the prescribed procedures or the degree of compliance with them does not provide reasonable assurance that errors or irregularities in amounts that would be material in the financial statements being audited would be prevented or detected within a timely period by employees in the normal course of performing their assigned functions.

The second standard of field work requires the auditor to review and evaluate internal accounting control. The auditors then test accounting controls if they intend to rely on them in restricting substantive testing. The auditor does not normally review, test, or evaluate internal accounting control for the specific purpose of communicating weaknesses or corrective action to management. However, such communications may result from the auditor's accounting control procedures. Communicating weaknesses either orally or in writing to management is not required for the auditor to state that the examination was made in accordance with GAAS. Such communications are incidental to the auditor's objective in reviewing, testing, and evaluating accounting controls, the purpose of which is to obtain sufficient competent evidential matter so as to form an overall opinion as to the fairness of the financial statements.

Establishing and maintaining a sound system of internal controls is the responsibility of management. Knowledge of material weaknesses that might exist in such a system is essential for management to discharge its responsibility. In reviewing, testing, and evaluating accounting controls the auditor may become aware of material weaknesses in the client's system. When aware of such weaknesses, the auditor should communicate them either orally or in writing to senior management and the board of directors (or its audit committee). If the auditor communicates findings regarding material weaknesses orally, this oral communication should be documented by appropriate notations in the audit working papers.

Auditors should communicate material weaknesses as soon as they come to their attention (probably orally, followed by a written communication at the conclusion of the audit in what is generally called an internal control letter). Material weaknesses communicated in writing at interim dates need not be repeated at year-end. However, the auditor should reference such interim communications in any year-end communications to management.

Material weaknesses communicated in prior examinations that have not been corrected by management should be repeated or referred to in subsequent communications made by the auditor.

If the auditors become aware of material weaknesses for which management believes corrective action is not practicable, they may refer to the circumstances and summarize the weaknesses. However, a detailed communication of the circumstances and related weaknesses is not required of the auditor.

Communications of weaknesses in accounting control will usually include comments regarding corrective action that may be taken by management. Also, if corrective action is currently being taken, the auditor's communication will usually so indicate.

An auditor may wish to communicate to management weaknesses in accounting control that are considered immaterial in relation to the fairness of the financial statements taken overall. However, such communication is not required by GAAS.

SPECIAL-PURPOSE REPORTS ON INTERNAL ACCOUNTING CONTROL AT SERVICE ORGANIZATIONS*

(Section 324, SAS No. 44)

Section 324 addresses the independent auditor's use of a special-purpose report on internal accounting control of a service organization that performs services for a client whose financial statements the auditor is examining. This section also addresses the service auditor's responsibilities for special-purpose reports.

Examples of service organizations are data processing centers, bank trust departments, mortgage bankers or savings and loan associations that service loans for others, shareowner accounting organizations for investment companies, and insurers that maintain the accounting for ceded reinsurance. This section applies to instances where the service organization provides the following services to the client organization: (1) executes transactions and maintains the related accountability, (2) records transactions and processes the related data, and (3) various combinations of these services. This section does not apply to services executed by service organizations at the specific authorization of the client, such as a bank processing checking account transactions or a broker administering securities transactions.

FACTORS AFFECTING THE DECISION TO OBTAIN A SERVICE AUDITOR'S REPORT

An auditor may need to consider the service organization's internal accounting controls when a client uses a service organization. An efficient approach would be to read a service auditor's report on the service organization's controls. The type of services performed by the service organization will determine the relationship between the service organization's controls and the client's controls.

---

* This section was written by Joann O'Brien, CPA and Graduate Student, Creighton University.

Service Organizations that Maintain Controls that Interact with Client Organization Controls

When a service organization records client transactions and processes the related data, the authorization of the transaction and the maintenance of the related accountability are done by the client. The service organization's controls interact with the client's controls. A data processing center that processes payrolls is an example of a service organization that records client transactions and processes the related data.

The auditor should understand the transaction flow through the entire accounting system, including both the client's system and the service organization's system. The auditor may improve his or her understanding of the service organization's system by reading a service auditor's report on the design of the system. This report may also help the auditor plan compliance and substantive tests of the client. The report cannot be used as a basis for relying on service organization controls because it provides no assurance regarding compliance.

The auditor should be interested in control procedures of both the client and the service organization. In the example of the data processing center that processes client payroll transactions, the client might recalculate payroll data on a test basis after it is returned from the data processing center. This client control procedure provides reasonable assurance that errors and irregularities in service center processing would be detected. The auditor can rely on the client's controls, assuming satisfactory compliance, and not perform a study of the service organization's controls.

In other instances, the control procedures required to achieve internal accounting control objectives may be performed at the service organization. If the auditor intends to rely on controls in planning the audit procedures, he or she should evaluate the service organization's controls. The auditor can perform appropriate procedures at the service organization, request the service auditor to perform procedures, or read a service auditor's report that contains information on both the design of the system and compliance tests of the control procedures. This report includes the service auditor's opinion on whether the control procedures and the degree of compliance with them provide reasonable assurance that control objectives are accomplished. If the report does not include procedures the auditor intends to rely on, the auditor should perform his or her own compliance tests or request the service auditor to perform compliance tests.

After reading the service auditor's report, the auditor should determine whether the client's controls and the service organization's controls together provide a basis for reliance in reducing substantive tests. Important control weaknesses in the service organization's system should be considered client weaknesses.

Service Organizations that Maintain Controls that do not Interact with Client Organization Controls

When a service organization executes transactions and maintains the related accountability, the client may not have its own records of the transactions; therefore, the client will not be able to maintain internal accounting control over these transactions. A bank trust department that invests and holds assets for an employee benefit plan under a discretionary trust arrangement is an example of a service organization that executes transactions without specific authorization of individual transactions. The auditor will decide whether to rely on service organization controls or perform substantive tests at the service organization.

A bank trust department that invests and holds assets for an employee benefit plan under a nondiscretionary trust arrangement must receive specific authorization to execute individual transactions. In this case, the client will be able to maintain internal accounting control over the transactions. The auditor might still decide to restrict substantive tests and rely on service organization controls.

The auditor should do one of the following to accomplish his or her study and evaluation of internal accounting control if the auditor plans to rely on the service organization's controls in either of the situations described above: (1) read a service auditor's opinion on the service organization's controls, (2) perform audit procedures at the service organization or (3) request the service auditor to perform audit procedures at the service organization.

CONSIDERATIONS IN USING A SERVICE AUDITOR'S REPORT

Obtaining and Evaluating a Service Auditor's Report

The auditor should contact the service organization through the client to determine the type of service auditor's report available, if any. The auditor may be able to influence the type of future report to be issued. The auditor should inquire about the service auditor's professional reputation through appropriate sources (as discussed in Section 543.10a).

The auditor may discuss the scope and the results of the work with the service auditor if he or she feels that the report may not be adequate to meet audit objectives. The auditor may request the service auditor to perform tests on the service organization's records that apply particularly to the type of transactions handled by the service organization for the client or the auditor may perform these tests himself or herself. The auditor should qualify the opinion or disclaim an opinion because of a scope limitation if he or she is unable to accomplish the audit objectives.

Timing of Service Auditor's Report

The period covered by a service auditor's report may not coincide with the period covered by the financial statements that the auditor is examining. The auditor should decide whether compliance tests are necessary for the period from the date of the service auditor's last report to the client's year-end and should inquire of the service auditor or the service organization about any significant changes in internal accounting control subsequent to the date of the service auditor's last report. The auditor should request additional procedures if he or she feels they are necessary.

Reference to a Service Auditor's Report

The auditor should not refer to the service auditor's report in the audit opinion on the client's financial statements. Although the service auditor's report is used in the audit, the service auditor is not responsible for examining part of the financial statements as of a particular date or period of time; therefore, the responsibility for the financial statements cannot be divided. However, an auditor may refer to a service auditor's report in an opinion on a client's internal accounting control system because the service auditor's responsibility can be specifically identified in that instance.

RESPONSIBILITIES OF SERVICE AUDITORS FOR SPECIAL-PURPOSE REPORTS

The service auditor is responsible for his or her representations in the report and for due care in applying procedures that support the representations. The service auditor's work differs from an examination of financial statements in accordance with generally accepted auditing standards; however, it should be done in accordance with the general standards and other relevant GAAS. The service auditor is not, however, required to be independent with regard to each client of the service organization.

The service organization should determine the type of engagement to be performed and the type of report to be prepared. If possible, the service organization and its clients may discuss the type of report that best meets the clients' needs.

The service auditor may prepare any of the following types of reports: (1) reports on the design of the system, (2) reports on both the design of the system and compliance tests that are directed to specific objectives of internal accounting control, and (3) reports on the system of a segment of the service organization. These reports refer to the internal accounting control system used to process client transactions rather than the system used in preparing the service organization's financial statements.

REPORTS ON DESIGN AND ON BOTH DESIGN AND CERTAIN COMPLIANCE TESTS

Section 642, *Reporting on Internal Accounting Control*, states that special-purpose reports on internal accounting control should: (1) describe the scope and nature of the accountant's procedures, (2) disclaim an opinion on whether the system as a whole meets the objectives of internal accounting control, (3) state the accountant's findings, and (4) state that the report is intended only for management or specified third parties.

Reports on the Design of a System

The service auditor may obtain information for this report through discussion with service organization personnel and reference to systems flowcharts and narratives. Compliance tests are not required for this type of report. The service auditor may trace a few transactions through the system by examining supporting documents and records at or near the report date. Although not a test of compliance, this improves the service auditor's understanding of the system.

The service auditor reports his or her opinion on the design of the system as of a specified date. The service auditor is not required to look for system changes that may have occurred prior to the beginning of fieldwork. If the service auditor becomes aware of changes that occurred prior to the beginning of fieldwork that may be significant to accomplishing control objectives, he or she should explain the changes in the report. Changes made more than twelve months prior to the report date are not normally considered significant because they generally would not affect the client auditor's procedures.

The service auditor may discover control procedures described by the service organization are nonexistent or control procedures that are necessary to accomplish a control objective are not included in the system design. The service auditor should describe those conditions in his or her report when certain control objectives are not accomplished.

In addition to the requirements of Section 642, the service auditor's report on the design of a system should include:

1. A description of the service organization's system to process client transactions and the related internal accounting control procedures.

2. A description of the specific control objectives and control procedures for each significant accounting application that relate to errors or irregularities in transactions.

3. A statement that the procedures were performed for the purpose of evaluating the design of control procedures and that the described control procedures were not compliance tested.

4. A statement of the inherent limitations of internal accounting control systems and the risk of projecting an evaluation to future periods.

5. The service auditor's opinion as to whether the control procedures described are suitably designed to provide reasonable assurance that the control objectives specified are achieved if the control procedures are complied with satisfactorily.

The service auditor may include the service organization's description of the system in an attachment to the report. If the service auditor writes the system description, the service organization still remains responsible for the representations in the description.

The following illustrative report is considered appropriate when an auditor reports on the design of internal accounting controls maintained by a service organization, in this example, an EDP service center.

> To the Blank Service Center:
>
> We have reviewed the accompanying description of the operations and control procedures of the Blank Service Center related to its payroll processing system as of (date) and identified specific control objectives and the procedures that achieve those objectives. Our review included procedures we considered necessary in the circumstances to evaluate the design of the control procedures specified in Section 2. We did not test compliance with the control procedures and, accordingly, we do not express an opinion on whether those controls were being applied as prescribed for any period of time or on whether the system, taken as a whole, meets the objectives of internal accounting control. A further description of our review and its objectives is attached.
>
> Because of inherent limitations in any system of internal accounting control, errors or irregularities may occur and not be detected. Also, projection of any evaluation of the system to future periods is subject to the risk that procedures may become inadequate because of changes in conditions.
>
> In our opinion, the control procedures included in the accompanying description of the payroll processing system of the Blank Service Center as of (date) are suitably designed to provide reasonable, but not absolute, assurance that the control objectives specified in Section 2 would be achieved if the control procedures were complied with satisfactorily.
>
> This report is intended solely for use by management of Blank Service Center, its customers, and the independent auditors of its customers.

REPORTS ON BOTH THE DESIGN OF A SYSTEM
AND CERTAIN COMPLIANCE TESTS

The service auditor is not required to report every deviation or error found during a compliance test of controls. If the occurrence rate of deviations and errors is not significant in relation to the number of records examined, or if deviations and errors have been detected and corrected in the system, the service auditor may conclude that a system's objectives are accomplished.

In addition to the requirements of Section 642 and the items mentioned above, the service auditor's report on both the design of a system and compliance tests should include the service auditor's opinion as to whether control procedures and the degree of compliance with them are sufficient to provide reasonable assurance that specific control objectives are achieved during the time period covered by the review.

Reports on the System of a Segment of the Service Organization

The purpose of the service auditor's report on the system of a segment of the service organization that executes transactions for others is to state the service auditor's opinion on the internal accounting controls applied by the segment to the execution and recording of those transactions. Section 642.03 through 642.46 should be used as a guide for this type of report. Section 642 explains the form of opinion on a system of internal accounting control—that the system taken as a whole was sufficient to meet the objectives of internal accounting control "insofar as those objectives pertain to the prevention or detection of errors or irregularities in amounts that would be material in relation to the (entity's) financial statements." The financial statements of the service organization rather than the segment should be used as the basis for determining the materiality of errors or irregularities.

The service auditor should consider the appropriateness of management's actions to correct errors and irregularities, even if the errors and irregularities discovered by the service auditor were not significant enough to change his overall evaluation. The service auditor should request the service organization to report the errors to the client if he feels the errors would be material to the assets held for the client. The service auditor should describe the errors in his or her report if the service organization does not report them to the client.

AUGUST 1979

Auditing Under the Foreign Corrupt Practices Act

Here is a review of the Foreign Corrupt Practices Act of
1977 and its impact on internal and external auditors.
Significant implications are highlighted to assist auditors
in responding to present needs and in planning for the
future. Questions that can only be resolved by future
events are raised.

Thomas E. McKee, CPA, Ph.D.

THE Foreign Corrupt Practices Act (FCPA) of 1977
became law in December 1977. It raises significant
questions for all parties connected with the financial reporting process of companies covered by the Act. This
article explores implications for auditors of the FCPA's
accounting provisions. Both internal and external auditors
need to be familiar with the FCPA, since they will be expected to assist in complying with it. External auditors
must be alert for violations (as with any other legislation)
to comply with AICPA SAS 17—Illegal Acts by Clients.

Background of Act

Post-Watergate investigations revealed that many
U.S. corporations, in addition to making illegal domestic
political contributions, had made questionable payments
to foreign governments and politicians to maintain or obtain business. Disclosure of these payments in the media
caused much public concern and unrest.

The SEC performed a study of 26 companies admitting to having made such questionable foreign payments.
They found that virtually every foreign bribery case was
characterized by significant weaknesses in the company's
internal accounting system. Activities of this type were
concealed by maintaining "off-the-books" bank accounts
or otherwise circumventing the system of internal accounting control.

In 1976 the SEC submitted a report to a Senate
Committee which included a recommendation that Congress enact legislation designed to increase the accuracy
of corporate books and records. The Senate Committee
conducted hearings on this recommendation and others
relating to the illegal and questionable payments problem.
These hearings eventually resulted in passage of FCPA.

*Thomas E. McKee, CPA, Ph.D., is an Associate Professor of Ac-
counting at East Tennessee State University. He was formerly on
the staff of Price Waterhouse & Co. and is a member of the
AICPA, NAA, AAA and Academy of Accounting Historians.*

The name of the Act is somewhat a misnomer. The
provisions of FCPA having most significance to U.S. corporate management do not deal with foreign corrupt practices at all. Rather, they concern FCPA's accounting provisions. These provisions may have created significant
new duties and liabilities for internal and external auditors.

Details of Act

The FCPA has two main sections, the Antibribery
Provisions, after which the Act was named and the Accounting Standards Provisions.

Antibribery Provisions

These provisions make it a criminal offense for any
SEC registrant or other "Domestic Concern" to use any
means or instrumentality of interstate commerce to offer
or pay anything of value to (a) any foreign official, (b) any
foreign political party or official thereof, or (c) a third person who would indirectly perform the same function, for
the purpose of obtaining, retaining or directing business
to any person. Companies convicted of violating these
provisions may be fined up to $1,000,000 and individuals
convicted may be fined up to $10,000 and imprisoned up
to five years.

The Antibribery Provisions *do* have accounting and
auditing implications. Although it is not the primary purpose of this article, some of these implications are described.

Aside from possible loss of business from not being
able to pay bribes, from a corporate viewpoint the major
concerns would be the fine of up to $1,000,000 and pos-
sible adverse publicity or loss of business if prosecuted.
To prosecute, the Justice Department would probably
have to believe that the company either condoned offering a bribe or provided an atmosphere conducive to offering a bribe. To guard against this eventuality, companies
can take steps such as:

• Adopting (or modifying an existing one) a written

code of conduct spelling out policies relative to FCPA and other areas of responsibility;

• Adequately communicating the code of conduct throughout the organization;

• Seeking written agreements from agents and others representing the company in foreign countries that they will comply with the code of conduct;

• Establishing adequate procedures for monitoring compliance with the code of conduct.[1]

The company's internal auditors and/or independent auditors should review the adequacy of such a code of conduct. They should also review and possibly test procedures for monitoring compliance. All recommendations as well as any illegal activities or questionable payments noted should be brought to the attention of the Audit Committee of the Board of Directors as well as an appropriate level of management.

Note that the Antibribery Provisions of FCPA prohibit the offer or payment of "*anything of value*" to foreign officials. This is at variance with the public auditor's observance of present auditing standards concerning illegal acts which emphasizes detection of illegal acts *materially* affecting the financial statements. Auditors may have to reconsider their materiality standards in relation to activities covered under this portion of FCPA.

Accounting Provisions

The two major sentences in the Accounting Provisions are:

• Make and keep books, records and accounts, which, in reasonable detail, accurately and fairly reflect the transactions and dispositions of the assets of the issuer; and

'The provisions of FCPA having most significance to U.S. corporate management do not deal with foreign corrupt practices at all.'

• Devise and maintain a system of internal accounting controls sufficient to provide reasonable assurances that:

1. Transactions are executed in accordance with management's general or specific authorization;

2. Transactions are recorded as necessary (1) to permit preparation of financial statements in conformity with generally accepted accounting principles or any other criteria applicable to such statements, and (2) to maintain accountability for assets;

3. Access to assets is permitted only in accordance with management's general or specific authorization; and

4. The recorded accountability for assets is compared with the existing assets at reasonable intervals and appropriate action is taken with respect to any differences.

There are a number of significant points. First, the FCPA applies only to companies registered under Section 12 of the 1934 SEC Act. These include business enterprises (regardless of form) listed on a national stock exchange or have at least one million dollars in assets and five hundred or more shareholders.

'Auditors may have to reconsider their materiality standards in relation to activities covered under this portion of FCPA.'

Willful violations of FCPA are subject to the general penalties contained under the SEC Act of 1934. These include a fine of up to $10,000 and/or imprisonment up to five years. Companies and their financial advisers might also be subject to the civil litigation by third parties based on failure to comply with accounting provisions or failure to disclose a material fact.

Securities and Exchange Commission Action

ASR No. 242, issued February 1978, shortly after passage of the Foreign Corrupt Practices Act of 1977, was primarily intended to notify issuers, accountants, attorneys and other interested persons of enactment of FCPA. The release reviews the requirements of FCPA. It notes that the requirement under the 1933 and 1934 Securities Acts to disclose all material facts necessary to keep financial statements from being misleading was not altered by FCPA. Transactions which are not unlawful under FCPA may still require disclosure under the federal securities laws. SEC also states that it does not "...intend to render interpretive advice on the applicability of the Act's proscriptions to particular factual situations." Thus accountants, both internal and external, will have to interpret the FCPA based on available data on Congressional intent until sufficient precedent is established to provide guidance on unresolved issues. SEC has also announced that they are likely to require, in reports filed with them, a representation that the issuer's system of internal accounting controls is in compliance with FCPA.

Evaluation of Internal Control Systems

The definition of internal accounting controls contained in FCPA should not be new to auditors. It comes

---

[1] Arthur Andersen and Company, *An Analysis of the Foreign Corrupt Practices Act of 1977* (Chicago: Arthur Andersen and Company, 1978).

practically verbatim from Section 320.28 of SAS No. 1. Since this definition came from SAS 1, it seems reasonable that other relevant sections of SAS 1 should be applied in interpreting the intent, even though not contained in FCPA. This was apparently intended by SEC in choosing SAS wording, for they stated that they believed the specification of the objectives of a system of internal accounting controls by reference to accounting literature would be readily understood by issuers and accountants.

It is important to recognize that the FCPA only prescribed that companies maintain a sufficient system of internal *accounting* controls. There is no reference to administrative controls as defined in SAS No. 1, Section 320.27-28.

A supposed distinction between the two types of controls has long been in the authoritative literature. Public auditors have historically concentrated primarily on accounting controls. A problem occurs in that some controls may be classified as both accounting and administrative. Since the distinction is not always clear, auditors may have to concentrate on internal administrative controls to a greater extent than in the past.

Lack of Specific Criteria for Evaluating Internal Control

FCPA did not specifically provide a requirement that companies go through a formal evaluation of their internal accounting controls, merely that they "devise and maintain" a sufficient system. Presumably, if a company believed its system to be adequate, no action was required. In ASR No. 242, SEC, however, took a slightly different position and stated that:

> ...it is important that issuers subject to the new requirements review their accounting procedures, systems of internal accounting controls and business practices in order that they may take any actions necessary to comply with the requirements contained in the Act.

SEC did not, however, specify exactly what such a review should involve. Also, the tentative report of the Special Advisory Committee on Internal Accounting Control stated, "The Committee believes that management should initiate a preliminary assessment of the internal accounting control environment and of the appropriateness and effectiveness of existing accounting control procedures and techniques..."

Some companies are having their external and/or internal auditors make comprehensive reviews of their existing systems in an attempt to comply with FCPA. The problem with such reviews is that there are no definitive criteria or standards for measuring an internal accounting control system. The FCPA states that the system should be sufficient to provide "reasonable assurances" that the four broad objectives of an internal control system are met. What does the term "reasonable assurances" really mean or imply? SAS 1 provides some assistance by explaining that the concept of reasonable assurances encompasses the notions that the cost of a control should not exceed the benefits likely to be derived and that the evaluation of costs and benefits requires estimates and judgments by management. This explanation is not much help in regard to many controls, because both costs and benefits of the control may be unknown or impossible to estimate with any accuracy.

What Materiality Level?

FCPA does not limit its coverage to material items in either the Antibribery or Accounting Provisions. As noted earlier the Antibribery Provisions prohibit giving or offering "anything of value." The Accounting Provisions use the term "in reasonable detail" in describing the requirement for maintaining books and records but do not provide guidance as to what is "reasonable detail." Also, the requirement to maintain a system of internal accounting control raises unanswered questions about materiality levels, especially in view of the fact that there are no definitive criteria for evaluating the adequacy of such systems.

'SEC did not . . . specify exactly what such a review should involve.'

Most companies have weaknesses in their internal control systems and deficiencies in their record keeping procedures. In a literal sense that means they are in violation of FCPA. It is clear that this was not the intent of Congress in passing FCPA. However, given the lack of materiality standards, it is not clear how severe a weakness or record keeping deficiency would have to be so as to be deemed a violation. Since SEC is not, at the moment, providing any guidance in this area, it is probable that this question will be answered in the courts in future years.

Implications for External Auditors

FCPA does not create expressed new duties for external auditors. However, because of its impact on officers, directors and management, generally, there are a number of possible points for external auditors to ponder.

Effect on Scope of Work

In accordance with the second standard of field work, auditors perform "a proper study and evaluation of existing internal control." Auditors may question whether, in light of FCPA, they are expected to expand the scope of their work beyond that required by the second standard of field work to detect irregularities.

The answer to this question is apparently negative according to an auditing interpretation issued by the AICPA Auditing Standards Division. They note that SAS 20, which interprets the second standard, states that "...there is no requirement under generally accepted auditing standards to evaluate each control or to identify every material weakness." Also noted was the fact that nothing in the FCPA itself or its legislative history "...purports to alter the auditor's duty to his client or the purpose of his study and evaluation of internal accounting control."

'FCPA does not limit its coverage to material items in either the Antibribery or Accounting Provisions.'

Assurances to Management

Management and directors of companies covered by FCPA naturally want to minimize their liability under the Act. Some may seek to do this by attempting to obtain reports from their external auditors that they *have complied* with the Accounting Provisions. According to an interpretation issued by the AICPA Auditing Standards Division, CPAs may not issue reports of this type. A statement that a company is in compliance with FCPA is a legal opinion and should not be issued by auditors. Auditors may, however, review companies' control systems to comment to management on material weaknesses. Currently, neither auditors nor management has a responsibility to publicly report possible violations.[2]

Reports to Public

FCPA appears to have given impetus for public reporting on the adequacy of companies' internal control systems. It has been suggested that the issuing party for such a report might be either the board of directors' audit committee, the chief financial officer or the director of internal auditing. Harold Williams, chairman of SEC, stated in June 1978, "But it is virtually certain that reporting on internal control will be a reality for public companies in the near future." Two months later he also stated, "...some degree of auditor involvement with that report is a corollary we will have to consider in light of the traditional familiarity and expertise in this area of the accounting profession." Thus it appears that, unless SEC changes its position, public reports on internal control of

---

[2] Price Waterhouse and Company, *Monitoring Compliance With Control Systems Under the Foreign Corrupt Practices Act* (New York: Price Waterhouse and Company, 1978).

systems will be a reality in the near future. The significant unanswered question is to what degree will external auditors be involved with such reports?

SAS 17—Illegal Acts by Clients

This standard provides guidance for auditors when they discover client acts that appear to be illegal during the course of an audit. Actions to be taken by an auditor per the SAS remain unchanged by FCPA and include inquiry of client's management and consultation with client's legal counsel. The major difference, as noted previously, is that materiality standards under FCPA may differ from traditional standards applied by an auditor in determining if a material weakness in internal accounting control exists. SAS 17 does not provide a general framework for reviewing the adequacy of internal control systems.

SAS 20—Required Communication of Material Weaknesses in Internal Accounting Control

As a result of this statement, auditors are required to communicate to senior management and the board of directors or its audit committee material weaknesses in internal accounting control that come to their attention during an audit. This requirement remains unchanged but FCPA has created several factors that the auditor should be aware of. First, because of different materiality levels and a different purpose in reviewing internal control during an audit, the audit may not have uncovered all weaknesses as contemplated in FCPA. This fact should be carefully conveyed to management both orally and in writing so that they will not place undue reliance on the accountant's report. Second, because of potential increased liability as a result of FCPA, management will probably be more concerned about weaknesses reported. The auditor should, where appropriate, note corrective actions taken or in progress. Also, if management believes corrective action is not practicable, the auditor should summarize the circumstances and management's position. This will ensure that management's best position is stated in writing and that it is not unnecessarily jeopardized by a report reflecting essentially only one viewpoint.

Responsibility for Subsidiaries

It is not clear under FCPA whether unconsolidated domestic subsidiaries and foreign subsidiaries are subject to FCPA. Until a precedent is established it would be prudent to proceed as if they are included.

Implications for Internal Auditors

The internal audit function has traditionally been viewed as a part of the system of internal control having responsibility for reviewing and monitoring other controls. This function has not changed under FCPA, but there are a number of important changes occurring in the operations of internal audit departments as a result.

Control System Evaluations

Many companies are turning to their internal auditors as opposed to their external auditors, because of cost and other reasons, to perform control system evaluations. Previous comments made about such evaluations concerning external auditors also apply to internal auditors. Any cost/benefit rationale previously employed by internal auditors may be outdated due to the penalties associated with FCPA.

Increased Prominence

Because of these penalties, management in many companies is attaching increasing importance to the activities and reports of the internal audit department. As a result, many such departments are experiencing increased attention to their recommendations. The prestige of such departments also appears to be increasing. Certainly FCPA will cause companies not having internal audit departments to re-evaluate their need for this function. FCPA will probably accelerate an existing trend toward having internal audit departments report to a higher level of management.

Additional Resources

The new emphasis on internal control should lead to an upgrading ar 1 expansion of the quality and size of internal audit departments. This is being done in response to efforts to show current compliance with FCPA and perhaps in anticipation of public reporting on control systems in the near future. Part of the resource increase is also attributable to the fact that in many companies internal audit penetration has heretofore been low in foreign operations, but because of FCPA, these areas are now receiving additional scrutiny.

Decreased Emphasis on Operational Auditing

Due to new pressures created by FCPA on limited internal audit staffs, it is probable that some shifting of resources away from operational auditing may take place. Traditional internal audit functions are more likely to be emphasized.

Increased Professionalism and Training

Increased responsibilities and prominence because of FCPA may accelerate the trend toward professional certification of internal auditors. Certainly if the profession is going to grow and attract qualified people, they will want to identify with it in a professional manner. Along with the trend toward professionalism will come increased training and continuing education since they are attributes of a professional. It is significant to note that some of this training may be at facilities of their company's external auditors.[3]

Auditing Corporate Codes of Conduct

The importance of a formal code of conduct and the establishment of procedures for monitoring such a code was previously mentioned. Many internal audit departments have already been performing such reviews. As a result of FCPA, additional attention will have to be devoted to such reviews.

'The new emphasis on internal control should lead to an upgrading and expansion of the quality and size of internal audit departments.'

Summary and Conclusions

The FCPA has created significant new responsibilities and opportunities for internal and external auditors. There are a number of unanswered questions that can only be resolved by future events. Principal among these are:
• Development of definitive standards for evaluation of internal accounting control systems;
• Question of public issuance of reports on internal accounting control systems;
• Further definition of FCPA terms through SEC and court actions.
Auditors need to acquaint themselves in detail with the provisions of FCPA so they may respond to present needs and plan for the future. Ω

---

[3] Arthur Andersen and Company, "A Cooperative Program to Reduce the Costs of Audits," *Arthur Andersen and Company Executive News Briefs* (Chicago: Arthur Andersen and Company, October 27, 1978), pp. 1–3.

EVALUATING INTERNAL CONTROL

The authors suggest a practical approach to meet the FCPA objectives.

by James K. Loebbecke and George R. Zuber

Passage of the Foreign Corrupt Practices Act of 1977 (FCPA) contributed to a more formal effort by U.S. companies to document and review their systems of internal accounting control, and proposed Securities and Exchange Commission regulations promise a continuation of this trend. Managements must evaluate whether they have internal accounting control systems that meet the objectives of internal accounting control as defined in the FCPA.

Each system is different for each company, and all are necessarily complex in design. A system may be composed of thousands of daily procedures performed by hundreds of employees throughout an international, decentralized company. As a result, companies are finding it difficult to relate those thousands of procedures to the objectives of internal accounting control.

JAMES K. LOEBBECKE, CPA, is a partner of Touche Ross & Co. in New York. A former chairman of the American Institute of CPAs statistical sampling subcommittee, he is a member of the internal control task force of the auditing standards board. Mr. Loebbecke is vice-chairman–practice of the auditing section of the American Accounting Association, on the board of governors of the New York Chapter of the Institute of Internal Auditors and a member of the New York State Society of CPAs. He is also the author of various articles which have appeared in professional publications and coauthor of two books on the auditing field. GEORGE R. ZUBER, CPA, is a manager in the AICPA auditing standards division and an adjunct professor at New York University. He is a member of the New York State Society of CPAs and of the AICPA.

This article describes an approach to evaluating the design of an internal accounting control system that should be practical both for a company's internal accountants who assist management in evaluating the system and for an independent accountant who is engaged to report on the company's internal accounting control system. This approach involves describing the system by identifying specific control objectives and then relating those objectives to the numerous specific procedures in effect.

What Is an Internal Accounting Control System?

Managing a company is a stewardship function. To fulfill that responsibility, management establishes procedures to be followed in the day-to-day operations of the company which, among other things, safeguard the company's assets and ensure reliable recording of the company's monetary transactions.

Some of these control procedures are designed to deter employees from making unintentional errors or committing irregularities. These procedures are often described as preventive controls. Other control procedures, generally referred to as detective controls, are primarily used to discover the occurrence of errors or irregularities. Effective detective controls may alert management to ineffective preventive controls and also contribute indirectly to prevention. Employees may be more careful about trying to avoid making mistakes or be less inclined to commit irregularities when they believe the error or irregularity will be discovered through detective controls.

Although the internal accounting control system can be distinguished from the accounting system, some procedures contribute to both systems. Many preventive controls, for instance, are built into the design of the accounting system and therefore serve a dual purpose—for example, forms for processing transactions may also be designed to provide numerical control over recording the transactions in the proper period. When the controls are incorporated in processing procedures, the control objectives may be achieved at little or no additional cost.

The sole purpose of other controls, which are not designed as part of the accounting system, is to contribute to achieving the broad objectives of internal accounting control. Many detective controls are of this type.

When designing an internal accounting control system, management must consider the trade-off between the costs of instituting controls and the benefits of those controls as well as the cost trade-off between alternative control procedures that may achieve the same objective. For example, management may believe that it is more desirable to rely on a monthly reconciliation of credits to customer accounts than to require a second review of all credits at the time of posting. However, in making that decision, management will have to consider both the cost of the reconciliation compared to the cost of an additional review and the cost of correcting errors and irregularities detected, but obviously not prevented, by the reconciliation.

Although management and accountants alike recognize a distinction between internal accounting and internal administrative controls, it is essential to realize that the distinction is not clear-cut. The distinguishing

> "An accountant should select the method of grouping classes of transactions and assets that enables him to make the most effective evaluation of the internal accounting control system."

factor is not the control's label but, rather, whether the control is necessary for the company to achieve the broad objectives of internal accounting control.

Grouping Transactions and Assets

The foundation of a control system is at the transactional level. Statement on Auditing Standards no. 1, *Codification of Auditing Standards and Procedures,* provides guidance to auditors performing a study and evaluation of an internal accounting control system. Section 320.20 of that statement says: "Transactions are the basic components of business operations and, therefore, are the primary subject matter of internal control."[1]

The accountant who is evaluating an internal accounting control system will need to identify specific control objectives relating to the entity's transactions. To do this the

---

[1] Statement on Auditing Standards no. 1, *Codification of Auditing Standards and Procedures* (New York: AICPA, 1973), sec. 320.20. See also *AICPA Professional Standards* (Chicago, Ill.: Commerce Clearing House, 1979), AU sec. 320.20.

accountant should first identify all material classes of transactions and then determine the related material classes of assets to be safeguarded by the system.

Many types of transactions and assets are similar and can be grouped into like classes without altering their control characteristics. For example, a truck manufacturer's purchases of inventory and purchases of repair parts and supplies may be identical transactions from the standpoint of the accounting process and related controls. Similarly, raw packaging materials and cases of finished goods may be identical assets from an asset safeguarding viewpoint. For example, a lens grinding company may safeguard both unground glass and finished lenses to be sold to a camera manufacturer by employing guards and closed-circuit TV to protect the warehouse.

Certain classes of transactions and assets may also be logically grouped because they are controlled by the use of many common mechanisms within an organization. For example, they may be processed by the same groups of employees, documented on the same or related forms, entered and maintained on the same accounting records and reported, showing natural relationships, on common reports.

In current practice, these logical groupings tend to be of two types:

☐ *Transaction cycles,* which group classes of transactions by related activity. For example, purchases, cash disbursements, raw materials and operating expenses might be grouped as one transaction cycle.

☐ *Business functions,* which group transactions by particular organizational units. For example, a purchasing department, a manufacturing division and a regional branch could all be identified as separate business functions for control purposes.

These two groupings are not necessarily mutually exclusive. For example, an electronics manufacturer may have identified several business functions, such as a small appliance manufacturing division, a calculator manufacturing division, a distribution division and a research division, for control purposes. However, within each division the company may group transactions by cycles such as an expenditures cycle, a production cycle and a revenue cycle.

An accountant should select the method of grouping classes of transactions and assets that enables him to make the most effective evaluation of the internal accounting control system. He would normally consider the company's organizational structure, the related methods of communicating responsibility and delegating authority and the system for reporting the results of operations. For example, a business function approach may be used in large, decentralized organizations where it reflects the flow of management authority and responsibility within the organization, and individual classes of transactions may be identified within those business functions.

Making the Broad Objectives Operational

As described in sec. 320.28 of SAS no. 1 and as legislatively enacted in sec. 102(2) of the FCPA, the broad objectives of an internal accounting control system include the execution of transactions in accordance with management's authorization, the recording of transactions, the limiting of access to assets and the periodic comparison of recorded assets to physical assets. These objectives, however, are necessarily composed of numerous, more detailed objectives that bridge the gap between the overall objectives of a system and the operational level of detailed transactions. Before an accountant can relate individual classes of transactions and assets to the objectives of internal accounting control, he must identify the general objectives underlying the four broad objectives.

These control objectives may be developed by dividing the four broad objectives into operational objectives applicable to all transactions and assets. For example, several operational objectives can be identified that underlie the following broad objective: "Transactions are recorded as necessary (1) to permit preparation of financial statements in conformity with generally accepted accounting principles or any other criteria applicable to such statements, and (2) to maintain accountability for assets."[2] They include the following operational objectives:

☐ All transactions are reported.

☐ Recorded transactions have substance.

☐ Transactions are recorded at correct amounts.

☐ Transactions are recorded in the correct period.

☐ Transactions are classified in the correct accounts.

☐ Transactions are accurately posted and summarized.

Column 2 of figure 1, page 52, illustrates the operational objectives underlying each of the four broad objectives.

Identifying Specific Control Objectives

Specific control objectives may now be identified by relating the identified classes of individual transactions and assets to the operational objectives. Each applicable operational objective should be restated for each class of transactions or assets within the selected transaction grouping. In column 2 of figure 1, for example, each of the objectives may be restated for an identified class of sales transactions to develop related specific control objectives. For example, the operational objective "recorded transactions have substance" could be restated in terms of a sales transaction as "recorded sales are for goods shipped or services performed."

Alternatively, the specific control objectives may be stated in terms of whether a particular type of error or irregularity could occur. To illustrate, the objective "recorded transactions have substance" could be restated, for a sales transaction, to identify a specific potential error as "sales could be recorded for goods not shipped or services not performed."

Column 3 of figure 1 illustrates the identification of specific control objectives by restating the operational objectives identified in column 2 in terms of sales transactions and column 4 illustrates the same specific control objectives in terms of potential errors.

Relating Specific Control Procedures to the Objectives of Internal Accounting Control

The identification of specific control objectives is the necessary first step in the process of evaluating an internal accounting control system. The accountant must also identify the prescribed control procedures that meet these objectives in order to be satisfied that the system is suitably designed to fulfill the broad objectives of internal accounting control. This is a complex step.

An individual specific control procedure may meet several specific control objectives to varying degrees. In addition, a single

---

[2] Foreign Corrupt Practices Act of 1977, sec. 102(2). Also Title 1 of PL 95-213, 91 Stat. 1494 (December 1977) (amending sec. 13(b) of the Securities Exchange Act of 1934, 15 U.S.C. 78m(b)).

Figure 1

Example of making the broad objectives operational to identify specific control objectives or problems for a sales transaction

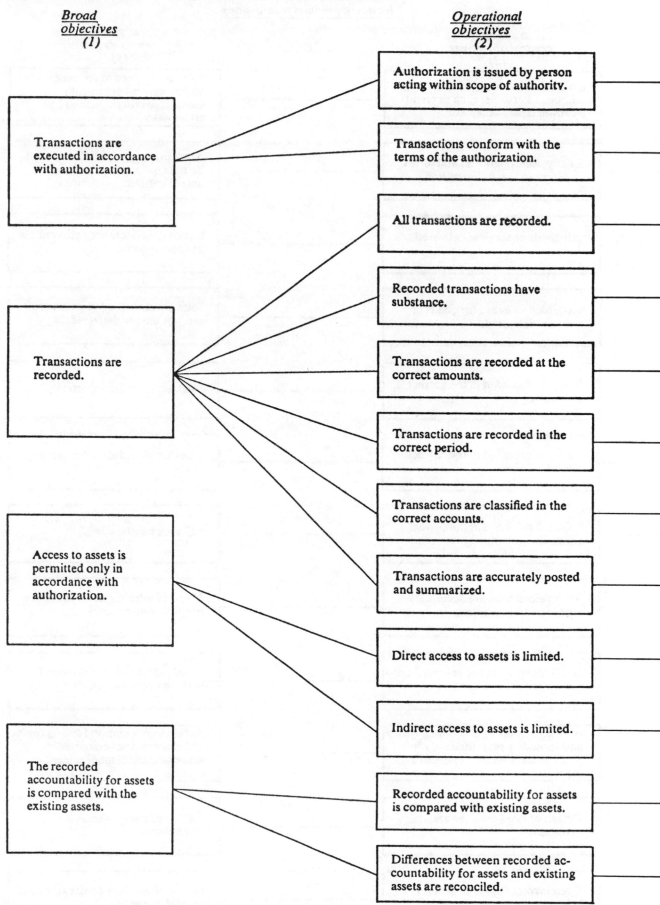

Restated for sales transactions

. . . as specific
control objectives
(3)

. . . or . . .

. . . as specific
control problems
(4)

. . . as specific control objectives (3)	. . . as specific control problems (4)
Only sales that meet management's authorized criteria, such as credit worthiness, are accepted.	Sales are shipped to customers who do not meet management's authorized criteria such as bad credit risks.
Sales prices, quantities and terms conform to the authorization.	Sales prices, quantities and terms do not conform to terms of authorization.
All goods or services delivered are invoiced.	Goods or services are delivered but are not invoiced.
Recorded sales are for goods or services delivered.	Sales are recorded but goods or services are not delivered.
Sales are recorded at the correct amounts.	Sales are recorded incorrectly.
Sales are recorded in the correct period.	Sales are recorded in the wrong period.
Sales are recorded in the correct accounts.	Sales are misclassified.
All invoiced sales are accurately posted and summarized.	Invoiced sales are not recorded or properly summarized.
Goods or services are delivered only with approved requests.	Goods or services are delivered without approved requests.
Access to shipping and billing forms and records is permitted only in accordance with management's criteria.	Access to shipping and billing forms and records is not restricted in accordance with management's criteria.
Details of open invoices are maintained.	Details of open invoices are not maintained.
Open invoices agree to general ledger.	Details of invoices do not agree with general ledger.

specific control objective may be met by one or more control procedures. In some cases, no one specific procedure may be adequate to achieve the specific control objective while several procedures working together do fulfill that objective.

A practical approach to this complex situation is to use a table that relates specific control procedures to identified specific control objectives or, alternatively, to potential types of errors. For example, some of the specific control objectives relating to a payroll department may include the following:

☐ Compensation is made at authorized rates.

☐ Payroll is recorded only for work performed.

☐ Payroll and related withholdings are correctly calculated.

☐ Payroll is recorded in the proper period. The entire set of specific control objectives related to a selected transaction grouping should be listed across the top of the table as headings to the vertical columns. The horizontal rows should be labeled with identified specific control procedures. The accountant would then check each box in the table to indicate where a specific control procedure achieves, or contributes to the achievement of, a specific control objective.

Some rows may have several check marks. For example, the identified cash disbursements control procedure "bank reconciliations are prepared on a timely basis" may contribute to meeting the following related specific control objectives, among others:

☐ All cash disbursements are recorded.

☐ All recorded payments have been made.

☐ Recorded payment amounts are correct. Also, the specific control objective "recorded payment amounts are correct" may be achieved in part or completely by the following control procedures, among others:

☐ Bank reconciliations are prepared on a timely basis.

☐ Check requests are used and totals are compared to check register.

☐ Prepared checks are compared to voucher package for accuracy of amount.

After all the specific control procedures have been considered and all the related specific control objectives that are partially or fully met by those procedures have been indicated by a check mark in the appropriate box, the accountant would identify procedures that are essential to achieving a specific control objective and distinguish them from controls that are less important by circling the appropriate check mark. If a procedure potentially contributes to the achievement of a specific control objective but is not essential to meeting the objective, it may be a redundant control or it may be only one of several control procedures required to fulfill the specific control objective.

Figure 2, page 55, is an illustration of a completed table. By using this approach, specific control objectives that have not been met by the designed control procedures would be readily identified because either no circled check marks would appear in the respective column or the aggregate effect of uncircled check marks is insufficient. A circled check mark for every specific control objective in every transaction group would indicate that the system has been designed with specific control procedures suitable for meeting the objectives of internal accounting control.

Primary and Secondary Levels of Control Procedures

The control procedures identified by the table approach are usually applied during the processing of transactions and handling of assets and may be referred to as "primary control procedures." Other control procedures may provide indirect control because they are applied after transaction processing has been completed. These control procedures may be referred to as "secondary control procedures."

When primary control procedures appear inadequate for achieving specific control objectives, the accountant may consider the impact of secondary control procedures. Secondary controls include, for example, a corporate control policy statement, an internal audit function and a budgeting and reporting system. A thorough investigation of deviations from such policies and variances from budgeted results may contribute to adequate overall assurance that material errors or irregularities will not occur or, if they do occur, that they will be detected within a timely period.

Benefits of a Table Evaluation

The table approach described in this article offers the accountant several benefits, including the following:

☐ The table is based on a logical approach of relating the broad objectives of internal accounting control to the company's trans-

Figure 2

Completed Evaluation Form

COMPANY: XYZ COMPANY, INC. .... Date _____

EVALUATION OF INTERNAL ACCOUNTING CONTROLS Prepared by _____ Reviewed by _____

PROCEDURE: ....

CHART: SALES ....

Control objectives checked (✓) are those partially or fully achieved by procedures; checks circled (Ⓥ) indicate those control procedures essential to meeting the objective. How many checks (✓) or circled checks (Ⓥ) are needed to produce a Ⓨⓔⓢ is dependent on the auditor's judgment.

Specific control objectives for a sales transaction

Control procedures description (Reference)	All sales authorized	Sales terms authorized	Shipments invoiced	Recorded sales shipped	Sales amount correct	Sale in correct period	Sale recorded in correct account	Sales correctly posted and summarized	Goods delivered on approved requests	Access to forms and records authorized	Details of accounts receivable maintained	Accounts receivable details agree to general ledger
1 Policy authorization of credit limits	Ⓥ											
2 Specific authorization required by credit manager for extension of credit limits	Ⓥ	Ⓥ										
3 Use of standard order forms		✓					✓		✓			
4 Use of standard list of accounts to be charged, prices, discounts, terms, customer numbers		Ⓥ			Ⓥ		Ⓥ	Ⓥ	Ⓥ			
5 Independent check of order form details		Ⓥ	Ⓥ		Ⓥ	✓	Ⓥ	✓	Ⓥ		✓	✓
6 Journal entries reviewed						✓						
7 Prenumbered shipping documents (copies of sales documents) used and followed up independently for serial continuity			Ⓥ	Ⓥ		Ⓥ			Ⓥ		✓	Ⓥ
8 Shipping function segregated from billing function			✓	✓					✓	✓		
9 Matching of sales invoices to shipping documents (packing slip signed by customer or product order validated by trucker)			Ⓥ	Ⓥ					Ⓥ	Ⓥ	✓	
10 Edit listing is agreed to shipping documents before files are updated			✓	✓					✓	✓	✓	✓
11 Control of access to shipping area			✓	✓					✓			
12 Aged accounts receivable trial balance reviewed, overdue balances investigated by controller, test checked to open invoice file	✓						✓			✓		✓
13 Review of aged unapplied payments list by controller	✓		✓		✓		✓	✓			✓	✓
14 Edit listing of sales order forms agreed to detail before invoice set prepared	✓		✓		✓		✓	✓			✓	✓
15 Acknowledgement copy of invoice mailed to customer	✓				✓			✓			✓	✓
16 Programs are validated and tested periodically	✓				✓		✓	✓		✓	✓	✓
17 All data processing functions are segregated from other major functions	✓				✓		✓	✓		✓	✓	✓
18 Billing function segregated from receivables function	✓	✓					✓			✓	✓	
19 Management review of weekly transaction register								✓				
20 Reconciliation of sales and accounts receivable postings						Ⓥ	Ⓥ	Ⓥ				Ⓥ
Evaluation—is the system adequately designed to achieve the control objective? (circle appropriate answer)	No (Yes)	No (Yes)	No (Yes)	No (Yes)	No (Yes)	No (Yes)	No (Yes)	No (Yes)	No (Yes)	No (Yes)	No (Yes)	No (Yes)

actions by identifying specific control objectives. The columnar headings of the tables should be a complete inventory of all identified specific control objectives. The accountant may be assured that if all the individual specific control objectives are fulfilled, the system as a whole is suitably designed to meet the broad objectives of internal accounting control.

☐ The table clearly shows, in a simple format, the complex relationship between specific control objectives and the voluminous control procedures established by the company. This approach may reduce the need for more complex approaches such as extensive flowcharts of the accounting and control systems or internal control questionnaires.

☐ Because the table approach focuses on specific control objectives, no standard form of the system description is required for this approach. Some approaches require system descriptions to be in a standardized format —for example, questionnaires or flowcharts. Reformatting existing procedural manuals and other descriptive documentation into a standard format can be costly and time-consuming.

☐ Because a table identifies both the minimum specific control procedures essential to achieving a specific control objective and other related specific control procedures, the accountant can readily determine if alternative control procedures are provided by the system in case he later finds that compliance with an essential procedure is not adequate.

☐ In addition to clearly illustrating whether the system is suitably designed to meet all specific control objectives, the approach may be used to identify control procedures that are redundant, ineffective or otherwise unnecessary. If procedures are not identified as essential to achieving any objectives, management may wish to review whether those specific control procedures can be eliminated.

Summary

This article has described an approach to evaluating the design of an internal accounting control system. The accountant's overall objective, however, is to evaluate both the design and the functioning of that system. Additional steps necessary to achieve that goal include testing compliance with control procedures prescribed by the system and forming an overall conclusion on the sufficiency of the system. Readers may find guidance for performing these remaining steps in sec. 320 of SAS no. 1, publications prepared by many public accounting firms and numerous articles and special reports. Although such guidance is beyond the scope of this article, using the table approach described in this article puts the accountant well along the road to meeting his overall goal of evaluating both the design and the functioning of the system. ■

CASE 7

THE CASE OF THE BROKEN ENGAGEMENT *

Razer, Back, Cobb & Corn, Certified Public Accountants, were engaged to examine the financial statements of Sooner and Switzer Manufacturing Company for the year ended November 30, 19x1. The partners have been practicing together in public accounting for several years. However, in recent months they have experienced, among themselves, some serious business and social problems. Due to the nature of these problems, the partners have decided to dissolve their partnership immediately and sell their practice to a firm in a nearby city. Each partner has also agreed that it is in the best interest of everyone involved to move out of the state and set up separate accounting practices.

Because of the time required in concluding the affairs of the partnership, the firm has withdrawn from the Sooner engagement and recommended your firm, Akers and Royal, to be the successor CPAs. Akers and Royal accepted the engagement on December 12, 19x1.

Mr. Akers, the senior audit partner, has assigned you to complete the examination of Sooner and Switzer's 19x1 financial statements. After reviewing the working papers prepared by Mr. Corn of the predecessor firm, you estimate that the engagement is about one-quarter complete. When Akers and Royal accepted the engagement, it was agreed that the examination would be completed and the finished report delivered to the client in approximately four weeks. Five staff accountants have been assigned to you for assistance on the audit. You estimate that with your staff and efficient use of the client's personnel that the audit can be completed on a timely basis.

Your review of the working papers prepared by Mr. Corn and his staff revealed several significant factors with respect to the work performed by his firm. The disposition of the engagement is as follows:

Work completed: Cash, Fixed Assets, Depreciation, and Mortgage Payable and Accounts Payable

Work partially completed: Inventories, Tests of Purchase Transactions, and Payrolls

Work to be done: Accounts Receivable—Trade, Inventory Receiving Cutoff and Price Testing, Accrued Expenses Payable, Analytic Review of Operations, Payroll-Deductions Test and Observation of Payroll Check Distribution, Tests of Sales Transactions, Other Expenses, Vouching of November Purchase Transactions, Auditor's Report, Internal Control Investigation, Internal Control Letter, Review of Board Minutes, Preparation of State and Federal Tax Returns, Procedural Recommendations for Management, Review of Subsequent Events, Supervision and Review

In reviewing the working papers prepared by Mr. Corn and his staff, you determine that the working papers are incomplete and that they were not reviewed by Corn. For example, working papers evidencing test counts of inventory included incomplete explanations. In addition, inventory working papers gave no indication of the observation of the client's inventory. Also, cash, fixed asset, inventory count procedures, and depreciation working papers were not properly indexed or cross-referenced.

CASE DISCUSSION QUESTIONS

1.   Discuss the first standard of field work with respect to the Sooner and Switzer Manufacturing engagement and the work performed by Mr. Corn and his staff.

2.   The second standard of field work requires the auditor to make "a proper study and evaluation of the existing internal control as a basis for reliance thereon . . ." From the information provided in the case, what conclusions can you draw with respect to the predecessor firm in discharging this responsibility? Discuss fully.

---

* Case adapted from AICPA Uniform CPA Examination Questions.

3. Define the terms "predecessor auditor" and "successor auditor."

   a. With whom does responsibility rest in initiating communication between the two auditors? In what form may the communication be?

   b. What communications should the successor auditor make before accepting an engagement?

4. The appointment of an auditor near or after the year-end date may present certain potential problems. Explain.

5. Accounting control is within the scope of the study and evaluation of internal control comprehended by GAAS, while administrative control is not. The basis for evaluation of internal control includes two phases.

   a. What terms describe these phases?

   b. What process does the auditor follow in reviewing the system of internal accounting control?

   c. Explain the purpose of performing tests of compliance.

   d. Discuss the documentation requirements, if any, when the auditor does not plan to rely on the client's system of internal accounting control.

6. Is the review of internal control to be correlated with the performance of other auditing procedures? If so, why? Discuss. In your discussion include some of the obvious problems raised by the Sooner and Switzer engagement.

7. There are several basic concepts of internal control that are implicit in the definition of accounting control. List and explain the meaning of each concept and its relation to internal accounting control. (Hint—you should be able to identify ten basic concepts.)

8. Outline a logical approach the auditor should follow in evaluating accounting control. In your answer include or identify procedures for accomplishing each step contained in your outline.

9. Assume that several material weaknesses in internal accounting control are discovered by you during the examination of the Sooner and Switzer Company. Also, several immaterial internal control weaknesses are noted in your working papers. What action would be required by your firm as a result of these identified weaknesses in internal control? Explain.

10. Discuss the extent to which the existence of an "internal audit function" may affect the work performed by external auditors in conducting an examination of financial statements.

11. Discuss the impact of the "Foreign Corrupt Practices Act" on the procedures followed by an independent auditor in examining the financial statements of a public company. What is the effect of the Act on internal control review and evaluation? What reports are required under the Act that the auditor will be concerned with? (The articles relating to the Foreign Corrupt Practices Act contained in this section should be considered for background reading material in responding to this question.)

CASE 8

SPECIAL-PURPOSE REPORTS ON INTERNAL ACCOUNTING CONTROL AT SERVICE ORGANIZATIONS

Your firm has been engaged to perform an audit of Health Care Cost Containment Coalition, Inc., for the year ended 19x1. Your client's primary objective is to promote lower health care costs in the State of Nebraska. To achieve this objective your client obtains major medical insurance claims data from insurance companies providing insurance to major employers in the state. Also, the employers, through their insurance claims department, provide major medical data to Health Care Cost Containment Coalition, Inc. The major medical data is provided to the Coalition in such a way as to not identify individual employees claiming insurance benefits.

Major employers pay a fee to the Coalition in return for information concerning:

a. Costs charged by individual doctors for certain surgical procedures.

b. Costs charged by individual hospitals for their various cost centers such as, operating room, labor and delivery, radiology, laboratory, physical therapy, emergency, etc.

With the above information, employers can recommend to their employees where the least expensive health care can be obtained within a given area of the state and thus, hopefully, reduce their health care costs.

Due to the nature of its operation Health Care Cost Containment Coalition, Inc. has need for many accounting-type reports in addition to its financial statements. In order to have the above reports on a timely basis, it uses an EDP service center to:

a. Process its payroll.

b. Prepare its financial statements.

c. Prepare health care reports for its subscribers

d. Process billings and collections.

CASE DISCUSSION QUESTIONS

1. Discuss when the auditor is required to test compliance with control procedures (Hint: See SAS No. 1, Section 320.49 through .55).

2. SAS No. 44 discusses factors affecting the user auditor's decision to obtain a service auditor's report. Assume the service organization maintains controls that interact with the client's organization controls. Can the user auditor rely on the service organization's system of internal accounting control? Does it matter where the control procedures are located? Discuss in detail.

3. (a) Is it possible for the service organization to maintain controls that do not interact with client organization controls? (b) If yes, what should the auditor do? Give an example from SAS No. 44 to support your answer.

4. With respect to question 3(a) above, would the user auditor ever rely on the controls at the service organization? Discuss fully.

5. (a) What considerations apply if the user auditor decides to use the service auditor's report? Include in your answer any consideration required with respect to the timing of the service auditor's report? (b) Should the user auditor refer to the service auditor's report?

6. Discuss the responsibilities of the service auditor for special-purpose reports for the following:

   a. Responsibility to the user auditor.

   b. The matter of independence with regard to each client organization.

   c. List the types of reports that a service auditor may issue.

7. Assume you are the service auditor for an EDP service center and you have reported on the design of the system of internal accounting control.

   a. How is this report useful to the user auditor?

   b. How does the service auditor obtain the required information for the report?

   c. Is the service auditor's report for a specified date? Discuss in detail.

   d. Section 642.61 describes certain elements of special-purpose reports. SAS No. 44 specifies additional elements of special-purpose reports. What are they? Explain fully.

8. Assume you are the service auditor for the EDP service center discussed in the case above and your report is on both the design of a system and certain compliance tests.

   a. How is your report useful to the user auditor?

   b. How does the service auditor obtain the required information for the report?

   c. What elements of special-purpose reports (in addition to those described in Section 642.61) should be included in your report?

9. A service auditor's report on the system of a segment of the service organization differs from a report where the auditor forms an opinion on the system of internal accounting control taken as a whole. Discuss and contrast the differences between these two types of reports. (Hint: Review Section 324.42 through 324.46 and Section 642.03 through 642.46).

THE ROLES OF INTERNAL AND EXTERNAL AUDITORS IN AUDITING EDP SYSTEMS

by Larry E. Rittenberg and Gordon B. Davis

The increasing complexity of data processing systems calls for new approaches to EDP auditing.

Internal audits of complex computer systems require internal auditors who are computer audit specialists. This philosophy is followed by an increasing number of internal audit departments. They have added specialized EDP audit sections staffed by auditors qualified in both auditing and EDP. These sections generally have a broad mandate for audit reviews of all major areas of computer data processing. The trend toward specialized EDP internal auditors has resulted in significant changes which should be considered by the CPA when determining the relationship between the auditors of the CPA firm and the internal audit department. Among the more significant trends to be considered are the following:

1 Increased internal audit participation during the design phase of new computer applications.

LARRY E. RITTENBERG, CPA, Ph.D., is assistant professor of accounting and information systems at the University of Wisconsin-Madison. He is a member of the AICPA, the Institute of Internal Auditors, the American Accounting Association and the EDP Auditors Association. **GORDON B. DAVIS**, CPA, Ph.D., is a professor of accounting and management information systems at the College of Business Administration of the University of Minnesota. He is a member of the AICPA, the AAA, the Minnesota Society of CPAs, the Association for Decision Sciences and the EDP Auditors Association. He has written several books on data processing.

2 The development and implementation of more sophisticated audit techniques by internal audit departments.

3 Increased internal audit review of major computer program changes.

4 Increased internal audit attention to the general data processing control environment.

These developments indicate the potential for substantial benefits to be received from greater internal and external audit cooperation in complex EDP environments. This article reports on a research study which investigated the EDP audit function in the internal audit departments of 39 major corporations.

Research Methodology

The authors identified 48 internal audit departments which were thought to be among the more advanced in the use of EDP audit techniques. Each of the organizations received a detailed questionnaire about their EDP audit activities. Thirty-nine of the 48 responded in the sample to the questionnaire. A summary of the distribution and response is shown in table 1, this page.

Table 1

Questionnaires sent to internal audit departments

Responses received:	
From those performing design phase audits	31
From those not performing design phase audits	8
Total responses	39
No response	9
Total questionnaires mailed	48
Response rate	81%

For each company participating in the study, two questionnaires were mailed to the company's external auditors, one to the CPA responsible for reviewing EDP internal control and one to the manager or partner in charge of the audit.

EDP Audit Activities Currently Performed by Internal Auditors

The investigation of the 39 EDP audit groups showed that EDP audit activities that are performed by internal auditors fall into three categories:

1 Audit activities relating to an EDP application after it is developed, i.e., *post-implementation audits.*

2 Audit activities relating to *data processing operations and management.*

3 Audit activities relating to an EDP application while it is being developed, i.e., *design phase audits.*

An EDP application is a specific processing function performed by a set of computer programs. Examples of EDP applications include payroll, inventory recordkeeping or marketing sales analysis. Thus, an audit of an existing payroll application using test data is classified as a post-implementation audit. An audit of data processing security is classified as a data processing operations and management audit. A review for the adequacy of controls being designed into a new payroll application is classified as a design phase audit.

In carrying out these three types of audits, the auditor examines two types of data

---

Table 2

Internal audit of existing EDP applications (post-implementation audits)*

Audit activities	Frequency (on a 1-5 point scale)
Most frequently performed activities (approximately ½ of the time)	
1 Use audit software to interrogate files, e.g., selecting samples, footing populations, etc.	3.34
2 Survey users about satisfaction with new accounting EDP application.	3.31
3 Audit around the computer by tracing transaction flows.	3.23
4 Review program changes for audit implications.	3.20
5 Survey users about satisfaction with recently implemented information system.	3.08
Occasionally performed (approximately ⅓ to ½ of the time)	
6 For a recently developed application, compare achieved results with objectives developed during feasibility study (post-audit).	2.42
7 Use test data to evaluate processing controls.	2.26
Seldom performed (⅓ of the time or less)	
8 Evaluate efficiency of particular EDP application.	1.97
9 Compare actual costs of development with budgeted costs and investigate differences.	1.90
10 Use integrated test facility to monitor processing controls.	1.47

*The average frequency is based on responses from 39 internal audit managers. The scale contained the following responses: (1) never, (2) occasionally (less than 35% of the time), (3) half (35-65%), (4) usually (65-95%) and (5) always (95-100%).

processing controls: general and application.[1] General controls relate to how things are done in EDP and consist of such items as the plan of organization, and policies or standards for documentation, systems development, data security, etc. Application controls relate to specific tasks performed by EDP and are often referred to as input, processing and output controls. The application controls operate within the control environment of general controls.

The scope of audit activities conducted by internal auditors will depend on the audit philosophy regarding the three categories of audit activities and the relative emphasis to be placed on general versus application controls.

Post-implementation EDP audit activities. The internal audit departments in our sample spent approximately 30 percent of their EDP audit time on existing EDP applications. The post-implementation audit activities performed on existing EDP applications are shown in table 2, page 52. These audit activities take on added significance when they are later compared with the activities most likely to affect the work of the external auditor.

The post-implementation audit activities performed most often by internal auditors include traditional approaches such as using audit software to interrogate computer files or tracing transaction flow around the computer to verify that transactions have been processed. The remaining audit activities shown in table 2 reflect an operational audit approach. for example, surveying users concerning their satisfaction with an existing system, or comparing achieved results with projected results. It should be noted that two audit approaches using the computer at a fairly high level of expertise—test data and the integrated test facility[2]—are among the least-performed audit activities.

The audit activities shown in table 2 are indicative of a comprehensive internal audit approach that deals with organizational risks and inefficiencies, and is broader in scope than the traditional audit of financial statements. The activities shown in table 2 indicate an audit approach directed at ensuring the integrity of EDP controls.

Data processing operations and management audit activities. A summary of internal audit activities related to data processing operations and management is presented in table 3, this page. These audit activities accounted for 18 percent of the sample firms' total EDP audit time. Most internal auditors in the sample evaluate data processing security and make recommendations as a regularly scheduled part of their audit activities. Clearly, this is in response to an organizational desire by management to reduce potential computer-based risks. The other activities shown in table 3 are performed at less frequent intervals by most of the sample internal audit departments. Of these activities, the one performed least often is the surprise inspection of data processing facilities to ensure adherence to company policy.

Table 3

Internal audit of data processing operations and management*

Audit activities	Frequency** (on a 4-point scale)
1 Evaluate data processing security and make recommendations.	3.80
2 Consult on audit implications of potential data processing changes.	2.85
3 Evaluate operating efficiency of data processing facilities.	2.77
4 Use surprise inspections to ensure adherence to company policies.	2.69

* Based on responses from 39 internal auditors.
** A rating of 4 indicates the activity is performed as a regular part of the audit program, while a rating of 3 indicates the activity is performed frequently, but not at regularly scheduled intervals.

---

[1] Statement on Auditing Standards no. 3, *The Effects of EDP on the Auditor's Study and Evaluation of Internal Control* (New York: AICPA, 1974), p.4.

[2] In the integrated test facility, also referred to as the "mini company" approach, the application is designed to operate on separate organizational units such as departments or companies. The auditor establishes a unit solely for audit purposes. The auditors prepare transaction data, submit the transactions and analyze results as processed on the audit unit. For example, a payroll application might process data for departments A, B, C, D and the audit test department at the same time, using the same program. In other words, testing is conducted concurrently with regular programming. For a further description, see Barry R. Chaiken and William E. Perry, "ITF: A Promising Computer Audit Technique," JofA, Feb.73, pp.74-78.

Table 4

Internal audit activities performed during design phase of new EDP application*

Audit activities	*Frequency (1-5 scale)*
Almost always performed	
1 Identify audit trail and control requirements.	4.64
Usually performed (over ⅔ of design phase audits)	
2 Review design documentation for compliance to company policy.	4.12
3 Assess and report potential risks of proposed application to management.	4.06
4 Prepare audit guide for future audits of the application.	3.79
5 Review design activities for compliance to company policy.	3.73
6 Sign off at end of each major phase noting approval or specifying deficiencies.	3.51
Occasionally performed (approximately ⅓ to ⅔ of design phase audits)	
7 Review conversion tests performed by others.	3.28
8 Review feasibility study for reasonableness, compatibility with present facilities, etc.	3.22
9 Participate as part of team performing conversion tests.	2.82
Seldom performed (⅓ of the time or less)	
10 Act as liaison between programmers, users and systems design personnel.	2.69
11 Design, or supervise development of, embedded audit routines to be included in application.	2.67
12 Participate as member of feasibility study committee to assess appropriateness of proposed applications.	2.01

*The average frequency is based on the responses of 31 companies who perform design phase audits. The other companies (approximately 20%) that do not perform any design phase auditing have been excluded from the table. The five-point response scale included the following captions: (1) never; (2) seldom (less than 35% of the time); (3) half (35-65%); (4) usually (65-95%); (5) always (95-100%).

Design phase EDP audit activities. One of the more significant recent changes in internal auditing has been the increased participation of internal auditors during the design phase of new EDP applications. Internal auditors are generally concerned with two audit questions during the design of new computer applications: Have adequate controls (both manual and program) been built into the system? Is the system development process well-controlled? The major internal audit emphasis has been directed toward adequacy of application controls, but more internal auditors are beginning to perform operational audits of the systems design process.[3]

The companies in the survey spent approximately 25 percent of their EDP audit time on design phase audit activities. However, some of the internal audit departments spent as much as 70 percent of their audit time during the design phase. A summary of design phase audit activities currently per-

[3] For a further description of the systems design process, see Gordon B. Davis, *Management Information Systems: Conceptual Foundations, Structure, and Development* (New York: McGraw-Hill Book Company, 1974), pp.413-20.

formed by the sample companies is presented in table 4, page 54.

The most commonly performed design phase audit activity consists of identifying audit trail and control requirements. Many of the other audit activities frequently performed by the sample companies concentrate on control standards over the development process, e.g., ascertaining the degree of documentation or compliance with company policies. Although at first glance, audits of these general controls (how things are done in data processing) might seem less important than audits of application controls (controls built into the system or computer program), quite the contrary may be true. If a data processing department develops a sound set of control and system development standards, then adherence to these standards should result in controlled, auditable systems.

Almost half (18 of 39) of the internal EDP auditors participating in our study have either formal or informal sign-off responsibilities during major application developments. Increasingly, however, internal auditors issue informal memos which identify potential control weaknesses to data processing management and users on an "as needed" basis. In most cases, internal auditors have avoided actual participation in the design process, e.g., performing conversion tests or participating as a member of a feasibility study.

Design phase participation vs. internal audit independence. Internal audit participation during the design of new EDP applications appears to produce a control consciousness that often doesn't exist in new developments. Even though such audit participation seems beneficial, some have questioned such involvement because of the possible impairment of internal audit independence. The results of a comprehensive study of this question involving internal auditors, data processing management, executive management and CPAs, indicate that design phase auditing will not impair internal independence under the following conditions:[4]

1 The internal auditor avoids design phase audit activities in which he or she might be perceived as a *designer,* or a *participant* in the design of the system. Rather, design phase audit activities should be limited to activities focusing on either compliance testing of systems design procedures or a review

for the adequacy of controls built into the new application.

2 The internal auditor must have the EDP technical competence to be self-reliant and thus independent of data processing personnel.

3 There is adequate supervision and review of staff work by internal audit managers.

4 There is top management support of internal audit activities. (This, of course, is always a requirement for an independent staff, but it was reemphasized in relation to EDP auditing.)

The trend toward separate EDP audit sections was also seen to have a positive effect on independence. The existence of the EDP audit section indicates a commitment to building EDP technical competence. In many organizations the EDP audit section concentrates on design phase audit activities while the remaining audit staff performs much of the post-implementation audit activities, thereby eliminating some potential conflicts which might impair independence.

Although there is a valid concern over internal audit independence, the evidence indicates that internal auditors can make substantial contributions during the design phase without losing their independence. The trend for internal audit involvement during the design phase is expected to continue.

Impact of Internal EDP Audits on the CPA

The 39 external auditors participating in our study expressed willingness to adjust the audit scope of their EDP-related activities when they were satisfied about the "independence" and "quality of work" of the internal auditor (see table 5, page 56). The CPAs felt strongly that internal auditors should participate in the design phase of new EDP applications so that they could assess the adequacy of controls. However, they were ambivalent on whether the internal auditor's contribution during the design phase was more important than post-implementation audit activities. The CPAs were also ambivalent on whether fraud detection/prevention should be a primary objective of the internal audit of EDP.

CPAs' use of internal audit work. Statement on Auditing Standards no. 9 indicates that the work performed by internal auditors may have limited, significant or direct impact on the scope of the external auditor's ex-

---

[4] Larry E. Rittenberg, *Auditor Independence and Systems Design* (Orlando, Fla.: The Institute of Internal Auditors, 1977).

Table 5

CPA attitudes toward internal audit of EDP activities*

Attitude toward internal audit of EDP	*Agreement with statement***
Strong agreement	
The CPA will be able to adjust the scope of audit activities in the EDP area when satisfied as to the "independence" and "quality of work" of the internal auditor.	4.82
Agreement to strong agreement	
The internal auditor should actively evaluate the adequacy of controls during the design phase of new EDP applications.	4.59
Mild agreement	
A representative of internal auditing should be a member of an EDP steering or EDP advisory committee.	3.82
Ambivalence to mild agreement	
Fraud detection and/or prevention should be one of the primary objectives of internal audit work in the EDP area.	3.50
Ambivalence	
The internal auditor's potential contribution during the design phase of new EDP applications is greater than post-implementation audit work.	3.26

* Based on 39 responses from CPAs actively involved in EDP auditing.
** A rating of 5 was labeled very strongly agree; 4—agree; 3—neither agree nor disagree; 2—disagree; and 1—very strongly disagree.

amination.[5] As applied to EDP auditing, the internal auditor's impact might be viewed as follows:

1 Limited—The internal auditor reviews data processing general controls and security.
2 Significant—The internal auditor reviews and tests both general and application data processing controls throughout the year. Tests of EDP application controls include significant accounting applications.
3 Direct—The internal auditor may perform either compliance or substantive tests ultimately used by the CPA as part of the total evidence gathered during the audit.

Our study of the relationship of the internal and external auditor dealt with only the first two categories and did not explore the direct use of internal audit work under the guidance of the CPA.

Internal audit activities likely to influence the CPA. The CPAs participating in the research study were asked whether various audit activities performed by internal auditors would have "no effect," "a minor effect," "a moderate effect" or a "significant effect" on the scope or approach of the CPA's audit examination. The results are summarized in table 6, page 57.

It is noteworthy that the two internal EDP audit activities most likely to affect the external auditor's work—embedded audit routines[6] and use of test data—are among the least-used of all EDP audit techniques. This suggests that the accounting profession should be encouraging development and im-

---

[5] Statement on Auditing Standards no. 9, *The Effect of an Internal Audit Function on the Scope of the Independent Auditor's Examination* (New York: AICPA, 1976).

[6] An embedded audit routine is a part of the processing program that does testing and collects data during processing for subsequent audit review.

Table 6

Internal audit activities likely to affect scope or approach of external auditor*

Effect of specific internal audit activities on CPA's scope or approach	Current internal audit performance (table reference)	Rating of effect (on 4 point scale)**
Moderate to significant effect		
1 Monitor processing controls using embedded audit routines.	Not frequently performed. (Table 4)	(3.28)
2 Use test data to evaluate processing controls.	Not frequently performed. (Table 2)	(3.10)
Moderate effect		
3 Participate during design phase by specifying audit trail and control requirements.	Frequently performed. (Table 4)	(2.74)
4 Review major program changes for audit implications.	Frequently performed. (Table 2)	(2.74)
5 Evaluate data processing security.	Regularly performed. (Table 3)	(2.69)
6 Surprise inspections of data processing facilities to ensure adherence to company policies.	Performed at irregular intervals. (Table 3)	(2.62)
7 Assist in design by identifying problem areas and control needs.	Regularly performed. (Table 4)	(2.56)
Minor to moderate effect		
8 Review conversion tests of new EDP application development.	Occasionally performed. (Table 4)	(2.39)
9 Consult on audit implications of potential data processing facilities change.	Performed as need arises. (Table 3)	(2.36)
10 Audit around the computer by tracing transactions.	Frequently performed. (Table 2)	(2.31)
Minor to no effect		
11 Evaluate efficiency of data processing facilities.	Performed, but not on regular basis. (Table 3)	(1.71)
12 Review feasibility study for reasonableness, compatibility with present facilities, etc.	Occasionally performed. (Table 4)	(1.51)
13 Participate as member of feasibility study committee to assess appropriateness of proposed application.	Seldom performed. (Table 4)	(1.28)

*Based on 39 responses from CPAs actively involved in EDP auditing.
**The following response scale was used:
1 No effect.
2 Minor effect—A positive effect on the EDP environment and a minor effect on the audit approach.
3 Moderate effect—Procedure increases reliability of system and would have a moderate effect on both audit scope and audit approach.
4 Significant effect—On both audit scope and audit approach.

plementation techniques such as embedded audit routines and the integrated test facility.[7]

The internal audit activities most likely to influence the CPA, as shown in table 6 (items 1-7) include audit activities in the three categories of existing computer applications, data processing operations and new EDP application developments. Embedded audit routines, test data and review of major program changes are internal audit activities related to existing computer applications that are rated important by CPAs. Audits of data security and compliance to company policies are the most influential activities related to audit reviews of data processing as a whole. The review of the adequacy of controls being built into new EDP applications is the most influential internal audit activity related to the review of new EDP application developments.

Table 6 reflects the external auditor's perceptions of audit needs in a rapidly changing computer environment. Computer hardware and software change rapidly, and there is constant development of new or revised applications or programs. Auditors need to know about the EDP system as it operates throughout the year. For example, the auditor needs to know if there were any changes in application controls during the year or whether general controls were so weak that an unauthorized or undocumented change to the system could go undetected. The unique contribution of the internal auditor is his or her ability to review the controls and changes in controls throughout the year.

The audit activities in table 6 that were rated highly by the CPAs also are the audit activities well-suited to a full-time internal EDP audit group. For example, internal auditors generally deal with only one computer system and can therefore devote time to understanding the system in detail. Because it has the expertise, and can use the techniques continually over a period of years and recoup development cost, the internal audit group is more likely to develop such sophisticated audit techniques as the integrated test facility or embedded audit routines. Likewise, the internal audit group is present throughout the year to review program changes, participate during the design of new systems, perform compliance tests of general controls (which may take on added importance in these more complex systems) and evaluate data security. The trend toward internal EDP audit efforts was dictated by the changing technology. There is no reason to believe that the need for audit activities like those described above will diminish in the future.

Summary

The increased complexity of EDP systems calls for new approaches to EDP auditing. As a member of the organization, the internal auditor has sufficient day-to-day contact with data processing to effectively design and carry out audit programs that should strengthen EDP controls. Internal auditors can be effective in a "preventive approach" to EDP auditing. Technically competent EDP auditors can perform post-implementation audits of existing applications and audits of data processing operations that can strengthen managerial controls as well as provide substantial design phase audit input to ensure the auditability of newly developed systems.

The following specific developments in internal EDP auditing were identified as beneficial to the external auditor:

☐ The continued trend toward specialized EDP audit functions within internal audit departments, and the development of greater EDP technical competence among all internal auditors.

☐ Increased participation by internal auditors during the design phase of new EDP applications to review for the adequacy of controls built into the application or ascertain compliance to policies regarding new developments.

☐ Continued development of sophisticated audit techniques, such as the integrated test facility, or other embedded audit routines.

☐ More internal audit reviews of major computer program changes.

☐ Increased audits of general controls surrounding data processing operations and data security evaluations.

The CPAs participating in the study are willing to use the work of the EDP internal auditor. There are, however, differences between the audit activities presently conducted and the activities most likely to affect the external auditor. These results provide a good starting point for cooperation between CPAs and internal auditors interested in advancing effective EDP auditing. ■

---

[7] As noted earlier, the integrated test facility allows the auditor to develop test data, but since it is in operation throughout the year, it overcomes many of the disadvantages of using test data alone.

The Vulnerability of Computer Auditing*

Bennet P. Lientz, Ph.D.,
and Ira R. Weiss, Ph.D.

Bennet P. Lientz, Ph.D., Associate Professor of Computers and Information Systems, Graduate School of Management, University of California, L.A., is author of many papers and a textbook on information systems. Ira R. Weiss, Ph.D. (pictured above), Assistant Professor of Accounting and Information Systems, Graduate School of Business, NYU, is currently developing an in-depth computer auditing course for NYU.

* This work was partially supported by the Information Systems Program, Office of Naval Research, under contract NOOO14-75-C-0266, project no. 049-345.

Some of the problems associated with computer auditing are related to AICPA Statement on Auditing Standard No. 3. The authors propose means for dealing with the problems until improved internal computer security methods are implemented.

Introduction

Most auditing procedures for computer-based systems relate only to those aspects that can be readily reviewed and understood. The problem, however, is much more general and includes the *total environment* of the system including operating systems and telecommunications. This environment has been shown to be vulnerable in such a way that it may affect the financial condition and life cycle of the firm. Examples of this vulnerability are cited in a report of Stanford Research Institute.[1] Even with the most sophisticated organizational and application controls, the remaining parts of the systems environment are substantial and the problems associated with these elements can be catastrophic to the organization.

From reviewing the AICPA Statement on Auditing Standards No. 3 (SAS No. 3) and some of the literature on computer auditing, it becomes evident that more is needed to insure the integrity of the systems being audited. Further auditing procedures must be instituted to insure compliance with the *intent* of SAS No. 3.

What Is SAS No. 3?

SAS No. 3 indicates that internal controls in the data processing installation should be evaluated when computers are used in processing a significant number of accounting applications. SAS No. 3 further points out that the auditing examination should be performed by persons with adequate technical training as auditors. In evaluating a computer-based system, this implies that auditors must not only be competent in understanding audit objectives, but also in understanding of computer concepts to be able to identify the strengths and weaknesses of the system.

SAS No. 3 points to several types of controls that should be evaluated, including the following:

1. Organizational plan and operation of activities;
2. Procedures relating to documentation, review, testing and approval of systems and systems changes;
3. Controls for hardware;
4. Access controls to equipment and files;
5. Application controls relating to input, processing and output;
6. Segregation of functions relating to both manual and computer operations (e.g., the same person should not be allowed to write a program to process vendor invoices and be able to submit transactions to that program for operational processing).

In concluding, the statement considers some procedures to review these controls.

Computer Auditing—State of the Art

Today, over 100,000 computers are in use worldwide with over 80 percent of these storing and processing financial records.[2] In terms of SAS No. 3, a good portion of these installations are processing a significant amount of accounting information and should be evaluated, as part of the organization, for strengths and weaknesses in the control functions. Yet, many companies are doing today's computer audit work with yesterday's auditing expertise in terms of experience and education.[3] The EDP environment has changed substantially in the last decade. Unit record equip-

[1] Donald B. Parker, "Report to the SRI Conference on Computer Abuse," Stanford Research Institute, 1973.

[2] Robert L. Stone, "Who Is Responsible for Computer Fraud," *Journal of Accountancy*, February 1975.

[3] Joseph Wasserman, "Selecting a Computer Audit Package," *Journal of Accountancy*, April 1974.

ment techniques have evolved into sophisticated operating systems, teleprocessing, data base systems, multiprogramming and multiprocessing environments.[4] We would expect the firm which possesses these processing capabilities to have more technical expertise in an operational sense than an independent auditor, when the auditor has not been trained as a technical computer information systems specialist.

What is the impact of this progress on the auditor? The traditional internal control evaluation becomes somewhat more complex. Areas of concern are segregation of duties which might be blurred by highly integrative systems and the partial or total disappearance of the audit trail.[5] These developments give rise to a multiplicity of interactions within advanced systems, on a real-time basis, widening the potential error rate and potential fraudulent activity at any given time. After-the-fact tests of compliance and control may be insufficient to meet present day audit requirements.[6] The number of transactions processed daily, projected to a monthly basis, could be so voluminous that a center undergoing undetected penetration or errors in processing could be so severely affected that the going concern concept for that company could become invalid prior to an in-depth audit. Therefore, the need for *continuous* system integrity reviews appears imperative.

Again, what are the implications of these problems to the auditor? The auditor in the attest function states that the financial statements fairly represent the financial position of the company. Given an unqualified statement the auditor by implication states that the firm's liquidity is adequate to support the going concern concept. Yet there have been many cases of documented computer abuse totaling in the millions of dollars. After the fact

auditing might in fact locate abuses, but there is still the issue of responsibility for loss if the firm cannot recover from these abuses. In Equity Funding management, auditors and computer vendors were all named as parties to a "computer" fraud.

What then is the current state of the art in computer auditing? Computer auditing may be considered as having two component parts. First, the computer is utilized in many audits as a *tool*. Extension testing, depreciation calculations, present values, footing, confirmations, aging, statistical sampling, etc. are some of the functions that can be accomplished through the computer on a timely and cost/effective basis. This aspect of computer auditing is being utilized with great frequency.[7] The auditor is able to identify direct benefits from this audit tool and the audit can then be a scientifically sampled verification of financial statements rather than a heavy clerical burden.

The second aspect of computer auditing can be referred to as *data center reviews*, which encompasses the main thrust of SAS No. 3. This entails a review and analysis of operations, security, applications and general internal control functional tests. Here the auditor is faced with some problems. Levine[8] depicts 11 basic concerns of the auditor in this area, highlighted by keeping current in EDP and its audit impact. He also addresses some aspects of what auditors need to enable them to address the audit with sufficient competency including utilization of monitoring systems, methods of evaluating systems' integrity and standard software controls. Weber[9] goes further by insisting that operating systems be audited periodically because the integrity of the entire system is controlled by the operating system. Yet, since the technical aspects of operating systems are so complex, the auditor views this aspect as a

low risk area. This *may be a critical error of the auditor* and will be discussed further in the next section.

To summarize the state of the art, the auditor utilizes the computer as a *tool* in a relatively efficient manner. But in a *data center review* the extent to which controls are evaluated is often limited to the visible physical security and applications controls. In doing this the auditor relies on technical systems such as telecommunication networks and operating systems that in fact might be used to override and change the very applications that have been audited, judged appropriate and outputs relied on without extensive substantive testing.

Problems Remaining

As pointed out in the previous two sections, there are areas of the systems environment that are not explicitly addressed by SAS No. 3. For example, suppose a system is operational within a computer mode and a penetrator is seeking to enter the system and gain access to data and/or programs by using a terminal. If the computer system is a general time-sharing system, the data and programs are available to authorized users during certain times. The data and programs could relate to accounts payable, inventory shipments, personnel data or product development.

The penetrator first attempts to enter the system using the telecommunications network. Even if the system is password protected, and the password cannot be broken, the penetrator can resort to masquerading (penetrator represents an authorized user), eavesdropping (listening in at random), wiretapping (listening at determined times and recording data over the lines), piggybacking or between lines (penetrator uses system when the authorized user is signed on but not active, or is given disguised messages). Alternatively, the penetrator may be able to deduce the authorized users' password by the characteristics of room location, initials, social security number, birthdate, address or other data obtainable pertaining to authorized users.

After the penetrator has successfully entered the system, an

[4] Editorial, "Technical Proficiency for Auditing Computer Processed Accounting Records," *Journal of Accountancy*, October 1975.

[5] Carl Pabst, "What's All the Fuss About EDP," *California CPA Quarterly*, June 1974.

[6] George Rittersbach and S. Harlan Jr., "Auditing Advanced Systems," *Journal of Accountancy*, June 1974.

[7] Everett C. Johnson, "The Computer As an Audit Tool," *California CPA Quarterly*.

[8] E. G. Levine, "Auditing Requirements for Advanced Systems," *Journal of Accountancy*, March 1974.

[9] Ron Weber, "An Audit Perspective of Operating System Security," *Journal of Accountancy*, September 1975.

attempt can be made to override the operating system and move into the privileged mode (where the penetrator has the ability to affect the system itself). At this point the penetrator disables or diverts the computer accounting system such that the activity (i.e., audit trail) of the system is blurred. Now the penetrator can initiate unauthorized transactions, alter program and systems logic, destroy information, obtain or view highly sensitive information or can accomplish all that is possible by his or her own creativity. The penetrator now having completed the above task signs off the computer system undetected.

There are several implications in this simple example. First, unauthorized transactions can seriously impair the operational integrity of the system. The financial statements, depending on the system, may not reflect the true state of affairs of the company. A second implication is the recognition that competition within an industry combined with precedents of lenient attitudes toward white collar crime and the available technology makes such approaches more attractive and limited in risk. A third implication is that if only the content of SAS No. 3 is followed, the internal controls could be judged sufficient, giving the auditor comfort in relying on the outputs generated, when in fact they were not due to the computer and communications environment of the system (i.e., possibility of penetration).

To summarize, these three implications may impact the firm which relies heavily on computer systems by indicating the threat, the effect on operations, financial statements and the on-going concern concept, and the need for additional and more sophisticated controls.

Security Measures

One study[10] has indicated that there are no secure operating systems commercially available and that there is no way today of certifying secure computer systems. It is essential then that interim measures be employed until secure operating systems become a reality.[11]

Exhibit I represents a table of penetration methods, recovery measures if penetrated, preventive security measures and cost elements of implementing the security measures. This Exhibit can be utilized to address the example presented earlier. To counteract penetration of communication lines: data can be encrypted (coded), system-generated random dialogues utilized (system queries user at random with regard to personal characteristics), alternate routing of messages and multiple passwords per transaction can be required. The techniques in the computer center itself include encrypted files and programs, automatic cancellations upon unauthorized attempted access, accounting programs that are not controlled by operating systems, but by input/output controllers, disk controllers that are hardwired for security techniques and access authorization.

The Exhibit is not all inclusive, but represents some techniques that can be employed when weaknesses are discovered in the operations of a data center. The auditor should be aware that there are interim techniques available to partially control access and penetration when these are considered high-risk areas.

In general, there should always be passwords on files when possible, read/write restrictions if appropriate, accounting systems, programs in load module form and counteractive systems measures when mistakes are made either in the log-on procedure or access procedure. Starting with the above measures, utilizing some methods given in the table and employing intelligent and alert personnel will insure more confidence and less risk within the computer system.

Developing Cost-Effective Approaches to Security

Implementing all possible countermeasures is not warranted or cost effective. Overkill to counteract improbable penetration can se-

verely affect the cost and performance of systems. Organizations and independent auditors can employ simulation techniques and risk analysis[12] to identify the highly sensitive and exposed areas where the major control efforts should be placed.

There are basically three areas to be observed when reviewing the internal controls of data centers: operations, physical security and software security. For operations, the same guidelines should be imposed as when reviewing manual systems. Typical functional areas are: input, operations, programming and maintenance, library and output. When the organizational framework is set-up in this manner, the review can be structured to look at segregation of duties and control functions. The librarian controls programs and data while the input section controls new transactions. The programming and maintenance functions are separate. Therefore, there is no possibility of changing programs to fit new data. Controls that can be implemented are logging procedures of programs utilized, authorization for programming changes, appropriate dissemination of output and explicit operational directions for operators. A wealth of literature is available describing adequate physical security.[13]

The approach to reviewing software security is not defined as precisely as the other areas. One reason for this is that, given the most sophisticated software security available, penetration may still be possible. The approach must be a probability technique accessing high risk areas. Once these areas have been identified, one can pick the measure available that would most satisfy, in cost and performance, that particular need.

The most effective approach might be the one most common to auditors today, the questionnaire. Through this method we try to quantify both the impact and proba-

---

[10] IBM, "Data Security and Data Processing," IBM Corporation, G320-1370-0, 1974.

[11] R. C. Canning, "Protecting Valuable Data: Part II," EDP Analyzer, February 1974.

[12] J. J. Martin, Security Accuracy and Privacy in Computer Systems, Englewood Cliffs, N. J., Prentice-Hall, 1973.
[13] "The Considerations of Physical Security in a Computer Environment," IBM Corporation Manual, G520-2700, 1972.

EXHIBIT I
Event List

Event	Recovery Measure	Preventive Measure	Elements of Cost
Attempts through communication lines (see definitions under "Problems Remaining")			
• Masquerading	Retain back-up files	Levels of Passwords Transformation Functions Random Dialogues Encrypted Files	Software costs Encryption/Decryption Devices (coding and decoding) Effect on System Performance—increased systems overhead
• Wiretapping/Eavesdropping	Retain back-up files	Cryptography Alternate Routing of Messages	Softward Costs Encryption/Decryption Devices Effect on System Performance
• Piggybacking or Between Lines	Retain back-up files	Cryptography Random Dialogues Levels of Passwords Continuous Passwords With Each Transaction Automatic Shut Offs After n Seconds of Nonuse	Software Costs Encryption/Decryption Devices Effect on System Performance
Attempts through Computer Systems			
• Unauthorized Attempt to Enter System	Retain back-up files	All Identification/Authorization Measures (a) passwords (b) dialogues (c) transformation functions (d) magnetically encoded cards If detected immediate disabling actions	Software Costs Effect on System Performance
• Browsing	Retain back-up files/none	Functional Passwords Transformations Read/Write Restrict Encrypted Files Intelligent Disk Controllers	Software Costs Hardware Costs Encryption/Decryption Devices Effect on System Performance
• Override Operating System	Retain back-up files/none	Automatic Cancellations Upon Unauthorized Action Accounting System Independent of Operating System System Monitors Encrypted Files	Software Costs Personnel Costs Encryption/Decryption Devices Effect on System Performance

bility of an occurrence. This enables the following questions to be addressed. Can the occurrence be tolerated? Can the dollar impact be lowered or can the probability be lessened? This type of analysis measures the value of an asset to the firm and the amount of resources to allocate to the asset for protection. For example, a system might contain two resident disk packs. On one, pack data pertaining to census information is stored. On the other, product development information is stored. Each disk has an equal probability of being penetrated. Yet the outcomes of suc-

cessful penetration are quite different depending on which pack is chosen. We can tolerate penetration of the census data. It is public information and at worst duplication would be the final outcome for the firm. It is obvious that the answer dramatically changes under the product development assumption. Here penetration cannot be tolerated, so that there is concern about the dollar impact and about lessening the probability of penetration. We have now put a new type of value on an asset. We might call it an *exposure value* or *cost of loss* of exclusive use. Though product

development information may be totally useless without proper demographics, the information, considering exposure value, is quite different.

Through Exhibit 2 we attempt to give the organization and independent auditor some points to consider and questions to answer to develop proper exposure values or probabilities of penetration. There is no clear-cut method of achieving these values since they are installation dependent. As the exposure of an asset widens through its uninterrupted accessibility, the risk of exposure is in-

EXHIBIT 2
Risk Analysis Questionnaire

Telecommunications
- Identify systems that are dependent on telecommunications
- What are the log-on procedures?
  - Do they remain constant or change?
- What type of data is transmitted?
- What is the sensitivity of the data?
- What is the frequency of data transmission?
- What is the volume of data transmission?
- What has been the experience with retransmission or lost messages?
- Are telecommunication systems data entry systems only or retrieval and processing systems as well?
- Is the system restricted to certain terminals or can the system be dialed up from any compatible terminal?
- What type of communication system?
- Are long time lags experienced between responses?
- Are the users of the system heterogeneous or homogeneous organizationally?
- What security procedures are currently employed?

Computer Operations
- Identify on-line systems
- What are the log-on procedures?
  - Do they remain constant or change?
- Are all programs/data protected in some manner?
  - Password protection?
  - Encryption?
  - Read/Write restrictions?
  - Do they remain constant or change?
- Does the operating system control the checking procedures for the protection methods?
- Has, to your knowledge, the operating system, either intentionally or accidently, been overridden?
- Have requests been made to your system which were answered by data irrelevant to the question, but considered sensitive data?
- Is there an up-to-date accounting program employed by your system?
  - Is it controlled by the operating system?
- Are there procedures employed to cancel programs that exceed their authority?
- Are all vendor supplied security features employed?
  - If not, why not?
- Are there periodic checks that current production programs conform to the authorized version?
- Can a program be run if it is not cataloged?
- Organizationally speaking, is the computer used by a heterogeneous or homogeneous set of people?
- What are the security features currently employed?

creased. It is then up to installation management or independent auditors to consider whether resources should be allocated to that asset.

This approach can serve as a guideline for the design and the continuous auditing of the system. The approach aims to identify where controls should be placed to assure reasonable processing of data in a cost effective manner.

Conclusion

With the development of SAS No. 3, the independent auditing firm that audits clients with significant accounting computer-based applications systems has more responsibility for assessing computer-based controls. The responsibility must be met with technical expertise and an understanding of the environment of application systems for computers and telecommunications. The scope of controls necessitated by this environment must be broadened and the auditing firm must be knowledgeable enough to audit the total system to address these elements of the environment. Ω

John O. Mason, Jr., CPA, Ph.D., and Jonathan J. Davies, DBA

Legal Implications of EDP Deficiencies

The *Adams* v. *Standard Knitting Mills* case raises a number of serious auditing issues, among them the responsibility of accountants in reporting on financials when a company's internal controls are inadequate.

John O. Mason, Jr., CPA, Ph.D., associate accounting professor, Director of Accounting Graduate Studies, University of Alabama, was with a major accounting firm. Member AICPA, Alabama Society of CPAs and AAA, he has published in professional journals. Jonathan J. Davies, DBA, assistant accounting professor at the same university, recently completed a faculty residency with Arthur Andersen & Company. Member of AAA, he has published in professional journals.

While the legal relationship between public accountants and financial statement users has been in a constant state of flux, the courts seldom have found it necessary (or desirable) to comment on the auditor's legal responsibilities in the examination of electronic data processing systems. In the recent case of *Adams* v. *Standard Knitting Mills, Inc.*[1] (*Standard Knitting Mills*), the federal court saw fit to break this legal silence, and thus, defined the basic legal responsibilities of those engaged in audits of computer-based accounting systems.

This article takes a three-step approach toward analyzing the ramifications of the *Standard Knitting Mills* case. The first section of the article presents a brief description of the facts that served as the basis of the litigation. The second section presents a discussion of the various legal issues decided by the court. The final section speculates on the effects that this decision will have on auditing practices. This three-step analysis provides the auditor with a base of information for a proper assessment of the legal responsibilities inherent in the provision of audit services where EDP is involved (as well as having implications for the reporting of internal control weaknesses in any accounting environment).

Basic Facts of the Litigation

In 1969, Chadbourn, Inc. engaged its auditor, Peat, Marwick, Mitchell & Co. (PMM & Co.), to prepare a proxy statement for filing with the Securities and Exchange Commission in connection with the proposed acquisition of *Standard Knitting Mills, Inc.* (Standard). The proxy statement that was subsequently prepared failed to accurately report two situations which Standard stockholders later alleged

---

[1] *Adams* v. *Standard Knitting Mills, Inc.,* 95,683 CCH Fed. Sec. Law Rei .. (E. D. Tenn., 1976).

to be material in relation to the merger decision.

The first of these inaccuracies concerned the ability of Chadbourn to pay dividends and redeem capital stock. In the preparation of the proxy statement, PMM & Co. noted at several different times that existent loan agreements contained severe restrictions with respect to all Chadbourn *capital* stock. Yet, the footnotes actually included in the audited financial statements indicated that these restrictions applied only to *common* stock. On realizing that the dividend and redemption restrictions also applied to the preferred stock that they had accepted under the merger agreement, Standard stockholders filed suit contending that PMM & Co. had violated generally accepted auditing standards and thus seriously misled them.

The second proxy statement inaccuracy (and the more generally significant one) concerned certain weaknesses in the Chadbourn *system of internal control*. While PMM & Co. did realize that several deficiencies and serious defects did exist in the Chadbourn EDP system, the proxy statement submitted to Standard shareholders made no mention of these problems.

In litigating this matter, Standard shareholders argued that PMM & Co.'s failure to disclose significant information about internal control weaknesses in the Chadbourn EDP system seriously impaired their ability to make informed judgments about the proposed merger transaction. Thus, the plaintiffs argued that PMM & Co. had again violated generally accepted auditing standards by failing to implement full and accurate disclosure.

Issues Decided by the Court

Since the *Standard Knitting Mills* case was predicated upon inaccuracies contained in a proxy statement filed with the Securities and Exchange Commission, the plaintiffs contended that liability should be imposed under Commission Rules 10(b)-5[2] and 14(a)-9.[3] In determining the applicability of these rules to this specific fact situation, the court embarked upon an analysis of several major factors that it considered prerequisite to the existence of such legal responsibility.

The first of the prerequisite factors to be dealt with by the *Standard Knitting Mills* Court was that of materiality. If the defendants were to be held legally responsible for violations of Federal Securities Law, it would have to be proven that the inaccuracies contained in the proxy statement were material.

Traditionally, a decision on the materiality of a particular fact is a judgment issue which centers around whether a reasonable man would have assigned significance to that fact in making his ultimate

---

[2] Rule 10b-5, C. F. R. Section 240.10b-5. The rule specifically reads:
"It shall be unlawful for any person, directly or indirectly, by the use of any means or instrumentality of interstate commerce, or of the mails or of any facility of any national securities exchange,
a) To employ any device, scheme, or artifice to defraud,
b) To make any untrue statement of a material fact or to omit to state a material fact necessary in order to make the statements made, in light of the circumstances under which they were made, not misleading, or
c) To engage in any act, practice, or course of business which operates or would operate as a fraud or deceit upon any person, in connection with the purchase or sale of any security."
[3] Rule 14a-9, 17 C. F. R. Section 249-14a-9. The rule specifically states:
"(a) No solicitation subject to this regulation shall be made by means of any proxy statement, form of proxy, notice of meeting or other communication, written or oral, containing any statement which, at the time and in the light of the circumstances under which it is made, is false or misleading with regard to any material fact necessary in order to make the statement therein not false or misleading or necessary to correct any statement in any earlier communication with respect to the solicitation of a proxy for the same meeting or subject matter which has become false or misleading.
(b) The fact that a proxy statement, form of proxy or other soliciting material has been filed with or examined by the Commission shall not be deemed a finding by the Commission that such material is accurate or complete or not false or misleading, or that the Commission has passed upon the merits of or approved any statement contained therein or any matter to be acted upon by security holders. No representation contrary to the foregoing shall be made."

decision.[4] With respect to the EDP problems existent at Chadbourn, the *Standard Knitting Mills* Court concluded:

The EDP deficiencies at Chadbourn were of such pervasive nature and importance that their existence did, or at a minimum, could have significantly affected the entire operation of Chadbourn and would therefore most directly relate to matters contained in the financial statements.[5]

Thus, the court reasoned that PMM & Co.'s failure to reveal significant EDP weaknesses constituted a misstatement of a material fact.

The second legal issue to be dealt with by the court was that of duty. Unless it could be shown that the public accountants had a legally enforceable responsibility to the third party proxy statement users, the imposition of liability for pecuniary losses would be precluded.

While the common law approach to such a legal question is directly dependent upon the existence of privity of contract or some similar state of plaintiff-defendant relationship,[6] the institution of the Securities Acts in the early 1930s did away with many such restrictions. In the *Standard Knitting Mills* case, the court agreed that an adequate degree of legal responsibility did exist by saying:

PMM & Co. had full knowledge of Standard shareholders' reliance on PMM & Co. represen-

---

[4] See generally: *SEC v. Texas Gulf Sulphur Company*, 401 F.2d 833 (2nd Cir. 1968).
[5] *Standard Knitting Mills.*
[6] Throughout the early part of this century, courts ruled that a contractual relationship between plaintiff and defendant is prerequisite to recovery of pecuniary losses. While the courts have sometimes relaxed this rule to allow recovery by those who were "the primary beneficiary" of a specific contract, the privity requirement remains entrenched in the common law. See generally: Prosser, William L., "Misrepresentations and Third Parties," *Vanderbilt Law Review*, 19 (March, 1966), 231-255; and *Glanzer v. Shepard*, 135 N.E. 275 (N.Y. 1922); and *Ultramares Corporation v. Touche, Niven and Company*, 174 N.E. 441 (N.Y. 1931); and *Rhode Island, Hospital Trust National Bank v. Swartz, Bresenoff, Yavner and Jacobs*, 455 F.2d 847 (4th Cir. 1972).

tations contained in the financial statements. In such a situation, PMM & Co. owed the Standard shareholders, including plaintiffs, the duty to perform and conduct the audit with due care and to observe and comply with applicable auditing standards. At a minimum, that was PMM & Co.'s duty to plaintiff. . .[7]

Beyond this basic statement of the facts inherent in the *Standard Knitting Mills* case, the court commented on the general duties of public accountants by saying, "Additionally, an accountant owes a duty to the public to be independent of his client and to report *fairly* the facts before him."[8] This broad statement of the court's perception of the accounting function not only established the existence of the prerequisite degree of responsibility, but also implied a legal precedent which, if later applied, would impose a degree of legal duty on the public accountant that has seldom, if ever, been sought by the courts.

The last major legal determination to be made by the *Standard Knitting Mills* court concerned the existence of scienter, or intent, on the part of the defendants. In March 1976, the Supreme Court ruled that proof of a defendant's intent to deceive was prerequisite to the imposition of liability under many of the provisions of the 1934 Securities Exchange Act.[9] Therefore, if PMM & Co. were to be held legally responsible under Rules 10b-5 and 14a-9, the prerequisite degree of intent would have to be proven.

With respect to PMM & Co.'s failure to adequately describe the EDP weaknesses existent in the Chadbourn system, the court concluded:

Defendant's agents documented Chadbourn's numerous EDP defects at the time of the 1969 audit and approximately one year later some corrections had been made but a consider-

---

[7] Standard Knitting Mills.
[8] Ibid.
[9] *Ernst & Ernst v. Hochfelder*, 96 S. Ct. 1375 (1976).

able number of deficiences still remained—yet defendant did not feel obligated to report this to plaintiffs. Finally, with full knowledge of Chadbourn's EDP and other internal weaknesses, defendant conducted its 1969 audit as though Chadbourn was as sound as a dollar used to be—clearly deviating from GAAP, GAAS and the provisions of PMM & Co.'s own audit manual. The court finds and holds the proof in this case clearly established that, with the knowledge defendant possessed prior to, during and after the 1969 audit compared against the content of the PMM & Co.'s 1969 Chadbourn financial statements, defendant acted wilfully, with intent to "deceive" and "manipulate and in reckless disregard for the truth." [10]

Thus, the court interpreted PMM & Co.'s failure to fully disclose all available financial information as evidence of an intent to mislead the users of the proxy statement.

The decisions of the *Standard Knitting Mills* court with respect to materiality, duty and scienter opened the door to third party liability under the provisions of the Securities Exchange Act. The imposition of such a degree of legal responsibility on those involved in EDP system audits should have several significant effects on members of the public accounting profession.

Implication for the Auditing Profession

If not reversed on appeal, the decision in *Standard Knitting Mills* is likely to stir as much controversy and comment as that of the recent *Hochfelder* case. From the standpoint of the members of the auditing profession, *Standard Knitting Mills* may mark the most painful crisis since the *Continental Vending* case[11] of the late sixties. Clearly, the *Standard Knitting Mills* decision

will have a multidimensional effect on auditing standards, accounting principles and the manner in which they both are applied.

Perhaps the most significant lesson to be learned from *Standard Knitting Mills* will deal with the process known as "auditing around the computer." For years the accounting profession has circumvented many of the problems associated with audits of computer based systems by relying upon an "informal understanding" that the ultimate extent of review and testing applied to an EDP system may vary as other optional audit procedures are applied.

Yet, while some practicing accountants were relying on this "informal understanding," the profession as a whole was moving toward more rigorous standards for EDP audits. In "Statement on Auditing Standards Number 1," the profession concluded that the auditor's study of internal control should produce:

1. A knowledge and understanding of the procedures and methods prescribed, and

2. A reasonable assurance that they are in use and operating as planned, regardless of the type of system employed by the firm for accounting purposes.[12]

The *Standard Knitting Mills* Court's firm adherence to professionally espoused auditing standards is exemplified by its conclusion that, "in areas of internal control. . . especially EDP. . . PMM & Co. violated the second. . . and third standard(s) of audit field work."[13] Such a conclusion, when combined with the court's rejection of any "real world" distinction between "accounting" and "administrative" controls,[14] clearly indicates that the professional accountant will soon be forced to place more emphasis on EDP controls when carrying out his audit function.

A second, and more puzzling, aspect of the *Standard Knitting Mills* case lies in the area of financial disclosure. While the accounting profession has generally felt that the audit opinion alleviated the need for statements about specific matters, the *Standard Knitting Mills* court reasoned that in this particular instance, *the EDP and internal control weaknesses* of Chadbourn were so *significant* as to *warrant specific disclosure*. In presenting this argument for full financial disclosure, the court reasoned:

> No experienced accounting firm can report a company's financial position today and ignore what it may be tomorrow. This is especially true when as in this instance, the accountant has knowledge of adverse information and conditions which obviously may significantly jeopardize the client company's future performance. . .[15]

The court's implication of such a full disclosure doctrine could easily introduce a strange twist to the accounting profession's going concern assumption. Under such a doctrine of legal responsibility, the professional auditor would no longer be allowed to make unilateral decisions about the future prospects of a given firm, but instead, he would be required to supply financial statement users with all information that might be inherent to the making of their own investment decisions. Such a shift in legal responsibility would definitely have a material impact on the performance of the audit function. In this connection, the proposed statement on auditing standards by AudSec "Required Communication of Material Weaknesses in Internal Accounting Control" indicates the profession's growing concern with reporting on internal control weaknesses.

Summary

As the computer became an integral part of the auditing environment, public accountants attempted to adapt their standards and techniques to deal with this new factor. Yet, while the account-

---

[10] Standard Knitting Mills.
[11] See generally: *U.S.* v. *Simon*, 425 F2d 796 (2nd Cir. 1969).

---

[12] "Statement on Auditing Standards No. 1," (New York: American Institute of Certified Public Accountants, 1973).
[13] Standard Knitting Mills.
[14] *Ibid.*

---

[15] *Ibid.*

ing profession took action to implement the necessary adaptations, the courts failed to provide an adequate definition of the auditor's legal responsibilities in EDP engagements.

In *Adams* v. *Standard Knitting Mills, Inc.*, the federal court took the first steps toward defining these legal responsibilities. If later applied, this decision should affect the auditing profession in two ways. First, the *Standard Knitting Mills* decision could place severe limitation on the use of "auditing around the computer" as a replacement for adequate evaluation and testing of EDP controls. Second, the *Standard Knitting Mills* decision should broaden the concept of "full financial disclosure" employed by the public accountant in the preparation of audited financial statements. Although this first statement of the courts may have a significant effect on the EDP-auditing environment, the public accountant can be relatively sure that this is only a precursor to future legal decisions.Ω

CASE 9

THE SOFT HARDWARE COMPANY

Ficke & Ficke, Certified Public Accountants, are preparing to audit the financial statements of Soft Hardware, Inc. for the current year. Soft Hardware (SH), a large wholesaler of hardware items, supplies local hardware stores (franchised stores) located throughout the United States, with merchandise to be sold to both homeowners and commercial customers. Your firm has acted as the auditors for SH for the last ten years. SH has been a pioneer both in marketing hardware items and in providing services to the franchised local hardware stores. For example, SH provides local stores with information as to which merchandise is expected to be a "hot item," when to reorder specific items in inventory, monthly profit and loss statements, etc.

SH maintains its home office in midtown U.S.A., where all accounting functions are performed by computer. All accounting records are entered from punch cards or direct terminal input. For example, direct terminal input is used to process payroll and to maintain inventory control procedures. Accounting information is stored in data files—that cannot be read or changed without the use of EDP, but can be changed through the use of EDP without visible evidence that a change has been made.

In addition to the above EDP application, SH makes use of an integrated system that processes accounting, production, marketing, and administrative information simultaneously. Its EDP operations are conducted by a separate department and its accounting control procedures are performed by personnel in several different departments. The EDP system is also capable of detecting errors and irregularities as well as providing specific authorization for selected transactions. As an example, a program for accounts payable has been designed to process a vendor's invoice for payment if it is accompanied by a purchase-order record agreeing with the invoice as to prices and quantities and a receiving record indicating receipt of the merchandise or service.

Because SH makes use of computer application in both accounting and administrative areas, it does not have all of the computer time that it needs. Therefore, certain of its computer applications, including accounting applications, are processed by the Last National Bank's computer center.

In view of recent computer fraud cases involving auditing firms, Ficke & Ficke has adopted a policy of taking every precaution with audit engagements involving computer applications. Specifically the firm is making an effort to assure itself that a careful review of internal control within the EDP system is made and that EDP accounting controls have been established and are operating as intended. To meet these goals and to provide assurance that the firm's audit staff is current on recent auditing pronouncements, a series of staff development meetings were conducted to review auditing pronouncements relating to internal control and EDP operations. In connection with the audit engagement several questions have been raised.

CASE DISCUSSION QUESTIONS

1. The first general auditing standard is as follows: "The examination is to be performed by a person or persons having adequate technical training and proficiency as an auditor." Discuss this standard as it relates to Soft Hardware Company.

2. What are general controls and application controls and how do they relate to EDP?

3. SH's EDP system includes an accounts-payable program designed to process a vendor's invoice for payment.

   a. Does this represent an incompatible function? If so, how?

   b. If there is a lack of adequate control over such a program, is there need for the auditor to be concerned? Does the fact that EDP files can be changed through the use of EDP without visible evidence that a change has occurred create any problems? Explain; write one answer for both questions.

4. What advantages does EDP offer in terms of internal accounting control and the recording of transactions?

5. Discuss the auditor's review of a client's system of internal control. Include in your answer a discussion of what may be included in the preliminary phase of Ficke & Ficke's review of Soft Hardware's internal accounting control.

6. What is the auditor's objective in the preliminary phase of the review of internal control? Your discussion should relate to the EDP system used by SH.

7. What is the purpose of tests of compliance?

    How can the auditor determine that the objective of tests of compliance are being met?

8. What effect does the processing of part of SH's records at the Last National Bank's computer center have on your responsibility to perform an audit in accordance with GAAS? In this regard, how is the review of internal accounting control affected?

AUDITING AND REPORTING

Internal Audit Function Effect on Scope of Examination

Larry H. Beard, Ph.D., and Stephen E. Loeb, CPA, Ph.D., University of Maryland.

In December 1975 the AICPA's Auditing Standards Executive Committee issued SAS No. 9, "The Effect of an Internal Audit Function on the Scope of the Independent Auditor's Examination." [1] This new statement supersedes SAS No. 1, Section 320.74, and is intended to provide guidance to the independent auditor in considering the work of an internal auditor. Since more and more companies have an internal audit function, SAS No. 9 will have an impact on independent auditors, their clients and ultimately

[1] Copyright © 1976 by the American Institute of Certified Public Accountants, Inc.

investors. It is our purpose to review selected portions of SAS No. 9 and discuss their implications.

A General Overview

In the opening paragraph of SAS No. 9, the Committee indicates that the work of the internal auditor cannot be a substitute for the work of the independent auditor. Nevertheless, it is indicated that the work of the internal auditors may be useful to the CPA in performing both compliance tests and substantive tests. This is acceptable whether the independent auditor is merely examining the normal work performed by the internal auditor or has requested that the internal auditor perform various tests and report directly to him. Essentially, SAS No. 9 states that the internal auditor may affect the work of the independent auditor in the following two ways:

1. An analysis of the work of the internal auditor will be a factor that the independent auditor should consider ". . . in determining the nature, timing, and extent . . . " of his audit procedures; and

2. The internal auditor may provide direct assistance to the independent auditor by performing various tests and activities considered appropriate.

Internal Auditors and Internal Control

The concept that the work of the internal auditor may affect the nature, timing and extent of the independent auditor's tests is not new. Historically, authorities have considered the internal audit function as an important factor contributing to effective internal control. SAS No. 9 recognizes that when internal auditors perform

compliance or substantive tests, this activity represents a special function that is greater than an elemental level within internal control systems. More specifically, SAS No. 9 notes that the internal auditors are acting " . . . as a separate, higher level of control to determine that the system is functioning effectively.

The independent auditor should carefully evaluate the personnel of the internal audit staff. SAS No. 9 indicates that this evaluation of the internal audit function should not include " . . . personnel with the title 'internal auditor' who do not perform such a function. Conversely, personnel with other titles who perform such a function should be considered internal auditors. . . . " In determining the extent of reliance which may be appropriate, the independent auditor may wish to refer to a definition promulgated by the Institute of Internal Auditors (IIA). In the "Statement of Responsibilities of the Internal Auditor," the IIA defines internal auditing as:

. . . an independent appraisal activity within an organization for the review of operations as a service to management. It is a managerial control which functions by measuring and evaluating the effectiveness of other controls.

In determining the degree that the internal auditor's work will affect his audit, SAS No. 9 suggests that the independent auditor review the competence and objectivity of the client's internal auditing function.

Competence

SAS No. 9 suggests that an

evaluation of the competency of internal auditors might include the following factors: the company's hiring practices, the company's training programs and the company's supervisory practices.

With regard to the hiring practices, the independent auditor could investigate general standards or criteria applicable specifically to the internal audit staff. For example, the educational and experience levels required of new employees at beginning and advanced levels would be signficant. In addition, the results of background investigations for new employees and job performance appraisals could be analyzed.

In evaluating training programs, a variety of questions may be posited. Does the company officially encourage continuing education? Does the company have a formal training program? If the company does not have a formal training program, does it subsidize training by giving release time to participate in external programs and/or by paying for the educational fees? Does the company encourage membership and activity in professional accounting organizations?

The independent auditor might evaluate the client's supervisory practices by examining corporate policies and procedures. Are employees properly instructed? Are working papers and reports adequately reviewed? Are standard audit forms, checklists and questionnaires used? (See SAS No. 4, para. 12.)

In addition, the independent auditor might inquire how many members of the internal audit staff are CPAs, CMAs, and/or CIAs. Finally, corporate advancement policies could be reviewed to discover historical trends in promotions and turnover rates.

Objectivity

SAS No. 9 implies that the internal auditor's objectivity is a function of the organizational level of the supervisor to whom the internal auditor (a) reports his findings and (b) is administratively responsible. Thus the Auditing Standards Executive Committee is suggesting that objectivity in this instance is related to the internal auditor's perceptions of his independence within the organization.

The necessity for independence within the organization has been a concern of internal auditors for some time. The IIA "Statement of Responsibilities" indicates that " . . . independence is essential to the effectiveness of internal auditing." Ideally the internal auditor should report to the board of directors; however, this is infrequently the case, and perhaps the independent auditor should use the IIA's suggested criterion as a guide when evaluating the internal audit staff. The IIA statement indicates that " . . . the head of the internal auditing function . . . should be responsible to an officer whose authority is sufficient to assure both a broad range of audit coverage and the adequate consideration of an effective action on the audit findings and recommendations."

Extent of Reliance

The independent auditor's evaluation of the internal auditor's work includes the following (SAS No. 9):
• An evaluation of documentary evidence of the work performed by the internal auditor.
• An evaluation of the scope of the internal auditor's work.
• An evaluation of audit programs, working papers and reports.
• Tests of the internal auditor's work.

SAS No. 9 does not offer an indication of the degree to which the independent auditor can rely on the work of the internal auditor in determining the nature, timing and extent of the auditing procedures. One member of the Auditing Standards Executive Committee emphasized this point in his dissent. Apparently this consideration remains a matter of individual professional judgment.

Direct Assistance

The types of direct assistance that an internal auditor can provide to independent auditors are diverse. One authority suggests that in large, complex businesses, independent auditors and internal auditors may alternate auditing various aspects of the business and exchange and make use of each other's working papers and findings.[2] Also, " . . . the two groups may undertake concurrent examinations of the same subject matter, dividing the tasks between them." [3]

SAS No. 9 states that it is permissible for the internal auditor to directly assist the independent auditor by performing both compliance tests and substantive tests. The Committee, however, indicated that the professional judgment of the independent auditor should control the extent and conditions under which the internal auditor would be permitted to participate. In situations where direct assistance is utilized, SAS No. 9 suggests that the independent auditor carefully supervise the internal auditor's activities and that all audit judgments be made by the independent auditor.

[2] Philip L. Defliese, Kenneth P. Johnson and Roderick K. Macleod, *Montgomery's Auditing*, 9th ed. (New York: The Ronald Press, 1975), p. 196.
[3] *Ibid.*

Internal Audit Function—Review Checklist

By Professor Thomas D. Hubbard, Virginia Polytechnic Institute and State University.

SAS No. 9, "The Effect of an Internal Audit Function on the Scope of the Independent Auditor's Examination," states that the independent auditor should consider the procedures, if any, performed by internal auditors in determining the nature, timing and extent of his own auditing procedures. Accordingly, the CPA should acquire an understanding of the internal audit function as it relates to his study and evaluation of internal accounting control. If the CPA decides that the work of the internal auditors may have a bearing on his own procedures, he should consider the competence and objectivity of internal auditors and evaluate their work.

During the course of developing an AICPA Continuing Professional Education course, the author developed the audit program shown for reviewing the internal audit function and work performed. The program is based on the experience of the author and incorporates the requirements of SAS No. 9. The program should be useful to all CPA firms that have clients with internal audit staffs. Ω

Review of Internal Audit Staff and Work Performed
Date of Examination ___

	Done by

1. Summarize the scope of the internal audit function.
2. Make inquiries concerning the competency of the internal audit staff, including consideration of the client's practices for hiring, training and supervision.
3. Examine, on a test basis, documentary evidence of the work performed by internal audit staff and consider:
   - Adequacy of scope;
   - Appropriateness of audit programs;
   - Appropriate documentation of work papers;
   - Whether conclusions reached are appropriate in the circumstances;
   - Whether reports are consistent with the work performed.
4. Depending on the types of transactions and materiality, perform tests of some of the work of the internal audit staff. These tests may be accomplished by: examining the transactions or balances examined by the internal audit staff or examining similar transactions or balances.
5. Did the internal audit staff observe requirements of a "surprise" examination, if planned on that basis?
6. Did the internal audit staff properly control activities in the office or department during the initial phase of their work?
7. Review recommendations made by the internal audit staff and the extent to which corrective action was taken.
8. With respect to selected reports prepared by the internal audit staff:
To whom were they submitted?
   - Did they set forth all exceptions disclosed by working papers?
   - Did they adequately summarize or describe scope and results of the work.
   - Did they contain comments or suggestions on internal accounting controls and accounting procedures and practices?
   - Was a written reply prepared by an officer with respect to all criticisms and exceptions contained in the reports?
   - Obtain copies for the work papers.
9. When the internal audit staff is to be relied on or used in the annual examination, inform them, early in the engagement, of the reports and work papers they will be asked to assist with.
10. Appraise the competency and objectivity of the internal audit staff.
11. In appraising objectivity, consider the organizational level to which internal auditors report the results of their work and the organizational level to which they report administratively.
12. Describe the internal aduit function as it relates to the study and evaluation of internal accounting control.
13. Consider the procedures performed by internal audit staff in determining the nature, timing and extent of independent procedures to be applied.
14. Prepare a brief conclusion as to the overall effectiveness of the internal auditors' function, indicating where applicable, any additional testing in the particular area performed by our representatives and the reasons therefor.

Reviewed by Sr._____ Mgr._____

CASE 10

THE INTERNAL AUDIT FUNCTION AND THE CPA'S EXAMINATION

Edwards and Brown, Certified Public Accountants, have been engaged to audit Keeler, Phibbs & Co., a poultry-producing firm. Keeler, Phibbs & Co. has ten internal audit staff members. Two of the internal auditors, one of which was a staff member with Edwards and Brown for five years, are CPAs with several years of public accounting experience. You are an audit senior with Edwards and Brown and have been assigned to the Keeler engagement. The audit partner, audit manager, and you have discussed the client's internal audit staff and you all are of the opinion that the client's staff is both competent and objective. You decide to rely on the internal auditors in performing your examination.

The decision to rely upon the internal auditors is based upon two factors. First, it is believed that there has been adequate training and supervision of the internal audit staff, and your staff has reviewed work performed by the internal auditors and concluded that they are objective in performing their duties.

CASE DISCUSSION QUESTIONS

1. Is it appropriate for Edwards and Brown to rely upon the work performed by Keeler's internal audit staff? Explain your answer.

2. What factors should the independent auditor consider in evaluating the competence of internal auditors?

3. What considerations should be given by the independent auditor in evaluating the objectivity of internal auditors?

4. The independent auditor is required to evaluate the work of internal auditors. Discuss the procedures the internal auditor should perform in the evaluation of the internal auditors.

5. Internal auditors often perform a number of services for management, including, but not limited to, studying and evaluating internal accounting control, reviewing operating practices to promote increased efficiency and economy, and making special inquiries at management's direction.

   Is SAS No. 9 applicable to situations in which internal auditors perform work as part of their normal duties?

6. SAS No. 9 states:

   > "The independent auditor should acquire an understanding of the internal audit function as it relates to his study and evaluation of internal accounting control. The work performed by internal auditors may be a factor in determining the nature, timing, and extent of the independent auditor's procedures . . ."

   In summarizing the scope of the internal audit function Edwards and Brown noted the following:

   > "The scope of the internal audit function includes verification of the mathematical accuracy of all invoices."

   Does SAS No. 9 consider this a proper internal audit function?

7. Is it appropriate for Edwards and Brown to rely on the judgment of internal auditors regarding the extent of tests they perform?

8

Evidential Matter

(Section 326, SAS No. 31, Sections 331 and 332, SAS No. 1, and Section 333, SAS No. 19)

EVIDENTIAL MATTER

The third standard of field work requires that sufficient competent evidential matter is to be obtained through inspection, observation, inquiries and confirmations to afford a reasonable basis for an opinion regarding the financial statements under examination.

The majority of work performed by an auditor is concerned with obtaining and evaluating information. This information is evidential matter accumulated in support of the assertions made in the financial statements. The nature of evidential matter includes underlying accounting data and all corroborating information. Underlying accounting data includes the client's books of original entry, general and subsidiary ledgers, accounting manuals, memorandums and worksheets, and computations and reconciliations. Corroborating evidence includes such sources as checks, invoices, contracts, minutes, confirmations, and information obtained by the auditor by means of inquiry, observation, inspection, and physical examination.

Evidential matter varies in quality. The degree to which the evidential matter can influence an auditor's opinion on the financial statements depends upon its pertinence, objectivity, timeliness, and existence, all of which impact upon the auditor's opinion of the assertions made in the financial statements.

NATURE OF ASSERTIONS

While the assertions made in the financial statements are those expressed by management, they may be explicit or implicit in nature. SAS No. 31 has classified these assertions into five catagories: existence or occurrence; completeness; rights and obligations; valuation or allocation; and presentation and disclosure. Examples of these assertions include the fact that inventory exists at year-end, liabilities are owed by the entity, valuations are proper, and that all necessary disclosures have been made and are properly classified. These assertions may also be used as an aid in developing audit objectives and designing substantive tests.

The auditor must develop audit objectives according to the specific assertions of the engagement. Items to be considered include the economic and industry environment in which the entity operates. Also, individual audit procedures may relate to several audit objectives. Consideration should be given to the reliance placed on internal control, effect of irregularities, and effectiveness of the substantive tests. All of these items should be incorporated into the auditor's judgments concerning the financial statements.

COMPETENCY OF EVIDENTIAL MATTER

To be competent, evidential matter must be both valid and relevant. Presumptions as to the validity and competency of evidential matter include the following:

Outside evidence is more reliable than evidence gathered entirely within an enterprise's own records

The soundness of internal controls influence the reliability of evidence

Direct personal knowledge obtained through physical examination, observation, computation, and inspection is more persuasive than indirect information

SUFFICIENCY OF EVIDENTIAL MATTER

Whether or not evidential matter obtained by the auditor is sufficient to warrant the expression of an opinion is, of course, a judgmental factor. In reaching a decision, regarding the sufficiency of evidential matter, the auditor should consider the nature of the item under consideration, its overall materiality, and the degree of risk associated with the item. The auditor must gather sufficient competent evidential matter to provide a reasonable basis for the expression of an opinion and usually must rely on evidence that is persuasive rather than convincing. If sufficient evidence cannot be obtained so as to remove substantial doubt as to any material item, the auditor must either express a qualified opinion or disclaim an opinion. An auditor cannot go to any length to obtain evidential matter as there must be some relationship between the cost of obtaining evidence and its usefulness; benefit must exceed cost.

EVIDENTIAL MATTER FOR RECEIVABLES AND INVENTORIES

Confirmation of receivables and observation of inventories are accepted auditing procedures. The auditors who issue an opinion when they have not employed these procedures must bear in mind that they have the burden of justifying any opinion expressed.

Receivables

Confirmation of receivables requires direct communication with debtors either during or after the period under audit. Factors to be considered by the auditor in selecting the information to be requested and the form of the confirmation and the extent and timing of his confirmation procedures include the following:

Effectiveness of internal control

Apparent possibility of disputes

Inaccuracies or irregularities in the accounts

The probability that requests will receive appropriate consideration or that the debtor will be able to confirm the information requested

Materiality of the amounts involved

Two forms of confirmation requests are the "positive" form of request, where the debtor is asked to respond to the confirmation whether or not he or she is in agreement with the information given, and the "negative" form of confirmation request, wherein the debtor is asked to respond only if he or she disagrees with the information given. The positive form of confirmation is preferable when individual account balances are relatively large, or there is reason to believe that there may be a substantial number of accounts in dispute, or the auditor believes that the accounts contain inaccuracies or irregularities.

The negative form of confirmation is particularly useful when internal control over accounts receivable is considered to be effective, a large number of accounts when relatively small balances are involved, and the auditor has no reason to believe that persons receiving the requests will not give them consideration. When the negative form is used, the number of requests sent or the extent of the other auditing procedures applied to the receivable balances should normally be greater to obtain the same degree of satisfaction as would be obtained from the use of positive confirmation requests.

A combination of positive and negative confirmations may be appropriate in most audit situations with the positive confirmations used for accounts with large balances and the negative confirmations for accounts with relatively small balances. Confirmation procedures may be directed toward account balances with debtors or toward individual items included in such balances. For example, an auditor could confirm either the amount a debtor owes to a client or he or she could confirm the amount of the last payment on account by the debtor. The auditor should follow up on nonreplies to positive confirmation requests with a second and sometimes a third confirmation. For those significant confirmation requests for which no replies are received, procedures may include examination of evidence of subsequent cash receipts, cash remittance advices, sales and shipping documents, and other records in order to support the balance in the account.

Inventories

When inventories are determined solely by means of a physical count, and all counts are made as of the balance sheet date or as of a single date within a reasonable time before or after the balance sheet date, it is ordinarily necessary for the independent auditors to be present at the time of count and, by suitable observation, tests, and inquiries satisfy themselves regarding the following:

> Effectiveness of the methods of inventory-taking

> Measure of reliance which may be placed upon the client's representations about the quantities and physical condition of the inventory

When well-kept perpetual inventory records are tested by the client periodically by comparisons with physical counts, the auditor's observation procedures usually can be performed either during or after the end of the period under audit.

When statistical sampling is used by a client in the taking of the physical inventory or in estimating the inventory, the auditor must be satisfied that:

> The sampling plan has statistical validity

> The plan has been properly applied

> The resulting precision and reliability are reasonable in the circumstances

It will always be necessary for the auditor to make, or observe, some physical counts of the inventory and apply appropriate tests of intervening transactions. Auditors may be asked to make an examination of financial statements covering the current period and one or more periods for which they have not observed or made some physical counts of prior inventories. In these cases they may be able to become satisfied as to inventories through appropriate procedures such as tests of prior transactions, reviews of the records of prior counts, and the application of gross profit tests, provided that they have been able to become satisfied as to the current inventory. In other words, auditing standards require auditors to satisfy themselves regarding the ending inventory, to make or observe some physical counts of inventory, but permit auditors to satisfy themselves regarding the beginning inventory by the application of auditing procedures other than direct physical count or observation.

INVENTORIES HELD IN PUBLIC WAREHOUSES

Sufficient evidential matter for inventories held in public warehouses may be obtained by direct confirmation in writing from warehouse custodians provided that, where the amounts involved represent a significant proportion of either current or total assets, supplemental inquiries are made to satisfy the auditor as to the bonafides of the situation. The supplementary inquiries should include:

> Discussion with the owner as to the control procedures in investigating the warehousemen, and tests of related evidential matter

> Review of owner's control procedures concerning performance of the warehouseman, and tests of related evidential matter

> Observation of physical counts of goods in the warehouse whenever practicable and reasonable

> Where warehouse receipts have been pledged as collateral, confirmation (on a test basis where appropriate) from lenders as to pertinent details of the pledged receipts

For inventories stored at outside warehouses, if the inventories make up a significant proportion of total or current assets, it may be desirable to obtain an independent CPA's report on the warehouseman's system of internal accounting control (see SAS No. 44, Section 324, *Special-Purpose Reports on Intenral Accounting Control at Service Organizations* for the content of such a report).

EVIDENTIAL MATTER FOR LONG-TERM INVESTMENTS

The objective of the auditor's examination of long-term investments is to ascertain whether they are being accounted for in conformity with GAAP, consistently applied, and whether the related financial statement disclosures are adequate.

The auditor should examine sufficient competent evidential matter supporting the existence, ownership, and cost of long-term investments. The carrying amount of investments, income and losses attributable to investments and any related disclosures in the investor's financial statements should also be examined. The auditor should gather sufficient evidence to support whether the investor should follow the equity method of accounting for investments or other appropriate methods.

Types of Evidence

Evidence as to the existence, ownership, and cost of long-term investments includes accounting records and documents of the investor relating to acquisition. Evidence should be corroborated by inspection of the securities and written confirmation when securities are held by third parties or when third parties can provide evidence as to the existence and ownership of the securities. Evidence pertaining to the carrying amount of long-term investments, income and losses attributable to such investments, and capital and other transactions of the investee may be available in the following forms:

> Audited financial statements (constitutes sufficient competent evidential matter as to the equity in underlying net assets and results of operations of the investee)

> Unaudited financial statements (provides information and evidence but unaudited statements do not, by themselves, provide sufficient competent evidential matter supporting long-term investments)

> Market quotations (constitutes sufficient competent evidential matter supporting investments if quotations are based on a reasonably broad and active market)

Equity Method of Accounting

The auditor has a responsibility to become satisfied with respect to the appropriateness of the accounting method adopted for investments in voting stock of an investee. An auditor should make inquiry of an investor's management as to:

Whether the investor has the ability to exercise significant influence over operating and financial policies of the investee under the criteria set forth in APB Opinion No. 18, and

The attendant circumstances which serve as a basis for management's conclusion that the equity method of accounting is appropriate

When an auditor accounts for an investment contrary to the presumptions established by APB Opinion No. 18, the auditor should examine sufficient evidence to become satisfied that such presumption has been overcome (APB Opinion No. 18 establishes the presumption that the equity method of accounting for an investment in common stock should be used when the investor owns 20 percent or more of the outstanding voting stock) and that appropriate disclosure is made regarding the reasons for not accounting for the investment in keeping with the presumption of control.

With respect to events and transactions of the investee from the date of the investee's financial statements to the date of the auditor's report (subsequent events period), the auditor should review available interim financial statements of the investee and make appropriate inquiries of the investor. The auditor should ascertain through such inquiries that the investor is aware of any material events or transactions arising subsequent to the date of the investee's financial statements. When the amounts of unrealized intercompany profits or losses could reasonably be expected to be material in relation to the investor's financial statements, unaudited data obtained from the investee ordinarily should be subjected to auditing procedures.

CLIENT REPRESENTATIONS

As part of the procedures performed in an audit of financial statements in accordance with GAAS, the auditor obtains certain written representations (SAS No. 19) from management. Oral and written representations are made to the auditor during the course of the examination covering a variety of matters such as the overall fairness of the financial statements, the completeness of the minutes of meetings of the board of directors and company committees, the value and saleability of the inventory, the adequacy of disclosures in the financial statements concerning related party transactions, legal matters, and so forth. Such representations are requested from management and provided because there are many matters regarding the financial statements that management alone has knowledge of and corroborating evidence is not ordinarily obtainable. Also, obtaining written representations impress upon management its responsibility for the overall fairness of the financial statements, including disclosure.

SAS No. 19, *Client Representations*, requires the auditor to obtain written representations as part of the examination of financial statements in accordance with GAAS. Such representations confirm the continuing appropriateness of oral representations given to the auditor during the course of the engagement. Also, by emphasizing management's responsibility for the overall fairness of the financial statements, such representations may bring attention to information or evidence that the auditor otherwise was not aware of, for example, an important subsequent event requiring disclosure in the financial statements such as a planned merger with another firm. Accordingly, written representations should be obtained by the auditor near the end of his or her field work (which is the date of the audit report) so as to cover the subsequent period.

Many representations obtained from management, as indicated, are not subject to corroboration. For example, a criteria for classification of marketable equity securities as current assets is management's intent to use the securities for working capital purposes during the coming operating cycle. By confirming the proper classification of marketable equity securities in the balance sheet, management is attesting to its intent to use the securities for working capital purposes. Unless audit evidence reveals conditions to the contrary, the auditor's reliance on the truthfulness of management's representations is reasonable.

Management's representations may be limited to matters that are considered material to the financial statements provided management and the auditor have reached an understanding as to the limits of materiality for such purposes.

Written representations should be addressed to the auditor and signed by members of management with responsibility for company operations (usually the chief executive officer and the controller). Individuals responsible for specific functions may be requested to provide separate written representations regarding their function. For example, the individual responsible for maintaining the minutes of the corporation may be asked to represent that they are complete. The representation letter is ordinarily prepared by the auditor for the client's signature.

Management's refusal to furnish written representations that the auditor believes are necessary or its refusal to permit the auditor to perform procedures considered necessary regarding matters in a representation letter is a scope limitation sufficient to preclude an unqualified opinion (probably a disclaimer of opinion would be called for).

The specific written representations obtained by the auditor will depend on the circumstances of the engagement and the nature and basis of presentation of the financial statements. According to SAS No. 19, the following matters ordinarily would be included in a representation letter:

1.   Management's acknowledgement of its responsibility for the fair presentation in the financial statements of financial position, results of operations, and changes in financial position in conformity with generally accepted accounting principles or other comprehensive basis of accounting.

2.   Availability of all financial records and related data.

3.   Completeness and availability of all minutes of meetings of stockholders, directors, and committees of directors.

4.   Absence of errors in the financial statements and unrecorded transactions.

5.   Information concerning related party transactions and related amounts receivable or payable.

6.   Noncompliance with aspects of contractual agreements that may affect the financial statements.

7.   Information concerning subsequent events.

8.   Irregularities involving management or employees.

9.   Communications from regulatory agencies concerning noncompliance with, or deficiencies in, financial reporting practices.

10.   Plans or intentions that may affect the carrying value or classification of assets or liabilities.

11.   Disclosure of compensating balances or other arrangements involving restrictions on cash balances, and disclosure of line-of-credit or similar arrangements.

12.   Reduction of excess or obsolete inventories to net realizable value.

13.   Losses from sales commitments.

14.   Satisfactory title to assets, liens on assets, and assets pledged as collateral.

15.   Agreements to repurchase assets previously sold.

16.   Losses from purchase commitments for inventory quantities in excess of requirements or at prices in excess of market.

17.   Violations or possible violations of laws or regulations whose effects should be considered for disclosure in the financial statements or as a basis for recording a loss contingency.

18.   Other liabilities and gain or loss contingencies that are required to be accrued or disclosed by Statement of Financial Accounting Standards No. 5.

19.   Unasserted claims or assessments that the client's lawyer has advised are probable of assertion and must be disclosed in accordance with Statement of Financial Accounting Standards No. 5.

20.   Capital stock repurchase options or agreements or capital stock reserved for options, warrants, conversions, or other requirements.

Following is an illustrative representation letter incorporating the above matters and other matters that could involve additions to the letter (note items 15 and 16 in the letter):

ABC Corporation
1000 Rosebud Ave.
Los Angeles, California 22233

January 29, 19x2

Anderson and Holdren
Certified Public Accountants
200 Life Building
Los Angeles, California 22244

Gentlemen:

In connection with your examination of the financial statements of ABC Corporation as of December 31, 19x1, and for the year then ended for the purpose of expressing an opinion as to whether the financial statements present fairly the financial position, results of operations, and changes in financial position of ABC Corporation, in conformity with generally accepted accounting principles, we confirm, to the best of our knowledge and belief, the following representations made to you during your examination.

1. We are responsible for the fair presentation in the statements of financial position, results of operations, and changes in financial position in conformity with generally accepted accounting principles.

2. We have made available to you, all —

   a. Financial records and related data.

   b. Minutes of the meetings of stockholders, directors, and committees of directors, or summaries of actions of recent meetings for which minutes have not yet been prepared.

3. There have been no —

   a. Irregularities involving management or employees who have significant roles in the system of internal accounting control.

   b. Irregularities involving other employees that could have a material effect on the financial statements.

4. We have no plans or intentions that may materially affect the carrying value or classification of assets and liabilities. (Except as stated in Item No. 15.)

5. The following have been properly recorded or disclosed in the financial statements:

   a. Related party transactions and related amounts receivable or payable, including sales, purchases, loans, transfers, leasing arrangements, and guarantees.

   b. Arrangements with financial institutions involving compensating balances or other arrangements involving restrictions on cash balances and line-of-credit or similar arrangements.

   c. Agreements to repurchase assets previously sold.

6. There are no —

   a. Violations or possible violations of laws or regulations whose effects should be considered for disclosure in the financial statements or as a basis for recording a loss contingency.

   b. Other material liabilities or gain or loss contingencies that are required to be accrued or disclosed by FASB Statement No. 5.

7. There are no unasserted claims or assessments that our lawyer has advised us are probable of assertion and must be disclosed in accordance with FASB Statement No. 5.

8. There are no material transactions that have not been properly recorded in the accounting records underlying the financial statements.

9. Provision, when material, has been made to reduce excess or obsolete inventories to their estimated net realizable value.

10. The company has satisfactory title to all owned assets, and there are no liens or encumbrances on such assets nor has any asset been pledged.

11. Provision has been made for any material loss to be sustained in the fulfillment of, or from inability to fulfill, any sales commitments.

12. Provision has been made for any material loss to be sustained as a result of purchase commitments for inventory quantities in excess of normal requirements or at prices in excess of the prevailing market prices.

13. We have complied with all aspects of contractual agreements that would have a material effect on the financial statements in the event of noncompliance.

14. No events have occurred subsequent to the balance sheet date that would require adjustment to, or disclosure in, the financial statements.

15. Short-term obligations have been excluded from current liabilities because it is the company's intention to refinance these obligations on a long-term basis and the company has demonstrated the ability to consummate such refinancing.

16. In the case of investments classified as marketable equity securities in the current asset section of the balance sheet, it is the company's intention to employ these securities as working capital during the next accounting period.

                                _____
                                        President

                                _____
                                        Controller

An Auditing Interpretation of Section 333 (SAS No. 19) considers the question of management representations on violations and possible violations of laws and regulations that is included in the client representation letter.

The Interpretation concerns the question as to "what representations regarding illegal acts" the auditor is asking management to attest to.

The Interpretation states that guidance on evaluating the need to disclose litigation, claims, and assessments that may result from possible violations of laws and regulations is provided by FASB Statement No. 5, *Accounting for Contingencies*. The client representations on illegal acts do not include matters beyond those described in FASB Statement No. 5. That is, matters that may require accrual or disclosure in accordance with FASB Statement No. 5.

In requesting the representation on illegal acts, the auditor is not requesting management's speculation on all possible legal challenges to its actions. Rather, the representation concerns matters that have come to management's attention and that are significant enough that they should be considered in determining whether financial statements should be adjusted or additional disclosure should be made.

ACCOUNTS RECEIVABLE CONFIRMATION—AN ALTERNATIVE AUDITING APPROACH

Using individual invoices instead of account balances solves many of the usual confirmation problems.

by Jack L. Krogstad
and Marshall B. Romney

One of the most deeply ingrained and widely practiced auditing procedures is the written confirmation of accounts receivable with third parties. Whether positive or negative confirmation requests are used, the amount confirmed is normally the account balance as of a specific date. However, recent studies have raised serious doubts about the efficacy of this audit procedure.[1] Practitioners frequently are plagued with low response rates, tedious reconciliations caused by routine items in transit and invoice processing lags, time-consuming alternative procedures and returned confirmations of dubious reliability.

This article describes a frequently overlooked alternative confirmation approach that mitigates each of these problems and offers other advantages to auditors, clients and third-party respondents in many audit situations. This approach is the confirmation of individual invoices in lieu of account bal-

ances. Statement on Auditing Standards no. 1, *Codification of Auditing Standards and Procedures*, reads:

"Confirmation procedures may be directed toward account balances with debtors or toward *individual items included in such balances*. The latter procedure may be particularly useful when the nature of the accounts or the debtors' records are not likely to permit successful confirmation of account balances." [Emphasis added.][2]

The provision emphasized in the above statement was inserted by the committee on auditing procedure of the American Institute of CPAs for the first time in Statement on Auditing Procedure no. 43, *Confirmation of Receivables and Observation of Inventories*.[3] Unfortunately, this confirmation alternative has not received attention in the accounting literature. The committee's foresight is rec-

---

[1] See Carl S. Warren, "Confirmation Reliability—The Evidence," JofA, Feb.75, pp.85-89, for a summary of field studies of the confirmation procedure.

[2] Statement on Auditing Standards no. 1, *Codification of Auditing Standards and Procedures* (New York: AICPA, 1973), section 331.07. Also see *AICPA Professional Standards* (Chicago, Ill.: Commerce Clearing House, Inc., 1979), AU sec. 331.07.

[3] Statement on Auditing Procedure no. 43, *Confirmation of Receivables and Observation of Inventories* (New York: AICPA, 1970).

JACK L. KROGSTAD, CPA, Ph.D., associate professor of accounting at Kansas State University, Manhattan, Kansas, presently is a visiting associate professor at the University of Michigan, Ann Arbor, Michigan. A member of the Texas Society of CPAs, the American Accounting Association, the American Institute of CPAs and the EDP Auditors Association, Dr. Krogstad is the editor of *The Auditor's Report,* the newsletter for a section of the AAA. He is also the coauthor of several articles which have appeared in professional journals. **MARSHALL B. ROMNEY,** CPA, Ph.D., is assistant professor of accounting at the Institute of Professional Accountancy, Brigham Young University, Provo, Utah. A member of the AAA, Dr. Romney is also a member of the AICPA and the EDPAA. He has written a number of articles which have appeared in various professional and academic publications.

ognized, however, when the environmental changes surrounding the confirmation procedure are considered.

Changes in the Confirmation Environment

Since McKesson & Robbins,[4] the environment in which accounts receivable confirmation is performed has changed in three significant ways. First, the computer age brought to business new methods of information processing, storage and retrieval. EDP capability, coupled with attention to cash management by both client and customer, has led to accounts receivable and accounts payable systems that are maintained on an invoice basis instead of an account basis. Accordingly, individual invoices have replaced monthly statements as the customer billing medium in many business entities.

Second, interim confirmation of accounts receivable has become generally accepted by the auditing profession when internal control permits roll-forward procedures at year-end. This timing of the confirmation procedure permits it to take on increasing significance in internal control compliance evaluations.

Third, statistical sampling has emerged as an acceptable approach to stratification of accounts receivable, sample size determination, sample selection and estimation of the accounts receivable balance. This has focused attention on audit efficiency, population variability and sample reliability and has permitted meaningful evaluations and comparisons of differing confirmation strategies employed in the audit of accounts receivable.

Despite these changes, most auditors continue attempting to confirm customers' account balances. Consequently, a growing number of confirmation requests are returned to auditors with the following notation: "Our records do not permit us to confirm this account balance." Frequently, returned confirmations contain disputes arising from invoices in transit and invoice processing lags, or the customer's frustration in attempting to

appropriately respond to a client's confirmation request leads to ill-considered or unwarranted sign-offs. Further, the confirmation procedure's articulation with internal control evaluations goes untapped. One gets the distinct impression that in many cases confirmation of accounts receivable has assumed a sterility perpetuated by mere mechanical compliance with accepted auditing practice.

These are some of the concerns that motivated one large office of an international CPA firm to begin experimenting with individual invoice confirmations in 1974.[5] The approach has been effective and the firm has used it on an increasing number of clients each year. Therefore, a tentative evaluation of its usefulness is possible. The remainder of this article is based on the actual experience of this office with invoice confirmations.

Description of Open Invoice Confirmation

Invoice confirmation of accounts receivable begins with the judgmental or statistical selection of individual invoices from the client's open invoice file. One approach is to make two copies of each invoice to be confirmed. One copy is enclosed with the confirmation request sent to the client's customer; the other is retained in the work papers. Exhibit 1, page 70, contrasts a standard positive confirmation request with the confirmation request that accompanies an open invoice. The differences in content are underscored. It should be noted that the invoice date replaces the audit date in the invoice confirmation request. An auditor can modify the suggested wording to fit any particular confirmation strategy. For example, it might be deemed undesirable to enclose a copy of the invoice and the confirmation wording would be changed accordingly.

Invoice confirmations address the same substantive audit objectives as account balance confirmations (for example, existence, valuation, cutoff, accounting propriety and reasonableness of sales) and, accordingly, can be used in conjunction with account balance confirmations. The auditor may wish to stratify accounts receivable by amount, type of customer, age or some other relevant criterion and use the invoice confirmation procedure only when it offers significant advantages in accomplishing audit objectives.

---

[4] Although direct confirmation of customer's accounts was advocated by some practitioners and writers before 1938, the McKesson & Robbins collapse resulted, in 1939, in SAP no. 1, *Extensions of Auditing Procedure,* (New York: American Institute of Accountants, 1914), which required confirmation of accounts receivable for the first time.

[5] The authors gratefully acknowledge the cooperation and staff support provided by the Houston office of Ernst & Whinney. Without the assistance of Larry E. Darst and K. Reid Lawrence, this article would not have been possible.

Exhibit 1

Standard positive confirmation request*
Our auditors are making an examination of our financial statements and wish to obtain direct confirmation of the correctness of the amount owed to us as of the date indicated.

Please compare the balance shown below with your records, noting details of any exceptions on the reverse side. Then sign this letter in the space provided and return it directly to our auditors. A reply envelope which requires no postage is enclosed for your convenience.

   This is not a request for payment and remittance should not be made to our auditors.

Audit date _____

Account balance _____

   The balance shown above was correct on the date indicated. (If not correct, check here ___ and indicate difference on reverse.)

Open invoice confirmation request*
Our auditors are making an examination of our financial statements and wish to obtain direct confirmation of the correctness of the invoice amount owed to us. Please compare the invoice amount shown below with your records, noting details of any exceptions on the reverse side. A copy of the invoice is enclosed to help you locate the requested information and identify any discrepancies. Then sign this letter in the space provided and return it directly to our auditors. A reply envelope which requires no postage is enclosed for your convenience.

   This is not a request for payment and remittance should not be made to our auditors. Your account balance with us may include other invoices; however, for purposes of confirmation, our auditors are interested in only this specific invoice.

Invoice no. _____

Invoice date _____

Invoice amount _____

   The invoice amount shown above is correct. (If not correct, check here ___ and indicate difference on reverse.)

* The differences in content between the two confirmation requests are underscored.

For example, many auditors are concerned with the dollar coverage of the confirmation procedure. Receivable account balances may be stratified and all customers with relatively large balances circularized with standard positive confirmations. The invoice confirmation procedure then could be used for the remaining accounts, probably on a sample basis. Alternatively, invoices might be stratified according to dollar amounts and sample sizes adjusted to reach the dollar coverage desired.

   The greatest benefits of invoice confirmations are realized when the procedure is used statistically. Exhibit 2, page 71, shows selected audit data from one client application. As can be seen from the comparison of account balance confirmations (1975) with invoice confirmations (1976), dollar coverage is permitted to decrease under the invoice approach from $871,000 to $380,000 (see "From sample population"). However, the increase in sample size leads to equal levels of confidence and precision. Thus, audit conclusions are reached using invoice confirmations that satisfy the same statistical parameters. In estimation sampling for variables, invoices merely replace account balances in deriving statistical projections.

   The invoice confirmation procedure should not be rejected as an inferior alternative to standard confirmation procedures. It should be evaluated on its merits and its ability to accomplish audit objectives in the context of specific client situations. In some cases, invoice confirmations may prove superior to standard confirmations, even in achieving desirable levels of dollar coverage. Accordingly, the determination of whether this alternative approach is appropriate requires some appreciation for the client and receivable properties that are conducive to its application.

Conducive Properties

Because of the limited experience with invoice confirmations, a comprehensive list of conducive client and receivable properties is not yet possible. However, the following four general questions can be used to supplement and guide the auditor's judgment as he considers the appropriateness of the procedure in specific audit situations:

☐ Is the account balance confirmation procedure producing unsatisfactory results in terms of low response rates, time-consuming alternative procedures or numerous immaterial reconciliations? If so, further consideration certainly should be given to the invoice confirmation approach. On the other hand, a negative response to this question is not a conclusive signal to disregard the invoice approach. Careful thought still should be given to the advantages it offers in terms of accomplishing specific audit objectives.

☐ Are customer account balances composed of many invoices? The more invoices composing an account balance, the more attractive invoice confirmations become. Conversely, if only a single purchase is made by a customer per client billing period, standard account balance confirmation probably is satisfactory.

☐ Are customer accounts payable systems maintained on an invoice basis? Most such systems are maintained according to invoices rather than to accounts. For example, accounts payable transactions normally are associated with supporting purchase requisitions, purchase orders, invoices and receiving reports. The more closely the requested confirmation information articulates with the customer's information system, the easier it is for the customer to respond reliably.

☐ Is the client's receivable information processing system on an invoice basis, and is it reliable and timely? It is important that the system match cash receipts, credit memos and other adjustments to specific invoices. Further, it is beneficial if supporting documentation for clicnt sales is organized and stored on an invoice basis.

Advantages of Open Invoice Confirmation

Many auditing situations are compatible with the practices implied by the questions above because such practices are recognized as

---

Exhibit 2

Illustrative invoice confirmation application
(Large manufacturing—commercial conglomerate)

	Confirmation of account balances (1975)		Confirmation of open invoices (1976)	
Sample plan				
Population	$.01 < accounts < $40,000		$.01 < invoices < $20,000	
Confidence level	95%		95%	
Precision	5%		5%	
Confirmation results	*Number*	*Amount (in 000s)*	*Number*	*Amount (in 000s)*
Total accounts receivable		$19,881		$22,895
Positive confirmations requested				
From sample population	105	871	181	380
From above upper sample boundary (100%)	82	9,566	119	7,752
Total	187	$10,437	300	$8,132
Dollar coverage	52.5%		35.5%	
Confirmations returned				
Without exception	59		149	
With exception	28		31	
Unable to respond	27		0	
Total	114		180	
Confirmations not returned	73		120	
Total	187		300	
Confirmation response rate	46.5%		60.0%	
Audit hours incurred	187		143	

sound business procedures in harmony with principles of strong internal control. Affirmative responses to the questions should bring the auditor to a consideration of the advantages of open invoice confirmations. Pertinent portions of exhibit 2 are noted for illustrative purposes in the following discussion of the advantages of invoice confirmations.

☐ *Increased response rate.* Response rates show a marked increase when invoice confirmation requests replace positive confirmations of account balances. Experience indicates that this increase can be expected to

"Instead of searching the files for documentation supporting . . . dozens of invoices that constitute a single nonresponding account balance confirmation, the auditor need vouch only a single invoice."

range from 25% to 75% depending on the circumstances. This means that a 40% response rate using standard positive confirmations might jump to the 50% to 70% range. Exhibit 2 shows a 29% increase in the overall response rate (46.5% to 60.0%). On other clients (not shown), the response rate has jumped by as much as 75%.

Why does this increase occur? Primarily because the invoice approach makes it much easier for the customer to respond. In many instances, customers had to reply to account balance confirmation requests by saying that they were unable to respond. Exhibit 2 illustrates this case very well. In 1975, 27 confirmations were returned that indicated an inability to respond. The use of invoice confirmations in 1976 reduced this number to zero, even though the sample size was larger. Though no "official" voice exists for governmental units, all state and federal governmental agency officials questioned have found invoice confirmations desirable and have said they would cooperate with attempts to confirm invoice amounts.

☐ *Efficient alternative procedures.* Alternative procedures required for nonresponses can be performed quickly and easily. Instead of searching the files for documentation supporting perhaps dozens of invoices that ·constitute a single nonresponding account balance confirmation, the auditor need vouch only a single invoice. Frequently, all the required supporting documentation is found attached to the invoice or at least filed for quick retrieval by invoice date or number. Supporting documentation for account balances is not organized this efficiently.

Further increases in efficiency result from the ease with which subsequent collections can be traced to individual invoices. Since customer payments typically relate to invoiced amounts, matching collections with specific invoices is a convenient procedure. With account balance confirmations, it can be quite an undertaking to match a number of subsequent collections with an accounts receivable balance as of a specific date.

☐ *Reduced reconciliation work.* Invoice confirmations eliminate most of the minor problems of trying to reconcile invoices when some are in transit and when there are invoice processing lags; these often are annoying problems with standard account balance confirmations. As illustrated in exhibit 2, the percentage of exceptions to total confirmations drops from 15% (28 of 187 confirmations) to 10% (31 of 300). Other applications of invoice confirmations (not shown) have reduced the number of such exceptions to zero.

Exhibit 2 also shows a 24% decrease in audit hours incurred in performing the accounts receivable work (from 187 hours to 143 hours). The number of hours saved through an increased response rate, more efficient alternative procedures and reduced reconciliation work actually exceeds the difference of 44 hours. However, certain pressures on audit time, such as the larger sample size, offset some of the time gain. Also, some start-up time requirements are incurred the first year that invoice confirmations are used. These vary from application to application depending on the client's information system, the audit procedures used in the previous audit, the composition of receivables, the audit objectives and the familiarity of the auditor with the invoice confirmation procedure. Accordingly, the time savings likely will increase in subsequent years.

☐ *Increased reliability of confirmation responses.* Two factors suggest that confirmation reliability may be increased with invoice confirmations. First, requesting information about a specific invoice removes much of the respondent's frustration by enabling him to respond quickly and meaningfully. In contrast, consider the situation in which the customer is asked to confirm an account balance of $1 million that is made up of approximately two hundred individual invoices. The customer's records show that as of the confirmation date the accounts payable balance owed to the client is $950,000. Aware of the time lags caused by in-transits and invoice and payment processing and because of the time involved and the difficulty in reconciling all the invoices to the client's balance, the customer may sign the confirmation without giving it the attention desired by the auditor. When confronted with a request for information about a specific invoice, however, it seems more likely that the customer will respond reliably, given the substantially reduced task of obtaining his copy of the invoice and reconciling it to the confirmation request.

A second, but related, factor concerns materiality. Since account balances normally are much larger than an invoice amount, larger discrepancies may be tolerated by respondents, as in the situation described above. When the customer sees detailed reconciliation as a formidable task, and especially when the customer–client relationship is based on trust and cooperation, a $50,000 discrepancy may seem unimportant. Correspondingly, the $50,000 may fall below the auditor's materiality threshold for overall fair presentation of the financial statements; yet, the same or a smaller discrepancy emerging from a properly reconciled response may contain valuable information for the auditor about lapping, discount policies, sales cut-offs, sales returns, consignments and overall reliability of the client's information system for sales, receivables and cash receipts. Invoice confirmations contain smaller amounts and provide sufficient detail to encourage customers to note much smaller discrepancies, if they exist.[6]

□ *Complementary to compliance evaluations.* The use of invoice confirmations is in keeping with the increasing attention accorded internal control evaluations and the emerging cycle-oriented approach to auditing.[7] Because of the specific nature of invoice confirmation requests, discrepancies tend to point directly to specific transactions, con-

trols or individual responsibilities. SAS no. 1, sec. 320.20, reads: "Transactions are the basic components of business operations and, therefore, are the primary subject matter of internal control." The sales-receivable–cash receipts transaction cycle is the heart of most business entities, and invoices articulate with the principal ingredients of information processing and transaction documentation in this cycle. Invoice confirmations thus dovetail with the primary functions of internal control involved in the revenue producing flow of transactions—authorization, execution, recording and accountability. An example further clarifies this advantage.

Errors can easily be made somewhere in the sales-collection transaction cycle. Suppose a client's clerk is to check prices on invoices before mailing to customers as an internal control procedure. The clerk is then to initial the client's file copy of the invoice. Assume the clerk is sometimes careless and, in one instance, overlooks a mistakenly entered price for a case of products when the customer received only one item. The customer's receiving clerk notes the discrepancy on the invoice, and later an accounting clerk telephones the client and obtains a credit adjustment to the accounts receivable balance.

"This [invoice confirmation] procedure directs accounts receivable confirmations to invoice amounts in lieu of account balances."

A credit memo is initiated by an accounting supervisor with the client, but the specific invoice is not pulled and corrected. The auditor happens to select this uncorrected open invoice for confirmation, and the returned confirmation from the customer clearly describes the discrepancy.

A compliance test verifying the requisite initials would reveal no breakdown in the internal control. Similarly, an account balance confirmation would not indicate any discrepancy (the credit memo has corrected the account balance). While a substantive test involving recomputation, retracing or vouching

---

[6] This is a behavioral hypothesis that deserves empirical testing.
[7] Auditors have viewed internal control in terms of transaction cycles such as sales-receivables-cash, purchases-payables-cash or payroll for many years. Recently, this approach has been extended to substantive work as well in an effort to more directly relate internal control evaluations to the audit program.

likely could disclose the breakdown, such audit activity normally is done on a very limited sample, if at all. However, the invoice confirmation would catch this breakdown in internal control as well as many similar control deviations. The reported discrepancy points directly to the specific transaction, the control deviation and the individual responsible. Thus, the invoice confirmation procedure can be used as a dual-purpose test yielding both substantive and compliance evidence. Recognizing this important contribution of invoice confirmation holds promise of improving auditing efficiency and needs further exploration.

It also should be noted that when invoice confirmations are to be interpreted in a compliance context, an attribute sampling plan is appropriate. Attribute sampling is easily implemented with simple manual calculations and the use of sample size tables. This opens an important area for statistical sampling applications to smaller CPA firms that may not have variable sampling capability.

Perhaps even more significant as auditors move toward systems or cycle auditing is the inverse of the above process. One of the most difficult problems confronting auditors is relating the system of internal control that is tested for compliance to the appropriate restriction of substantive work. From the previous discussion, the direct linkage between internal controls and invoice confirmations is apparent. Thus, relating specific internal control strengths and weaknesses to sample size and population stratification determinations is facilitated.

Conclusion

The invoice confirmation procedure offers the auditor a promising alternative that is well adapted to the recent changes in the confirmation environment and that is in accordance with generally accepted auditing standards. This procedure directs accounts receivable confirmations to invoice amounts in lieu of account balances. Invoice confirmations are practical when receivables consist of numerous individual invoices and when customer accounts payable systems are maintained on an invoice basis. The advantages associated with the procedure are increased confirmation response rates, ease of alternative procedures for nonresponses, reduced reconciliation work, increased confirmation reliability and generation of compliance evidence. ∎

Self-regulation and Caesar's wife

It is imperative that the accounting profession ensure not only that its self-regulation is [as] effective as we know it can be but also that public perception of our role and its implementation is clear. Caeser's wife must not only be pure in her heart [but also] she must be above stain before her critics. The alternative is governmental regulation, a constraint which would prohibit us from fulfilling our obligations to our clients and would gradually strangle the financial capability of American business.

From an address by Joseph P. Cummings
1978-79 chairman of the American Institute of CPAs
at the University of Hartford Center for the Study
of Professional Accounting, May 1, 1979

CASE 11

NEWTON BUILDERS, INC.

Your new client, Newton Builders, Inc., owns several subsidiary companies including six lumber yards. The parent and subsidiaries all have December 31 closings. You have been assigned to the December 31, 19x1 audit.

Each of the subsidiary lumber yards is located in a different town. You decide to make a preliminary scope review as part of your initial planning of the examination. You study the operations of the lumber yards and develop the following information:

1. Each lumber yard has its own manager and is located within a fifty mile radius of the parent company. Each manager receives a salary plus a bonus at year-end based on net income. All merchandise inventory is maintained on a periodic system. The yard manager is responsible for purchasing inventory and supplies. When merchandise is received, a copy of the purchase order, receiving report, bill of lading, and vendor's invoice is forwarded to the parent (home office), Newton Builders. These documents are reviewed by home office personnel for clerical accuracy and the receiving report, bill of lading, vendor's invoice and purchase order are compared to assure that all merchandise ordered was received. Upon completion of these review procedures, the invoice is approved for payment. Payment is made by check, drawn on the respective yard's bank account. Each subsidiary lumber yard maintains a bank account in its town.

2. Each yard manager, while not trained in accounting procedures, is aware of the effect inventory has on net income. You determine that personnel from each yard will count the year-end inventory and that these counts will require a day for each lumber yard. You ascertain that the first yard will count its inventory on Friday, December 15, 19x1 and that inventory in the last yard to be counted will be taken on Friday, December 22, 19x1. During the planning phase of the audit you note that almost all lumber is received by railroad car (there is a railroad siding at each lumber yard location). Also, it is determined that there will probably be one or more box cars containing lumber on the premises of each yard when inventory counts are made. It is determined that counting of the inventory will begin at 8:00 a.m. on each count day. Accordingly, you make arrangements to arrive at the yard offices on each count day at 7:00 a.m. to establish a clean cutoff with respect to both purchases and sales and to be ready to observe the counting procedures and make planned test counts.

3. Sales are recorded on prenumbered invoices and processed as follows:

    a. The customer is given the original copy.

    b. A second copy is given to the yard bookkeeper for posting to subsidiary ledgers (for credit sales), after which it is filed alphabetically by customer name.

    c. The third copy is filed numerically and sent to the home office with a remittance advice on a daily basis.

    All cash receipts at each lumber yard are deposited intact daily and a copy of the validated deposit slip is sent to the home office.

4. The books of original entry and the general ledger are maintained at the parent company's office. You also learn that all insurance policies for each lumber yard are paid by the parent and charged to a general insurance account. At year-end, an adjusting entry allocates insurance expense and general administrative expense to each of the six lumber yards.

5. While each lumber yard has a considerable volume of cash transactions, a major portion of each yard's sales are made to local contractors on credit terms. The bookkeepers at the respective lumber yards bill each account receivable at the end of the month. Contractor sales are made at a discount based on the volume of business each contractor has conducted with the company during the past year. Terms are n/30.

6. During your preliminary scope review, you have reached the conclusion that internal control appears to be sound with respect to merchandise purchases, accounts receivable, and cash collections.

CASE DISCUSSION QUESTIONS

1. The third generally accepted auditing standard of field work requires that the auditor obtain sufficient competent evidential matter to afford a reasonable basis for an opinion regarding the financial statements under examination. In considering what constitutes sufficient competent evidential matter, a distinction should be made between underlying accounting data and all corroborating information available to the auditor.

    a. Discuss the nature of evidential matter to be considered by the auditor in terms of the underlying accounting data, all corroborating information available to the auditor, and the methods by which the auditor tests or gathers competent evidential matter.

    b. What general presumptions can be made about the validity of evidential matter with respect to comparative assurance, persuasiveness, and reliability?

    c. Discuss direct and indirect types of audit evidence and sufficiency of audit evidence (see the related article preceding this case).

2. Confirmation of receivables and observation of inventories are generally accepted auditing procedures.

    a. With respect to receivables, the confirmation date, the method of requesting confirmations, and the number of confirmations to be requested are determined by the independent auditor.

    (1) Two forms of confirmation requests are used in audit engagements, positive and negative. Under what conditions is the positive form preferred? When is it appropriate to use the negative form?

    (2) What other confirmation procedures are available to the auditor?

    b. Newton Builders determines its inventory balances solely by means of a physical count.

    (1) Given the information in the case, what must you do to satisfy yourself as to the effectiveness of the inventory method used by the client and representations concerning the quantity and physical condition of the inventory?

    (2) When a client maintains well-kept perpetual inventory records, what alternatives does the CPA have regarding inventory observation procedures?

3. Assume a client uses statistical sampling techniques which are sufficiently reliable to make an annual physical count of each inventory item unnecessary. What procedures does the independent auditor need to perform?

4. In those cases where inventories are held in public warehouses the auditor is required to perform certain procedures. Discuss fully.

5. An examination of the financial statements of Newton Builders, Inc., the parent company, revealed long-term investments of $6,480,000 solely related to investments in stocks of its subsidiary companies. None of the stocks are actively traded.

    a. What is the auditor's objective in examining long-term investments?

    b. Evidential matter pertaining to the existence, ownership, and cost of long-term investments includes accounting records and documents of the investor relating to the acquisition of the investments. In the case of securities (such as stocks, bonds, and notes), this evidential matter should be corroborated by inspection, or in appropriate circumstances, by written confirmation from an independent custodian of securities on deposit, pledged, or in safekeeping. In the case of loans, advances, and registered bonds and similar debt obligations, evidential matter obtained from accounting records and documents also should be corroborated by written confirmation from the debtor or trustee.

    What forms of evidence would be appropriate to satisfy the auditor regarding long-term investments?

6. Explain the purpose of a representation letter. In what way, if any, does the letter relieve the auditor from performing auditing procedures that are considered necessary in accordance with GAAS?

7. Who prepares the representation letter? When should it be dated?

8. Why would an auditor consider obtaining additional representations from individuals responsible for specific functions within a company—the person responsible for keeping the minutes of meetings of the board of directors, for example.

9. What is the impact on the auditor's examination, if any, if management refuses to provide written representations? Discuss any effects on the auditor's opinion.

CASE 12

McKESSON & ROBBINS LIABILITY CASE*

The Man — Philip Musica

Philip Musica was born and grew up in New York City. The McKesson & Robbins case is tied into the character of this man. Musica's life in the world of fraud began in 1901 at the age of 25 when he was indicted for bribery of customs officials as they recorded the cheese imported for the Musica family store at a weight less than actual, therefore reducing the tariffs.

After his release from prison, Musica once again became involved in the business world, organizing the U.S. Hair Co. Using the international banking system and the import-export business, which he understood thoroughly despite his lack of training, Musica created a fictitious company around a "large" non-existent inventory of lengths of human hair and operated it for approximately a year. U.S. Hair Co. was incorporated and its shares were traded on the New York Curb Exchange. When the fraud was discovered in 1913, seventy-eight creditors filed claims against the bankrupt company. (The four largest claims totaled $251,000.)

After this stage in his life, Philip Musica changed his image and his name—first to Frank D. Costa and, more premanently, to F. Donald Coster. He did not change his basic means of operating, however.

During Prohibition Coster/Musica conferred upon himself a medical degree and opened a pharmaceutical firm—Girard & Co. This firm manufactured drugs of high alcoholic content. Part of these drugs was sold legitimately to customers while a larger volume part was sold to bootleggers at twice the price. The firm maintained meticulous records showing a large volume of business so as to keep their permit for the amount of alcohol they needed for their more widespread "business." It was during this successful period, 1924, that Coster requested an audit by the firm of Price Waterhouse.

The Company — McKesson & Robbins

In 1926 Coster learned of the opportunity of acquiring the firm of McKesson & Robbins. This was a well thought of drug manufacturing and wholesaling firm which had, in the past, been known for its innovation and far-reaching distribution system. In recent years the firm had split and was doing poorly. Coster purchased McKesson & Robbins for $1,000,000.

He then organized underwriters and bankers and sold $1,650,000 worth of stock in the company which he moved to Fairfield and renamed McKesson & Robbins of Connecticut. McKesson & Robbins continued in the illegal alcohol business. The merchandise was channeled through W.W. Smith Co.—a sales agency which Coster established for that purpose. This company and, later, the Manning Bank, were located in New York but were primarily mail drops for the fake documents Coster circulated to substantiate the fictitious business transactions recorded by McKesson & Robbins, Inc.

---

*This case was originally prepared by Sai-Hor Chan, Bob Freeman, and Sarah Harriman, Master of Accountancy students, Virginia Polytechnic Institute and State University.

In 1927 McKesson & Robbins, Ltd. of Canada was organized as a totally owned subsidiary involved in the crude drug industry outside of the United States. This business was handled exclusively by F. Donald Coster (Philip Musica) and his brother George Dietrich (Musica) who was employed as assistant treasurer of McKesson & Robbins. Also, in 1927 Coster reached his goal of having his firm's securities traded on the Big Board.

In 1928 Coster organized and put into operation a plan merging the retailers and distributors of McKesson & Robbins products under the new parent company of McKesson & Robbins, Inc. (chartered in Maryland).

The Fraud

As previously mentioned, Coster and Dietrich handled all of the crude drug "affairs." The entire fraud was based on the mailing of false documents. The chart in Appendix A indicates the supposed flow of the documents for the crude drug subsidiary.

McKesson & Robbins would prepare a purchase order and "send" it to a vendor who would return an invoice and "ship" the goods to one of the warehouses. These warehouses in turn sent McKesson & Robbins a receipt for the goods. Finally, the Manning Bank would send payment to the vendor. It must be emphasized that for the crude drug operations the vendors never received the orders and the warehouses never received any goods. All these transactions consisted solely of documents mailed between Coster and his brother.

A similar arrangement was used for sales and receipts. "Customer" orders were channeled through the W.W. Smith & Co. sales agency to the warehouses. The warehouses would "ship" the goods to the customers and mail notice of shipping to W.W. Smith who in turn notified McKesson & Robbins. McKesson & Robbins sent billings to the customers who would send payment to the Manning Bank. Manning would send McKesson & Robbins notification of payments by customers and the balance in the firms' "accounts." These documents were completely false, having been forged by Coster or his brothers. They also prepared monthly accounting reports of the Canadian subsidiary which were "sent" to Connecticut for inclusion in the financial statements.

McKesson & Robbins' prime year was 1937. At the end of the fiscal year, December 31, 1937, the financial statements (Certified by Price Waterhouse) reported total assets of $88,000,000 including inventories of $44,000,000 and sales were reported at $174,000,000 for the year.[1] (For figures compiled after the fraud was uncovered, see Appendix B.)

The Fraud Uncovered

It was after the audit of 1937 that Julian Thompson, Treasurer for McKesson & Robbins, Inc. began to become suspicious concerning the management of the crude drug subsidiary. His suspicions were the result of the following practices and events:

1. The Canadian firm reinvested all of its profits in its crude drug trade. It did not pay the fees owed by it to W.W. Smith Co.; McKesson & Robbins of Connecticut paid them.

2. The crude drug firm stockpiled huge inventories according to the records.

3. When Thompson traveled to the Canadian warehouses to check on the physical inventory, Coster hindered him by calling him back for nonexistent, urgent business.

4. When the board of directors voted to reduce all inventories, Coster ignored the policy for the Canadian firm and instead continued to increase them.

5. The reports from Dun & Bradstreet which Thompson and Price Waterhouse received on W.W. Smith Co. were false. Dun & Bradstreet had no record of the Smith Co. whatsoever.

6. Upon checking with the five Canadian warehouses, he found them to be small with little activity.

---

[1] Charles Keats, *Magnificent Masquerade* (New York: Funk & Wagnalls Company, Inc., 1964), p. 153, serves as the basis for this background discussion of McKesson & Robbins.

7.   Whenever he questioned Coster on the crude drug subsidiary, he received no answers.

8.   Coster placed the company into receivership so the records would be impounded and Thompson would be denied access to them.

As a result, Thompson and the executive committee went to the Stock Exchange and had trading suspended. The Securities and Exchange Commission began an investigation. The board asked for Coster's resignation. The records of Coster's past as Philip Musica were uncovered. Also, the company was reorganized under Chapter X of the Chandler Act and was placed under the control of a trustee who was responsible for preparing a plan of reorganization, running the business with no stockholder assistance, and recovering all missing assets.[2]

Finally, on December 16, 1938, F. Donald Coster, still president of McKesson & Robbins of Connecticut, committed suicide.[3]

AUDIT IMPLICATIONS

As a result of the McKesson & Robbins fraud, both the American Institute of Accountants (AIA) (forerunner of the AICPA) and the Securities and Exchange Commission (SEC) issued statements addressing themselves to the deficiencies of the Price Waterhouse audit which mirrored the standard of the profession at that time.

Extensions of Auditing Procedure was issued by the AIA in 1939. It dealt with (1) examination of inventories, (2) examination of receivables, (3) appointment of independent certified public accountants, and (4) form of independent certified public accountants' report. The final version of this bulletin was later adopted as Statement on Auditing Procedures No. 1.

In 1941 the SEC issued its *Summary of Findings and Conclusions* which also emphasized these four areas.

Examination of Inventories

Prior to 1939 audit examinations did not include procedures intended to determine the existence or count of inventory. Management usually certified the existence and count of inventory. The SEC found that the Price Waterhouse audit complied with the generally accepted auditing practices of the period which confined inventory verification to the accounting records. They also felt that these procedures were inadequate and commended the profession for subsequently adopting extended procedures.

Extension of Auditing Procedure states:

> That hereafter, where the independent certified public accountant intends to report over his signature on the financial statements of a concern in which inventories are a material factor, it should be generally accepted auditing procedure that, in addition to making auditing tests and checks of the inventory accounts and records, he shall, wherever practicable and reasonable, be present, either in person or by his representatives, at the inventory taking and by suitable observation and inquiry satisfy himself as to the effectiveness of the methods of inventory taking and as to the measure of reliance which may be placed upon the client's representations as to inventories and upon the records thereof.[4]

It further states that for physical inventory systems the procedures should be followed at the time of inventory taking. For perpetual inventory systems with complete records and physical inventories taken during the year, the outlined procedures may be accomplished at any interim date.

Also stated:

> That hereafter, in the case of inventories which in the ordinary course of business are in the hands of public warehouses or other outside custodians, direct confirmation in writing from such custodians is acceptable procedure; except that, where the amount involved represents a significant proportion of the current assets or of the total assets of a concern, the independent certified public accountant shall make supplementary inquiries.[5]

---

[2] Keats, pp. 181-182.
[3] Keats, p. 206.
[4] American Institute of Accountants, *American Institute of Accountants Yearbook* (New York: American Institute of Accountants, 1939), p. 174.
[5] American Institute of Accountants, p. 175.

Examination of Receivables

Also in the area of accounts receivable the SEC found that Price Waterhouse had followed the generally accepted auditing practices of the period. These practices included no procedures to determine whether the receivables were valid obligations of existing concerns but rather relied on management certification of their validity. The SEC felt the McKesson case demonstrated the wisdom of adopting confirmation of accounts receivable and notes receivable as required procedures.

> *Extension of Auditing Procedure* recommends:
>
> That hereafter, wherever practicable and reasonable, and where the aggregate amount of notes and accounts receivable represents a significant proportion of the current assets or of the total assets of a concern, confirmation of notes and accounts receivable by direct communication with the debtors shall be regarded as generally accepted auditing procedure in the examination of the accounts of a concern whose financial statements are accompanied by an independent certified public accountant's report; . . .[6]

The method, extent, and timing of the confirmation is to be determined by the CPA.

Appointment of Independent Certified Public Accountants

In the McKesson & Robbins audit the appointment of Price Waterhouse was made by either Coster (President) or McGloon (Comptroller) near the close of the year. The SEC findings indicated that the board of directors, with rare exceptions, had no role in arranging the audit and did not know the content of the letter of engagement or the long-form report which was addressed to Coster. The SEC felt this practice did not insure the degree of independence needed for the protection of investors. They suggested that auditors be elected by the stockholders, the details arranged by a committee of non-officer board members, and the report be addressed to stockholders. The *Extensions of Auditing Procedure* suggests that the auditor be appointed early in the fiscal year so that he or she may carry out part of his or her work, such as inventory observation, during the year.

Form of Independent Certified Public Accountant's Report or Opinion

Much discussion and a few alterations in the auditor's report resulted from the McKesson & Robbins experience. First, the phrase "obtained information and explanations from officers and employees of the company" was dropped from the opinion because it is inherent in audit procedures and it led to misconceptions concerning reliance on management's statements.

> *Extensions of Auditing Procedure* states:
>
> Assuming that normal procedures have been carried out, it is not considered necessary to describe the details of the examination in this form of report. Any such details as are given should be included in separate paragraphs of the report.[7]

This leads to a more general report which sums up the details of the audit in the phrase " . . . by methods and to the extent we deemed appropriate."

The SEC felt that any generally accepted auditing procedures omitted should be identified and reasons given. These exceptions and exceptions to scope should be clearly labeled. The AIA continues by saying that these exceptions should be included in a separate paragraph and be referred to in the opinion paragraph.

The AIA in *Extensions of Auditing Procedure* makes a final point that the scope of the examination is the auditor's responsibility and his or her judgment is required to decide whether generally accepted auditing procedures have been met and any exceptions are clearly marked.

---

[6] *Ibid.*

[7] American Institute of Accountants, p. 177.

Conclusions

Recently the Equity Funding insurance fraud has proven that massive management-perpetrated fraud still remains a problem for auditing firms. The Equity Funding fraud included three major areas: (1) creation and inflation of assets in the balance sheet; (2) the borrowing of cash without recording the corresponding liability; and (3) the creation of phony insurance which was "sold" to other insurance companies. In especially the first category there are similarities to McKesson & Robbins.

> The principal lesson of the McKesson and Equity Funding frauds is that auditor reliance on the representations of management must be coupled with auditor alertness to any signals that such reliance is unwarranted.[8]

The profession has been showing signs of increased auditor alertness in the area of fraud detection. Touche Ross recently published guidelines to alert auditors of possible fraud. In a broader sense, alertness increases as an Exposure Draft of a new Statement of Auditing Standards is prepared on the detection of fraud.[9]

CASE DISCUSSION QUESTIONS

1. What was the overall impact of the uncovering of the fraud of McKesson & Robbins on the accounting profession? How did this effect the CPA's relationship with the public?

2. What audit recommendations were made by the SEC in their report on McKesson & Robbins? What impact did these "recommendations" have on the profession?

3. What audit standards or procedures are directly or indirectly related to this case?

4. What charges, if any, were brought against Price Waterhouse for their audit of McKesson & Robbins?

5. What parallels can be drawn between McKesson & Robbins and Equity Funding?

6. Should auditors be held liable for fraud that materially misstates the financial position and results of operation of the company being audited when they failed to uncover the fraud?

APPENDIX A

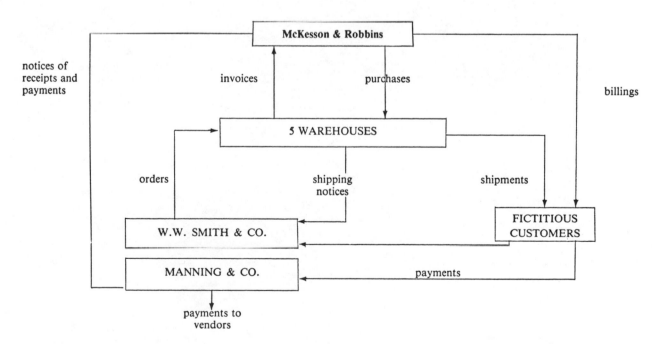

---

[8] Kerry Cooper & Steven Flory, "Lessons from McKesson and Equity Funding," *CPA Journal*, April 1976, p. 23.

[9] "The Touche Ross Manual for Spotting Fraud," *Business Week*, February 17, 1975, p. 52.

APPENDIX B

Audited Total Assets............................		$ 88,000,000
Fictitious Cash in Bank........................	$ 75,000	
Fictitious Accounts Receivable.................	9,000,000	
Fictitious Inventories.........................	10,000,000	19,075,000
Actual Total Assets.............................		$ 68,925,000
Audited Gross Income..........................		$174,000,000
Fictitious Sales (crude drug subsidiary)..........		18,250,000
Actual Gross Income...........................		$155,750,000

REFERENCES

American Institute of Accountants, *American Institute of Accountants Yearbook* (New York: American Institute of Accountants, 1939).

Cooper, Kerry & Flory, Steven, "Lessons from McKesson and Equity Funding," *CPA Journal*, April 1976.

Committee on Professional Ethics (AICPA), "Special Report on McKesson & Robbins," *Journal of Accountancy*, July 1941.

Keats, Charles, *Magnificent Masquerade* (New York: Funk & Wagnalls Company, Inc., 1964).

Securities and Exchange Commission, "Findings and Opinions; McKesson & Robbins, Inc.," *Journal of Accountancy*, January 1941.

Stettler, Howard F., *Auditing Principles: objectives, procedures, working papers,* (Englewood Clifffs, N.J.: Prentice-Hall, Inc., 1961).

Kerry Cooper, Ph.D., and Steven Flory, CPA

Lessons from McKesson and Equity Funding

The degree of responsibility for management fraud is one of the most vexing and critical problems facing the auditing profession. Two landmark cases, 35 years apart, focus on this issue.*

Kerry Cooper, Ph.D., is Associate Professor of Accounting at Texas A&M University. He is coauthor of a financial accounting textbook and has published articles in numerous professional journals. Steven Flory, CPA, is Assistant Professor of Accounting, University of Alabama in Birmingham, graduated from Louisiana State University, and is a doctoral candidate there. He formerly was with Arthur Andersen & Co.

The revelations of the massive management-perpetrated fraud in Equity Funding Corporation pose very serious questions for our business institutions and practices. These include the regulation of insurance companies, the role of financial analysts with regard to "insider" information, and the capacity of the independent auditor to perform meaningfully the attest function for corporate financial statements in an increasingly complex business environment.

The Equity Funding case has been called the greatest crisis for the public accounting profession since the McKesson & Robbins fraud of the 1930s, which it resembles in many ways. The similarities of these two fraud cases include the involvement of top-level management, the fact that neither was detected for a number of years, the widespread publicity given both, and the questions each raised regarding fundamental audit standards and procedures and auditor responsibility for the detection of management fraud. The impact of the McKesson & Robbins case on the auditor is now a matter of record. It is quite possible that the Equity Funding fraud will have at least as great an impact, particularly in regard to the issue of management fraud. This article recounts and contrasts these two sensational fraud cases in an effort to assess and evaluate this potential impact. To obtain perspective for such an analysis, it is helpful to consider briefly the first formal response of the profession to the Equity Funding case. This is the report of the AICPA special committee which studied the Equity Funding case for almost two years.

Report of the Special Committee on Equity Funding

In May 1973 the AICPA appointed a special committee to "study whether the auditing standards which are currently considered appropriate and sufficient in the examination of financial statements should be changed in the light of Equity Funding and report its conclusions to the Board of Directors and the auditing standards executive committee."

The special committee's report, dated February 1975, was released to the public in June. In regard to the crucial question of whether customary auditing procedures should have resulted in detection of the fraud, the committee concluded that:

> Customary audit procedures properly applied would have provided a reasonable degree of assurance that the existence of fraud at Equity Funding would be detected.

The Committee concluded further that:

> Except for certain observations relating to confirmation of insurance in force and auditing related party transactions, generally accepted auditing standards are adequate and no changes are called for in the procedures commonly used by auditors.

The committee carefully refrained from attributing fault to Equity Funding's auditors. It is surely not coincidental that the release of the report (dated February 1975) came only *after* the verdict (guilty) was rendered on May 20, 1975 by a federal district court jury in a criminal trial of three of the accountants involved with Equity Funding. Even then, two committee members dissented to publication of the report prior to the termination of the civil litigation growing out of the fraud.

The committee avoided with equal care endorsing of an enlargement of auditor responsibility for detection of fraud. It devoted a chapter of its report to this issue, however, and recommended a restatement of those sections of SAS No. 1 relating to this responsibility.

The committee concluded:

> It seems clear that the auditor has an obligation to discover material frauds that are discoverable through application of customary auditing procedures applied in accordance with generally accepted auditing standards. The auditing profession should, on an ongoing basis, continue to improve the efficiency of customary audit procedures to the end that probability of discovery of material frauds continues to increase within the limits of practicability.

The profession has thus given a formal response to the Equity Funding disclosures. The ultimate impact of the case, however, is far from resolved.

The McKesson & Robbins Fraud

A February 1939 *Journal of Accountancy* editorial included the following comment:

> Accustomed to relative obscurity in the public prints, accountants have been startled to find their procedures, their principles and their professional standards the subject of sensational and generally unsympathetic headlines.

The source of accountancy's sudden notoriety was the uncovering, in December 1938, of the McKesson & Robbins fraud. This fraud, which had been carried on for more than a decade without detection by the firm's auditors, was conducted by the firm's president, Philip Musica, alias F. Donald Coster. Musica's three brothers assisted him in the scheme to channel a portion of the firm's profits into his own pockets, two of them occupying high positions in the firm and the third serving as the front man for dummy companies created by Musica.[1]

---

[1] For a highly readable account of Philip Musica's criminal career and the McKesson & Robbins fraud in particular, see Charles Keats, *Magnificent Masquerade* (New York: Funk & Wagnalls, 1964).

Dummy companies were the key feature of Musica's scheme, particularly McKesson & Robbins, Ltd., ostensibly a Canadian corporation established to trade in crude drugs outside the United States. Musica's control of McKesson's financial operations permitted him to "pay out" the firm's cash for fictitious purchases of crude drugs for the Canadian subsidiary. Part of the cash thus diverted from the McKesson treasury was later returned as pretended collections of fictitious sales of the crude drug inventories. (This scenario varied somewhat over the life of the fraud.)

The Musica brothers maintained a continuous flow of sham documents to lend the appearance of reality to the pretended transactions and thus deceive McKesson's auditors. Invoices, inventory schedules, contracts, etc., relating to transactions of the nonexistent company went through the accounting department of McKesson & Robbins. The charade allowed Musica to ultimately sluice $120 million through phony accounts, most (but not all) simply flowing in and out of the McKesson treasury.

The hoax had the effect of grossly overstating accounts receivable, inventories, sales and net income. According to the report of the accountant for the trustee, it appeared that fictitious transactions resulted in cash payments of almost $25 million, of which about $22 million came back to the company as collections of fictitious receivables or as cash transfers. The last year-end report filed with the SEC (1937) had reported total assets of approximately $87 million.

The details of the fraud were developed in 1938 by Julian Thompson, the McKesson & Robbins treasurer. Musica committed suicide. A total of eight investigations were launched, the most significant of which was that conducted by the SEC.

The executive committee of the AI(CP)A held a special meeting in New York in December 1938, and issued a statement announcing the undertaking of a "careful review" of customary auditing procedure in the light of the McKesson & Robbins case. The statement went on to say that:

Auditing procedure has evolved over the years, and it naturally remains in the process of evolution. It will be the task of the American Institute of Accountants to determine what, if any, changes in procedure should be adopted by the profession in the light of the revelations in the McKesson & Robbins case.

The basic question confronting the AI(CP)A was what to do about inventories and receivables, the key items in the McKesson & Robbins fraud, although a number of peripheral points also claimed attention—methods of selecting auditors, proposed revisions of the short-form report, investigation of new clients, etc.

The AI(CP)A's 1936 pronouncement, "Examination of Financial Statements by Independent Public Accountants," stated that confirmation of receivables by direct communication with the debtor was unnecessary in the case of companies having an adequate system of internal control. In the case of inventories, the auditor was obliged to "rely principally for information upon the responsible officers and employees of the company." The SEC investigation ultimately concluded that the auditing procedures followed in the audit of McKesson were in accordance with then accepted standards.

The AI(CP)A committee report issued in May 1939 recommended that auditors observe the taking of the physical inventory and make test counts where it was considered practicable and reasonable to do so. With regard to receivables, the report stated that direct confirmation from the debtor should be regarded as a normal audit procedure in all cases where receivables constituted a significant proportion of total assets. The final version of this report was subsequently adopted as the first of the Statements on Auditing Procedures series.

The summary, findings and conclusions of the SEC in its investigation of the McKesson & Robbins fraud were released in 1940. It was reported that, on the basis of the report issued by the public accounting firm which made the post-fraud audit of McKesson & Robbins for its trustee, Coster (Musica) had caused almost $3 million to be abstracted from the firm. The SEC report commended the accounting profession for adopting its extensions of auditing procedure and expressed confidence that no specific rules and regulations governing auditing steps to be performed were necessary.[2]

While this fraud was a tragedy of considerable proportions, it is likely that the sensational case did the accounting profession more good than harm. A prediction of such an outcome was included in an editorial in the February 1939, *Journal of Accountancy*:

> While the numerous uncomplimentary allusions to accounting and auditing appearing in the press have caused members of the profession a great deal of discomfort, we feel that in the long run this publicity will not be entirely harmful to the profession . . . . The importance of independent audits and of accounting procedure will not be forgotten. If this incident reveals weaknesses in customary auditing procedure, those weaknesses can be corrected. We predict that in the future auditors will encounter less resistance to examinations of wider scope and less effort to place limitations on their work than in the past.

The Equity Funding Case

While all the facts relating to the Equity Funding fraud are not yet a matter of public record, a great deal has become known as the result of the various investigations to date. Perhaps the most thorough of these was that of Robert Loeffler, court-appointed trustee for the company under Chapter X bankruptcy proceedings. The trustee's report was filed in November 1974. The report is extemely critical of the various individuals and firms who had been re-

sponsible for past audits of Equity Fundings and its affiliated firms.[3]

The trustee's report groups the fraudulent activities conducted by members of Equity Funding's management into three major categories:

1. The creation and inflation of assets in the balance sheet;
2. The borrowing of cash without recording the corresponding liability; and
3. The creation of phony insurance which was "sold" to other insurance companies.

From 1964 to 1972 more than $143 million of fictitious earnings were reported. The effect of these activities was to give the appearance of rapid, steady earnings growth, thus facilitating the obtaining of cash via loans and the sale of securities. The sale of the nonexistent insurance policies also served to provide cash.

A former financial vice president of the firm has testified that he was ordered on many occasions by the firm's chairman to falsely inflate its profits.[4] Beginning in 1964 he was periodically directed to make Equity's books reflect a specific earnings-per-share figure.

A number of asset accounts were inflated, but the most significant amount related to loans supposedly made to participants in Equity's mutual fund-life insurance package. Equity Funding and its subsidiaries sold a package that involved both life insurance and mutual fund shares. The mutual fund shares were used as collateral for a loan from Equity that was used to pay the premium on the insurance policy. The policies, then, were often sold to various "reinsurers." The fraudulent entries on Equity's books reflected fictitious sales of such packages to individuals.

The practice of reinsuring (or coinsuring) involves the sale of a life insurance policy to another company, referred to as the coin-

surer, for a sum equal to about 180 percent to 190 percent of the first-year premium. The issuing company continues to service the policy and to collect the customer's premium, of which about 90 percent is remitted to the coinsurer. Since the sale of bogus policies by Equity involved no actual receipt of annual premiums from customers, these periodic remittance requirements created a continuing cash crisis. The company thus found itself in a position of constantly creating more and more fictitious assets to generate needed cash (and maintain the illusion of steady earnings growth).

Thus the "funded loans and accounts receivable" account on Equity Funding's balance sheet grew steadily larger. At the end of 1972 the balance amounted to $117 million, more than half of it fictitious.

The fraud was discovered in early 1973, when a former employee of Equity reported it to the New York State Department of Insurance and to an insurance stock analyst. Within a few weeks, the SEC had suspended trading in all EFCA securities on all markets, a petition for protection under Chapter X of the Bankruptcy Act had been filed and approved, and the business and popular press was reporting the most sensational fraud in the history of American business. The unraveling of the many facets of the case and an assessment and interpretation of its impact remained to be accomplished.

The Fraud Cases Compared

An assessment of the implications for the auditor of the differences and similarities in the two cases follows.

The Differences

The McKesson & Robbins fraud was essentially a family affair; it was devised, perpetrated and concealed by the Musica brothers. The Equity Funding case involved a much larger number of unrelated individuals. Nineteen former Equity executives have pleaded guilty to stock-fraud charges. It is apparent that many other employees of the company were aware of the fraud but "passively colluded" by, at a

[2] *United States of America before the Securities and Exchange Commission in the Matter of McKesson & Robbins, Inc.—Report on Investigation* (Washington, D.C.: U.S. Government Printing Office, 1940), p. 24.

[3] "Equity Funding Trustee Calls the Fraud an Inept, Slapdash, Pyramiding Scheme," *Wall Street Journal*, November 4, 1974, p. 4.

[4] "Equity Funding Chief Ordered False Figures, Ex-Officer Testifies," *The Wall Street Journal*, October 7, 1974, p. 14.

minimum, failing to expose it. The dissimilarity between the two cases is a troubling one for auditors, since internal controls will generally be rendered ineffective by such widespread collusion, passive or active. The McKesson & Robbins case was in an old, albeit unfortunate, tradition of what might be called "entrepreneurial fraud." The Equity Funding case is in a different mold; the energies and expertise of a top corporate management team were devoted to fraudulent rather than legitimate activities. The implications for the American business system, if such a phenomenon became widespread, are nothing less than appalling. In any event, the Equity Funding case brings into question the auditor's traditional reliance on the representations of management to a much greater degree than did the McKesson case.

Another dissimilarity between the two cases is the prominence of the computer as an instrument of deceit in the Equity Funding fraud. This has drawn particularly sharp attention in both the popular and the business press. As a result of this aspect of the fraud, audit procedures relating to computerized accounting systems are being reexamined in many quarters. The Special Committee on Equity Funding asserted, however, that:

> The fraud was not based on a sophisticated application of data processing technology. The principal falsifications were achieved by manually preparing fictitious journal entries and recording them on the books of certain Equity Funding companies. However, the computer was used to prepare records in support of some of the fictitious account balances. An enormous amount of clerical effort would have been required to create the supporting detail manually. . . .
> The computer was an important factor in carrying out measures to conceal the fraud, but was not essential to the commission of the basic fraudulent acts.

A third major dissimilarity is in the specialized nature of some of the manipulative items in the Equity fraud. Receivables and inventories were the principal elements of the McKesson fraud—one or both of which are likely to be found on the balance sheets of most business firms. The Equity case generally involved business practices peculiar to the insurance industry, although it is also sprinkled with more widely applicable manipulations (such as failure to record liabilities and creation of fictitious securities). It is possible, then, that a proper response to the case by the accounting profession may involve a focus on *industry* audit procedures rather than on overall audit standards. The Special Committee offered a recommendation in this regard to the AICPA's Auditing Standards Executive Committee. The recommendation concerned possible clarification of the Life Insurance Audit Guide with regard to the confirmation of policies with policyholders.[5]

A possible dissimilarity, which involves an unresolved and certainly sensitive issue, is the degree of adherence to existing audit standards and procedures which marked the performance of the audit tasks in the two fraud cases. The report of the SEC investigation of the McKesson case in 1939 absolved the auditors of any dereliction in their performance of the audit procedures required under existing standards. It would appear that a different conclusion may emerge from the Equity Funding fraud. Three Equity Funding auditors have been found guilty on multiple criminal counts of securities fraud. Robert M. Toeffler, Equity Funding's trustee in bankruptcy, concluded in his November 1974, report that, "Had the auditors properly discharged their obligations, the fraud would have been caught years ago."[6]

The lesson of the apparent contrast is clear: No matter how efficacious a prescribed body of audit standards and procedures may be when they are employed in a properly conducted audit, the auditors must adhere to them if they are to be effective. If the Equity Funding audit was simply a "bum job," *it may be appropriate to reassess the institutional and organizational arrangements relating to audit engagements rather than the framework of auditing principles.* The failure of the Special Committee to consider this issue is understandable in view of the nature of their basic charge and given the circumstances (especially the existence of pending litigation) in which their report was issued. This should not, however, be a prelude to ostrich-like behavior on the part of accountants in regard to this issue. All our experience indicates that it would be far better for the profession itself to address such problems, rather than leaving them to the courts and the government. The recent increased attention given to "quality control" in auditing by public accounting firms is an encouraging indication of efforts in this direction.

The Similarities

Despite the dissimilarities of the McKesson and Equity Funding cases, the similarities are striking. One is the parallel in the business environment in which the two frauds were disclosed. The revelations of the McKesson case broke during the continuing economic malaise of the 1930s in which the prestige of business was at a very low ebb. It should be recalled that the question of whether the audit function should be performed in the private or public sector was still an issue in the wake of the securities legislation enacted a few years earlier. It was something less than a comfortable time for the accounting profession to grapple with a sensational fraud case.

The Equity Funding fraud also broke at an awkward time for accountants. Already besieged by the demands and retributions of investors in an age of consumerism, and pressured by an activist SEC, the profession could only view this new scandal with trepidation. That a similar crisis was safely weathered in another trying period may reassure accountants. Such reassurance, however, should be coupled with a determination to respond as quickly and as effectively as the

---

[5] *Report of the Special Committee*, p. 31.

[6] "As Trial of Three Equity Funding Auditors Opens, Responsibility of CPA is Debated," *Wall Street Journal*, January 8, 1975, p. 30.

profession did in 1939. The report of the Special Committee should only mark the beginning, not the end, of this response.

A dreary similarity between the two cases is the way they both dramatically raised the issue of fraud detection by the auditor. In both cases, the conventional argument that routine audit procedures are not designed to detect fraud, particularly fraud perpetrated by top management, sounded rather hollow to lay observers. Whether this perspective can endure after Equity Funding, given its prior battering in a series of recent lesser frauds, remains to be seen.

The AICPA's Statement on Auditing Standards No. 1 includes this section on detection of fraud:

> In making the ordinary examination, the independent auditor is aware of the possibility that fraud may exist. Financial statements may be misstated as the result of defalcations and similar irregularities, or deliberate misrepresentation by management, or both . . . . However, the ordinary examination directed to the expression of an opinion on financial statements is not primarily or specifically designed, and cannot be relied upon, to disclose defalcations and other similar irregularities, although their discovery may result. Similarly, although the discovery of deliberate misrepresentation by management is usually more closely associated with the objective of the ordinary examination, such examination cannot be relied upon to assure its discovery.

This cautious approach to auditor responsibility for fraud detection inevitably draws attack in the wake of such scandals as the McKesson and Equity Funding cases. The auditor's desire to avoid responsibility for detection of all varieties of fraud is highly defensible, however, quite aside from his own self-interest. An examination designed to bring all possible cases of defalcation to light would be extremely expensive, could never provide absolute assurance, and the added costs would almost certainly exceed the benefits both at the level of the individual firm and in the aggregate. The issue of auditor detection of the type of fraud which was executed in the McKesson and Equity cases—massive, management-perpetrated fraud—cannot be so readily dismissed in light of current pressures. SEC Chairman Ray Garrett, Jr., for example, at the AICPA's 1973 annual meeting, stated flatly that he thought accountants should be willing to assume responsibility for the detection of management fraud.

The issue, simply stated, is whether auditor responsibility should differ for the relatively petty variety of embezzlement and defalcation as opposed to the kind of massive fraud which results in financial statements which are essentially fictional documents. The Special Committee explicitly rejected such a dichotomy:

> The question may be raised, whether, even if in ordinary circumstances audits cannot reasonably be expected to detect all material fraud, the expectation should not be different when, as in Equity Funding, the fraud is a "massive" one. In other words, it might be suggested that, assuming the term "massive" could be given a concrete definition, auditing standards should be such that an auditor's opinion would invariably constitute a reasonable assurance that no "massive" fraud existed such as in Equity Funding. The committee does not believe that such a suggestion is sound.

The Special Committee indicated that *massive* might mean the *magnitude of falsified figures* (or the losses of those relying on them), the *extent of collusion*, or the *number of accounts* affected. The chances of auditor detection generally increase directly with increases in any of these three. The fact remains, however, that skillful collusion, the use of forged documents and the failure to record transactions may result in an escape from detection at varying degrees of "massiveness" as defined in any of these fashions. In the committee's view, therefore, it is impracticable to prescribe auditing standards or procedures which would provide absolute assurance with respect to detection for any defined degree of massiveness. Thus the committee endorsed the extant position of the profession in regard to fraud detection and only urged the rephrasing of the formal expression of that position.

The Lessons of the Fraud Cases

The principal lesson of the McKesson and Equity Funding frauds is that auditor reliance on the representations of management must be coupled with auditor alertness to any signals that such reliance is unwarranted. There is evidence that the accounting profession is moving quickly to encourage such vigilance on the part of auditors.

The recommendations of the Auditing Standards Executive Committee of the AICPA in regard to related party transactions should serve to foster a greater degree of such wariness among auditors. Transactions between related entities were key features of both the McKesson and Equity frauds. The proposed statement directs the auditor to examine related party transactions with an eye toward the disclosure of their substantive economic effects rather than just their legal form. Procedures relating to related party transactions include audit steps that depart somewhat from conventional patterns. These include checks of the records of the related contracting party in a transaction, and reference to various other documents outside the traditional "audit trail." While a related party transaction is generally to be accounted for as any other transaction, these audit steps are meant to help assure full and substantive disclosure.

One large CPA firm has developed a set of guidelines for its audit personnel which are intended to alert them to the possibility of management fraud.[7] A number of "warning signals" are cited in these guidelines relating to conditions which might possibly tempt management to tamper with its financial

---

[7] "Spotting the Fraud Cases," *Business Week*, February 17, 1975.

records, including a strained cash position, the existence of strong pressures to maintain a good earnings trend, dependence on a small number of products or customers, customer collection difficulties and management domination by a small number of individuals. The firm's auditors are advised to pay special attention to transactions that occur very near the end of a reporting period.

The SEC, in ASR No. 174, has also urged auditors to be on the alert for signals that indicate management might be seeking to conceal a deterioration in the financial position of a firm. Such signals include the recognition of income from transactions which do not reflect actual economic changes, unwarranted attempts to defer expense recognition or to avoid recognition of losses, and timing of major transactions so as to achieve apparent improvements in the financial statements.

The major remedial steps taken in the wake of the McKesson case—new requirements relating to confirmation of receivables by direct communication with debtors and observation of the taking of the inventory—constituted a step away from complete reliance on the representations of management. It appears that the Equity Funding fraud has served to trigger additional steps in the same direction. In addition to the measures referred to above, these may encompass such "loophole-closing" measures as requiring confirmation of insurance policies by communication with policyholders[8] and more extensive employment of existing tests of asset existence.Ω

---

[8] Auditors of insurance firms have generally relied on tests of premium income to obtain evidence regarding the existence of policies. This was done in the case of Equity Funding but, since the architects of the fraud had duly recorded premium receipts for the nonexistent policies, the procedure was ineffective.

9

Related Parties

(Section 334, SAS No. 45)

SAS No. 45, *Related Parties* provides guidance as to those procedures that should be considered when auditors perform an examination of financial statements in accordance with GAAS to identify related party transactions and to satisfy themselves as to the substance of these transactions as well as financial statement disclosure.

The term *related parties* denotes the reporting entity; its affiliates; principal owners, management, and members of their immediate families; entities for which investments are accounted for by the equity method; and any other party with which the reporting entity may deal when one party is prevented from fully pursuing its own separate interests. Usually it would consist of members of the board of directors, the president, secretary, treasurer, any vice-president directing a principal business function, and any other individual who performs similar policy-making functions.

Related party transactions include transactions between a parent and its subsidiary, transactions between subsidiaries of a common parent, and transactions the reporting entity engages in with other affiliated businesses, with management, or with principal stockholders. Transactions between or among the above parties are deemed to be related party transactions, even when accounting recognition is not given. Compensation arrangements, expense allowances, and similar transactions performed in the normal course of business between an enterprise and its management are not deemed to be related party transactions. This is also true of transactions eliminated in preparing consolidated or combined financial statements.

AUDIT PROCEDURES

An independent auditor conducting an examination in accordance with GAAS cannot expect to be assured that all related party transactions will be discovered. However, in the course of the examination, the auditor should be alert for the possible existence of material related party transactions. In this connection other audit procedures are used, specifically directed to related party transactions.

The possibility of related party transactions necessitates the auditor obtaining an understanding of management's responsibilities and the relationship of each component to the entity as a whole in order to ascertain the scope of the work to be performed. The auditor should evaluate internal accounting controls over management activities as well as considering the business purpose of the various components of the entity. Generally, the style and structure of business operations are developed considering such factors as the abilities of management, tax and legal considerations, product diversification, and geographical location. However, experience has proven that on occasion business structure and operating style have been deliberately designed to conceal related party transactions. Unless otherwise indicated, transactions with related parties should be assumed to be in the ordinary course of business. (An audit program for related party transactions is presented in an accompanying article.)

DISCLOSURE

The auditor, to obtain assurance that the client has made adequate disclosure in the financial statements with respect to related party transactions should ascertain whether sufficient competent evidential matter has been obtained so as to understand the relationship of the parties and the substance of the transaction. The auditor should, at this point, evaluate all information available concerning the transaction and be satisfied on the basis of professional judgment that the transaction is adequately disclosed.

A reporting entity that has participated in related party transactions that are material in nature should, as specified by *Statement of Financial Accounting Standards* No. 57, "Related Party Disclosures," disclose in its financial statements the following information:

Nature of the relationship

A description of transactions for the period, including amounts, if any, and such other information as is deemed appropriate for an understanding of the effects on the financial statements

Dollar amount of transactions and the effects of any change in the method of establishing terms from that used in the preceding period

Amounts due from or to related parties and, when not apparent, terms and manner of settlement

In nonroutine transactions, it will generally not be possible to ascertain whether a particular transaction would have occurred if the parties had not been related, or, given that it would have occurred, what the terms and manner of settlement might have been. Accordingly, representations to the effect that a transaction was made on terms no less favorable than those that would have been obtained if the transaction had been with a nonrelated party are difficult to substantiate. If such representation appears in the client's financial statements and the auditor cannot reach a conclusion as to the propriety thereof, consideration should be given to including in the auditor's report a comment to that effect and expressing a qualified opinion or disclaiming an opinion. If it is believed that the representation is misleading, the auditor should express a qualified or adverse opinion, depending on materiality.

CASE 13

"ARE BOB AND CAROL AND TED AND ALICE RELATED PARTIES?"

Your firm is conducting the annual audit of Robert H. Perry Manufacturing Company, for the year ended June 30, 19x7. Perry is a relatively small candy manufacturing company that produces a variety of assorted packaged candies sold primarily through a department store chain and to several independent candy stores.

The Company, which is owned by Bob Perry and his wife Carol, has been in operation for several years. Bob is the principal stockholder, Chairman of the Board and the President, and he runs the manufacturing operations of the business. Carol, who is also a principal stockholder, is the Secretary of the Corporation and handles financial and accounting matters.

In addition to Bob and Carol, there are five other stockholders all related to the Perrys in one way or another. The salaries that Bob and Carol receive from the Company vary considerably from year to year, depending on earnings of the Company and their personal financial and tax status.

The Company's primary source of income is derived from sales to the department store chain, which constitutes approximately 60 percent of total revenue. The sales made to the independent candy stores, none of which are material in relation to overall operations, comprise approximately 15 percent of total revenue. The remaining sales are made through a local candy store owned exclusively by Ted Reem, a 12 percent minority stockholder in Perry Manufacturing Company and Bob's brother-in-law. Ted's wife Alice is a 20 percent stockholder in Perry.

Perry is the sole franchise manufacturer of "chocolate delight," a brand of chocolate candy bar. This product constitutes approximately 20 percent of all candy sales and a royalty is paid to Hershman Candy Company based on gross sales.

CASE DISCUSSION QUESTIONS

1. Explain, in your own words, the meaning of the term *related parties*.

2. SAS No. 45 includes the terms *affiliate*, *control*, *principal owner*, and *management*. Discuss the meaning of each of these terms.

3. Identify the related parties in the case. Explain why you consider them to be related parties.

4. Your audit working papers contain the following information:

   An account receivable in the amount of $29,000 appears on the aging schedule. The receivable represents credit sales made to a local candy store owned by Ted Reem. The balance in the receivable account has accumulated over a five year period. Cash payments have been received from Reem's store each year, but credit sales have always exceeded cash received. When questioned concerning the receivable, both Bob and Carol indicated that Reem has been unable to keep his account current. However, both insist that the amount will eventually be collected.

   a. Is this a related party transaction?

   b. Do GAAP require special accounting treatment for this transaction?

5. What related party disclosure requirements are required for Perry Manufacturing's financial statements?

6. What kinds of transactions may indicate the existence of related parties?

7. What procedures should independent auditors use to satisfy themselves as to the purpose, nature, and extent of identified related party transactions and their effect on the financial statements?

PRACTITIONERS FORUM

An audit program for related party transactions

In the July 1977 issue of the Practitioners Forum, Dan M. Guy and Raymond J. Clay gave us a flowchart of SAS no. 6. Drs. Courtenay L. Granger and Thomas D. Hubbard, professors of accounting at Virginia Polytechnic Institute, have prepared an audit program for SAS no. 6. Hubbard is the author of the AICPA course manual, Accounting and Auditing Annual Updating Workshop. *Currently, Granger is on academic leave from VPI and is working with the firm of Andrews, Burket & Co., Box 13445, Roanoke, Virginia 24034, which has used his program.*

The purpose of Statement on Auditing Standards (SAS) no. 6, *Related Party Transactions,* is to set up guidelines for financial audit procedures that can assist the auditor in the identification of related party transactions so that the economic substance of these transactions and the adequacy of their disclosure in financial statements may be evaluated.

Accounting data is the result of a process designed to measure the substance of economic events that affect an enterprise's financial affairs. It is important to recognize that the validity of the accounting process is dependent upon certain assumptions regarding the way the entity operates. An important consideration underlying the validity of financial statements is the separate-entity assumption. That is, the entity reported on is assumed to have independent discretionary power over the resources committed to it and is an identifiable accounting unit whose transactions and interests are clearly separate from the transactions and interests of owners, managers and others. Whenever the assumption of separateness becomes

invalid, then the economic substance represented by traditional accounting entries based on this assumption may also be invalid and could result in financial statement users' being misled.

In cases where common ownership or management control exists, revenues and cost can be allocated between or among two or more entities without the economic considerations which normally prevail in separate entities' pursuing their own separate interests. For example, services may be provided to a related party without charge or sales to unrelated parties may be allocated among the related parties based upon other than economic considerations. Obviously, related party transactions are not at arm's length as is the case with unrelated party transactions. Although the accounting form of the entry remains the same in each situation, the economic substance of the exchange between related parties does not necessarily follow the accounting form.

At some point during the course of a financial audit, the auditor has always had to satisfy himself that the economic substance of the events recorded is reflected in the firm's financial statements. Since December 26, 1975, the effective date of SAS no. 6, this judgment has become even more important in auditing. Consequently, the preparation of an audit program for the determination of the existence of related parties and the identification of related party transactions can be crucial for any examination made in accordance with generally accepted auditing standards.

The audit program presented below is not intended to specify the form or detailed procedures which will fit all related party transaction audit programs. Such audit programs should be designed to meet the circumstances and auditor's needs on the individual engagement. Nonetheless, we believe that the audit program beginning on page 50 can serve as a useful guide and checklist for compliance with the auditing procedures outlined in SAS no. 6 regarding related party transactions.

Audit program: Related party transactions
Client:
Date of examination:

Audit objectives and definitions. Related party transactions are required disclosures by promulgated auditing standards as set forth in SAS no. 6. This pronouncement and related interpretations should be reviewed by the staff prior to the audit.

The term "related party" means the reporting entity and its affiliates (an affiliate is an entity that is directly or indirectly controlled by the reporting entity or controls the reporting entity), principal owners (an owner or known beneficial owner of more than 10 percent of the voting interests of the reporting entity), management, members of the immediate family of a principal owner or member of management,[1] entities for which investments are accounted for by the equity method and other entities where economic or other operating relationships may create situations where one party has the ability to significantly influence the management or operating policies of the other.

The audit should identify the existence of related parties, identify related party transactions that may have a material impact on the financial statements and ensure appropriate reporting and disclosure of such transactions.

Audit personnel should obtain an understanding of management's responsibilities and the relationship of each corporate component to the total business entity. The auditors should carefully consider the business purpose served by the various components of the entity. Staff should be aware that business structure and operating style are occasionally deliberately designed to obscure related party transactions.

In identifying possible related parties and corresponding transactions, staff should be aware of the possibility that transactions with related parties may have been motivated solely, or in large measure, by particular business or industry

conditions. The following conditions, for example, may indicate related party situations:

☐ Lack of sufficient working capital or credit to continue the business.

☐ An urgent desire for a continued favorable earnings record to support the price of the company's stock.

☐ An overly optimistic earnings forecast.

☐ Dependence on relatively few products, customers or transactions for the ongoing success of the venture.

☐ A declining industry, characterized by a large number of business failures.

☐ Excess capacity.

☐ Significant litigation, especially litigation between stockholders and management.

☐ Significant obsolescence dangers if the company is in a high-technology industry.

Staff should be satisfied as to the adequacy of disclosure about related party transactions. Sufficient evidence should be gathered to provide an understanding of the relationship of the parties, the substance of the transactions and the effects on the financial statements. Adequate disclosure should include the following:

☐ The nature of the relationship(s).

☐ A description of the transactions (summarized when appropriate) for the reported period, including amounts and such other information necessary to an understanding of the effects on the financial statements.

☐ The dollar volume of transactions and the effects of any change in the method of establishing terms from that used in the preceding period (consistency of treatment).

☐ Amounts due from or to related parties and, if not otherwise apparent, the terms and manner of settlement.[2]

Audit procedures. Each of the following procedures should be reviewed and initialed by the staff:

1 Evaluate internal accounting controls over management activities.

2 Evaluate the company's procedures for identifying and properly accounting for related party transactions.

3 Ask appropriate management personnel for the names of all related parties and any transactions with these parties during the period.

4 Review the reporting entity's filings with the SEC and with other regulatory agencies for the names of related parties and for other businesses in which officers and directors occupy directorships or management positions.

5 Determine the names of all pension and other trusts established for the benefit of employees and the names of the officers and trustees thereof. (If the trusts are managed by or under the trusteeship of management, they should be deemed to be related parties.)

6 Review stockholder listings of closely held companies in order to identify principal stockholders.

7 Review workpapers of prior years for the names of known related parties.

8 Ask predecessor, principal or other auditors of related entities about their knowledge of existing relationships and the extent of management's involvement in material transactions.

9 Review material investment transactions during the period under examination to determine whether the nature and extent of investments during the period create related parties.

10 A list of known related parties should be provided to all audit personnel working on the engagement so that they may become aware of transactions with such parties during their examinations.

11 Review the minutes of meetings of the board of directors and executive operating committees for information as to material transactions authorized or discussed at their meetings.

12 Review proxy and other material filed with the SEC and comparable data filed with other regulatory agencies for information as to material transactions with related parties.

13 Review conflict-of-interest statements obtained by the company from its management.

14 Review the extent and nature of business transacted with major customers, suppliers, borrowers and lenders for indications of previously undisclosed relationships.

15 Consider whether any transac-

---

[1] "Auditing Interpretations," JofA, Mar. 76, p.70.

[2] Ibid.

tions are occurring that are not being given accounting recognition, such as receiving or providing accounting, management or other services at no charge or a major stockholder's absorbing corporate expenses.

16 Review accounting records for large, unusual or nonrecurring transactions or balances, paying particular attention to transactions recognized at or near the end of the reporting period.

17 Review confirmations of compensating balance arrangements for indications that balances are or were maintained for or by related parties.

18 Review invoices from law firms and response to lawyers' inquiry letters for indication of the existence of related parties or related party transactions.

19 Review confirmations of loans receivable and payable for indications of guarantees. When guarantees are indicated, determine their nature and the relationships, if any, of the guarantors to the reporting entity.

20 In examining related party transactions, obtain an understanding of the business purpose of the transaction (a discussion of the purpose of certain transactions with the specific parties involved may be necessary to a full understanding).

21 Examine invoices, executed copies of agreements, contracts and other pertinent documents, such as receiving reports and shipping documents.

22 Determine whether related party transactions have been approved by the board of directors or other appropriate officials.

23 Test for reasonableness the compilation of amounts to be disclosed, or considered for disclosure, in the financial statements.

24 Arrange for the audits of intercompany account balances to be performed as of concurrent dates, even if fiscal years differ. Ensure examination of specified, important and representative related party transactions by the auditors of each of the parties, with an appropriate exchange of relevant information.

25 Inspect or confirm and obtain satisfaction as to the transferability and value of collateral supporting related party transactions.

26 When necessary to fully understand the business purpose or substance of related party transactions. perform the following extended procedures:

a Confirm transaction amount and terms, including guarantees and other significant data, with the other party(s) to the transaction.

b Inspect evidence in possession of the other party(s) to the transaction.

c Confirm or discuss significant information with intermediaries, such as banks, guarantors, agents or attorneys.

d Refer to financial publications, trade journals, credit agencies and other sources if there is reason to believe that customers, suppliers or other enterprises with which material amounts of business have been transacted may be financially unstable.

e For material uncollected balances, guarantees and other obligations, obtain information as to the financial capability of the other party(s) to the transaction (such information may be obtained from audited financial statements, unaudited financial statements, income tax returns and reports issued by regulatory agencies, taxing authorities, financial publications or credit agencies).

Using the Work
of a Specialist

(Section 336, SAS No. 11)

SAS No. 11 defines a specialist, for purposes of employment by an independent auditor, as a person (or firm) possessing special skill or knowledge in a particular field other than accounting or auditing. Examples of specialists working with accountants include actuaries, appraisers, attorneys, engineers, and geologists. The definition of a specialist is further qualified by SAS No. 11 in that the term does not apply to a specialist who is a member of the auditor's staff (except as explained later) or to a client's lawyer in his or her capacity as the respondent to an auditor's inquiry letter concerning legal matters involving a client. Also, the term specialist, as used in SAS No. 11, does not apply to a person whose special skill or knowledge relates to the internal affairs or business practices of the client, such as a credit or plant manager.

DECISION TO USE THE WORK OF A SPECIALIST

Auditors are specialists in their field and as such, are expected to exercise professional judgment in performing an examination of financial statements. The auditor cannot rely on another person, no matter how well qualified, in making judgmental decisions in the areas of accounting and auditing. For example, the CPA is required by GAAS to observe the inventory-taking and confirm accounts receivable. Others cannot be employed to perform these functions for the auditor. On the other hand, the auditor is not expected to be a valuer of merchandise and, in those matters that require special knowledge, the services of a specialist may be appropriate. Examples of situations that the auditor may decide require using the work of a specialist include the following:

Valuation (works of art, special drugs, and restricted securities)

Determination of physical characteristics relating to quantity on hand or condition (mineral reserves or materials stored in piles above ground)

Determination of amounts derived by using specialized techniques or methods (certain actuarial determinations)

Interpretation of technical requirements, regulations, or agreements (the potential significance of contracts or other legal documents, or legal title to property)

SELECTING A SPECIALIST

When auditors find it necessary to employ the services of a specialist, they must satisfy themselves concerning the professional qualifications and reputation of the specialist. This is accomplished by inquiry or other procedures, as appropriate. The auditors should consider:

The professional certification, license, or other recognition of the competence of the specialist in his or her field, as appropriate

The reputation and standing of the specialist in the views of his or her peers and others familiar with his or her capability or performance

The relationship, if any, of the specialist to the client

Using the work of a specialist related to the client is acceptable. However, an auditor ordinarily should attempt to employ the services of an outside specialist as the work of an independent specialist would require less corroborating evidence than would the work of a specialist in the client's employment.

An understanding should exist between the client, the specialist, and the CPA as to the nature of the work to be performed by the specialist. This understanding should be documented in the auditor's working papers and the form and content of the specialist's report should be such that it will enable the auditor to make the intended use of the specialist's work.

USING THE FINDINGS OF THE SPECIALIST

An auditor should obtain an understanding of the methods or assumptions used by the specialist to determine whether the findings are suitable for corroborating the representations included in the client's financial statements. This does not indicate that the CPA must understand all of the formulas or other technical material used by the specialist. It does mean, however, that the CPA should be assured that any data used by the specialist that is taken from the client's records or assumptions made concerning business transactions, ratios, interest rates, and so forth, are both reasonable and representative. The CPA should consider whether the specialist's findings support the representations included in the statements and make appropriate tests of the accounting data provided to the specialist by the client. Ordinarily, an auditor will use the work of a specialist unless circumstances indicate that the findings are unreasonable in the circumstances.

EFFECT OF THE SPECIALIST'S WORK ON THE CPA'S REPORT

An auditor may rely on the work of a specialist in issuing an opinion when the specialist's findings have been sufficiently corroborated. The CPA should apply additional auditing procedures when there is a material difference between the specialist's findings and the representations included in the financial statements, or if the auditor believes that the determinations made by the specialist are unreasonable. If the CPA is unable to resolve the matter it is ordinarily necessary to qualify the opinion or disclaim an opinion because of a scope restriction—an inability to obtain sufficient competent evidential matter concerning a material item. If the CPA, as a result of performing additional auditing procedures, concludes that the financial statements are materially misstated, a qualified or an adverse opinion should be expressed because of a lack of fair presentation.

The CPA should not refer to the work of a specialist in expressing an unqualified opinion as such reference might detract from the purpose of the opinion. It is permissible, however, to refer to the specialist when the auditor decides to modify the opinion based on the findings of the specialist.

APPLICABILITY OF SAS NO. 11 TO SPECIALISTS ON AUDIT STAFF

SAS No. 11 states that the provisions of that Statement do not apply to using the work of a specialist who is a member of the auditor's staff. This exclusion, according to an Auditing Interpretation of SAS No. 11, relates to a specialist who is also serving as a member of the audit staff. For example, an actuary who is also an auditor and performs actuarial services for an audit client and also participates in the examination of that client's financial statements. SAS No. 11 is applicable to the work of a specialist in the employ of an auditor who is not simultaneously engaged in the examination of the financial statements of the client he or she is performing services for as a specialist.

CASE 14

USING THE WORK OF A SPECIALIST

Wilson & Wilson (WW), Certified Public Accountants, are conducting their annual audit of Burke Roofing, Inc., for the year ended January 31, 19x1. Burke is a small but very successful industrial roofing contractor. The firm's success is attributed to the owner's ability to hire and retain key employees. In order to maintain high quality personnel, Mr. John Burke established an attractive pension plan several years ago.

To assure themselves that the annual pension cost provision is accounted for in accordance with APB Opinion No. 8, "Accounting for the Cost of Pension Plans," WW has engaged the services of Mulligan & Harrington, Inc., a firm of consulting actuaries. The actuaries were informed that their findings would support financial statement amounts regarding current pension costs.

Mulligan & Harrington's study revealed that the annual charge for pension cost for Burke Roofing, Inc. for the year ended January 31, 19x1 should be $135,650, which includes normal cost, an amount equivalent to interest, at an appropriate rate, on unfunded prior service costs, and a provision for vested benefits. In their report Mulligan & Harrington explained the objectives and scope of their work and further stated that they were not related to Burke Roofing, Inc. The report also contained a description of the methods and assumptions used in arriving at the annual charge for pension costs as well as a comparison with the methods and assumptions applied in the preceding period. Mulligan & Harrington concluded discussion of the nature of their work with a statement of their understanding of the corroborative use of their findings in relation to representations made in the financial statements.

CASE DISCUSSION QUESTIONS

1. Should Wilson & Wilson accept, at face value, the report issued by the consulting actuaries? Justify your answer.

2. Give examples of specialists and examples of the types of matters that may require the independent auditor to use the work of a specialist.

3. Are there situations in which the independent auditor would make reference to the specialist in his or her report? If so, why?

4. Assume that WW believes that the charge for pension costs, as determined by Mulligan & Harrington, is unreasonable.

    a. What course of action should they take?

    b. What course of action should WW take if they are unable to resolve the matter?

    c. What position should WW take if after performing additional procedures and using another specialist, it is determined that the representations are not in conformity with GAAP?

Inquiry of a Client's Lawyer

(Section 337, SAS No. 12)

Requesting that a client send a letter to its legal counsel concerning litigation, claims, and assessments that may require recognition in the financial statements is a generally accepted auditing procedure (SAS No. 12).

ACCOUNTING AND AUDITING CONSIDERATIONS

Management is responsible for adopting policies and procedures to identify, evaluate, and account for litigation, claims, and assessments. FASB Statement No. 5, *Accounting for Contingencies*, outlines the procedures to be followed in accounting for loss contingencies, including those arising from legal considerations.* The auditor's responsibility is to obtain evidential matter relevant to:

The existence of a condition, situation, or set of circumstances indicating an uncertainty as to the possible loss to an entity arising from litigation, claims, and assessments

The period in which the underlying cause for legal action occurred

The degree of probability of an unfavorable outcome

The amount or range of potential loss

---

*FASB No. 5 defines a contingency as an existing condition, situation, or set of circumstances involving uncertainty as to possible gain (a gain contingency) or loss (a loss contingency) to an enterprise that will ultimately be resolved when one or more future events occur or fail to occur. Resolution of the uncertainty may confirm the acquisition of an asset or the reduction of a liability or the loss or impairment of an asset or the incurrence of a liability. When a loss contingency exists, the likelihood that the future event or events will confirm the loss or impairment of an asset or the incurrence of a liability can range from *probable to remote*. *Probable* means the future event or events are likely to occur. *Reasonably possible* means the chance of the future event or events occurring is more than remote but less than likely. *Remote* means the chance of the future event or events occurring is slight.

FASB No. 5 requires an estimated loss from a loss contingency to be accrued by a charge to income if information available prior to issuance of the financial statements indicates that it is *probable* that an asset had been impaired or a liability had been incurred at the date of the financial statements and the amount of loss can be reasonably estimated. If accrual of a loss contingency is not made because the conditions for accrual are not met, disclosure of the contingency is required when there is at least a *reasonable possibility* that a loss may have been incurred. Disclosure is not required for a loss contingency involving an unasserted claim or assessment when there has been no manifestation by a potential claimant of an awareness of a possible claim or assessment unless it is considered *probable* that a claim will be asserted and there is a *reasonable possibility* that the outcome will be unfavorable.

An auditor looks primarily to management and its legal counsel as sources of information concerning litigation, claims, and assessments. Accordingly, the CPA's procedures should include the following:

Inquiry of and discuss with management concerning the policies and procedures adopted for identifying, evaluating, and accounting for litigation, claims, and assessments

Obtain from management a description and evaluation of litigation, claims, and assessments that existed at the date of the balance sheet being reported on, and during the period from the balance sheet date to the date the information is furnished, including an identification of those matters referred to legal counsel, and obtain assurances from management, ordinarily in writing, that they have disclosed all such matters required to be disclosed by FASB No. 5

Examine documents in the client's possession concerning litigation, claims, and assessments, including correspondence and invoices from lawyers

Obtain assurance from management, ordinarily in writing, that it has disclosed all unasserted claims that the lawyer has advised them are probable of assertion and must be disclosed in accordance with FASB No. 5. Also the auditor, with the client's permission, should inform the lawyer that the client has given the auditor this assurance. This client representation may be communicated by the client in the inquiry letter or by the auditor in a separate letter.

Procedures the auditor ordinarily performs as a regular part of every examination that may disclose pending or threatened litigation, claims against the client, or assessments made against the client as a result of legal action, include:

Requests that the client's management send a letter of inquiry to those lawyers with whom they consulted concerning litigation, claims, and assessments

Reviewing minutes of meetings of stockholders, directors, and appropriate committees held during and subsequent to the period being examined

Reviewing contracts, loan agreements, leases, and correspondence from taxing or other governmental agencies, and similar documents

Obtaining information concerning guarantees from bank confirmation forms

Inspecting other documents for possible guarantees by the client

INQUIRY OF A CLIENT'S LAWYER

The auditor's role of evidence-gathering regarding litigation, claims, and assessments is primarily one of corroborating information provided by the client and information obtained from performing auditing procedures. A letter of inquiry to the client's lawyer is the CPA's primary means of corroboration of the information furnished by management. Evidential matter obtained from the client's inside general counsel or legal department may provide the necessary corroboration. However, the use of inside counsel is not considered a substitute for any information outside counsel refuses to furnish.

The matters that should be covered in a letter of audit inquiry include, but are not limited to, the following:

Identification of the company (including subsidiaries) covered by the auditor's opinion and the date of the examination.

A list of pending or threatened litigation, claims, and assessments with respect to which the lawyer has been engaged and to which he or she has devoted substantive attention on behalf of the company in the form of legal consultation or representation. The list may be prepared by the client or the client may request the lawyer to prepare the list.

A list, which must be prepared by the client, that describes and evaluates unasserted claims and assessments that management considers to be *probable* of assertion, and that, if asserted, would have at least a *reasonable possibility* of an unfavorable outcome. This list should include matters to which the lawyer has devoted substantive attention.

As to each threatened or pending litigation, claim, or assessment listed in the letter, a request that the lawyer either furnish the following information or comment on those matters as to which his or her views differ from those stated by management:

> A description of the nature of the matter, the progress of the case to date, and the action the company intends to take

> An evaluation of the likelihood of an unfavorable outcome and an estimate, if one can be made, of the amount or range of potential loss

> With respect to a list prepared by management, an identification of the omission of any pending or threatened litigation, claims, and assessments or a statement that the list of such matters is complete

As to unasserted claims listed by management, a request that the lawyer comment on those matters as to which his or her views concerning the description or evaluation of the matter may differ from those stated by management

A statement by the client, that the client understands that the lawyer will advise him or her of unasserted possible claims or assessments that may require disclosure in accordance with the requirements of FASB No. 5. The letter should include a request that the lawyer confirm whether this understanding is correct

A request that the lawyer specifically identify the nature of and reasons for limitations on his or her response

Inquiry need not be made of the client's legal counsel regarding items that are considered to be immaterial. However, the CPA, in requesting the lawyer to comment on material items, should come to an understanding with the client's lawyer concerning what the CPA considers to be material for financial statement presentation.

ILLUSTRATIVE INQUIRY LETTER

Presented below is an illustrative lawyer's inquiry letter that incorporates the requirements of SAS No. 12:

M A R A   M A N U F A C T U R I N G   C O M P A N Y

1537 West Atlantic Street, Springfield, Missouri 21304

December 31, 19x1

John Marshall, Attorney at Law
1600 Kearney Avenue
Springfield, Missouri 21304

Dear Sir:

Holdren & Co., 2140 Lee Street, Springfield, Missouri 21304, are making their usual annual examination of our accounts, and we will appreciate your furnishing them with information concerning the following matters as of December 31, 19x1 and as of the date of your reply:

1. A list of all open engagements you are now handling, including a description of the matter and its present status, the action the company intends to take, an evaluation of the likelihood of an unfavorable outcome and an estimate of the amount or range of potential loss, including court costs and legal fees.

2. Any explanation that you consider necessary to supplement our representations to Holdren & Co. that there are no unasserted claims against the company that are probable of assertion and, if asserted, would have at least a reasonable possibility of an unfavorable outcome.

   We understand that whenever, in the course of performing legal services for us with respect to a matter recognized to involve an unasserted possible claim or assessment that may call for financial statement disclosure, if you have formed a professional conclusion that we should disclose or consider disclosure concerning such possible claim or assessment, as a matter of professional responsibility to us, you will so advise us and will consult with us concerning the question of such disclosure and the applicable requirements of Statement of Financial Accounting Standards No. 5. Please specifically confirm to our auditors that our understanding is correct.

3. Any stock option agreements, subordination agreements, leases, guarantees of company debts by stockholders, officers or others, and any matters affecting title to assets of which you have knowledge.

4. A listing of companies of which you have knowledge, that may be deemed to be affiliates or related parties of the company.

5. Any amount due you for services and expenses.

Please specifically identify the nature of and reasons for any limitation on your response.

With respect to items (3) and (4), you need to report only items which have not previously been reported or which have been modified since your last letter replying to our request for this information.

The scheduled completion date of our auditors' examination is such that you should send your letter to Holdren & Co. on or about February 15, 19x2.

Sincerely,

Richard A. Mara
President

In special situations, involving technical points of law, the CPA may obtain the information normally included in the inquiry letter in a conference with the client's attorney. In such cases, the conclusions reached concerning the need for accounting or for disclosure of litigations, claims, and assessments should be appropriately documented in the auditor's working papers.

When a client has terminated a relationship with an attorney, the CPA should consider inquiries as to the reasons for the termination of the relationship as it may affect financial statement disclosures.

LIMITATIONS ON A LAWYER'S RESPONSE

A lawyer may limit the response to a letter of inquiry to those matters to which he or she has given substantive attention. Also, the response may be limited for other reasons. For example, a lawyer may not be able to respond as to the outcome of a pending matter under litigation because there is insufficient experience in trying matters of this nature or because the client or other firms in the client's industry are not experienced with this kind of litigation. Such restrictions are not considered limitations on the scope of the auditor's examination. In such circumstances, the auditor ordinarily will normally conclude that the financial statements are affected by an uncertainty concerning the outcome of a future event which is not susceptible of reasonable estimation. If the effect of the matter is material, the CPA ordinarily will issue a qualified opinion.

When a lawyer has devoted substantive effort to matters covered in the inquiry letter and refuses to furnish the information requested in the letter, such limitation would be considered a limitation on the scope of the auditor's examination sufficient to prohibit the issuance of an unqualified opinion.

The American Bar Association has approved a statement of policy regarding lawyers' responses to auditors' requests for information.

CASE 15

"LET'S TALK TO HECTOR'S MOUTHPIECE"

A client and his or her lawyer have a "privileged" relationship—the attorney is prohibited by law from revealing to others confidential information imparted by the client. Corporation lawyers, however, are now being held responsible by some courts when their clients, upon their advice, fail to disclose information in their financial statements that was deemed to be required in order to make the statements not misleading. Lawyers now have a responsibility to advise their clients regarding financial statement disclosure involving litigation, claims, and assessments and to respond to proper inquiries addressed to them by CPAs in an attorney's letter.

You are performing the annual audit of Hector, Inc., a local manufacturing company. As a result of inquiry and discussion with client personnel concerning the company's policies and procedures adopted for identifying, evaluating, and accounting for litigation, claims, and assessments, the following was noted:

> Hector is presently being sued by a consumer organization for damages alleged suffered from using the company's product. The amount of damages claimed in the suit is very material in relation to both results of operations and financial position. Hector, however, carries an insurance policy that its legal counsel has determined will cover any damages sustained. Furthermore, Hector's legal counsel is of the opinion that the claims are without foundation and Hector will not sustain any loss as a result of the suit.

Peter Lorre, President of Hector, when confronted with the possibility of disclosing the litigation in the financial statements responded that disclosure was not required as there would be no loss to the Company. He took the position that disclosure may, in fact, damage the company's financial status with local bankers and thus impair its ability to obtain necessary short-term bank loans for working capital purposes. Mr. Lorre feels that the suit will be dropped and nothing will come of the matter.

CASE DISCUSSION QUESTIONS

1. SAS No. 12, "Inquiry of a Client's Lawyer Concerning Litigation, Claims, and Assessments," provides guidance on the procedures an auditor should follow in identifying litigation, claims, and assessments relating to the client's financial statements. These procedures apply when an auditor is performing an examination in accordance with generally accepted auditing standards.

   What is the client's responsibility regarding accounting for litigation, claims, and assessments?

2. With regard to the lawsuit facing Hector, what accounting and reporting is required by FASB No. 5, *Accounting for Contingencies*?

3. The contingency relating to the lawsuit was brought to the attention of the auditor as a result of inquiry and discussion with client personnel concerning Hector's policies regarding accounting for litigation, claims, and assessments. The auditor's examination normally includes certain procedures undertaken for different purposes that might also disclose litigation, claims, and assessments.

   a. What "other procedures" might disclose litigation, claims, and assessments?

   b. What evidential matter should an auditor obtain with respect to client litigation, claims, and assessments?

4. Assume that Peter Lorre informs you that there are no unasserted claims requiring disclosure in conformity with the requirements of FASB No. 5. He states that he reached this conclusion based on discussions with his legal counsel.

   a. Should you communicate with Hector's legal counsel regarding this assurance?

   b. Assuming communication is appropriate, what format would you follow?

5. An auditor ordinarily does not possess legal skills and, therefore, cannot make legal judgments concerning information coming to his or her attention. Accordingly, the auditor should request the client's management to send a letter of inquiry to those lawyers with whom they consulted concerning litigation, claims, and assessments.

   a. Is evidential matter obtained from a client's inside counsel sufficient for corroboration of management assertions regarding legal matters?

   b. What matters should be covered in a letter of audit inquiry?

6. Assume an auditor becomes aware that the client, during the period covered by the financial statements being examined, has changed legal counsel. Will such information influence procedures performed by the auditor regarding legal matters?

7. A lawyer's response regarding information requested in an inquiry letter may be limited for a number of reasons. Consider the following and indicate the effect, if any, on the auditor's reporting responsibilities:

   a. Hector's lawyer has not given substantive attention to a matter that was listed in the inquiry letter involving threatened litigation.

b.   Hector's lawyer refuses to comment on the lawsuit involving consumer damages, even though he has devoted substantive attention to this matter in the form of legal consultation with the client.

c.   Assume Hector's lawyer believves the consumer lawsuit has merit. However, because of inherent uncertainties he is unable to respond to an inquiry letter concerning the amount of range of potential loss resulting from the suit.

12

Working Papers

(Section 339, SAS No. 41)

Careful documentation and review of work performed is the basis of public accounting. GAAS require the auditor to gather sufficient competent evidential matter to support an opinion as to the overall fair presentation of financial position, results of operations, and changes in financial position, in conformity with GAAP or another comprehensive basis of accounting. Not only must sufficient competent evidential matter be obtained, but the auditor must document this evidence in the working papers. If called upon to testify in court concerning the adequacy of the audit examination and to demonstrate that an examination was performed in accordance with GAAS, the working papers will constitute the major defense and the auditor generally will successfully defend the work done or be found wanting almost entirely on the content of the working papers. The old adage that "The CPA is convicted by his own words" is often confirmed because CPAs sometimes tend to slight the importance of proper working paper documentation.

Working papers should be designed so as to meet the particular circumstances at hand and the auditor's needs on individual engagements. Working papers serve mainly to assist the auditor in the conduct of the audit work and provide an important support for the auditor's opinion, including the representation as to compliance with GAAS. Working papers are the records maintained by the auditor during the course of the examination of the client's financial statements and they generally include the procedures followed, the tests performed, the information obtained, and the conclusions reached. Working papers generally include such documentation as audit programs for each major audit area which identify the procedures performed, analyses made, memoranda, letters of confirmation, documented client representations, abstracts of company documents, and schedules or commentaries prepared or obtained by the auditor.

Factors affecting the auditor's judgment as to the quantity, type, and content of working papers desirable for a particular engagement include:

> The nature of the auditor's report

> The nature of the financial statements, schedules, or other information upon which the auditor is reporting

> The nature and condition of the client's records and internal controls

> The needs in the particular circumstances for supervision and review of the work performed by any assistants

Although the quantity, type, and content of working papers will vary with the circumstances, they generally would include or demonstrate the following:

Data sufficient to demonstrate that the financial statements or other information upon which the auditor is reporting were in agreement with (or reconciled with) the client's records

That the engagement has been planned, such as by use of work programs, and that the work of any assistants has been supervised and reviewed (compliance with the first standard of field work)

That the client's system of internal control had been reviewed and evaluated in determining the extent of the tests to which auditing procedures were restricted (compliance with the second standard of field work)

The auditing procedures followed and testing performed in obtaining evidential matter (compliance with the third standard of field work)

How exceptions and unusual matters, if any, disclosed by the procedures were resolved or treated

Appropriate commentaries prepared by the auditor indicating his or her conclusions concerning significant aspects of the engagement

The working papers are and remain the property of the auditor. The auditor's rights of ownership of working papers, however, are subject to certain ethical limitations designed to prevent improper disclosures by the auditor of confidential matters relating to the clients' affairs. The working papers should not be regarded as constituting a part of, or as a substitute for, the client's own accounting records. However, certain information usually appearing in the working papers should be provided to the client. For example, the auditor should give the client a copy of all adjusting journal entries affecting balances appearing on the client's financial statements. Also, if the client does not maintain detailed records regarding certain matters and the auditor computes amounts appearing in the financial statements, this information should also be provided to the client. For example, assuming the client's property records are incomplete, the auditor may prepare a schedule of property, plant, and equipment and compute depreciation expense. Copies of such working paper information is then considered part of the client's records and should be provided to the client.

The auditor should adopt reasonable procedures for the safe custody of the working papers at all times and retain them for a period of time sufficient to meet the needs of his or her practice and satisfy any legal requirements for retention.

SEPTEMBER 1978

Prior Year's Working Papers: Uses and Dangers

Last year's working papers are an essential audit tool,
but they must be used with caution or they can lead
to serious traps.

Manuel A. Tipgos, CPA, Ph.D.

IN the last few years, practically every aspect of the auditor's work has been subjected to close scrutiny, not only in terms of procedures, policies, and quality, but also in terms of the fundamental principles and concepts upon which the whole accounting function is based. Two of these serious appraisals stood quite prominently in the minds of accountants. First was the congressional investigations which threatened the free and independent functioning of the accounting profession in the private sector. Second was the significant successes of legal actions brought against public accountants which put to test the adequacy and reasonableness of the auditing standards, principles, procedures, and methods employed by the auditor as well as the resulting quality of the work performed. As a result, the accounting profession pledged to institute self-policing measures in an effort to calm down an apparently well-founded clamor for government intervention and control, and to reassure the public that it has attained a certain degree of maturity capable of improving and disciplining itself.

One of these significant self-policing measures is the periodic quality control reviews (or peer review) which the AICPA and the various state societies have adopted to attempt to insure the quality of the work performed by public accountants. As a result, major areas of the auditor's work have received renewed interest and discussion in the accounting literature. However, one aspect of the audit that appears to have escaped this discussion is the use of last year's working papers in performing the examination. A cursory review of accounting literature in the last five years does not reveal, except for a superficial commentary by Professor C. W. Bastable,[1] any significant discourse on the subject. This situation is disturbing because failure to understand the role of the prior year's working papers in an audit engagement may create serious problems for the auditor.

This article will discuss the positive and negative aspects of the auditor's reliance on last year's working papers. The discussion will start with the the potential dangers that may result from such reliance, and will move on to identify the benefits that can be derived from the intelligent and imaginative use of prior year's working papers.

Violation of Auditing Standards

The indiscriminate and unimaginative use of previous year's working papers may result in the violation of the first two standards of field work and the third general standard which requires professional care in the performance of the engagement.

Planning and supervision of assistants. The first standard of field work states: "The work is to be adequately planned and assistants, if any, are to be properly supervised.[2] This planning requirement is not, however, diligently followed, particularly on repeat engagements where last year's audit experience did not indicate any significant and unusual findings. In fact, in various situations encountered by this writer, planning was left to the "heavy" staff assigned to the audit whose planning horizon was seriously constrained by "what was done last year."

This situation could also result not only in lack or inadequate supervision of assistants as required by the first standard of field work, but also in inefficiency and waste in undertaking the audit. In one instance, the senior accountant on the job thought that the assistant

Manuel A. Tipgos, CPA, Ph.D., associate professor of accounting, University of Kentucky, is partly assigned to its Mara Institute of Technology, Kuala Lumpur, Malaysia. He was previously with Price Waterhouse & Co. and is a member of many professional societies. His article "Offensive Auditing" in the CPA Journal, September 1976, won the "Max Block" Award.

[1] C. W. Bastable, "Accounting and the Status Quo," *Journal of Accountancy*, (October 1977), pp. 47–48.
[2] *Codification of Statements on Auditing Standards* (New York: AICPA, 1977), p. 33.

auditor engaged to assist him was a "heavy" one. The latter was directed to carry on with the audit with minimal supervision. Asked what to do, the senior directed him to follow "what was done last year." When the deadline was fast approaching, the senior came to review the working papers only to find that the work performed was inadequate in relation to the objectives of the examination. (Incidentally, the objectives of the current year's audit were not discussed with the assistant). As a consequence, certain aspects of the audit had to be redone, and overtime work had to be undertaken resulting in a budget overrun which the auditor was unable to bill to the client.

Evaluation of internal control. The second standard of field work requires that:

> There is to be a proper study and evaluation of the existing internal control as a basis for reliance thereon and for the determination of the resultant extent of the tests to which auditing procedures are to be restricted.[3]

Undue reliance on last year's working papers may violate this standard. It is not uncommon in repeat engagements to complete the detail examination of certain accounts or functions before completing the review of internal control. If the auditor uses an internal control questionnaire, previous answers to the questionnaire as well as a superficial question and answer type of discussion with the client's staff is the primary basis for accomplishing the current year's review of internal control. In certain instances, an inexperienced audit assistant would request the client to read the questionnaire and to indicate his answers to the specific question addressed thereon. Naturally, the answer would be favorable and the answer which the auditor would want to hear. This writer once described the review of internal control in his first audit assignment as follows:

> In the classroom, we were told that the review of existing internal control determines the scope of the examination and the resulting extent of the tests to be performed by the auditor. In practice, however, "what was done last year" determines the extent of the work to be undertaken by the auditor.

Due care in performing the audit. The third general standard states: "Due professional care is to be exercised in the performance of the examination and the preparation of the report."[4] This standard requires that the auditor and/or his audit assistants should observe

---

[3] *Ibid.*, p. 41.
[4] *Ibid.*, p. 27.

the standards of field work, and, more particularly, that every aspect of the examination and at every level of supervision must be critically reviewed and supervised. It follows that any violation committed against the first two standards of field work as discussed in the preceding paragraphs would constitute a violation of the general standard of due professional care. Undoubtedly the situation could seriously damage the auditor's position if court litigation affecting his work would arise.

> ## 'It is not uncommon in repeat engagements to complete the detail examination of certain accounts or functions before completing the review of internal control.'

Complacency and "Satisficing" Audit

The auditor must guard against complacency based on the result of his reliance on last year's working papers. In a pre-audit meeting with the client, it is not uncommon for the auditor to ask the chief financial officer these questions: Is there anything significant or unusual that happened in your operation this year which we should be concerned about? Is there any area of your operation this year which you want us to pay close attention? Is there anything in particular that you would like us to do this year? Negative answers to these questions may create complacency on the part of the auditor and is considerably reinforced if there was nothing unusual or any significant areas of concern in the previous audit. But the fact is that, if the client or its financial officer has something to hide, negative answers to these questions would most likely be provided rather than risk a potential thorough audit.

Unfortunately, complacency on the part of the auditor may lead to a "satisficing" audit, particularly if deadlines are tight and the auditor's overall staffing requirements are creating certain problems. A "satisficing" audit may take the form of reducing the scope and extent of this year's examination in relation to last year's or "doing a little more" on top of what was done last year. This type of audit is not normally done to satisfy the professional curiosity or the professional skepticism or apprehensiveness of the auditor. For instance, in one audit engagement, the auditor has, for a number of years, concentrated the detail examination of inventories on a number of major product lines, the reason being that a considerable percentage of annual sales was accounted for by these product lines. The results of the examination in previous years were satisfactory, and no unusual or significant problems were noted. During the current year's audit, the same audit approach was followed, but the senior accountant directed his staff auditor to select one more product to be subjected to similar examination. Queried about this decision, (i.e., why add just one product, why not two or three, etc.) he stated that he wanted an added satisfaction and assurance that the inventory was in order. Unfortunately, a few months after the completion of the audit, the client discovered that about $200,000 of inventory of the product selected by the auditor for an extended examination was omitted from final inventory. The reason was that due to certain technical problems with the computer program, the accumulation of a number of products for final pricing was done manually and, apparently, such products were inadvertently left out.

Undeniably, the failure on the part of the auditor to detect such an error may have been caused by a number of reasons. However, there was no doubt that the complacency of the auditors and the "satisficing" audit performed on inventories had contributed to the failure in detecting the error. The decision to select one additional product for detail examination did not stem from the professional curiosity or professional skepticism of the auditor, but was merely intended to reinforce the auditor's predisposition to the presumed positive outcome of the audit as influenced by the favorable experiences with the client in previous engagements.[5] *The proper attitude, however, is that every audit engagement, regardless of whether it is a new client or a repeat engagement, must be considered as a new undertaking in itself.* This condition enables the auditor to take a fresh viewpoint and an independent approach to the circumstances of his client.

Usefulness of Prior Year's Working Papers

Historical events have more value to historians than to laymen. This is equally true of the auditor's working papers as the historical record of the financial and operating facts of the client as seen from the professional perspective of an expert accountant. Used with imagination and due professional care, last year's working papers are an indispensable tool in undertaking the audit in subsequent periods.

The usefulness of these working papers is demonstrated in the following areas: in planning the current year's audit; as a training aid for new staff accountants on the job; in controlling the course of the audit; as a

valuable tool in various aspects of the actual field work; as an aid in the auditor's self-appraisal and self-improvement in undertaking his audit work; as an indispensable basis for quality control reviews; as the auditor's salvation (or conversely "electric chair") in times of court litigation; and in a variety of other uses.

'The auditor must guard against complacency based on the result of this reliance on last year's working papers.'

Planning tool—As a planning aid, last year's working papers have various significant uses not only in defining the scope of this year's examination and budget determination but also in highlighting potential exposure, vulnerability, and other problem areas of the audit engagement. For example, before approving the tentative scope and budget for the current audit, a former manager of an international accounting firm, used to require his senior accountants to review the scope of the previous year's examination, paying close attention to areas of the audit in which the firm exposed itself due to inadequate choices or applications of audit procedures or to performing a "satisficing" audit. Additionally, in situations of serious budget overruns, a review of last year's working papers may uncover inefficiencies in the audit or "over audits" which may have contributed to such overruns.

'The proper attitude, however, is that every audit engagement, regardless of whether it is a new client or a repeat engagement, must be considered as a new undertaking in itself.'

Training aid for new accountants on the job— Knowledge of the client's operation is an important ingredient in performing a good audit. Because of staffing constraints, it is often not possible to retain the staff accountants who were involved in the previous audits of the same client. For this reason, working papers are an indispensable aid in providing new staff auditors on the job with valuable information and understanding of the client's operation as well as the particular audit philosophy and strategy being em-

---

[5] The amount of this inventory error was not material in relation to net income and total inventory at year end. But this case has created certain strain in the auditor-client relationship at the functional level for some time.

ployed in undertaking the examination. The knowledge acquired from reviewing last year's working papers is reinforced by pre-audit meetings among the staff accountants engaged in the current year's examination.

Aid in controlling the audit — For audit engagements with tight schedules and deadlines, last year's working papers are an important aid in completing the examination on time. For instance, comparing the amount of work done and the number of hours charged up to a certain date with the same information for the comparable period in the past will tell the senior accountant how the audit is progressing and whether overtime and/or additional staff is needed to meet the deadline.

Valuable aid during the actual field work — Experienced auditors have found the various uses of last year's working papers during the actual field work as necessary in the efficient and effective conduct of the examination. In fact, when the client changes auditors, the incoming ones would always request that the outgoing accountants lend them their last year's working papers. An example: The auditor follows a rotation procedure in the examination of fixed assets in such a way that after a number of years all major fixed asset categories would be subjected to detailed examination. This could be accomplished in a number of ways. One of them is similar to the ABC method of handling inventory which starts by classifying the fixed assets into groups according to their activity, i.e., in terms of the number of transactions, additions and disposals during the year. The most active fixed assets are assigned to Group A; the less active ones get the "B" category; and the least active fixed assets are included in the "C" group. Assuming that the auditor decides to concentrate on the most active fixed assets, Group A, for the rotation program, the next step is to ascertain the number of years for which it would be carried out and the corresponding number of assets to be examined within the group each year, the objective being that when the program is completed all fixed assets under this group would be subjected to detailed examination. For the remaining fixed assets classified under Groups B and C, the auditor can continue the usual audit procedures.

Undoubtedly, prior year's working papers are indispensable in providing accurate information about the fixed assets which were examined in previous periods during the rotation program. Incidentally, this rotation approach may prove valuable in examining other accounts such as inventories , accounts receivable, and even revenue and expense accounts (on top of the usual comparison of this year's and last year's income and expense accounts), particularly those which, by their nature, are a potential haven for errors, irregularities, and even for so-called questionable or sensitive payments.

Other areas in which last year's working papers will prove useful are answers to questions such as: Were there any significant findings resulting from last year's audit of a particular account? Were there any discrepancies noted and brought to the attention of the client? Were there any internal control breakdowns in handling a particular account not significant enough for inclusion in the internal control memorandum but brought to the attention of the client? Were they acted on? What are the records kept by the client pertaining to a particular account, and who is keeping them? These and many more questions can be answered by referring to last year's working papers.

Valuable aid for self-appraisal — A good auditor will not file a completed working paper without reviewing it for accuracy, conciseness and completeness. For most auditors, this final step is quite hard to perform because of certain mental fixations, biases, or even mental blocks that developed in completing the audit and in preparing the working papers. One useful approach is to use prior year's working papers as a starting point for such self-review or self-appraisal, the reason being that, if last year's working papers were accepted as adequate, they must have at least met minimum quality standards.

This self-review or self-appraisal may be done in two stages. The first stage can be done before starting the audit of a given account in order to familiarize the auditor with the specific objective of the specific portion of the audit as well as the audit procedures used to accomplish it. Based on this review, the auditor can reach certain conclusions regarding the quality of the working paper, formulate guidelines to accomplish it, and decide on the specific audit procedures to be used consistent with the current objective of the particular portion of the audit (this latter objective being consistent with the specific and overall goals of the audit engagement). The second stage of such a self review is done after its completion to insure that the accuracy and completeness, or, at least, the minimum quality of the working paper is met.

Basis for quality control reviews — The importance of prior year's working papers in relation to quality control reviews depends on the type of program being instituted by the auditor. Fundamentally, there are three types of quality control reviews, one supplementing the other. The first type is internal in nature, and this is undertaken by a committee of experienced auditors within the firm. The primary objective is to ascertain the adequacy of the scope and the reasonableness of audit procedures employed in the examination, working paper documentation, resolution of review notes ("to do" items), disposition of findings, and other related matters of interest. In this type of quality control review, the indispensability of prior year's working papers is beyond question. The second type which is commonly referred to as peer review has a much broader scope and objective, and is undertaken by outsiders appointed by the auditor or by the AICPA (if undertaken in conjunction with the peer review program sponsored by the Institute). The main thrust of this review extends not only to matters directly related to the conduct of the audit as reflected in last year's working papers, but also to matters relating to the auditor's firm policies and other administrative practices.

The third type of quality control review, just like the first type, has a limited scope and objective, and is undertaken by highly prominent figures in the professions and the business community, including, but not necessarily, former top government officials, both local and foreign.[6] Its primary objective is to insure the adequacy and reasonableness of the auditor's firm-wide audit philosophy, policies, and other administrative practices. The best example of this type is the Public Review Board of Arthur Andersen & Co. which was referred to by the former head of the Federal Communications Commission, Newton Minow, a current member of the Board, as sort of outside directors of public accounting.[7] A very significant aspect of this type of quality control review is the resources involved, particularly prominence and material resources, which only the larger accounting firms can reasonably afford. Last Year's working papers probably have little or no value at all in this type of review.

Aid in defending the auditor during court litigation — Last year's working papers represent the record of the examination done by the auditor, and are significant

evidence brought to bear in court litigations involving the audit. For accountants who have experienced the trauma of court litigation involving their work, prior year's working papers can be a salvation if done with due professional care or an "electric chair" if done poorly and sloppily.

Other uses — Being a record of significant financial information about the client, prior year's working papers serve a variety of purposes. It is not uncommon, for example, for a client to request from the auditor an analysis of certain accounts covering a number of years in the past. In one case, prior year's working papers were used to reconstruct certain accounting records which were burned resulting from a fire that razed the client's premises.

Perhaps, one of the most important uses of last year's working papers is to satisfy the professional curiosity or professional skepticism of the auditor. In one case, an auditor went through the several years working papers of a client which was dependent on imported raw materials so as to satisfy his curiosity regarding the potential impact of the deteriorating trade imbalances and overall economic condition of the country on that client's business.

Concluding Note

It is not uncommon to hear arguments discounting the value of history or historical data as a guide to future actions. Perhaps, one of these few records of the past with unquestionable importance, at least to the auditor, is last year's working papers. However, using them unimaginatively and indiscriminately has serious dangers which the auditor must guard against. Ω

---

[6] "A Wider Public Look at What CPAs Do." *Business Week*, (January 30, 1978), p. 71
[7] *Ibid.*

CASE 16

COVER-UP IN D.C.

Cover-up in D.C. is a play in four acts illustrating the role of the auditor in gathering evidence and documenting working papers with adequate support for the auditor's opinion. This play is designed to stress the importance of working paper documentation and compliance with generally accepted auditing standards. The play may be assigned for reading and discussion, or it may be performed in class with students assuming the roles of the CPAs and then leading the class in a panel discussion.

The first and third acts take place in the offices of the CPA firm and involve discussions of evidential matter, working papers, and support for the auditor's opinion. The second and fourth acts are panel discussions of the problems encountered by the CPA firm.

PROGRAM

Act I   — *"Review of Working Papers"*

Act II   — *"Panel Discussion"*

Act III   — *"It's Cover-up Time"*

Act IV   — *"Panel Discussion"*

PLAYERS

The panel should be composed of about three students (or other experts) who discuss the problems encountered by the CPA firm in the first act and the results of their efforts in the third act. The players consist of Dick the partner, Bev the manager, and John the senior. In the third act, the players are joined by Karen, the firm's lawyer.

As the first act unfolds, Partner Dick is discussing with Manager Bev and Senior John the evidence included in the working papers for their new audit client, D.C. Security Company, Inc.

ACT I — "Review of Working Papers"

Dick: Bev, John, I've called this meeting to discuss the working papers for the DCS audit.

Bev: Oh, yes, D.C. Security Company, our new audit client in Washington. I think we did a pretty good job on that audit, all things considered.

Dick: Well, I'm not so sure. I've been reviewing the working papers and they don't seem to fully support a clean opinion. I noticed some of the comments and exceptions noted in the working papers were not fully explained. Also, some of the audit steps have not been performed, or at least the working papers do not indicate that they were.

Bev: I think we did a fair job. If we use our imagination and read between the lines, we can get by. What do you think, John, you supervised most of the work?

John: As you know, DCS is a new client and we were not appointed as auditors until near the year-end. This fact alone made it difficult for us to plan the audit so that we could gather sufficient evidence to support a clean opinion.

Dick: I know all of that John, but you also know I promised a clean opinion as one of the conditions in getting this audit.

John: Yes sir, but if the evidence is incomplete or indicates a qualified opinion or other type of opinion, then what?

Dick: Let's not talk about that! A promise is a promise.

Bev: John, you seem to be implying that the working papers are incomplete. I realize you were pushed a little on this job, but taking that into consideration the papers looked O.K. when I reviewed them.

Dick: Did you review them—I don't see your initials any place?

Bev: Guess I forgot that.

Dick: Seems like you've been forgetting a lot of things lately. The most important thing, you know, is for me to be covered in case of trouble. John, if you think something is wrong, speak up, you know I value your opinion.

John: Well, sir, for one thing the working papers do not contain sufficient evidence to support a clean opinion in accordance with the second and third standards of field work.

Dick: What's he talking about, Bev?

Bev: I don't know. I guess it's that professional development course we sent him to.

Dick: I certainly hope the state society doesn't adopt that continuing education requirement for CPAs. If they do, we will all have to start taking those P.D. courses and I haven't cracked a book since college.

Bev: I think that just applies to new men. You and I don't need that stuff!

Dick: John, you know if the working papers are incomplete, it's your fault, not mine. Did you send out confirmations?

John: Yes sir, but we didn't get a chance to follow-up on the non-responses.

Dick: Well, I can understand that! What about the general ledger, does it balance?

John: Well, not exactly. We couldn't get the cash to reconcile—you know they have several bank accounts, including one in Mexico.

Dick: We won't worry about that, all the cash will be lumped together in the balance sheet anyway. How do you guys explain the incompleteness of the working papers?

John: Well, I don't think there were enough hours budgeted for this engagement. You know, with a new client there is a lot of extra work that must be done and the records of DCS were not exactly up-to-date. We had to do a lot of bookkeeping work before we even got into the audit.

Dick: Although I promised a clean opinion, maybe we should consider issuing unaudited statements this year—especially if there are problems with cash. You didn't find any indication of fraud, did you? On second thought, don't answer that.

John: I don't think unaudited statements would be appropriate when we undertook an audit engagement and had evidence indicating possible lack of fairness.

Bev: Listen, unaudited statements are always appropriate—we use them to get off the hook!

John: Well, I think the proper thing would be to spend more time on the audit and develop sufficient evidence to support whatever opinion is warranted in the circumstances. You know, on this job, time was our biggest problem.

Bev: Yes, I'm aware of that. You know, I tried to get some more time.

Dick: You must think this firm has unlimited resources. To get the DCS audit I had to give a pretty low bid and we have to cut some corners or not make a dime on this job.

John: Yes, sir, but we still have to gather sufficient, competent evidential matter before we can express an opinion and we have to have time to document the evidence in the working papers. Statement on Auditing Standards No. 1 says that we must review, test, and evaluate internal accounting control and gather evidence in support of our opinion.

Dick: There he goes again. Just tell me if these working papers will support a clean opinion or not.

Bev: Well, I think they will. I know they're not complete in every respect, but who else knows that?

Dick: If I give a clean opinion, is there any way we might get in trouble?

John: Well sir, I think you would be running a big risk. The working papers are incomplete, the evidence is not documented and sufficient planning, supervision, and compliance with other generally accepted auditing standards are not indicated.

Bev: I think you can assume everything is O.K. I spent a couple of days out on the job and nothing came to my attention to indicate that the statements are not fairly presented.

Dick: O.K., that's what I wanted to hear. I'm sorry John, but I've got to go with experience. I'll sign the opinion and if anything comes up we can always clean up the working papers.

(END FIRST ACT)

Act II — "Panel Discussion"

The panel discusses the important problems indicated by Act I. The following outline indicates those topics that may be discussed:

Responsibility of CPA

Professional qualifications of CPA

Education and experience to practice as an auditor and continuing education

The importance of adhering to GAAS

The importance of planning and supervision and desirability of early appointment of the auditor. Problems in appointment of auditor near or after year-end

Importance of the study and evaluation of internal control

Gathering sufficient evidential matter to support the opinion

Competence of evidential matter

Presumptions as to the validity of evidence

Sufficiency of evidential matter

Importance of working papers and the documentation of evidential matter

Function and nature of working papers

What working papers should generally show

Definition of unaudited financial statements in accordance with Section 516 of SAS No. 1

When negative assurance is appropriate

Act III — "It's Cover-Up Time"

In Act III, Partner Dick, Manager Bev, and Senior John are joined by the firm's attorney. The audit of DCS has gone sour and the firm is faced with possible legal action regarding their expression of opinion on the financial statements. As the scene opens, Partner Dick is explaining the situation to Attorney Karen.

Dick: Karen, it looks like the DCS audit may give us some trouble. We certainly did everything we could to provide them with good service. It's just one of those things—the client is in weak financial position, a few things go wrong, and bang—they are in bankruptcy.

Karen:	Well, there should be no problem if your firm performed in accordance with the standards of the accounting profession. Just because a client is forced into bankruptcy, there is no responsibility on the auditor's part if his opinion was based on sound auditing procedures and the financial statements contained sufficient disclosures.
Bev:	That all sounds good, Karen, but that's not the way it goes. You see, the client gets into trouble and the hounds come after the auditors—no matter what kind of job they did.
Dick:	Yes, Karen, I think Bev hit the nail right on the head. With the current rash in liability suits, it is obvious that the auditor hasn't got a chance in court.
John:	Uncovering that sizable fraud won't help our position.
Karen:	You know, I have considerable experience in liability cases involving auditors and it has been my experience that when the CPA loses one of these cases, it is usually because he did a sloppy job on the audit.
Dick:	Well, we were pushed for time on this job—we had to take the engagement at a minimum fee—and therefore did not devote as much time as we normally would.
Karen:	You know you can't justify substandard work on the basis of substandard fees. One of your standards requires the auditor to exercise due professional care in the performance of the examination and the preparation of the report. John, I understand you were the senior on the audit.
John:	Yes, that's right.
Karen:	Will you explain what you consider to be weaknesses in the audit?
John:	It has been my feeling all along that the working papers were incomplete and did not contain sufficient evidence to support the opinion.
Dick:	Now, don't bring that up again! You know we can doctor those papers up if we have to.
Bev:	Besides, a slick attorney like Karen can get us off without any sweat.
Karen:	You've been watching too many late movies, Bev. You may have a serious problem here.
Dick:	That's right, Bev, this is no time for a joke. Besides, I'm not in a very good mood. I was all set to go on vacation and now I have to deal with this mess.
Karen:	John, I've been reading your auditing standards and they indicate that although the quantity, type, and content of working papers may vary with the circumstances, they generally should include certain information. For example, do the working papers show that the client's financial statements agree with the books or were reconciled with the client's records?
John:	Well, that was a problem we discussed in reviewing the working papers. There were several areas where the statements did not agree with the records. We were unable, for example, to reconcile cash.
Karen:	Why not?
John:	Well, DCS maintains several cash accounts in various banks and their bank reconciliations were not complete and the cash accounts in the ledger did not agree with the bank confirmations. We were finding some mistakes when we exceeded the budget and had to back off. Also, the client was getting very upset with our fooling around in the cash records.
Karen:	What about planning? Do the working papers show that the engagement was planned and the work of assistants supervised and reviewed?
Dick:	Oh, we had planning and supervision alright! Didn't we, Bev?
Bev:	That statement was uncalled for. We had some time constraints on this job, as John has already stated, and therefore we had to cut short the review of internal control and use work programs from a similar engagement.

Karen: If I remember correctly, one of your standards requires that the system of internal control be reviewed and evaluated in determining the extent to which auditing procedures will be applied. Are you telling me the working papers don't show compliance with this standard?

John: We didn't have much time to review internal control and as Bev indicated, we used this work program from another engagement and did most of the required steps, although many were not fully completed.

Karen: Did you indicate that the steps not done were not applicable to this engagement?

John: No.

Dick: That's something we can correct now.

Karen: At least, I hope your working papers show the auditing procedures that you did follow in obtaining evidence and how exceptions and unusual matters were resolved or treated.

Bev: I hate to keep throwing water on your ideas, Karen, but I'm afraid you've got us there too.

John: I made that point very clear to Dick and Bev in discussing the signing of the opinion. I don't believe I got through to them.

Dick: He never made that clear!

Karen: Well, you know, if this case goes to court your working papers will be subpoenaed as evidence of the kind of audit that was performed and the court is not likely to permit oral testimony in support of deficiencies found in the working papers.

Dick: That's not fair. You lawyers always twist things around.

Bev: Maybe we can buy them off.

Dick: With your money or mine?

Karen: That might be the best approach. Settling out of court would keep this thing out of the papers and protect your reputation and that of the profession. You know, your Code of Ethics says that violation of generally accepted auditing standards represents substandard work.

Dick: Let's don't get into that. My ethics are unquestionable—just ask Bev about that.

Karen: Well, my advice is for you to take a loss on this client and try to profit from your experience.

John: Maybe if we all had been more willing to attend some professional development courses, we could have prevented this mess.

Dick: You know, you may have something there, John.

(END ACT THREE)

Act IV — "Panel Discussion"

The panel discusses the important points brought out in the third act involving auditing standards, ethics, and the accountant's legal liability. This portion of the program should be brief, only indicating the importance of the following:

> CPA's responsibility for fairness of financial statements including adequate disclosure (SEC stated position)
>
> Meaning of due care
>
> The auditor's responsibility in connection with issuing an opinion on a client in weak financial position—when does the auditor abandon the going concern assumption in favor of liquidation

Some discussion of recent liability cases and the reasons auditors found themselves in trouble (support for Karen's statement)

The auditor's responsibility for the discovery of fraud

What the auditor should do when he suspects fraud

The impact of the relatively new ethics ruling (Rule 202 and 203) on generally accepted accounting principles and generally accepted auditing standards

Continuing education and professional development

AICPA professional development courses

State Society and local chapter programs

In-house staff training

The Auditor's Considerations When a Question Arises About an Entity's Continued Existence

(Section 340, SAS No. 34)

SAS No. 34 is concerned with the auditor's considerations in those situations where the "going concern" concept is imperiled. While most of these instances will involve the entity's inability to meet its financial obligations, other factors may also be present. These other factors include loss of key personnel or key customers, shortage of resources or supply blockage, etc. Auditors typically do not search for information regarding these considerations, but should be aware of their possible existence, and be able to spot information that may signal that further investigation is required.

Information that may signal a decline in "going concern" may take several forms. Negative trends, defaults, dividend in arrears, and denial of credit are all examples of possible indications. Non-financial information such as legal proceedings, labor stoppages, etc., are also possible indicators. These indicators should be explored fully by the auditor, typically by consulting management and legal council, if necessary. This review should carry over into the area of forecasts and projections.

Effect on the Auditor's Report

Upon researching possible contrary information, the auditor may extend his or her substantive test, modify the audit report, or determine that a modification is not warranted. Guidance as to the reporting considerations are provided in SAS No. 2. Modification of the report should be made for the current period only, the period in which the uncertainty arose.

An example of a report qualified for an uncertainty concerning the recoverability and classification of recorded asset amounts or the amounts and classification of liabilities because of a substantial doubt about an entity's ability to continue in existence follows:

(Explanatory paragraph)

As shown in the financial statements, the company incurred a net loss of $. . . . during the year ended December 31, 19xx, and, as of that date, the company's current liabilities exceeded its current assets by $. . . . and its total liabilities exceeded its total assets by $. . . . These factors, among others, as discussed in Note X, indicate that the company may be unable to continue in existence. The financial statements do not include any adjustments relating to the recoverability and classification of recorded asset amounts or the amounts and classification of liabilities that might be necessary should the company be unable to continue in existence.

(Opinion paragraph)

In our opinion, subject to the effects on the financial statements of such adjustments, if any, as might have been required had the outcome of the uncertainty about the recoverability and classification of recorded asset amounts and the amounts and classification of liabilities referred to in the preceding paragraph been known, the financial statements referred to above present fairly the financial position of X Company as of December 31, 19xx, and the results of its operations and the changes in its financial position for the year then ended, in conformity with generally accepted accounting principles applied on a basis consistent with that of the preceding year.

Auditors, at times, in trying to judge the going concern of their clients and their associated reporting responsibility may be inclined to defer to language such as the following:

"Auditor's Report"

We have audited this balance sheet and say in our report:

> That the cash is overstated, the cashier being short;
> That the customer's receivables are very much past due;
> And that if there are some good ones, they are very, very few;
> The inventories are out of date and principally junk;
> And the method of their pricing is very largely bunk;
> The investments are all worthless and the prepaids are a mess;
> The amount of liabilities is anybody's guess;
> So, according to our figures, the undertaking's wrecked,
> But, subject to these comments, the balance sheet's correct.

(Taken from the Montana CPA)

AUGUST 1981

Going Concern Questions

The increasing frequency of financial difficulties of businesses has caused auditors to consider the auditing procedures that are relevant when a question arises about an entity's continued existence. The authors present an analysis of and related commentary on SAS No. 34, the AICPA's recent pronouncement on this subject. A flowchart is included to assist auditors dealing with this problem, which involves significant application of informed judgment.

Paul Munter, CPA, DBA, and Thomas A. Ratcliffe, CPA, Ph.D.

IT has been argued frequently in the accounting literature that going concern is a basic postulate of accounting. The position has been espoused in AICPA publications such as APB Statement No. 4 "Basic Concepts and Accounting Principles Underlying Financial Statements of Business Enterprises," and Accounting Research Study No. 1 "The Basic Postulates of Accounting," as well as in a number of other professional publications. As such, the continued existence of the enterprise typically is assumed when the financial statements are being prepared.

At times, however, enterprises do not plan on continuing, and thus the assumption of going concern is not valid. Such would be the case when, for example, the enterprise is in the process of liquidation or the owners have agreed to commence liquidation. In these circumstances, when it is certain that going concern is an invalid assumption, GAAP is abandoned in favor of liquidation values for purposes of preparing the financial statements.

An auditor performing the attest function on the financial statements has no unusual problems when the assumption of going concern is correct. Likewise, when liquidation is in progress and the financial statements are prepared accordingly, few problems in this circumstance arise. The primary problem for the auditor is when there is significant uncertainty about the continued existence of the enterprise. SAS No. 2 "Reports on Audited Financial Statements" suggests that a "subject to" qualification be used in these circumstances, although the auditor is allowed to issue a disclaimer of opinion. Previously, however, little guidance was provided to the auditor in assessing whether the uncertainty about the continued existence of enterprise was great enough to result in a qualification of the audit opinion or a disclaimer.

Paul Munter, CPA, DBA, and Thomas A. Ratcliffe, CPA, Ph.D., are Associate Professors of Accounting at Texas Tech University. They have published several articles in the professional literature, including The CPA Journal. *Both are involved in continuing education programs for accountants on a nationwide basis.*

In view of this, the ASB issued SAS No. 34 "The Auditor's Considerations When a Question Arises About an Entity's Continued Existence" in March 1981. The purpose of this document is to provide guidance to the auditor in assessing the continued existence of the enterprise. This article discusses the guidelines established by SAS No. 34 and shows how the going concern assessment can relate to other aspects of the audit. The substantive provisions of SAS No. 34 are depicted in Exhibit I.

Factors Affecting Going Concern

A question about the enterprise's continued existence may arise primarily from two sources. First, there are questions about the solvency of the enterprise. These considerations relate to the ability of the enterprise to generate cash from its ongoing operations to meet its obligations as they come due. Indications that the enterprise may have to dispose of a significant portion of its operating assets, restructure debts, or obtain additional capital to meet its current obligations raise doubt as to the future solvency of the enterprise.

Other factors which do not directly impact solvency may cause the auditor to question the continued existence of the enterprise. These factors may have a potential impact on the solvency of the enterprise in the future. These other factors include, for example, loss of key personnel, loss of principal supply source and an unfavorable rate ruling by a regulatory agency.

As we noted earlier, the continued existence of the enterprise is usually assumed in the preparation of financial statements. Therefore, when the auditor is examining the financial statements in accordance with GAAS, he would not search for evidential matter relating specifically to the continued existence of the enterprise. However, neither can the auditor ignore any evidential matter obtained in the examination (see SAS No. 31 "Evidential Matter"). As a consequence, the auditor must be aware that auditing procedures applied primarily for other pur-

EXHIBIT I

Flowchart Summary of SAS No. 34

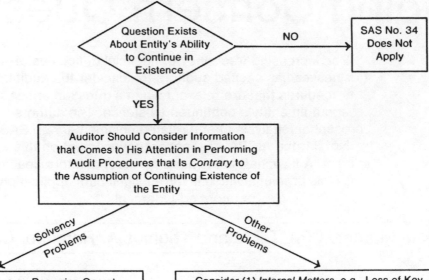

Question Exists About Entity's Ability to Continue in Existence

NO → SAS No. 34 Does Not Apply

YES

Auditor Should Consider Information that Comes to His Attention in Performing Audit Procedures that Is *Contrary* to the Assumption of Continuing Existence of the Entity

Solvency Problems

Other Problems

Consider (1) *Negative Trends*, e.g., Recurring Operating Losses, Working Capital Deficiencies, Negative Cash Flows, and Adverse Key Financial Ratios, and (2) *Other Indications*, e.g., Loan Defaults, Dividend Arrearages, Denial of Trade Credit, Noncompliance in the Capital Requirements, and Necessity to Seek New Means of Financing

Consider (1) *Internal Matters*, e.g., Loss of Key Personnel, Work Stoppages or Other Labor Difficulties, Substantial Dependence on Success of a Particular Project and Uneconomic Long-Term Commitments, and (2) *External Matters*, e.g., Legal Proceedings, Litigation, Legislation, Loss of Key Franchise, License, or Patent, Loss of Principal Customer or Supplier, and Uninsured Catastrophes

Auditor Should Consider Information that Mitigates the Significance of Contrary Information

Related to Solvency Problems

Related to Other Problems

Consider (1) *Asset Factors*, e.g., Disposability, Sale-Leasebacks, (2) *Debt Factors*, e.g., Unused Lines of Credit, Capability of Reviewing or Extending Due Dates, (3) *Cost Factors*, e.g., Postponing Expenditures, Reducing Overhead Administrative Expenditures, and (4) *Equity Factors*, e.g., Variability of Dividend Requirements, Capability of Obtaining Additional Equity Capital

Consider Capacity to Adopt *Alternative Courses of Action*, e.g., Replace Key Personnel, Lost Customers or Suppliers, Assets Seized or Destroyed, and Capability to Operate at Reduced Level or of Redeploying Resources

EXHIBIT I—*Continued*

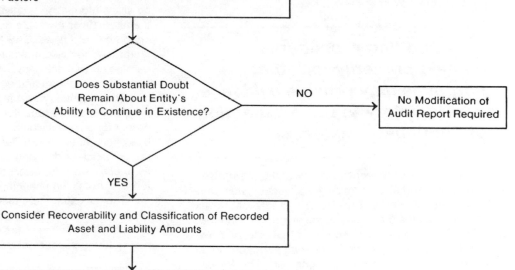

Initial Consideration: (1) Contrary Information—Focus on Underlying Conditions that Resulted in Contrary Information, (2) Mitigating Factors—Based Primarily on Nature of Entity's Business, Discussions with Principal Officers, Understanding Possible Legal Implications

Additional Considerations: Consider Plans to Liquidate Assets, Plans to Borrow Money or Restructure Debt, Plans to Reduce or Delay Expenditures, Plans to Increase Ownership Equity, and Management Forecasts, Projections, Budgets, or Other Prospective Data

Auditor Should Consider Need for, and Adequacy of, Disclosure of Principal Conditions that Raise Questions About the Entity's Continued Existence, Possible Effects of Such Conditions and Management's Evaluation of the Significance of Those Conditions and Mitigating Factors

Does Substantial Doubt Remain About Entity's Ability to Continue in Existence?

NO

No Modification of Audit Report Required

YES

Consider Recoverability and Classification of Recorded Asset and Liability Amounts

Professional Judgment Should Be Used to Determine Point Where Uncertainties Surrounding Recoverability and Classification Require Auditor to Modify Report (See Exhibit II)

poses may provide evidence contradictory to the assumption of continued existence. Therefore, in forming an opinion on the financial statements taken as a whole, the auditor must evaluate the contrary information in light of any factors tending to mitigate the contrary information and also evaluate management's plans for resolving these economic conditions.

Contrary Information

For purposes of determining the ability of the enterprise to continue in existence, contrary information is any evidence obtained during the course of the engagement up to the date of the audit report which relates to the enterprise's ability to continue in existence. Thus all such information, regardless of the source it is derived from, must be evaluated if it relates to the continuity of the enterprise as of the date of the financial statements on which the auditor is reporting.

Sources of Contrary Information

As noted, contrary information is primarily of two types: information about the current solvency of the enterprise and other information which does not directly impact the current solvency of the enterprise.

' . . . auditing procedures applied primarily for other purposes may provide evidence contradictory to the assumption of continued existence.'

In assessing the current solvency of the enterprise, the auditor may be able to employ analytical review procedures quite effectively. SAS No. 23 ''Analytical Review Procedures'' states that a basic premise underlying the use of analytical review procedures is that relationships among data can be expected to exist and continue in the absence of known contrary conditions. SAS No. 23 further requires that, when analytical review procedures identify unexpected fluctuations or the absence of expected fluctuations, the auditor should investigate further if he believes that they are indicative of matters which can have a significant effect on the examination.

If the use of analytical review procedures reveals negative trends which cause the auditor to question the continued existence of the enterprise, he also may need to look for other indications of solvency problems. Other indications of solvency problems could be dividends in arrears, attempts to establish new lines of credit, and default or restructuring of debt during the period under examination.

The other information which may indirectly impact solvency may be obtained from various sources. Loss of key personnel may be documented in the corporate minutes which the auditor should read. The auditor also may discover this loss through an examination of the payroll records. The auditor is required to obtain information about litigation, claims, assessments and unasserted claims by SAS No. 12 ''Inquiry of Client's Lawyer Concerning Litigation, Claims and Assessments.'' In these inquiries, the auditor may obtain information which raises a question about the continued existence of the enterprise.

As can be seen, the sources of information which raise a question about the continued existence of the enterprise are varied. The auditor does not search for such information, rather, he obtains it through his search for evidential matter about other information. Thus, the auditor must be alert for this information. When the auditor obtains contrary information about the ability of the enterprise to continue operating, he must consider any mitigating factors and how these factors impact the auditor's going concern assessment.

Mitigating Factors

Factors which tend to mitigate the significance of the contrary information relative to current solvency relate to the alternatives available to the enterprise for maintaining adequate cash flows. SAS No. 34 identifies four types of factors which could mitigate the contrary information concerning current solvency. These are asset factors, debt factors, cost factors and equity factors.

The mitigating asset factors which the auditor would need to consider are factors such as the availability of assets for disposal which would not impact the continuing operations of the enterprise. Other factors would include the potential for delaying asset replacements and the ability to use assets for factoring, sale-leaseback, or other forms of obtaining financing.

The mitigating debt factors would include the availability of unused lines of credits, the capability of renewing or extending the due dates of debt, and the potential for restructuring the current debt agreements.

' . . . contrary information is any evidence . . . which relates to the enterprise's ability to continue in existence.'

The mitigating cost factors relate to the ability of the enterprise to delay cash outflows. These could include the separability of operations producing negative cash flows—which could include disposing of a segment of the business. Other cost factors include the ability of the enterprise to postpone nonessential expenditures such as maintenance and advertising and the possibility of reducing overhead (such as an agreement with the labor union to accept a cut in pay) and administrative costs.

The equity factors could include the ability to vary dividend payments and the capability of the enterprise to obtain additional funds through an issuance of equity securities.

> ## 'In assessing the current solvency . . . the auditor may be able to employ analytical review procedures . . . '

For the other contrary information, mitigating factors relate primarily to the ability of the enterprise to adopt alternative courses of action. For example, the loss of key personnel may be mitigated by the availability of qualified persons to fill the vacated position and the loss of a rate increase request may be mitigated by the availability of more cost-efficient productive facilities.

Auditor's Evaluation of the Contrary Information and Mitigating Factors

The auditor initially must consider the nature of the contrary information. Primarily, that consideration is one of whether the contrary information is indicative of underlying conditions which are of enough significance to threaten the continued existence of the enterprise. Likewise, the auditor must give initial consideration to the mitigating factors and how those factors impact the initial assessment of the contrary information. The auditor's consideration of the mitigating factors is based on:

• Knowledge of the nature of the business and its operating characteristics, including items affecting the industry and the impact of general economic factors;
• Discussions with appropriate management personnel; and
• Understanding of legal implications based on discussions with legal counsel.

> ## ' . . . mitigating factors relate primarily to the ability of the enterprise to adopt alternative courses of action.'

If, after an initial consideration of the contrary information and mitigating factors, the auditor still believes there is reason to question the continued existence of the enterprise, the auditor must consider other factors. The additional considerations typically focus on the plans of management which are responsive to the contrary information. In considering the plans, the auditor will give greater weight to those plans which can be instituted the quickest. As the time frame increases, the relevance of the plans to the auditor's consideration decreases. However, in assessing the relevance of the plan, the auditor should evaluate the time frame in light of the operating cycle of the enterprise.

The auditor should discuss with management each of the mitigating factors (e.g., asset factors, debt factors, cost factors and equity factors) and give consideration to the ability of management to carry out its plans and the effect those plans can have on the continued existence of the enterprise. The auditor also should discuss with management any forecasts, projections, budgets or other prospective data as it relates to the cash flow availability of the enterprise. In evaluating the prospective data, the auditor should consider the support for assumptions underlying the prospective data when the assumptions can have a material impact on the prospective data.

Effect on Auditor's Report

The auditor must consider the need for and the adequacy of the disclosure of principal conditions that raised a question about the ability of the enterprise to continue in existence, the possible effects of such conditions and management's evaluation of the significance of those conditions and any mitigating factors. The third standard of reporting states that:

Informative disclosures in the financial statements are to be regarded as reasonably adequate unless otherwise stated in the report.

'Now this is a going concern – except for their delivery van'

EXHIBIT II

**Reporting Guidance for Questions Concerning Entity's Continuing Existence
As Shown in SAS No. 34**

Example Explanatory Paragraph (SAS No. 34, para. 12)

As shown in the financial statements, the company incurred a net loss of $ . . . during the year ended December 31, 19XX, and, as of that date, the company's current liabilities exceeded its current assets by $ . . . and its total liabilities exceeded its total assets by $ . . . These factors, among others, as discussed in Note X, indicate that the company may be unable to continue in existence. The financial statements do not include any adjustments relating to the recoverability and classification of recorded asset amounts or the amounts and classification of liabilities that might be necessary should the company be unable to continue in existence.

Example Opinion Paragraph (SAS No. 34, para. 12)

In our opinion, subject to the effects on the financial statements of such adjustments, if any, as might have been required had the outcome of the uncertainty about the recoverability and classification of recorded asset amounts and the amounts and classification of liabilities referred to in the preceding paragraph been known, the financial statement referred to above presents fairly the financial position of X Company as of December 31, 19XX, and the results of its operations and the changes in its financial position for the year then ended, in conformity with generally accepted accounting principles applied on a basis consistent with that of the preceding year.

SAS No. 32 "Adequacy of Disclosure in Financial Statements" amplifies this by requiring that the auditor must qualify his opinion (or issue an adverse opinion) and provide the omitted information if disclosure in the financial statements, including the notes thereto, is lacking. Thus, if the auditor believes there are *significant economic conditions which should be and are not disclosed*, the auditor is *required to give an "except for" qualification.*

Even if the auditor is satisfied about the adequacy of the informative disclosures, the audit report still may need modification. After giving consideration to the contrary information and the mitigating factors discussing the plans, prospective data, and other information with management, and making any substantive tests necessary, the auditor may conclude that a modification of his report for reason of going concern is not necessary. However, if, after performing all tests the auditor believes to be necessary, substantial doubt remains about the enterprise's ability to continue in existence, the audit report should contain a "subject to" qualification (or issue a disclaimer of opinion) for reason of uncertainty (see SAS No. 2). When the auditor is reporting on comparative financial statements, the qualification for reason of uncertainty due to the substantial doubt about the continued existence of the enterprise typically should refer only to the current period financial statements and not the financial statements of the prior period(s). Illustrative reports are provided in Exhibit II.

Conclusion

Due to the problems in assessing business failures, the ASB issued SAS No. 34, which provides guidance to auditors to determine when the audit report should be modified. Since financial statements typically are prepared under the assumption that the enterprise will continue to exist, the auditor will not necessarily search for evidence which is contrary to that assumption. However, if contrary information is obtained in the course of the audit, the auditor must evaluate the contrary information to assess whether it creates significant doubt of the continued existence of the enterprise.

'If significant doubt remains, the auditor should determine whether informative disclosure . . . is adequate . . . '

After due consideration of the contrary information in light of the mitigating factors, the auditor should perform other such substantive tests as are necessary and practicable. If significant doubt remains, the auditor should determine whether informative disclosure of the economic condition is adequate (giving an "except for" qualification if disclosure is inadequate) and qualify the audit report due to the uncertainty.

When the auditor qualifies his report due to the uncertainty, he is not saying that he expects the enterprise to liquidate—rather, such a qualification alerts financial statement readers to the doubt which exists. Conversely, if the auditor believes that a modification of the audit report is not necessary, this is not an assurance that the enterprise will continue, but that there is not a great enough uncertainty to seriously question the assumption of continued existence. Thus, the auditor would qualify his report only when he *cannot* resolve the question about continued existence to his satisfaction. Ω

Audit Sampling

(Section 350, SAS No. 39)

SAS No. 39, *Auditing Sampling*, provides guidance for planning, performing, and evaluating audit samples. Audit sampling is the application of an audit procedure to less than 100 percent of the items within an account balance or class of transactions for the purpose of evaluating some characteristic of the balance or class. SAS No. 39 does not cover situations in which an auditor may examine only a few transactions from an account balance or class of transactions to (a) gain an understanding of the nature of an entity's operations or (b) clarify his or her understanding of the design of the entity's internal accounting control.

The auditor often is aware of account balances and transactions that may be more likely to contain errors—something he or she must consider in planning audit procedures, including audit sampling. On the other hand, other account balances and transactions, which the auditor usually will have no special knowledge of, will require testing to meet audit objectives. Under these circumstances, audit sampling is especially helpful.

Both nonstatistical and statistical sampling are considered by SAS No. 39. The auditing student should be aware that both of these approaches require the auditor to exercise professional judgment in planning, performing, and evaluating a sample and in relating evidence produced by the sample to other evidential matter when forming a conclusion about the related account balance or class of transactions.

Audit sampling is covered by the third standard of field work which requires sufficient, competent evidential matter to be acquired to afford a reasonable basis for an opinion regarding the financial statements under examination. Sufficiency of evidential matter relates to the design and size of an audit sample. The size of the sample depends on both the objective and the efficiency of the sample.

The auditor must rely on his or her judgment in evaluating the competence of evidential matter obtained by audit sampling and not on the design or evaluation of the audit sample. Simply put, the auditor should ascertain whether the sample is representative of the population. Thus, the selection of nonstatistical or statistical sampling does not directly affect the auditor's decisions about the auditing procedures to be applied, the competence of the evidential matter obtained with respect to individual items in the sample, or the actions that might be taken in light of the nature and cause of particular errors.

UNCERTAINTY AND AUDIT SAMPLING

Some degree of uncertainty is implicit in the concept of "a reasonable basis for an opinion" referred to in the third standard of field work—something that has allowed the basic concept of sampling to become well established in auditing practice. But there are some items that do not justify the acceptance of some uncertainty, in which case the only alternative is to examine all of the data.

SAS No. 39 refers to uncertainty inherent in applying auditing procedures as *audit risk*.* Audit risk is a combination of the risk that material errors will occur in the accounting process used to develop the financial statements and the risk that any material errors that occur will not be detected by the auditor. The independent CPA may use internal accounting control to reduce the first risk and substantive tests to reduce the second risk. Audit risk includes uncertainties due to sampling (sampling risk) and uncertainties due to factors other than sampling (nonsampling risk).

Sampling risk arises from the possibility that, when a compliance or a substantive test is restricted to a sample, the auditor's conclusions may be different from the conclusions he or she would reach if the test were applied in the same way to all items in the account balance or class of transactions. That is, the sample is not representative of the population. For a sample of a given design, sampling risk varies inversely with the sample size.

Nonsampling risk includes all the elements of audit risk that are not due to sampling. For example, the CPA may select audit procedures that are not appropriate to achieve the desired objective. Nonsampling risk also arises because the CPA may fail to recognize errors included in documents that he or she examines. The risk of nonsampling error can be reduced through adequate planning and supervision (see Section 311, *Planning and Supervision*) and proper conduct of a firm's audit practice (see Section 161, *Quality Control).*

SAMPLING RISK

The independent CPA should exercise professional judgment in assessing sampling risk. In performing substantive tests of details the auditor is concerned with two aspects of sampling risk:

> The risk of incorrect acceptance

> The risk of incorrect rejection

In performing compliance tests of internal accounting control, the auditor is concerned with two aspects of sampling control:

> The risk of overreliance on internal accounting control

> The risk of underreliance on internal accounting control

The risk of incorrect rejection and the risk of underreliance on internal accounting control relate to the efficiency of the audit. The risk of incorrect acceptance and the risk of overreliance on internal accounting control relate to the effectiveness of an audit in detecting an existing material misstatement.

SAMPLING IN SUBSTANTIVE TESTS OF DETAILS

Planning Samples

When planning a particular sample for a substantive test of details, the CPA should consider:

> The relationship of the sample to the relevant audit objective (see Section 326, *Evidential Matter*)

> Preliminary estimates of materiality levels (the maximum error is called *tolerable error* for the sample)

> The auditor's allowable risk of incorrect acceptance

> Characteristics of the population, that is, the items comprising the account balance or class of transactions of interest.

---

*Section 1020, SAS No. 45 amends Section 350, SAS No. 39, by substituting the term "audit risk" for "ultimate risk."

In planning a sample, the CPA needs to evaluate the specific audit objective to be achieved and at the same time be sure that the audit procedure(s) to be applied will achieve that objective. Also, the CPA must be certain that the population to be sampled is appropriate for the specific audit objective. For example, an understatement due to omission could not be discovered by sampling recorded transactions. As an illustration, cash disbursements made subsequent to the period under examination might be sampled to test for unrecorded liabilities.

In planning a sample for a substantive test of details, the CPA should consider how much monetary error in the related account balance or class of transactions may exist without causing the financial statements to be materially misstated. This maximum dollar error is called the tolerable error for the sample. Tolerable error is a planning concept and is related to the auditor's preliminary estimates of materiality levels in such a way that tolerable error, combined for the entire audit plan does not exceed those estimates.

The extent of substantive tests required to obtain sufficient evidence under the third standard of field work should vary inversely with the auditor's reliance on internal accounting control. The greater the reliance on internal accounting control or on other substantive tests directed toward the same specific audit objective, the greater the allowable risk of incorrect acceptance for the substantive test of details being planned—something allowing for a smaller sample size for the substantive test of details.

The auditor is to exercise professional judgment in ascertaining which items should be individually examined and which items, if any, should be sampled. Concerning the sample, the CPA may be able to reduce the required sample size by separating items subject to sampling into relatively homogeneous groups based on some characteristic related to the specific audit objective. Some examples of common bases for such groupings are the recorded or book value of the items, the nature of internal accounting control related to processing the items, and special considerations associated with certain items.

SAMPLE SELECTION

The sample must be representative of the population and all items should have an opportunity to be selected. One means of obtaining a sample is through random based selection techniques. Random-based selection includes, for example, random sampling, stratified random sampling, sampling with probability proportional to size and systematic sampling with one or more random starts.

PERFORMANCE AND EVALUATION

Given the audit objective, the appropriate auditing procedures should be applied to each sample item. When the auditor is unable to apply planned audit procedures caused by circumstances such as missing documents, he or she should ascertain the effect of not being able to complete such audit procedures and take the appropriate action. For example, assume that those missing documents are misstated and that such an error would lead the auditor to the conclusion that the balance or class is materially in error, the independent CPA should consider alternative procedures that would provide him or her with sufficient evidence to form a conclusion as to the effect of a misstatement. In those cases where the auditor is not able to examine items he or she must consider the implications, if any, that such an event will have on planned reliance on internal accounting control or the degree of reliance on management representations.

The auditor should project the error results of the sample to the items from which the sample was taken. The projected errors should be added to the errors discovered in any items examined 100 percent. The sum of the two errors should be compared with the tolerable error for the account balance or class of transactions and then weighted against the sampling risk.

The auditor must also consider the qualitative aspects of any errors. Qualitative aspects include (a) the nature and cause of misstatements, and (b) the possible relationship of the misstatements to other phases of the audit. The auditor may discover irregularities during his or her examination—something ordinarily requiring broader consideration of possible implications than does the discovery of an error.

The auditor should relate evidence obtained by sample to other relevant audit evidence when forming a conclusion about the related account balance or class of transaction. Projected error results for all sampling and nonsampling applications should be considered in the aggregate along with other relevant audit evidence when the auditor evaluates whether the financial statements taken as a whole may be misstated.

SAMPLING IN COMPLIANCE TESTS OF INTERNAL ACCOUNTING CONTROLS

Planning Samples

When planning a sample the auditor should consider:

The relationship of the sample to the objective of the compliance test

The maximum rate of deviations from prescribed control procedures that would support his planned reliance

The auditor's allowable risk of overreliance

Characteristics of the population, that is, the items comprising the account balance or class of transactions of interest.

Sampling normally is not applicable to tests of compliance with internal accounting control procedures that depend primarily on appropriate segregation of duties or that otherwise provide no documentary evidence of performance. When designing samples for the purpose of testing compliance with internal accounting control procedures that leave an audit trail, the auditor normally should plan to evaluate compliance in terms of deviations from pertinent control procedures, as to either the rate of such deviations or the monetary amount of the related transactions.

SAS No. 39 defines the term, *tolerable rate*, as the maximum rate of deviations from a prescribed control procedure that the auditor would be willing to accept without altering his planned reliance on the control. In evaluating the tolerable rate, the auditor must consider the relationship of procedural deviations to (a) the accounting records being tested, (b) any related internal accounting control procedures, and (c) the purpose of the auditor's examination. As an illustration, if significant reliance is to be placed on the control procedures, the auditor may decide that a tolerable rate of 5 percent or less would be reasonable; if less reliance is planned, the auditor may decide that a tolerable rate of 10 percent is reasonable. It is important to note that while deviations from pertinent control procedures increase the risk of material errors in the accounting records, such deviations do not necessarily result in errors. For example, a recorded receipt that does not contain the necessary documentation may nevertheless be a transaction that is properly accounted for. Deviations would result in errors in the accounting records only if the deviations and the errors occurred on the same transactions. Deviations from pertinent control procedures at a given rate normally would be expected to result in errors at a lower rate.

When conducting compliance tests, the auditor uses sampling as a basis for determining whether internal accounting control procedures are being applied as prescribed. Since the compliance test is the primary source of evidence of whether the procedure is being applied as prescribed, the auditor should allow for a low level of risk of overreliance. In quantitative terms the auditor may consider 5 percent to 10 percent risk of overreliance on internal accounting control as acceptable.

The number of items selected for a particular sample for a compliance test depends on the tolerable rate of deviation from the control(s) being tested. (Note: In this regard, the auditor must consider the planned degree of reliance, the likely rate of deviations; and the allowable risk of overreliance on internal accounting controls.)

SAMPLE SELECTION

Sample selection should be made in a way that insures that the sample is representative of the population and that all items have an equal opportunity to be chosen. Random-based selection of items represents one means of obtaining such samples. The selection method used should be one that allows for selecting items from the entire period covered by the audit.

PERFORMANCE AND EVALUATION

Appropriate auditing procedures should be applied to achieve the objective of the compliance test. If the auditor is unable to apply planned audit procedures or appropriate alternative procedures to selected items, he or she should evaluate the reasons for this limitation. In this regard, the selected items referred to above should be considered to be deviations from planned procedures for the purpose of evaluating the sample.

The sample deviation rate represents the auditor's best estimate of the deviation rate in the population. If the estimated deviation rate is less than the tolerable rate for the population, the auditor should consider the risk that such a result might be obtained even though the true deviation rate for the population is greater than the tolerable rate for the population. For example, if the tolerable rate for a population is 10 percent and no deviations are found in a sample size of 60 items, the CPA may determine that there is an acceptably low sampling risk that the actual deviation rate in the population exceeds the tolerable risk rate of 10 percent. It is important that the auditor also consider qualitative aspects of any deviations. Finally, if the auditor determines that he or she is unable to rely on internal controls, the planned substantive test should be altered.

DUAL-PURPOSE SAMPLES

There are instances when the auditor may want to design a sample that will be used for dual-purposes—to test compliance with a control procedure (compliance tests) and to test whether the recorded dollar amounts of a transaction are accurate (substantive tests). Normally, an auditor planning to use a dual-purpose sample would assume that there is an acceptably low risk of compliance deviations in the population being greater than the tolerable rate. Concerning dual-purpose samples, the sample size should be the larger of the samples that would otherwise have been designed for the two separate purposes.

SELECTING A SAMPLE APPROACH

As discussed earlier, either a nonstatistical or statistical approach to audit sampling can provide sufficient evidential matter. Statistical sampling helps the CPA (a) to design an efficient sample, (b) to measure the sufficiency of the evidential matter obtained, and (c) to evaluate the sample results. Statistical sampling allows the auditor to quantify sampling risk and thus permits him or her to determine an acceptable level of risk. However, statistical sampling may require additional training on the part of the auditor, resulting in additional training costs.

Sample size should be determined by combining professional judgment with formulas, tables, or computer programs. Sampling risk is inversely related to sample size, so an auditor can reduce this risk by examining more items. Planned reliance, the tolerable error rate, the allowable risk of over-reliance, and the likely rate of deviations should be considered when computing an appropriate sample size. Of course, to assure a representative sample, all items in the population should have an equal chance of being selected.

Evaluating Compliance Test Results

Auditing procedures should be applied to all the sample items, and a sample error rate should be computed.[7] An estimated population error rate is then projected and compared to the tolerable error rate. If the population rate is higher, planned reliance on internal control should probably be adjusted downward, and substantive testing would have to be modified accordingly. Even if the tolerable rate is the larger of the two, the auditor should assess the risk that this result was obtained in error. The closeness of the population deviation rate to the tolerable error rate is an important factor in making this assessment.

In addition to the number or rate of errors, various qualitative factors need to be considered when evaluating compliance test results. Auditors should consider the kinds of deviations and the probable reasons for their occurrence. Obviously, intentional deviations from controls are of greater concern than unintentional departures. Additionally, the auditor needs to relate deviations to other aspects of the audit and other evidence obtained.

In the final analysis, whether statistical or nonstatistical sampling is used, the auditor's conclusions concerning reliance on internal controls is a matter of professional judgment.

SUBSTANTIVE TESTS OF TRANSACTIONS AND BALANCES

An inverse relationship exists between the auditor's reliance on internal controls and the extent of substantive testing of transactions and balances. In other words, the more the auditor can rely on the internal control system to produce accurate accounting information, the less he or she needs to rely on substantive testing of the details that make up the amounts in the financial statements.

Planning a Substantive Test

Many substantive tests of transactions and balances lend themselves well to audit sampling. When planning a substantive test, the auditor contemplates, in particular, his or her objectives, the allowable risk of incorrectly accepting a population that is in error, and preliminary estimates of materiality levels. Additionally, the auditor must use judgment to decide on an appropriate tolerable error for each application. This decision should be based on the auditor's assessment of the maximum monetary error possible before the financial statements become misleading.

TABLE 3
SAMPLING RISKS
SUBSTANTIVE TESTS OF DETAILS

Risk	Effect	Severity
Incorrect rejection of population	Decreased audit efficiency	Not critical
Incorrect acceptance of population	Decreased audit effectiveness	Critical

The sufficiency of substantive tests is very much related to the individual significance of the items in question and their potential for causing material financial statement misstatements. Of course, there could be some items for which the auditor believes no sampling risk can be accepted. These items should be examined 100 percent and should not be considered part of the population subject to sampling.

Appropriate selection requires that all items in a population have an equal chance of selection. Whether statistical or nonstatistical sampling is used, the auditor should consider the tolerable error, the allowable risk of an incorrect population acceptance, and the characteristics of the population when deciding on a sample size. Frequently, sample size can be reduced if populations are stratified and sampled individually. Stratification refers to the process of dividing a population into more homogeneous subpopulations. For example, a client's account receivable population might be stratified into subpopulations based on the size of individual account balances.

Evaluating Substantive Test Results

When audit procedures have been applied to all items in the sample, the auditor needs to project the sample error results to the population.[8] If the population was stratified, each subpopulation should be projected separately and then the results summed. If statistical sampling is used, the auditor can usually make an explicit statement expressing the uncertainty and risk inherent in the projection. For example, a substantive test of inventory might result in statements like the following:

> I estimate the value of the client's inventory to be between $750,000 and $754,000. The risk that the true unknown inventory value lies outside this range is 5 percent.

The range of inventory values in the above example would be compared to the inventory book value to determine the projected population error.

If statistical sampling is not used, it is more difficult to express one's uncertainty in quantitative terms. Likewise, it is not as easy to specify the population error possibilities.

Whether statistical or nonstatistical sampling is used, the auditor needs to compare the projected population error with the predetermined tolerable error. If the projected error exceeds the tolerable error, the auditor has cause for concern. Even if the projected error is less than the tolerable error, closeness should be considered. The possibility that this result was obtained even though the population monetary error actually exceeds the tolerable error deserves investigation.

The projected error results from all sampling applications, along with known errors from non-sampling applications, need to be viewed together when forming an opinion on the financial statements. Of course, other factors should be considered as well. The auditor needs to seek the nature and causes of errors, the impact of errors on other phases of the audit, and the relationship of errors to other audit evidence. For example, it could be that the auditor initially placed an inappropriate degree of reliance on internal controls.

CONCLUSION

In many situations an auditor recognizes early in an engagement that certain items, transactions, or accounts require particularly intense scrutiny or 100 percent examination. In other cases the auditor has no specific advance knowledge. SAS No. 39, *Audit Sampling*, is especially helpful in these latter instances as the Statement provides guidance in employing sampling procedures.

SAS No. 39, however, by no means eliminates the need for professional judgment when sampling. Regardless of whether statistical or nonstatistical sampling is used, judgment is necessary when planning the sample, performing the audit procedures, and evaluating the sampling results. Likewise, judgment is required to relate sampling results to other audit evidence when forming an overall opinion on the financial statements.

Auditors can consider sampling for both compliance and substantive testing. Each type of test has been described in this article, along with a general overview of sampling and its relationship to the entire audit process. ▪

FOOTNOTES

[1] SAS No. 39, "Audit Sampling," supersedes SAS No. 1, sections 320A, "Relationship of Statistical Sampling to Generally Accepted Auditing Standards," and 320B, "Precision and Reliability for Statistical Sampling in Auditing."

[2] SAS No. 31, "Evidential Matter."

[3] Some data, of course, should be subject to a 100 percent examination. For example, board of directors' minutes are normally examined in full. Both the cost and time required to examine all of the board of directors' minutes are minimal when compared to the consequences that might result from only sampling them. The auditor must use professional judgment to determine which audit areas, or items within an area, require individual investigation and which can be subject to sampling.

[4] The auditor needs to be concerned with "nonsampling risk" as well. Using inappropriate audit procedures and failing to detect errors that appear in the sample examined are two examples of nonsampling risk. This risk can best be minimized by instituting appropriate firm-wide quality controls and by proper planning and supervision.

[5] SAS No. 1, "Codification of Auditing Standards and Procedures," section 320.

[6] It should be recognized, however, that control deviations do not necessarily signal the existence of errors or irregularities. For example, a paid voucher lacking evidence of prescribed dual approval could still be recorded accurately in the accounting records and represent a bona fide disbursement.

[7] If audit procedures cannot be applied to a particular sample item, the auditor should consider the reasons why and should probably consider the item to be equivalent to an internal control departure.

[8] If audit procedures cannot be applied to some items in a sample, the auditor should determine what the impact would be if he or she considered the items to be in error. If considering them in error would result in the conclusion that the account balance or class of transactions are materially in error, the auditor should apply alternative auditing procedures. If considering the items in question to be in error would not result in a conclusion of material misstatement, there would not be any need for further examination. The auditor should consider why auditing procedures could not be applied, however.

AUDIT SAMPLING: A PRACTICAL APPROACH

How to implement nonstatistical sampling under SAS no. 39.

by Carl S. Warren, Stephen V. N. Yates and George R. Zuber

The implications on practice of Statement on Auditing Standards no. 39, *Audit Sampling*,[1] are more far-reaching than some accountants might think. In the area of nonstatistical sampling, the auditor should know how to estimate sample size, what selection methods are available and how to evaluate the sample results.

SAS no. 39 identifies several factors that the auditor must consider when designing, performing and evaluating audit samples. This article provides practical guidance for the auditor in considering those factors as they apply to nonstatistical samples.[2] For example, it discusses

☐ Which factors are most important in determining a sample size.

☐ The influence of those factors on sample size.

☐ Four methods of selecting samples.

☐ How the auditor should consider sampling risk in evaluating nonstatistical sampling.

SAS no. 39 has implications for the planning and conduct of an entire audit. Therefore, this article also describes how

[1] Statement on Auditing Standards no. 39, *Audit Sampling* (New York: AICPA, 1981). See also *AICPA Professional Standards*, vol. 1 (Chicago, Ill.: Commerce Clearing House, Inc.), AU section 350.

[2] This article does not consider specific guidance on statistical sampling plans because of the numerous reference materials available on this topic. However, the auditor using statistical sampling should find the general framework of audit sampling set forth in this article useful.

SAS no. 39 fits into the audit plan. Exhibit 1, page 4, provides a flowchart illustrating the decision process for applying audit sampling.

The Decision Process in Audit Sampling

An auditor generally uses audit sampling when a complete examination of every item in an account balance or a class of transactions would be too costly. However, when an auditor samples only a portion of the items making up a balance or class, he or she may obtain a sample that is not representative of that balance or class. This sampling risk reflects the fact that the sample may not contain the same proportion of error that exists in the balance or class as a whole. Therefore, the time and dollar savings achieved from sampling bear an implicit cost—because of sampling risk, the auditor may make an incorrect audit decision about the balance or class.

The following procedures are consistent with SAS no. 39 and should aid the auditor at each stage of the decision process:

Specify audit objectives. As shown in exhibit 1, the audit sampling process begins with an identification of audit objectives. The auditor develops these objectives to verify financial statement assertions and designs substantive tests to meet the objectives. For example, for finished goods inventory of a manufacturing company, one of management's assertions is that the inventory is properly valued. The auditor designs substantive tests to verify the audit

CARL S. WARREN, CPA, Ph.D., is a professor in the School of Accounting at the College of Business Administration of the University of Georgia, Athens, Georgia. A member of the American Institute of CPAs, the American Accounting Association and the Georgia Society of CPAs, Dr. Warren has written numerous articles which have appeared in professional publications. STEPHEN V. N. YATES, CPA, is partner in charge of statistical sampling at Peat, Marwick, Mitchell & Co., New York. Mr. Yates serves on the AICPA statistical sampling subcommittee and is a member of the New Mexico Society of CPAs and the New York State Society of CPAs. GEORGE R. ZUBER, CPA, is a manager in the AICPA auditing standards division and an adjunct professor at New York University. A member of the New York State Society of CPAs, Mr. Zuber wrote, with Abraham D. Akresh, "Exploring Statistical Sampling," which appeared in the February 1981 *Journal*.

objective that the finished goods inventory is properly stated at the lower of cost or market.

When designing substantive tests, the auditor also must consider the nature of the errors or irregularities that may occur in the financial statements. For example, the finished goods inventory cost may be misstated because of incorrectly allocated overhead. A substantive test designed to detect this error might require a recomputation or review of overhead allocations.

Consider factors that determine audit scope. In determining the scope (that is, the nature, timing and extent) of a substantive test, the auditor considers the relative riskiness and materiality of the account balance or class of transactions on which a conclusion is to be reached. Audit risk depends on such factors as the nature of the entity's business and the nature of the items under audit. For example, the overhead allocation for finished goods inventory for a chemical manufacturer is more complex than that for a manufacturer of business signs, and, therefore, the risk that the finished goods inventory might be misstated would be higher for the chemical company. The nature of the items under audit also may affect the risk of misstatement. For example, an inventory of highly marketable radio equipment items is more susceptible to theft than an inventory of manufacturing equipment such as tool dies. Therefore, the risk that the inventory balance of radio equipment is overstated is greater than that for the tool die inventory.

The materiality of an account balance or a class of transactions to the financial statements as a whole affects the scope of the audit. According to SAS no. 22, *Planning and Supervision,*[3] an auditor should make preliminary estimates of materiality when planning the audit. SAS no. 39 implies that these preliminary estimates of materiality for the financial statements as a whole should be allocated to the individual account balances or classes of transactions. In allocating materiality, the auditor should consider how much misstatement, or "tolerable error," may exist in a balance or class without causing the financial statements to be materially misstated.

[3]SAS no. 22, *Planning and Supervision* (New York: AICPA, 1978). See also *AICPA Professional Standards,* AU sec. 311.

Exhibit 1

The decision process for applying and sampling

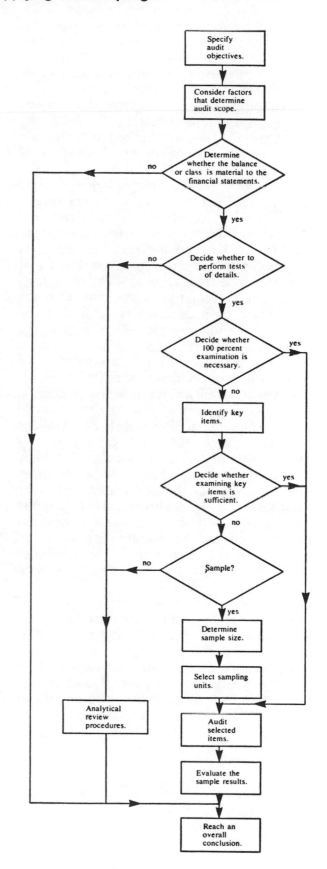

In addition, the auditor should consider how different allocations of materiality would affect the efficiency of the audit. Consequently, the amount of tolerable error for each balance or class may not be equal. Finally, materiality should be allocated by the auditor in such a way that the tolerable error aggregated across the entire audit plan does not exceed the estimate of materiality for the financial statements taken as a whole.[4]

Although scope refers to the nature, timing and extent of testing, the following discussion is primarily limited to the impact of risk and materiality on the extent of testing.

Determine whether the balance or class is material to the financial statements. If after the auditor considers audit risk and materiality the tolerable error allocated to an account balance or class of transactions is greater than or equal to the book value of the recorded transactions, substantive tests may not be required. For example, if the allocation of materiality is such that the auditor can tolerate $50,000 of error in the prepaid insurance account which has a balance of only $40,000, no substantive tests on prepaid insurance are required. However, even when a balance or class is not individually material to the financial statements, the auditor still should consider whether any potential errors or irregularities in the balance or class would be material when aggregated with misstatements in other balances or classes of transactions. In addition, auditors must always be alert to special risk considerations such as the possible existence of related party transactions or the possibility that the recorded book values are substantially understated.

Decide whether to perform tests of details. Substantive tests include both tests of details and analytical review procedures. Auditors often test a balance or class by a combination of the two. Because analytical review procedures in general do not provide as much assurance to the auditor as tests of details, auditors usually rely solely

on analytical review procedures only when the risk that a financial statement misstatement will exceed the tolerable error for a balance or class is low. For example, it is not unusual for an analytical review procedure of the office (or prepaid) supplies account between two years to suffice as the sole substantive test even though the dollar balance exceeds the tolerable error for the account.

Decide whether a 100 percent examination is necessary. The auditor's decision to perform tests of details on an account balance or class of transactions presents him with a choice between a complete examination or sampling. When making this choice, the auditor should consider whether the cost of a 100 percent examination of all the items in the balance or class is justified. Of course, if the auditor examines only a portion of the items in a balance or class, sampling risk exists.

When performing substantive tests of details, the auditor is concerned with the risk of two types of incorrect decisions. As set forth in SAS no. 39, the risks are

1 Incorrect rejection—"the risk that the sample supports the conclusion that the recorded account balance [or class of transactions] is materially misstated when it is not materially misstated."

2 Incorrect acceptance—"the risk that the sample supports the conclusion that the recorded account balance [or class of transactions] is not materially misstated when it is materially misstated."[5]

"The risk of incorrect rejection . . . relate[s] to the efficiency of the audit. For example, if the auditor's evaluation of an audit sample leads him to the initial erroneous conclusion that a balance is materially misstated when it is not, the application of additional audit procedures and consideration of other audit evidence would ordinarily lead the auditor to the correct conclusion. . . . The risk of incorrect acceptance . . . relate[s] to the effectiveness of an audit in detecting an existing material misstatement."[6]

The following sections discuss how the auditor can control the latter risk in audit sampling. Of course, in situations when the auditor cannot accept any sampling risk, a 100 percent examination of all the items in the balance or class of transactions must be

---

[4]An American Institute of CPAs task force on materiality and audit risk currently is considering guidance on how auditors determine materiality levels and how auditors should allocate preliminary estimates of materiality to account balances and classes of transactions that make up the financial statements.

[5]SAS no. 39, par. 12. See also *AICPA Professional Standards,* AU sec. 350.12.

[6]Ibid., par. 13-14. See also *AICPA Professional Standards,* AU sec. 350.13-14.

performed. For example, if the activity in an investment account consists of only a few large transactions, auditors usually will examine all the investment activity. The auditor usually is willing to accept some sampling risk in testing accounts receivable and inventory.

Identify key items. Even when the auditor has decided to test the account balance or class of transactions using audit sampling, some items in the balance or class might be individually significant, and the auditor should examine these individually. The auditor should identify these key items and separate them from the other items in the balance or class before he begins sampling. Key items may include any items that have large book values or items that have special risks associated with them. For example, auditors usually identify all high-dollar items for complete examination. What constitutes a high-dollar item depends on audit judgment. However, any item for which the book value individually exceeds the amount of tolerable error allocated to the account or class would generally qualify as a high-dollar (key) item. An auditor may also identify unusual items as key items.

Decide whether examining key items is sufficient. After all the key items have been identified, the items that remain in the population may not be significant enough in the aggregate to warrant any additional testing; examination of the key items may be sufficient to achieve the audit objectives. If not, the auditor must choose among examining a sample of the remaining items in the population, performing an analytical review procedure on these items or performing both substantive tests. This choice should be based on the approach that, under the circumstances, is most effective and efficient in providing sufficient, competent evidential matter.

Sample? If the auditor decides to sample the remaining portion of the items in the account balance or class of transactions, he must determine a sample size, select and examine the items and evaluate the results. Each of these steps is briefly described in the following sections.

Determine the sample size. Reliance on other audit procedures, the tolerable error, the expected size and frequency of errors and the division of the population into

homogeneous groups influence how many items the auditor should sample.

Because an audit includes many tests that are interrelated, the sample size for a given substantive test depends to a degree on the extent to which the auditor is planning reliance on other audit procedures. These other audit procedures include planned reliance on internal accounting controls and reliance on other substantive tests including analytical review procedures. The greater the reliance on other audit procedures, the smaller the substantive test sample size needs to be and vice versa. For example, when determining the sample size for confirmation of accounts receivable, the auditor should consider the reliance to be placed on related internal accounting controls and tests such as subsequent cash collection procedures and a review of collectibility. An expansion of subsequent collection procedures would reduce the necessary sample size for the confirmation of accounts receivable.

As the amount of tolerable error the auditor is willing to accept for a balance or class of transaction increases, the sample size decreases. For example, if the tolerable error for the finished goods inventory increases from $50,000 to $60,000, the sample size will decrease if all other planning considerations remain the same. Conversely, if the tolerable error decreases from $50,000 to $30,000, the sample size will increase. Ultimately, if the tolerable error is reduced to zero, a 100 percent examination of all items will be required.

As the size and frequency of errors in the account balance or class of transactions increases, the likelihood becomes greater that the total amount of error in the balance or class exceeds tolerable error. Consequently, an auditor would need more information from his sample to verify the accuracy of the account balance or recorded amount of transactions, and the sample size would increase. In effect, the auditor is less willing to accept sampling risk knowing that the initial risk of error is high.

An auditor who is planning a sampling application as part of his substantive testing also should consider the possibility of dividing the population into relatively homogeneous groups for sampling purposes. When an auditor uses sampling, he usually bases inferences about the balance or class on an average value related to the sample items. By dividing the items making up the balance or class of transactions into relatively homogeneous groups (generally by dollar amount) and selecting a sample from each group, the audit objective usually can be achieved with a smaller overall sample size. This process is called stratification. Because the auditor's interest generally is directed to large dollar amounts, stratification allows the auditor to focus more attention on items with large book values. The identification of key items, discussed earlier, is a form of stratification.

One characteristic of an account balance or class of transactions whose effect on sample size generally is overstated is the effect of the number of items making up the balance or class (the population size). This is because the incremental information obtained from adding items to a sample decreases as the sample size becomes larger. For example, the added information obtained from examining an additional item when the auditor already has examined 200 items generally is small. Consequently, population size in general should be ignored as a significant factor influencing sample size unless the population size is very small.

Exhibit 2, page 8, summarizes the effect of each of the factors that influence sample size. Determining an appropriate sample size based on these factors requires professional judgment. The appendix to this article, page 9, provides some additional guidance on estimating appropriate sample size to the auditor using nonstatistical sampling.

Select a sample. After determining an appropriate sample size, SAS no. 39 requires the auditor to select a sample that is expected to be representative of the account balance or class of transactions of interest. *Representative* means that the sample should exhibit the same characteristics of interest (generally dollars in error) as the balance or class it was selected from. SAS no. 39 does not require the auditor to prove that a sample is representative of the balance or class. As a matter of fact, because of sampling risk a sample rarely will perfectly represent the balance or class from which it is selected. However, SAS no. 39 does imply a need for auditors to understand which selection plans are more likely to result in representative samples. Descriptions of four types of selection plans follow:

1 Random number sampling—uses random numbers taken from a random number table or generated by a computer. The auditor matches items subject to sampling to random numbers in the same order that the random numbers are generated until he has identified enough items to equal the desired sample size. Because each item in the account balance or class of transactions has an equal chance of selection, a random sample will, on average, be representative of the balance or class from which it was selected. Of course, any one sample might not be representative—sampling risk is inherent in all sampling applications.

2 Systematic sampling—uses one or more fixed intervals to select a sample. For example, if an auditor wishes to select a sample of 100 items from the 1,000 items that make up an account balance, every tenth item would be selected after choosing a random starting point. An auditor using systematic sampling should be careful to avoid selecting a sample that coincides with any pattern of error that might exist in the balance or class. An auditor can reduce the chance of selecting an unrepresentative sample that is caused by a pattern of errors in the balance or class by selecting several random starts.

3 Haphazard selection—relies on the auditor's judgment to select items in a "random fashion" without the assistance of random numbers. The auditor selects items from an account balance or class of transactions without any special reason for

Exhibit 2

Factors influencing sample size*

Factor	Conditions leading to smaller sample size	Conditions leading to larger sample size
Reliance on internal accounting controls	Greater reliance on internal accounting controls	Less reliance on internal accounting controls
Reliance on other substantive tests (including analytical review procedures)	Substantial reliance	Little or no reliance
Measure of tolerable error for a specific account or class of transactions	Larger tolerable error	Smaller tolerable error
Expected size and frequency of errors	Smaller errors or lower frequency	Larger errors or higher frequency
Division of population into homogeneous groups	Larger number of homogeneous groups	Smaller number of or no homogeneous groups
Number of items in population	Little effect on sample size unless the population is small	

*This table is consistent with the appendix of SAS no. 39, *Audit Sampling*.

selecting or omitting any specific items. If an auditor can avoid unintentionally selecting or omitting items such as the first or last item, or physically large or small items in a balance or class, a haphazard sample can be expected to be representative.

4 Block sampling—uses groups of contiguous items selected from an account balance or class of transactions. For example, examining one month of sales with the objective of reaching a conclusion about sales for the year would be a block sampling application. Items in the other months of the year would not have a chance of selection. Although conceivably a block sample might be representative of the account balance or class of transactions from which it was selected if the block, or blocks, selected happen to contain errors or irregularities in the same proportion as the balance or class as a whole, in general there is little basis for this assumption. Consequently, extreme caution should be used with block sampling.

Examine selected items. The auditor should apply his planned procedures to each item selected as part of the sample. The choice of procedures is an ordinary audit decision and is not determined by the auditor's decision to sample or to examine 100 percent of an account balance or class

of transactions. If the auditor is unable to apply the planned procedures to some items in the sample, he usually applies alternative procedures to those items. If neither planned nor alternative procedures can be applied to an item or a portion of an item, that item may conservatively be considered to be in error for the purposes of evaluating the sample results.

Evaluate the sample results and reach an overall conclusion. If the auditor discovers errors or irregularities in a sample, it is likely that additional errors or irregularities exist in the other items that make up the balance or class. SAS no. 39 requires the auditor to project the identified errors and irregularities to the balance or class from which the sample was selected to estimate the total amount of misstatement in that balance or class. There are several acceptable ways to project errors from a sample. For example, assume that an auditor identified a $1,000 error in a sample. If the sample included 10 percent of the account balance, the error in that balance could be projected to be $10,000. Any amount of error discovered in the individually significant (key) items should be added to the estimated total projected error in the population subject to sampling. For example, if $500 in error was discovered in the audit of key items, the total estimated error for the preceding illustration would be $10,500.

The auditor also should consider sampling risk when evaluating sample results. Although sampling risk cannot be accurately measured by an auditor using nonstatistical sampling, it exists nonetheless. SAS no. 39 requires the auditor to consider the likelihood that the difference between the total projected error and the tolerable error could be accounted for by allowance for sampling risk. In general, the larger the sample size, the smaller the needed allowance for sampling risk. If the total projected error is close to the tolerable error, the auditor might consider examining an additional sample to gain additional insurance that the true error in the account balance or class of transactions is less than the tolerable error. For example, if the tolerable error in the preceding example was $12,000, the allowance for sampling risk would be only $1,500 ($12,000–$10,500). When the projected error is close to the tolerable error, the sample results in general would not be considered as supporting the book value. However, if the auditor's understanding of the business or the results of other related audit procedures suggest that the balance is not materially misstated, the auditor should consider expanding the sample or performing additional audit procedures to satisfy himself about the book value. If, on the other hand, the tolerable error had been $50,000 in the preceding example, the sample results generally would be considered as supporting the book value and no further work would be required.

In addition to making a quantitative evaluation of the sample results, auditors also should consider the qualitative aspects of any errors or irregularities that are identified in the sample. The auditor should consider the nature and cause of all misstatements identified as a result of the sampling procedure. In some cases, qualitative considerations override quantitative findings. For example, the discovery of only one error in a sample might lead to an acceptable quantitative conclusion. However, further investigation of the error might reveal a related party transaction or a fraudulent transaction that might cause the auditor to perform additional procedures.

The auditor should consider the results of sampling procedures along with all other audit procedures, such as analytical review procedures or a complete examination of an account balance, when forming an opinion on the presentation of the financial statement in accordance with generally accepted accounting principles.

Summary

The issuance of SAS no. 39 has caused practitioners to focus their attention on the proper use of sampling in auditing. To help the auditor in implementing that statement, this article presents—in nontechnical general terms—a framework for planning, performing and evaluating audit sampling. In addition, the article's appendix should help the auditor using nonstatistical sampling to determine appropriate sample sizes.

Appendix
A model to assist the auditor using nonstatistical sampling to determine sample sizes for substantive tests*

Although an understanding of the relative effect of various planning considerations on sample size is essential to designing a nonstatistical sampling application (see exhibit 2), the auditor also should have some understanding of appropriate sample sizes in applying those considerations. The auditor using nonstatistical sampling to determine appropriate sample sizes may find useful a model based on a sampling technique known as dollar-unit sampling (DUS).

DUS is useful for this purpose because knowledge of the inherent characteristics of a population is not required to estimate sample sizes. However, the selection technique required by a strict application of DUS in general differs from that used by the nonstatistical sampler. Because of this, the nonstatistical sample size generally should be larger than the sample size for a strict DUS sample. Accordingly, the non-

---

*This model is currently being used in practice by a national public accounting firm and in general has proved to be satisfactory for nonstatistical applications.

statistical sample sizes presented in the following model are somewhat larger than strict DUS sample sizes.

The following model illustrates the relative effect of different planning considerations on sample size and is not intended to be a substitute for the auditor's professional judgment.

Step one

Classify the degree of audit assurance desired for the sample as follows:

a Substantial—a relatively high level of assurance generally indicating little or no reliance is placed on internal accounting control or other related substantive procedures.

b Moderate—an average degree of assurance generally indicating some reliance is placed on internal accounting control or other related substantive procedures.

c Little—the minimal assurance generally indicating considerable reliance is placed on internal accounting controls or other related substantive procedures.

Step two

Choose an appropriate "assurance factor" as follows:

	Assurance factors	
Degree of audit assurance	*Where little error is anticipated*[1]	*Where some error is anticipated*
Substantial	6	12
Moderate	4	8
Little	2	4

[1]Little error means that the auditor judgmentally assesses that the probable total monetary error in the account being tested does not exceed one-third of tolerable error.

Step three

Estimate the book value of the account balance or class of transactions after deducting any items examined 100 percent.

Step four

Computer sample size as equal to

$$\frac{\text{Balance or class book value}}{\text{Tolerable error}} \times \text{Assurance factor}$$

Step five

The nonstatistical sample size selected should be reasonably close to the sample computed in step four.

For example, assume that an auditor is designing a sample of accounts receivable with a book value of $150,000 and desires "moderate" audit assurance. First the auditor should identify those key items to examine 100 percent—in this case, assume there were 12 key items with a total book value of $70,000. The remaining items with a book value of $80,000 would be subject to sampling. If the auditor assesses the tolerable error as $8,000, and if no errors are anticipated, the estimated sample size is

$$\frac{\text{Balance or class book value}}{\text{Tolerable error}} \times \text{Assurance factor}$$

$$\frac{\$80,000}{\$8,000} \times 4 = 40 \text{ sampling units}$$

In this case, the auditor would examine a total of 52 items—12 individually significant items with a book value of $70,000 and 40 sampling units.

The above sample size of 40 items is appropriate if the auditor has identified key items to be examined 100 percent and uses some minimum stratification of the account balance or class of transactions in selecting the items to be sampled. For example, minimum stratification could be achieved by dividing the balance or class subject to sampling into at least two groups: two-thirds of the sample from the higher-dollar items and the remainder from the lower-dollar items. If stratification is not cost-effective, then the calculated sample size should be increased to compensate for the lack of stratification. We recommend that in this latter situation the computed sample size be doubled. ■

Ronald M. Copeland, Ph.D., and Ted D. Englebrecht

Statistical Sampling: An Uncertain Defense Against Legal Liability

In some situations statistical sampling may provide an important legal defense for the auditor. However, as the authors point out, there are serious pitfalls to be avoided in the design and application of the sampling techniques.

Ronald M. Copeland, Ph.D., is Professor of Business Administration, University of South Carolina. A member of the American Accounting Association and the Financial Executives Institute, he has authored numerous books and articles. Ted D. Englebrecht is Instructor of Accounting, University of South Carolina. A member of the American Accounting Association, he has written extensively.

Legal liability cases involving auditors have mushroomed in recent years. Hardly a day passes without the financial press reporting new litigation directed against an auditor. References in *The Accountants' Index* to "accountants' liability" jumped over sevenfold from 1961 to 1973. Litigation is being filed against auditors under traditional common law grounds, alleged statutory violations, and on grounds from emerging case law that reflect society's expanded view of auditing responsibility in defending the public interest.

Surprisingly enough, statistical sampling has not been raised as a primary issue in any recent case. We say surprisingly, because auditors increasingly use statistical sampling as an inherent part of many audit programs. Statistical sampling technology offers a sound defense against some types of allegations, although its incorrect use expands the auditors' vulnerability. The objective of this article is to discuss statistical samping as a possible defense against legal liability.

Nature of Statistical Sampling in Auditing

Sampling involves selecting a part of a population and using characteristics of that part to draw inferences about the entire population. It is common procedure to draw inferences about a population attribute from a sampling. The sommelier who tastes a bottle of wine to determine the acceptability of a particular bottling employs sampling. The difference between common uses of sampling and that used in audits is in the methodology of choosing the sample.[1]

Judgmental sampling for auditing purposes is very like the sommelier sampling the wine. Statistical sampling for audit purposes requires random selection of items to be evaluated: the results of this evaluation may be tested on the basis of mathematical laws of probability.

Purposes of Statistical Sampling in Auditing

Modern auditors readily adopt statistical sampling methods in their programs. This acceptance of statistical sampling reflects, in part, a desire to achieve greater objectivity than attainable through more traditional judgmental sampling. Auditors strive for this objectivity, both to provide better services for their clients, and to produce demonstrable evidence of professional diligence in an audit engagement. A consensus of current auditing thought favors statistical sampling, since it allows auditors to state the specific levels of reliability and precision used to formulate their opinion. Furthermore, many users report that statistical sampling often entails much smaller sample sizes than previously needed to provide the required degree of confidence: this too increases the popularity of statistical technology.

The statistical determination of samples aids the professional auditor in each of the following interrelated areas: specifying risks, eliminating judgmental bias, forcing auditing discipline, evidencing compliance with auditing standards and defending the scope of work effort.

Sampling risks can be controlled and specified. Statistical estimation provides the auditor with a tool which allows him to specify the degree of precision and reliability of his estimates, i.e., the range of values within which the true value is expected to fall and

---

[1] John R. Stockton and Charles T. Clark, *Introduction to Business & Economic Statistics*, fourth ed. (1971), p. 235.

the degree of confidence that the true value would be contained within that range. Additionally the use of statistical technology allows the auditor to make explicit trade-offs between risk and amount of sampling effort, an advantage not available when he relies upon traditional judgmental sampling plans.

Statistical sampling eliminates some judgmental bias. Unrestricted random sampling plans require that each and every element in the population be given an equal chance of being selected.[2] Once an element has been selected, it cannot be ignored or excluded for any reason. Thus, statistical sampling plans offer the best chance that the sample will represent the population and produce the best estimate. While statistical samples rest upon certain long-run laws of chance, judgmental samples do not. A jury of laypeople may be more easily convinced that scientifically valid methods based upon long-run laws of chance can produce more appropriate indicators of underlying values than judgmental sampling plans can produce.

Statistical sampling forces discipline in auditing. Statistical sampling plans force more discipline on the total auditing function than normally required in judgmental sampling. If pressed for time by either exigencies of his own staff or the impatience of the client, an auditor might be able to rationalize reduction in a judgmental sample, since its scope was originally set by an intuitive process. But once the size of a statistical sample is determined, the sampling procedure specified, and the desired precision/reliability limits stated, the auditor has no justification for curtailing the scope of his procedure. Furthermore, auditing discipline provides the audit supervisor with direct evidence of internal compliance by staff personnel.

Sampling working papers pro-

vide courts with evidence of compliance with generally accepted auditing procedures. The standards of accuracy are no different for estimates based upon statistical samples than those based on judgmental samples. In either case, the auditor would be concerned with compliance to the first and third auditing standards of field work.[3] Typical work sheets underlying a statistical sample might provide convincing evidence of audit planning, supervision and competence relative to the first standard. Compliance with the third standard of field work on the sufficiency of evidential matter may be evaluated in terms of the sample size and specification of precision and reliability levels. Auditors are in a stronger defensive position with a sample that has been scientifically drawn; the precision and reliability levels can be quantified, and sample size is commensurate with the chosen levels of reliability and precision.

The size of sample can be determined rationally. Traditional judgmental sampling is inherently vague about the specific number of items to sample. Usually the sample size is fixed as a stated proportion of a population. Many auditors continue to fix sample size as a proportion of the total population by, for example, auditing one month's vouchers out of the total for the year. But proportional samples fail on two counts: they may not be representative (as previously discussed) and they may not be economical. Statistically drawn samples are less vulnerable to this type of criticism.

Statistical Sampling—A Defense for the Auditor

While statistical sampling has yet to become an issue in a legal liability case involving accountants, we can reasonably expect one in the not too distant future. If and when this happens, the accountant will face four major hurdles: (1) getting the sample data admitted as evidence, (2) getting the evidence accepted as having significant

weight, (3) using the evidence to convince the judge and jury, and (4) avoiding pitfalls that extend liability beyond that which would have existed if statistical sampling had not been introduced. Regarding these issues, the accountant must be concerned with two types of considerations—prior and prospective. Prior considerations relate to issues with which the auditor ought to have been concerned before and during the planning and implementation stage of his statistical sampling effort. Prospective considerations relate to those issues that may arise after the audit but before or during the trial.

Admissibility of Sampling Data as Evidence

Statistical sampling data must be admitted as evidence by the court before it can provide a valuable defense for the auditor. Federal courts have recognized since 1870 that samples based on mathematical probability statistics can be admitted as evidence.[4,5] Unfortunately, there is a paucity of cases in which sample evidence on economic data posed a contested issue to the courts.

Courts give substantial weight to certain prior factors in admitting sample data as evidence. These factors should be directly incorporated into an audit sampling plan to enhance the legal admissibility of statistical sampling results. Major factors considered essential by the courts in determining the admissibility of sample evidence are as follows:

1. Population should be definable.

2. Sample data should be representative of the population.

3. Sampling results may be regarded as business records.

4. Sample data may be considered as a recorded past recollection.

5. Verification of sample results should not require an excessive amount of time nor raise numerous side issues.

---

[2] Throughout this article we shall assume that unrestricted random sampling is appropriate. Our conclusions change only slightly where this assumption is relaxed. If the auditor believes that unrestricted random sampling will produce a sample that is not representative of the population, he should redefine his population to make it more homogeneous or he should choose another sampling plan.

[3] See Appendix A, pp. 36–42, Statement on Auditing Standards, No. 1, (New York: AICPA, 1973).

[4] The *Howland Will* case, 4 Am. L. Rev. 625, 648–50 (1870).

[5] Fred M. Kecker, "Admissibility in Courts of Economic Data Based on Samples," *28 Journal of Business*, p. 114.

The importance of homogeneity in sampling has been recognized repeatedly by the courts in cases tried under the Federal Food and Drug Acts.[6] John Henry Wigmore, an authority on legal evidence, concluded the following about homogeneity in sampling:

Samples are admissible as evidence of the whole lot from which they were drawn only where the mass is substantially uniform with reference to the quality in question and where the sample portion is of such a nature as to be fairly representative.[7]

The definability of the population is a factor cited frequently by the courts as essential for admission of sampling results.[8] The Federal Judicial Council's *Manual for Complex and Multi-District Litigation* states that the party offering the survey data as evidence has the burden of proving that the survey was administered in accordance with accepted principles of survey research, a vital part being examination of the proper universe.[9] Hearsay evidence is not admissible under most circumstances. Consequently, the hearsay evidence rule may preclude an auditor from offering his recollection of the sampling results as evidence in court. However, he may be able to avoid the hearsay rule if he previously included the methodology and the results of the statistical sampling process in the working papers.[10]

The "business record" exception should enable the sampling results, as recorded in the working papers, to be classified as business records of the auditor used to support his audit opinion. If the business record exception is denied, then "the past recollection recorded" exemption should be used. Under this rule, the court would admit a written record (working papers) as evidence if it was prepared when the events were fresh in the witness's (auditor's) mind.[11]

Although statistical sampling results may be admitted under the technical rules of evidence, they may, nonetheless, still be excluded if the court rules that an offer of proof and counterproof will require an excessive amount of time. The court may also exclude sample evidence if the offer of proof and counterproof is likely to raise marginal issues which will unjustly distract the jury from the principal issues in the case. Thus, the method of admitting sample data becomes a problem: How to introduce complex concepts without using undue time or raising peripheral issues.[12]

Evidence Accepted as Having Significant Weight

Even though the Supreme Court ruled favorably on the admissibility of sampling data, other courts may not automatically follow this lead. Some may first seek an alternative source of evidence. The acceptability of sample data basically reduces to an economics problem. For example, a trial judge may accept a sampling procedure in lieu of a complete enumeration when no alternative is reasonable and practical.[13] Obtaining complete information for a large firm may well be unreasonable and impractical. In the recent *Bar Chris*[14] case, the court states that a complete examination is not needed by auditors before an opinion can be expressed. Whenever a complete examination is not performed, the auditor would have the burden of proving that the

scope and depth of his examination was sufficient. The critical factors considered by courts in appraising the significance of sample findings are as follows:

1. Sample plan should be designed in conformity with objective statistical methods.
2. Sample data should be gathered by skilled technicians.
3. There should be supportable evidence of homogeneity in the population.

In *State Wholesale Grocery* v. *Great Atlantic & Pacific Tea Company*,[15] a sample survey was held to conform to generally accepted standards of objective procedure in the field of opinion surveys. The trial court concluded in *People* v. *Franklin National Bank of Franklin Square*[16] that the design of the sample must conform to accepted statistical methods, and the sampling process should be carried out by people who are careful, intelligent and unbiased in their application of the sampling technique. The court also indicated that random sampling with no human judgment in the choice of sample elements is essential.

The above decisions imply that accountants who adhere closely to the first and third auditing standards of fieldwork should not encounter any difficulty concerning the admissibility of their sample data. Therefore, statistical sampling plans that are based upon sound mathematical principles, that are meticulously planned and executed, and that are fully documented in the working papers should provide significant evidence in defense of any audit when properly introduced and admitted. For example, audit sample size is one item upon which statistical methodology can provide conclusive evidence.

Using Sample Evidence to Convince

Successful use of statistical technology to defend an audit opinion requires two ingredients—that the auditor *has a case* and that he

[6] See *A. O. Andersen* v. *United States*, 284 Fed. 542 (9th Cir. 1922); *United States* v. *935 Cases of Tomato Puree*, 65 F.Supp. 503 (N.D. Ohio 1946); *United States* v *1459 Cases of Canned Salmon*. Decisions of courts in cases under the federal Food and Drug Acts 995 (W. D. Wash. 1921).

[7] 2 Wigmore, Sec. 439.

[8] *United States* v. *88 Cases, More or Less*, 187 F.2d 967 (C.A. 3, 1951), cert. denied 342 U.S. 861 (1951); *United States* v. *United Shoe Machinery Corp.*, 110 F.Supp. 295 (D.C. Mass., 1953).

[9] Board of Editors, Federal Judicial Center, *Manual for Complex and Multi-District Litigation* (1970), p. 38.

[10] Allan H. McCoid, "The Admissibility of Sample Data into a Court of Law: Some Further Thoughts," *UCLA Law Review*, (February 1957), pp. 238–239.

[11] *Ibid.*

[12] *Ibid.*, pp. 248–249.

[13] R. Clay Sprawls, "The Admissibility of Sample Data into a Court of Law: A Case History," *UCLA Law Review*, (February 1957), p. 230.

[14] *Escott* v. *Bar Chris Construction Corp.*, 283 F.Supp. 643 (S.D.N.Y., 1968).

[15] 154 F.Supp. 471 (1957).

[16] 347 U.S. 373, rev'd. 113 N.E. 2d 796 and 118 N.Y.S. ed 210, aff'd. 105 N.Y.S. 2d 81.

presents his case. Having a case depends upon the actions taken before and during the audit while the presentation depends upon skill at marshalling evidence and defending it from counterattack. Presentation hinges upon form, approach and substance.

Form has to do with theatrics. Many a case has been won simply because a witness appeared to know what he was talking about or because the attorney appeared to have demonstrated a particular point. Appearances are extremely important in jury trials and may be important in nonjury trials as well. The lesson for accountants is that the expert witness on statistical matters must have a manner of presentation that commands respect, is open and honest, patient and has all the other attributes that will cause a listener to have faith in him.

Approach has to do with the direction and ordering of testimony. On statistical matters, auditors and attorneys must take an educative approach, since much of the material is technically beyond the average listener.

Substance is of utmost importance in determining the viability of the auditor's presentation. Consequently, the methodology employed by the auditor should be based on objective (mathematically sound) techniques of statistical sampling. It is essential to employ methods suited to the task and to be able to defend these methods upon critical examination of the following factors:

The circumstances were appropriate for statistical sampling;

The auditor's judgment was exercised correctly in determining the sample size, or precision/reliability limits;

The decisions pertaining to judgment problems (management and audit significance) were appropriate in evaluating the sample results.

Interpretive Problem

A judge or jury may have difficulty determining the degree of compliance with auditing standards. These standards are stated in qualitative terms, but audit quality is measured in quantitative terms. In the Continental Vending[17] case, accounting experts testifying before the court disagreed on the degree of compliance with auditing standards. When accountants cannot agree among themselves, judges are bound to be perplexed. This dilemma is compounded whenever a court establishes new auditing standards and/or accounting principles, as was done in Continental Vending and *Bar Chris*. Statistical methodology allows an auditor to establish quantitative standards for determining the extent of the audit examination. Pre-specification of precision and reliability limits provide courts with objective criteria for appraising the sample results. Additionally, the court would also be able to quantitatively measure the extent to which compliance with auditing standards was accomplished.

Sample data has long been accepted as evidence before administrative tribunals. However, these tribunals are distinctly different from courts, in that their decision-making body is composed of "experts" in an administrative area as contrasted to "nonexpert" judges and juries.[18] Administrative tribunals have technical expertise over their area of administration. But courts typically lack understanding of statistical sampling methods, a point noted by Joel Dean as the greatest single obstruction to enlarging judicial reliance on statistical sampling data.[19] Albert Sawyer, a lawyer experienced in submitting sample data before the courts, labels the risk of introducing sample data as "the tyranny of ignorance."[20] While the problem of statistical sampling knowledge in court is real, increased exposure to results of political polls, opinion surveys and marketing surveys tend to heighten the sophistication of the general population.

Avoiding Pitfalls

Reliance on purely mechanical applications of statistical sampling techniques may leave auditors more vulnerable than if they had employed judgmental sampling techniques. An auditor's professional competence can be easily shattered in the court's eyes when opposing counsel demonstrates that the design or application of the statistical procedure was faulty. The sufficiency of sample evidence is open to query when the sample size is extremely sensitive to minor changes in any of the input variables, especially the projection of the universe standard deviation. Undoubtedly, auditors attempting to support their position on a given sample size would encounter great difficulty trying to convince a judge, jury of laypeople or an irate client of their proper auditing standards, if a simple sensitivity analysis demonstrates sizable fluctuations in sample sizes with only negligible changes in the variables.

By taking the following steps, the auditor should be able to reduce the questions raised by sensitivity analysis:

After compiling a sample, the auditor would be well advised to determine the shape of the sample distribution.[21] Estimates of population parameters based on statistics from extremely skewed samples may not be representative of the true population parameters. (a) Where the sample is skewed, the auditor should immediately consider increasing the sample size to produce a more normal distribution; (b) Where the expanded sample is still skewed, the auditor should reexamine his assumption that the population is normally distributed and should redefine the population being sampled, or abandon unrestricted random sampling; (c) In any event, the audit workpapers should reflect the shape of the original preliminary or expanded sample distribution.

The auditor should compare the

---

[17] *United States* v. *Simon*, 425 F.2d 796 (2d Cir. 1969), cert. denied, 397 U.S. 1006 (1970).

[18] Sprawls, *op. cit.*, p. 222.

[19] Joel Dean, "Sampling to Produce Evidence on Which Courts Will Rely," *Current Business Studies*, (October 1954), p. 11.

[20] Albert E. Sawyer, "Commentary in Seminar," *Current Business Studies*, (October 1954), p. 62.

[21] See Sidney Siegel, *Nonparametric Statistics* (New York: McGraw Hill Book Co., 1956), pp. 47–58, for a discussion of the Kolmogorov-Smirnov test for normality.

pilot sample mean and estimated population distributions with those determined from the ultimate sample. Large differences indicate that the preliminary sample produced nonrepresentative data.

The audit work papers should contain a simple sensitivity analysis of the affect that differences in any of the statistical inputs have on parameter estimates. If major differences are found, the auditor would be well advised to supplement the statistical work with additional audit procedures, e.g., more intensive review of internal control or more detailed analysis of transactions.

Whenever auditors modify statistical procedures applied to ongoing audit engagements, they subject themselves to potential wounds from a two-edged sword, as happened in a recent nonaccounting context. Time Inc. charged W. R. Simmons & Associates with using "biased and unreliable statistics" in preparing a magazine audience study. The current figures prepared by Simmons are at variance with those prepared during the period 1962–73, and reflected an alleged change in procedures. Time Inc. charges that either the current figures and procedures are defective, invalid and unreliable or else the past figures and procedures were defective, invalid and unreliable.[22]

Implications

Many independent auditors are discovering with alarm that auditing is far from a safe and secure profession. This uneasiness is due in large part to the ability of third parties not in privity to the audit contract to challenge auditors with class actions in heretofore untested situations. Several cases have found auditors failing to adhere to generally accepted auditing standards.[23] However, other cases imperil auditors with audit standards introduced by the courts,[24] and with new accounting principles that have not received prior authoritative support.[25] Additionally, the accounting profession may find itself responsible for discovering fraud, as suggested by John C. Burton, the Chief Accountant of the SEC.

I think the question of the auditor and fraud is one that has to be attacked this year. The historical posture of the auditor, which seems to be that fraud is not what the CPA is responsible for finding, has to be reconsidered.[26]

Undoubtedly, Mr. Burton's viewpoint reflects society's enlarged view that the auditor's duty is to safeguard the public interest, not that of his client.

The authors see statistical sampling as a defense in this expanded legal liability arena. Admittedly, statistical sampling is not without some perplexities and difficulties. However, these problems can be overcome, so that objective measures of statistical sampling can provide auditors with a worthwhile and viable defense.

Conclusions

Statistical sampling results, based on objective and accepted methodology (such as long-run laws of chance), provide the auditor with data readily defensible in court. This data reduces the vulnerability of the auditor to legal liability claims, because it gives the court *quantitative* standards to measure *quantitative* results, and the probability that deviations from the universe are not included in the results has been mathematically determined.

Statistical sampling, however, is not without some problems. Auditors, therefore, whenever employing statistical sampling should remember that:

Statistical sampling can be a double-edged sword;

Areas of vulnerability must be carefully checked by: (a) utilizing sensitivity analysis in the audit work papers, (b) investigating any violations of assumptions, such as randomness, stratification, skewness, nonnormality, etc., and (c) adhering at all times to auditing standards;

The available measures to strengthen sample results should be fully utilized.

The authors feel that auditors cannot afford to overlook the objective techniques of statistical sampling as a viable defense in legal liability situations. Ω

[22] As reported in "Time Inc. Sues W. R. Simmons, Charges Audience-Study Statistics Are Unreliable," *Wall Street Journal*, January 16, 1975, p. 15.

[23] *Escott* v. *Bar Chris Construction Corp.*, 283 F.Supp. 643 (S.D.N.Y., 1968); Note: "U.S. Financial Inc. Accused of Fraud to Create Profit," *Wall Street Journal* (February 26, 1974), p. 4.; Carl S. Hawkins, "Professional Negligence Liability of Public Accountants," *Contemporary Accounting and Its Environment*, edited by John W. Buckley (1969), pp. 91–96.

[24] *Rhode Island Hospital Trust National Bank* v. *Swartz*, 455 F.2d 847 (4th Cir. 1972); *United States* v. *Simon*, 425 F.2d 796 (2d Cir. 1969), cert. denied, 397 U.S. 1006 (1970).

[25] See *Bar Chris*, note 15 supra.

[26] Note: "The SEC and the World of Accounting in 1974," the *Journal of Accountancy*, (July 1974), p. 59.

CASE 17

AUDIT SAMPLING

You are a CPA who has been employed by a large national accounting firm for seven years. During the last two years, you have been responsible for developing several of the national firm's staff training programs including a course on audit sampling. Due to your experience, the regional CPA firm of Seim, Sestak and Johnson, in your hometown, made you a job offer at a salary substantially more than you were making with the national firm. You have accepted their offer and have just reported for work. The personnel partner, Mr. Mark Jilek, has asked you to develop a staff training course in audit sampling for new staff members who have recently graduated from college. You and Mr. Jilek determine that the course should cover only the concepts and terms contained in SAS No. 39. In this regard, you developed questions which Mr. Jilek has asked you to present at next week's partners' meeting for their review. The discussion questions are as follows:

CASE DISCUSSION QUESTIONS

1. Discuss the purpose of SAS No. 39 and the two general approaches to audit sampling.

2. The use of audit sampling relates to the third standard of field work which requires sufficient, competent evidential matter to be obtained to afford a reasonable basis for an opinion. Discuss and relate the terms *sufficient* and *competent* to audit sampling.

3. The third standard of field work implies a certain element of uncertainty is involved. Discuss uncertainty as it relates to audit sampling.

4. Auditor judgment is required in assessing sampling risk. In performing substantive tests of details and compliance tests of internal accounting control the auditor is concerned with certain aspects of sampling risk. Discuss the aspects of sampling risk that the auditor is concerned with.

5. When planning a particular sample for a substantive test of details, the auditor must consider relevant audit objectives, materiality levels, etc. Discuss fully the relevancy of audit objectives, materiality and other considerations that relate to sampling in substantive tests of details.

6. SAS No. 39 provides guidance concerning the performance and evaluation of sampling in substantive tests of details (paragraphs 25-30 of the SAS). Outline what the auditor should do with respect to:

    a. Performing audit procedures.

    b. Evaluating sample results (include in your discussion the qualitative aspects of errors).

7. Discuss fully the planning involved with respect to sampling and compliance tests of internal accounting controls. Your answer should include a discussion of the auditor's allowable risk of overreliance and the characteristics of the population of interest.

8. Discuss the term, *tolerable risk*.

9. What are Dual-Purpose Samples? Discuss.

10. Explain the sample selection and performance evaluation as they relate to compliance tests of internal accounting controls.

(Question 11 may be assigned when students have read the article "Audit Sampling: A Practical Approach," by Warren, Yates, and Zuber)

11. Assume that you are conducting an audit of a small manufacturing client and you are designing a sample as part of your audit procedures to be applied to accounts receivable. You determine that accounts receivable have a book value of $1,500,000. Based on your study of internal accounting control you conclude that you can place "moderate" audit assurance on the client's internal accounting control. You have identified those key items to examine 100 percent—in this case, assume there are 36 key items with a total book value of $700,000. The remaining items with a book value of $800,000 are subject to sampling. Assume you assess the tolerable error as $60,000. Also, assuming no errors are anticipated, what is the estimated sample size?

The First, Second, and Third Standards of Reporting

(Sections 410 and 420, SAS No. 1, Section 411, SAS No. 5, Section 431, SAS No. 32, and Section 435, SAS No. 21)

The first three standards of reporting are as follows:

1. The report shall state whether the financial statements are presented in accordance with generally accepted accounting principles.

2. The report shall state whether such principles have been consistently observed in the current period in relation to the preceding period.

3. Informative disclosures in the financial statements are to be regarded as reasonably adequate unless otherwise stated in the report.

The first two standards of reporting require the auditor to make declarative statements in the audit report. The third standard does not require such a statement, however. The auditor's standard short-form report, therefore, implies that the financial statements include adequate disclosure unless the auditor takes exception to disclosure in the report. When an auditor takes exception to disclosure, a qualified or adverse opinion may be required, depending upon the effect on the overall fairness of the financial statements. If modification is required, the auditor should include the information in his or her report if practicable. In order to be practicable, the information should be easily obtainable, and not place "preparer" responsibility on the auditor.

SAS No. 2 presents the auditor's standard short-form report. The report includes a scope paragraph (first paragraph) which identifies the statements examined by the auditor, the period covered by the examination, and states that the examination was made in accordance with GAAS and includes such other tests that the auditor considered necessary in the circumstances. The opinion paragraph (second paragraph) states that the financial statements present fairly (or do not present fairly) financial position, results of operations, and changes in financial position, and includes the declarative statements required by the first and second reporting standards. The auditor's standard short-form report is presented below, with reference to the first and second reporting standards italicized:

(Scope paragraph)

We have examined the balance sheet of X Company as of (at) December 31, 19xx, and the related statements of income, retained earnings and changes in financial position for the year then ended. Our examination was made in accordance with generally accepted auditing standards and, accordingly, included such tests of the accounting records and such other auditing procedures as we considered necessary in the circumstances.

(Opinion paragraph)

In our opinion, the financial statements referred to above present fairly the financial position of X Company as of (at) December 31, 19xx, and the results of its operations and the changes in its financial position for the year then ended, *in conformity with generally accepted accounting principles applied on a basis consistent with that of the preceding year.*

THE FIRST STANDARD OF REPORTING

The term GAAP as used in the reporting standards is construed to include not only accounting principles and practices but also the methods of application. The first reporting standard requires that the financial statements be presented in conformity with GAAP. If limitations on the scope of the examination prevent the auditor from forming an opinion on the conformity of the statements with GAAP, the auditor is required to qualify the opinion or to disclaim an opinion because of a scope restriction. The materiality of the matter at hand will determine the appropriateness of the opinion to be used.

THE MEANING OF PRESENT FAIRLY

The auditor states in the short-form report (opinion paragraph) whether or not the statements are "presented fairly" in conformity with GAAP. The determination of whether statements are presented in accordance with GAAP requires the exercise of judgment and familiarity with alternative principles and promulgated principles. SAS No. 5 attempts to explain the meaning of the phrase "present fairly . . . in conformity with GAAP" as used in the CPA's standard report. The phrase GAAP encompasses the conventions, rules, and procedures necessary to define accepted practice at a particular time. These conventions, rules, and procedures provide a standard for measuring financial presentations and include (as presented and discussed in APB Statement No. 4) pervasive measurement principles, broad operating principles, and detailed principles.

Pervasive measurement principles relate to financial accounting as a whole and serve as a foundation for the other principles. They are broad in application, develop through a slow evolutionary process, and usually stand the test of time. Broad operating principles guide the recording, measuring, and communicating processes of financial accounting and are developed from and relate to pervasive measurement principles. The detailed principles indicate the practical application of the pervasive and broad operating principles. These three types of principles form a hierarchy. The pervasive principles are few in number and fundamental in nature. The broad operating principles derived from the pervasive principles are more numerous and more specific and guide the application of a series of detailed principles. The detailed principles are both numerous and specific. Judgments concerning the fairness of overall financial presentation should be applied within the framework of GAAP, as GAAP provide a uniform standard for judging fairness. The auditor's opinion as to fair presentation of financial position, results of operations, and changes in financial position should be based on the auditor's judgment as to whether:

The accounting principles selected and applied have general acceptance

They are appropriate in the circumstances

The statements, including the notes, are informative of matters that may affect their use, understanding, and interpretation

The information presented is classified and summarized in a reasonable manner (not too detailed or too condensed)

The financial statements reflect financial position, results of operations, and changes within a range of acceptable limits (means reasonable and practicable to attain)

Independent CPAs agree on the existence of a body of GAAP, and they are experts in those accounting principles and determination of their general acceptance. However, the determination that a given accounting principle is generally accepted may be difficult because there are several sources for such principles.

SAS No. 43 (Section 1010.07) amends SAS No. 5, regarding the sources of GAAP. This amendment clarifies the order of authority of sources of estabished accounting principles that an auditor should follow in ascertaining whether an accounting principle is generally accepted. The amendment also adds to the sources of established accounting principles certain types of pronouncements that did not exist when SAS No. 5 was issued. Sources of established accounting principles have been categorized as follows: (a) pronouncements of an authoritative body designated by the AICPA Council to establish accounting principles, pursuant to Rule 203 of the AICPA Code of Professional Ethics; (b) pronouncements of bodies composed of expert accountants that follow a due process procedure, including broad dissemination of proposed accounting principles for public comment, for the intended purpose of establishing accounting principles or describing current practices that are generally accepted; (c) practices or pronouncements that are widely recognized as being generally accepted because they represent prevalent practice in a particular industry or the knowledgeable application to specific circumstances of pronouncements that are generally accepted; (d) other accounting literature.

Category (a) includes the following pronouncements:

FASB Statements of Financial Accounting Standards

FASB Interpretations

APB Opinions

Accounting Research Bulletins

Category (b) includes the following pronouncements:

AICPA Industry Audit Guides and Accounting Guides

AICPA Statements of Position

Category (c) includes the following practices and pronouncements:

Industry practices

AICPA Accounting Interpretations

FASB Technical Bulletins

Category (d) includes the following:

APB Statements

AICPA Issues Papers

Textbooks and Articles

FASB Statement No. 32, *Specialized Accounting and Reporting Principles and Practices in AICPA Statements of Position and Guides on Accounting and Auditing Matters*, issued in September 1979 now recognized certain Statements of Position issued by the AICPA Accounting Standards Executive Committee and certain Accounting and Auditing Guides issued by Committees of the AICPA as promulgated accounting principles under Rule 203. FASB No. 33 should be consulted as to which SOPs, Accounting Guides, and Auditing Guides are included.

CPAs should be alert for any pronouncements that change accounting principles and to changes that become acceptable as a result of common usage in business. Also, the CPA should examine carefully the application of accounting principles by looking at the substance of transactions as well as their form.

Accounting principles may have only limited usage but have general acceptance and GAAS permits the use of alternative accounting principles where no body designated by Council of the AICPA has designated a specific principle or method of accounting. For example, different methods for determining depreciation expense are generally accepted.

An Auditing Interpretation of Section 410 (SAS No. 1) considers the impact on an Auditor's report of an FASB Statement prior to the statement's effective date. The Interpretation considers the impact on the auditor's unqualified opinion, which states that the client's statements are presented in conformity with GAAP, when the FASB has issued a statement of financial accounting standards that will, after its effective date, require retroactive application of its provisions by prior period adjustment. Should the client follow currently existing standards or should the client's statements reflect the newly approved FASB Statement?

According to the Interpretation, the auditor's report may be effected in any of three ways. First, if the client does not consider the forthcoming FASB Statement and presents the financial statements in conformity with currently existing standards, then there is no effect on the auditor's report. However, if the auditor feels that the forthcoming FASB Statement will have such an impact on the client's financial statements that current disclosure of the future effect of the FASB Statement is required and such disclosure is not made, the auditor would qualify his or her opinion because of the lack of disclosure.

Second, if the forthcoming FASB Statement reduces existing alternative accounting principles and will require retroactive application, for example, like FASB No. 2, which requires all R&D costs to be expensed and required retroactive application, it may be advisable to change to the FASB Standard that will be required in future statements. In this situation, the auditor would qualify his or her opinion because of the inconsistency. The change would, of course, be justified by the forthcoming FASB Statement.

Third, an option always open to an auditor is to emphasize a matter regarding the financial statements in his or her audit report. Accordingly, for the situation posed by a forthcoming FASB Statement that will have retroactive application, an auditor may, whether the client disclosed the future effect of the FASB Statement or not, include a middle paragraph(s) in his or her report to emphasize the matter.

THE SECOND STANDARD OF REPORTING

The objective of the consistency standard (second standard of reporting) is to provide assurance that the comparability of financial statements between and among periods has not been materially affected by changes in accounting principles. If comparability has been materially affected by such changes, the standard requires appropriate modification of the auditor's report.

A comparison of the financial statements of an entity between years may be affected by accounting changes, an error in previously issued financial statements, changes in classification, or events or transactions substantially different from those accounted for in previously issued statements.

An accounting change, as defined in APB Opinion No. 20, indicates a change in an accounting principle, a change in an accounting estimate, or a change in the reporting entity. Changes in accounting principles having a material effect on the financial statements require recognition in the auditor's opinion as to consistency. Other factors affecting comparability in financial statements may require disclosure, but they would not ordinarily be commented upon in the auditor's report.

ACCOUNTING CHANGES AFFECTING CONSISTENCY

Change in Accounting Principle

A change in an accounting principle results from the adoption of GAAP which differ from that used previously for reporting purposes. The consistency standard is applicable to this type of change and requires recognition in the auditor's opinion. The opinion would be qualified by the auditor as to consistency, the auditor would state the GAAP that had been followed in the past, state the newly adopted GAAP, and explain the effect of the changes on financial position, results of operations, and changes in financial position. APB Opinion No. 20 requires the client to justify the change in a note to the financial statements or the auditor must indicate that the change was made without proper justification.

Change in Reporting Entity

A change in the reporting entity is a special type of accounting change and is considered to be a change in accounting principles by APB Opinion No. 20. The consistency standard is, therefore, applicable. Changes in the reporting entity that require recognition in the auditor's opinion include:

Presenting consolidated or combined statements in place of statements of individual companies

Changing specific subsidiaries comprising the group of companies for which consolidated statements are presented

Changing the companies included in combined financial statements

Changing among the cost, equity, and consolidation methods of accounting for subsidiaries or other investments in common stock

A business combination accounted for by the pooling-of-interests method would also result in a change in the reporting entity. For purposes of application of the consistency standard, a change in the reporting entity does not result from the creation, cessation, purchase, or disposition of a subsidiary or other business unit.

Correction of an Error in Principle

A change from an accounting principle that is not generally accepted to one that is generally accepted, including a correction of an error in the application of a principle, is considered to be a correction of an error in the application of accounting principles. This type of change should be accounted for as a prior period adjustment. The change *does* require recognition in the auditor's opinion as it is an inconsistency. Also, a change in an accounting principle that is inseparable from a change in an estimate is considered an inconsistency and requires recognition in the auditor's opinion. An example would be changing the estimated life of a depreciable asset and, as a result of changing the estimated life, changing the method of determining depreciation expense.

ACCOUNTING CHANGES NOT AFFECTING CONSISTENCY

Change in Accounting Estimate

A change in an accounting estimate may be required by altered conditions that affect comparability but do not involve changes in accounting principles and, therefore, do not involve inconsistency. An example of a change in an accounting estimate would be changing the estimated useful life of an asset. APB Opinion No. 20 requires that such changes be accounted for by allocating the effect of the change over the current and future periods of the remaining life of the asset. The auditor need not comment on such changes in the report as they do not affect consistency. A change of this type having a material effect may, however, require disclosure in a note to the financial statements.

Error Correction not Involving a Principle

The correction of an error in previously issued financial statements resulting from mathematical mistakes, oversight, or misuse of facts that existed at the time the statements were originally prepared does not involve the consistency standard. Such changes may, however, require disclosure.

Changes in Classification and Reclassifications

Material changes in the classification of accounts should be explained in the financial statements or notes thereto. Such changes do not afect the consistency standard.

Variations in Format and Presentation of Statement of Changes in Financial Position

Variations between periods in the format of the statement of changes, such as changing to or from a balanced form, are deemed to be reclassifications. If such variations materially affect comparability, they should be disclosed in the financial statements. However, they ordinarily will not be referred to in the auditor's report.

Also considered reclassifications are variations from period to period in the concept of funds followed in the preparation of the statement. As for example, following a working capital concept in one period and changing to a cash concept in the following period. The CPA need not refer to such changes in his or her report if they have been applied retroactively to all prior periods presented and have been adequately disclosed in the financial statements (see SAS No. 43, *Omnibus Statement on Auditing Standards*).

Substantially Different Transactions or Events

The modification or adoption of an accounting principle necessitated by transactions or events that are clearly different in substance from those previously occurring, does not involve the consistency standard. However, disclosure may be required in the statements or notes.

Changes Expected to Have a Material Future Effect

If a change in an accounting principle or the method of its application has no material effect in the current year, but is reasonably certain to have a substantial effect in later years, there is no effect on consistency in the current period. The change, however, should be disclosed in the notes to the statements for the period of change.

DISCLOSURE OF CHANGES NOT AFFECTING CONSISTENCY

As indicated in the previous discussion, changes that do not affect consistency may require disclosure in the statements or notes. When the auditor feels that such changes do require disclosure and the necessary disclosures are not made, a qualified opinion or an adverse opinion should be expressed, as appropriate, because of a lack of fairness.

PERIODS TO WHICH THE CONSISTENCY STANDARD RELATES

When an auditor is reporting only on the current financial period, the report should comment on the consistency of the application of accounting principles in relation to the preceding period, regardless of whether statements for the preceding period are presented. When the auditor is reporting on two or more years, the report should comment on the consistency of the application of accounting principles between such years and on the consistency of such years with the year prior thereto if such prior year is presented.

CONSISTENCY EXPRESSION

When an auditor is expressing an opinion on the financial statements of a single year, the appropriate consistency expression is "on a basis consistent with that of the preceding year." If the auditor's report includes two or more years, the consistency expression should be "applied on a consistent basis." If the report covers two or more years and the year preceding the earliest year being reported upon is also presented, the consistency expression should be "consistently applied during the period and on a basis consistent with that of the preceding year."

THE THIRD STANDARD OF REPORTING

The third standard of reporting establishes the requirement that financial statements include all necessary informative disclosures. Informative disclosure means that the financial statements and the related notes contain all the information that would tend to influence the opinion or decisions of an informed reader of the statements. Verbosity should not be mistaken for adequate disclosure. Disclosure should be accomplished in a clear and consise manner. Whether or not a particular matter requires disclosure is an issue for the auditor to decide in the exercise of professional judgment in light of the circumstances and facts available at the time of the issuance of the statements. If matters which the auditor believes require disclosure are omitted from the financial statements, these matters should be included in the report and the auditor should appropriately qualify the opinion as to lack of fairness. Disclosures should not be considered to require publicizing certain kinds of information that would be detrimental to either the company or its stockholders.

SEGMENT INFORMATION

(SAS No. 21)

SAS No. 21 provides guidance to the independent auditor examining and reporting on financial statements in those circumstances where segment information is included in accordance with the provisions of FASB Statement No. 14.

Auditing procedures are applied to segment information with the objective of providing the auditor with a reasonable basis for ascertaining whether the information is presented in conformity with GAAP. The independent auditor, in conducting an examination in accordance with GAAS, views segment information, as all other disclosures, in relation to the financial statements taken as a whole. Thus, it is not necessary to apply auditing procedures that would be required to express a separate opinion on the segment information alone.

In the event the client indicates to the auditor that it does not have industry segments, foreign operations, or major customers required to be disclosed under the provisions of FASB Statement No. 14, in most circumstances the auditor would be able to determine, given previously obtained knowledge of the client's business, whether it has reportable segments. If however, the audiitor is unable to arrive at a conclusion and the client refuses to make available the necessary information, the auditor should indicate in the scope paragraph of the report the limitation on the examination imposed by the client and qualify the opinion on the statements taken as a whole (an example of such a qualifed report is presented later in this section).

The concept of materiality is basic to the work of the auditor, as discussed in SAS No. 1, in ascertaining the nature, timing, and extent of auditing procedures to be used in an examination of financial statements. Segment information, in terms of materiality, is evaluated by comparing the dollar amount of the information to the financial statements taken as a whole. As is the case with other areas of the auditor's examination, the materiality of segment information depends on both qualitative and quantitative judgments.

The auditor, in planning the examination, may deem it necessary to modify certain audit tests to be applied to the financial statements taken as a whole. For example, physical observation of inventories may be conducted on the basis of industry segments or geographic areas. The auditor must consider factors such as the following in determining whether the audit procedures should be modified:

Internal accounting control and level of integration, centralization, and uniformity of accounting records

Nature, number and relative size of industry segments and geographic areas

Nature and number of subsidiaries or divisions in each industry segment and geographic area, as well as accounting principles in use by the industry segments and geographic areas

The tests of the underlying accounting records usually performed by the auditor in the examination of financial statements should be accomplished so as to allow a determination to be made as to whether the client's revenue, operating expenses, and identifiable assets are appropriately classified among industry segments and geographic areas.

The standard report prepared by the auditor implies that segment information is presented in accordance with GAAP—the same as other informative disclosures that are not clearly marked as "unaudited" (as noted above, FASB

---

* Except as amended by FASB Statement No. 18, *Financial Reporting for Segments of a Business Enterprise—Interim Financial Statements* and FASB Statement No. 21, *Suspension of the Reporting of Earnings per Share and Segment Information by Nonpublic Enterprises.*

No. 21 suspended the reporting of segment information by nonpublic enterprises). If a client presents comparative segment information for fiscal years beginning prior to December 15, 1976, that information should be reported as "unaudited," assuming the auditor did not perform the auditing procedures as prescribed in SAS No. 21. If the auditor determines, on the basis of the available information, that the "unaudited" segment information is not presented in conformity with GAAP and the client declines to make appropriate revision the auditor should express appropriate reservations and disclaim an opinion.

Segment information should not be mentioned in the standard report unless the auditor's examination reveals either a misstatement or omission, or a change in accounting principle affecting segment information that is material in relation to the financial statements taken as a whole. Also, the auditor would refer to segment information when the auditing procedures considered necessary in the circumstances were not performed. The auditor must evaluate several factors in determining whether an item relating to segment information is material to the statements. For example, the importance of a matter to a particular enterprise (such as, an incorrect presentation of revenue and operating profit of a small segment deemed by management to be significant to future profitability of the enterprise), or the pervasiveness of an item (such as whether it affects amounts and reporting of several items in the segment information), or the impact of an item (such as whether it misrepresents trends indicated in segment information) are all factors which should be examined in evaluating whether an item pertaining to segment information is material to the statements taken as a whole.

With respect to material misstatements or omissions of segment information that are not corrected, the auditor should express a qualified or adverse opinion due to a departure from GAAP. An example of an auditor's report that is qualified due to a misstatement of segment information follows:

(Explanatory paragraph)

With respect to the segment information in Note X, $ . . . . of the operating expenses of Industry A were incurred jointly by Industries A and B. In our opinion, Statement No. 14 of the Financial Accounting Standards Board requires that those operating expenses be allocated between Industries A and B. The effect of the failure to allocate those operating expenses has been to understate the operating profit of Industry A and to overstate the operating profit of Industry B by an amount that has not been determined.

(Opinion paragraph)

In our opinion, except for the effects of not allocating certain common operating expenses between Industries A and B, as discussed in the preceding paragraph, the financial statements referred to above present fairly . . .

An example of an auditor's report that is qualified due to an omission of segment information follows:

(Explanatory paragraph)

The Company declined to present segment information for the year ended December 31, 19xx. In our opinion, presentation of segment information concerning the Company's operations in different industries, its foreign operations and export sales, and its major customers is required by Statement No. 14 of the Financial Accounting Standards Board. The omission of segment information results in an incomplete presentation of the Company's financial statements.

(Opinion paragraph)

In our opinion, except for the omission of segment information, as discussed in the preceding paragraph, the financial statements referred to above present fairly . . .

As indicated in the above examples, the explanatory paragraph of the auditor's report for both misstatements and omissions of segment information should describe the type of information omitted but the auditor is not required to provide the omitted information in the report.

An inconsistency in segment information may occur because of such factors as the following:

A different basis of accounting for sales or transfers between industry segments or between geographic areas, or in the methods of allocating operating expenses or identifiable assets among industry segments or geographic areas

A change in the method of determining or presenting a measure of profitability for part or all of the segments

A change in accounting principles as delineated in APB Opinion No. 20

A change requiring restatement for prior periods as discussed below

GAAP requires that segment information for previous periods that is disclosed in comparative statements be retroactively restated if:

The entity's financial statements have been restated for previous years

The method of classifying goods and services into industry segments or of classifying foreign operations in geographic areas is changed and the change affects the segment information presented

GAAP requires that the nature and effect of these changes be disclosed in the period of change. The auditor should modify the opinion whenever there is a departure from GAAP. An example of an auditor's report that is qualified due to an entity's failure to disclose the nature and effect of a change in the method of accounting for sales between reportable segments follows:

(Explanatory paragraph)

In 19xx, the Company changed the basis of accounting for sales between its industry segments from the market price method to the negotiated price method, but declined to disclose the nature and effect of this change on its segment information. In our opinion, disclosure of the nature and effect of this change, which has not been determined, is required by Statement No. 14 of the Financial Accounting Standards Board.

(Opinion paragraph)

In our opinion, except for the omission of the information discussed in the preceding paragraph, the financial statements referred to above present fairly . . .

With respect to consistency, the auditor is not required to modify the audit report for the changes outlined above, except in the case of a change in accounting principle affecting the financial statements taken as a whole.

As was mentioned earlier in this section, when the auditor is unable to determine whether the client is required to report segment information, the limitation on the examination should be indicated in the scope paragraph of the report and the opinion on the financial statements taken as a whole qualified. An example of the auditor's report when the scope of the examination is limited is as follows:

(Scope paragraph)

. . . Except as explained in the following paragraph, our examination . . . and such other auditing procedures as we considered necessary in the circumstances.

(Explanatory paragraph)

The Company has not developed the information we consider necessary to reach a conclusion as to whether the presentation of segment information concerning the Company's operations in different industries, its foreign operations andd export sales, and its major customers is necessary to conform with Statement No. 14 of the Financial Accounting Standards Board.

(Opinion paragraph)

In our opinion, except for the possible omission of segment information, the financial statements referred to above present fairly . . .

A qualified opinion should be given on the statements taken as a whole if the auditor is prohibited from applying to reported segment information auditing procedures considered necessary in the circumstances. An example of a qualified auditor's report under these circumstances is as follows:

(Scope paragraph)

. . . Except as explained in the following paragraph, our examination . . . and such other auditing procedures as we considered necessary in the circumstances.

(Explanatory paragraph)

In accordance with the Company's request, our examination of the financial statements did not include the segment information presented in Note X concerning the Company's operations in different industries, its foreign operations and export sales, and its major customers.

(Opinion paragraph)

In our opinion, except for the effects of such adjustments or disclosures, if any, as might have been determined to be necessary had we applied to the segment information the procedures we considered necessary in the circumstances, the financial statements referred to above present fairly . . .

The auditor may be asked, on occasion, to report on segment information apart from the normal audit report on the financial statements taken as a whole or in a special report. When an examination of this nature is performed, the determination of materiality should be associated with segment information only and not to the financial statements taken as a whole. Thus, the independent auditor must undertake a more extensive examination of segment information reported on separately than would be the case if the same information were considered in conjunction with an examination of the financial statements taken as a whole.

SAS No. 14, *Special Reports*, provides guidance that is appropriate to segment information reported on separately. However, since disclosure of segment information is required by GAAP, all GAAS also apply to an examination of segment information reported separately. Thus, the audit report should state whether, in the opinion of the auditor, segment information is presented in accordance with the first and second standards of reporting.

accounting & auditing

Editor:
D. R. Carmichael, CPA, Ph.D.
Director, Auditing Standards
American Institute of CPAs

What does the independent auditor's opinion really mean?

The editor discusses the meaning of the phrase "present fairly . . . in conformity with GAAP" as used in the standard form of auditor's report. Following that discussion is an auditing interpretation.

For over 35 years the standard form of auditor's report used in the United States has expressed the auditor's opinion that financial statements "present fairly . . . in conformity with generally accepted accounting principles." After using that phrase for so long, why should there be any doubt about its meaning?

Why is the meaning elusive?
The meaning is difficult to define for two basic reasons. First, the meaning is a moving target. It depends as much on the nature of generally accepted accounting prin-

ciples (GAAP) as it does on the meaning of "present fairly," and the nature of GAAP has changed—most dramatically—in the last ten years.

Second, a careful study of what has recently been written and said about the subject shows that the controversy is not about what the phrase means, but what the responsibility of the independent auditor *should be* in reporting on financial statements.[1] In 1965, a special committee on Opinions of the Accounting Principles Board suggested that the meaning of "presented fairly in conformity with GAAP" was open to several possible interpretations. Since then the meaning has been debated by accountants and others, including the courts, securities regulators and the financial press. If the

---

[1] Paul Rosenfield and Leonard Lorensen, "Auditor's Responsibilities and the Audit Report," JofA, Sept. 74, pp. 73-83, identify several possible interpretations of "present fairly . . . in conformity with GAAP" and review some of the recent discussions of the subject.

question were one of original intent, we could look back to the inception of our present report wording.

What does history tell us?
The present wording of the standard report seems to have originated in correspondence between the New York Stock Exchange and the American Institute. In January 1933, the president of the Exchange sent a letter to all listed corporations specifying requirements for auditors' reports. Among the requirements was one that an audit report state: "Whether in their opinion the form of the balance sheet and of the income, or profit and loss, account is such as fairly to present the financial position and the results of operations."

After correspondence between the Institute and the Exchange, a new form of opinion paragraph was recommended: "In our opinion . . . the [financial statements] fairly present, in accordance with accepted principles of accounting consistently maintained by the company during the year under review, its position at December 31, 1933, and the results of its operations for the year." Thus, the Institute committee was apparently opposed to using the phrase "fairly present" without modification.

In 1939 the Institute's senior committee on auditing recommended a new standard form of report. The opinion paragraph of that report was essentially the same as the one used today. The committee transposed the words "fair" and "present" and separated "in conformity with GAAP" from "present fairly." The reason for repositioning the reference to GAAP was to clarify the meaning of the reference to consistency.[2] Some accountants apparently believed that "consistently maintained during the year" did not relate the principles for the current year to those for the prior year. The changed wording removed that confusion, but may have clouded the relationship between fair presentation and GAAP.

During the years since 1939 and up to the time prior to the present controversy, the words "present fairly" had an accepted meaning that can be deduced from the use of that phrase in the writings of CPAs, though I would be hard-pressed to defend that meaning as authoritatively established. The accepted meaning concerns the "accuracy" of financial statements. The phrase has simply meant that adherence to professional standards—both accounting and auditing—cannot assure absolute accuracy. That meaning does not imply that professional standards are inadequate; it is intended only to convey the thought that an assurance of absolute accuracy is impossible, given the nature of financial statements.

GAAP comprise the body of conventions that permit the summarization of business activity in the familiar form of financial statements. Generally accepted auditing standards govern the independent auditor's investigation and his method of reporting. Without those professional standards, audited financial statements could not be prepared, but even with those standards an auditor's report does not connote absolute accuracy.

[2] Samuel J. Broad, "The Accountant's Report and Certificate," JofA, July39, pp. 17-22.

Indeed, on those occasions when the organized profession has attempted to interpret the meaning of the auditor's report for users of financial statements the explanation has been that the estimates, evaluations and judgments required in preparing financial statements preclude the use of words such as "true" or "correct." For example, the AICPA booklet, *Forty Questions and Answers About Audit Reports,* published in 1956 (p. 11), stated: "What is the significance of the expression 'present fairly' in the CPA's report? . . . No one can be in a position to state that a company's financial statements 'exactly present' financial position or results of operations. Accordingly, the CPA usually states that the financial statements 'present fairly' in the sense that he believes they are substantially correct. For the same reason, his findings are expressed in the form of an opinion. However, it should be borne in mind that the judgment involved is an informed one, and is guided by generally accepted accounting principles."

A similar booklet, *The Auditor's Report,* published by the AICPA in 1967, also emphasized that accounting for business transactions requires approximations and estimates and that financial statements cannot be exact.

If the significance of "present fairly" is commonly understood, why do we not simply change the wording and substitute a new phrase that better expresses the uncertainties, such as "reasonably stated" or "presents in all material respects"?

The Institute's auditing committee for several years had a project underway to revise the standard form of auditor's report. Among other changes, the committee considered a more descriptive phrase than "present fairly," such as those mentioned above. That project was halted, in part, because it became apparent that any new wording would have to do more than convey the problems in accounting measurement. Removing "present fairly" might seem to be a reduction of the auditor's responsibility and the replacement would have to be accompanied by a more positive statement of responsibility.

More recently, the AICPA's auditing standards executive committee has once again been studying

the meaning of "present fairly." From the beginning, these deliberations have focused on the nature of an auditor's responsibility in expressing an opinion. Until the committee is ready to report its conclusions, I can offer only my own views. Identifying what I think has been rejected is easier than explaining the accepted position.

What interpretations of responsibility have been rejected?

The auditor's responsibility in expressing an opinion is complex. Not surprisingly, simple explanations of responsibility have been rejected.

An opinion on fairness. Asking independent auditors to express an opinion on the fairness of financial statements without specifying a standard of measurement, such as GAAP, would lead to chaos. If each individual auditor formulated his own view of what was fair, an auditor's opinion would be so personal and unique that comparability of financial statements could not even be approached. A framework is necessary to attain a universal level of quality; GAAP provide that framework.

The notion that fairness alone should be substituted for GAAP in establishing an independent auditor's responsibility may stem from a misinterpretation of recent legal decisions. The most prominent of those is *Continental Vending (U.S. v. Simon,* 425 F.2d 706 (2d Cir. 1969), cert. den. 397 U.S. 1006 (1970)).

Continental Vending did not set a new responsibility for auditors in expressing opinions on financial statements. The decision simply held that conformity with GAAP, if established, does not by itself preclude a jury from inferring criminal intent from other evidence of the auditor's conduct, particularly if GAAP are not specific in the circumstances in question.

Continental Vending concerned a footnote that was alleged to be affirmatively misleading. No authoritatively established accounting principles specifically applied to the disclosure in question. Expert witnesses testified that the financial statements were otherwise in conformity with GAAP, but that was not found to be a conclusive defense. The instructions to the jury indicated only that the good faith of auditors cannot be left exclusively to the testimony of other expert auditors, but must be in the province of the jury to decide. *Continental Vending* did not reject GAAP and substitute fairness.

Other practical reasons support rejecting fairness alone as the standard for expressing an opinion. Members of public accounting firms might find it difficult to agree on a universal standard of fairness and sign opinions in the firm name. Undesirable competition among firms might grow, based on whose personal ideas on accounting theory agreed with those of a client.[3] Similar problems may exist today, but the problems would be worse if opinions were based on a personal judgment of fairness.

A dual opinion. Requiring auditors to express two opinions—one on fairness and one on conformity with GAAP—might be as chaotic as using fairness alone. The state of confusion would be blatantly apparent in auditor's reports.

An individual auditor might have a personal opinion that a presentation was in conformity with GAAP but not fair, or fair but not in conformity with GAAP. The results could only be to undermine GAAP and undermine confidence in financial statements. Auditors might be forced to include treatises on accounting theory in their reports to defend their views. GAAP would be constantly challenged publicly and the benefits of comparability and a universal level of quality would be lost.

Individual auditors and firms of independent auditors who disagree with GAAP should work to change GAAP. Requiring them, however, to publicize their disagreements in every report they sign would not seem to be in the public interest.

An opinion on conformity with GAAP. Objections to the use of conformity with GAAP as the sole basis of the auditor's responsibility rest on the imperfections of GAAP. Those who reject this standard may do so because they equate GAAP with accounting principles that have been expressed in official pronouncements. If GAAP were defined as the whole body of pronouncements and customs and con-

ventions, written and unwritten, technical and ethical, that guide the presentation of financial statements, then I would support this standard. However, a more definitive explanation of such a standard is necessary.

If GAAP is regarded as a list of published rules and if conformity with GAAP means only technical compliance with those rules, then the standard of conformity with GAAP would have to be rejected. The imperfections of GAAP are well-known to independent auditors, but those imperfections have diminished in the last decade. In the early sixties, most auditors would, I think, have agreed with the attitude toward GAAP then expressed by Mautz and Sharaf:

"It seems to us that any careful analysis of the nature of generally accepted accounting principles, as the term is used at the present time, unavoidably stresses the auditor's duty to accept them with care and caution. Because they are not complete, have no absolute authority, do not require even majority support, tend to lag behind the appearance of the problems they are intended to solve, and can no more than presume to reflect actual events and conditions, he must never accept and apply them blindly. To do so would be a violation of his professional responsibility to bring to his work the benefits of his judgment and experience."[4]

In the early sixties, the organized profession in the United States undertook, through the Accounting Principles Board, a vigorous campaign to narrow the range of choices in accounting principles. The volume of authoritatively established accounting principles greatly increased and the pronouncements changed in nature from those of the APB's predecessor to become increasingly more detailed and specific. The APB also issued a comprehensive body of accounting principles in Statement No. 4. Taken together the AICPA's pronouncements on accounting constitute an impressive body of accounting knowledge, certainly more complete than that existing a little over a decade ago.

In 1973 the AICPA's membership adopted a new Code of Profes-

sional Ethics that delegated the power to establish authoritative accounting principles to a body to be designated by the AICPA's Council. The Council recognized the existing pronouncements of the APB and its predecessor and the pronouncements to be issued by the Financial Accounting Standards Board as having that authority.

As the written expression of accounting principles becomes more extensive and gains more authority, the danger may increase that a pronouncement will be applied blindly. For example, if a uniform point for revenue recognition were established, such as point of sale, the blind application of that rule could lead to inappropriate results. Some would contend that that is precisely what happened in recognizing revenue on franchise fees in the recent past.

The importance of such a danger depends on how the development of accounting principles progresses. If that development leads to better identification of the circumstances in which a specific accounting principle is to be used, then adherence to established accounting principles will produce appropriate results.

The number of instances in which a choice from among alternative accounting principles is not influenced by the circumstances may be smaller than is generally recognized. A response of the AICPA's accounting standards division to a recent proposal of the Securities and Exchange Commission is pertinent. The SEC proposed that financial statements disclose the effect of applying certain alternate principles. The accounting standards division in discussions with the SEC agreed to prepare a list of alternate accounting principles for which comparison disclosures might be useful. The response, in part, stated that:

"As a result of the work of the task force the Division has concluded that meaningful disclosure to users of financial statements cannot be accomplished by rules that compare differences in income resulting from differences in the application of accounting principles. Our view is based primarily on the belief that *the effect of circumstances on the selection of accounting principles applied in preparation of financial statements is so pervasive* that meaningful comparisons among

---

[3] Some of the same arguments are identified by Rosenfield and Lorensen.

[4] R. K. Mautz and Hussein Sharaf, *The Philosophy of Auditing* (Madison, Wis: American Accounting Association, 1961), p. 166.

companies cannot be made simply by disclosing alternative income measures on the assumption that different accounting principles might have been applied. Moreover, the Division feels that the number of areas where alternatives may exist and comparison disclosure might be accomplished is so limited that comparison disclosures in these areas would be of little value to users of financial statements."[5]

For example, the letter noted that any of three accounting methods might be used for recording installment sales—the accrual, installment and cost recovery methods. However, the use of each method is governed by the circumstances as specified in criteria contained in Accounting Research Bulletins, APB Opinions or AICPA Industry Audit or Accounting Guides. The letter listed only the following areas in which use of alternative accounting principles is not governed by the circumstances: (1) the investment credit, (2) deferred research and development costs, preoperating costs, start-up costs and similar deferrals, (3) inventories, (4) depreciation and (5) goodwill and other purchased or acquired intangibles.

Recently, the FASB has acted to remove research and development costs from the list. Even though the list might have to be expanded in the future because of new business developments, in most instances the choice among accounting principles is not discretionary. If GAAP includes appropriate application of accounting methods in the circumstances, then conformity with GAAP is an appropriate standard for the auditor's responsibility. However, that standard requires some elaboration.

What is the auditor's responsibility in expressing an opinion?

The only recent direct definition of "present fairly in conformity with GAAP" in an AICPA pronouncement provides a starting point for further discussion of the auditor's responsibility. APB Statement No. 4 (paragraph 189) contains the following definition: "Financial statements 'present fairly in conformity

with generally accepted accounting principles' if a number of conditions are met: (1) generally accepted accounting principles applicable in the circumstances have been applied in accumulating and processing the financial accounting information, (2) changes from period to period in generally accepted accounting principles have been appropriately disclosed, (3) the information in the underlying records is properly reflected and described in the financial statements in conformity with generally accepted accounting principles, and (4) a proper balance has been achieved between the conflicting needs to disclose important aspects of financial position and results of operations in accordance with conventional concepts and to summarize the voluminous underlying data into a limited number of financial statement captions and supporting notes."

That definition recognizes the difficulty of deciding whether disclosure is adequate. The narrative description necessary for meaningful interpretation of the numbers in financial statements cannot be delineated by a set of detailed instructions. Authoritative pronouncements give some guidance, but a large amount of individual judgment will probably always be necessary.

The portion of the definition that most requires elaboration is the condition that "generally accepted accounting principles applicable in the circumstances have been applied. . . ." The nature of the auditor's appraisal of the application of GAAP is the heart of an acceptable explanation of the auditor's responsibility in expressing an opinion.

An independent auditor should appraise whether the accounting principles applied, in addition to being generally accepted in the abstract, are applicable to the facts of a particular transaction and have been applied appropriately. He should also appraise whether management's decisions in the selection and application of individual accounting principles have resulted cumulatively in the preparation of financial statements that taken as a whole are not misleading. It is not enough to weigh the application of accounting principles item by item without considering the cumulative impact of the choices.

An auditor should consider

whether an accounting principle selected is applied to the transaction in a manner that properly recognizes the economic impact of the transaction in terms of its present and future cash flows. I believe that auditors have a general conception of how the success or failure of a business should be measured. That general conception runs through accounting theory and gives some idea of the purpose of accounting. It is a simple guide by reference to which it can be seen whether the chosen accounting principles are operating satisfactorily. To succeed, a business must ultimately take in more cash than it spends. If the business is failing by that simple guideline, the financial statements should not portray a picture of success.

One example of the application of that guideline should be sufficient. The basic activities of financial institutions—banks or loan companies—are quite simple. They borrow money from the public at one rate of interest and then loan funds out or otherwise invest them at a higher return. A financial institution that does not invest money it borrows from the public but uses it to meet earlier obligations or invests it at a marginal return is not succeeding. Its financial statements should make that lack of success abundantly clear, but some of our financial institutions that have recently gotten into trouble have had less than illuminating annual reports.

Concluding remarks

In summary, the essential meaning of the auditor's opinion that financial statements are fairly presented in conformity with GAAP is that the accounting principles a company uses are appropriate for the circumstances to which they are applied. GAAP are not perfect and management sometimes has undesirable latitude in selecting and applying alternate accounting principles, but the cure for that problem is to improve GAAP.

As the written expression of accounting principles progresses, those charged with that task should bear in mind the relationship between GAAP and the auditor's responsibility. Pronouncements on accounting principles should identify the circumstances in which a particular accounting principle is to be applied. Those pronouncements should

---

[5] Letter to John C. Burton, Chief Accountant, Securities and Exchange Commission, February 20, 1974. (Emphasis added.)

also identify the objectives of accounting principles so that an auditor can appraise conformity with the spirit of GAAP as well as its letter.

CASE 18

THE MEANING OF PRESENT FAIRLY

You have accepted an engagement to examine the financial statements of Northview Corporation, a relatively small and closely-held manufacturer of CB radios. The Corporation has experienced a tremendous growth in sales volume with the recent craze sweeping the CB radio market. Northview needs an audit both because it plans to go public in the near future and because it has already borrowed substantial funds from financial institutions for the expansion of its facilities to meet growing market demands.

The Company usually experiences excess cash flow at year-end. This condition being a temporary one, Northview usually invests the surplus cash in marketable equity securities. The controller, Harry Brown, is concerned about the application of FASB Statement No. 12, *Accounting for Certain Marketable Securities*, to Northview's portfolio of current marketable securities. In order to present a sound and stable financial position, the controller wishes to carry the marketable equity securities at market value in the year-end balance sheet, with offsetting gains or losses recognized in the equity section of the balance sheet. Brown has made a careful study of the requirements of FASB No. 12 and has concluded that, since Northview is not in an industry with specialized accounting practices for marketable securities, the Company probably should carry their securities at the lower of cost or market. You agree that this is the proper method of accounting as called for by FASB No. 12.

Brown, being concerned that Northview receive an unqualified opinion, has raised a number of questions concerning the auditor's standard report, failure of a client to follow generally accepted principles of accounting promulgated by the FASB, and the meaning of the phrase "present fairly in conformity with GAAP" appearing in the auditor's report.

CASE DISCUSSION QUESTIONS

1. Where does the FASB obtain its authority to require business firms to follow its pronouncements?

2. What would be the probable course of action for your firm if Northview decides to present its marketable equity securities portfolio in its balance sheet at market value?

3. What does the phrase "present fairly . . . in conformity with generally accepted accounting principles" mean?

4. What factors should an auditor consider in judging whether the financial statements are presented fairly within the framework of GAAP? Would the auditor consider, for example, whether the accounting principles followed have general acceptance within a particular industry or in general?

5. A few years ago Brown worked for a company that received an adverse opinion from its CPA. He explains that the company was delisted by the stock exchange, got in trouble with the SEC, and eventually was liquidated in bankruptcy proceedings because of continuing operating losses. The company had written-off a considerable amount of obsolete inventory and charged the loss against retained earnings. By doing this, the company was able to report a nominal amount of earnings. The CPA, however, took exception to the charge to retained earnings and issued an adverse opinion, quoting an APB in support of his opinion.

   Brown would like for you to explain what sources a CPA consults in determining whether an accounting principle is generally accepted. What are the primary sources and what are other possible sources?

CASE 19

CONSISTENCY AND DISCLOSURE

You have been in public accounting practice for ten years. All of that time has been spent with a local CPA firm of which you are now a partner. Your primary responsibility in the firm (which has three area offices and 72 staff persons) is concerned with the review of working papers for compliance with firm quality control standards and GAAS.

You are a member of the AICPA and of the state society of CPAs and have been involved in numerous professional development courses as both a discussion leader and a participant. You have developed a reputation throughout the state as somewhat of an expert in the review of working papers and their compliance with GAAS.

As a result of your reputation, the planning committee for the annual meeting of the state society of CPAs has asked you to serve on a general accounting and auditing panel discussion. You agree, and during the meeting several questions are raised concerning consistency and disclosure.

CASE DISCUSSION QUESTIONS

1. Why is the independent auditor required to state whether GAAP have been consistently observed in the current period in relation to the preceding period?

2. What is the relationship between the consistency standard and comparability?

3. How does a change in accounting that is material, as defined in APB Opinion No. 20, affect the independent auditor's report?

4. What does the term *accounting principles* mean or include? Are both consistency and comparability involved? Explain.

5. APB Opinion No. 20 defines a change in the reporting entity as a special type of change in accounting principle.

   a. Does the consistency standard apply to this special type of change in accounting principle? Explain the application of the consistency standard, if in fact it applies, and give examples of such changes.

   b. Assume you have a client that created a subsidiary for marketing a new product. The subsidiary is included in consolidated financial statements. For purposes of application of the consistency standard, is this a change in a reporting entity?

6. GAAP provides guidance in the accounting for the correction of an error in accounting principle, including the correction of an error in the application of an accounting principle.

   a. How should this type of change in accounting principle be accounted for?

   b. Should the auditor's report recognize the correction of an error in accounting principle? If so, how?

7. Assume that your client constructed a new brick building late in 1976 and estimated its useful life to be 50 years. The client's bookkeeper recorded the transaction and is depreciating the building over a five-year period. You are conducting the audit of the client for the year ending December 31, 1979 and discover the error.

   a. Should the error be accounted for as a change in accounting estimate? If not, how should it be accounted for?

   b. Should the change be recognized in the auditor's opinion?

8. When the independent auditor encounters a change in principle that is inseparable from a change in estimate, how should it be accounted for? What effect, if any, does this type of change in accounting principle have on the independent auditor's report?

9. You are performing an audit on the Uptown Holiday Inn. Since it began operations three years ago, Uptown has depreciated all its buildings and land improvements over a twenty-five year period. For the fiscal year beginning July 1, 19x4, Uptown changed the estimated life of its buildings and land improvements

from twenty-five years to fifty years. The Uptown Holiday Inn reported a net income of $60,000 for the year ended June 30, 19x5. For each of the previous three years it had reported a net loss. You determine that the change from a loss situation to that of reporting net income of $60,000 is due solely to the change in economic life years of the buildings and land improvements for depreciation purposes. Uptown has refused to disclose the effect of the change on this year's net income. Discuss the above, giving consideration to changes in accounting estimate as well as adequacy of informative disclosure (the third standard of reporting).

10.   Discuss the influence on the auditor's report of changes in classification and reclassification in the financial statements.

11.   Assume that your client presents the statement of changes in financial position on a working capital basis instead of the cash basis which was used in previous years. The client has also converted the previous period's statement of changes in financial position to a working capital basis. These changes are deemed to be material. What action should be taken with regard to the independent auditor's report and disclosure?

12.   Your client began operations in February of the current year. What reference, if any, should you, as the independent auditor, make in referring to consistency in your report? Explain.

AUDITING
AND
REPORTING

Segment information — audit
procedure checklist

Segment Information — Audit Procedure Checklist

By David J. Ellison, Ph.D., Assistant Professor, University of Nebraska.

SAS No. 21, "Segment Information," requires that the auditor have "a reasonable basis" for concluding whether an entity's segment information is presented in conformity with FASB Statement No. 14, "Financial Reporting for Segments of a Business Enterprise."[1] FASB No. 14 specifies that the financial statements of an entity include disclosure information concerning its operations in different industries, foreign operations and export sales, and major customers. Statement No. 14 also requires a business operating in a single industry to identify that industry.[2]

The FASB has issued a Proposed Statement of Financial Accounting Standards that would suspend the application of FASB Statement No. 14 in the financial statements of nonpublic enterprises. The Board's action was taken in response to pressure received from the public and from within the profession concerning burdensome financial statement disclosure requirements on small or closely held businesses. However, businesses issuing financial statements to be filed with a regulatory agency in ad-

vance of the sale of debt or equity securities in a public market would be considered a public enterprise, under the proposed Statement, and would be required to present financial statements in accordance with FASB Statement No. 14. The exposure draft states the "Statement shall be effective (upon issuance) for financial statements issued on or after that date."

Because of FASB No. 14, small and medium sized CPA firms will, perhaps, for the first time have to consider segment reporting rules and related audit procedures in the case of a client "going public" and in those cases where clients are required to file financial statements with a regulatory agency. It should be noted that FASB, SEC and FTC rules are different for certain segment requirements (e.g., the test to determine if a segment is significant and reportable). Since Statement No. 14 requires that segment information be included in financial statements for certain types of businesses (as amended), the CPA, in an audit engagement, must perform specific procedures to support the fairness of presentation of segment disclosures.

The auditor should review accounting records of SEC clients and clients who are preparing to issue securities publicly to determine whether they have reportable segment information. The auditor should perform his review as soon as possible (effective for closings after December 15, 1977) because of the potential need to obtain new data and to evaluate the client's methods of data classification. The client may indicate that he does not have industry segments, foreign operations, export sales or major customers requiring disclosure in accordance with FASB No. 14. Gener-

[1] SAS No. 21, "Segment Information" (New York: AICPA, December 31, 1977), paragraph 3.
[2] SFAS No. 14, "Financial Reporting for Segments of a Business Enterprise," paragraph 1. Statement No. 14 has been amended to eliminate its application to interim financial statements. See Statement No. 18, "Financial Reporting for Segments of a Business Enterprise — Interim Financial Sate ments — an amendment of FASB Statement No. 14".

ally, the auditor would be able to ascertain, based on his knowledge of the client's business, whether the client has reportable segment information. If the auditor is unable to determine whether the client has reportable segments and the client refuses to provide the information he considers necessary to reach a conclusion, the auditor may have a scope restriction sufficient to prohibit issuance of an unqualified opinion on the financial statements taken as a whole.

The auditor's objective in examining financial statements containing segment information is the expression of an opinion on the statements taken as a whole. In the course of the examination the auditor should develop working papers that will aid him in the conduct of his work, and provide support for his opinion, including his representation as to compliance with gener-

ally accepted auditing standards.[3] It is expected that the amount, kind and content of working papers will differ with circumstances. However, working papers normally would provide the following:

• Enough information to indicate that the financial statements or other data the auditor is reporting on agrees with the client's books or can be reconciled thereto;

• Evidence that the audit work was planned (e.g., use of work program checklists) and that the duties performed by any assistants had been supervised and reviewed;

• Evidence that the client's system of internal control was examined in determining the extent of the tests to which the auditor's procedures were restricted;

---

[3] Statement on Auditing Standards No. 1, Section 338, "Working Papers" (New York: AICPA, November 1972), paragraph 2.

• Auditing procedures used and tests performed in developing evidence;

• Explanation of how any exceptions and unusual items discovered by the auditor's procedures were resolved;

• Necessary written comments made by the auditor in presenting his conclusions concerning significant aspects of the work performed.[4]

Procedure Checklist

Audit Objectives and Planning. The audit objective for segment information is to provide a reasonable basis for concluding whether the segment information is presented in conformity with GAAP (FASB No. 14) in relation to the financial statements taken as a whole. Segment information, as other informative disclosures, is to be considered in relation to the financial statements taken as a whole; the auditor is not required to apply auditing procedures that would be necessary to express a separate opinion on segment information.

Materiality for segment information is evaluated primarily by relating the dollar magnitude of the information to the financial statements taken as a whole. However, as with other elements of financial statements, the materiality of segment information does not depend on relative size; qualitative as well as quantitative judgments need consideration.[5]

In planning the audit, it may be necessary to modify or redirect selected audit tests to be applied to the financial statements because of segment information. For example, inventories may be selected for physical observation on the basis of industry segments or geographical areas. A decision on redirecting audit procedures because of segment information should be based on such factors as the following:

• Internal accounting control and the degree of integration, centralization, and uniformity of the accounting records;

---

[4] SAS No. 1, paragraph 5.
[5] See SAS No. 2, paragraph 16 and SAS 21, paragraph 5 for a discussion of qualitative characteristics for materiality.

- The nature, number and relative size of industry segments and geographic areas;
- The nature and number of subsidiaries or divisions in each industry segment and geographic area;
- The accounting principles used for the industry segments and geographic areas.

Audit Procedures

The following procedures, as a minimum, should be applied to segment information to be presented in the financial statements.

1. Inquire of management concerning its methods of determining segment information. Summarize methods and evaluate reasonableness in relation to factors identified in FASB No. 14 (paragraphs 11-21 and Appendix D).
2. Inquire as to bases of recording sales or transfers between industry segments and between geographic areas and test to extent considered necessary for conformity with the bases of accounting disclosed. For example, vouch transfer pricing information and trace to the board of directors' minutes or other appropriate sources.
3. Test disaggregation of segment information.
   A. Evaluate percentage tests specified in paragraphs 15-20 and 31-39 of FASB No. 14 to ascertain reportable segments. Usually a segment is reportable if it meets any of the following three tests:
      - Revenue is 10 percent or more of the combined revenue of all segments, including intersegment sales. The dollar amount of operating profit or loss is 10 percent or more of the greater of:
        1. Combined operating profit of all profitable segments, or
        2. Combined operating loss of all segments with losses.
      - Identifiable assets are 10 percent or more of the combined identifiable assets of all segments.[6]
   B. The percentage tests are to be applied each year, with the results evaluated to assure interperiod comparability.
      - For segments not meeting significance test in current period determine:
        1. If segment was significant in prior years, and
        2. If segment is expected to be significant in future years—If both conditions are met, the segment is reportable.
      - To eliminate reporting insignificant segments, determine if there are any segments that meet one or more tests of significance in the current year, but were not significant in prior years and are not expected to be significant in future years.

Determine that segments which meet the 10 percent test of significance account for at least 75 percent of combined sales to unaffiliated customers.
      1. Identify additional segments if the 75 percent test is not met.

---

[6] *Accounting and Auditing Update Workshop,* Thomas D. Hubbard, AICPA, N.Y. 1978.

2. Note: Reportable segments should not exceed 10. To comply with the 75 percent test and at the same time avoid disclosing more than 10 segments, closely related segments should be combined.

C. Perform analytical review of segment information and make inquiry concerning relationships and items that appear unusual. Analytical review should include:
   • Comparing current-year segment information with that of the previous year and any available related budget information for the current year.
   • Considering interrelationships of elements of the segment information that would be expected to conform to a predictable pattern based on the enterprise's experience (such as operating profit as a percentage of both total revenue and identifiable assets by industry segment or geographic area), and
   • Considering types of matters that in the preceding year have required accounting adjustments.

4. Inquire as to methods of allocating operating expenses and identifiable assets used jointly by two or more segments. Evaluate the reasonableness and test allocations to the extent considered necessary.

5. Determine whether segment information has been presented on a consistent basis. If not, is the nature and effect of the inconsistency disclosed and, if applicable, has information been retroactively restated (in conformity with paragraph 40 of FASB No. 14).

A. An inconsistency in segment information may occur because of:
   • A change in the bases of accounting for intersegment sales or transfers or in the method of allocating operating expenses or identifiable assets.
   • A change in the method of reporting or determining the measure of profitability for one or more segments.
   • A change in accounting principle(s) as defined in APB Opinion No. 20, paragraph 7.
   • A change requiring retroactive restatement, as discussed in FASB No. 14, paragraph 40.

B. FASB No. 14 requires disclosure of the nature and effect of changes and restatements (see SAS No. 21, paragraphs 11, 12 and 13 and FASB No. 14, paragraph 40).

6. Concurrent with tests of revenue or sales, accounts receivable, cash receipts, and other related accounts (or when testing related party transactions) review transactions and supporting documentation to identify major customers (disclosure is required when 10 percent or more of the revenue of an enterprise is derived from sales to any single customer, a group of customers under common control, sales to domestic government agencies, or to foreign governments in the aggregate).

CASE 20

A&M, INC.

You are an audit partner with a national CPA firm which, for the last few years, has conducted the audit of A&M, Inc. This client develops, manufactures, and sells numerous products in the electrical and electronics industry for industrial, consumer, and government markets. These products consist of components (semiconductors such as integrated circuits, and electrical and electronic control devices), digital products (such as minicomputers, data terminals and electronic calculators and watches) and government electronics (such as radar, infrared surveillance systems, and missile guidance and control systems).

The company also manufactures metallurgical materials for use in a number of applications including automotive equipment, appliances and telecommunications equipment and provides services, primarily through the collection and electronic processing of seismic data in connection with petroleum exploration.

The following information on 19x2 operations is required by FASB No. 14. Information on 19x1 net sales billed and profit is *presented for purposes of comparison only*.

	Millions of Dollars	
Net Sales Billed	*19x2*	*19x1*
Components		
Trade	$ 857	$ 736
Intersegment	101	100
	958	836
Digital Products		
Trade	512	368
Intersegment	47	28
	559	396
Government Electronics		
Trade	376	312
Intersegment	17	19
	393	331
Metallurgical Materials		
Trade	120	98
Intersegment	28	29
	148	127
Services		
Trade	175	138
Intersegment	0	0
	175	138
Eliminations and Adjustments	(187)	(169)
Total Net Sales Billed	$2,046	$1,659
Geographic Profit		
United States	$ 164	$ 151
Europe	39	28
Other Areas	47	33
Eliminations and Corporate Items	(39)	(34)
Income Before Provisions for Income Taxes	$ 211	$ 178
Identifiable Assets		
United States	$ 734	
Europe	188	
Other Areas	144	
Eliminations and Corporate Items	189	
	$1,255	

Industry segment and geographic area profits for 19x5 and 19x4 were determined by taking total revenue less associated operating expenses, which include general corporate expenses, currency gains and losses, interest income and expense, and income taxes. Identifiable assets are those assets of the company related with industry segment or geographic operations and exclude unallocated cash and short-term investments, internal company receivables, treasury stock held for awards under incentive programs and net accumulated income tax timing differences. Normally, net sales billed between industry segments and geographic areas are based on prevailing market prices or an approximation thereof arrived at through negotiations between independent profit centers.

The portion of consolidated assets net of liabilities outside the U.S. was 28% at December 31, 19x5 and 34% at December 31, 19x4.

	Millions of Dollars	
Segment Profit	19x5	19x4
Components	$ 121	$ 112
Digital Products	54	30
Government Electronics	39	33
Metallurgical Materials	22	20
Services	14	2
Eliminations and Corporate Items	(39)	(19)
Income Before Provision for Income Taxes	$ 211	$ 178

	19x5 Millions of Dollars		
Identifiable Assets	Identifiable Assets	Depreciation	Additions (Net) to Property, Plant and Equipment
Components	$ 529	$ 58	$ 94
Digital Products	270	17	44
Government Electronics	114	17	37
Metallurgical Materials	60	3	10
Services	61	11	13
Eliminations and Corporate Items	221	2	1
Totals	$1,255	$108	$199

Net sales billed to federal, state and local government agencies in the United States, made principally by the government electronics segment totaled $296,512,000 for 19x5.

Information about the company's operations by geographic area is as follows (intersegment sales represents sales between geographic areas):

	Millions of Dollars	
Net Sales Billed	19x5	19x4
United States		
Trade	$1,431	$1,138
Intersegment	138	133
	1,569	1,271
Europe		
Trade	403	336
Intersegment	7	8
	410	344
Other Areas		
Trade	212	185
Intersegment	251	202
	463	387
Eliminations and Adjustments	(396)	(343)
Total Net Sales Billed	$2,046	$1,659

You have completed your review of the audit working papers, the financial statements, and related footnote disclosures for the A&M audit. The firm has scheduled you to conduct a one-day seminar for supervisory audit staff members on the topic of generally accepted auditing standards as they relate to reporting segment information. In conjunction with this seminar you prepared the above disclosures and are ready to develop case questions to be used in illustrating decisions faced by the auditor in examining and reporting on financial statements that are required to include segment information in conformity with FASB Statement No. 14.

CASE DISCUSSION QUESTIONS

1. What is the auditor's objective in applying audit procedures with respect to segment information required under FASB No. 14?

2. Discuss the concept of materiality as it relates to segment information.

3. In planning the audit, you may be required to either modify or redirect selected audit tests to be applied to the financial statements taken as a whole.

   a. Give examples, mentioned in SAS No. 21, with respect to modifying or redirecting selected audit tests.

   b. A decision to redirect audit procedures because of segment information should be based on certain factors. What factors are specified by SAS No. 21?

4. SAS No. 21 provides guidance as to auditing procedures when financial statements include segment information to be presented in the financial statements. What auditing procedures should be applied by the independent auditor? Relate your answer, where possible, to the disclosures provided in the A&M case. (Hint: See the audit procedure checklist included in the readings.)

5. Under what conditions, if any, would the auditor's standard report refer to segment information?

6. Footnote No. 3 in SAS No. 21 states "if an entity discloses comparative segment information for fiscal years beginning prior to December 15, 19x4, that information should be clearly marked as 'unaudited' unless the auditor has applied to that segment information the auditing procedures set forth in this Statement."

   a. Are the disclosures presented in the A&M case in compliance with SAS No. 21? Support your answer with logical reasoning.

   b. Assume that A&M presented additional information as follows:

   The following unaudited information indicates the contribution to consolidated net sales billed and income in the years indicated by electrical and electronic products, the "line of business" reported in the company's annual report to the Securities and Exchange Commission on Form 10-K:

	(Unaudited)		
	19x3	19x2	19x1
Net sales billed..............	83%	86%	86%
Income...................	93%	89%	90%

Income has been calculated before unallocated general corporate expenses not directly related to the individual "lines of business" and before provision for income taxes. *For comparison* with the industry segment information set forth in the case above pursuant to Statement of Financial Accounting Standards No. 14, in the years shown in the table the electrical and electronic products "line of business" included all except an immaterial portion of the net sales billed and profit of components and all of the net sales billed and profit of digital products, government electronics and metallurgical materials.

Would this additional information alter your answer in 6? If not, why not?

7. Assume that A&M has misstated depreciation expense for the Components and Digital Products segments but you are unable to determine the amount of the misstatement and A&M declines to make the information available to you. What should you do? Include in your answer discussion of the auditor's report.

8. Assume that the "Segment Profit" included in the case was not available and the client refused to include it in its financial statements. What action, if any, should the auditor take with respect to the opinion on the financial statements? Include in your answer the "explanatory and opinion paragraph" of the auditor's report.

9. The auditor is required to test disaggregation of segment information.

   a. What tests should be included for purposes of determining whether there is a reportable segment?

   b. Are the tests applied each year?

   c. Would a segment not meeting "significance test" in the current year be included as a reportable segment? Explain.

10. SAS No. 21 addresses inconsistency in reporting segment information.

   a. What are some examples of accounting methods that would result in an inconsistency of segment information?

   b. How is the auditor's report affected?

11. Assume that A&M has asked your firm to prepare a special report for segment information as well as a report on the financial statements taken as a whole. How would this request influence the engagement?

16

The Fourth Standard of Reporting

(Section 505, SAS No. 15, Section 509, SAS No. 2, and Sections 542, 544, and 545, SAS No. 1)

The fourth reporting standard requires that whenever the auditor is associated with financial statements, an opinion or a disclaimer of an opinion be expressed and all of the substantive reasons for the disclaimer be stated. The objective of the fourth standard is to prevent misinterpretation of the degree of responsibility assumed when the auditor is associated with financial statements. The standard reads as follows:

> The report shall either contain an expression of opinion regarding the financial statements, taken as a whole, or an assertion to the effect that an opinion cannot be expressed. When an overall opinion cannot be expressed, the reasons should be stated. In all cases wherein an auditor's name is associated with financial statements, the report should contain a clear-cut indication of the character of the auditor's examination, if any, and the degree of responsibility he is taking.

The fourth standard is intended to apply equally to a complete set of financial statements and to an individual financial statement. For example, an auditor may disclaim or express an adverse opinion on one or more statements and express an unqualified opinion on another. Or the auditor may be engaged to report only upon a single financial statement—a balance sheet, for example.

REPORTS ON COMPARATIVE FINANCIAL STATEMENTS

SAS No. 15, *Reports on Comparative Financial Statements*, provides guidance for reporting when financial statements are presented for comparative purposes. The basic concept underlying this Statement is that the fourth standard of reporting applies to the statements of one or more prior periods presented on a comparative basis with those of the current period. The fourth standard of reporting requires an opinion or disclaimer of opinion whenever the auditor is associated with financial statements.

A "continuing auditor" is required to "update" the opinion on prior-period statements presented for comparative purposes. A *continuing auditor* is one who has examined the financial statements of the current period and those of one or more immediately preceding periods. An auditor *updates* a prior opinion by re-expressing the previous opinion or, depending on the circumstances, expressing a different opinion. An updated opinion differs from a reissued opinion since the updated opinion is influenced by information the auditor becomes aware of during the examination of the current-period financial statements and is issued in conjunction with the current-period statements.

The following example illustrates a continuing auditor's standard report involving comparative financial statements for two fiscal periods.

We have examined the balance sheets of ABC Company as of (at) December 31, 19x2 and 19x1, and the related statements of income, retained earnings, and changes in financial position for the years then ended. Our examinations were made in accordance with generally accepted auditing standards and, accordingly, included such tests of the accounting records and such other auditing procedures as we considered necessary in the circumstances.

In our opinion, the financial statements referred to above present fairly the financial position of ABC Company as of (at) December 31, 19x2 and 19x1, and the results of its operations and the changes in its financial position for the years then ended, in conformity with generally accepted accounting principles applied on a consistent basis.

A report on comparative statements applies to the individual statements and the auditor may, therefore, modify the opinion (qualify or express an adverse opinion) or disclaim an opinion with respect to one or more of the statements presented. In the case of a modified opinion or a disclaimer of opinion, the auditor should disclose all the substantive reasons in a separate explanatory paragraph(s) and the modified opinion or disclaimer should refer to the explanatory paragraph. An explanatory paragraph is not required for an opinion modified because of a change in accounting principle. A continuing auditor need not report on prior-period statements when only summarized comparative information is presented. If the auditor is requested to express an opinion on such data, consideration should be given to whether the data includes sufficient detail to constitute a fair presentation in conformity with GAAP. Generally, the auditor's report on comparative financial statements should be dated as of the date of completion of the field work on the most recent examination.

The following circumstances or events would ordinarily result in an opinion different from that previously expressed:

Subsequent Resolution of an Uncertainty

The resolution of an uncertainty in the current period that resulted in a subject-to opinion modification (or disclaimer of opinion) in the statements of a prior period presented for comparative purposes will result in the auditor updating his prior opinion to an unqualified opinion.

Discovery of an Uncertainty in a Subsequent Period

When the auditor discovers an uncertainty in his current examination that relates to statements of a prior period presented for comparative purposes, he should consider modifying his opinion (or disclaiming) in the updated report because of the newly discovered uncertainty.

Subsequent Restatement of Prior-Period Financial Statements

When prior-period statements which were not in conformity with GAAP are, for comparative purposes, restated to conform with GAAP, the auditor should update his prior modified opinion to an unqualified opinion. The updated opinion should indicate that the statements have been restated.

When an auditor's updated opinion is other than unqualified, the opinion (or disclaimer) paragraph should include a reference to the explanatory paragraph(s) in the report. The explanatory paragraph(s) should disclose the following information:

The date of the auditor's previous report

The type of opinion previously expressed

The circumstances or events that caused the auditor to update his opinion, and

That the auditor's updated opinion is different from the previous opinion

Following are illustrative examples of explanatory paragraphs:

Resolution in the Current Period of an Uncertainty Existing in a Prior Period Requiring Recognition in the Current Financial Statements In our report dated March 1, 19x2, our opinion on the 19x1 financial statements was qualified as being subject to the realization of the investment in DEF Company. As explained in Note X, the carrying amount of that investment has been charged to operations in the current year as required by generally accepted accounting principles. Accordingly, our present opinion on the 19x1 financial statements, as presented herein, is different from that expressed in our previous report.

A New Uncertainty Affecting Both the Current- and Prior-Period Financial Statements As discussed in Note X, a number of legal actions were filed against the Company subsequent to the date of our report on the 19x1 financial statements. These actions claim substantial damages as a result of alleged violations of antitrust laws during prior years. The Company is in the process of litigating these actions, but the ultimate outcome is uncertain at this time. In our report dated March 1, 19x2, our opinion on the 19x1 financial statements was unqualified; however, in view of the litigation referred to above, our present opinion on the 19x1 financial statements, as presented herein, is different from that expressed in our previous report.

Subsequent Restatement of Prior-Period Financial Statements to Conform with Generally Accepted Accounting Principles In our report dated March 1, 19x2, we expressed an opinion that the 19x1 financial statements did not fairly present financial position, results of operations, and changes in financial position in conformity with generally accepted accounting principles because of two departures from such principles: (1) the Company carried its property, plant and equipment at appraisal values, and provided for depreciation on the basis of such values, and (2) the Company did not provide for deferred income taxes with respect to differences between income for financial reporting purposes and taxable income. As described in Note X, the Company has restated its 19x1 financial statements to conform with generally accepted accounting principles. Accordingly, our present opinion on the 19x1 financial statements, as presented herein, is different from that expressed in our previous report.

A predecessor auditor may be requested by a former client to reissue the report on prior-period statements presented for comparative purposes. Before agreeing to reissue his report, a predecessor auditor should consider whether the previous opinion is still appropriate. Either the current form or manner of presentation of the financial statements of the prior period or subsequent events might make a predecessor's previous opinion inappropriate. Therefore, before reissuing the report, a predecessor auditor should:

Review the statements of the current period

Compare the statements previously reported on with the statements to be presented for comparative purposes

Obtain a letter of representation from the successor auditor

The letter of representation should state whether the successor's examination revealed any matters that, in the successor's opinion, might have a material effect or require disclosure in the statements reported on by the predecessor. The predecessor, in the reissued report, should not refer to the report or work of the successor auditor.

When the predecessor becomes aware of matters that may affect the opinion, inquiries should be made and the auditor should perform such other procedures considered necessary. For example, the auditor may wish to review the working papers of the successor. The predecessor should decide on the basis of evidence obtained whether to revise the opinion. The predecessor's reissued report should carry the original date. If the report is revised, dual dating should be used.

When statements of a prior period are presented for comparative purposes and those statements were examined by a predecessor auditor whose report is not presented, the successor auditor should indicate the following in the scope paragraph of the report:

That the statements of the prior period were examined by other auditors (the predecessor auditor should not be named)

The date of the predecessor auditor's report

The type of opinion expressed by the predecessor

The substantive reasons for the predecessor's opinion if it is other than unqualified

An example of a successor auditor's report when the predecessor auditor's report is omitted is as follows:

> We have examined the balance sheet of ABC Company as of December 31, 19x2, and the related statements of income, retained earnings, and changes in financial position for the year then ended. Our examination was made in accordance with generally accepted auditing standards and, accordingly, included such tests of the accounting records and such other auditing procedures as we considered necessary in the circumstances. The financial statements of ABC Company for the year ended December 31, 19x1, were examined by other auditors whose report dated March 1, 19x2, expressed an unqualified opinion on those statements.

> In our opinion, the 19x2 financial statements referred to above present fairly the financial position of ABC Company as of December 31, 19x2, and the results of its operations and the changes in its financial position for the year then ended, in conformity with generally accepted accounting principles applied on a basis consistent with that of the preceding year.

If the statements of the prior period have been restated, the scope paragraph of the successor's report should indicate that the predecessor reported on the statements of the prior period before restatement.

REPORTS ON AUDITED FINANCIAL STATEMENTS

SAS No. 2, *Reports on Audited Financial Statements*, applied to the auditor's report issued in connection with an examination of financial statements that are intended to present financial position, results of operations, or changes in financial position in conformity with GAAP. The Statement does not apply to unaudited statements issued in connection with an accounting service engagement. The Statement is concerned primarily with the relationship of the fourth reporting standard to the language of the CPA's report.

Auditor's Standard Report

SAS No. 2 presents the format and language of the auditor's standard unqualified short-form report. This Statement requires that a separate "statement of changes in stockholders' equity accounts" be identified in the scope paragraph of the report, but need not be reported on separately in the opinion paragraph. The report may be addressed to the company, its board of directors, or stockholders. A report to an unincorporated entity should be addressed as particular circumstances dictate, for example, to the partners, to the general partner, or the proprietor.

The recommended form and language of the report is presented below.

(Scope paragraph)

> We have examined the balance sheet of X Company as of (at) December 31, 19xx, and the related statements of income, retained earnings and changes in financial position for the year then ended. Our examination was made in accordance with generally accepted auditing standards and, accordingly, included such tests of the accounting records and such other auditing procedures as we considered necessary in the circumstances.

(Opinion paragraph)

> In our opinion, the financial statements referred to above present fairly the financial position of X Company as of (at) December 31, 19xx, and the results of its operations and the changes in its finan-

cial position for the year then ended, in conformity with generally accepted accounting principles applied on a basis consistent with that of the preceding year.

Auditors are cautioned against deviating from the accepted language of the standard short-form report when issuing an unqualified opinion as such deviation often involves making unwarranted assertions or assuming inappropriate responsibility.

Circumstances Resulting in Departures from Auditor's Standard Report

Circumstances that may result in the auditor departing from the language of the standard short-form report include the following:

Scope limitations

Opinion based in part on the report of another auditor

Departure from GAAP

Departure from a promulgated accounting principle

Accounting principles not consistently applied

Uncertainties and emphasis of a matter

Scope Limitation   Scope restrictions tend to preclude the application of one or more GAAS or auditing procedures considered necessary in the circumstances and thereby, prevent the auditor from gathering sufficient evidence to express an unqualified opinion. The scope of the auditor's examination may be limited for a number of reasons, including the following:

Time of the engagement—the auditor is not employed until near or after year-end

The condition of the client's accounting records

The client prohibits the auditor from gathering evidence in certain areas

The materiality (or potential materiality) of the item or items to which the scope restriction relates will determine whether the opinion is qualified or whether a disclaimer of opinion is appropriate. When the auditor does qualify or disclaim an opinion because of a scope restriction, his report should describe all of the substantive reasons for the qualification or disclaimer.

Common restrictions and the scope of the examination include *observation of inventory* and *confirmation of receivables*. Since these auditing procedures are considered essential to the auditor's examination, material restrictions regarding them will generally require the auditor to disclaim an opinion on the financial statements. Moreover, restrictions imposed by the client that relate to these or other material areas of the examination will generally result in a disclaimer of opinion. The disclaimer usually results because the auditor is prohibited from gathering evidence in the restricted area and, therefore, has no idea of the significance of the matter to overall fairness of presentation.

An auditor may be asked to report on a single basic financial statement and not on others—a balance sheet for example. Such engagements are permissible and are not considered scope limitations but, rather, are engagements involving limited reporting objectives. The auditor's scope of examination may not, however, be restricted by the client so that related accounts or records may not be examined.

Opinion Based in Part on the Report of Another Auditor   When an auditor is the principal auditor and decides to refer to the work of another auditor, this fact should be disclosed in the scope paragraph. The principal auditor should also refer to the report of the other auditor in his or her opinion. This situation may arise when a principal auditor refers to the work of another auditor who has audited a subsidiary and the principal CPA is reporting on the consolidated financial statements. Although such a reference is a departure from the standard short-form report, it does not indicate a qualification, but merely provides information by referring to the division of responsibility for the examination.

Departure from GAAP   When the financial statements are affected by a departure from GAAP and the effects are material, the auditor should express a qualified opinion or an adverse opinion and state the basis for this opinion. In deciding on the materiality of the departure, the auditor should consider the dollar magnitude and significance of the item to the particular enterprise, the pervasiveness of the misstatement, and the impact on the financial statements taken as a whole. For example, a departure from GAAP in presenting inventories in the financial statements of a manufacturing company would likely have a significant monetary effect; the misstatement would be pervasive, affecting many accounts; and the impact would be felt in all financial statements presented.

Departure from a Promulgated Accounting Principle   When there are departures from promulgated accounting principles, Rule 203 of the AICPA Code of Professional Ethics applies. Promulgated accounting principles are those principles and practices issued by the body designated by Council of the AICPA to issue such principles. They include ARBs (Accounting Research Bulletins), APBs (Accounting Principles Board Opinions), and Statements and Interpretations of the FASB (Financial Accounting Standards Board). When a client does not follow these pronouncements, Rule 203 requires that the auditor state in the report that the client has departed from a promulgated accounting principle, state the effect of the departure, and include the information required by the promulgated principle, if known to the auditor. Although they usually result in a qualification, such departures do not necessarily prohibit the expression of an unqualified opinion.

Accounting Principles Not Consistently Applied   When there is a change in accounting principles, the auditor should modify the opinion as to the consistency violation. A qualified opinion would usually be issued, although the auditor may, under some circumstances, issue an adverse opinion.

Uncertainties   In preparing financial statements, management is expected to use its estimates of the outcome of future events. For example, management is expected to estimate the useful lives of depreciable assets, the collectibility of accounts receivable, and the realizable value of inventory. When the auditor disagrees with management's estimates and the related effects on the financial statements are material, a qualified or an adverse opinion should be expressed because of a departure from GAAP. The outcome of certain matters that may affect the financial statement amounts or disclosures are not, however, susceptible to reasonable estimation. These matters are defined as uncertainties. When there are uncertainties affecting financial presentation that are not susceptible to reasonable estimation, their nature and possible effects on the statements should be disclosed. The auditor's function in forming an opinion on financial statements does not include estimating the outcome of future events if management is unable to do so. The auditor need not modify the opinion because of the existence of an uncertainty when it is concluded that there is only minimal likelihood that resolution of the uncertainty will have a material effect on the statements.

In cases involving uncertainty, the auditor should be able to form an opinion whether the statement items have been stated in conformity with GAAP in all respects other than those contingent on the outcome of the uncertainty. If the auditor is satisfied that they have been so stated, an opinion qualified by reason of the uncertainty may be expressed. Although auditing standards do not specifically prohibit disclaiming an opinion because of an uncertainty, a "subject-to" qualified opinion is the usual type of opinion modification. An example of an auditor's report qualified because of an uncertainty affecting the financial statements is as follows:

(Standard scope paragraph)
(Separate middle explanatory paragraph)

As discussed in Note X to the financial statements, the Company is defendant in a lawsuit alleging infringement of certain patent rights and claiming royalties and punitive damages. The Company has filed a counter action, and preliminary hearings and discovery proceedings on both actions are in progress. Company officers and counsel believe the Company has a good chance of prevailing, but the ultimate outcome of the lawsuits cannot presently be determined, and no provision for any liability that may result has been made in the financial statements.

(Opinion paragraph)

In our opinion, subject to the effects, if any, on the financial statements of the ultimate resolution of the matter discussed in the preceding paragraph, the financial statements referred to above present fairly . . .

or

In our opinion, subject to the effects of such adjustments, if any, as might have been required had the outcome of the uncertainty referred to in the preceding paragraph been known, the financial statements referred to above present fairly . . .

The subsequent resolution of an uncertainty that led to qualification of an auditor's report will result in adjustment of the financial statements, be recognized in subsequent statements, or result in a conclusion that the matter has no monetary effect.

Emphasis of a Matter   An auditor may wish to call attention to a matter such as an unusually important subsequent event, fact that an entity is a component of a larger business, or that the entity engages in transactions with related parties. Such information may be presented in a separate middle paragraph(s) of the auditor's report. Although the standard short-form report is modified by giving emphasis to a matter, the auditor may still issue an unqualified opinion.

Type of Opinions

An auditor, when associated with the financial statements of a public company,* must either express an *unqualified opinion*, a *qualified opinion*, an *adverse opinion*, or he or she must *disclaim an opinion*. The following discussion outlines the general conditions under which the four types of opinions are appropriate.

Unqualified Opinion   The unqualified opinion may be given when the following conditions exist:

The financial statements present fairly financial position, results of operations, changes in financial position in conformity with GAAP

The financial statements include informative disclosures

GAAP have been consistently applied

The auditor has formed an opinion based on an examination in accordance with GAAS

Qualified Opinion   A qualified opinion may be given under any of the following conditions:

Restriction on the scope of examination imposed by circumstance, timing of engagement, condition of the records, or by the client. (Restrictions imposed by the client will, however, usually result in a disclaimer of opinion.)

Financial statements contain a material departure from GAAP

There has been a material change in GAAP or their application

There are significant uncertainties affecting the financial statements (SAS No. 43 amends this section. The amendment is discussed below.)

And, the auditor has decided not to express an adverse opinion or to disclaim an opinion, as appropriate

---

*Reporting on the financial statements of a nonpublic client is discussed in a subsequent section of this text.

SAS No. 43 (Section 1010.06) modifies the language of the example "subject to" qualification contained in Section 509.39. SAS No. 43, states that reports qualified due to an uncertainty should not contain language referring to "the effects, if any," on the financial statements "of the ultimate resolution" because of the requirements of FASB Statement 16, *Prior Period Adjustments*. The amendment removes the reference to a prior period adjustment, except in those rare instances when a resolution of an uncertainty will be accounted for as a prior period adjustment. (Note that the accounting issue involving uncertainties is normally prospective in nature and will not, therefore, result in a prior period adjustment under FASB Statement 16.)

A qualified opinion states that, "except for" or "subject-to" the effects of the matter to which the qualification relates, the statements present fairly financial position, results of operations, and changes in financial position in conformity with GAAP. Ordinarily the auditor should not modify the language of the opinion paragraph unless the opinion is qualified. Reference to another auditor's report as a basis, in part, for the principal auditor's opinion is not considered to be a qualification. Unaudited information, pro forma calculations or other similar disclosures, where appropriately identified as "unaudited" or as "not covered by auditor's report," need not be referred to in the auditor's opinion.

When the auditor intends to qualify an opinion all substantive reasons therefore should be disclosed in a separate explanatory paragraph(s) and in the opinion paragraph appropriate qualifying language should be used, referring to the subject matter of the qualification, and to the explanatory paragraph(s). A separate explanatory paragraph is not required in the auditor's report when it is qualified because of a change in accounting principles. The auditor may refer to a note that explains the reason for the change. The explanatory paragraph(s) should disclose the effects of the subject of the qualification on financial position, income statement, and changes in financial position, if reasonably determinable, or state that the effects are not determinable. Such disclosures may, however, be made in a note and referred to in the explanatory paragraph. The explanation for the qualification should make clear whether the matter is a result of difference of opinion between the auditor and the client and whether the auditor believes an adjustment should be made or whether the matter involves an uncertainty that depends on future events.

When a qualified opinion results from a scope limitation or insufficiency of evidence, this information should be described in the explanatory paragraph(s) and not in a note and it should be referred to in both the scope and opinion paragraphs of the report.

Qualifying language should include the word "except" or "exception" in the phrase "except for" or "with the exception of" and the phrase "subject-to" when the qualification relates to an uncertainty. When the qualification arises because of an inconsistency, the qualifying language should be included in the opinion paragraph. When the auditor qualifies the opinion because of a scope limitation, the opinion paragraph should indicate that the qualification pertains to possible effects on the statements and not to the scope limitation. Appropriate language would be as follows:

(Scope paragraph)

Except as explained in the following paragraph, our examination . . . and such other auditing procedures as we considered necessary in the circumstances . . .

(Separate paragraph)

We did not observe the taking of the physical inventories as of December 31, 19xx (stated at $ . . . .), and December 31, 19x1 (stated at $ . . . .), since those dates were prior to the time we were initially engaged as auditors for the Company. Due to the nature of the Company's records, we were unable to satisfy ourselves as to the inventory quantities by means of other auditing procedures.

(Opinion paragraph)

In our opinion, except for the effects of such adjustments, if any, as might have been determined to be necessary had we been able to observe the physical inventories . . .

Adverse Opinion   There is only one reason for issuing an adverse opinion—when in the auditor's judgment the financial statements taken as a whole are not fair presentations in conformity with GAAP. An adverse opinion resulting from lack of fairness must be based on an examination in accordance with GAAS. When the auditor expresses an adverse opinion, disclosure should be made in a separate paragraph of all substantive reasons for the adverse opinion, and the effects of the subject matter of the adverse on financial position, results of operations, and changes in financial position, if reasonably determinable, or state that the effects are not reasonably determinable and report any other reservations he or she has as to fairness. The opinion paragraph should include a direct reference to the separate paragraph(s) and no reference to consistency should be made as such reference might imply fair presentation in accordance with GAAP.

Disclaimer of Opinion   SAS No. 2 requires a disclaimer of opinion in an audit engagement when the scope of an auditor's examination has been so restricted that an opinion, even one of limited usefulness, cannot be given. This is a two-paragraph disclaimer (scope and opinion disclaimer) that must include a middle paragraph(s) explaining all of the substantive reasons for the disclaimer.*

Piecemeal Opinion   A piecemeal opinion is an opinion on a part of a financial statement (such as working capital) that was given in the past when an overall adverse opinion or disclaimer of opinion had been given. Because piecemeal opinions tend to overshadow or may appear to contradict a disclaimer or adverse opinion, SAS No. 2 states that they are inappropriate and should not be issued.

OTHER CONDITIONS WHICH PRECLUDE THE APPLICATION OF NECESSARY AUDITING PROCEDURES

Receivables and Inventories

As previously noted, the confirmation of receivables and the observation of inventories are important audit procedures. When an auditor is unable to become satisfied regarding these procedures, the auditor will usually issue a disclaimer of opinion. However, in some cases a qualified opinion may be appropriate.

If the auditor has not become satisfied by means of other auditing procedures with respect to opening inventories, the auditor should either disclaim an opinion on the statement of income, retained earnings, and statement of changes, or qualify the opinion on these statements, depending on the degree of materiality of the amounts involved. The auditor may express an unqualified opinion on the balance sheet. An illustration of such a disclaimer follows:

(Scope paragraph)

We have examined the balance sheet of X Company as of September 30, 19x2, and the related statements of income and retained earnings and changes in financial position for the year then ended. Our examination was made in accordance with generally accepted auditing standards, and accordingly included such tests of the accounting records and such other auditing procedures as we considered necessary in the circumstances, except as stated in the following paragraph.

(Middle paragraph)

Because we were not engaged as auditors until after September 30, 19x1, we were not present to observe the physical inventory taken at that date and we have not satisfied ourselves by means of other procedures concerning inventory quantities. The amount of the inventory at September 30, 19x1, enters materially into the determination of the results of operations and changes in financial position for the year ended September 30, 19x2. Therefore, we do not express an opinion on the accompanying statements of income and retained earnings and changes in financial position for the year ended September 30, 19x2.

(Opinion paragraph)

In our opinion, the accompanying balance sheet presents fairly the financial position of X Company at September 30, 19x2, in conformity with generally accepted accounting principles applied on a basis consistent with that of the preceding year.

---

*A disclaimer of opinion for a public company when financial statements are unaudited because of an accounting service engagement is discussed in a subsequent section of this text.

An Auditing Interpretation of Section 509 (SAS No. 2) considers reporting problems involved when an outside inventory-taking firm is employed to count a client's ending inventory. Outside firms of nonaccountants specializing in the taking of physical inventories are used at times by some companies, such as retail stores, hospitals, and automobile dealers, to count, list, price and subsequently compute the total dollar amount of inventory on hand at the date of the physical count. The question considered in the Auditing Interpretation is "Would obtaining the report of an outside inventory-taking firm be an acceptable alternative procedure to the independent auditor's own observation of physical inventories?"

The Interpretation states that the fact that the inventory is counted by an outside inventory firm of nonaccountants is not, by itself, a satisfactory substitute for the auditor's own observation or taking of some physical counts. The auditor's concern, in this respect, is to satisfy himself or herself as to the effectiveness of the counting procedures used. If the client engages an outside inventory firm to take the inventory, the auditor's primary concern would be to evaluate the effectiveness of the procedures used by the outside firm and his or her auditing procedures would be applied accordingly.

Long-Term Investments

When the effects of accounting for long-term investments are material, the auditor is not in a position to express an unqualified opinion on the investor's financial statements unless sufficient competent evidential matter has been obtained in support of the objectives of the audit. That is, that investments have been properly accounted for and are presented in accordance with GAAP. There may be situations where there is an effective limitation on the scope of the auditor's examination because sufficient evidential matter is not available. Examples of such scope limitations, generally with respect to investments accounted for under the equity method, would include the following:

The auditor not being able to obtain audited financial statements of an investee or to apply auditing procedures to unaudited financial statements of an investee

The auditor not being able to examine sufficient evidential matter relating to the elimination of unrealized profits and losses resulting from transactions between the investor and investee

In situations involving scope limitations for long-term investments, such as those mentioned above, the auditor should indicate in the scope paragraph of the report any limitations on the examination and, depending on materiality of the amounts involved, the auditor should either qualify his or her opinion or disclaim an opinion.

LACK OF CONFORMITY WITH GAAP—REGULATED COMPANIES

GAAP apply equally to business enterprises in general and to companies whose accounting practices are prescribed by governmental regulatory authorities or commissions. Examples of companies that follow accounting and reporting systems prescribed by government authorities include public utilities, common carriers, insurance companies, and certain financial institutions. The first standard of reporting, which requires the auditor to state whether the financial statements are presented in conformity with GAAP, is applicable to opinions on financial statements of regulated companies presented for purposes other than filings with their respective supervisory agencies. Because such regulated companies do not necessarily follow GAAP, the first reporting standard will usually require a qualified or an adverse opinion as to fair presentation in conformity with GAAP. An adverse opinion on the statements of a regulatory company may, however, be accompanied by an opinion on supplementary data which are presented in conformity with GAAP. This is not a piecemeal opinion as the opinion relates to supplemental data and is not an opinion on a part of the basic financial statements. (SAS No. 14, Section 621, discusses special reports to regulatory authorities based on statements prepared on a basis of accounting specified by a regulatory authority.)

INADEQUATE DISCLOSURE

When a client declines to disclose information in the financial statements that is essential for an understanding of financial position, results of operations, or changes in financial position, or to incorporate the essential information by reference in the notes, the auditor should provide the necessary information in the report, usually in a middle paragraph(s), and issue a qualified opinion or an adverse opinion, as appropriate. An illustration of appropriate wording in such instances follows:

(Standard scope paragraph)
(Middle paragraph)

On January 15, 19x2, the company issued debentures in the amount of $ . . . . for the purpose of financing plant expansion. The debenture agreement restricts the payment of future cash dividends to earnings after December 31, 19x1.

(Opinion paragraph)

In our opinion, except for the omission of the information in the preceding paragraph, the aforementioned financial statements present fairly . . .

Omission of Statement of Changes in Financial Position

When a client issues financial statements that purport to present financial position and results of operations but omits the related statement of changes in financial position, the auditor will normally conclude that the omission requires a qualified opinion.

A client's failure to disclose required information in its financial statements normally requires the auditor to include the omitted information in the report and appropriately qualify the opinion. This disclosure requirement does not, however, require the auditor to include a basic financial statement in the report when management has declined to present the statement. Accordingly, when the statement of changes in financial position is omitted the auditor should qualify the report ordinarily in the following manner:

We have examined the balance sheet of X Company as of December 31, 19xx, and the related statements of income and retained earnings for the year then ended. Our examination was made in accordance with generally accepted auditing standards, and accordingly included such tests of the accounting records and such other auditing procedures as we considered necessary in the circumstances.

The company declined to present a statement of changes in financial position for the year ended December 31, 19xx. Presentation of such statement summarizing the company's financing and investing activities and other changes in its financial position is required by Opinion No. 19 of the Accounting Principles Board.

In our opinion, except that the omission of a statement of changes in financial position results in an incomplete presentation as explained in the preceding paragraph, the aforementioned financial statements present fairly the financial position of X Company at December 31, 19xx, and the results of its operations for the year then ended, in conformity with generally accepted accounting principles applied on a basis consistent with that of the preceding year.

A Flow Chart Conceptualization of Auditors' Reports on Financial Statements

Richard A. Epaves, Laurence R. Paquette and Michael A. Pearson

ENZIL Causey's recent article [Causey, 1976] includes a table that is useful for classroom discussions on the topic of audit report variations. Expanding on the Causey table, we have developed a flow chart (Figure 1) that covers most reporting situations confronted by certified public accountants. (Reports on incomplete statements, capsule information or other special presentations are not included.)

The purpose of the flow chart is to provide students of auditing with an easy-to-digest, logical model of the major reporting possibilities. A definitive understanding of related sections of the *Codification of Statements on Auditing Standards, Numbers 1 to 7* [AICPA, 1976], however, requires careful reading and study; the flow chart presented here is not intended to relieve students of that task. Relevant sections and paragraphs of the *Codification* are referenced to emphasize this point.

Figure 1 uses American National Standards Institute (ANSI) symbols. The oval represents a terminal point, and the diamond indicates that the auditor must make a decision.

LACK OF INDEPENDENCE AND UNAUDITED ENGAGEMENTS

The first horizontal branch stemming from the "start" instruction sorts out disclaimers required for lack of independence and unaudited engagements. If two "yes" answers are obtained along this branch, the undertaking is considered to be an audit.

CIRCUMSTANCES REQUIRING DEPARTURE FROM AN UNQUALIFIED OPTION

The second horizontal branch reads from right to left and sorts out those circumstances which require a deviation from an unqualified opinion. If a "yes" answer is obtained, the appropriate vertical branch should be followed to determine what type of departure is necessary. Of course, an unqualified opinion still can be issued when any of these circumstances exist if its effect is immaterial. In all cases, more than one action is possible; the ultimate opinion rendered depends on the auditor's assessment of each individual situation.

Starting from the right, the first vertical branch identifies the reporting options available if scope limitations exist. The reasons for the scope limitation, the

Richard A. Epaves is Associate Professor of Accounting at The Cleveland State University; Laurence R. Paquette is Associate Professor of Statistics and Data Processing at Western New England; and Michael A. Pearson is a doctoral student at Kent State University.

THE ACCOUNTING REVIEW
Vol. LI, No. 4
October 1976

FIGURE 1
SUMMARY OF REPORTING POSSIBILITIES

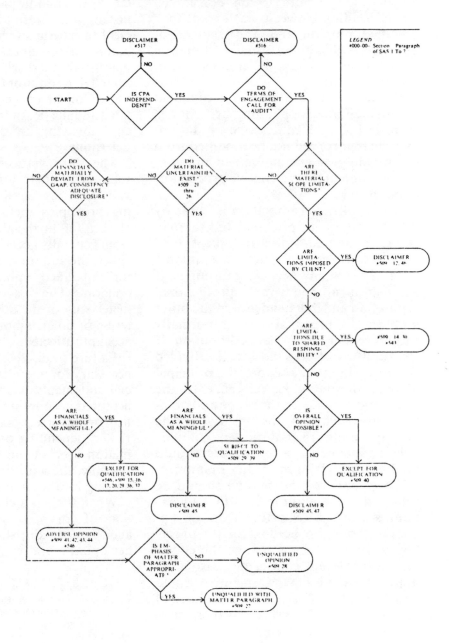

effect of any omitted procedures on the auditor's ability to form an opinion, and the size and number of account balances affected are factors to be considered when deciding between an "except-for" qualified opinion and a disclaimer of opinion. A disclaimer usually should be issued when restrictions are client-imposed.

If sufficient evidence is obtained through alternative auditing procedures, there is no significant scope limitation, and the report need not be modified from the wording of an unqualified opinion. No mention of the alternative procedures is necessary.

If part of the examination is made by other auditors, the principal auditor may issue an unqualified, an "except for" qualified, or a disclaimer of opinion.[1] After making any necessary inquiries, if he or she is satisfied with the professional reputation and independence of the other auditor, the principal auditor normally should render an unqualified opinion. If the auditor wishes to indicate the divided responsibility in the report, the principal auditor should make reference to the other auditor in both the scope and opinion paragraphs. If the results of the principal auditor's inquiries are unfavorable or inconclusive, he or she should qualify or disclaim his or her opinion.

The second vertical branch should be followed if the auditor feels that uncertainties exist. A departure from an unqualified opinion because of an uncertainty is only necessary when the effects of a future event cannot be reasonably approximated by management. A qualified ("subject to" type) or disclaimer of opinion should be written in these situations.

When deciding whether to render a qualified or a disclaimer of opinion, the auditor should consider the significance and complexity of the possible effects of

the uncertainty on the financial statements. It is the belief of the Auditing Standards Executive Committee that a descriptive middle paragraph and a qualified opinion normally should be sufficient to inform statement users as to the nature of the uncertainty. However, it appears that a disclaimer would be warranted if the auditor feels that the possible impact of the uncertainty cannot be isolated and the possible effects on the financial statements are difficult for a user to determine.

The third vertical branch should be followed if there are inconsistencies or violations of generally accepted accounting principles including adequate disclosure. If financial statements deviate from generally accepted accounting principles, the auditor may render an "except for" qualified opinion or an adverse opinion.[2] The selection depends on the materiality of the deviation expressed in terms of dollar amounts and number of accounts affected.

Failure to disclose information that is necessary for a fair presentation of financial statements is contrary to generally accepted accounting principles. A qualified or adverse opinion would be warranted depending on the omitted information's effect on the statements. If possible, the auditor should provide the missing information in his or her report.

When there is a change in the application of an accounting principle, the auditor normally should qualify his or her opinion and explicitly state concur-

---

[1] One would infer from Causey's table that an unqualified opinion always would be appropriate. Section 543, paragraph 11 of the *Codification* indicates that there are circumstances when an auditor either should qualify or disclaim his or her opinion.

[2] Note, however, that an unqualified opinion would be justified if there were a departure from a promulgated accounting principle (with which the auditor concurs) because, due to an unusual situation, complying with the principle would produce misleading results.

rence. If the new principle or the method of accounting for the effect of the change to the new principle is not generally accepted, the auditor should express a qualified or adverse opinion because of a deviation from generally accepted accounting principles.[3]

UNQUALIFIED OPINION

If three "no" answers are obtained when passing through the second horizontal branch, an unqualified opinion is justified. If the auditor wishes to emphasize a particular matter, he or she should do so in a separate middle paragraph. This paragraph should not be referred to in other sections of the report, and it would not constitute a qualification of opinion.

[3] Causey's table calls for a qualified opinion or a "disclaimer as to consistency." Section 546 of the *Codification* specifically states that either a qualified or an *adverse* opinion should be issued if inconsistencies are present.

REFERENCES

American Institute of Certified Public Accountants, Auditing Standards Executive Committee, *Codification of Statements on Auditing Standards, Numbers 1 to 7* (1976).
Causey, D. Y., "Newly Emerging Standards of Auditor Responsibility," THE ACCOUNTING REVIEW (January 1976), pp. 19–30.

The AICPA's legal counsel and its technical research
director discuss the legal principles used by a court
in determining that the defendant accountants
were negligent in their auditing procedures.

DISCLAIMERS AND LIABILITY—
THE RHODE ISLAND TRUST CASE

BY DAVID B. ISBELL AND D. R. CARMICHAEL

ANY CPA who reports on financial statements
could learn several valuable lessons from the
recent decision of the United States Court of Appeals for the Fourth Circuit which is reprinted in
full in this issue (Official Releases, p. 63).

HIGHLIGHTS OF THE CASE

Briefly, the plaintiff bank extended credit to the
defendant accountants' client, a cement importer, in
asserted reliance upon representations that the
company had made improvements to certain leasehold shipping facilities. Audited financial statements of the client, which were submitted to the
bank together with the accountants' long-form report containing a disclaimer of opinion, attributed
to these improvements $212,000 out of a total of
approximately $610,000 of expenditures during
1964. The capitalization of these improvements accounted for approximately two-thirds of the company's net worth shown on the balance sheet and
resulted in the statement of operations showing a
$9,000 profit rather than a substantial operating
loss. In fact, the leasehold improvements thus reflected on the financial statements had not been
made at all. The crucial question was whether the
representations made or implied by the accountants' report suggested that they had.

The lower court, after trial, dismissed the complaint, having concluded that the evidence failed to
establish "fraud or collusion on the part of the accountants, any lack of good faith, misrepresentation, breach of duty, negligence or failure to use
reasonable care in the preparation and issuance of
the financial statements." The Court of Appeals reversed, holding that there was negligence by the
accountants in failing either to take adequate measures to determine whether the leasehold improvements existed or to give notice that their existence
had not been verified. As a result of such negligence, the Court held, the accountants would be
liable to the bank if the bank could show reliance
upon the accountants' report; and it remanded the
case to the trial court for determination of this issue.
(The trial court has since held for the defendants
on the issue of reliance, and the case is once more
on appeal to the Court of Appeals.)

PRELIMINARY COMMENTS

The Court of Appeals' opinion is not as clear or
as solid as might be wished, but its legal premises
appear to be familiar enough. The Court's application of these legal principles to the facts of the case
as the Court states them also appears on the whole
to be sound. The interplay of familiar legal principles and a factual situation that, though perhaps
not a common one, will nonetheless be readily rec-
ognizable to most practitioners makes the decision
one from which some useful practical lessons can
be drawn.

The general legal principle which underlies the
decision is that an accountant who issues an audit
report on financial statements will be assumed to
have exercised reasonable care as to all matters
necessary to permit him to express an opinion, in
the absence of clear notice in his report of any matter on which he was not able to satisfy himself. In
this case, the Court held the accountants had failed
to exercise adequate care in verifying the existence

of the improvements, and had not only failed to give adequate notice of those respects in which such care could not be exercised but had affirmatively implied in their report that they were satisfied that the improvements existed.

NEGLIGENCE IN THE AUDIT

The Court's determination that the accountants were negligent in their auditing procedures on the facts set out in the decision, viewed independently of the audit report, is no surprise. The workpapers, the Court said, gave no indication that the accountants had themselves inspected the improvements or asked correspondent accountants (who had been used for other purposes) to do so. They showed that the accountants had examined the client's records with respect to the labor costs purportedly attributable to the improvements but gave no indication of their having identified the material costs, which would necessarily have been incurred if the improvements had in fact been made.

Although on such evidence a finding that the accountants were negligent in failing to discover the nonexistence of the improvements is not surprising, nonetheless, this branch of the decision may offer an important practical lesson. The defendants in the case appear to have been in the very uncomfortable position of being unable to establish what was in fact done with respect to the crucial matter of the leasehold improvements, because the workpapers did not provide a complete record and because the partner concerned with the engagement had died, so that there was no way of filling in the gaps with testimony. The lesson is an obvious one: it is important that workpapers be complete.

THE AUDIT REPORT

The other, more important branch of the Court's holding is that the accountants had represented in

DAVID B. ISBELL *is a partner in the law firm of Covington & Burling in Washington, D.C. He is admitted to practice in the District of Columbia and in Connecticut and before the Supreme Court of the United States. Mr. Isbell is a member of the American Bar Association and the Bar Association of the District of Columbia. He received his baccalaureate and law degrees from Yale University.* D. R. CARMICHAEL, *CPA, Ph.D., is director of the technical research division of the AICPA and an editor of the Accounting & Auditing column of* THE JOURNAL. *He is in charge of the Institute's research program for all technical areas—accounting, auditing, international practice, taxation and management advisory services. He also serves as adjunct professor of accounting at Baruch College of The City University of New York.*

their report that the leasehold improvements existed, not only because the report failed to give adequate notice of the limitations on their audit relating to the leasehold improvements but also because it seemed to imply that the accountants were satisfied as to the existence of the improvements. Here the Court was recognizing the perfectly sound and familiar legal principle that an auditor will not be held responsible for limitations on his audit if his report gives adequate notice of such limitations.[1] However, in determining whether such notice was adequately given by the limitations described in the accountants' report and the disclaimer with which the report concluded, the Court was reading the accountants' language strictly—in effect, from the viewpoint of an uninformed and unsophisticated reader. An accountant should recognize that any disclaimer or qualification or other limitation referred to in his report may be so strictly viewed.

REPORT HELD AS MISLEADING

Given that viewpoint, it was easy for the Court to conclude that the accountants' report failed to convey the pertinent limitations on the audit with respect to the leasehold improvements, and, indeed, carried a suggestion that the improvements had, in fact, been made. Several passages in the accountants' report, which the Court quoted with emphasis, could well be read as implying that the leasehold improvements existed:

> *Additions* to fixed assets in 1963 *were found* to include principally warehouse improvements and installation of machinery and equipment in Providence, Rhode Island, Brunswick, Georgia, and Palm Beach, Florida. Practically *all of this work was done by company employees and materials and overhead were borne by the International Trading Corporation and its affiliates.* Unfortunately, fully complete detailed cost records were not kept of these capital improvements and no exact determination could be made as to the actual cost of said improvements. (Emphasis added by the Court.)

The only passages in the report which the accountants could claim gave notice of the limitations of their audit in respect of the leasehold improvements were their disavowal, in the last sentence just quoted, of any "exact determination" of the "actual cost"; and the disclaimer with which they concluded their report:

> Because of the limitations upon our examination expressed in the preceding paragraphs and the material nature of the items not confirmed directly to

---

[1]For example, *Stephens Industries, Inc. v. Haskins & Sells,* 438 F.2d 357 (10 Cir. 1971).

us, we are unable to express an opinion as to the fairness of the accompanying statements.

The Court's discussion of the weight to be given to these references is instructive:

> . . . Accountants certified the financial statements, saying overall only that they could not express an opinion with regard to their fairness. This disclaimer, however, followed other reference to the purported leasehold improvements which expressed no reservation about their existence but only their precise value. We think that a fair reading of Accountants' covering letter and disclaimer indicates that while the leasehold improvements may have had a value of more or less than $212,000, there was no question but that they existed and that they had substantial value.

The lesson to be learned here is also obvious: an accountant disclaiming or qualifying an opinion, or otherwise seeking to give notice to a reader of limitations on the responsibilities he is assuming, should do his best to be sure that the language he uses will make those limitations clear even to an uninformed and unsophisticated reader.

HAZARDS OF THE LONG-FORM REPORT

The case also illustrates the hazards inherent in using a long-form report. The portion of the Court's opinion that considers the language of the accountants' report clearly rested less on the insufficiency of the disclaimer than on the language used in the body of the report, which tended to convey the impression that the leasehold improvements in fact existed. Without this language, indeed, it is probable that the decision would have gone otherwise than it did.[2]

Although the profession has adopted a standard form of report for an unqualified opinion on financial statements, no such forms have yet been adopted for many of the special situations faced when an unqualified opinion cannot be expressed. The use of special phraseology often bearing little resemblance to standard phraseology can be hazardous. Variety of expression may be a desirable

---

[2] An instructive example of affirmative representations overriding a disclaimer is the case of *Ryan v. Kanne*, 170 N.W. 2d 395 (Iowa 1969), where the accountants had prepared unaudited financial statements, adequately marked them as such and appended to them a disclaimer of opinion substantially in the form required by SAP No. 38—but also represented in an accompanying letter that they had confirmed accounts payable-trade, and, in addition, orally represented them to be correct within $5,000. These accounts proved to be materially understated, and it was shown that the accountants had not adequately confirmed them. As a result, they were held liable despite their disclaimer.

goal for literary style, but it can lead to serious difficulties in a technical report.

SOME GUIDES TO PRACTICE

When disclaiming an opinion an accountant should first consider whether the financial statements are audited within the meaning of paragraphs 8 through 16 and 22 through 25 of Chapter 10 of SAP No. 33. If the financial statements are unaudited, then the standard wording of the disclaimer of opinion recommended in paragraph 3 of SAP No. 38 should be followed. If the financial statements are audited but the accountant has concluded that a disclaimer of opinion is still called for because of the limited nature of his examination, he should carefully adhere to the following guides in writing his report:

1. The absence of compliance with generally accepted auditing standards should be reported directly and not left to inference.
2. The report should state that the examination was performed in conformity with generally accepted auditing standards *except* for certain specific procedures which should be enumerated in the report. The alternative practice of enumerating the procedures performed, as was followed by the accountants in the case under discussion, is fraught with too many hazards of hindsight interpretation.
3. The description of the scope of the examination in the accountants' report should not be interwoven with comments on the financial statements or comments on the operations of the company; any such comments that are needed should be footnotes, which are representations of the company, not the accountant.

PROFESSIONAL STANDARDS AND THE LAW

Although the conclusions of the Court with respect to the adequacy of the notice given by the accountants' report did not rest on the standards of the profession, they were, the Court said, "reinforced" by reference to such standards. This branch of the Court's opinion deserves some comment regarding both the general rule of law applied and the specific interpretation of various provisions of SAP No. 33.

The general principle, the Court stated, is that "while industry standards may not always be the maximum test of liability, certainly they should be deemed the minimum standard by which liability should be determined"; and the Court looked to SAP No. 33 to determine what the "industry standard" is. The Court's formulation is one that accountants should keep in mind. It is surely the general rule that the courts will hold accountants to the standards of their profession[3] and will look for those standards in the pronouncements of the committee on auditing procedure,[4] the APB and other Institute bodies of similar authority.[5]

What of the Court's assertion that such standards "may not always be the maximum test of liability"? Should the Court be understood as embracing a different rule from the one pronounced in the *BarChris* case: "Accountants should not be held to a standard higher than that recognized in their profession"?[6] The Court did not explain what it meant by this phrase; it had no need to do so, since it found that the accountants had failed to meet the minimum standards.

It appears to the authors that the Court need not be understood as saying anything more than that if there had not been a professional standard against which the accountants' report could be tested, the accountants still would have been held liable. In any event, it is clear that technical pronouncements like those of the committee on auditing procedure, while they establish the standards to which accountants will be held on those matters to which they speak, do not necessarily provide comprehensive guidance on every problem. An accountant must be prepared not only to show compliance with official pronouncements but also to justify the manner in which he has dealt with matters not specifically covered in pronouncements.[7]

In testing what the defendants in this case had done against the requirements of SAP No. 33, the Court found two grounds on which they had failed to comply with the standards therein set forth. As to one of these, the Court was on solid ground; but as to the other, it appears to the authors that the Court went astray.

The first ground is the requirement of Chapter 10, paragraph 16, of SAP No. 33 that "whenever the independent auditor disclaims an opinion, he should give *all* substantive reasons for doing so." The stated grounds of disclaimer referred to in the accountants' report in this case were limitations upon their examination expressed in the report, and the material nature of the items not confirmed by them. There was, however, no reference—at least, not in terms obvious to a lay reader—to any inability to verify the existence of the leasehold improvements, let alone any grounds for doubting their existence.

In the opinion of the authors, the Court's reading of this requirement of SAP No. 33 and its application to the disclaimer in question were correct. The lesson cannot be put more concisely than is already done in SAP No. 33: "Whenever the independent auditor disclaims an opinion, he should give *all* substantive reasons for doing so." The emphasis in this phrase, it should be pointed out, appears in the Statement itself.

The Court also referred to the requirement of paragraph 9 of Chapter 10 of SAP No. 33, which, dealing with a qualified opinion, asserts that the opinion "should refer specifically to the subject of the qualification and *should give a clear explanation of the reasons for the qualification* and of the effect on financial position and results of operations, if reasonably determinable." The emphasis in the foregoing passage was supplied by the Court, and its opinion in this regard rested upon what it deemed to be a failure of the accountants to disclose the reasons why "appraisals" were resorted to. Here the Court was surely mistaken in its understanding of what professional standards require. For one thing, paragraph 9 of Chapter 10 of SAP No. 33 deals with qualifications of opinions, not disclaimers. Further, and more fundamentally, the Court was here applying the phrase "clear explanation" much more broadly than would be the general understanding of the accounting profession. If the Court had a valid point here, it was the point that is made in the footnote accompanying this portion of the text of the opinion, that is, that the "appraisals" were not really appraisals at all, but estimates. The difference is obviously significant in this case, since an appraisal would not have been conducted without actually ascertaining the extent of the improvements being appraised.

To the extent that the Court here misunderstood and therefore misapplied the provision of SAP No. 33 under discussion, there is, of course, no useful lesson to be learned, since there is no way an accountant can guard against all possibilities of such misinterpretation. The point does not appear to have been material in the context of this case, however, for the same result was reached by the Court on two independent grounds, and, as indicated, its conclusion on both grounds appears right as a matter of law in one instance and of professional standards in the other. It bears repeating, however, that the crux of the defendants' problem in this case lies in the loose language of their report and

---

[3] The rule is the same for all professions, as well as trades. See *Restatement (Second) of Torts*, §299A (1965).

[4] For example, *Escott* v. *BarChris Construction Corp.*, 283 F. Supp. 643, 701 (S.D. N.Y. 1968) (S-1 review program found to conform to generally accepted auditing standards).

[5] For example, *Stanley L. Block, Inc.* v. *Klein*, 45 Misc. 2d 1054, 258 N.Y.S. 2d 501, 506 (Sup. Ct. 1965) (AICPA Code of Ethics "without any doubt, fixes the existing and accepted standards of their profession").

[6] *Escott* v. *BarChris Construction Corp.*, supra, at 703.

[7] See *United States* v. *Simon*, 425 F.2d 796, 806 (2d Cir. 1969).

disclaimer. But for this, there would have been no occasion for the Court to err on the point under discussion.

LIABILITY TO THIRD PARTIES

One further point with respect to the legal rules applied in the Court of Appeals' decision deserves brief consideration: the scope of an accountant's liability for negligence to persons other than his client. The Court, applying the common law of Rhode Island (since that was where the bank had received and assertedly relied on the financial statements) as interpreted in an earlier case by the Federal District Court there,[8] held the rule to be that "an accountant should be liable in negligence for careless financial representations relied upon by actually foreseen and limited classes of persons." In this case, the Court held, the accountants "not only knew but acknowledged that Bank sought Borrower's financial statements in connection with loans," and therefore would be liable for negligence rather than, as is the case with respect to most third parties, only for fraud. The Court recognized that this drawing of the line which describes the circle of those to whom an accountant owes a duty of care as distinct from a duty of honesty went somewhat beyond the holding of the *Ultramares* case.[9] In that case, the Court by Judge (later Justice) Cardozo, laid down the general common law rule that accountants and others making representations in the course of their profession or calling owe a duty of care only to those with whom they are in privity; and only honesty to all others. The Court in *Ultramares* recognized an exception to this rule which is sometimes designated the "primary benefit rule."

This rule holds that an accountant is also liable for negligence to those whose use of the information he supplies is the "end and aim of the transaction" in which he supplies it—that is, his engagement.[10] That formulation may not have been applicable in the case under discussion, since it does not appear from the Court's opinion that the audited financials were prepared primarily for use by the plaintiff bank.[11]

However, the rule applied by the Court is well within the formulation developed by the American Law Institute in the *Restatement of Torts*[12] a few

years after the *Ultramares* decision as well as the more precise formulation in the draft of *Restatement (Second) of Torts*, which is still under consideration.[13] Even though the *Restatement* rule extends third-party liability beyond *Ultramares*, which still appears to be the law in most states,[14] it nonetheless confines third-party liability for negligence to a limited group of immediately intended users of information in specifically foreseen transactions. The vast group of merely foreseeable but unidentified third-party users is still beyond the scope of an accountant's responsibility for negligence. It is significant that no court in a reported case involving accountants has extended common law liability for negligence to that larger group.

The Federal District Court in Rhode Island, in the decision on which the Court of Appeals relied in the case under discussion, expressed agreement with the views of some commentators who would eliminate the third-party limitation on liability for negligence.[15] These views, however, were simply dictum, and the rule actually applied in the case was the relatively narrow one applied by the Court in the case under discussion.[16] In fact, the Court need not have gone even that far, for as the Rhode Island Court recognized, the circumstances were such as to come squarely within the primary benefit rule as enunciated by Judge Cardozo in *Ultramares*.[17]

The Supreme Court of Iowa has also recently treated, in less than illuminating fashion, the question of the extent of accountants' liability to third parties for negligence, in a rather curious case.[18] There the suit was instituted by accountants seeking to recover, from the corporate successor to a

---

[8] *Rusch Factors, Inc. v. Levin*, 284 F. Supp. 85 (D.R.I. 1968).

[9] *Ultramares Corp. v. Touche*, 255 N.Y. 170, 174 N.E. 441 (1931).

[10] *Idem*, 174 N.E. at 445.

[11] Contrast the case of *Rusch Factors, Inc. v. Levin, supra*, where the audit was performed at the specific insistence of the plaintiff lender.

[12] The formulation of *Restatement of Torts*, § 552 (1938), is that a person who, in the course of his profession, supplies

information for the guidance of others is subject to liability for negligence to "the person or one of the class of persons for whose guidance the information was supplied" where such person justifiably relies upon it in a "transaction in which it was intended to influence his conduct or in a transaction substantially identical therewith."

[13] *Restatement (Second) of Torts*, § 552 (Tent. Draft No. 12, 1966), somewhat more narrowly states that liability for negligence runs to "the person or one of the persons for whose benefit and guidance [the professional person] intends to supply the information, or knows the recipient intends to supply it," for loss suffered "through reliance upon it in a transaction which he intends the information to influence, or knows that the recipient so intends, or in a substantially similar transaction."

[14] For example, *Stephens Industries, Inc. v. Haskins & Sells, supra; Investment Corp. of Fla. v. Buchman*, 208 So. 2d, 291 (Fla. Dist. Ct. of App. 1968); *Koch Industries, Inc. v. Vosko*, CCH Fed. Sec. L. Rep. § 93,705 (U.S.D.C.D. Kan. 1972).

[15] *Rusch Factors v. Levin, supra*, 284 F. Supp. at 90-91.

[16] See text following note 8, *supra*.

[17] *Rusch Factors, Inc. v. Levin, supra*, 284 F. Supp. at 91, 93.

[18] *Ryan v. Kanne, supra*.

sole proprietorship which had been their client, their fees for services performed in preparing un-audited financial statements which were to be used in soliciting subscriptions to the stock of the cor-poration. The issue of accountants' liability to third parties for negligence arose because the defendant corporation counterclaimed, seeking damages for negligence in the accountants' work. The Court applied the formulation of *Restatement (Second)* and held the accountants liable for negligence on the counterclaim. It is hard to see why the corporate defendant should have been treated as a third party at all, however, since the accountants, in suing the corporation for their fees, were treating it as sub-stantially identical to the client, or at least as a successor in interest, which indeed it was. More-over, even if the corporation was a third party it was clearly one within the scope of the primary benefit rule, for the solicitation of subscriptions to stock of the corporation that was to be formed was the "end and aim" of the accountants' engagement.

CONCLUSION

It is probably fair to say that many accountants have believed that disclaiming an opinion on finan-cial statements which they have audited relieved them of liability for errors in the financial state-ments unless a plaintiff could demonstrate that the accountants had knowledge of such error. This belief is a dangerous oversimplification. Account-ants issuing long-form reports, with or without dis-claimer, should consider their language with care; and, when a disclaimer is issued, the reasons for it should be spelled out fully and with care. Particu-lar care should be taken to be sure that in the course of explaining reasons for a disclaimer, the account-ant does not make statements that unwittingly con-tain implications that are affirmatively misleading.

CASE 21

JWD, CPAs

You are a member of the firm of JWD, CPAs (Jurgens, Winningham, and Dukeman). Your firm has grown rapidly since its formation in 19x1. Presently it has fifteen partners and ninety staff accountants. The firm has an excellent reputation due to the high professional standards it has maintained over the years. JWD has a wide variety of clients and performs services ranging from audits of public and nonpublic companies to preparation of unaudited statements that involve compilation and review services, tax work, and management services engagements. Because of the variety of its practice, the firm is a member of both the public and private practice sections of the AICPA.

JWD has just had its first quality control review, as required of members in the public practice section of the AICPA, and generally received a good report. However, there were some problems identified with respect to the firm's audit engagements. The following points of criticism were noted in the quality control review team's report:

1. The language contained in various audit reports issued by the firm does not conform to the standard report language established by Statement on Auditing Standards Nos. 2 and 15.

2. Working paper documentation for certain audit reports is incomplete in supporting the types of opinions given.

3. A prior audit report was reissued, with portions of the related financial statements being revised, and an improper report date was used.

4. The firm has improperly reported as continuing auditors on financial statements presented in comparative form.

5. The firm has not properly updated a prior-period report in connection with comparative financial statements for a public company.

Because of these identified reporting problems, the firm has been encouraged to conduct several in-house professional development programs related to the auditor's reporting responsibilities. The following questions have been prepared for discussion. Consider each question and develop an appropriate answer based on the reporting requirements of SASs Nos. 2 and 15.

CASE DISCUSSION QUESTIONS

1. What is a continuing auditor? When must a continuing auditor update his or her report on prior-period financial statements? How does an updated report differ from a reissued report?

2. What would be JWD's reporting responsibilities in the following situations:

   a. Comparative financial statements will be presented by the client for the current year. JWD has audited the current year's statements and are considered continuing auditors. They previously issued a subject-to qualified opinion on the prior-period financial statements. As a result of their current engagement, JWD determines that the uncertainty giving rise to the subject-to opinion on the prior-year's statements has been resolved.

   b. Another client has restated the prior-year's financial statements presented in comparative form with the current year's statements to reflect a change in accounting principle. The change in principle was made because the accounting principle followed in the prior year was not generally accepted. JWD qualified their opinion in the previous period because of the departure from GAAP. JWD has performed an examination of the current period financial statements and are prepared to issue their report.

    c.   JWD are predecessor auditors and have been asked to reissue their report on the prior-period statements that will be presented in comparative form with the current period statements. The current auditor is Anderson Coopers, CPA.

3.   What conditions or situations must exist before an auditor will be in a position to issue:

    a.   An unqualified opinion?

    b.   A qualified opinion?

    c.   An adverse opinion?

    d.   A disclaimer of opinion resulting from an audit engagement?

4.   What is the objective of the fourth standard of reporting? If a client decided to issue only a balance sheet, how does the fourth standard of reporting apply if the auditor has examined the financial statements? Explain.

5.   Regarding the auditor's standard short-form report, respond to the following questions:

    a.   When should the report be dated?

    b.   To whom should the report be addressed?

    c.   Who should sign the report?

    d.   An auditor wishes to emphasize a matter regarding the financial statements. How is this done? Is the report qualified or unqualified? Explain.

    e.   The auditor is reporting on consolidated statements. He or she wishes to divide responsibility between himself or herself and another auditor who has examined a significant subsidiary. How is this done? What is the effect on an unqualified opinion when there is a division of responsibility between a principal auditor and other auditors?

6.   A client has departed from GAAP in two respects. First, there is a departure from a promulgated accounting standard (the client has failed to capitalize interest related to certain qualifying assets under FASB Statement No. 34). Second, the client has followed an accounting principle that is contrary to what is generally accepted in the client's industry because of general business usage. What is the effect on the auditor's reporting responsibility:

    a.   When there is a departure from a promulgated accounting standard?

    b.   When there is a departure from GAAP that has not been promulgated but has become generally accepted because of business usage?

7.   Explain the effect on the auditor's report when there is a client-imposed scope restriction on:

    a.   The confirmation of receivables.

    b.   The observation of inventory.

        Would the effect on the auditor's report, in the above instances, be the same if the scope restriction resulted from the timing of the engagement or the condition of the client's records, rather than being imposed by the client? Explain.

8.   Why is a subject-to qualified opinion given when a material uncertainty exists regarding the financial statements? Are the statements considered to be fair presentations, the uncertainty notwithstanding? Explain.

9.   During the past year, JWD was unable to observe the taking of the physical inventory of Joe's Clothing Store and a qualified opinion was issued:

   a.   Write the separate paragraph and opinion paragraph for a qualified opinion (assume 12/31/x1 was the date of the financial statements).

   b.   Give examples of phrases that would not be acceptable for use in an opinion qualified because of a scope restriction.

An examination of the Continental Vending case
to determine (1) what its implications
for the accounting profession probably are
and (2) what legal rules the Court has
authoritatively said will apply

THE CONTINENTAL VENDING CASE:
LESSONS FOR THE PROFESSION

BY DAVID B. ISBELL

O N November 12, 1969, the United States Court of Appeals for the Second Circuit issued its opinion affirming the convictions of the three accountant-defendants in the *Continental Vending* case, *United States* v. *Simon*, F.2d, CCH Fed. Sec. L. Rep., ¶ 92,511 (2nd Cir. 1969) (see JofA, Feb.70, p.61). Although review by the Supreme Court was sought through the discretionary writ of *certiorari*, on March 31, 1970, that Court denied the writ, thus leaving in effect the decision of the Court of Appeals. 397 U.S. 1006 (1970).

Because of the potential importance of certain aspects of the case to the accounting profession at large, the American Institute of CPAs submitted briefs as *amicus curiae* to the District Court (see JofA, Nov.68, p.54), to the Court of Appeals and to the Supreme Court (see JofA, May70, p.69). Those briefs viewed the case from the standpoint of what its implications might be for the accounting profession, and of what legal rules ought, from the profession's point of view, to apply. Now that the case has come to rest it must be viewed from a different perspective, for the pertinent questions now are not what the implications *might* be, but what they probably are; and not what legal rules *should* ap-

ply, but what rules the Court has authoritatively said will apply. This article is an attempt to examine the case from that new perspective.

I

RESUME OF THE CASE

Because the opinion of the Court of Appeals, which has been printed in the February 1970 JOURNAL (p.61), describes fully the history of the case and the facts that were pertinent to the Court's opinion, no elaborate description of the case is necessary here. A brief summary should suffice to set the framework for the discussion that follows.

The defendants, two partners and a manager in Lybrand, Ross Bros. & Montgomery, were charged with fraud in the preparation of the 1962 balance sheet of Continental Vending Machine Corporation. Harold Roth was Continental's founder and president and held 25 per cent of its outstanding stock. Roth was also an officer, director and major stockholder of Valley Commercial Corporation, which was thereby an affiliate of Continental. Valley had other auditors. Continental made substantial advances to Valley, resulting in the "Valley receivable"; and Valley, in turn, made substantial advances to Roth, which he used for transactions in the stock market. It was conceded that the defendants knew of these advances to Roth before they issued their opinion on Continental's 1962 financial statements. The defendants also knew that Roth could not repay to Valley the loans then outstanding, and that Valley could not repay Conti-

DAVID B. ISBELL *is a partner in the law firm of Covington & Burling in Washington, D.C. He is admitted to practice in the District of Columbia, in Connecticut and before the Supreme Court of the United States. Mr. Isbell is a member of the American Bar Association and the Bar Association of the District of Columbia. He received his baccalaureate and law degrees from Yale University.*

nental. In order to insure collectibility of the Valley receivable, collateralization was undertaken by hypothecation of securities held by Roth and his family. Eighty per cent of the securities pledged were the common stock and convertible debentures of Continental itself.

The defendants issued an opinion on the 1962 financial statements of Continental, which represented that the financials "present fairly the consolidated financial position of Continental . . . in conformity with generally accepted accounting principles." The financial statements disclosed, *inter alia*, the loans to Valley, the fact that Roth was an officer, director and stockholder of Valley, and that the loans were secured by Valley's equity in "certain marketable securities." The financial statements showed a large net loss, and trading in Continental stock was suspended shortly after the annual report containing the financial statements was issued.

Roth and the defendant accountants were indicted for fraud and conspiracy to commit fraud. Roth pleaded guilty to one count and testified against the accountants (hereinafter "the defendants") at their trial.

The charges with which the trial was concerned were these:

1. The principal charge was that the balance sheet was fraudulent in failing to disclose that Roth had received from Valley sums which Valley had received from Continental.

2. Footnote 2 to the financial statements was charged to be false and misleading generally in representing that the Valley receivable was adequately secured, and specifically

    a. In representing that the Valley receivable and Valley payable could be netted.

    b. In failing to disclose that a substantial part of the collateral consisted of securities of Continental itself.

    c. In failing to disclose a post year-end increase from $3.4 to $3.9 million in the amount of the Valley receivable.

All but one of these charges raised sharp issues regarding proper accounting practice. The exception was the netting of the Valley payable and receivable, which the defendants conceded could not be netted because the payable was represented by notes which Valley had discounted with banks. The defendants also conceded that footnote 2 erroneously implied that the payable and receivable might be netted but asserted that this was innocent error.

Eight defense experts testified that none of the disclosures was required by generally accepted accounting principles and that the statements taken as a whole did present the financial position and results of operation fairly in accordance with generally accepted accounting principles. Two prosecution experts testified to the contrary. After two trials (the first having ended in a hung jury) the defendants were convicted. No jail sentences were imposed; the defendants were fined $5,000 to $7,000 each.

Post-trial motions for acquittal and new trial, on which the Institute made its first *amicus curiae* submission, were denied, and as has been mentioned, the United States Court of Appeals affirmed and the Supreme Court denied *certiorari*.

II
GENERAL SIGNIFICANCE OF CASE

The decision of the Court of Appeals is an important one for the accounting profession. It is significant in two prime respects: first, for what it says about the weight the law will attach to the standards of the accounting profession; second, for what it says about obligations, over and above those imposed by the standards of the profession itself, which the law will impose upon accountants in the course of their professional work.

The case is also instructive. The decision of the Court of Appeals tells much of a practical nature about how accountants can get into legal trouble and by the same token suggests ways in which at least some risks may be avoided.

In the perspective in which the case must now be viewed, an aspect that rendered it particularly shocking when it was brought—and while it was pending—becomes virtually without significance. That is the fact that it was a criminal case rather than a civil case. None of the major lessons of the case turns on the fact that it was a criminal rather than a civil proceeding. The major implications of the case to be discussed below apply as fully to the risk of civil as to criminal liability.

The fact that the case was a criminal matter did, of course, give particular poignancy to the fate of the individual defendants. It also serves as an important warning of the gravity of the hazards with which professional life is fraught. There are also some peculiar twists related to the criminal nature of the proceeding which deserve a preliminary word or two.

One such twist lies in the fact that the criminal prosecution certainly served as leverage to force the settlement of the companion civil suit, in the amount of $2.1 million. Another is the peculiar irony that the specific charges in this particular case would not have supported a civil damage action even though they did support a criminal action. The reason for this is that no one was damaged by the failures of disclosure in Continental's 1962 balance sheet for which the defendants were held responsible. To be sure, the market for Continental stock collapsed as soon as the financials appeared, and people were hurt by its collapse, but this was because of what the financial statements showed and not because of what the jury found they had wrongfully concealed.[1]

III

IMPLICATIONS OF THE CASE FOR THE ACCOUNTING PROFESSION

As has been mentioned, the case appears to have general significance to the accounting profession in three areas: (1) the weight to be given professional standards, (2) the standards of inquiry and disclosure proclaimed by the Court and (3) the practical lessons taught by the case.

A. WEIGHT OF PROFESSIONAL STANDARDS

The case is significant in what it says about the weight that the courts will give, where liability is concerned, to the standards of the accounting profession. The defendants offered eight expert witnesses, all eminent in the profession, to testify that Continental's balance sheet, which was charged to be fraudulent, fairly presented the financial position of Continental in conformity with generally accepted accounting principles. Two prosecution witnesses testified to the contrary, but the Court of Appeals observed that:

> With due respect to [the latter] . . . , they hardly compared with defendants' witnesses in aggregate auditing experience or professional eminence.

There were thus critical factual issues for the jury, as to which of the expert witnesses should be believed (on which issues the Institute took no position); and, underlying these, there was a critical legal issue, on which the Institute moved to participate at all three levels of the proceeding, as to the weight to be given to the standards of the profession. That issue was framed in terms of the instructions to the jury.

The defendants had asked the trial court for instructions that would have required the jury to acquit if it found that the balance sheet was in con-

formity with generally accepted accounting principles. The trial court instead gave instructions which said that the "critical test" was whether the balance sheet fairly presented the financial position without reference to generally accepted accounting principles.

The trial court also said in its instructions that evidence of compliance with generally accepted accounting principles would be very persuasive, but not conclusive. It also gave other instructions which the jury might have taken as an invitation to test the fairness of presentation, not against generally accepted accounting principles, but against their idea of what an investor or other layman might want to know.

It was this seeming invitation to apply a lay standard rather than to look at the balance sheet as an accountant does—and as the defendants by their opinion on the Continental financials had represented that they had—that prompted the Institute's concern.

The position of the Institute in its submissions was not quite the same as that which had been proposed by the defendants' instructions. If the Institute had proposed instructions embodying its position, they would have required the jury to test the balance sheet against generally accepted accounting principles and to acquit if they found it in conformity with generally accepted accounting principles, *unless* the jury found from evidence beyond the financials themselves that the defendants had an intent to defraud. The Institute's position thus recognized the possibility of formal compliance with all professional standards which is a mere sham or subterfuge. As the Institute's brief in the Supreme Court specifically recognized, the jury might have convicted the defendants in this case even under such instructions because of the evidence (to be discussed below) which the jury could have taken as showing wrongful intent. The problem was that the instructions actually given by the trial court allowed, if they did not invite, the jury to take what the Institute considered to be an improper route (of appraising the financials in purely lay terms) in reaching that result.

The Court of Appeals, however, substantially narrowed the possibility which the trial court had left open, of a jury's being allowed to take a purely layman's view and to disregard the standards of the profession in a future case, whether civil or criminal.

The Court of Appeals emphasized that fair presentation was the "critical test"; indeed, it equated the trial court's emphasis on fair presentation with that of the defendants themselves. The Court of Appeals gave no emphasis to—in fact, did not refer to—the lay investor's standard which had been men-

---

[1] Lybrand's opinion was withdrawn within a week after it was published and the SEC contacted because the collateral supporting the loans in question had fallen in value.

tioned in the instructions of the trial court:

> We do not think the jury was . . . required to accept the accountants' evaluation whether a given fact was material to overall fair presentation, at least not when the accountants' testimony was not based on specific rules or prohibitions to which they could point, but only on the need for the auditor to make an honest judgment and their conclusion that nothing in the financial statements themselves negated the conclusion that an honest judgment had been made. Such evidence may be highly persuasive, but it is not conclusive, and so the trial judge correctly charged.

Thus, the Court of Appeals seems to cast the difference between the accountants' view and the view permitted the jury in terms of materiality—i.e., in terms of the relative weight to be given to different factors—rather than in terms of potentially wholly differing standards of accountants and laymen.

Moreover, the Court of Appeals in the passage quoted is limiting its holding that less than conclusive weight may be given to professional standards to cases where such standards involve no specific rules on prohibitions but leave the matter to the judgment of the individual auditor. The Court's "at least" implies that in cases where there are specific rules or prohibitions they may be conclusive. This also is what the *BarChris* case suggests: "Accountants should not be held to a standard higher than that recognized in their profession." (*Escott* v. *BarChris Construction Corp.*, 283 F. Supp. 643, 703 (S.D.N.Y. 1968)).

The Institute would, of course, have preferred a rule requiring more conclusively that a jury weigh matters from the perspective of the accountant. Moreover, the areas where judgment alone applies —so that evidence as to professional standards is, under the Court of Appeals' formulation, only "persuasive" and not "conclusive"—will remain large. Nonetheless, the rule enunciated by the Court of Appeals does not appear to be one that the profession cannot live with.

Two practical lessons can be drawn from this point: one for the profession as a whole, and the other for individual practitioners. For the profession the case points out once more the very real advantage, at least from the point of view of legal responsibility, in having professional standards spelled out. Had there been specific rules or prohibitions governing the matters about which there was dispute among the expert witnesses in this case, to which the defendants could refer, it is quite probable the result would have been different. There would very possibly have been different instructions; very likely a different verdict; and altogether likely, if neither of those had occurred, a different decision by the Court of Appeals.

For the practitioner, the opinion of the Court of Appeals suggests the desirability of adopting a procedure whereby, at least in cases where pure judgment does govern, a special review is made to determine whether disclosures are adequate and understandable from a layman's point of view. The Lybrand firm has adopted a procedure requiring in every case, prior to release of a published report, a "cold look" by a partner unassociated with the engagement with a view to whether the disclosures made are understandable to laymen. This is certainly a sensible course, although it is not one that is required by the Court of Appeals' decision.

B. INQUIRY AND DISCLOSURE

The case has further significance in the rules of inquiry and disclosure laid down by the Court of Appeals. There were four issues of this nature on which the expert testimony was divided:

1. Whether disclosure had to be made of the fact that sums advanced by Continental to Valley had in turn been lent to Continental's president, Roth.

2. Whether there was a duty on the defendants to make inquiry into the affairs of Valley, Continental's affiliate, which had its own auditors.

3. Whether disclosure was required to be made of the composition of the collateral which was pledged to secure the Valley receivable, which collateral consisted largely of stock and debentures of Continental which was owned by and pledged by Roth.

4. Whether disclosure should have been made of the post-fiscal year-end increase in the Valley receivable from $3.4 million to $3.9 million.

1. Loans by Valley to Roth. It is the first of these issues, i.e., whether disclosure had to be made of the fact that money advanced by Continental to Valley had been lent to Roth, about which the Court had most to say, and on which its holding is, for precedential purposes, most important. Unfortunately, its language on this point is not altogether clear:

> We join defendants' counsel in assuming that the mere fact that a company had made advances to an affiliate does not ordinarily impose a duty on an accountant to investigate what the affiliate has done with them or even to disclose that the affiliate has made a loan to a common officer if this has come to his attention. But it simply cannot be true that an accountant is under no duty to disclose what he knows when he has reason to believe that, to a material extent, a corporation is being operated not to carry out its business in

the interest of all the stockholders but for the private benefit of its president. For a court to say that all this is immaterial as a matter of law if only such loans are thought to be collectible would be to say that independent accountants have no responsibility to reveal known dishonesty by a high corporate officer. If certification does not at least imply that the corporation has not been looted by insiders so far as the accountants know, or if it has been, that the diversion has been made good beyond peradventure (or adequately reserved against) and effective steps taken to prevent a recurrence, it would mean nothing, and the reliance placed on it by the public would be a snare and a delusion. Generally accepted accounting principles instruct an accountant what to do in the usual case where he has no reason to doubt that the affairs of the corporation are being honestly conducted. Once he has reason to believe that this basic assumption is false, an entirely different situation confronts him. Then, as the Lybrand firm stated in its letter accepting the Continental engagement, he must "extend his procedures to determine whether or not such suspicions are justified." If, as a result of such extension or, as here, without it, he finds his suspicions to be confirmed, full disclosure must be the rule unless he has made sure the wrong has been righted and procedures to avoid a repetition have been established. At least this must be true when the dishonesty he has discovered is not some minor peccadillo, but a diversion so large as to imperil if not destroy the very solvency of the enterprise.

The Court says too much here, and in language too pungent, to leave the meaning of this crucial passage as clear as its importance warrants. Careful analysis, however, suggests its proper interpretation.

First of all, it seems clear enough that the Court is saying that there is *not ordinarily* a duty on an auditor to disclose the disposition of funds advanced by its client to an affiliate. It is only in certain circumstances where the Court says such a duty of disclosure arises. Unfortunately, the uncertainty arises when the Court comes to identifying those circumstances.

The Court's language in the passage quoted suggests four possible definitions of the circumstances giving rise to the duty of disclosure. First, the Court refers to "looting"—and elsewhere in its opinion repeatedly uses that term. Second, the Court refers to dishonesty—"known dishonesty by a high corporate officer." Third, the Court refers to a corporation being operated to a material extent for the private benefit of its president. Finally, the Court refers to diversion of funds.

Which of these, in the Court's view, gave rise to the additional duty of disclosure here involved? I suggest that it is only the last—that is, diversion of funds—which gives rise to such a duty of disclosure.

"Looting" is no more a term of art or certain meaning in the law than it is in accountancy. It is not clear in this case when, in the Court's view, Roth's borrowings became looting. Looting, presumably, does not mean illegality, since the trial court instructed the jury, in this case, that Roth's borrowings were not illegal. It thus appears that the word "looting" is merely a literary touch rather than an operative analytical element of the Court's opinion.

The Court's second possible test for bringing into play the duty of disclosure is operation of a corporation, to a material extent, for the private benefit of the president. This is even less helpful than the "looting" test for analytical purposes, at least as a formulation divorced from the facts of this particular case.

Virtually every corporation is operated, to some extent, for the benefit of its officers and other insiders. Indeed, it is quite proper and usual for a corporation to attempt to link the self-interest of the principal officers and employees to the corporation: that, of course, is the governing principle of stock options. Moreover, especially in smaller corporations and those which have recently gone public, the officers are likely to be the principal stockholders themselves. (In the case of Continental, the president owned about 25 per cent of the outstanding stock.) And in corporations of all sizes the insiders, rather than the stockholders as a group, typically control the corporation. To require the accountant to make judgments as to the extent to which the decisions of the principal corporate officers are governed by self-interest rather than stockholder interest, and to draw lines short of specifically prohibited conduct, would indeed be to launch accountants on an uncharted and perhaps unchartable sea.

The third phrase, "known dishonesty by a high corporate officer," in itself is surely not the key, either. The accountant may know that his client's president has cheated the Internal Revenue Service, or fellow investors in a different enterprise, or has been convicted of a crime, but the Court was surely not saying that the accountant has a duty to pass along such information to his client's stockholders.

The key factor bringing into play the special duty of disclosure, it seems to me, is the diversion of funds. The Court defines what sort of diversion of funds it is talking about: a *dishonest* (though not necessarily illegal) diversion, and one "so large as to imperil if not destroy the very solvency of the enterprise." By these terms the Court describes the situation in which a special rule of disclosure applies sufficiently precisely so that there should not be inordinate difficulty in following the rule.

Where disclosure is so required, what should its

content be? The Court of Appeals' opinion indicates that "full disclosure" must be the rule—but what does this mean? The Court does not say in general terms, but it does in specific terms: it sets out a version of footnote 2 which, it says, presents the disclosure which the government claims should have been made, and which the Court by implication indicates would have been sufficient in this case. Comparison of that footnote with the footnotes and pertinent excerpts of the Continental balance sheet quoted in the Court of Appeals' opinion offer, I suggest, a clear enough idea as a practical matter of what the Court means by full disclosure. It does not mean that there should be a characterization made of the transactions being disclosed, or an opinion expressed upon them; the Court does not suggest that the labels "diversion," or "dishonest" or "looting" should be used. But the disclosure made includes all the facts, quite neutrally stated, which a reader of the note would have to be apprised of in order to make his own evaluation of the "diversion of funds" in question.

Two further, and important, points should be made about this aspect of the Court's opinion: about a contingency that could possibly render disclosure unnecessary, and about the timing of disclosure.

In the passage of the opinion quoted above, the Court twice makes reference to a situation where the diversion has been made good or adequately secured against and procedures have been established to prevent a repetition. In such a situation, the Court quite clearly says, the special rule of disclosure does *not* apply. With respect to this exception to the general rule of disclosure, the Court indicates that more is required than a reasonable assurance of collectibility. The defense experts said, in effect, that collectibility made disclosure in this case unnecessary, and the Court specifically rejected this contention. Of course, an accountant may not always be able easily to determine what steps should be taken to prevent the recurrence of a dishonest diversion, or whether steps taken are sufficiently effective to meet the Court's test so that disclosure is no longer necessary. The Court offers no guidance on this problem. This may, perhaps, be a subject deserving study by an appropriate body of the Institute.

The other point to be noted about this part of the Court's opinion is the clear implication that an accountant's duty of disclosure applies only at the time that his opinion is issued. This is an important point, because it has been suggested that the *Continental Vending* case implies a general duty on the part of accountants to disclose improprieties on the part of their clients or their clients' officers, no matter when they learn of them and no matter when they occur. I believe the case carries no such implication.

In this case, the Court of Appeals accepted the prosecution's evidence (which the defendants denied) that all three defendants knew at least as early as December 1962 that the funds advanced to Valley had wound up with Roth. Although the Lybrand opinion was not issued until more than two months later, the Court does not suggest that disclosure should have been made prior to the issuance of the opinion. Moreover, when the Court talks about disclosure it is clearly talking about disclosures as of the time when the opinion was issued. Still further, the Court is clearly saying that if as of that time the diversion had been made good and steps taken to prevent a repetition, then it need not be disclosed. Thus, there are no grounds in the opinion for asserting that accountants have a duty of disclosure with respect to the activities of their clients apart from the issuance of their opinion on the client's financial statements.

In a recent case, a federal district court and court of appeals held that an insurance company which had knowledge of fraudulent conduct by a broker making a market in the company's stock was liable to investors under Section 10 of the Securities and Exchange Act of 1934 and the SEC Rule 10b-5 thereunder, in part by reason of its failure to report the broker's activities to the State Securities Commission (*Brennan* v. *Midwestern United Life Ins. Co.*, 286 F. Supp. 702 (N.D. Ind. 1968, *aff'd*, 417 F.2d 147 (7th Cir. 1969), *cert. denied*, 397 U.S. 989 (1970).). It might be suggested that the *Brennan* case implies a similar duty of accountants to report to public authority all improper activities of their clients, quite apart from the accountants' responsibility with respect to their opinion. This, however, would be reading the *Brennan* case too broadly. For one thing, the Court of Appeals there found active participation by the insurance company in the broker's fraud. More importantly, the relationship of the insurance company to the broker there was quite different from that of an accountant to his client. The accountant has a professional obligation of confidence with respect to his client, wholly absent in the relationship of corporate issuer to its market maker. Moreover, the issuer in that case stood to benefit by the broker's improper activities.

Thus, it seems clear that an accountant's obligation with respect to disclosure or reporting of improper activities by the client or the client's officers is limited to matters affecting the accountant's opinion on the client's financial statements (or, if no opinion is issued, his association therewith: see AICPA committee on professional ethics, Opinion No. 8, "Denial of Opinion Does Not Discharge Responsibility in All Cases"; and AICPA committee on auditing procedure, Statement on Auditing Procedure No. 38, "Unaudited Financial Statements"). Such an obligation may, of course, arise not only with respect to an opinion being issued, which is what the *Continental Vending* case was concerned with, but also with respect to an opinion previously issued, which was the problem raised in the *Yale Express* case (*Fischer v. Kletz*, 266 F. Supp. 180 (S.D.N.Y. 1967)), and which is more fully dealt with in SAP No. 41, "Subsequent Discovery of Facts Existing at the Date of the Auditor's Report."

2. Inquiry Into Affairs of Valley. The second issue on which the expert witnesses disagreed was whether accountants are under a duty of inquiry into the affairs of affiliates to which advances are made.

The passage from the opinion quoted above suggests that where there is reason to believe that a material dishonest diversion of funds has occurred, an auditor may well have an obligation to investigate the affiliate through which the suspected diversion was made to see if his suspicions are well founded. The Court clearly indicates, however, that this duty of investigation arises only in such exceptional circumstances. There is no implication in this decision that in ordinary circumstances an auditor has an obligation to inquire into the affairs of an affiliate which is audited by other auditors. It may be noted, however, that the committee on auditing procedure has under study the question of an auditor's obligation with respect to such transactions with affiliated companies.

It is also of interest in this connection that the Lybrand firm has now adopted the policy of requiring, as a condition of engagement, that it be engaged to audit not only the principal company but also that company's affiliates.

3. Composition of Collateral. The third question of a technical nature as to which the expert witnesses disagreed involved disclosure of the composition of the collateral pledged against the loans to Valley. The ruling of the Court on this point is quite narrow. It did not hold that collateral must always be described, or even that collateral must always be described where it consists in large part of securities of the creditor entity. Rather, the Court held that failure to describe the collateral in this case must "be judged in light of [the defendants'] failure to reveal the looting by Roth"; and that the jury might infer that this failure to disclose "was part of a deliberate effort to conceal what defendants knew of the diversion of corporate funds that Roth had perpetrated."

An accountant, however, would be well advised to disclose the make-up of the collateral securing a loan in a case such as *Continental Vending*, i.e., where the collectibility of the loan is essential to avoiding an excess of current liabilities over current assets (particularly where there is a serious operating loss), and where the collateral consists in substantial part of the stock of the lending company, whose value is necessarily dependent on the perceived financial condition of the company itself. As the Court observed, the securities of the company whose solvency is at issue are "the one kind of property ideally unsuitable" to collateralize a receivable such as the Valley receivable.

4. Increase in Valley Receivable. The final technical question as to which the expert witnesses disagreed concerned the nondisclosure of the increase in the Valley receivable from $3.4 million to $3.9 million between the fiscal year-end and the date of the auditors' opinion.

The Court treated this question in the same fashion as the question of disclosure of the composition of collateral: that is, not in terms of any general principle of disclosure, but in terms of the light which the jury might think that the nondisclosure cast upon the defendants' purposes, given the central fact that the known diversion of the funds was not disclosed.

Thus, so far as standards of professional conduct are concerned, the Court of Appeals' opinion enunciates only one general rule that is, to any significant degree, a new one. The rule is that where the auditor knows of or suspects a dishonest diversion of funds sufficiently large to imperil his client's solvency, there must either be exceptional disclosure or exceptional measures to make it good and to prevent a recurrence.

C. PRACTICAL IMPLICATIONS

The third major group of lessons to be learned from the case are practical, rather than legal, in nature.

First, the case suggests two general rules of a practical character whose implications may be seen throughout the Court's opinion. One is that where an accountant discovers such a diversion as was involved in this case (and, I would suggest, whether or not the diversion is made good), he would do well to consider every action that he takes thereafter, every disclosure or nondisclosure, and every contact with the client, in the light of how it may subsequently appear in a court of law. The other is that the accountant in such circumstances, in order to protect himself, should as a practical matter exercise an extraordinary degree of caution: a much higher degree of caution than, to their misfortune, was exercised by the defendants in this case.

The case illustrates why such extra care and circumspection are called for: conduct that could well have been less than negligent was, in the light of hindsight, made to appear to be deliberately fraudulent and, indeed, criminal. Thus, for example, the Court of Appeals makes specific reference to

• The fact that, as the defendants conceded, footnote 2 to the Continental Vending financials erroneously implied that the Valley payable and Valley receivable could be netted.

• The fact that the defendants apparently did not consult with a partner in their firm with whom problems in audits were supposed to be discussed.

• The fact that two of the defendants failed to tell the assistant who confirmed the collateral about liens on the collateral at certain banks.

• The fact that the defendants failed to require effectuation of Roth's promised pledge of his house and furnishings.

• The fact that although the defendants asked to have Continental's board approve the transactions involved in securing the Valley receivable, they did not, before issuing their opinion, see to it that this had been done.[2]

The case also suggests some more specific practical rules, applicable where a problem of a potentially serious nature is discovered:

1. The accountant should not be rushed by supposedly urgent deadlines. The client can stand a little delay in issuing its annual report, or in filing its 10-K, much better than the accountant can bear the blame for the economic misfortunes of the client or its stockholders.
2. The accountant should not rely on promises of the client's officers as to important matters; he should see to it that they are carried out.
3. The accountant should not rely on representations made by the client with regard to such important matters if they are matters which the accountant can check for himself.
4. The accountant should consult with a partner or a colleague who can bring objectivity to bear on the matter before he issues his opinion.
5. Finally, it may be useful for the accountant to consult his attorney, if he has one. Such consultation should not take place merely after the accountant has issued his opinion or after trouble has developed, but while trouble—or at least legal involvement of the accountant in such trouble—may still be avoided. The attorney may not be able to bring great expertise to bear. Unfortunately, expertise in accounting matters is not widely spread in the legal fraternity, in part because accountants have not until recently consulted attorneys much. But the attorney, even if he does not possess accounting expertise, should be able at least to bring judgment to bear as to how the accountant's opinion and his conduct will look to a lay jury, a judge and a prospective plaintiff's attorney in the event that trouble develops.

---

[2] At both trials, the defendant who had been in charge of the audit testified without contradiction that Roth had told him of the board's "reluctant" approval at a meeting two days before certification. The draft of the minutes of that meeting, indicating disapproval, was not received until after the collapse of the company and notification to the SEC.

CASE 22

CONTINENTAL VENDING LIABILITY CASE*

General Background   In 1966 two partners and a manager of Lybrand, Ross Brothers and Montgomery were indicted on criminal charges for mail fraud and violation of the Securities and Exchange Act of 1934 (see Appendix I). Lybrand had served as auditors for Continental Vending Machine Corporation (hereafter referred to as "Continental") since 1956, and the charges were related to the examination of the financial statements of Continental for the year ended September 30, 1962.

The trial focused on the financial relationships that had developed between Continental and its affiliate, Valley Commercial Corporation (hereafter referred to as "Valley"), which was operated from a single office on the premises of Continental. At the center of the financial arrangements was Harold Roth, founder and president of Continental, officer and director of Valley, and a major stockholder in both companies. He owned 22% of Continental's and 25% of Valley's outstanding stock.

The year 1956 marked the beginning of what came to be known as "the Valley Payable." This account resulted from business transactions between the companies. Valley transferred funds to Continental who would in turn issue negotiable notes to Valley. Valley would then discount the notes at one of two New York banks to obtain cash which was generally funnelled back to Continental for additional notes. Another account, "the Valley Receivable," developed in mid-1957 when Continental began advancing funds to Valley which then loaned the money to Harold Roth to finance his personal stock market activities.

The financial transactions between and among the companies and Roth are illustrated in the following diagram.

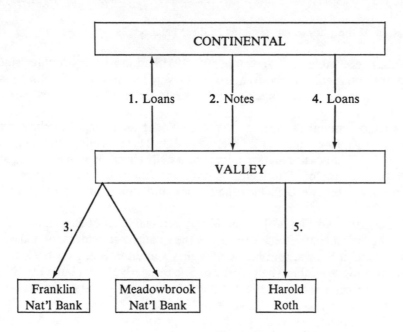

Figure 1

1.   Valley advances cash to Continental, a "Valley Payable" transaction.

2.   Continental issues notes to Valley, a "Valley Payable" transaction.

3.   Valley discounts notes and step 1 repeated.

4.   Continental advances funds to Valley, a "Valley Receivable" transaction.

5.   Valley advances funds to Roth.

---

*The original draft of this case was prepared by Nathan Kranowski, Susan Paul, Ed Spede and John Vincie, Master of Accountancy students, Virginia Polytechnic Institute and State University.

Continental's Financial Statements

Lybrand had first noted the Valley accounts in 1958 and Mr. Yoder, then manager of the Continental audit, discussed them with Roth. Yoder later wrote in the workpapers that in fiscal 1958 Continental had made cash payments to Valley of $1,185,790 which "appeared to be for no other purpose than to provide Valley with cash."[1] He also noted that since year-end Continental had made additional payments to Valley totaling $824,752 which were used "to finance the acquisition of capital stock of U.S. Hoffman Machine Corporation by Mr. Roth or for loans by Valley to U.S. Hoffman."[2]

In a memorandum written in 1960 to Carl Simon, a senior partner in Lybrand and one of the defendants at the trial, Yoder indicated that payments to Valley were frequent, in round amounts, and unaccompanied by written explanations. In 1961 and 1962 such payments continued. The table below shows the increase of the Valley receivable and payable accounts from 1960 to 1962.

Table I*

Year Ended	Valley Receivable Balance	Valley Payable Balance
9/30/60	$ 397,996	$ 949,852
9/30/61	848,006	780,472
9/30/62	3,543,335	1,029,475

*Refer to Figure I for an illustration of the transactions resulting in these balances.

As indicated in the table, the Valley receivable as of September 30, 1961 had more than doubled since the previous year, but the 1961 statements did not comment on this situation. However, Simon then told Roth that if the Valley receivable was as large in 1962, an examination of Valley's books would be required. (Valley was not audited by Lybrand.)

In 1962, Melvin Fishman, another defendant at the trial, replaced Yoder as manager of the Continental audit. When he visited Continental in September 1962, he was told that as of July 31, the Valley receivable had reached 3.6 million dollars and the company was in a tight cash situation operating a daily check float in excess of $500,000. When Fishman asked why Valley needed these monies, Continental's Assistant Controller stated that "Roth needed the money to maintain the margin accounts on the U.S. Hoffman stock and bonds and the Continental stock and bonds."[3]

In December 1962, after Fishman informed Simon that the Valley receivable as of September 30 was about 3.5 million dollars, Roth was told that the auditors would have to review the financial statements of Valley to evaluate the collectibility of the receivable. Roth called Simon, told him that Valley's audit had not yet been completed but indicated that the statements would be made available when received. Subsequently, he explained to Simon that Valley was not able to repay the advance from Continental because it (Valley) had loaned him about the same amount and he was unable to repay. Roth suggested that the borrowings from Valley be secured by his posting as collateral his stocks and bonds of Continental and U.S. Hoffman. Therefore, because the collectibility of the Valley receivable was assured, Continental's statements could be examined and an unqualified opinion could be rendered without a review of Valley's statements. Simon agreed if the following conditions were met: (1) the collateral must be adequate; (2) a satisfactory legal opinion must be obtained; and (3) Continental's Board of Directors must approve the transactions.

These conditions were accepted by Roth and the collateral was assigned to a trustee for Valley and Continental. However, one of the conditions had not been met. Roth informed Simon that the reluctant approval of the Board had been obtained when, in fact, they had disapproved of the loans to Valley. In early February the auditors were able to confirm a total of 3.1 million dollars in collateral. The confirmation was made by telephone by James Harris, a Lybrand supervisor who had no previous connection with the Continental audit. By February 15, the date of the

---

[1] *The Journal of Accountancy*, Continental Vending Decision Affirmed, February, 1970, p. 63.
[2] *Ibid.*
[3] *Ibid.*

auditor's report, the market value of the collateral had fallen to $2,978,000. In reality, its value as collateral was substantially less because of prior liens totaling $1,000,000. These liens had not been discovered by Harris in the process of his confirmation. On this same day, the Valley receivable had reached $3.9 million.

The financial statements mailed on February 20, 1963 were, to say the least, discouraging. Continental reported an operating loss of $867,000 for fiscal 1962 compared to a net income after taxes of $1,249,000 for fiscal 1961. Current assets barely exceeded current liabilities. Other relevant items taken from the 1962 financial statements follow:

ASSETS

Current assets:

. . . .

Accounts and notes receivable:

. . . .

Valley Commercial Corp., affiliate (Note 2) . . . $2,143,335

. . . .

Noncurrent accounts and notes receivable:
Valley Commerical Corp., affiliate (Note 2) . . . $1,400,000

. . . .

LIABILITIES

Current Liabilities:

. . . .

Long-term debt, portion due within one year . . . $8,203,788

. . . .

Long-term debt (Note 7)

. . . .

Valley Commercial Corp., affiliate (Note 2) . . . $486,130

. . . .

NOTES TO CONSOLIDATED FINANCIAL STATEMENTS

2.   The amount receivable from Valley Commercial Corp. (an affiliated company of which Mr. Harold Roth is an officer, director and stockholder) bears interest at 12% a year. Such amount, less the balance of the notes payable to that company, is secured by the assignment to the company of Valley's equity in certain marketable securities. As of February 15, 1963, the amount of such equity at current market quotations exceeded the net amount receivable.

7.   . . . . The amounts of long-term debt, including the portion due within one year, on which interest is payable currently or has been discounted in advance, are as follows:

. . . .

Valley Commercial Corp., affiliate . . . $1,029,475

Five days after the statements were mailed, the market in Continental's stock dropped sharply. The quoted price fell to such an extent that the market value of the collateral (80% of which was Continental securities) dropped to $395,000. As a result, Lybrand, which had given an unqualified opinion on the financial statements, refused to do the same for the 10-K filing. On the same day, Continental's check to the IRS was returned NSF and two days later the government padlocked the plant. Investigations by the SEC and bankruptcy soon followed.

The Trials

The trustee for Continental's debenture holders brought a civil suit of $41 million against the auditors. This suit was eventually settled out of court for $2 million. In an extraordinary development, the government indicted three Lybrand personnel associated with the audit. Roth was also charged but pleaded guilty and subsequently testified against the accountants.

The trial of the auditors, *United States* vs. *Simon*, began in 1966. There were actually two trials. The initial trial resulted in a hung jury in 1968. The retrial lasted only a month and a verdict of guilty was returned. Defendants were fined $5,000 to $7,000 each but no jail sentences were imposed. The U.S. Appeals Court upheld the verdict and the Supreme Court denied *certiorari*. In 1973, the defendants received a full presidential pardon.

The Issue

Eight eminent defense witnesses testified that there had been no departure from generally accepted accounting principles or generally accepted auditing standards in the presentation of the statements or the conduct of the audit. Two prosecution witnesses stated that such departures had occurred. The judge in the second trial declared that conformity to standards and principles may be persuasive but, it was not conclusive evidence. His charge to the jury was that they, not expert witnesses, were to decide if the financial statements were presented fairly.

The AICPA filed a brief with the U.S. Court of Appeals as *amicus curiae*. This brief questioned whether a professional may be judged by standards which were not those of his or her profession (a layman's standards). Judge Friendly, the Appeals magistrate, was unconvinced by either the testimony of the defense witnesses or the Institute's brief. In affirming the jury's verdict, he said:

> We do not think the jury was also required to accept the accountants' evaluation whether a given fact was material to overall fair presentation, at least not when the accountants' testimony was not based on specific rules or prohibitions to which they could point, but only on the need for the auditor to make an honest judgment and their conclusion that nothing in the financial statements themselves negated the conclusion that an honest judgment had been made. Such evidence may be highly persuasive, but it is not conclusive, and so the trial judge correctly charged.[4]

CASE DISCUSSION QUESTIONS

1. The prosecution made the point that the Valley receivable and payable amounts could not be offset as indicated in footnote 2. Is this contention correct? Under what circumstances may assets and liabilities be offset?

2. If, instead of footnote 2, the following footnote had been used, would the requirement of adequate disclosure have been met?

    "2. The amount receivable from Valley Commercial Corp. (an affiliated company of which Mr. Harold Roth is an officer, director and stockholder), which bears interest at 12% a year, was uncollectible at September 30, 1962, since Valley had loaned approximately the same amount to Mr. Roth who was unable to pay. Since that date Mr. Roth and others have pledged as security for the repayment of his obligation to Valley and its obligation to Continental (now $3,900,000, against which Continental's liability to Valley cannot be offset) securities which, as of February 15, 1963, had a market value of $2,978,000. Approximately 80% of such securities are stock and convertible debentures of the company."

---

[4] The case is cited U.S. vs. Simon, et al., 425 F. 2d. 796 (2nd Civ. 1969).

3. Should the auditors have secured information sufficient to determine the collectibility of Valley's receivable? In what manner (audit, obtaining a copy of Valley's financial statements, inquiry with Valley's auditors, etc.)?

4. Was sufficient competent evidential matter gathered by the auditors to confirm the collateral pledged as security on the Valley receivable? Discuss.

5. SAS No. 5 discusses the meaning of present fairly in conformity with GAAP. In what manner is this statement relevant to the circumstances in the Continental Vending Case? Discuss.

6. With reference to the accounting profession, what is the particular importance of the Continental Vending Case? Explain.

APPENDIX I

The opinion of the Court of Appeals states that the defendants were convicted "of conspiring to violate 18 U.S.C. paragraphs 1001 and 1341 and paragraph 32 of the Securities Exchange Act of 1934, 15 U.S.C. paragraph 78ff., by knowingly drawing up and certifying a false and misleading financial statement of Continental Vending Machine Corporation for the year ending September 30, 1962, and of using the mails to distribute the statement in violation of 18 U.S.C. paragraph 1341." Reproduced in this appendix are the relevant portions of the United States Code and of the Securities Exchange Act.

18 U.S.C.

1001: Whoever, in any matter within the jurisdiction of any department or agency of the United States knowingly and willfully falsifies, conceals or covers up by any trick, scheme, or device a material fact, or makes any false, fictitious or fraudulent statements or representations, or makes or uses any false writing or document knowing the same to contain any false, fictitious or fraudulent statement or entry, shall be fined not more than $10,000 or imprisoned not more than five years, or both.

1341: Whoever, having devised or intending to devise any scheme or artifice to defraud, or for obtaining money or property by means of false or fraudulent pretenses, representations, or promises, or to sell, dispose of, loan, exchange, alter, give away, distribute, supply, or furnish or procure for unlawful use any counterfeit or spurious coin, obligation, security, or other article, or anything represented to be or intimated or held out to be such counterfeit or spurious article, for the purpose of executing such scheme or artifice or attempting so to do, places in any post office or authorized depository for mail matter, any matter or thing whatever to be sent or delivered by the Post Office Department, or takes or receives therefrom, any such matter or thing, or knowingly causes to be delivered by mail according to the direction thereon, or at the place at which it is directed to be delivered by the person to whom it is addressed, any such matter or thing, shall be fined not more than $1,000 or imprisoned not more than five years, or both.

15 U.S.C.

78 ff.(a) Any person who willfully violates any provision of this chapter, or any rule or regulation thereunder the violation of which is made unlawful or the observance of which is required under the terms of this chapter, or any person who willfully and knowingly makes, or causes to be made, any statement in any application, report, or document required to be filed under this chapter or any rule or regulation thereunder or any undertaking contained in a registration statement as provided in subsection (d) of Section 78o of this title, which statement was false or misleading with respect to any material fact, shall upon conviction be fined not more than $10,000, or imprisoned not more than two years, or both, except that when such person is an exchange, a fine not exceeding $500,000 may be imposed; but no person shall be subject to imprisonment under this section for the violation of any rule or regulation if he or she proves that he or she had no knowledge of such rule or regulation.

(b) Any issuer which fails to file information, documents, or reports required to be filed under subsection (d) of Section 78o of this title or any rule or regulation thereunder shall forfeit to the United States the sum of $100 for each and every day such failure to file shall continue. Such forfeiture, which shall be in lieu of any criminal penalty for such failure to file which might be deemed to arise under subsection (a) of this section, shall be payable into the Treasury of the United States and shall be recoverable in a civil suit in the name of the United States.

(c) The provisions of this section shall not apply in the case of any violation of any rule or regulation prescribed pursuant to paragraph (3) of subsection (c) of Section 78o of this title, except a violation which consists of making, or causing to be made, any statement in any report or document required to be filed under such rule or regulation, which statement was at the time and in the light of the circumstances under which it was made false or misleading with respect to any material fact.

Unaudited Financial Statements

(Section AU 504, SAS No. 26, and Sections AR 100, AR 200, AR 300, AR 400, and AR 500, SSARS No. 1, 2, 3, 4, and 5)

Reporting when an accountant is associated with the unaudited financial statements of his or her client depends on the classification of the client as public or nonpublic. SAS No. 26, *Association With Financial Statements*, now establishes reporting standards when a CPA is associated with the financial statements of a public client and the statements have not been audited. Statements on Standards for Accounting and Review Services (SSARSs) issued by the Accounting and Review Services Committee of the AICPA now establish reporting standards for financial statements of a nonpublic company that have been compiled or reviewed by a CPA. The SAS is applicable to the audited financial statements of a public or nonpublic company.

This section provides a review of SAS No. 26 and SSARS Nos. 1, 2, 3, 4, and 5 as they relate to unaudited financial statements of public and nonpublic clients.

Association with Financial Statements (SAS No. 26)

SAS No. 26 provides guidance on reporting when an accountant is associated with the financial statements of a public entity or with a nonpublic entity's financial statements that he or she has been engaged to audit.

SAS No. 26 supersedes Sections 516, 517, and 518 of SAS No. 1 and paragraphs 13-15 of SAS No. 15 regarding unaudited statements.

SAS No. 26 defines a public entity (using the same concept as in SSARS No. 1) as an entity (a) whose securities trade in a public market either on a stock exchange (domestic or foreign) or in the over-the-counter market, including securities quoted only locally or regionally, (b) that makes a filing with a regulatory agency in preparation for the sale of any class of its securities in a public market, or (c) a subsidiary, corporate joint venture or other entity controlled by an entity covered by (a) or (b).

An accountant is associated with financial statements when he or she has consented to the use of his or her name in a report, document, or written communication containing the statements. Also, when an accountant submits to his or her client or others, statements that he or she has prepared or assisted in preparing, the accountant is deemed to be associated even though the accountant does not append his or her name to the statements. An accountant may be associated with audited or unaudited statements. Financial statements are audited if the accountant has applied auditing procedures sufficient to permit a report on them as described in SAS No. 2, *Reports on Audited Financial Statements*. The unaudited interim statements (or information) of a public entity are reviewed when the accountant has applied procedures sufficient to permit a report on them as described in SAS No. 36, *Review of Interim Financial Information*.

When an accountant is associated with the statements of a public entity and has not audited or reviewed the statements, a disclaimer of opinion should be issued. The disclaimer would read as follows:

The accompanying balance sheet of X Company as of December 31, 19x1, and the related statements of income, retained earnings, and changes in financial position for the year then ended were not audited by us and, accordingly, we do not express an opinion on them.

(Signature and date)

The disclaimer may accompany the statements or it may be placed directly on them. Each page of the statements should be clearly and conspicuously marked as unaudited. The accountant has no responsibility to apply any procedures other than reading the statements for obvious material errors. Any procedures that may have been applied should not be described in the disclaimer as it might cause the reader to believe the statements have been audited or reviewed.

The disclaimer establishes the accountant's responsibility for complying with the fourth standard of reporting. The fourth standard reads as follows:

The report shall either contain an expression of opinion regarding the financial statements, taken as a whole, or an assertion to the effect that an opinion cannot be expressed. When an overall opinion cannot be expressed, the reasons therefore should be stated. In all cases when an auditor's name is associated with financial statements, the report should contain a clear-cut indication of the character of the auditor's examination, if any, and the degree of responsibility he or she is taking.

When an accountant is aware that his or her name is to be included in a client-prepared communication of a public entity containing financial statements that have not been audited or reviewed, the accountant should request that his or her name not be included.

When an accountant is associated with unaudited statements prepared in accordance with a comprehensive basis of accounting other than GAAP he or she should modify the identification of the statements in the disclaimer. For example, a disclaimer on cash basis statements might read as follows:

The accompanying statement of assets and liabilities resulting from cash transactions of XYZ Corporation as of December 31, 19x1, and the related statement of revenues collected and expenses paid during the year then ended were not audited by us and, accordingly, we do not express an opinion on them.

(Signature and date)

A note to the statements should describe how the basis of presentation differs from GAAP, but the monetary effect of such differences need not be stated.

When an accountant is not independent, he or she would be precluded from expressing an opinion because any procedures that might be performed would not be in accordance with GAAS. Accordingly, the accountant should disclaim an opinion with respect to the financial statements and should state specifically that he or she is not independent. The disclaimer would read as follows:

We are not independent with respect to XYZ Company, and the accompanying balance sheet as of December 31, 19x1, and the related statements of income, retained earnings, and changes in financial position for the year then ended were not audited by us and, accordingly, we do not express an opinion on them.

(Signature and date)

Each page of the statements, of course, should be marked as unaudited and any procedures that may have been performed should not be described. If the statements are those of a nonpublic entity, the accountant should look for guidance to SSARS No. 1.

An Auditing Interpretation of Section 504 (SAS No. 26) responds to the question "What should a CPA consider in determining whether he or she is independent with respect to a client's financial statements?" The Interpretation explains that the CPA should consider the AICPA's Code of Professional Ethics, its Rules of Conduct, Interpretations under the Rules and Ethics rulings in determining whether he or she is independent and whether the reporting requirements of SAS No. 26 are applicable. Also, the CPA should consider the ethical requirements of his or her state

CPA society or state board of accountancy. Consideration of independence should be the same whether financial statements are audited or unaudited. However, if the statements are those of a nonpublic entity, the accountant should look to the guidance in SSARS No. 1.

If an accountant concludes, on the basis of facts known to him or her that unaudited statements with which he or she is associated are not in conformity with GAAP (or other comprehensive basis of accounting), the accountant should suggest appropriate revision. If the statements are not revised, the accountant should describe the departure in his or her disclaimer. This description should refer specifically to the nature of the departure and, if practicable, state the effects on the statements or include the necessary information for adequate disclosure. Generally, a reservation paragraph would be added to the disclaimer that states:

> What GAAP (or other comprehensive basis) requires
>
> What the client has done
>
> The effect on the financial statements (if known)

When the effects of the departure on the statements are not reasonably determinable, the disclaimer should so state. When a departure from GAAP involves inadequate disclosure, it may not be feasible for the accountant to include the omitted disclosures in the report. For example, when management has elected to omit substantially all of the disclosures, the accountant should clearly indicate that in his or her report, but the accountant would not be expected to include such information in the report.

If a client will not agree to revision of the statements for a departure from GAAP (or other basis of accounting) or will not accept the accountant's disclaimer with the reservations added, the accountant should refuse to be associated with the statements and, perhaps, withdraw from the engagement.

When unaudited statements are presented in comparative form with audited statements in documents filed with the SEC, such statements should be clearly marked as "unaudited," but should not be referred to in the auditor's report. When unaudited statements are presented in comparative form with audited statements in any document other than an SEC filing, the statements that have not been audited should be clearly marked to indicate their status and either (a) the report on the prior period should be reissued or (b) the report on the current period should include, as a separate paragraph, an appropriate description of the responsibility assumed for the statements of the prior period.

When the statements of the prior period have been audited and the report on the current period is to contain a separate paragraph, it should read as follows:

> The financial statements for the year ended December 31, 19x1, were examined by us (other accountants) and we (they) expressed an unqualified opinion on them in our (their) report dated March 1, 19x2, but we (they) have not performed any auditing procedures since that date.

When statements of the prior period have not been audited and the report on the current period is to contain a separate paragraph, it should include (a) a statement of the service performed in the prior period, (b) the date of the report on that service, (c) a description of any material modifications noted in that report, and (d) a statement that the service was less in scope than an audit and does not provide a basis for the expression of an opinion on the statements taken as a whole. When the statements are those of a public entity, the separate paragraph should include a disclaimer, or a description of a review. When the statements are those of a nonpublic entity and the statements were compiled or reviewed, the separate paragraph should contain an appropriate description of the compilation or review. For example, a separate paragraph describing a review might read as follows:

> The 19x1 financial statements were reviewed by us (other accountants) and our (their) report thereon, dated March 1, 19x2, stated we (they) were not aware of any material modifications that should be made to those statements for them to be in conformity with generally accepted accounting principles. However, a review is substantially less in scope than an audit and does not provide a basis for the expression of an opinion on the financial statements taken as a whole.

A separate paragraph describing a compilation might read as follows:

> The 19x1 financial statements were compiled by us (other accountants) and our (their) report thereon, dated March 1, 19x2, stated we (they) did not audit or review those financial statements and, accordingly, express no opinion or other form of assurance on them.

When an accountant disclaims an opinion, his or her disclaimer should not be contradicted by the inclusion of expressions of assurance on the absence of knowledge of departures from GAAP (negative assurance) except as provided by GAAS. Negative assurances, for example, are permissible in letters for underwriters.

Compilation and Review of Financial Statements (SSARS No. 1)

Although a variety of services may be performed by a CPA for a nonpublic client, such as income tax work, write-up involving keeping books for the client, preparing adjusting entries and year-end closing of the books, SSARS No. 1 recognizes compilation and review as the only services an accountant can offer with respect to the unaudited statements of a nonpublic client.

A compilation involves presenting in the form of financial statements information that is the representation of management (owners) without undertaking to express any assurance on the statements. An audit and a review disclaimer are included in a compilation report. SAS No. 1 formerly permitted an accountant to perform accommodation services for clients that involved typing or reproducing statements that were prepared by the client. Such services are now prohibited by SSARS No. 1 as any service performed for a client that results in the issuance of financial statements is considered a compilation and the accountant must report accordingly.

There are three standard compilation reports. First, a compilation engagement may involve presenting financial statements that are in conformity with GAAP, including full disclosure. The appropriate report for such statements would be:

I (We) have compiled the accompanying balance sheet of XYZ Company as of December 31, 19xx, and the related statements of income, retained earnings, and changes in financial position for the year then ended in accordance with standards established by the American Institute of Certified Public Accountants.

A compilation is limited to presenting in the form of financial statements information that is the representation of management (owners). I (We) have not audited or reviewed the accompanying financial statements and, accordingly, do not express an opinion or any other form of assurance on them.

The first paragraph in the above report establishes the accountant's responsibility for the scope of his or her work. It should contain a statement that—A compilation has been performed in accordance with standards established by the American Institute of Certified Public Accountants. The second paragraph describes a compilation of financial statements and disclaims an audit opinion and a review assurance. The accompanying statements may be marked "unaudited," although this is not required by SSARS No. 1. The statements must, however, include a notation on each page "see accountant's compilation report."

The second standard compilation report is issued when the financial statements are presented on a GAAP basis, but substantially all disclosures required by GAAP, including those normally appearing in the body of the statements themselves, are omitted. These so called "bob-tail" statements were formerly permitted by SAS No. 1 as statements restricted to internal-use only by client personnel. Internal-use only statements are no longer appropriate and the client can issue compiled statements that omit disclosures to anyone providing the omission of the disclosures are not intended to make the statements misleading for the purpose of their intended use. The standard compilation report for bob-tail statements is as follows:

I (We) have compiled the accompanying balance sheet of XYZ Company as of December 31, 19xx, and the related statements of income, retained earnings, and changes in financial position for the year then ended in accordance with standards established by the American Institute of Certified Public Accountants.

A compilation is limited to presenting in the form of financial statements information that is the representation of management (owners). I (we) have not audited or reviewed the accompanying financial statements and, accordingly, do not express an opinion or any other form of assurance on them.

Management has elected to omit substantially all of the disclosures (and the statement of changes in financial position—if omitted) required by generally accepted accounting principles. If the omitted disclosures were included in the financial statements, they might influence the user's conclusions about the company's financial position. Accordingly, these financial statements are not designed for those who are not informed about such matters.

The first two paragraphs of the above report are the same as the standard compilation report on a full disclosure basis. The third paragraph notes the omission of disclosures and warns the reader of the limited usefulness of the statements.

In addition to omitting all significant financial statement disclosures, SSARS No. 1 permits reporting, based on a compilation, when only selected disclosures are included in the financial statement presentations. For this type of reporting the selected disclosures that are included must be titled "Selected information—substantially all disclosures required by GAAP are not included." Also, the accountant may not be associated with such statements if he believes that the inclusion of selected disclosures and the omission of others is being done with the intent to mislead users of the financial statements.

The third form of standard compilation report is issued when a CPA is performing a compilation engagement for a nonpublic client and he or she is not independent with respect to the client's financial statements. SSARS No. 1 permits a compilation when the CPA is not independent (but not a review or audit) providing the compilation report is modified to indicate the lack of independence. The standard report in such circumstances would be exactly the same as the first two paragraphs of the above reports and would include the warning paragraph regarding the omission of disclosures, if appropriate. In addition, a paragraph would be added that reads as follows:

I am (We are) not independent with respect to XYZ Company.

Reporting on a comprehensive basis of accounting other than GAAP (as defined in SAS No. 14, which is covered in a subsequent section of this text) is permitted by SSARS No. 1. A compilation or review on a comprehensive basis of accounting other than GAAP (cash basis, tax basis, regulatory basis, or other basis) would result in issuance of a report that incorporates the standard report language of a compilation report or a review report except that the titles of the financial statements would reflect the basis of accounting being followed. For example, a cash basis balance sheet would be a "statement of assets and liabilities resulting from cash transactions" and a cash basis income statement would be a "statement of revenues collected and expenses paid." A statement of changes in financial position is, of course, not required unless both a balance sheet and an income statement are presented on a GAAP basis. SSARS No. 1 relaxes the rules of reporting on a comprehensive basis of accounting other than GAAP as established in SAS No. 14. Contrary to the SAS No. 14 requirements for audited statements, a compilation or review report on a non-GAAP basis need not identify the basis of accounting followed unless it is not identified in the statements or notes. Also, another difference is that describing how the basis of accounting being followed differs from GAAP is not required.

A review of the financial statements of a nonpublic client involves performing inquiry and analytical procedures that provide a reasonable basis for expressing limited assurance that there are no material modifications that should be made to the statements for them to be in conformity with GAAP (or other comprehensive basis of accounting).

Reviewed financial statements ordinarily must include full disclosure and the accountant must be independent. An interpretation of SSARS No. 1 states that an accountant ordinarily would not accept an engagement to review financial statements unless it was the intention of the client to present full disclosure in the statements. However, the interpretation does state that if, after performing significant procedures in connection with a review engagement, a client decides to omit substantially all financial statement disclosures, including those normally presented in the body of the statements, it would be appropriate for the accountant to issue a review report with a warning paragraph, regarding the omission of disclosures, added to his or her report. Presumably the warning paragraph would follow the wording of the bob-tail report for a compilation engagement presented above.

If an accountant is unable to perform procedures he or she considers necessary in a review engagement he or she has no basis for reporting and would be forced to withdraw from the engagement. After careful consideration of the effects of the limitations on the scope of his or her review engagement, it may be possible for the accountant to step-down and issue a compilation report. Before doing so the accountant should, however, carefully consider the reasons for the restriction on the scope of his or her review engagement.

An accountant may perform a compilation or review involving only one financial statement—for example, a balance sheet. SSARS No. 1 considers this to be an engagement involving limited reporting objectives. In the case of a review, the accountant must be permitted to perform all of the inquiry and analytical review procedures he or she considers necessary for the limited reporting engagement.

The accountant's standard review report, as specified in SSARS No. 1, is as follows:

> I (We) have reviewed the accompanying balance sheet of XYZ Company as of December 31, 19xx, and the related statements of income, retained earnings, and changes in financial position for the year then ended, in accordance with standards established by the American Institute of Certified Public Accountants. All information included in these financial statements is the representation of the management (owners) of XYZ Company.
>
> A review consists principally of inquiries of company personnel and analytical procedures applied to financial data. It is substantially less in scope than an examination in accordance with generally accepted auditing standards, the objective of which is the expression of an opinion regarding the financial statements taken as a whole. Accordingly, I (we) do not express such an opinion.
>
> Based on my (our) review, I am (we are) not aware of any material modifications that should be made to the accompanying financial statements in order for them to be in conformity with generally accepted accounting principles (or other comprehensive basis).

The first paragraph of the above review report establishes the accountant's scope of work, the second paragraph describes a review service and disclaims an audit opinion, and the third paragraph expresses limited assurance that the statements are presented in conformity with GAAP (or another basis of accounting). The financial statements may be marked as "unaudited" and each page of the statements must include a reference "see accountant's review report."

A reporting problem exists in a compilation or review engagement when there are departures from GAAP or another basis of accounting, other than the omission of disclosures in a bob-tail report. The accountant, in such situations, must decide whether modification of his or her report is sufficient to disclose the departure. If the accountant decides that it is not, he or she should not be associated with the financial statements as they are misleading.

Normally neither an inconsistency nor an uncertainty in compiled or reviewed financial statements will require a modification of the accountant's report. If the inconsistency or the uncertainty is appropriately disclosed in the financial statements and properly accounted for, the accountant will not modify his or her compilation or review report other than, perhaps, including a paragraph in his or her report to emphasize the inconsistency or the uncertainty. However, such emphasis is not required.

Other departures from GAAP should be recognized in the accountant's report if they are not corrected by the client. This is accomplished by adding a reservation paragraph (as previously discussed in connection with SAS No. 26). The reservation paragraph will state the requirements of GAAP, what the client has done, and the effect of the departure, if known. The accountant is not obligated to determine the effect of a departure from GAAP if such information is not provided by the client. If the effect of the departure has not been determined, the accountant's report should so state.

Step-downs in engagement objectives are permitted by SSARS No. 1. It is, for example, permissible for an accountant to agree to review the financial statements and then, subsequently, agree to change the engagement objective to a compilation. Likewise, a step-down from an audit to a review or a compilation is permitted. When step-downs in engagement objectives occur, the accountant should not refer in the report to any procedures previously performed in connection with the original engagement objective. A request for a change in engagement objective may result from a misunderstanding with the client (for example, the client did not understand the purpose of audit, review, or compilation when it was decided that an audit was needed), changed circumstances (for example, the client needed an audit in connection with a loan agreement, but during the audit engagement the loan is paid and audited statements are no longer necessary), or, perhaps, a scope restriction. Before agreeing to change the engagement objective the accountant should carefully consider the reason given for the change and the amount of work already completed on the original engagement. For example, it would not be proper to step-down from an audit to a review if substantially all of the work in connection with the audit engagement had been completed.

SSARS No. 1 applies, in effect, the procedures in Section 561 to compilation and review engagements when information comes to the attention of the accountant subsequent to the issuance of his or her report that indicates that the statements and his and her report may no longer be appropriate. Also, SSARS No. 1 suggests that Section 560, subsequent event procedures, may be appropriate in compilation and review engagements.

SSARS No. 1 requires that the accountant reach an understanding with his or her client regarding the nature of the engagement. This understanding should be documented in the working papers (perhaps in the form of an engagement letter). The understanding should provide that the engagement (compilation or review) cannot be relied upon to disclose errors, irregularities, or illegal acts.

The accountant is required by SSARS No. 1 to report only according to the highest level of work performed. According to an interpretation of SSARS No. 1, this means that in a review engagement only a review report would be issued, even though a review engagement also involves a compilation of the financial statements. The agreement reached with the client, that should be documented, will normally dictate the appropriate reporting responsibility.

The accountant should possess an understanding of the client's business operations and the accounting principles and practices followed in the client's industry that will enable him or her to compile financial statements in suitable form. This understanding of the client's business and industry is also important in a review because it provides a basis for making appropriate inquiries and performing analytical review procedures that will provide a basis for expressing limited assurance regarding the presentation of the statements in conformity with GAAP (or other comprehensive basis of accounting).

When basic financial statements are accompanied by supplementary information, the accountant should clearly indicate the degree of responsibility he or she is assuming for the supplementary information, if any. For example, the accountant would at least report that he or she has compiled the supplementary information. If the accountant has reviewed the supplementary information this fact should be indicated. This may be accomplished by expanding the scope paragraph of the compilation or review report to cover the supplementary information (such as long-form information like detailed summaries of operating expenses, cost of goods sold, ratios, etc.) or the accountant may report on the supplementary information in a separate report that accompanies the data.

Analytical procedures required in a review engagement generally parallel those identified by SAS No. 23 (in a previous section of this text). The accountant should make inquiries concerning the client's accounting principles and practices and the methods followed in applying them in the financial statements. Inquiries should also be made concerning the entity's procedures for recording, classifying, and summarizing transactions, and accumulating information for disclosure in the financial statements.

Analytical procedures that are designed to identify relationships and individual items that appear to be unusual should be applied in a review. Such procedures consist of:

> Comparison of the financial statements with statements for comparable prior period(s)
>
> Comparison of the financial statements with anticipated results (if available) such as, for example, budgets and forecasts
>
> Study of the relationships of the elements of the financial statements that would be expected to conform to a predictable pattern based on the entity's experience

SSARS No. 1 indicates that an accountant performing a review engagement should carefully consider the desirability of obtaining a management representation letter similar to what is required by SAS No. 19 for audit engagements.

In summary, SSARS No. 1 provides guidance considered necessary to enable the accountant to comply with the general standards of the profession as set forth in Rule 201 of the AICPA Code of Professional Ethics in the context of a compilation engagement or a review engagement and establishes additional standards deemed appropriate for such engagements. Rule 201—General Standards—reads as follows:

> A member (of the AICPA) shall comply with the following general standards as interpreted by bodies designated by Council (of the AICPA), and must justify any departures therefrom.
>
> A. Professional competence. A member shall undertake only those engagements which he or she or his or her firm can reasonably expect to complete with professional competence.
>
> B. Due professional care. A member shall exercise due professional care in the performance of an engagement.
>
> C. Planning and supervision. A member shall adequately plan and supervise an engagement.
>
> D. Sufficient relevant data. A member shall obtain sufficient relevant data to afford a reasonable basis for conclusions or recommendations in relation to an engagement.

E.   Forecasts. A member shall not permit his or her name to be used in conjunction with any forecast of future transactions in a manner which may lead to the belief that the member vouches for the achievability of the forecast. (The standard on forecasts is not applicable to accounting and review engagements.)

Reporting on Comparative Financial Statements (SSARS No. 2)

SSARS No. 2 establishes standards for reporting on comparative financial statements of a nonpublic entity when one or more periods have been compiled or reviewed in accordance with SSARS No. 1.

SSARS No. 2 amends SSARS No. 1 regarding the definition of a nonpublic company. A nonpublic company is any company other than (a) one whose securities trade in a public market either on a stock exchange (domestic or foreign) or in the over-the-counter market, including securities quoted only locally or regionally, (b) one that makes a filing with a regulatory agency in preparation for the sale of any class of its securities in a public market, or (c) a subsidiary, corporate joint venture, or other entity controlled by an entity covered by (a) or (b).

SSARS No. 2 defines the terms "continuing accountant" and "updating." A continuing accountant is an accountant who has been engaged to audit, review, or compile, and report on the financial statements of the current period and one or more consecutive periods immediately prior to the current period.

Updating means taking into consideration information the accountant becomes aware of during his or her current engagement and reexpressing his or her previous conclusion (with a current report date) or depending on the circumstances, expressing different conclusions on the statements of a prior period (with a current report date). An updated report differs from a reissued report in that a reissued report bears the same date as the original report and it is not based on a subsequent engagement. If a reissued report is revised, SSARS No. 2 requires that dual-dating be used by the accountant.

A continuing accountant who performs the same or a higher level of service with respect to the financial statements of the current period should update his or her report on the prior-period statements that are presented for comparative purposes.

A continuing accountant who performs a lower level of service with respect to the current period statements should reissue his or her report on the prior period statements when they are presented for comparative purposes or the accountant would include paragraph in the current period's report establishing the degree of responsibility he or she is taking regarding the prior-period statements. Such a paragraph would, of course, describe the previous engagement—review or audit.

The following standard reports on comparative financial statements, from SSARS No. 2, are presented as examples of the continuing accountant's reporting responsibility.

1.   *Compilation each period*

    I (We) have compiled the accompanying balance sheets of XYZ Company as of December 31, 19x2 and 19x1, and the related statements of income, retained earnings, and changes in financial position for the years then ended, in accordance with standards established by the American Institute of Certified Public Accountants.

    A compilation is limited to presenting in the form of financial statements information that is the representation of management (owners). I (We) have not audited or reviewed the accompanying financial statements and, accordingly, do not express an opinion or any other form of assurance on them.

    February 1, 19x3

2.   *Review each period*

    I (We) have reviewed the accompanying balance sheets of XYZ Company as of December 31, 19x2 and 19x1, and the related statements of income, retained earnings, and changes in financial position for the years then ended, in accordance with standards established by the American Institute of Certified Public Accountants. All information included in these financial statements is the representation of the management (owners) of XYZ Company.

A review consists principally of inquiries of company personnel and analytical procedures applied to financial data. It is substantially less in scope than an examination in accordance with generally accepted auditing standards, the objective of which is the expression of an opinion regarding the financial statements taken as a whole. Accordingly, I (we) do not express an opinion.

Based on my (our) reviews, I am (we are) not aware of any material modifications that should be made to the accompanying financial statements in order for them to be in conformity with generally accepted accounting principles.

March 1, 19x3

3. *Review in current period and compilation in prior period*

I (We) have reviewed the accompanying balance sheet of XYZ Company as of December 31, 19x2, and the related statements of income, retained earnings, and changes in financial position for the year then ended, in accordance with standards established by the American Institute of Certified Public Accountants. All information included in these financial statements is the representation of the management (owners) of XYZ Company.

A review consists principally of inquiries of company personnel and analytical procedures applied to financial data. It is substantially less in scope than an examination in accordance with generally accepted auditing standards, the objective of which is the expression of an opinion regarding the financial statements taken as a whole. Accordingly, I (we) do not express such an opinion.

Based on my (our) review, I am (we are) not aware of any material modifications that should be made to the 19x2 financial statements in order for them to be in conformity with generally accepted accounting principles.

The accompanying 19x1 financial statements of XYZ Company were compiled by me (us). A compilation is limited to presenting in the form of financial statements information that is the representation of management (owners). I (we) have not audited or reviewed the 19x1 financial statements and, accordingly, do not express an opinion or any other form of assurance on them.

March 1, 19x3

A continuing accountant who performs a compilation in the current period and has previously reviewed one or more prior-period financial statements that are presented for comparative purposes should either describe his or her responsibility for the prior-period reviewed statements in the compilation report or reissue the review report on the prior-period statements. In either case, the accountant should state that he or she has not performed any procedures in connection with the prior-period review engagement since the date of his or her review report. Following is an example of a paragraph that may be added to a current compilation report establishing responsibility for a prior-period review:

The accompanying 19x1 financial statements of XYZ Company were previously reviewed by me (us) and my (our) report dated March 1, 19x2, stated that I was (we were) not aware of any material modifications that should be made to those statements in order for them to be in conformity with generally accepted accounting principles. I (we) have not performed any procedures in connection with that review engagement after the date of my (our) report on the 19x1 financial statements.

A continuing accountant is required to update his or her report on the prior-period statements presented for comparative purposes if information obtained in the current engagement so indicates. A changed reference may involve, for example, the addition of a reservation paragraph regarding a departure from GAAP discovered in the current period that also affects the prior-period statements presented for comparative purposes. Or, a changed reference could involve deletion of a reservation paragraph regarding a departure from GAAP noted in the prior period that has been corrected by the client through restatement. When there is a changed reference to a departure from GAAP regarding the prior-period statements, the accountant's current report should include a separate explanatory paragraph indicating:

The date of the accountant's previous report

The circumstances or events that caused the reference to be changed

When applicable, that the financial statements of the prior period have been changed

Following is an example of such a paragraph:

> In my (our) previous (compilation) (review) report dated March 1, 19x2, on the 19x1 financial statements, I (we) referred to a departure from generally accepted accounting principles because the company carried its land at appraised values. However, as disclosed in Note X, the company has restated its 19x1 financial statements to reflect its land at cost in accordance with generally accepted accounting principles.

When the financial statements of a prior period or periods have been compiled, reviewed, or audited by a predecessor accountant and they are to be presented for comparative purposes with the current period statements, the predecessor accountant may be requested to reissue his or her report on the prior-period statements or the successor accountant may make references to the report of the predecessor in the current report, or he or she may compile, review, or audit the prior-period statements and report accordingly. When there is a successor-predecessor accountant relationship, the successor accountant should consider the guidance provided in SAS No. 7, *Communications Between Predecessor and Successor Auditors*, as applicable to compilation or review engagements.

A predecessor accountant, even though requested to do so, may decide, for various reasons, not to reissue his or her report. If the report of the predecessor is not reissued and the successor has not compiled, reviewed, or audited the prior-period statements, the successor should refer to the report of the predecessor in the current report. The following information should be included:

A statement that the financial statements of the prior period, which are presented for comparative purposes, were compiled or reviewed by another accountant (other accountants) (the other accountants should not be named)

The date of his or her (their) report

A description of the standard form of disclaimer or limited assurance, as applicable, included in the report

A description or a quotation of any modifications of the standard report and of any paragraphs emphasizing a matter regarding the financial statements

Before agreeing to reissue the report on a prior-period's financial statements, a predecessor should consider whether his or her report is still appropriate. He or she should consider the current form and manner of presentation of the prior-period statements, subsequent events, and changes in the statements that require the addition or deletion of modifications to the standard report. Accordingly, the predecessor should read the current period statements and the successor's report, compare the current period statements with those he or she reported on, and obtain a letter of representation from the successor. The letter should indicate whether the successor is aware of any matter that may materially affect the prior-period statements. If the predecessor becomes aware of information that may affect the current presentation of the statements he or she reported upon, the predecessor should perform other procedures before reissuing the report. Such other procedures may include discussions with the successor and reviewing the working papers of the successor. A predecessor accountant who agrees to reissue his or her report is required to update that report for information learned from the successor that materially affects the statements reported upon. A predecessor who reissues a report on the prior-period statements should use the original reporting date. If the report is revised, based on information learned from the successor, dual-dating would be used (see Section 530, SAS No. 1).

When financial statements that have been compiled or reviewed are presented with comparative statements that have been audited, the accountant should follow the guidance provided by SAS No. 26.

SSARS No. 2 prohibits the presentation in comparative form of financial statements that include full disclosure with those that omit substantially all of the disclosures required by GAAP (bob-tail statements). However, it is permissible to make such statement comparable by omission of previously presented financial statement disclosures. For example, current period bob-tail compiled statements may be presented in comparative form with prior-period compiled or reviewed statements that included full disclosure providing the disclosures for the prior-period statements are omitted and the accountant's report on the comparative statements indicates the nature of the previous engagement. Following is an example of an appropriate report when prior-period statements that omit substantially all disclosures have been compiled from previously reviewed statements for the same period:

(Standard three paragraph compilation report in comparative form for bob-tail statements)

(Fourth paragraph)

The accompanying 19x1 financial statements were compiled by me (us) from financial statements that did not omit substantially all of the disclosures required by generally accepted accounting principles and that I (we) previously reviewed as indicated in my (our) report dated March 1, 19x2.

February 1, 19x3

When reporting on comparative statements, the current reporting status of the client determines the applicable reporting standards. A report for a public company that was a nonpublic company in the prior period, for example, should follow SAS No. 26 and other applicable SASs. A report for a nonpublic company that was a public company in the prior period is covered by the SSARSs. A previously issued report that is not appropriate for the current status of the reporting entity should not be reissued or referred to in the current report. This means, for example, that an accountant reporting on the current period statements of a nonpublic company that was a public company in the prior period must compile, review, or audit the prior-period statements if they are presented for comparative purposes. Reissue of an SAS No. 26 disclaimer of opinion or reference to such a disclaimer would not be appropriate.

The following table, "Comparative Reporting Requirements (nonpublic companies)" identifies the various comparative reporting situations that one might encounter.[1]

COMPARATIVE REPORTING REQUIREMENTS (NONPUBLIC COMPANY)

	Comparative Statements		*Reporting*
	12/31/x2	*12/31/x1*	*Authority*
1.	Compiled	Compiled	SSARS No. 2
2.	Compiled	Reviewed	SSARS No. 2
3.	Compiled	Audited	SSARS No. 2
4.	Reviewed	Compiled	SSARS No. 2
5.	Reviewed	Reviewed	SSARS No. 2
6.	Reviewed	Audited	SSARS No. 2
7.	Audited	Compiled	SAS No. 26
8.	Audited	Reviewed	SAS No. 26
9.	Audited	Audited	SAS No. 15
10.	Compiled—Disclosures Omitted	Compiled	SSARS No. 2
11.	Compiled—Disclosures Omitted	Reviewed	SSARS No. 2
12.	Compiled—Disclosures Omitted	Audited	SSARS No. 2
13.	Compiled, Reviewed, or Audited	Compiled—Disclosures Omitted	SSARS No. 2 SSARS No. 2 SAS No. 26

[1] Source: *Accounting and Auditing Annual Updating Workshop*, 1980, Thomas D. Hubbard, Continuing Professional Education Group, American Institute of Certified Public Accountants, New York, page 3-2-13.

For items 1, 4, 5, and 9 in the table, when the same level of service or a higher level of service has been rendered in the current period compared to the preceding period, the continuing accountant's report must cover both periods and he or she must update the report on the prior period. Regarding item 9, SAS No. 15 governs reporting on comparative audited statements. The continuing auditor would issue one report, with a current date, covering both periods.

For items 2, 3, and 6 in the table, a continuing accountant performing a lower level of service in the current period should either describe his or her responsibility for the prior-period statements in the current report or reissue the previous report.

Regarding items 7 and 8 in the table, when the current-period statements have been audited and those for one or more prior periods have been compiled or reviewed the provisions of SAS No. 26, "Association with Financial Statements," govern reporting. Generally, the auditor would reissue the compilation or review report or include a separate paragraph in his or her current audit report describing the reporting responsibilities.

For items 10, 11, 12, and 13 in the table, SSARS No. 2 prohibits presenting in comparative form statements that omit substantially all disclosures with statements that include such disclosures. However, in these circumstances, the accountant may report on such statements as comparative compiled statements and omit disclosures if he or she includes in the report an additional paragraph indicating the nature of his or her previous service and the date of the previous report.[2]

Compilation Reports on Financial Statements Included in Certain Prescribed Forms (SSARS No. 3)

SSARS No. 3 was developed to provide alternative reporting format for financial statements included in certain prescribed forms. The statement provides a standard compilation report that may be used when a prescribed form requests financial statement information that is not in conformity with GAAP or other comprehensive basis of accounting. A SSARS No. 1 compilation report, modified to reflect departures from GAAP, may also be used as SSARS No. 3 provides alternative reporting—not required reporting format for prescribed forms. A prescribed form is any standard preprinted form designed or adopted by the entity to which it is to be submitted. Examples of organizations that typically design or adopt such forms are industry trade associations, credit agencies, banks, and governmental and regulatory bodies other than those dealing with the sale or trading of securities.

A presumption made in SSARS No. 3 is that the information included in a prescribed form is the information needed by the entity requesting the information and there is no need to modify the form or the accountant's report to present any additional information even though GAAP or another comprehensive basis of accounting typically requests such additional information. For example, if a prescribed form does not request market value disclosure regarding investments that are presented at cost, there is no need to modify the form or the accountant's report to include such information.

Following is a standard compilation report (from SSARS No. 3) that may be used when an accountant submits to his or her client or others a prescribed form that requests financial statement information containing departures from GAAP (or other comprehensive basis of accounting):

> I (We) have compiled the (identification of financial statements, including period covered and name of entity) included in the accompanying prescribed form in accordance with standards established by the American Institute of Certified Public Accountants.
>
> My (Our) compilation was limited to presenting in the form prescribed by (name of body) information that is the representation of management (owners). I (We) have not audited or reviewed the financial statements referred to above and, accordingly, do not express an opinion or any other form of assurance on them.
>
> These financial statements (including related disclosures) are presented in accordance with the requirements of (name of body), which differ from generally accepted accounting principles. Accordingly, these financial statements are not designed for those who are not informed about such differences.

---

[2] *Accounting and Auditing Updating Workshop*, page 3-2-11 - 3-2-12.

The accountant should add a reservation to the report, if he or she discovers any departure from GAAP or from the requirements of the form other than departures required by the form. The following sentence may be used to introduce the reservation paragraph of disclosing the departure:

> "However, I did become aware of a departure from generally accepted accounting principles that is not called for by the prescribed form or related instructions (or departure from the requirements of the form), as described in the following paragraph."

The accountant should consider any departure from the requirements of the prescribed form as the equivalent of a departure from generally accepted accounting principles in evaluating its effect on his or her report.

Communications Between Predecessor and Successor Accountants (SSARS No. 4)

SSARS No. 4 covers two types of communication between successor and predecessor accountants: (1) inquiries regarding acceptance of an engagement to compile or review the financial statements of a nonpublic entity, and (2) inquiries regarding the conduct of the compilation or review engagement.

Inquiries Regarding Acceptance of an Engagement

SSARS No. 4 does not require a successor accountant to communicate with a predecessor. However, the following situations may influence a successor accountant to communicate with a predecessor accountant: (1) information about the prospective client and its management and principals is limited or appears to warrant special attention, (2) the change in accountants occurs substantially after the end of the accounting period for which financial statements are to be compiled or reviewed, and (3) frequent changes in accountants have been made.

If a successor decides to initiate communications, the successor accountant should request the client to (1) allow him or her to inquire of the predecessor accountant and (2) authorize the predecessor accountant to respond completely to the inquiries. The successor accountant should consider the reasons for, and effects of, a client's refusal to comply with this request, in connection with the acceptance of the engagement as it may be a signal of possible serious problems.

The successor accountant's communication with the predecessor may be oral or written. Information about the following matters is commonly requested: (1) management integrity, (2) conflicts with management about accounting principles or the need for performing certain procedures, (3) management cooperation in providing additional or revised information, and (4) predecessor accountant's understanding of the reason for the change in accountants. The predecessor accountant should reply promptly and completely to a successor accountant's proper inquiries. There are situations, however, such as impending litigation, which may cause the predecessor accountant to limit response. In this case, he or she should explain that the response is limited. The successor accountant should consider the reasons for, and effects of, the limited response in connection with acceptance of the engagement, as this is also an indication of potential serious problems.

Other Inquiries

The successor accountant may decide to initiate other inquiries of the predecessor. For example, questions about the compilation or review engagement in the prior period. Such questions may be directed to the predecessor when the successor is concerned about (1) insufficient financial data, (2) performing other necessary accounting services, and (3) spending excessive time in problem areas. These inquiries may be made either before or after the successor accountant has accepted the engagement.

If the successor accountant wants to review the predecessor accountant's working papers, he or she should ask the client to authorize the predecessor accountant to make the working papers available. Some sections of the working papers may only be reviewed and others may be copied, depending on the agreement between the predecessor accountant and successor accountant. The successor accountant should have access to working papers for items of continuing accounting significance and those relating to contingencies. The predecessor accountant may, however, have valid business reasons for refusing access to the working papers. If more than one accountant is considering accepting an engagement, the predecessor accountant is not obligated to make the working papers available until the client has selected the successor accountant.

The successor accountant should not refer to the predecessor accountant in his or her report, unless the reference is made to financial statements of a prior period as covered by SSARS No. 2 or SAS No. 26 (reporting on comparative statements).

Financial Statements Reported on by Predecessor Accountant

If the successor accountant discovers information that would require the revision of financial statements reported on by the predecessor accountant, he or she should request that the client explain this information to the predecessor accountant. The predecessor accountant should then follow the guidance provided in SAS No. 1 regarding subsequent discovery of information (see Section 516) as the statements and the accountant's report may require revision. The successor accountant should consult his or her attorney if the client refuses to communicate with the predecessor regarding subsequently discovered information or if he or she is not satisfied with the predecessor accountant's course of action.

Reporting on Compiled Financial Statements (SSARS No. 5)

SSARS No. 5 amends the reporting standard set forth in SSARS No. 1 as well as changing the wording of the first paragraph of the standard compilation report to conform to the wording of review and audit reports. These amendments have been included in the summary of SSARS No. 1 above.

CPa   SEPTEMBER 1980

Liability Exposure in Compilation and Review

Here is an analysis of possible legal exposure presented
by compilation and review engagements. The author
describes and develops problem areas that he perceives
and offers suggestions to assist practitioners and their
clients to avoid opening themselves to law suits.

Dan L. Goldwasser, LL.B.

IN December 1978, the Accounting and Review Services Committee of the AICPA issued Statement on Standards for Accounting and Review Services No. 1 (SSARS 1) which established standards for compilation and review engagements. Although this statement is far superior to the exposure draft dated January 20, 1978, it, nevertheless, presents a number of liability pitfalls for practitioners.[1]

In large measure, SSARS 1 is aimed at adding a measure of professionalism to the services of accountants on nonaudit engagements with private companies. In this regard it creates, with respect to nonaudit financial statement engagements for nonpublic companies, two distinct classes of services: a compilation wherein the public accountant assembles and prepares financial statements from the records of his client, and a review wherein the public accountant performs a limited review of financial statements prepared by him or his client.[2] Prior to the publication of SSARS 1 such services were treated as an "unaudited" engagement, the scope of which remained largely undefined in professional pronouncements.

There can be no doubt that the greater precision of professional standards as enunciated in SSARS 1 will enhance the professional character of an accountant's work; however, that very precision will also create added liability exposure.[3] SSARS 1 offers certain guidance in avoiding some of the liability pitfalls. Apart from the greater particularity of professional standards, SSARS 1 also creates liability with the review concept which imposes responsibilities that remain to be defined.

Prior to the adoption of SSARS 1, financial statement services performed by an accountant were divided into two major classes: audit engagements and nonaudit engagements. It was generally held that an accountant associated with unaudited financial statements had no liability except for known inaccuracies.[4] Moreover, the accountant assumed no responsibility for the completeness of those statements; i.e., whether they contained all the disclosures necessary under generally accepted accounting principles (GAAP).[5] Similarly, it was not even clear whether an accountant performing services with respect to unaudited statements had any duty to ascertain whether those statements were presented in accordance with GAAP.[6] Accordingly, to avoid liability on unaudited financial statements, an accountant usually had only to observe the following precautions: (1) that he labeled the statement clearly as being "unaudited" to avoid the legal presumption that unlabeled statements were deemed to be audited; and (2) that his client understood that he was not performing an audit and could not be expected to uncover errors and irregularities which an audit might reveal. Because SSARS 1 establishes (or merely formalizes) explicit requirements, it opens up new vistas of liability in the event the accountant fails to observe one or more of those requirements.

Dan L. Goldwasser, LL.B., is an attorney and a member of Solinger & Gordon (New York City) which serves as counsel to the Professional Liability Insurance Committee of the New York State Society of Certified Public Accountants. Mr. Goldwasser has written numerous articles on accountants' liability as well as the NYSSCPA and AICPA continuing professional education materials on accountants' legal responsibilities.

[1] The Exposure Draft was issued on January 20, 1978 by AICPA's Accounting and Review Services Committee. See Thomas P. Kelley "Compilation and Review—A Revolution in Practice," *The CPA Journal*, April 1979.

[2] Although SSARS No. 1 provides that a review may be performed on financial statements prepared by the reviewing accountant, the CPA must, nevertheless, be "independent." Under the standards of the SEC (which generally do not apply to nonpublic companies) an accountant is not independent with respect to financial statements which he has prepared.

[3] The courts have generally viewed unaudited work as not being professional in nature because of the heretofore absence of established standards of conduct. The adoption of SSARS 1 will provide the courts with standards against which an accountant's work can be measured.

[4] Common law concepts of fraud apply to unaudited financial statement. Under a fraud theory liability may be found for knowing or intentional misstatements of fact.

[5] See, Gold v. DCL, Incorporated, CCH Fed. Sec. L. Rep. ¶94,036 (S.D.N.Y. 1973).

[6] It can be argued from the language of the 2nd Circuit's opinion in U.S. v. Simon, 425 F.2d 796 (1969) that an accountant associated with financial statements has a duty to cause them to fairly present the financial status and operating results of the company even if he does not audit the accuracy of the financial data.

Compilation Engagements

Prior to the adoption of SSARS 1, one of the few liability problems involved client misunderstandings relating to the scope of the accountant's engagement. In the *Max Rothenberg* case[7] an accountant was held liable for failing to detect a defalcation by his client's managing agent. The case turned on the question of whether the accountant had undertaken to perform an audit, which question the court answered in the affirmative based on the testimony of the client's managing agent and certain audit procedures undertaken by the accountant. In order to overcome this problem, SSARS 1 provides a form of engagement letter which, if used, should preclude Max

> ## 'Because SSARS 1 establishes . . . explicit requirements, it opens up new vistas of liability in the event the accountant fails to observe one or more of those requirements.'

Rothenberg-type liability. On the other hand if the accountant fails to use such an engagement letter, he will not only find himself in the Max Rothenberg dilemma but perhaps in greater danger, since even the performance of any analytical procedures might be sufficient to deem him to have undertaken a review engagement, even if he is not found to have undertaken an audit. Moreover, since the professional literature expressly encourages the use of an engagement letter to avoid such misunderstandings, the courts may be prone to decide such issues against the accountant who fails to use the engagement letter.

Another common liability problem prior to the adoption of SSARS 1 was the issuance by an accountant of financial statements which were not clearly labeled in terms of the accountant's engagement. Thus, if the accountant was associated with financial statements and failed to disclose that they were "unaudited," the courts would presume that they had been audited and would hold the accountant responsible to third parties for audited work.[8] To overcome this hazard, accountants have adopted the practice of not only specifying in their report that the attached financial statements are unaudited but also noting on each page of the financial statements that no audit has been conducted. SSARS 1 adopts this procedure and in paragraph 16 provides that "each page of the financial statements compiled by the accountant

should include a reference such as 'see accountant's compilation report'."

Naturally, the failure to take these precautions in the face of express professional standards will subject the accountant to the inference that the financial statements bearing his name were audited. Because SSARS 1 specifically requires such language to be placed on every page of a compilation report, the courts might have little sympathy for an accountant in a situation in which management removes his report and reproduces financial statements printed on his stationery. While it is not clear that the accountant would be held to the standards of an audit engagement in such circumstances, it is not out of the realm of possibility.

SSARS 1 imposes a number of new duties in connection with a compilation engagement. One such requirement is contained in paragraph 10 which provides that the accountant should have

> a knowledge of the accounting principles and practices of the industry in which the entity operates that will enable him to compile financial statements that are appropriate in form for an entity operating in that industry.

Paragraph 10 goes on to provide, however, that an accountant may accept a compilation engagement for an entity in an industry with which he has no previous experience. Thus, it merely places upon him the responsibility to obtain the required level of knowledge prior to·or during the course of his engagement.

> ## 'SSARS 1 seems to advance that principle one step further by requiring knowledge of those accounting principles and practices which pertain to the industry which is the subject of the engagement.'

Before the adoption of SSARS 1 the professional literature generally provided that an accountant was responsible for knowledge of the professional standards pertaining to a given area of practice.[9] Accordingly, if he were to accept a tax advisory engagement he would have to have a familiarity with the tax laws and the rules and regulations adopted by the IRS. Similarly, in an audit engagement he would have been required to have a knowledge of generally accepted accounting principles as well as generally accepted auditing standards. SSARS 1

---

[7] 1136 Tenants' Corp. v. Max Rothenberg & Co., 319 NYS2d 1007 (1971), aff'd 330 NYS2d 800 (1972).

[8] See, Stanley L. Bloch, Inc. v. Klein, 258 NYS2d 501 (1965).

[9] See, Rule 201 of the AICPA Code of Professional Ethics and Interpretation 201-1 thereunder.

seems to advance that principle one step further by requiring knowledge of those accounting principles and practices which pertain to the industry which is the subject of the engagement. Accordingly, it may not be sufficient for an accountant charged with malpractice to demonstrate that he merely had the competence and technical knowledge of other practitioners in the area; he may also have to show that he had such knowledge and competence insofar as applied to this particular industry. The greater precision of SSARS 1 thus imposes a higher degree of skill and responsibility on the accountant.

In addition, paragraph 11 of SSARS 1 provides that

the account should possess a general understanding of the nature of the entity's business transactions, the form of its accounting records, the stated qualifications of its personnel, the accounting basis on which the financial statements are to be presented, and the form and content of the financial statements.

SSARS 1 thus formalizes and records that type of knowledge regarding a client's business affairs which an accountant should obtain before embarking on any financial statement engagement. From the point of view of advancing the standards of the profession, this provision represents a significant contribution. On the other hand, it will increase the liability exposure of those practitioners who merely go through the motions of preparing financial statements without giving serious consideration to the adequacy of their client's accounting systems and personnel. To see this one need only envision an accountant being cross-examined on his knowledge of his client's business practices and the educational experience and business background of his client's accounting personnel. Every "I don't know" elicited from him by plaintiff's attorney will have a devastating cumulative impact in undermining the accountant's defense.

Before the adoption of SSARS 1 an accountant could be held liable if he knew that unaudited financial statements with which he was associated contained a material misstatement of fact. Such a misstatement might consist of a known numerical error or a known failure to comply with GAAP. Historically, "unaudited" statements have contained rather spotty note disclosures with most such disclosures required under GAAP being frequently omitted. Nevertheless, the courts have rarely imposed liability as a result of such omissions.

Although SSARS 1 tries to encourage accountants to include in all financial statements compiled by them such information (including footnote information) as may be required under GAAP, paragraph 19 expressly provides that financial statements may omit substantially all the disclosures required by GAAP, including disclosures that might appear in the body of financial statements. In such cases, however, the accountant must clearly indicate in his report that those matters have been omitted and must satisfy himself they are not being omitted with the intention of misleading those who might reasonably be expected to rely upon them. Therefore, whereas in the past an ac-

countant would generally have no liability exposure for financial statements compiled by him which contain inadequate footnote disclosure, under SSARS 1 he may have such liability exposure if the footnotes do not contain the prescribed GAAP disclosure, depending on whether he discloses the omission and whether such omissions were intended to mislead.

It is not even clear that a simple statement that "all GAAP disclosures have not been made" will suffice in this situation. The footnote disclosures mandated by GAAP, by definition, are "material." Accordingly, their omission in almost every case may be deemed to be misleading. The only question then is whether that omission was effected *for the purpose* or *with the intention* of misleading the user. Unfortunately, almost any knowledge on the part of the accountant that management was not particularly anxious to have potential readers of its financial statement aware of the omitted information might give rise to a finding of the requisite misleading intent. For this reason, paragraph 19 may go a long way toward reversing prior cases with respect to omitted footnote disclosures.

'It is not even clear that a simple statement that all GAAP disclosures have not been made *will suffice in this situation.*'

Before the adoption of SSARS 1, the general rule was that an accountant was not liable for errors in financial statements he prepared unless he knew of those errors. Paragraph 13 of SSARS 1 transcends this standard and also requires that such statements must be free of "obvious material errors." This requirement raises certain problems because what is "obvious" to a knowledgeable accountant may not be obvious to one who has not taken the trouble to update himself on current accounting practices. Moreover, since the accountant himself has compiled the financial statements, any error in the application of GAAP would probably constitute an obvious material error if the use of the erroneous accounting principle materially affects the statements. Thus, SSARS 1 would seemingly impose liability for failures to apply GAAP in the preparation of the financial statements themselves as well as failure to make the footnote disclosures required by GAAP.

Review Engagements

The review concept is relatively new, having first been introduced in SAS 10 (December 1975) which outlines procedures for limited reviews. Because of its novelty, it is not clear which standard of care the courts will apply. One can only imagine that the applicable standard of care will be higher than that for a compilation engagement but lower than that required for an audit engagement.

Because the review falls somewhere between audited and nonaudited engagements as we previously knew them, it is likely to be an elastic concept covering virtually all engagements ranging from financial statement work in which the CPA merely reconciles the issuer's bank statement to those in which the accountant performs substantial analytical procedures. For this reason it is important that the accountant undertaking a review explain to his client (as well as those who might rely on his report) the extent of his services and the responsibilities which he is assuming.[10] To this end, Exhibit C of SSARS 1 sets forth a sample engagement letter designed to avoid such misunderstandings. Such a form letter is indeed helpful if used. If not used, it can be not only a source of embarrassment but also a source of potential liability.

> ‘. . . it is important that the accountant undertaking a review explain to his client (as well as those who might rely on his report) the extent of his services and the responsibilities which he is assuming.’

SSARS 1 also provides, with respect to a review, requirements similar to those noted for compilation engagements. Accordingly, the potential liability problems for a compilation engagement apply equally (if not with greater force) to review engagements.

One of the more troublesome concepts in audit and review engagements is the problem of the degree of assurance needed by an accountant to render an opinion or report. The standards of the profession require that the auditor must obtain sufficient competent audit evidence to allow him to render an opinion. In a review, however, the accountant does not form an opinion on the financial statements, but rather merely states that on the basis of his limited review he has no reason to believe that material modifications are required to be made to the financial statements in order for them to comply with GAAP or some other applicable guideline. It may require several years to clarify under what circumstances an accountant may make this statement.

The liability potential of this uncertainty can be seen as follows. Assume that a company's principal asset con-

sists of certain patent rights and the company carries them at a high value. May a CPA render a review report if he knows that sales of the patented items have been modest? Does he have to ascertain the size of the market for the products represented by the patent rights? May he accept management's representation that the company has clear title to those patent rights when he knows that other manufacturers are selling similar products? Does he have to explore to what extent competing technologies exist? While these and other measures may be necessary to render an audit opinion, at what point may he cease his inquiry to issue a review report? Moreover, may he issue a review report even in circumstances in which he might feel constrained to issue a "subject to" opinion if he had been engaged to perform an audit?

A similar issue exists for material items on which the CPA develops doubts. For example, assume that a major asset of a corporation consists of an account receivable which, on the date of the issuance of the accountant's report, are 150 days old and remain unpaid. Moreover, the company has issued instructions that all further shipments are to be made on a C.O.D. basis and that this particular customer has just assigned all its assets to secure its indebtedness to its major creditor. In recognition of these factors, the company has decided to take a 25 percent reserve against this receivable. Paragraph 29 of SSARS 1 provides that the CPA must extend his procedure if he "becomes aware that information is incorrect, incomplete or otherwise unsatisfactory." What steps, if any, must the accountant take in these circumstances to issue a review report? Unfortunately, if the answers to these questions are not decided by the accounting profession in the near future, they may be decided by a court that has little, if any, familiarity with audit standards or with the purposes and intents of a review engagement.

> ‘One of the more troublesome concepts in audit and review engagements is the problem of the degree of assurance needed by an accountant to render an opinion or report.’

Appendix A to SSARS 1 provides a "laundry list" of recommended procedures in performing a review. Such a list, while perhaps helpful to the CPA, poses two distinct problems. First, mere compliance with those listed procedures may not be sufficient to avoid liability under certain circumstances. Second, the accountant who fails to follow that list in rendering a review report on financial statements which prove materially inaccurate will be hardpressed to prove that he was not negligent, particularly if it can be argued that one or more of those procedures would have led to the discovery of the misstated facts.

---

[10] There is presently a wide scope of views as to the role of an accountant in performing review work and it may be many years before there is a general understanding among accountants and others as to the role of the accountant in a review engagement. See, D. Raymond Bainbridge, "Unaudited Statements—Bankers' and CPAs' Perceptions," *The CPA Journal*, December 1979.

Thus, SSARS 1 creates a trap for the accountant who insists on continuing his present way of conducting his business.

In dealing with nonpublic company clients, liability frequently results from a misunderstanding with the client himself. Paragraph 36 of SSARS 1 sows the seeds for many such disputes. It provides that:

> When an accountant is unable to perform the inquiry and analytic procedures he considers necessary to achieve limited assurance contemplated by a review, his review will be incomplete. A review that is incomplete is not an adequate basis for issuing a review report. In such a situation, the accountant should consider whether the circumstance resulting in an incomplete review also preclude him from issuing a compilation report on the entity's financial statement.

In an audit engagement, should the accountant run into unforeseen problems precluding him from rendering an unqualified report, he has the option of either rendering a qualified report, disclaiming an opinion or rendering an adverse opinion. Should the accountant face a similar situation in a review engagement, SSARS 1 states that he may not be able to render any report. Accordingly, the illustrative engagement letter for a review engagement provides "if, for any reason, we are unable to complete our review of your financial statements we will not issue a report on such statements as a result of this engagement." While as a matter of contract law the accountant probably has a good argument that he has performed his contract even though he renders no report and is, therefore, still entitled to receive his fees, that prospect will not be particularly well received by the client who will require little encouragement to assert a counterclaim should the accountant commence legal action to collect his fees. Because of the lack of flexibility provided by SSARS 1, the accountant should think twice about embarking on a review engagement if, at the outset, there is any significant likelihood that he will be unable to render a review report.

Paragraph 37 of SSARS 1 provides that an accountant may issue a review report for a single financial statement, such as the balance sheet, rather than a full set of statements as required by GAAP. While this provision in itself provides no particular liability exposure it may well lead to liability. In conducting a review, the accountant must undertake certain analytical procedures so as to be in a position to render a report. In reviewing only one financial statement and completely ignoring data underly-ing related financial statements, the accountant may find that he has not undertaken sufficient steps to even pass on the one financial statement which is the subject of his report. For example, in a review engagement relating only to a balance sheet, failure to analyze (and in some measure verify) the operating results of his client may prevent him from rendering a report on that balance sheet. This might occur when the valuation of certain material assets are a function of their income generating ability which could have been ascertained from a review of the operating statements. Therefore, even though SSARS 1 permits review engagements with respect to single financial statements, such engagements should not be undertaken without giving hard consideration to the extent to which the related statements bear on the one which is to be the subject of the accountant's report.

In a review engagement the financial statements are not required to include all of the note disclosures that would be required under generally accepted accounting principles. The accompanying footnotes or report should, however, specify the nature of the information required under GAAP which has been omitted. Unlike audited financial statements, such disclosure need not set forth the actual or particular *effects* on the financial statements as reported of each such item. It is not clear from paragraph 40 the extent of such required disclosure. For example, need the notes to an accountant's review report specify each particular item of note disclosure which has been omitted or may it simply state that certain additional disclosures required by GAAP have been omitted? While the latter would seem perhaps sufficient for a compilation report, in a review engagement itemization of the omitted disclosures would seem more appropriate.

Conclusion

All in all, SSARS 1 represents a significant advance in professionalism with respect to unaudited financial statements. It not only adds uniformity of presentation but also tends to quantify (even if only in a general fashion) the participation of the independent accountant associated with those statements. In this way the reader can better evaluate their content. These gains, however, are not without their price in that they clearly expose the accountant to a higher degree of liability. Such greater liability results from the greater precision of effort required in complying with SSARS 1 and also through the injection of new and still largely undefined concepts. Ω

CASE 23

1136 TENANTS' CORPORATION LIABILITY CASE*

In 1939 the AIA (American Institute of Accountants) approved Statement on Auditing Procedure (SAP) No. 1. If an examination was lacking in scope or if financial statements did not follow generally accepted accounting principles, the accountant was not to express an opinion that such statements were fairly presented. In 1947 SAP No. 23 required that reasons be stated for failing to express an opinion. Statement No. 23 created much confusion and was revised in 1949, when Council issued the following clarification concerning unaudited statements:

> . . . when financial statements prepared without audit are presented on the accountant's stationery without comment by the accountant, a warning, such as "Prepared from the Books Without Audit," appearing prominently on each page of the financial statements is considered sufficient.[3]

In September 1962, the Committee on Auditing Procedure issued SAP No. 32, a clarification of reporting standards. Paragraphs 16 and 17 dealt entirely with unaudited financial statements. It was preferred that all unaudited statements be accompanied by a disclaimer of opinion, but a disclaimer was required only when the statements were accompanied by comments. It was also stated that if the auditor believed the statements were false or misleading, he or she should refuse to be associated with them in any way.

1136 Tenants' Corporation vs. Max Rothenberg & Company

In August 1963, I. Jerome Riker, manager of Riker and Company, Inc., and others purchased a building located at 1136 Fifth Avenue, New York City. The apartments were subsequently sold. Riker incorporated and became the owner of the property. He also, according to legal contract, became the managing agent of the tenants' property.

Max Rothenberg & Company, a small local accounting firm, was engaged to perform limited accounting services by an oral agreement. Payment for Rothenberg's services was established at $600 per year.

When Rothenberg submitted periodic financial statements to 1136 Tenants' Corporation, a letter of transmittal was enclosed. The letter began:

> Pursuant to our engagement, we have reviewed and summarized the statements of your managing agent and other data submitted to us by (the managing agents) pertaining to 1136 Tenants' Corporation.

The letter concluded:

> The following statements (the financial statements and appended schedules) were prepared from the books and records of the Corporation. No independent verifications were undertaken thereon.[4]

The financial statements themselves were marked, "Subject to comments in letter of transmittal."

By March of 1965, it was discovered that Riker & Company, Inc. was in severe financial difficulty. Tenants' obligations which had been reported as "paid" in Riker's monthly statements were in fact unpaid.

---

*An original draft of this case was prepared by Rhoda Myers, Mark Noftsinger, and Laurie Penner, Master of Accountancy students, Virginia Polytechnic Institute and State University.

[3] Marlene K. Minnich, "Legal Responsibility—Unaudited Statements," *Ohio C.P.A.*, Winter 1975, pp. 11-21.

[4] Michael H. Granoff, "Recents Legal Developments in the U.S.," *The Chartered Accountant in Australia*, April 1963, pp. 6-10.

Riker had drawn checks in payment of the cooperative's bills. He had held back the release of the checks until he received further payment from both Tenants' Corporation and other firms which were managed by him. These funds were siphoned off to support other real estate investments. Ultimately Riker was in debt to the various cooperative corporations to the extent of more than $1 million.

Since Riker was bankrupt, the 1136 Tenants' Corporation sued Max Rothenberg & Company.

The Plaintiff

The plaintiff, 1136 Tenants' Corporation, claimed that Max Rothenberg & Company had been engaged for auditing services, including verification of bank statements, invoices, vouchers, and other evidences of payment of bills. Consequently, the plaintiff charged the defendant with breach of contract, negligence in adhering to professional standards, and lack of disclosure of the existing financial position.

The Tenants' Corporation further weakened the defendant's case by getting a senior partner to admit in court that some audit procedures were applied beyond general write-up work. A work-sheet entitled "Missing Invoices 1/1/63-12/31/63" totaling $44,000 was introduced as evidence. Use of the term "audit" in the financial statements and "audit notes" in the working papers also damaged the defendant's case.

The Defendant

The defendant, Max Rothenberg & Company, stated that they had been engaged to perform "write-up" work and prepared unaudited statements solely from the information provided by Riker without verification. In addition, they were to prepare a letter containing tax deductions for mortgage interest and real estate taxes applicable to each of the tenants as well as the federal and state tax returns of the corporation. Each set of financial statements was accompanied by a letter stating that they were prepared according to information submitted by Riker with no independent verification. Each page of the financial statements was marked, "Subject to comments in letter of transmittal."

The Decision

On July 1, 1970, the trial court held that on the basis of testimony the defendant had been engaged to confirm and verify the books and records provided by Riker. The court found negligence in the performance of professional duties. Justice Riccobono awarded the plaintiff $174,066.93 plus interest, costs, and disbursements for a total of $237,278.83. He awarded the defendant $1,000 for additional accounting services rendered with interest and other costs, totaling $1,349.51.

On April 8, 1971, the Appellate Division of the Supreme Court of New York, by a four-to-one decision, upheld the 1970 decision of the trial court by stating:

> . . . even if a firm of certified public accountants was hired only to perform "write-up" services for owners of (an) apartment building, when accountants became aware that material invoices purportedly paid by (the) manager of (the) building were missing, the accountants were negligent in failing to inform owners of (the) building of that fact.[5]

Justice Stewer rendered the only dissenting vote. He stated that the plaintiff's loss was due to the actions of Riker. Riker had given contradictory testimony as to the terms of the engagement. It seemed improbable that Riker would hire a CPA for an audit that would detect his own embezzlement. The statements issued by the defendant indicated that there were "no independent verifications" and were appropriately labeled to that effect. The amount of the annual fee would have been larger had the engagement actually included a full audit.

In March 1972, the decision of the Appellate Division was appealed to the court of Appeals of the State of New York (the state's highest court) and a brief as *amicus curiae* was filed jointly by the AICPA and the New York State Society of CPAs. On this second appeal, the decision of the lower court was unanimously upheld.

---

[5] Marlene K. Minnich, *op. cit.*, p. 15.

Consequences

Before the Tenants' case had come to court, SAP, *Statement on Auditing Procedure*, No. 38 was issued, which detailed an accountant's reporting responsibilities when associated with unaudited financial statements. SAP No. 38 was subsequently incorporated into SAS No. 1 as Sections 516 and 517. Currently, SAS No. 26 establishes the accountant's reporting responsibilities when associated with the unaudited financial statements of a public client.

In 1972 a Task Force was appointed by the Chairman of the AICPA Committee on Auditing Procedure (now the Auditing Standards Board) to consider the ramifications of the 1136 Tenants' decision and its effect on the accounting profession. In 1975 the Task Force issued a Guide on Unaudited Statements as a result of their consideration of the problems in the Tenants' case. That Guide has now been replaced with the current reporting standards for compilation and review services (SSARS No. 1) in connection with the unaudited statements of nonpublic clients and, as indicated above, with SAS No. 26 regarding the unaudited statements of public clients.

REFERENCES

Bab, Donald Stuart. "The CPA's Expanding Legal Liability," *Practical Accountant* (March/April 1973), pp. 43-53.

Chazen, Charles. "Unaudited Financial Statements—Beware of Hidden Dangers," *California CPA Quarterly* (December 1974), pp. 8-12.

_____and Solomon, Kenneth. "The 'Unaudited' State of Affairs," *Journal of Accountancy* (December 1972), pp. 41-5.

Guy, Dan M. and Winters, Alan J. "Unaudited Financial Statements: A Survey," *Journal of Accountancy* (December 1972), pp. 46-53.

Minnich, Marlene K. "Legal Responsibility—Unaudited Statements," *Ohio CPA* (Winter 1975), pp. 11-24.

CASE DISCUSSION QUESTIONS

1.   When are financial statements unaudited?

2.   When is a CPA associated with financial statements?

3.   When are the following types of accountant's reports (disclaimers) appropriate?

   a.   SAS No. 2 disclaimers?

   b.   SAS No. 26 disclaimers?

   c.   SSARS No. 1 disclaimers?

4.   When should a CPA be responsible for fraud and defalcation in an accounting service engagement?

5.   What inquiries or procedures should a CPA utilize in an accounting service engagement for the preparation of compiled statements? Review report? Unaudited statements for a public client?

6.   Due to the possible importance of working papers, what factors should an accountant consider as to the quantity, scope, type, and content of working papers desirable for a particular engagement?

7.   In what circumstances should the CPA's disclaimer of opinion (or other appropriate report) on unaudited financial statements contain a reference to the absence of necessary disclosures and restrictions of the statements to internal use?

8.   Do GAAP apply to unaudited statements? When an accountant finds accounting in an unaudited statement not in conformity with GAAP and his or her name is associated with the statements, what should be done?

CASE 24

ASSOCIATION WITH FINANCIAL STATEMENTS

You are a partner in the firm of Landry, Phillips and Co., Certified Public Accountants. A potential client, who owns and operates several restaurants, Joe Theisman, is visiting with you to discuss the services that your firm may render for his organization; you have discussed alternatives ranging from advice and assistance in the preparation of financial statements to an audit examination. Mr. Theisman's background has been entirely in the restaurant business and professional sports, so he is unfamiliar with many aspects of the CPA's involvement with financial statements.

CASE DISCUSSION QUESTIONS

1. Outline for Mr. Theisman the circumstances under which Landry, Phillips and Co. would be deemed to be "associated" with financial statements?

2. Is it possible for Landry, Phillips and Co. to be associated with both audited and unaudited financial statements?

3. Would it be possible for Landry, Phillips and Co. to be associated with Theisman's financial statements even though the name of the firm will not appear with the statements? Explain.

4. What action should Landry, Phillips and Co. take when they are associated with financial statements but have not audited or reviewed such statements? (Write out an example of any necessary report.)

5. What is meant by the CPA's independence? Why is independence important? How does one decide whether or not the CPA is independent?

6. Outline the circumstances under which Landry, Phillips and Co. would be required to modify a disclaimer on Theisman's unaudited statements.

7. When is "negative assurance" permissible?

CASE 25

COMPILATION AND REVIEW OF FINANCIAL STATEMENTS

Your firm, Campbell and Stabler, Certified Public Accountants, has been approached by Larry Lee, owner and operator of Jewelry Brokers, Inc. Lee wishes to meet with you to discuss services that your firm may provide for him and his organization.

Jewelry Brokers is currently engaged in the wholesale and retail sale of diamonds, various other precious stones, gold and silver. What began as a part-time business operated from Larry's home has developed into an expanding operation with a total of four locations in Texas, Illinois, California and Thailand. Several additional sites are currently in the planning stages and at least two new offices will be in operation during the next twelve months. Net income (before taxes) was $515,000 on approximately $1 million of sales last year. Lee has indicated to you that he will be disappointed " . . . with anything less than a 100% increase in both sales and earnings this year."

After considerable discussion, you determine that Lee is interested in a wide range of services, excluding an audit examination.

CASE DISCUSSION QUESTIONS

1. Draft a paragraph which will explain to Lee the basic differences between:

    a.   An audit examination.

    b.   A compilation.

    c.   A review.

2.   If your firm performed both a compilation and a review for Jewelry Brokers, what type of report would you issue? Explain.

3.   In performing a compilation of financial statements for a client, the accountant is concerned with both the form of the statements and whether they are free from obvious error. In this context:

    a.   What qualifications should the accountant possess?

    b.   What procedures should the accountant employ in the compilation?

    c.   What does the term "error" mean to the auditor in a compilation? Give examples.

4.   The concerns of the accountant performing a review of financial statements differ from those in a compilation only. In this regard:

    a.   What qualifications should the accountant possess?

    b.   What procedures should the accountant employ in the review?

    c.   Does the auditor study and evaluate the client's system of internal control during a review of financial statements? Explain.

    d.   Outline the content of the report issued by the accountant after completing a review of the financial statements for the client.

5.   Distinguish between an updated and a reissued report.

6.   What report(s) should be issued by the accountant when the current-period financial statements have been compiled or reviewed and those of the prior period have been audited? Explain.

7.   SSARS No. 3 provides guidance applicable to reports presented in a prescribed form. It also provides an alternative compilation report form when a prescribed form or related instructions call for a departure from GAAP.

    a.   Discuss the prescribed form of financial statement referred to in SSARS No. 3. What type of entities or organizations provide these statements?

    b.   Discuss the presumption about information required by a prescribed form.

    c.   Discuss the accountant's reporting requirements concerning a prescribed form.

8.   SSARS No. 4 provides direction to a successor accountant who decides to communicate with a predecessor accountant concerning acceptance of a compilation or review engagement.

    a.   Discuss when it is appropriate for the successor accountant to make inquiries of the predecessor accountant.

    b.   List and discuss the information that the successor accountant normally would want to obtain from the predecessor accountant.

c. Would there be times when the succcessor accountant would want access to the predecessor accountant's working papers? Discuss.

d. Is the predecessor accountant always required to make his or her working papers available to the successor accountant? Explain fully.

e. What should the successor accountant do if he or she believes that financial statements reported on by the predecessor accountant need to be revised? Explain in detail.

f. Should the successor accountant refer to the report or work of a predecessor accountant in his or her report? (Hint: See SSARS No. 2 or SAS No. 26).

9. SSARS No. 5 amends SSARS No. 1. Discuss the amendments.

CASE 26

MORGAN, CABELL & CO.

Joe Morgan, CPA, is a partner in the firm of Morgan, Cabell & Co., a regional CPA firm with offices located in Houston, Austin and Bryan-College Station, Texas. Among the clients for which Joe has responsibility are two non-public clients, Bryan Furniture Sales and Aggie Products.

Bryan Furniture Sales is a furniture store located in Bryan, Texas. Joe prepares income tax returns, maintains the books, and prepares quarterly and annual financial statements without audit. Because Joe is very familiar with Bryan's operations, he normally does not perform any procedures in connection with the preparation of the financial statements other than reading the statements, determining that they are in the appropriate format and free from obvious material arithmetical or clerical errors.

Aggie Products is a general merchandising store located in Austin, Texas. As is the case with Bryan Furniture, Joe prepares income tax returns and quarterly and annual financial statements without audit for Aggie Products, but he does not keep Aggie's books. Because Joe is not as familiar with the operations of the Company as he feels he should be and because he does not maintain books, he performs additional procedures in connection with the preparation of the financial statements. The procedures performed by Joe on the books and records of Aggie Products normally include:

1. Reconciling all bank accounts.

2. Testing postings from the books of original entry to the general ledgers.

3. Testing the arithmetical accuracy of the general ledger.

4. Confirming cash balances directly with local banks.

5. Testing the reasonableness of the allowance for doubtful accounts (but not confirming accounts receivable).

6. Testing the computation of depreciation.

7. Reviewing Aggie's inventory count records (but not observing the inventory count).

8. Making inquiries concerning the accounting principles followed by Aggie for inventory, long-term assets, sales, and selected other financial statement items.

9. Performing selected analytical procedures that include making comparisons of statement amounts with amounts reported for preceding periods; computation of ratios and comparison with industry norms; and comparison of operating results with budget amounts.

10. Completing a financial statement disclosure checklist.

CASE DISCUSSION QUESTIONS

1.   What is Joe's reporting responsibility regarding the financial statements of Bryan Furniture Sales? Discuss.

2.   How does Joe's reporting responsibility for Aggie Products differ from that for Bryan Furniture Sales? Explain.

18

Reporting on Inconsistency

(Section 546, SAS No. 1)

The auditor's reporting responsibilities regarding the second standard of reporting and inconsistency are related to:

Reporting a change in an accounting principle

Reporting on changes in accounting principles that are not in conformity with GAAP

Reports following a pooling of interests

Reports on first examinations

Reports on pro forma effects of accounting changes

Change in Accounting Principle

When a client has made a change in an accounting principle the auditor should modify the opinion as to consistency, indicating the nature of the change. Concurrence with a change in accounting principles is implicit unless the auditor takes exception to the change in expressing the opinion. To be more informative, however, the auditor should make this concurrence explicit by using the expression "with which we concur." Such concurrence is not required for changes that involve the correction of an error.

The form of modification of the auditor's opinion for an accounting change depends on the method of accounting for the change. For example, if there has been a change in accounting principle which should be reported by restating the prior year's financial statements, the appropriate reference to consistency is that the statements are consistent after giving effect to the change, as illustrated below:

(Opinion paragraph covering one year)

. . . applied on a basis consistent with that of the preceding year after giving retroactive effect to the change, with which we concur, in the method of accounting for long-term construction contracts as described in Note X to the financial statements.

333

(Opinion paragraph covering two years)

. . . applied on a consistent basis after restatement for the change with which we concur, in the method of accounting for long-term construction contracts as described in Note X to the financial statements.

The auditor's report need not refer to a change in accounting principles and restatement made in conformity with GAAP when such statements are presented with subsequent statements for comparative purposes.

Following is an example of reporting an accounting change which does not involve restatement of prior years' financial statements:

(Opinion paragraph)

. . . in conformity with generally accepted accounting principles which, except for the change, with which we concur, in the method of computing depreciation as described in Note X to the financial statements, have been applied on a basis consistent with that of the preceding year.

APB Opinion No. 20 describes the proper accounting for changes in accounting principles. Certain changes are reflected in the current period by reporting the cumulative effect of the change in current income, disclosing the earnings per share effect, and indicating pro forma amounts. Also, footnote disclosure is required justifying the change and reporting the effects of the change on financial position, results of operations, and changes in financial position. APB No. 20 requires certain accounting changes to be reflected by prior period adjustment.

When a CPA is reporting on two or more years, reference should be made to a change in accounting principles as long as the year of change is included in the years being reported upon. If the year of change is other than the earliest year being reported on, the following example would be an appropriate reporting form:

(Opinion paragraph)

. . . in conformity with generally accepted accounting principles consistently applied during the period except for the change, with which we concur, in the method of computing depreciation as described in Note X to the financial statements.

There is no inconsistency when the year of an accounting change is the earliest year being reported on. However, the CPA should make reference to the change. Following is an illustration of such a disclosure:

(Opinion paragraph)

. . . in conformity with generally accepted accounting principles consistently applied during the period subsequent to the change, with which we concur, made as of January 1, 19xx, in the method of computing depreciation as described in Note X to the financial statements.

Reference to a change in accounting principles in the year preceding the earliest year being reported upon is not necessary.

Reporting on Changes in Accounting Principles That are Not in Conformity with GAAP

The CPA should evaluate an accounting change to become satisfied that the newly adopted principle is generally accepted, the method of accounting for the effect of the change is proper, and management has provided reasonable justification for the change. When a client adopts a change in accounting principles that is not generally accepted or if the method of accounting for the effect of the change is not in conformity with GAAP, the CPA should express a qualified opinion or an adverse opinion, depending on the materiality of the items involved. When a qualified opinion is expressed, the qualification would relate both to conformity with GAAP and to the consistency of the application. An example of such a qualified opinion follows:

(Middle paragraph)

The company previously recorded its land at cost but adjusted the amounts to appraised values during the year, with a corresponding increase in stockholders' equity in the amount of $ . . . . In our opinion, the new basis on which land is recorded is not in conformity with generally accepted accounting principles.

(Opinion paragraph)

In our opinion, except for the change to recording appraised values as described above, the aforementioned financial statements present fairly the financial position of X Company at December 31, 19xx, and the results of its operations and changes in its financial position for the year then ended, in conformity with generally accepted accounting principles applied on a basis consistent with that of the preceding year.

When the CPA expresses an adverse opinion because the change resulted in accounting principles not in conformity with GAAP, reference to consistency should not be made.

When management adopts an accounting change without providing reasonable justification for the change, the auditor should express an exception to the change having been made without reasonable justification. An illustration of the expression of such an exception is presented below:

(Middle paragraph)

As disclosed in Note X to the financial statements, the company has adopted (description of newly adopted method), whereas it previously used (description of previous method). Although use of the (description of newly adopted method) is in conformity with generally accepted accounting principles, in our opinion the company has not provided reasonable justification for making a change as required by Opinion No. 20 of the Accounting Principles Board.

(Opinion paragraph)

In our opinion, except for the change in accounting principles as stated above, the aforementioned financial statements present fairly the financial position of X Company at December 31, 19xx, and the results of its operations and changes in its financial position for the year then ended, in conformity with generally accepted accounting principles applied on a basis consistent with that of the preceding year.

Reports Following a Pooling of Interests

When companies have merged or combined their operations as a "pooling of interests," the appropriate effects of the pooling should be disclosed in the presentation of financial position, results of operations, changes in financial position, and other historical financial data for the year in which the combination is consummated and, in comparative financial statements, for years prior to the year of pooling. If prior year statements are not restated so as to give appropriate recognition to a pooling, the comparative financial statements are not presented on a consistent basis. In this case, the inconsistency arises not from a change in the application of an accounting principle in the current year, but from the lack of such application to prior years. Such inconsistency would require a qualification of the CPA's report.

When single-year statements only are presented for the year in which a combination is consummated, a note to the statements should adequately disclose the pooling transaction and state the revenues, extraordinary items, and net income of the pooled companies for the preceding year on a combined basis.

Initial Examinations

When a CPA has not audited the statements of a company for the preceding year, procedures should be adopted that are both practicable and reasonable in the circumstances to be assured that the accounting principles employed are consistent between the current and the preceding year. Inadequate records or limitations on the scope of the examination may prevent the CPA from forming an opinion as to consistency. Following is an example of reporting that may be used when the client's records are inadequate:

(Scope paragraph)

. . . and such other auditing procedures as we considered necessary in the circumstances, except as indicated in the following paragraph.

(Middle paragraph)

Because of major inadequacies in the Company's accounting records for the previous year, it was not practicable to extend our auditing procedures to enable us to express an opinion on results of operations and changes in financial position for the year ended (current year) or on the consistency of application of accounting principles with the preceding year.

(Opinion paragraph)

In our opinion, the accompanying balance sheet presents fairly the financial position of X Company as of (current year-end) in conformity with generally accepted accounting principles.

If the accounting records for prior years were maintained on a basis that did not result in fair presentation in conformity with GAAP and it is not practical to restate for those years, the CPA should omit the customary reference to consistency. The report would appear as follows:

(Middle paragraph)

The Company has kept its records and has prepared its financial statements for previous years on the cash basis with no recognition having been accorded accounts receivable, accounts payable, or accrued expenses. At the beginning of the current year, the Company adopted the accrual basis of accounting. Although appropriate adjustments have been made to retained earnings as of the beginning of the year, it was not practicable to determine what adjustments would be necessary in the financial statements of the preceding year to restate results of operations and changes in financial position in conformity with the accounting principles used in the current year.

(Opinion paragraph)

In our opinion, the aforementioned financial statements present fairly the financial position of X Company as of October 31, 19xx, and the results of its operations and the changes in its financial position for the year then ended, in conformity with generally accepted accounting principles.

The reference to consistency in the CPA's opinion would be omitted when expressing an opinion on the financial statements of a company for the initial year of the company's operations.

Pro Forma Effects of Accounting Changes

In single-year financial statements the pro forma effects of retroactive application of accounting changes should be disclosed.

CASE 27

REPORTING ON INCONSISTENCY

You are the partner in charge of the audit of Conglomerate Enterprises, Inc., an international company with approximately 70 subsidiary companies. You are reviewing your firm's working papers for the parent company and several of the subsidiaries for the current years examination. You are concerned with proper reporting in the separate statements of the subsidiaries regarding a number of apparent inconsistencies relating to accounting principles and other matters. The companies with apparent inconsistent reporting problems and the facts involved are listed below:

Western Development Corporation, a subsidiary in the long-term construction industry, changed its method of accounting for long-term contracts from the completed-contract method to the percentage-of-completion method. The effect of the change is material to financial position and results of operations. Prior years' financial statements, presented for comparative purposes, have been restated, in conformity with APB Opinion No. 20, to give appropriate recognition to the change.

Seaboard, Inc., a retail store chain on the east coast, changed its method of pricing inventories from Fifo to Lifo at the beginning of the current year. The effect of the change is material, you concur in the change, and the change has been appropriately disclosed in Note X to the financial statements, including justification. Prior period statements were not restated.

Penn Manufacturing Company is a newly acquired subsidiary of Conglomerate Enterprises that has not been previously audited. Your firm will be performing the initial audit of Penn this year. Financial records in prior years have been maintained on the cash basis. Although Penn has adopted the accrual basis of accounting for the current year, it was not practicable to restate prior years on that basis.

Patten Industries and Mitchell Enterprises, two partially owned subsidiaries of Conglomerate Enterprises, were merged during the current year in a business combination (Patten and Mitchell, Inc.) accounted for, in accordance with APB Opinion No. 16, as a pooling of interests. In preparing financial statements for the minority stockholders, prior year's financial statements presented in comparison with the current year's statements are not restated to give appropriate recognition to the pooling.

Shenandoah Federal, a financial subsidiary, has changed during the current period from an accounting principle that is considered generally accepted to one that is not.

Blacksburg Coal Company has made a change in accounting principles during the current period without establishing preferability. APB Opinion No. 20, paragraph 16, states: "The presumption that an entity should not change an accounting principle may be overcome only if the enterprise justifies the use of an alternative acceptable accounting principle on the basis that it is preferable."

CASE DISCUSSION QUESTIONS

1. Answer the following questions regarding the accounting change made by Western Development Corporation:

    a. Assuming you concur with the change, what would be your reporting responsibility? Draft the opinion paragraph of your report.

    b. Assume that in the year following the change, the statements for the year of change will be presented, for comparative purposes, with those of the current period. Should the change in accounting principle be referred to in your report which, in conformity with SAS No. 2, covers both years?

2.   With respect to the change in accounting principles made by Seaboard, Inc.:

    a.   What would be your reporting responsibility in reporting only on the year of change? Draft the opinion paragraph of your report.

    b.   What would be your reporting responsibility, regarding the change, in subsequent years? Draft the opinion paragraph of your report.

3.   The application of the consistency standard to first examinations and the resulting reporting responsibility of the auditor depends on the circumstances. Discuss the CPA's reporting responsibility in the following situations:

    a.   Initial examination of a new company. The audit is for the first year of the client's operation.

    b.   Initial examination of a company that has been operating for several years. Adequate accrual basis accounting records have been maintained by the client in prior years.

    c.   Initial audit by your firm of a company that was audited previously by other CPAs. Adequate records have been maintained by the client in previous years.

    d.   Initial examination of a company that has been in business for some time, but not been audited previously. The client has not maintained adequate financial records in prior years.

    e.   What would be your reporting responsibility regarding the inconsistency in the Penn Manufacturing Company's financial statements? Draft the opinion paragraph of your report.

4.   With respect to the financial statements of Patten and Mitchell, Inc.:

    a.   What is your reporting responsibility regarding consistency?

    b.   Would your responsibility differ if single-year statements only were presented by Patten and Mitchell?

5.   Regarding the accounting change made by Shenandoah Federal:

    a.   What is your reporting responsibility in the current year (the year of change)?

    b.   What is your reporting responsibility regarding the change made by Shenandoah Federal in subsequent years?

6.   What is your reporting responsibility regarding the accounting change made by Blacksburg Coal Company (change made without proper justification)? Draft the opinion paragraph of your report.

Other Information in Documents Containing Audited Financial Statements

(Section 550, SAS No. 8, Section 551, SAS No. 29, Section 552, SAS No. 42, Section 553, SAS No. 27, Section 554, SAS No. 28, Section 555, SAS No. 33, and Section 556, SAS No. 40)

The AICPA Council has designated the Auditing Standards Board as the body to establish through statements on auditing standards the reporting responsibilities of CPAs with respect to standards for disclosure of financial information outside the basic financial statements. The AICPA recognizes the FASB as the body under Rule 204 to establish standards for the disclosure of such information.

With the issuance of SAS No. 29 (which replaced previous long-form reporting standards) and other previously issued statements, the auditor now has the responsibility to report on all information included with financial statements issued by him or her to clients or others. When the auditor's standard report is included in a client-prepared document and he or she has not been engaged to report on information accompanying the basic financial statements, the auditor's responsibility is limited to reading the other information and considering whether there are any material inconsistencies or misstatements with respect to the basic financial statements. The auditor's responsibility for reporting on additional information, other information, and supplementary information accompanying the basic financial statements is now established by the following:

SAS No. 8, *Other Information in Documents Containing Audited Financial Statements*

SAS No. 27, *Supplementary Information Required by the Financial Accounting Standards Board*

SAS No. 28, *Supplementary Information on the Effects of Changing Prices*

SAS No. 29, *Reporting on Information Accompanying the Basic Financial Statements in Auditor-Submitted Documents*

SAS No. 33, *Supplementary Oil and Gas Reserve Information*

SAS No. 40, *Supplementary Mineral Reserve Information*

SAS No. 42, *Reporting on Condensed Financial Statements and Selected Financial Data*

These SASs are covered in this section.

OTHER INFORMATION IN DOCUMENTS CONTAINING AUDITED FINANCIAL STATEMENTS

(Section 550, SAS No. 8)

An enterprise may present documents containing other information in addition to audited financial statements and the independent auditor's report thereon. SAS No. 8 provides guidance for the independent auditor concerning the information included in such documents. This statement applies only to other information presented in (1) annual reports to holders of securities or beneficial interests, annual reports of organizations for charitable or philanthropic purposes distributed to the public, and annual reports filed with regulatory authorities under the Securities Exchange Act of 1934 or (2) other documents examined by the auditor on behalf of the client. This statement does not apply to financial statements and reports included in a registration statement filed in accordance with the Securities Act of 1933.

SUPPLEMENTAL INFORMATION REQUIRED BY THE FASB

(Section 553, SAS No. 27)

SAS No. 27 provides guidance as to the procedures to be used in connection with supplementary information required by the FASB, and describes the circumstances that would require the auditor to report concerning such information. SAS No. 27 provides for exception reporting. The auditor must expand his or her report to call attention to the omission of supplementary information required by the FASB, material departures from FASB guidelines on measurement or presentation of such information, or his or her inability to complete procedures delineated by SAS No. 27.

SAS No. 27 is applicable only to audited statements and does not apply when the auditor has been engaged to audit the supplementary information. The statement, however, is applicable to supplementary information voluntarily included in financial statements unless the client indicates that the auditor has not applied the procedures prescribed by SAS No. 27 or the auditor expands his or her report to include a disclaimer on the supplementary information. In either case, provisions of SAS No. 8, *Other Information in Documents Containing Audited Financial Statements*, are applicable. Normally, this means that the auditor must read the other information and consider whether such information, or the manner of its presentation, is materially inconsistent with information, or the manner of its presentation, as presented in the audited financial statements. As a result of the auditor's consideration of the other information, as required by SAS No. 8, the financial statements, the auditor's report, or both, may require revision because of a material misstatement of fact or an inconsistency between the presentation of other information and the information presented in the financial statements. The auditor's responsibility for other information not required by the FASB as supplementary information, but included in certain annual reports (like a president's letter that provides an analysis of the year's results of operations), is also covered by SAS No. 8.

SAS No. 27 requires the auditor to apply certain limited procedures to supplementary information required by the FASB and report deficiencies in, or the omission of, such information (for example, the information on changing prices required for large companies by FASB Statement No. 33). The auditor is required to report on supplementary disclosures only when:

1.   The supplementary information required by the FASB is omitted,

2.   The auditor has concluded that the measurement or presentation of the supplementary information departs materially from guidelines prescribed by the FASB, or

3.   The auditor is unable to complete the prescribed procedures.

(SAS No. 29 amends SAS No. 27 to require a disclaimer of opinion on unaudited supplementary information required by the FASB that is presented outside the basic financial statements in an *auditor-submitted document*. An example of such a disclaimer is presented in SAS No. 29, covered later in the section).

When situations (1), (2), or (3) above exist, the auditor should expand his or her report on the basic financial statements to include an explanatory paragraph to describe the circumstances. However, since supplementary information does not change the standards of financial accounting and reporting in the basic statements, the auditor's opinion would not be affected by the omission of supplementary information or deficiencies in its presentation.

The following are examples of additional paragraphs that would be added to the auditor's report when supplementary information is omitted:

Omission of Supplementary Information Required by the FASB:

> The company has not presented (describe the supplementary information required by the FASB in the circumstances) that the Financial Accounting Standards Board has determined is necessary to supplement, although not required to be part of, the basic financial statements.

Prescribed Procedures not Completed:

> The (specifically identify the supplementary information) on page xx is not a required part of the basic financial statements, and we did not audit and do not express an opinion on such information. Further, we were unable to apply to the information certain procedures prescribed by professional standards because (state the reasons).

Even though an auditor is unable to complete the procedures prescribed by SAS No. 27, if he or she is aware that supplementary information has not been measured or presented within FASB guidelines, the auditor should suggest appropriate revision. If the information is not revised, he or she should describe the nature of any material departure(s) in the audit report.

Ordinarily supplementary information should be presented distinct from audited statements and separately identifiable from other information presented outside the financial statements that is not required by the FASB. However, if the information is not placed outside the audited financial statements, it should be clearly marked as unaudited or the auditor's report should be expanded to include a disclaimer on the information.

SUPPLEMENTARY INFORMATION ON THE EFFECTS OF CHANGING PRICES

SAS No. 28, which was issued as a supplement to SAS No. 27, identifies additional procedures that should be applied to changing price information provided in financial statements in accordance with FASB No. 33, *Financial Reporting and Changing Prices.*

FASB No. 33 requires certain large public companies to present information on the effects of changing prices (as supplementary information) along with their basic historical cost financial statements. The FASB encourages other companies to voluntarily present the information specified in FASB No. 33

SAS No. 28 is applicable in an examination in accordance with GAAS of financial statements of an entity that presents the FASB No. 33 disclosures, whether the entity is required to do so or voluntarily presents the information. The auditor should, accordingly, apply the procedures specified by SAS No. 27. In applying those procedures the auditor's inquiries should be directed to, among other things, the judgments made by management concerning measurement and presentation of the FASB No. 33 disclosures.

FASB No. 33 requires explanations of the information disclosed on changing prices and discussions of its significance in the circumstances of the entity. It also encourages providing additional information to help users understand the effects of changing prices on the activities of the entity. The auditor should read this information and compare such narrative explanations and discussions with the audited statements and related supplementary information on changing prices. If the auditor concludes, after discussing the matter with the client, that the narrative is materially inconsistent with either the audited statements or the other supplementary information, or contains a material misstatement of fact, he or she should expand the audit report to describe the nature of the inconsistency or misstatement (as indicated in SAS No. 27).

REPORTING ON INFORMATION ACCOMPANYING THE BASIC
FINANCIAL STATEMENTS IN AUDITOR-SUBMITTED DOCUMENTS

SAS No. 29 supersedes SAS No. 1, Section 610, *Long-Form Reports*, and provides guidance on reporting when the auditor submits to his or her client or others a document that contains information in addition to the client's basic financial statements and the auditor's report thereon.*

Basic financial statements are defined by SAS No. 29 as:

1.   Balance sheet, statement of income, statement of retained earnings or changes in stockholders' equity, and statement of changes in financial position, and

2.   Descriptions of accounting policies, notes to financial statements, and schedules and explanatory material that are identified as being part of the basic financial statements.

The concept of basic statements also includes the issuance of an individual financial statement, such as a balance sheet, resulting from a limited reporting engagement, and financial statements prepared in accordance with a comprehensive basis of accounting other than GAAP, such as the income tax or cash basis of accounting.

Information covered by SAS No. 29 is presented outside the basic financial statements and is not considered necessary for presentation of financial position, results of operations, or changes in financial position in accordance with GAAP. Such information includes additional details or explanations related to the basic statements, consolidating information, historical summaries, statistical data, etc.

Reporting Responsibility—Accompanying Information

The auditor's report on accompanying information must establish the degree of responsibility he or she is assuming regarding the information. Although the auditor may prepare the basic financial statements and the accompanying information, or assist the client in their preparation, the statements and accompanying information are the representations of the client. The following guidelines are applicable in reporting on accompanying information in auditor-submitted documents:

1.   The auditor's report should state that the examination was made for the purpose of forming an opinion on the basic financial statements taken as a whole.

2.   The auditor's report should identify accompanying information. Identification may be by descriptive title or page number of the document.

3.   The auditor's report should state that the accompanying information is presented for purposes of additional analysis and is not a required part of the basic financial statements. The auditor may refer to any regulatory agency requirements applicable to the information presented.

4.   The auditor should either express an opinion on whether the accompanying information is fairly stated in all material respects in relation to the basic statements taken as a whole or disclaim an opinion, depending on whether the information has been subjected to the auditing procedures applied in the examination of the basic financial statements. The auditor may express an opinion on a portion of the accompanying information and disclaim on the remainder.

5.   The auditor's report on the accompanying information may be added to his or her standard report on the basic statements or it may appear separately in the *auditor-submitted* document.

---

*SAS No.. 29 also supersedes the auditing interpretation on *Reports on Consolidated Financial Statements that Include Supplementary consolidating Information*, March 1979 (AU 9509.15-20). SAS No. 29 is appllicable when an auditor is engaged to report on consolidating or combining information.

When reporting in the manner described above, the auditor is not expressing an opinion on the accompanying information taken alone. His or her opinion applies to the financial statements and, accordingly, his or her measure of materiality regarding accompanying information is the same as that used in forming an opinion on the statements. Reporting on specified elements, accounts, or items of financial statements for the purpose of a separate presentation is covered by SAS No. 14, *Special Reports*.

If the auditor concludes, on the basis of facts known to him or her that accompanying information is materially misstated in relation to the basic statements taken as a whole, the auditor should discuss the matter with the client and propose appropriate revision of the information. Failing revision, the auditor should either modify his or her report on the accompanying information and describe the misstatement or refuse to include the information in the document.

When the auditor expresses a qualified opinion on the basic statements, he or she should make clear the effects, if any, on accompanying information. When the auditor expresses an adverse opinion or disclaims an opinion on the basic statements, he or she should not express an opinion on the accompanying information. An expression of an opinion in these circumstances would be considered a piecemeal opinion and may tend to overshadow or contradict the disclaimer or adverse on the basic statements.

An auditor, at the request of his or her client, may include certain nonaccounting information or accounting information not directly related to the basic statements in an *auditor-submitted* document. When such information ins included, the auditor should disclaim an opinion on it.

Reporting Examples—Accompanying Information

The auditor is faced with several different possibilities in which he or she may have to report on accompanying information. The following reporting formats are presented as examples in SAS No. 29.

1. *Expression of opinion on accompany information*—Our examination was made for the purpose of forming an opinion on the basic financial statements taken as a whole. The (identify accompanying information) is presented for purposes of additional analysis and is not a required part of the basic financial statements. Such information has been subjected to the auditing procedures applied in the examination of the basic financial statements and, in our opinion, is fairly stated in all material respects in relation to the basic financial statements taken as a whole.

2. *Disclaimer of opinion on accompanying information*—Our examination was made for the purpose of forming an opinion on the basic financial statements taken as a whole. The (identify accompanying information) is presented for purposes of additional analysis and is not a required part of the basic financial statements. Such information has not been subjected to the auditing procedures applied in the examination of the basic financial statements, and, accordingly, we express no opinion on it.

3. *Disclaimer of opinion on part of accompanying information*—Our examination was made for the purpose of forming an opinion on the basic financial statements taken as a whole. The information on pages xx-xx is presented for purposes of additional analysis and is not a required part of the basic financial statements. Such information, except for that portion marked "unaudited," on which we express no opinion, has been subjected to the auditing procedures applied in the examination of the basic financial statements; and, in our opinion, the information is fairly stated in all material respects in relation to the basic financial statements taken as a whole.

    When the CPA disclaims an opinion on all or part of the accompanying information, such information should either be marked as unaudited or should include a reference to the CPA's disclaimer.)

4. *Reporting on accompanying information to which a qualification in the auditor's report on the basic statements applies*—Our examination was made for the purpose of forming an opinion on the basic financial statements taken as a whole. The schedules of investments (page 7), property (page 8), and other assets (page 9) as of December 31, 19xx, are presented for purposes of additional analysis and are not a required part of the basic financial statements. The information in such schedules has been subjected to the auditing procedures applied in the examination of the basic financial statements; and, in our opinion, except for the effects on the schedule of investments of not accounting for the investments in certain companies by the equity method as explained in the second preceding paragraph (second paragraph of our report on page 1), such information is fairly stated in all material respects in relation to the basic financial statements taken as a whole.

An auditor may be requested to describe the procedures applied to specific items in the financial statements. Such additional comments should not contradict or detract from the description of the scope of his or her examination in the standard audit report. Also, they should be set forth separately rather than interspersed with the accompanying information.

Supplementary Information Required by FASB Pronouncements

SAS No. 29 amends SAS No. 27, *Supplementary Information Required by the Financial Accounting Standards Board*, to require explicit reporting when supplementary information required by the FASB is presented outside the basic financial statements in an *auditor-submitted* document. When such information has not been audited, a disclaimer is required. Following is an example:

> The (identify the supplementary information) on page xx is not a required part of the basic financial statements but is supplementary information required by the Financial Accounting Standards Board. We have applied certain limited procedures, which consisted principally of inquiries of management regarding the methods of measurement and presentation of the supplementary information. However, we did not audit the information and express no opinion on it.

Consolidating Information

Consolidated statements, or combined statements, may include consolidating, or combining information, or the presentation of separate financial statements of one or more components of the consolidated or combined group of companies. When the auditor is engaged to express an opinion on the consolidated, or combined, financial statements and consolidated or combining information or schedules are included in the report, the auditor should be satisfied that the consolidating or combining information is suitably identified. For example, when the consolidated statements include columns of information about the components of the consolidated group, the balance sheet might be titled "Consolidated Balance Sheet—December 31, 19x1, with Consolidating Information," and the columns including the consolidating information might be marked, "Consolidating Information." When the consolidating information is presented in separate schedules, the schedules presenting balance sheet information might be titled "Consolidating Schedule, Balance Sheet Information, December 31, 19x1." Following is an example of the auditor's report on consolidated statements that include consolidating information that has not been separately audited:

> Our examination was made for the purpose of forming an opinion on the consolidated financial statements taken as a whole. The consolidating information is presented for purposes of additional analysis of the consolidated financial statements rather than to present the financial position, results of operations, and changes in financial position of the individual companies. The consolidating information has been subjected to the auditing procedures applied in the examination of the consolidated financial statements and, in our opinion, is fairly stated in all material respects in relation to the consolidated financial statements taken as a whole.

Co-Existing Financial Statements

Co-existing financial statements may result from an auditor's report on financial statements and accompanying information. For example, the client may submit only the basic financial statements (omitting accompanying information) and the auditor's report to various financial statement users. When this occurs, the basic statements should include all the information considered necessary for presentation in conformity with GAAP in all co-existing documents.

REPORTING ON CONDENSED FINANCIAL STATEMENTS AND SELECTED FINANCIAL DATA

(Section 552, SAS No. 42)

SAS No. 42 addresses auditors' reports on condensed financial statements and selected financial data in client-prepared documents. SAS No. 42 covers (a) condensed financial statements that are prepared from audited financial statements of a public entity that is required to file complete audited financial statements with a regulatory agency; (b) selected financial data that are prepared from audited financial statements of either a public or a nonpublic entity and that are included in a document with audited financial statements; and (c) selected financial data that are prepared from audited financial statements of a public entity that makes reference to audited financial statements filed with a regulatory agency.

Guidance on reporting on condensed financial statements or selected financial data that accompany audited financial statements in *an auditor-submitted document* is provided in Section 551 (SAS No. 29), *Reporting on Information Accompanying the Basic Financial Statements in Auditor-Submitted Documents.*

CONDENSED FINANCIAL STATEMENTS

An auditor is not required to report on condensed financial statements if they are included in a document with audited financial statements or if a reference is made to audited financial statements filed with a regulatory agency. A client may engage an auditor to report on condensed financial statements that are prepared from audited financial statements.

Condensed financial statements are less detailed than complete financial statements. This lack of detailed information prevents a fair presentation of financial position, results of operations, and changes in financial position in conformity with generally accepted accounting principles. Two steps should be taken to eliminate the possibility of mistaking condensed financial statements for complete financial statements. First, the user should read condensed financial statements in conjunction with the entity's most recent complete financial statements. Second, the auditor should issue a report for condensed financial statements that highlights their limitations.

The auditor's report on condensed financial statements that are prepared from financial statements that he or she has audited should include the following four items:

1.   A statement that the auditor has examined and expressed an opinion on the complete financial statements.

2.   The date of the auditor's report on the complete financial statements.

3.   The type of opinion expressed on the complete financial statements. If the auditor's opinion on the complete financial statements was other than unqualified, the report should specify the nature of, and the reasons for, the qualifications. Also, if the auditor's opinion on the complete financial statements referred to another auditor, the report on the condensed financial statements should indicate that fact. However, no reference to consistency is required if a change in accounting referred to in the auditor's report on the complete financial statements does not affect the comparability of the information being presented. The auditor should consider the effect that any modification of the opinion on the complete financial statements might have on the opinion on the condensed financial statements or selected financial data.

4.   The auditor's opinion on whether the information in the condensed financial statements is fairly stated in all material respects in relation to the complete financial statements from which it has been prepared.

Following is an example of an auditor's report on condensed financial statements that are prepared from complete financial statements on which the auditor has expressed an unqualified opinion:

> We have examined, in accordance with generally accepted auditing standards, the balance sheet of X Company as of December 31, 19x0, and the related statements of income, retained earnings, and changes in financial position for the year then ended (not presented herein); and in our report dated February 15, 19x1, we expressed an unqualified opinion on those financial statements. In our opinion, the information set forth in the accompanying financial statements is fairly stated in all material respects in relation to the financial statements from which it has been derived.

If a client-prepared document of a public entity, names the auditor and states that condensed financial statements are prepared from audited financial statements when the document does not contain audited financial statements or a reference to audited financial statements filed with a regulatory agency, the auditor should request that the client either delete the auditor's name from the document or include the auditor's report on condensed financial statements.

If the client will not agree to the auditor's request, it may be appropriate for the auditor to consult his or her legal counsel for guidance as to an appropriate course of action.

If such a statement is made in a client-prepared document that excludes the audited financial statements and the client is a nonpublic entity that is required to file complete audited statements with a regulatory agency, at least annually, the CPA would normally express an adverse opinion on the condensed financial statements due to inadequate disclosure (see Section 509.17). The following is an example of an acceptable report on condensed financial statements when the auditor has previously examined and reported on the complete financial statements:

> We have examined the consolidated balance sheet of X Company and subsidiaries as of December 31, 19x0, and the related consolidated statements of income, retained earnings, and changes in financial position for the year then ended (not presented herein). Our examination was made in accordance with generally accepted auditing standards and, accordingly, included such tests of the accounting records and such other auditing procedures as we considered necessary in the circumstances.
>
> The condensed consolidated balance sheet as of December 31, 19x0, and the related condensed consolidated statements of income, retained earnings, and changes in financial position for the year then ended, presented on pages xx-xx, are presented as a summary and therefore do not include all of the disclosures required by generally accepted accounting principles.
>
> In our opinion, because of the significance of the omission of the information referred to in the preceding paragraph, the condensed consolidated financial statements referred to above do not present fairly, in conformity with generally accepted accounting principles, the financial position of X Company and subsidiaries as of December 31, 19x0, or the results of their operations and changes in their financial position for the year then ended.

SELECTED FINANCIAL DATA

An auditor may only report on selected financial data that are prepared from audited financial statements. A comprehensive five-year summary of selected financial data for Schering-Plough Corporation is presented in Figure 1.

Figure 1.

Schering-Plough Corporation (Dollars in millions, except per share figures)	**Five-Year Selected Financial and Statistical Data**				
	1981	1980	1979	1978	1977
Operations					
Sales	**$1,808.8**	$1,738.8	$1,432.6	$1,080.7	$939.8
Operating income	**256.5**	302.4	284.2	248.6	230.3
Income before income taxes	**245.6**	324.8	306.1	270.1	239.6
Net income	**179.3**	237.1	220.4	191.8	165.2
Net income per common share	**3.31**	4.41	4.08	3.58	3.05
Dividends per common share	**1.66**	1.56	1.39	1.21	1.09
Dividends on common shares	**88.3**	82.8	74.3	64.8	59.0
Average number of common shares outstanding (in millions)	**53.2**	53.1	53.4	53.5	54.1
Balance Sheet					
Working capital	**$ 720.5**	$ 561.9	$ 514.2	$ 481.8	$ 381.8
Current ratio	**2.1**	1.9	2.1	2.8	2.6
Property, net	**$ 654.6**	$ 524.8	$ 415.4	$ 319.6	$ 295.3
Total assets	**2,285.5**	1,978.6	1,588.2	1,192.9	1,063.7
Long-term debt	**241.8**	41.2	7.6	1.6	.2
Redeemable preferred shares	**39.4**	39.4	39.4	—	—
Common shareholders' equity	**1,285.8**	1,196.3	1,042.4	908.4	804.7
Net book value per common share	**24.18**	22.52	19.65	17.05	14.88
Financial Statistics					
Operating income as a percent of sales	**14.2%**	17.4%	19.8%	23.0%	24.5%
Net income as a percent of sales	**9.9%**	13.6%	15.4%	17.7%	17.6%
Return on common shareholders' equity	**14.2%**	20.9%	22.3%	22.4%	22.0%
Effective tax rate	**27.0%**	27.0%	28.0%	29.0%	31.0%
Other Data					
Research and development	**$109.1**	$ 90.0	$74.8	$65.7	$58.6
Property additions	**170.3**	130.9	68.3	51.3	51.6
Annual depreciation	**43.1**	36.0	29.7	24.7	22.8
Number of employees	**27,000**	27,400	25,900	17,900	17,100

Effective for 1980 financial statements, the Company adopted the LIFO method of inventory valuation for substantially all domestic inventories.
Years prior to 1981 have been restated for the changes in methods of accounting for compensated absences and sales returns.

Source: Principles & Presentation, A Reivew of 1981 Annual Reports, Cosmetics, Peat, Marwick, Mitchell & Co., New York, N.Y.

If data prepared from audited financial statements and other information (such as number of employees) are both included in the selected financial data, the auditor should specifically identify the data on which he or she is reporting. If any of the selected financial data for the years presented are prepared from financial statements audited by another independent auditor, the auditor's report should state that fact, and the auditor should not express an opinion on that data.

The auditor's report on selected financial data that are prepared from financial statements that he or she has audited should include the following three items:

1.   A statement that the auditor has examined and expressed an opinion on the complete financial statements.

2.   The type of opinion expressed on the complete financial statements.

3.   The auditor's opinion on whether the information in the selected financial data is fairly stated in all material respects in relation to the complete financial statements from which it has been prepared.

If a client-prepared document names the auditor and states that selected financial data are prepared from audited financial statements when the document does not contain audited financial statements or a reference to audited financial statements filed with a regulatory agency, the auditor should request that the client either delete the auditor's name from the document or include a disclaimer of opinion on the selected financial data.

SAS No. 42 suggests the following auditor's report when the auditor is reporting on selected financial data that is included in a client-prepared document that includes audited financial statements.

> We have examined the consolidated balance sheets of ABC Company and subsidiaries as of December 31, 19x5, and 19x4, and the related consolidated statements of income, retained earnings, and changes in financial position for each of the three years in the period ended December 31, 19x5. Our examinations were made in accordance with generally accepted auditing standards and, accordingly, included such tests of the accounting records and such other auditing procedures as we considered necessary in the circumstances.
>
> In our opinion, the consolidated financial statements referred to above present fairly the financial position of the ABC Company and subsidiaries as of December 31, 19x5 and 19x4, and the results of their operations and the changes in their financial position for each of the three years in the period ended December 31, 19x5, in conformity with generally accepted accounting principles applied on a consistent basis.
>
> We have also previously examined, in accordance with generally accepted auditing standards, the consolidated balance sheets as of December 31, 19x3, 19x2, and 19x1, and the related consolidated statements of income, retained earnings, and changes in financial position for the years ended December 31, 19x2 and 19x1 (none of which are presented herein); and we expressed unqualified opinions on those consolidated financial statements. In our opinion, the information set forth in the selected financial data for each of the five years in the period ended December 31, 19x5, appearing on page xx, is fairly stated in all material respects in relation to the consolidated financial statements from which it has been derived.

The above report is for selected financial data covering a five-year period. In many cases, the auditor may be reporting on selected financial data covering a period, such as ten years. Under those circumstances, the auditor would revise his or her report to reflect the ten-year period reported on.

SAS No. 42 allows the client to name the auditor and present selected financial data taken from financial statements examined by the auditor and not require the auditor to report on the selected financial data. That is, providing that such data are presented in a document that contains audited financial statements (or, with respect to a public entity, that incorporates such statements by reference to information filed with a regulatory agency). If a client-prepared document names the auditor that does not include (or incorporate by reference) audited financial statements, the CPA should request that neither his or her name nor reference to him or her be associated with the information, or the CPA should disclaim an opinion on the selected financial data and request that a disclaimer be included in the document. If the client will not conform to the auditor's request, he or she should notify the client that he or she does not consent to either the use of his or her name or the reference to him or her and consider legal action, if appropriate.

SUPPLEMENTARY OIL AND GAS RESERVE INFORMATION

(Section 555, SAS No. 33)

FASB No. 19, *Financial Accounting and Reporting by Oil and Gas Producing Companies*, requires an entity engaged in oil and gas producing activities to include in a complete set of annual financial statements disclosure of oil and gas reserve quantities and changes in reserve quantities. FASB No. 25, *Suspension of Certain Accounting Requirements for Oil and Gas Producing Companies*, permits the disclosure of such reserve quantities to be made as supplementary information accompanying, but outside, the basic financial statements. The SEC, through Regulation S-X, requires that in addition to reserve quantities and changes therein, the disclosure of oil and gas reserve information should include the estimated future net revenues from proved oil and gas reserves, the present value of such net revenues and changes therein, and a summary of oil and gas activities prepared on the basis of reserve recognition accounting. These disclosures may be made as supplementary information outside the basic statements. The provisions of both SAS No. 27 and SAS No. 33 apply to these disclosures.

SAS No. 33 states that, in applying the procedures specified in SAS No. 27, the auditor's inquiries should be directed to management's understanding of the specific requirements for disclosure of the supplementary oil and gas reserve information.

SUPPLEMENTARY MINERAL RESERVE INFORMATION*

(Section 556, SAS No. 40)

Section 556 applies Section 553, Supplementary Information Required by the Financial Accounting Standards Board, to mineral reserve information. FASB Statement No. 39, *Financial Reporting and Changing Prices: Specialized Assets - Mining and Oil and Gas*, requires disclosure of quantity and price information for certain sized entities with mineral reserves other than oil and gas. The availability, completeness and accuracy of data, combined with the experience and judgment of a specialist determine the quality of the estimate of proved, or proved and probable, reserves for a particular ore body.

The auditor should inquire about management's understanding of the following supplementary mineral reserve information disclosures:

1. Estimated quantities of proved, or proved and probable, mineral reserves, whichever is used for cost amortization.

2. Estimated quantities, in physical units or in percentages of ore reserves, of significant mineral products in mineral reserves.

3. Quantities of each significant mineral product extracted and quantities of significant mineral product produced by milling or like process.

4. Quantity of mineral reserves bought or sold in place during the year.

5. Average market price for each significant mineral product.

Also, the auditor should inquire about factors considered in determining the reserve quantity information, such as reserves attributed to consolidated subsidiaries and proportionate share of reserves of proportionately consolidated investees. Finally, the auditor should inquire about the separate disclosure of the entity's proportionate interest in reserves of investees accounted for by the equity method.

---

*This section was written by Joann O'Brien, CPA and Graduate Student, Creighton University.

Following is a list of the auditor's procedures:

1.   Ask who estimated the reserve quantity information—mining engineer, geologist, or other specialist.

2.   Ask if methods and bases for estimating reserve information are documented and reviewed on a current basis.

3.   Compare recent production with reserve estimates of significant properties.

4.   Compare reserve quantity information with depletion and amortization.

5.   Compare production information with corresponding information used to prepare financial statements.

6.   Compare mineral reserves bought or sold in place with corresponding information used to prepare financial statements.

7.   Ask about method and bases used to calculate market price information and compare to sales prices or published mineral prices.

8.   Investigate any significant differences noted during comparisons.

The auditor should make further inquiries if he or she believes that any information is not properly presented. Due to the nature of estimates of mineral reserve information, the auditor may be unable to evaluate the additional responses. In this case, the auditor should report the limitation on the procedures prescribed by professional standards.

CASE 28

AUDITOR'S RESPONSIBILITY FOR OTHER INFORMATION

Your firm, Rose and Kite, CPAs, is conducting an audit of the financial statements of Carlson, Inc., for the year ending December 31, 19x2. The chairman of the board has provided you with a draft of the annual report to the stockholders containing the following information, in addition to the audited financial statements.

1.   Financial highlights for the years 19x1 and 19x2.

2.   Market price range of Carlson's common stock.

3.   Location of facilities.

4.   Chairman's message which includes a statement on how successful the company has been in terms of both financial and management performance. A statement that the firm's earnings reached a record level for the tenth consecutive year and information as to the capital expenditures made in 19x2.

5.   Operating considerations such as new facilities, participation in the federal government's voluntary energy program as well as environmental protection standards.

6.   Financial review for the last five years.

7.   Management's discussion and analysis of operations.

8.   Five-year summary of operations.

CASE DISCUSSION QUESTIONS

1. Does SAS No. 8 apply to the other information, outlined above, that Carlson, Inc., plans to include in their annual report?

2. What affect, if any, does SAS No. 8 have on a registration statement filed by Carlson under the Securities Act of 1933 (the corporation has included its financial statements and report in the registration statement)?

3. Other information contained in a document such as that included by Carlson in its annual report may be relevant to the CPA's examination or to the continuing propriety of the audit report.

    a. What responsibility, if any, does Rose and Kite have concerning information appearing in such a document?

    b. What course of action should Rose and Kite take if other information or the way it is presented, is materially inconsistent with the presentation of such information (the information itself or its manner of presentation) appearing in the financial statements? Include in your answer a discussion of Rose and Kite's obligation, if any, to perform procedures to corroborate other information contained in such documents as an annual report.

    c. Should Rose and Kite revise their report, the financial statements, or both? Explain in detail.

4. If Rose and Kite are not required to perform procedures to corroborate other information such as that presented in Carlson's annual report, what procedures should they perform concerning such information?

CASE 29*

REPORTING ON OTHER INFORMATION IN DOCUMENTS CONTAINING AUDITED FINANCIAL STATEMENTS

Deloitte Haskins & Sells audited the statements of consolidated financial position of Union Pacific Corporation and subsidiary companies as of December 31, 1981, 1980, and 1979 and the related statements of consolidated income, consolidated changes in stockholders' equity, and consolidated changes in financial position for the years then ended.

Deloitte Haskins & Sells (DH&S') audit report stated that their examination was made in accordance with GAAS and that Union Pacific Corporation and subsidiary companies' financial statements conform to GAAP.

Union Pacific Corporation's (UPC's) annual report includes financial highlights, report on operations, a financial review, supplementary information, ten-year summary, and a letter to the stockholders.

Included below is the letter to the stockholders, selected supplementary information and selected financial information.

---

*Adapted from the Union Pacific Corporation's 1981 Annual Report.

To Our Stockholders

Union Pacific Corporation achieved a new high in earnings in 1981 despite the deepening recession, a profit squeeze in refining, and declining rail traffic. The year was highlighted by significant growth in exploration and production income accompanied by our fourth consecutive annual gain in liquid hydrocarbon and natural gas reserves.

Net income in 1981 was $410.7 million, up 2 percent over 1980 earnings of $404.5 million. Earnings per share were $4.27 compared to $4.22 in 1980. For the third consecutive year, the corporation's energy and natural resource businesses accounted for more than half of its total earnings, contributing 60 percent to Union Pacific's 1981 net income. Revenues reached $6.38 billion, up 31 percent over 1980 revenues of $4.87 billion.

Three of our four operating companies reported 1981 earnings ahead of 1980. Although Union Pacific Railroad experienced a marked slowdown in traffic in the latter part of the year, it posted a 1 percent gain in net income to $167.1 million. Strong coal shipments, stringent cost control programs and freight rate increases offset a decline in consumer-related traffic and the first falloff in grain shipments since 1977.

Champlin Petroleum's net income declined 16 percent to $160.1 million because of a severe cost/price squeeze on refinery margins. However, it is significant to note that Champlin achieved a 40 percent gain in exploration and production operating income,

spurred by the sixth consecutive year of higher production of hydrocarbons. And for the fourth year in a row, Champlin increased proved reserves of liquid hydrocarbons—10 percent to 142 million barrels; and natural gas—14 percent to 2 trillion cubic feet.

Rocky Mountain Energy's earnings climbed 20 percent to $60.0 million through increased joint-venture coal production and higher prices for coal and natural soda ash.

Upland Industries' net income of $28.2 million, up 91 percent, stemmed largely from major land sales in western states. A detailed discussion of our operating companies' activities starts on page 6.

On November 19, the Board of Directors increased the quarterly dividend 12.5 percent, from 40 to 45 cents. This represented the ninth consecutive year the dividend has been raised and reflects the corporation's confidence in its future prospects, a confidence based to a large extent on the inventory of resources and capabilities described on pages 2 and 3.

To continue the development of these assets, in December we budgeted a record $1.3 billion for capital investments in 1982, with over $1 billion assigned to petroleum operations. The Railroad will have record outlays for roadway improvements, Rocky Mountain Energy will launch a new coal mine in 1982, and Upland Industries will open up or expand five industrial parks.

Merger Developments

Hearings before the Interstate Commerce Commission for authority to acquire the Missouri Pacific and Western Pacific Railroads were completed in early January, 1982. Legal briefs are due to be filed this spring, and we expect a decision by the Commission this fall.

Our applications have received broad-based support from shippers, state governments and the U.S. Department of Transportation. Preliminary comments and testimony by the Department of Justice have not identified significant competitive problems, and we are optimistic that the Commission will approve our applications.

If approved, the new system would provide single-system service linking Los Angeles, Oakland, Portland, Seattle, Spokane and Salt Lake City with the eastern gateways of St. Louis and Memphis, and such major Gulf ports as New Orleans, Houston and Galveston. This would be an important competitive feature, since economic deregulation stemming from the Staggers Rail Act places a greater premium on independent pricing and a flexible marketing strategy.

Energy Developments

During the year, the nation continued to make substantial progress toward developing a sound energy policy. In January, 1981, domestic crude oil prices were fully decontrolled, accelerating a process in which oil was being decontrolled more slowly over a 28 month period.

This action helped keep exploratory drilling at record levels for the second year in a row. Again it was demonstrated that producers will take on the substantial risks involved in searching for hydrocarbons if domestic crude oil is allowed to sell at world-market prices. Nearly 79,000 exploration and development wells were drilled by the industry last year, a 68 percent increase over 1978 when virtually all domestic crude oil was still subject to price controls and was selling well below world-market prices.

And, after several years in which the leasing of Federal lands for oil and gas exploration had been restricted, the Department of Interior moved expeditiously to open up lands to determine the existence of hydrocarbons and other minerals. Of special note, seven offshore sales were held during 1981, resulting in the leasing of 2.2 million acres.

Although the Administration has clearly formed a more cohesive energy policy, other energy issues need to be addressed.

In 1978 Congress passed the Natural Gas Policy Act, which provides for the phased decontrol of most categories of natural gas by 1985. Nevertheless, about one-third of the nation's natural gas will still be subject to price controls after 1985. Thus, if left unchanged, the law will leave the nation with a two-tiered pricing system that will inevitably produce awkward and uneconomic approaches to the development of natural gas reserves, just as the existing system of price controls has. Last fall an interagency cabinet-level task force recommended the total decontrol of natural gas prices. We strongly believe this proposal should be adopted.

Decontrol of natural gas prices should, however, be accompanied by the termination of the market use restraints on natural gas imposed by the Industrial Fuel Use Act of 1978. This law—which was intended to limit, and eventually terminate, the use of natural gas as a boiler fuel for utilities—has so far proven to be both unworkable and impractical. Market forces provide a far better way to determine fuel use.

Congress also is reviewing the Clean Air Act, which has affected coal consumption by requiring that all newly built, coal-fired utilities use "scrubbers," very costly emissions control devices, to achieve a percentage reduction in the amount of sulfur dioxide emitted in flue gases. The same emissions level can be achieved more cheaply by burning low-sulfur coal and by using other relatively inexpensive methods to treat coal before burning. The Reagan Administration has advocated that industry be given greater latitude as long as a single, uniform sulfur dioxide limit is met. We strongly endorse this approach, which will have the effect of encouraging construction of new, cleaner power plants.

Management and Board Changes

John R. Meyer, professor of transportation, logistics and distribution at the Harvard Graduate School of Business Administration, and a director of Union Pacific Corporation since 1978, was elected vice chairman of the Board, effective January 1, 1982. Mr. Meyer will develop an economics staff and assist the Chairman and President in the general management of the corporation.

We also are pleased to welcome as a member of the corporation's Board of Directors, Richard D. Simmons, president, The Washington Post Company, who was elected to the Board on January 28, 1982. Before joining The Washington Post Company in 1981, Mr. Simmons was vice chairman of The Dun & Bradstreet Corporation.

George S. Eccles, chairman and chief executive officer of the First Security Corporation, who retired as a director on April 17, 1981, after 33 years of service to the corporation, died on January 20, 1982. His long and distinguished financial career included service as a member of the International Monetary Commission and as a consultant to the Marshall Plan. His counsel to senior management was an invaluable cornerstone in the formation and growth of the modern Union Pacific Corporation.

Courtney C. Brown, dean emeritus of The Columbia University Business School, also retired as a director on April 17 after a quarter century of service. Dean Brown served the State Department, the Commodity Credit Corporation and the War Production Board with great distinction, and, at Union Pacific, his wisdom, insight and keen judgment will long be remembered.

Outlook

The nation has entered a recession of uncertain length, but most economists expect the economy to pick up by the middle of the year. Inflation has abated, and the Administration's economic programs should contribute to increasing the tempo of business activity as the year unfolds. Because of these factors, we believe the corporation will achieve improved earnings in 1982, although we expect the recession will cause us to get off to a slow start in the early months of the year.

A healthier economy should stimulate the Railroad's traffic later in the year. Champlin's refineries were profitable during the second half of 1981, and the company anticipates another strong year in 1982 in exploration and production, with increasing output of crude oil, plant liquids and natural gas. Champlin's outlook is further enhanced by its strengthening oil and gas reserves. As the recession eases, Rocky Mountain Energy anticipates increased sales of coal and natural soda ash. And Upland expects an improved climate for industrial real estate sales should interest rates decline.

On behalf of the Board of Directors, we thank our stockholders, customers, dealers, suppliers and our 32,000 employees for their loyalty and help in enabling the corporation to surmount the problems and challenges of a difficult year and thereby contribute to the building of an even stronger Union Pacific.

James H. Evans
Chairman

William S. Cook
President

Elbridge T. Gerry
Chairman of the
Executive Committee

February 9, 1982
New York, New York

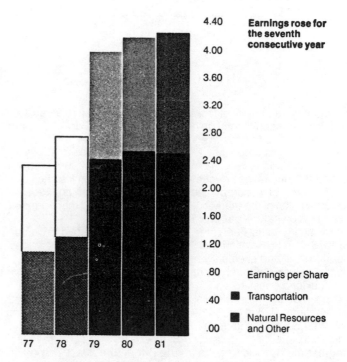

Earnings rose for the seventh consecutive year

Earnings per Share
- ■ Transportation
- ■ Natural Resources and Other

77 78 79 80 81

Financial Review

This review discusses principal reasons for changes in results of operations and sources and uses of funds. The review should be read in conjunction with the financial statements and their notes and related supplementary information.

Consolidated Results of Operations
1981 Compared to 1980

Consolidated earnings advanced to $410.7 million in 1981 from $404.5 million in 1980. Although the economic downturn which characterized much of 1980 recurred in 1981, earnings increased for three of the Corporation's four business segments. Transportation earnings of $167.1 million in 1981 were slightly ahead of the $165.1 million earned in 1980 as strong coal shipments, cost control measures and rate increases offset the effects of recession-induced traffic declines and an unexpected reduction in grain traffic during the last half of 1981. Oil and gas earnings were $160.1 million, down 16 percent from $191.0 million in 1980. Record exploration and production operating income in 1981, reflecting strong gains in production volumes and full decontrol of domestic crude oil prices, was offset by a loss for the manufacturing, marketing and petrochemical business as a result of higher crude oil and feedstock costs together with soft product prices. Mining earnings rose $9.8 million to $60.0 million with higher volumes and improved prices for coal and soda ash contributing to this advance; income from uranium operations declined from 1980 as a result of continued supply/demand imbalance in U.S. markets. Earnings from land operations almost doubled to $28.2 million as a result of several major land sales. A discussion of results by segment is included in commentary under separate operating company sections.

Return on average stockholders' equity was 13.9 percent for 1981 compared to 15.0 percent for 1980. Revenues rose to $6.4 billion in 1981 from $4.9 billion in 1980 and net income as a percent of revenues for 1981 was 6.4 percent compared with 8.3 percent for 1980.

1980 Compared to 1979

Consolidated earnings advanced to $404.5 million in 1980 from $382.5 million in 1979, despite the economic slowdown which began in early 1980. While freight rates and bulk commodity shipments improved during 1980, the effects of the economic slowdown together with certain inflationary costs held the increase in transportation earnings to $14.4 million. Oil and gas earnings advanced by $8.9 million, as significantly improved revenues resulting from the phased decontrol of domestic crude oil prices and increased production of liquid hydrocarbons and natural gas

more than offset depressed refinery margins. Mining earnings rose by $13.0 million, or 35 percent, due principally to higher volumes and improved prices for coal and soda ash; 1980 earnings include a full year's production from a joint-venture coal mine that commenced operations in 1979, production from another mine that reached commercial production late in 1980 and a write-off relating to uneconomic mineral resource assets. Earnings from land operations declined by $3.7 million from 1979 which included two major sales in Southern California.

Return on average stockholders' equity was 15.0 percent for 1980 compared to 15.8 percent for 1979. Net income as a percent of revenues for 1980 was 8.3 percent compared with 9.5 percent for 1979.

Revenues

Consolidated revenues rose $843.6 million or 21 percent to $4.9 billion in 1980. Oil and gas sales advanced $542.2 million primarily because of improved prices for crude oil and refined products. Transportation revenues increased $267.9 million principally as a result of improved freight rates. Revenue ton-miles increased 7 percent in 1980 due to substantial growth in the two largest traffic categories, coal and grain, while a recession adversely affected traffic levels for motor vehicles, forest products and a wide range of other products.

Costs and Expenses

Consolidated expenses advanced $821.6 million in 1980. Rising prices increased refinery crude oil and feedstock costs by $296.3 million, railroad fuel costs by $89.4 million and refinery utility costs by $65.3 million.

Expanded oil and gas exploration activities caused a $47.9 million increase in depreciation and related costs, while the new Windfall Profit Tax added $36.7 million to oil and gas expenses. Transportation salaries and benefits climbed $46.2 million and materials and supplies were up $39.7 million, due primarily to the effects of inflation.

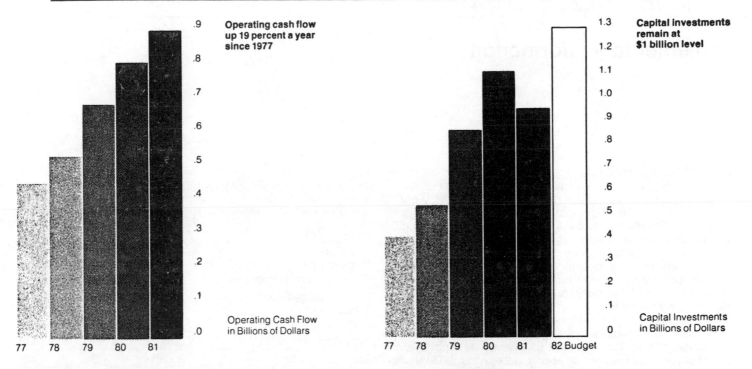

**Operating cash flow
up 19 percent a year
since 1977**

Operating Cash Flow
in Billions of Dollars

77   78   79   80   81

**Capital investments
remain at
$1 billion level**

Capital Investments
in Billions of Dollars

77   78   79   80   81   82 Budget

Funds Flow and Liquidity
The Past Five Years

The primary source of funds for the Corporation during this period was operating cash flow which provided $3.4 billion. These funds increased in each year to $895.5 million in 1981, growing at a compound rate of 19 percent since 1977. This consistent performance reflects the Corporation's ongoing commitment to capital investment programs designed to expand, modernize and maintain the productive capacity of its businesses.

Capital investments during the past five years were $3.9 billion and represented the single largest use of funds. Since 1977 these investments advanced at a compound rate of 23 percent to $954.1 million in 1981. Dividends amounted to $596.6 million during this period, increasing in each year and nearly doubling since 1977.

Funds required in excess of operating cash flow have been obtained mostly from outside financings. At December 31, 1981, debt due after one year was $1.7 billion, compared to $784.2 million at year-end 1976. The ratio of debt to total capitalization at year-end 1981 of 29.9 percent has remained within acceptable levels in view of the capital-intensive nature of the Corporation's businesses.

At year-end 1981, the Corporation had short-term and long-term credit facilities with various banks totaling $300 million and $460 million, respectively. These facilities supported commercial paper outstanding of $420 million.

1981 and 1980

During 1981, the Corporation expended $954.1 million on capital investment programs and declared dividends of $158.8 million. Operating cash flow aggregated $895.5 million, increasing 12 percent over 1980, enhanced by benefits associated with the Economic Recovery Tax Act. This cash flow was 94 percent of funds required for capital investments and 80 percent of requirements for investments and dividends combined. Debt due after one year increased by $376.0 million in 1981, compared to a $451.7 million increase in 1980. Commercial paper was a significant source of financing in 1981, augmented by a foreign-denominated borrowing and issuance of several tax-exempt debt securities.

In 1980, capital investments were $1.1 billion and dividends were $139.0 million. Operating cash flow was $801.2 million, or 71 percent of capital investments and 63 percent for total investments and dividends. Long-term debt financing during 1980 included $250 million of 30-year debentures which were rated "AA" and a note placement aggregating $150 million.

Capital Investments

Capital investments in 1981 were slightly below the record 1980 investments of $1.1 billion; direct capital expenditures totaled $902.6 million in 1981 compared with $965.6 million in 1980. Champlin invested $744.4 million in 1981, a 16 percent increase over 1980, including $498.8 million for acreage acquisition, exploration and development projects and $233.1 million for expansion and modernization at the Wilmington and Corpus Christi refineries. In 1980, Champlin invested $379.1 million for lease acquisition, exploration and development programs and $168.0 million for its refineries. Railroad expenditures for roadway and structures were $86.9 million in 1981 and $96.7 million in 1980. Equipment acquisitions of $47.5 million in 1981 were $240.9 million below 1980 expenditures, reflecting the return of 76 locomotives and 2,509 cars from the Rock Island Railroad and the acquisition in 1980 of 80 locomotives originally scheduled for delivery in 1981. Mining investments in 1981 were $56.4 million, including $27.0 million for development of coal properties and $19.3 million for expansion of soda ash capacity.

In December, the Corporation budgeted its 1982 capital investment program at a record $1.3 billion. Planned oil and gas investments of $1.0 billion include $628 million for lease acquisitions, exploration and development projects and natural gas processing plants as well as $371 million, primarily for modernization of the Wilmington and Corpus Christi refineries. Approximately $240 million is planned beyond 1982, essentially for refinery projects and development projects. The Railroad's budget of $163 million includes $128 million for roadway programs. Equipment acquisitions of $35 million are below traditional levels, reflecting the Railroad's equipment purchases and other additions over the past two years and the current traffic slow-down. Mining investments of $63 million include $25 million for the development of coal properties, including the first wholly-owned surface coal mine, and $20 million for the Corporation's share of energy conservation and pollution control projects of its trona affiliate. Land expenditures are budgeted at $25 million.

The Corporation intends to finance these capital investments primarily with internally generated funds with the balance from short- and long-term borrowings as appropriate.

Supplementary Information

Measuring Inflationary Impacts

There is general consensus that traditional accounting disclosures based on historical cost do not appropriately portray, particularly for capital-intensive companies such as Union Pacific, the cost of doing business and the capital required to maintain existing productive capacity in times of severe inflation. In response to this concern, the following experimental disclosures of certain financial information, adjusted for changes in the general price level (constant dollar data) and for changes in specific price levels (current cost data), are intended to supplement the traditional financial statements.

The constant dollar data presented measure selected financial information in terms of dollars having equivalent purchasing power. Under this approach properties, inventories, depreciation and cost of sales are restated by applying the average Consumer Price Index for all Urban Consumers (CPI-U) for 1981.

The current cost data presented reflect the same information measured in terms of specific price changes, which are influenced by technological improvements and by other supply and demand factors, as well as by changes in the general purchasing power of the dollar. The objective is to measure the estimated effects of inflation in terms of today's costs for inventories and productive capacity used in operations.

Current costs for properties were obtained from various sources. Those for road property of the Railroad were derived by using industry indexes and internal engineering estimates. Railroad equipment costs were developed from recent purchase prices and quotations. Oil and gas exploration and producing properties were adjusted by applying industry indexes and internally-developed unit prices derived from recent costs. Refineries and gas plants were restated by using industry indexes. The remaining properties were adjusted by using similar methods.

The traditional rate-regulated environment for the railroad industry has contemplated recovery of historical asset costs only. Although the Staggers Act of 1980 now allows somewhat more timely recovery of certain inflationary costs, resulting rates are subject to either competitive market conditions or to regulatory restraints against substantial increases. Thus, full recovery of inflation-adjusted costs for track structure (at December 31, 1981, $2.7 billion constant dollar and $4.8 billion current cost) from future cash flows is doubtful. The actual extent to which track asset costs will be recovered through future cash flows cannot be estimated since recovery will depend on many factors substantially beyond the control of the Railroad. Therefore, track structure and related right of way have been reflected in net assets at book value ($684 million at December 31, 1981). Nonetheless, income approximates the current cost of operations because the Railroad, together with most other rail carriers, follows the replacement accounting method for track structure and related right of way assets. The cost of replacing track in kind is expensed currently under this method, and since the track is being replaced on a planned program basis, the charge to income approximates the current cost of operations. The replacement method also is required currently for all regulatory reporting.

Crude oil and refined products inventories have been restated to a FIFO basis, which generally approximates current cost. Land held for development and sale has been restated to reflect current replacement costs. Cost of crude oil and refined products sales are determined on a LIFO basis, which approximate current costs. The costs of land sales have been restated to reflect their replacement cost at the dates of sale.

1981

The following constant dollar and current cost amounts are stated in average 1981 dollars.

Millions of Dollars	Historical Amounts	Constant Dollar	Current Cost
Revenues	$6,381	$6,381	$6,381
Depreciation	302	459	590
Other costs and expenses	5,507	5,518	5,513
Income before Federal income taxes	572	404	278
Federal income taxes[a]	161	161	161
Net Income	$ 411	$ 243	$ 117
Effective tax rate	28%	40%	58%
Purchasing power gain		$ 226	$ 226

[a]Federal income taxes have not been adjusted since the additional depreciation and other inflationary costs and expenses are not deductible under current tax law.

The current cost of inventories and properties, net of accumulated depreciation, depletion and amortization are $602 million and $9,448 million, respectively, at December 31, 1981. During 1981, the specific prices for these assets increased $1,054 million, of which $780 million was attributable to general inflation.

Constant dollar net income for 1981 was less than historical earnings, chiefly as a result of the inflationary costs reflected in depreciation. The majority of this effect is attributable to the long-lived assets of the Railroad which experience the most significant upward adjustment of historical costs. Net margin (net income as a percentage of revenues) on a constant dollar basis was 3.8 percent compared with 6.4 percent on the basis of historical amounts.

Current cost earnings for 1981 were significantly less than the constant dollar amount because the estimated costs at today's prices for Union Pacific's assets have risen, for the most part, at a rate higher than general inflation. Consequently, the current cost net margin of 1.8 percent is less than the constant dollar margin. This is due principally to current cost depreciation being $131 million more than the $459 million charged against constant dollar earnings. The increase in depreciation relates principally to Champlin and the Railroad.

These inflation-adjusted costs produce a dollar-for-dollar reduction in net income since no tax benefit is available under present income tax law. Thus, constant dollar and current cost effective tax rates of 40 and 58 percent, respectively, are significantly higher than the historical rate.

CASE DISCUSSION QUESTIONS

1. Concerning the president's letter,

   a. What procedures, if any, would DH&S have applied?

   b. What effect, if any, does the inclusion of the letter in the annual report have on DH&S's reporting responsibilities?

   c. What particular comments on the president's letter would be of concern to DH&S?

2. DH&S issued an unqualified opinion on the financial statements of UPC. A third paragraph of their report relates to the financial review information contained on pages 28 and 29 of UPC's annual report.

   a. Write the third paragraph of DH&S's report to comply with SAS No. 29.

   b. Where should additional information appear in a financial report?

3. DH&S issued an unqualified opinion on UPC. What information does SAS No. 29 require regarding the accompanying information?

4. What specific auditing procedures, if any, are required for accompanying information in order for an auditor to be in a position to express an opinion on such information?

5. Suppose the accompanying information in the UPC annual report includes comments on procedures applied by DH&S in the examination of the basic financial statements. Is it appropriate for DH&S to make such comments regarding the scope of their examination?

6. What action should an auditor take when he or she concludes that accompanying information is materially misstated?

7. How does a qualification in the auditor's standard report on the basic financial statements affect reporting on related accompanying information?

CASE 30

REPORTING ON CONDENSED FINANCIAL STATEMENTS AND SELECTED FINANCIAL DATA

Cosmetic Incorporated, a public entity, is required to file condensed financial statements and selected financial data with the Securities and Exchange Commission on an annual basis. The selected financial data required in Cosmetic's report to the Securities and Exchange Commission must cover the current and comparative fiscal years and the three years previous to the comparative fiscal year. For an illustration of selective financial data, refer to Figure 1, Section 552 of the text.

CASE DISCUSSION QUESTIONS

1. SAS No. 29 provides guidance on reporting on condensed financial statements and selected financial data accompanying audited statements in an auditor—submitted document. Discuss the objective of such an auditor's report and the guidelines the auditor is to follow in preparing the report (Hint: See the summary of the SAS, paragraphs five and six).

2. Should the auditor report on condensed financial statements in the same manner as he or she reports on complete financial statements from which they are derived? If not, why not?

3. What should an auditor's report on condensed financial statements indicate when the auditor has performed a complete financial statement audit? Discuss in detail.

4. Is the auditor required to report on condensed financial statements when the client names the auditor and states that the condensed financial statements are derived from audited financial statements? Explain.

5. When selected financial data are presented in the auditor's report, is the auditor limited concerning his or her source of such data? For example, assume the auditor has not prepared audited financial statements. Discuss fully.

6. SAS No. 42 states if selected financial data presented by management includes both data taken from audited statements and other information such as number of employees or square footage of facilities that the auditor's report should specifically identify the data on which he or she is reporting. Specifically what should the auditor's report indicate with respect to selected financial data?

7. Would the auditor, under any circumstances, disclaim an opinion on selected financial data included in a client-prepared document? Discuss.

20

Subsequent Events and Subsequent Discovery of Facts

(Sections 560 and 561, SAS No. 1)

Section 560, *Subsequent Events*, establishes auditing procedures to be applied in a subsequent period and defines two types of subsequent events. The subsequent period extends from the date of the financial statements to the date that the auditor's report is issued. The auditor is responsible for performing a limited review during the subsequent period to discover any items that may require adjustment or disclosure in the financial statements. Although the subsequent period extends to the date the auditor's report is issued the auditor's responsibility for reviewing subsequent events ends with the completion of the field work. Accordingly, the CPA should date the audit report as of the completion of the field work as the date of the report established the responsibility for performing a subsequent events review.

TYPES OF SUBSEQUENT EVENTS

There are two types of subsequent events that require consideration by management and evaluation by the CPA. The initial type consists of those events that provide additional evidence with respect to conditions that existed as of the date of the balance sheet and affect the estimates inherent in the process of preparing financial statements. All information that becomes available prior to the issuance of the financial statements should be used by management in its evaluation of the conditions on which the estimates were based. The statements should be adjusted for any changes in estimates resulting from the use of such evidence. Type-I subsequent events thus require an adjusting journal entry to reflect the effects of the event in the financial statement accounts. For example, a loss on an uncollectible trade account receivable as a result of a customer's deteriorating financial condition leading to bankruptcy subsequent to the balance-sheet date would be indicative of conditions existing at the balance-sheet date and would, accordingly, be a Type-I subsequent event requiring an adjusting journal entry to write-off the bad account. A similar loss resulting from a customer's major casualty such as a fire or flood subsequent to the balance-sheet date would not be indicative of conditions existing at the balance-sheet date.

The second type of subsequent event, Type-II, consists of events that provide evidence with respect to conditions that did not exist as of the date of the balance sheet being reported on but arose subsequent to that date. These events should not result in adjustments of the financial statements. Certain of these events, however, may be of such a nature that disclosure is required to keep the financial statements from being misleading. Examples of Type-II subsequent events include the following:

Sale of a bond or capital stock issue during the subsequent period

Purchase of a business during the subsequent period

Settlement of litigation when the event giving rise to the claim took place subsequent to the balance-sheet date

Loss of plant or inventories as a result of fire or flood during the subsequent period

Losses on receivables resulting from conditions (such as a customer's major casualty) arising subsequent to the balance-sheet date

When financial statements are reissued, for example, in reports filed with the SEC, events that require disclosure in the reissued statements to keep them from being misleading may have occurred subsequent to the original issuance of the statements. These events generally are Type-II subsequent events and would not result in adjustment, but may require disclosure.

AUDITING PROCEDURES IN THE SUBSEQUENT PERIOD

The CPA should perform procedures with respect to the period after the balance-sheet date for the purpose of ascertaining the occurrence of subsequent events that may require adjustment or disclosure in the financial statements. These procedures should be performed at or near the completion of the field work. They generally would include such procedures as reviewing interim financial statements, making inquiries of officers and other appropriate executives, reviewing available minutes of stockholders, directors, and appropriate committees, obtaining letters from legal counsel, and obtaining a letter of representation from the client as to whether any events occurred subsequent to the date of the financial statements being reported on that in the client's opinion would require adjustment or disclosure in the financial statements (the representation letter, as described in SAS No. 19).

SUBSEQUENT DISCOVERY OF FACTS

Section 561 is concerned with the subsequent discovery of facts that existed at the date of the auditor's report. This section applies to events arising after the CPA has issued a report on the client's financial statements. It establishes a continuing responsibility on the CPA to take action when information comes to his or her attention which indicates that the financial statements upon which an opinion has been expressed may be false or misleading.

When information discovered subsequent to the date of the CPA's report is found to be reliable and to have existed at the date of the auditor's report, the CPA should take action if the nature and effect of the matter are such that the audit report would have been affected if the information had been known at the date of the report and had not been reflected in the statements and it is believed there are persons currently relying or likely to rely on the financial statements who would attach importance to the information. When the CPA concludes that action should be taken to prevent future reliance on his or her report, the client should be advised to make appropriate disclosure of the newly discovered facts and the impact of these facts on the statements. The disclosure should be made to those persons who are known to be currently relying or who are likely to rely on the financial statements and the related auditor's report.

ACTION WHEN THE CLIENT COOPERATES

When the client undertakes to make appropriate disclosure, the method used and the disclosure made will depend on the particular circumstances.

When the effect on the statements or auditor's report can promptly be determined, disclosure should consist of issuing, as soon as practicable, revised financial statements and auditor's report. The reasons for the revision usually should be described in a note to the statements and referred to in the revised auditor's report. Generally, only the most recent issued audited statements would need to be revised, even though the revision resulted from events that had occurred in prior years.

When issuance of statements accompanied by the CPA's report for a subsequent period is imminent, so that disclosure is not delayed, appropriate disclosure of the revision may be made in such statements.

When the effect on the statements of the subsequently discovered information cannot be determined without a prolonged investigation, appropriate disclosure would consist of notification by the client to persons who are known to be relying or who are likely to rely on the statements and the related report of the auditor that they should not be relied upon, and that revised statements and a revised auditor's report will be issued upon completion of an investigation.

The client should be advised, if applicable, to discuss with the SEC, stock exchanges, and appropriate regulatory agencies the disclosure to be made or other measures to be taken in the circumstances.

ACTION WHEN THE CLIENT DOES NOT COOPERATE

When a client refuses to permit the auditor to make an investigation and refuses to make the disclosures that may be required, the CPA should notify each member of the client's board of directors of such refusal and of the fact that, in the absence of disclosure by the client, the CPA will take steps to prevent future reliance on the audit report. Unless the CPA's attorney recommends a different course of action, the CPA should take the following steps to the extent applicable:

1. Notification to the client that the auditor's report must no longer be associated with the financial statements.

2. Notification to regulatory agencies having jurisdiction over the client that the auditor's report should no longer be relied upon.

3. Notification to each person known to the auditor to be relying on the statements that the audit report should no longer be relied upon.

Because the CPA does not have knowledge of those to whom the client may have distributed the financial statements and the related report, notification to a regulatory agency having jurisdiction over the client will usually be the only practicable manner for the auditor to provide appropriate disclosure.

CONTENT OF DISCLOSURES

When the CPA has been able to make a satisfactory investigation of the subsequently discovered information and has determined that the information is reliable, the disclosure should describe the effect the information would have had on the audit report if it had been known at the date the opinion was issued and had not been reflected in the financial statements. The disclosure should include a description of the nature of the subsequently acquired information and of its effect on the financial statements. The information disclosed should be as precise and factual as possible and should not go beyond that which is reasonably necessary to accomplish the purpose of disclosure. Comments concerning the conduct or motives of any person should be avoided.

When the client has not cooperated in the examination of the subsequently discovered information, the auditor's disclosure need not detail the specific information but can merely indicate that information has become available which the client has not cooperated in attempting to substantiate and that, if the information is true, the auditor believes that the report must no longer be relied upon or be associated with the financial statements.

CASE 31

THE AUDITOR AND THE SUBSEQUENT PERIOD

Your firm, Anderson and Raymond, CPAs, acts as the independent auditor for Norton and McCall, Inc., one of the nation's leading manufacturers and marketers of quality products and services in the foods, cosmetics, fashion, soft drinks, vehicle rental and leasing, and packaging fields.

Norton's accounting year ends May 31. You are the audit manager responsible for the Norton engagement and you and your staff are in the process of completing the field work. As part of your normal audit program, you perform the following subsequent events auditing procedures:

> You have reviewed the most recent interim financial statements and compared these with the financial statements under examination.

> You have inquired of the corporate officers and other executives as to such matters as:

>> Whether any significant contingent liabilities or commitments existed as of May 31, 19x1 or at the date of your inquiry;

>> Whether any substantial change has occurred with respect to capital stock, long-term debt, or working capital through the date of your examination.

> You read the minutes of the board of directors, stockholders and other appropriate committees. In reviewing the minutes of the board of directors, you note that in June 19x1, the company purchased at a price of $22 per share, 3,744,000 shares (47% of the outstanding capital stock) of Davis, Inc. Davis, with its licensees has the largest rent-a-car fleet in the world.

> Furthermore, you determine that Norton, in July 19x1, will acquire the remaining 4,193,000 outstanding shares of Davis, Inc., at a price of $22 per share. The July acquisition is to be financed by cash and short-term investments included in the May 31, 19x1 balance sheet.

> The latest audited financial statements of Davis, Inc., as of December 31, 19x0, and for the year then ended, indicate revenues of $432,963,000, net income of $16,426,000, and shareholders' equity of $112,595,000, including intangibles of $15,113,000.

CASE DISCUSSION QUESTIONS

1. Two types of subsequent events require consideration by management and evaluation by the independent accountant.

    a. Discuss both types of subsequent events and the related accounting treatment for each type.

    b. Explain the type of subsequent event involved in the acquisition of Davis, Inc.

2. Assume that during your examination of Norton and McCall several of the following events were discovered during the subsequent period.

    a. An account receivable due from a major customer of Norton and McCall has been determined to be uncollectible. The customer has not been able to compete with foreign manufacturers and has been forced into bankruptcy.

    b. Another customer's plant and operations were shut down due to severe flooding in the month of June. Since the customer's loss was not insured, Norton does not expect to collect a material receivable due on May 31, 19x1.

c. Norton and McCall issued a large secondary stock offering during the subsequent period.

d. Norton and McCall reached a settlement with the IRS for $10,000,000 more in federal income taxes than was anticipated at May 31, 19x1.

For each of the subsequent events listed above identify those that would require an adjustment to the financial statements and identify those that would require disclosure. Explain each answer in detail.

3. Assume that you complete the field work on the Norton engagement July 15, 19x1 and the financial report is issued on July 20, 19x1. Identify the subsequent period.

4. In conjunction with the acquisition of the Davis, Inc. securities, would it be appropriate to supplement the historical financial statements with pro forma financial data giving effect to the event as if it had occurred on the date of the balance sheet? Discuss.

5. Discuss other auditing procedures, not mentioned in the text of the Norton and McCall case, that should be carried out by the independent auditor with respect to the "subsequent period."

6. Assume that after Anderson and Raymond issue their report to Norton and McCall, they become aware of facts that existed at the date of the report and would have affected their report had they known of such facts (assume that the information is reliable).

a. Should they seek legal counsel? If so, why?

b. What other steps should Anderson and Raymond take?

7. What advice should Anderson and Raymond give to Norton to prevent future reliance on their report?

8. Assume that Norton refuses to make the proper disclosures. Explain what Anderson and Raymond should do in such circumstances. Support your answer by outlining the steps they should follow in making the necessary disclosure(s).

CASE 32

BARCHRIS LIABILITY CASE*

The BarChris Construction Corporation Case of 1968 is perhaps the most comprehensive decision in a lawsuit involving civil liability under the Securities Act of 1933. The significance of the BarChris decision is based upon several factors. First, the plaintiff's case was based on alleged falsity or misleading omissions as of the date of the financial statements and it clarifies the criteria to be used for judging the existence of falsity or misleading omissions. Second, the case involves the failure to disclose important matters which occurred between the date of the certified financial statements and the effective date of the registration statement. And third, the decision involved a clarification of the criteria for judging the auditor's defense of due diligence.[1]

BarChris grew out of a business begun in 1946 by two men, Vitolo and Pugliesi, who at the time the case came to trial in the 1960's were the president and vice-president of the company, respectively. In 1955 the company entered the field of bowling alley construction. The increasing popularity of bowling in the 1950's caused BarChris's sales to rise from $800,000 in 1956 to over $3.3 million in 1959. In 1960, the company's financial statements indicated sales of over $9 million. However, the legal action against BarChris cast doubt as to the accuracy of these figures.

---

* An original draft of this case was prepared by John Royster, Richard Schreiber, Brady Sheffer, and Martin Stein, Master of Accountancy students, Virginia Polytechnic Institute and State University.

[1] Ernst & Ernst, SEC Reporting Conference Reading and Case Studies Manual (E&E Professional Development Series, 1975), p. 155.

Business Methods[2]

BarChris's method of doing business was to enter into a contract with a customer, receive a down payment, and proceed with the construction of the bowling center. Upon completion of construction, the customer would give Bar-Chris a note for the balance due; in turn, BarChris would discount the note to a factor, but continue to serve as an indorser of the note. Hence, if the customer were to default, BarChris was liable for the proceeds of the note to the factor. In 1960, BarChris began practicing an alternative method of financing which in substance was a sale and lease-back arrangement. Under this method, BarChris would construct and install bowling equipment in a building and would sell the "interior" to a factor, who would pay BarChris the full contract price. The factor then proceeded to lease the interior either directly to BarChris's customer or back to a subsidiary of BarChris which in turn would lease it to the customer. Under both financing methods BarChris spent considerable sums before it received payment and, as a consequence thereof, was in a constant cash squeeze. The need for cash became more pressing as the company's operations grew larger.

SEC Filing

The need for cash increased until in 1959 BarChris sold 560,000 shares of common stock to the public at $3.00 per share. By early 1961, BarChris needed additional working capital and the company began procedures to sell an issue of 5½ percent, 15-year convertible subordinated debentures. The registration statement for the issue was filed on March 30, 1961, with the SEC and became effective on May 16. Net proceeds on the issue were received on May 24.

Subsequent Events Affecting the Filing

The early 1960's saw the results of overbuilding in the bowling alley industry. BarChris was having difficulty collecting amounts due from its customers. Likewise, the factor was having problems in collecting the notes. Even though these difficulties existed, BarChris continued building bowling alleys in 1961 and 1962. On October 29, 1962, BarChris filed under the Bankruptcy Act. Four days previously (October 25, 1962) a civil suit was instituted under Section 11 of the 1933 Act against the Company, its Officers and Directors, the Underwriters, and the independent public accountants concerning the registration of the 1961 debentures issue. Nine plaintiffs began the action; however, by the trial date, over sixty plaintiffs were joined in a class action suit.

Plaintiff's Case

As noted previously, the suit was brought under Section 11 of the 1933 Securities Act. Section 11(a) provides that any person acquiring securities may sue "every accountant" who has certified any part of the registration statement which, "when such part of the registration statement became effective, contained an untrue statement of material fact or omitted to state a material fact required to be stated therein or necessary to make the statements therein not misleading." The action may be instituted by any purchaser and the purchaser need not prove reliance thereon. It is sufficient for the misstatement or omission to occur in the registration statement. Further, the Act speaks of the veracity of the registration statement at the effective date.

The Act, however, does not place an irrefutable burden on the accountant. The Act provides that no person, other than the issuer, shall be liable who shall sustain the burden of proof that the portions of the statement which he "expertized" were believed by him to be true and contained "no omission to state a material fact required to be stated therein or necessary to make the statements therein not misleading." Such belief must arise as the result of a "reasonable investigation" which gave rise to a "reasonable ground to believe."

Registration Statement

The registration statement contained a prospectus as well as other information. The plaintiff's case was based solely on the claims of falsities and omissions in the prospectus. The elements of the prospectus which were challenged are briefly discussed below (see Appendix A for a summary of omissions and misstatements).

---

[2] Background information and case data contained in this paper was obtained from: Federal Securities Law Report, Escott, et al. vs. BarChris Construction Corp., et al., 283 F. Supp. 643 (S.D. N.Y. 1968).

1. **Audited Financial Statements of 1960.**   The plaintiffs charged that sales, and consequently earnings and therefore earnings per share, was grossly overstated. After an investigation made by the court, the alleged overstatement of sales of $2.5 million was reduced to an overstatement of $650,000. This inaccuracy was due to the incorrect application of the percentage of completion method of accounting for construction contracts and the inclusion of sales representing bowling alleys which were in fact not sold to an outside customer. In two instances, BarChris, after constructing a bowling alley, sold it to a factor who subsequently leased it back to a wholly owned subsidiary of Bar-Chris. However, BarChris recorded the transaction by including the entire sales price in the 1960 figures. The court held that these sales amounts should not have been included in the 1960 figures.[3] The overall effect was to overstate net operating income by 14%. For reasons not apparent in the court's decision, it held that this overstatement was *not* material.

Plaintiff charges also included misstatements of balance sheet amounts. In December, 1960, the company, through a wholly owned subsidiary, arranged with its factor to loan $147,000 of reserves which the factor was holding against BarChris's discounted notes. The subsidiary received the funds and transferred $145,000 to the parent company which included that amount in its cash. The court held this not to be a current asset of BarChris and the judge stated that:

> Plaintiff's claim that this transaction was arranged . . . in order to increase BarChris's cash temporarily, so that its financial condition would look better on December 31, 1960. No other explanation was offered by the defendants and I can see none.

The court stated that treating this as cash on hand without an explanation was misleading and that the transaction cast doubt on the credibility of certain of BarChris's officers.

Evidence that several of the notes held by BarChris were worthless prompted the judge to rule that the company should have had a reserve of "at least $50,000" to match against potential losses on the notes.

Other matters to which the court directed comment included the classification of liabilities. It was ruled that contingent liabilities were understated by approximately $400,000 and direct liabilities of $325,000 were improperly classified as contingent.

2. **Unaudited 1961 Figures.**   The prospectus also included unaudited figures as to sales, earnings, contingent liabilities, and representations of the company's backlog of orders for the quarter ended March 31, 1961. The sales and gross profit figures were amended by the court (sales reduced by $519,810 and gross profit reduced by $230,755) to reflect the intercompany transactions which were improperly recorded. Also, contingent liabilities of the first quarter were understated by $618,853. The company's representation of the backlog on orders included contracts that were mere designations of geographic areas of proposed construction. While the backlog of orders spoke as of March 31, 1961, many of the orders were not built until long after May 16, 1961, the effective date. Several of the "ordered" bowling alleys which were built were eventually run by a corporation that was organized in May, 1961. Of $6,905,000 in orders, the judge held that $4,490,000 should not have been included.

3. **Text of the Prospectus.**   The court then began an evaluation of the text of the prospectus. The following issues were considered:

a.   *Officer Loans.*   The prospectus stated that while loans were made from time to time by officers to the corporation, all had been repaid. The court determined that in fact there were loans of $386,615 outstanding as of May 16, 1967 (effective date of registration statement). Certain of these loans had been "repaid" and the officers were merely "holding" the checks (this was due to insufficient cash on hand) while others were new loans which were to be repaid out of the proceeds of the bond issue.

b.   *Application of Proceeds.*   The prospectus stated that $150,000 of the proceeds was to be used for the construction of a new plant, $250,000 to develop new equipment, and $500,000 loaned to a subsidiary. The balance of $1,745,000 was to be used for additional working capital. Actually, $386,000 was destined to be used to repay officer loans, $826,000 to pay off negative cash balances created by postdated checks, and $120,000 was loaned to friends of BarChris's executive vice-president. The court held that the company used over 60 percent of proceeds to pay prior debts, and therefore was false and misleading.

---

[3] Reader's attention is directed to the appropriate sections of FASB No. 13 which establishes the criterion for accounting for sale/leaseback transactions.

c.   *Customer Delinquencies.*   In the narrative portion of the prospectus, BarChris stated that it had been required to repurchase only one-half of 1 percent of its discounted promissory notes since 1955. The plaintiffs charged and the court upheld that this statement, although literally true, was misleading in light of the current customer difficulties and the fact that BarChris had been able to forestall the factor's "informal" demands on payment of defaulted notes.

The Accountant's Defense

The independent accountants based their defense on the portion of Section 11(b) of the 1933 Securities Act which deals with the due diligence defense of an "expert" (see Appendix B).

The court ruled that the only experts involved in the case were the independent accountants and that the only expertized portion of the registration statement was the consolidated financial statements of December 31, 1960. The court emphatically pointed out that the unaudited financial information for the first quarter of 1961 was not purported to have been certified by the accountants. The court also pointed out that because the statute requires the court to determine the accountant's belief and the grounds thereof, "at the time such part of the registration statement became effective," the entire matter would be viewed as of May 16, 1961. Specifically, the court would consider not only the 1960 audit but also the subsequent "S-1 Review."

With respect to the 1960 audit, the court found that the accountants erred in several areas. As previously discussed, incorrect sales and earnings were reported as a result of intercompany transactions, transactions which never took place and errors in the percentage of completion computations. The senior accountant assigned to the BarChris audit did not, in the opinion of the court, conduct a reasonable investigation in light of the fact that much of the information regarding the contracts was obtained by inquiries made of company officers and little or no attempt was made to verify the information by other methods. As for the understatement of liabilities, it was held that the amounts for the 1960 statements would not have deterred a prospective purchaser of debentures but it led BarChris to further misstate the liabilities for the interim period.

The most damaging evidence against the accountants was related to the S-1 Review made in May, 1961. The purpose of the S-1 Review is to ascertain whether any material change has occurred in the company's financial position which should be disclosed in order to prevent the balance sheet figures from becoming misleading. At the time the review was conducted, an outline of procedures to be followed was set forth in Statements on Auditing Procedures No. 25, "Events Subsequent to the Date of Financial Statements" (see Appendix C).

The accountant's review program was held to be in accordance with the generally accepted auditing standards appreciable at that time. The question to which the court addressed itself was whether the review was properly carried out, and even though the misstatements were not discovered, whether the investigation was reasonable within the meaning of the statute (see Appendix B for definition of reasonable investigation).

The senior accountant assigned to the S-1 Review looked at the consolidated trial balance as of March 31, 1961, and compared it with the audited December 31, 1960, figures. He did not examine any other "important financial records." The senior reviewed the minutes of the Board of Directors meeting provided to him by officers of BarChris. He did not review or inquire about minutes of executive committee meetings or board meetings of subsidiaries.

In questioning company officials about increasing notes payable he accepted the explanation that "we are a bit slow in paying our bills" and made no further inquiries. Also, no attempt was made to contact the factors concerning the substantial amounts of discounted notes, some of which were delinquent.

In ruling on the accountant's defense of due diligence in conducting a reasonable investigation, the judge made the following remarks:

> There had been a material change for the worse in BarChris's financial position. That change was sufficiently serious so that the failure to disclose it made the 1960 figures misleading. Berardi did not discover it. As far as results were concerned, his S-1 Review was useless.

> Accountants should not be held to a standard higher than that recognized in their profession. I do not do so here. Berardi's review did not come up to that standard. He did not take some of the steps which (the accounting firm's) written program prescribed. He did not spend an adequate amount of time on a task of this magnitude. Most important of all, he was too easily satisfied with glib answers to his inquiries.

> This is not to say that he should have made a complete audit. But there were enough danger signals in the materials which he did examine to require some further investigation on his part. Generally ac-

cepted accounting standards required such further investigation under these circumstances. It is not always sufficient merely to ask questions.

Here again, the burden of proof is on (the accounting firm). I find that that burden has not been satisfied. I conclude that (the accounting firm) has not established its due diligence defense.

CASE DISCUSSION QUESTIONS

1. What are the statutory requirements under Section 11(b) of the 1933 Act for the due diligence defense of both "experts" and "non-experts?"

2. Who was considered an "expert" in the BarChris case and what information were they responsible for "expertising?"

3. Explain the differences in the accounting treatment of sale/leaseback transactions in 1961 and the present. What disclosures should have been made with respect to the BarChris sale/leaseback transactions?

4. In the BarChris decision the court determined that the accounting firm's audit program conformed with generally accepted auditing standards. In light of this, what was the basis for the court's adverse decision against the firm?

5. How did the court define materiality with respect to the omissions and misstatements in the registration statement?

6. Why should BarChris have eliminated the profit in the consolidated statements on its sale of a bowling alley to a factor after the alley was leased back by a subsidiary?

7. What is the independent accountant's responsibility with respect to capsule information contained in the registration statements?

APPENDIX A

Summary of omissions and misstatements in the 1960 audited financial statements and subsequent period.

1. *1960 Earnings*

    a. *Sales*

As per prospectus	$9,165,320
Correct amount	8,511,420
Overstatement	$ 653,900

    b. *Net Operating Income*

As per prospectus	$1,742,801
Correct amount	1,496,196
Overstatement	$ 246,605

    c. *Earnings per share*

As per prospectus	$.75
Correct amount	.65
Overstatement	$.10

2. *1960 Balance Sheet*
   Current Assets
   As per prospectus.................................... $4,524,021
   Correct amount...................................... 3,914,332
   Overstatement .... $ 609,689

3. *Contingent Liabilities as of December 31, 1960*
   on Alternative Method of Financing
   As per prospectus................................... $ 750,000
   Correct amount...................................... 1,125,795
   Understatement................................... $ 375,795

   Capital Lanes should have been shown
   as a direct liability............................... $ 325,000

4. *Contingent Liabilities as of April 30, 1961*
   As per prospectus................................... $ 825,000
   Correct amount...................................... 1,443,853
   Understatement................................... $ 618,853

   Capital Lanes should have been shown
   as a direct liability.............................. $ 314,166

5. *Earnings Figures for Quarter ending March 31, 1961*

   a. *Sales*
       As per prospectus............................ $2,138,455
       Correct amount.............................. 1,618,645
       Overstatement............................. $ 519,810

   b. *Gross Profit*
       As per prospectus............................ $ 483,121
       Correct amount.............................. 252,366
       Overstatement............................. $ 230,755

6. *Backlog as of March 31, 1961*
   As per prospectus................................... $6,905,000
   Correct amount...................................... 2,415,000
   Overstatement $4,490,000

7. *Failure to Disclose Officers' Loans*
   Outstanding and Unpaid on May 16, 1961............. $ 386,615

8. *Failure to Disclose Use of Proceeds in*
   Manner not Revealed in Prospectus
   Approximately.................................... $1,160,000

9. *Failure to Disclose Customers' Delinquencies*
   in May 1961 and BarChris's Potential Liability
   with Respect Thereto........................*Over* $1,350,000

10. *Failure to Disclose the Fact that BarChris*
    was Already Engaged and was about to be
    More Heavily Engaged, in the Operation
    of Bowling Alleys

APPENDIX B

Accountants' Liabilities Under the 1933 Act

Section 11(a) of the Securities Act of 1933 contains the provisions relating to civil liabilities of persons who sign the registration statement, directors of the issuer, underwriters, and "experts" (including accountants). This section provides, in part, as follows:

> In case any part of the registration statement, when such part became effective contained an untrue statement of a material fact or omitted to state a material fact required to be stated therein or necessary to make the statements therein not misleading, any person acquiring such security . . . may . . . sue . . . every accountant . . . who has with his or her consent been named as having . . . certified any part of the registration statement . . . with respect to the statement in such registration statement . . . which purports to have been . . . certified by him or her.

Section 11(b) provides the due diligence defense for an "expert." It states:

> Notwithstanding the provisions of subsection (a) above, no person . . . shall be liable as provided therein who shall sustain the burden of proof—that as regards any part of the registration statement purporting to be made upon his or her authority as an expert . . . he or she had, after reasonable investigation reasonable ground to believe and did believe at the time such part of the registration statement became effective, that the statements therein were true and that there was no omission to state a material fact to be stated therein or necessary to make the statements therein not misleading . . .

Section 11 (c) of the 1933 Act provides that:

> In determining, for the purpose of . . . subsection (b), what constitutes reasonable investigation and reasonable ground for belief, the standard of reasonableness shall be required of a prudent man in the management of his or her own property.

APPENDIX C

At the time the independent accountants certified the financial statements of BarChris and performed the "S-1 Review" in May, 1961, Statements on Auditing Procedures No. 25 (October, 1954), entitled "Events Subsequent to the Date of Financial Statements" outlined the special requirements under the 1933 Securities Act. Note the statutory requirement in paragraph 30 and the audit committee's opinion expressed in paragraph 34(a).

SPECIAL REQUIREMENTS UNDER SECURITIES ACT OF 1933

29.   The committee believes that attention should be directed to special problems resulting from timing and availability of recorded financial information, which arise in connection with reports included in registration statements filed under the Securities Act of 1933.

30.   Section 11 of the Act provides that, other than the issuer, no person shall be liable as provided therein if such person shall sustain the burden of proof that as to the part of the registration statement purporting to be made on his authority as an expert.

> "he had, *after reasonable investigation*, reasonable ground to believe and did believe, *at the time such part of the registration statement became effective*, that the statements therein were true and that there was no omission to state a material fact required to be stated therein or necessary to make the statements therein not misleading" (emphasis supplied).

Section 11 further provides that in determining what constitutes reasonable investigation and reasonable ground for belief,

> "the standard of reasonableness shall be that required of a prudent man in the management of his own property."

31.   In discussing such key phrases as "after reasonable investigation" and "at the time such part of the registration statement became effective" it is not the intention of this committee to offer a legal interpretation of these statutory terms. Until the courts have interpreted such terms it can proceed only in accordance with its understanding of their meaning in accordance with accounting and auditing standards and procedures. Accordingly, the opinion of the members of this committee is here submitted to these matters subject to any judicial interpretation which may issue in the course of time.

32.   After a registration statement has been filed, the processing may be delayed by administration procedures. There may be other causes brought about by issuers or underwriters necessitating continued deferral of the effective date. It is obvious that the accountant may encounter serious problems in keeping currently informed as to the happening of any extraordinary transactions or events bearing on the financial statements, and the procedures which may be unreasonably costly and impractical.

33.   There are additional difficulties involved in keeping currently informed up to the time of the effective date by reason of the lack of recorded financial information during the period immediately preceding the effective date. Depending on the size of the company and the complexity of its operations this period of time may be substantial.

34.   The committee therefore is of the opinion that a "reasonable investigation" (a) as to point of time, should be construed as referring to a period ending sufficiently prior to the actual effective date as is consistent with the practical availability of financial information, etc., and (b) as to procedures, should comprise the following:

1.   The reading of available minutes of meetings of stockholders, directors, and finance or executive committees, as applicable.

2.   Reading of such available interim financial statements as are regularly prepared by the client.

3.   The reading of the full text of the prospectus and review of pertinent portions of the rest of the registration statement.

4.   Inquiry of one or more officers or key employees and of legal counsel, where appropriate, as to happenings which may be considered material in relation to the financial statements reported upon by the auditor and included in the registration statement. Such happenings, or the absence thereof, should be the subject of written representations.

5.   Any other steps which the auditor deems necessary for a "reasonable investigation" under the particular circumstances.

35.   It is obvious that the responsibility for the disclosure of post-balance-sheet events must, as a practical and reasonable matter, decrease following the close of the field work and that subsequent to that time the accountant must rely, for the most part, on inquiries of officers and key employees. In the case of an issuer with multiple offices and wide-spread operations, the officers and employees would be those at the home office level.

CASE 33

YALE EXPRESS LIABILITY CASE*

"B-but Mr. Jimson, I w-want to be an (accountant)."

"of course you do, everybody does once. But they get over it, thank God, like the measles and the chickenpox. Go home and go to bed and take some hot lemonade and put on three blankets and sweat it out."

"But Mr. J-Jimson, there must be (accountants)."

"Yes, and lunatics and lepers, but why go and live in an asylum before you're sent for? If you find life a bit dull at home and want to amuse yourself, put a stick of dynamite in the kitchen fire, or shoot a policeman. Volunteer for a test pilot, or dive off Tower Bridge with five bob's worth of roman candles in each pocket. You'd get twice the fun at about one-tenth of the risk."

—paraphrased from *The Horse's Mouth*
Joyce Cory (Harper & Brothers; New
York), 1944, pp. 15-16.

---

*An original draft of this case was prepared by Susan Jolles and Steve Martin, Master of Accountancy students, Virginia Polytechnic Institute and State University.

Increasing litigation against public accountants in the last thirty-five years has stimulated controversy with respect to the proper limits of accountants' liabilities for damages which result from their certified audits. The passage of the Securities Acts extended financial reporting requirements and thus caused the role of the accountants' services to increase even further.

The Yale Express case has become a landmark case because it raises interesting issues with respect to the duties of accountants to persons other than their clients. It is also unusual because it involves a situation in which insiders become their own principal victims.

The Yale Motor Transport Company was a New York based short-haul trucker and freight forwarder which was founded in 1938 by Benjamin Eskow. Its troubles began when it acquired the Republic Carloading and Distributing Company in May, 1963.

In *Fischer* vs. *Kletz*, the defendant accountants, Peat, Marwick, Mitchell and Company (PM&M), audited and certified the 1963 financial statements of the Yale Motor Transport Company. These statements, reporting a profit of $1,140,000 were submitted to Yale stockholders in April, 1964. A Form 10-K Report, containing the same annual financial statements, was filed with the Securities and Exchange Commission (SEC) in June of that year.

Shortly afterwards, Yale engaged PM&M to conduct "special studies" of Yale's past and current income and expenses to be used for internal purposes. In the course of this special study, PM&M discovered that Yale has misstated its financial position and thus the annual report was false and misleading. PM&M alerted Yale Express to its discovery but neither PM&M nor Yale Express took further action.

Furthermore, during the course of the "special studies" engagement, Yale informed PM&M that it was issuing interim statements and reports of the company's 1964 financial performance. In the later part of 1964, Yale Express reported nine months' earnings of $904,000. It was not until March, 1965 that Yale Express reported that its interim report on profits was incorrect and that a loss of $3,306,000 was estimated for 1964. It was also disclosed that the 1963 financial statements should have shown a loss of $1,200,000.

The public accountants did not make any disclosures concerning the 1963 financial statements until May 5, 1965. In conjunction with its 1964 audit report, PM&M reported a loss of $1,880,000 for 1963. Yale Express also filed for Chapter X Bankruptcy in late May, 1965.

Purchasers who had acquired Yale's securities after PM&M's discovery, that the 1963 audited financial statements were false and misleading brought suit for damages against PM&M under common law for deceit, under Section 10(b) and Section 18 of the Securities Exchange Commission Rule 10b-5. PM&M made a motion to dismiss the case contending that accountants do not have a duty to disclose misrepresentations discovered after the distribution of the audited financial statements.

Since the case involved so many unsettled questions concerning the auditor's liability, Judge Tyler overruled PM&M's pretrial motion to dismiss the complaint. Although PM&M settled out of court by paying $650,000 of the $1,010,000 settlement fund, this case raised many pertinent questions that could not be resolved by relying on precedent. One of PM&M's main problems was that it wore "two hats" in its dealing with Yale Express. Their responsibility as the independent auditors of the 1963 annual report and Form 10-K was:

> . . . not only to the client who pays his fee, but also to investors, creditors, and others who may rely on the financial statements which he certifies . . . The public accountant must report fairly on the facts as he finds them whether favorable or unfavorable to his client. His duty is to safeguard the public interest, not that of his client [in the matter of Touche, Niven, Bailey, and Smart, 37 SEC 629, 670-671 (1957)].

PM&M donned its second hat when they agreed to undertake the "special studies" assignment which was necessitated by business demands. Its new role was that of a "independent public accountant" whose primary obligation was to its client.

Yale Express is also a landmark case, along with McKesson and Robbins, because it raised the possibility that an auditor may be held liable even though he followed generally accepted auditing standards. At the time of Yale, there were no authoritative guidelines for a public accountant to follow when there was a subsequent discovery of facts existing at the date of his or her report. It was not until October, 1969 that the American Institute of Certified Public Accountants issued Statement on Auditing Procedure Number 41 (SAP No. 41) entitled, "Subsequent Discovery of Facts Existing at the Date of the Auditor's Report." SAP No. 41 was later incorporated into Statement on Auditing Standards Number 1 (SAS No. 1). Its issuance was probably a direct result of the events in the Yale Express case.

The Securities and Exchange Commission filed an *amicae curiae* brief in which it contended:

> The accountant has a continuing duty to disclose any material information about false information in financial statements that the accountant has certified . . . Failure to disclose that the financial statements are false, when he or she becomes aware of that fact, is a fraud on persons in connection with the purchase or sale of securities (*Journal of Accountancy*, January 1967).

PM&M filed a reply memorandum with the court in which it contended that Congress and the courts had not "intended to impose such an extensive obligation on independent auditors" (*Journal of Accountancy*, January 1967). The firm contended that the SEC was attempting to apply the detailed provisions of the 1933 Act which extended the independent auditor's responsibility up to the effective date of the registration statement to annual financial statements filed under the 1934 Act.

CONCLUSIONS

Since the case was settled out of court, many of the questions were not completely answered. However, from the Opinion by Judge H.R. Tyler, Jr. on PM&M's motion for dismissal, some important conclusions and implications can be drawn.

1. Accounting firms can no longer rely on the privity defense available under the *Ultramares* doctrine. Judge Tyler no longer accepted this defense because he compared the act of certification to representations made in a business transaction. He continued that "(t)he elements of 'good faith and common honesty' which govern the businessman presumably should also apply to the statutory independent public accountant" (*Fischer* vs. *Kletz*).

2. When an accounting firm wears "two hats" in his relations to a client, the public interest must have controlling priority.

3. When GAAS is not specific, then once again the accountant must give the public interest controlling priority.

CASE DISCUSSION QUESTIONS

1. Assume that an accounting firm does not benefit directly or indirectly from the failure of its client to present financial statements that are considered fair presentations. Is this a valid defense in reducing or eliminating the firm's liability?

2. What effect, if any, does the presence or absence of common law fraud have to do with accountants' liability to non-privy third parties under Rule 10b-5?

3. Discuss the accountant's liability to Yale's creditors under the 1934 Act. Were the accountants liable under common law?

4. What is the auditor's responsibility to disclose facts discovered subsequent to the date of the financial statements when such facts tend to make the financial statements materially false or misleading? What disclosures would be required?

5. What is the auditor's responsibility to disclose facts discovered subsequent to the date of interim financial statements when such facts tend to make the statements materially false or misleading? Is this responsibility the same for interim financial statements to stockholders and those filed with the SEC in Form 10-Q?

6. What is the effect, if any, of the Yale Express case on the role of an auditor in a management services engagement?

21

Part of Examination Made by Other CPAs and Dating the Auditor's Report

(Sections 530 and 543, SAS No. 1)

DATING THE INDEPENDENT AUDITOR'S REPORT

Generally, the date of completion of the auditor's field work should be the date of the auditor's report. Although the subsequent period extends to the date the auditor issues the report, the auditor has no responsibility to make any audit inquiries or carry out any procedures for the period after the date of the report.

Events Occurring After Completion of Field Work but Before Issuance of Report

When a subsequent event of the type that requires adjustment of the financial statements (Type-I) occurs after the date of the auditor's report but prior to its issuance, and this event comes to the attention of the auditor, either the financial statements should be appropriately adjusted or the auditor should qualify the opinion expressed. When the adjustment is made without disclosure of the event, the CPA ordinarily should date the report as of the completion of the field work. If disclosure of the event is made or adjustment is not made and the CPA qualifies the opinion, two alternatives are available for dating the report. *Dual dating* may be used. Under this method the CPA would date the report as of the completion of the field work, except for the subsequently discovered event, which would be dated as of the date of its discovery. Such procedure would limit the CPA's responsibility for performing a subsequent events review (see Section 360, SAS No. 1) to the date of completion of the field work. A CPA may choose, however, to date the report as of the date following the completion of the field work when a subsequent event is discovered. In this case, responsibility for a subsequent events review would be extended up to this latter date and the auditor would be required to return to the client's premises and update the review of subsequent events.

When a Type-II subsequent event, one that requires disclosure, occurs after the date of the completion of the auditor's field work but prior to the issuance of the report, and the event comes to the attention of the auditor, it should be disclosed in a note to the financial statements or the auditor should qualify the opinion. The auditor would date the report using dual dating or would use the latter date and extend the subsequent events review.

Reissuance of the Auditor's Report

A CPA may reissue a report on statements included in annual reports filed with the SEC or other regulatory agencies or in a long-form report prepared for the client or for others. The CPA may also be requested by the client to furnish additional copies of a previously issued report. Use of the original report date in a reissued report removes any implication that the statements have been examined or reviewed after the date of their original issuance. When the original date is used, the CPA has no responsibility to make further investigation or inquiry as to events which may have occurred subsequent to the original issue date. The CPA may, however, become aware of an event that occurred subsequent to the date of the original report that requires either adjustment or disclosure. In this case, the CPA should consider the effect of these matters on the opinion and should re-date the report or use dual dating.

If an event of the type requiring disclosure only (Type-II subsequent event) occurs between the date of the original report and the reissuance of the report, and the event comes to the attention of the auditor, the event may be disclosed in a separate note to the financial statements captioned "Event (unaudited) subsequent to the date of the report of independent auditor." The auditor's report would then carry the original reporting date.

PART OF EXAMINATION MADE BY OTHER CPAs

Product line diversification and related business combinations and mergers have created situations where more than one CPA may be involved in auditing the financial statements of companies that are consolidated. Section 543 of SAS No. 1 establishes criteria for a CPA to consider in determining whether sufficient work has been performed to express an opinion on a consolidated group of companies and procedures that should be followed in relying on or using the work of other CPAs who have audited a part of the consolidated group.

Principal Auditor's Course of Action

The auditors of the parent company, or principal auditors, must decide whether their participation in the examination of the consolidated group of companies is sufficient to enable them to serve as the principal auditors. In making this decision, they should consider the materiality of the portion of the financial statements they have examined in comparison with the portion examined by other CPAs. The principal CPAs should consider the extent of their knowledge of the overall financial statements and the importance of the components they examined in relation to the enterprise as a whole.

When principal CPAs decide that they have examined a sufficient portion of the overall financial statements, they must then decide whether to make reference in their report to the examination by another auditor. If the principal auditors decide to assume responsibility for the work of the other auditor, no reference should be made to the other auditor's examination. However, if the principal auditors decide not to assume responsibility, their report should make reference to the examination of the other auditor and indicate clearly the division of responsibility.

Decision Not to Make Reference

Principal auditors would ordinarily be in a position to assume responsibility for the work of another CPA and, accordingly, not make reference to the other CPA, when any of the following conditions are met:

Part of the examination is made by another CPA, who is an associated or correspondent firm and whose work is acceptable to the principals based on their knowledge of the professional standards and competence of that firm

The other auditor was retained by the principal auditors and the work performed under the principals' guidance and control

The principal auditors, whether or not they selected the other auditor, take steps they consider necessary to satisfy themselves as to the other auditor's examination and are satisfied as to the reasonableness of the accounts for the purpose of inclusion in the financial statements on which they are expressing their opinion

The portion of the statements examined by the other auditor is not material to the financial statements covered by the principal auditors' opinion

Decision to Make Reference

When the principal auditors decide that they will make reference to the examination of another CPA, which is the usual situation, their report should indicate clearly, in both the scope and opinion paragraphs, the division of responsibility. The report should disclose the magnitude of the portion of the financial statements examined by the other CPA. This may be done by stating the dollar amounts or percentages of one or more of the following: total assets, total revenues, or other appropriate criteria, whichever most clearly reveals the portion of the financial statements examined by the other CPA. The other auditor may be named, but only with his or her expressed permission and provided his or her report is presented together with that of the principal auditors.

Reference in the report of the principal auditors to the fact that a part of the examination was made by another CPA is not to be construed as an opinion qualification, but rather as an indication of the divided responsibility.

Procedures Applicable to Both Methods of Reporting

Whether principal auditors intend to make reference to the work of another CPA or not, they should perform certain procedures to assure themselves as to the professional reputation and standing of the other CPA. The procedures are required even though the principal auditors are assuming responsibility for the work of the other CPA. The principal CPAs should:

Make inquiries as to the professional reputation and standing of the other auditor to one or more of the following:

a.   Other practitioners

b.   Bankers and other credit grantors

c.   Other appropriate sources (such as business associates)

Obtain a representation from the other CPA that he or she is independent under the requirements of the AICPA and, if appropriate, the requirements of the SEC

Ascertain through communication with the other CPA:

That he or she is aware that the statements which he or she is to examine or has examined are to be included in the statements on which the principal auditor will report and that the other auditor's report thereon will be relied upon (and, where applicable, referred to) by the principal auditor

That he or she is familiar with accounting principles generally accepted in the United States and with the GAAS promulgated by the AICPA and will conduct his or her examination (or has conducted the examination) and will report in accordance therewith

That he or she has knowledge of the relevant financial reporting requirements for statements and schedules to be filed with regulatory agencies (if applicable)

That a review will be made of matters affecting elimination of intercompany transactions and accounts and, if appropriate in the circumstances, the uniformity of accounting practices among the components included in the financial statements

Additional Procedures Under Decision Not to Make Reference

When the principal auditors decide to assume responsibility for the work of another CPA and, accordingly, not to make reference to the other CPA's work, they should perform procedures in addition to those outlined above. The principal auditor should:

Visit the other auditor and discuss the audit procedures followed and results obtained

Review the audit programs of the other auditor. In some cases, it may be appropriate to issue instructions to the other auditor as to scope of the audit work

Review the working papers of the other auditor, including the evaluation of internal control and the conclusions reached as to other significant aspects of the engagement

The principal auditor may consider it appropriate to participate in discussions regarding the accounts with management personnel whose statements are being examined by the other CPA and/or to make supplemental tests of such accounts

Qualifications in the Other CPA's Report

When the opinion of another CPA is qualified, the principal auditors should decide whether the subject of the qualification is of such nature and significance in relation to the financial statements on which they are reporting that it would require qualification of their own report. If the subject of the qualification is not material to the consolidated financial statements and the other CPA's report is not presented, the principal auditors need not make reference in their report to the qualification. If the other CPA's report is presented, the principal auditors may wish to explain the qualification and its disposition.

Restated Financial Statements of Prior Years Following a Pooling of Interests

Following a pooling-of-interests transaction, auditors may be asked to report on restated financial statements for one or more prior years when other auditors have examined one or more of the entities included in such financial statements. In certain of these situations the auditors may decide that they have not examined a sufficient portion of the financial statements for such prior year or years to enable them to serve as principal auditors. In these circumstances it may be appropriate for them to express their opinion solely with respect to the compilation of such statements. No opinion should be expressed unless the auditors have examined the statements of at least one of the entities included in the restatement for at least the latest period presented.

In reporting on the compilation of restated financial statements, auditors do not assume responsibility for the work of other auditors nor the responsibility for expressing an opinion on the restated financial statements. Their review is directed toward procedures which will enable them to express an opinion as to proper compilation only. These procedures include checking the compilation for mathematical accuracy and for conformity of the compilation methods with GAAP. The auditors should review and make inquiries regarding such matters as the following:

Elimination of intercompany transactions and accounts

Combining adjustments and reclassifications

Adjustments to treat like items in a comparable manner, if appropriate

The manner and extent of presentation of disclosure matters in the restated financial statements and notes

Using the Work and Reports of Other Auditors

By DENNIS S. NEIER, *CPA*

The practice of utilizing other auditors to participate in an engagement is a practical method of overcoming problems of travel, staff inadequacy, time urgencies and the need for specialized services. However, embarrassments to the principal auditors have resulted from flaws in the arrangements for and supervision of the auxiliary auditor's work, and from misconceptions as to the sharing of responsibility. SAP No. 45 was designed to provide guidelines for such arrangements and their observance will minimize the chances of embarrassment.

*I*n July 1971, the Committee on Auditing Procedure of the American Institute of Certified Public Accountants issued Statement on Auditing Procedure (SAP) No. 45: "Using the Work and Reports of Other Auditors." This SAP establishes guidelines for reporting on financial statements when the independent auditor (referred to herein as the principal auditor) utilizes the work and reports of other auditors who have examined the financial statements of one or more subsidiaries, divisions, branches or other components included in the financial statements on which the principal auditor is reporting.

This article reviews and analyzes the provisions of SAP No. 45. It points out their implications and compares the new provisions with those set forth in Paragraphs 32 to 36 of Chapter 10 of SAP No. 33, the paragraphs which are superseded by the new Statement. It also discusses the reporting requirements set forth in SAP No. 45.

Because of the complexity of the subject and the limitation of space no attempt has here been made to cover all aspects of the new provisions;

DENNIS S. NEIER, CPA, is a Manager with the firm of *Oppenheim Appel Dixon & Co.* and is an Adjunct Lecturer in Accounting at the *Herbert H. Lehman College* (C. U. N. Y.).

and, because the kinds of arrangements that can be made between the principal auditor and other auditors are almost endless, and since the circumstances in each case will be different, no attempt has been made to cover all the possible variations and questions that might arise. Since the concerned auditor should fully understand and comply with its provisions, it is worth emphasizing the importance of actually reading and working with the new SAP itself. What the principal auditor should do in a particular situation and what he should say in his report is a matter of professional judgment but should be based on the guidelines contained in this SAP as they apply to the circumstances in his particular case. Some embarrassments have resulted from laxity in "other auditor" services and the Statement is directed to their future avoidance.

Principal Auditor's Course of Action

It is not unusual for a public accountant, as the principal auditor, to report on financial statements where part of the examination has been made by other public accountants. The principal auditor may have performed all but a minor portion of the work, or significant parts of the examination may have been performed by other auditors. This form of collaboration between two or more public accountants for the purpose of reporting on one set of financial statements gives rise to several courses of action available to the principal auditor.

He must first decide whether his own participation is sufficient to enable him appropriately to serve as the principal auditor and to report as such on the financial statements taken as a whole. Among other things, this decision should be based on the materiality of the portion of the financial statements he has examined in comparison with that examined by other auditors, the extent of the knowledge he has of the overall financial statements and the importance of the components examined by him in relation to the enterprise as a whole.

Once he decides, based on the above considerations, that it is appropriate for him to serve as the principal auditor, he has to decide whether or not he will make reference in his report to the examination made by the other auditor or auditors. The guidelines upon which this decision should be made, and the effect that such reference or lack thereof would have on the responsibility assumed by the principal auditor are discussed later in this article.

Recommended Procedures

Before the principal auditor utilizes the report of another independent auditor, regardless of whether or not he has decided to make reference to the examination of the other auditors, he should carry out certain procedures. He should make inquiries concerning the independence and professional reputation and standing of the other auditor. In this respect he could make inquiries of professional societies, other practitioners, bankers and credit grantors. He could obtain written representation from the other auditor that he is independent as defined by the American Institute of CPAs, and if appropriate, as defined by the Securities and Exchange Commission.

The principal auditor should take whatever action he deems essential to ascertain that the coordination of his activities with those of the other auditor is sufficient to permit a proper review of the matters affecting consolidation of the financial statements or combining of accounts in the financial statements. In this respect he could ascertain through communication with the other auditor:

> That he is aware that the financial statements of the component which he is to examine are to be included in the financial statements on which the principal auditor will report and that the other auditor's report thereon will be relied

upon (and, where applicable, referred to) by the principal auditor.

> That he is familiar with accounting principles generally accepted in the United States and with the generally accepted auditing standards promulgated by the American Institute of Certified Public Accountants, and will conduct his examination and will report in accordance therewith.

> That he has knowledge of the relevant financial reporting requirements for statements and schedules to be filed with regulatory agencies such as the Securities and Exchange Commission, if appropriate.

> That a review will be made of matters affecting elimination of intercompany transactions and accounts and, if appropriate in the circumstances, the uniformity of accounting practices among the components included in the financial statements.

In addition to satisfying himself as to the matters described above (and especially when the principal auditor assumes responsibility for the examination of the other auditor to the same extent as though he had performed the work himself, as discussed later), the principal auditor may want to undertake measures to satisfy himself that the scope of the other accountant's examination was adequate. Some of the measures are as follows:

> Visit the other auditor and discuss the audit procedures followed and the results thereof.

> Review the audit programs of the other auditor. In some cases it may be appropriate to issue instructions to the other auditor as to the scope of his audit work.

> Review working papers of the other auditor, including his evaluation of internal control and his conclusions as to other significant aspects of the enagagement.

> Participate in discussions with management personnel of the component whose financial statements are being examined by the other auditor regarding any significant or contentious aspects of the audit or financial statements.

> Make supplemental tests of a portion or all of the accounts examined by the other auditor.

The Assumption of Total Attestation Responsibility

If the principal auditor is satisfied, based on the procedures discussed above, as to the independence, professional reputation, and adequacy of the other auditor's examination he may be willing to assume the responsibility for the examination of the other auditor to the same extent as though he had performed the work himself. When he so decides, he *should not* make reference to the other independent auditor in his report. In this respect, SAP No. 45 is stronger and more definite than was SAP No. 33. Paragraph 36 of Chapter 10 of SAP No. 33 states that when the principal auditor is willing to assume the responsibility for the examination of the other auditor to the same extent as though he had performed the work himself, the principal auditor "need make no reference to the other independent auditor in . . . his report. If reference is made, he should state that he is assuming the responsibility for such work." SAP No. 45 holds that such reference, when the principal auditor is assuming full responsibility, may cause a reader to misinterpret the degree of responsibility being assumed, and should not be made.

The Assumption of Limited Attestation Responsibility

In many cases the principal auditor is unwilling to assume responsibility for the performance of the other auditor's work (to the same extent as though he had performed that work himself) but is willing to utilize the report of the other independent auditor for the purpose of expressing his opinion on consolidated or combined statements. In such cases the principal auditor may utilize other reports, and may appropriately express an unqualified opinion on the fairness of the consolidated or combined financial statements without assuming responsibility for the report or work of the other independent auditor, provided the basis for his opinion is adequately described. The principal auditor should indicate clearly in *both* the scope and opinion paragraphs of his report the division of responsibility between that portion of the financial statements covered by his own examination and that covered by the examination of the other auditor.

Here again, SAP No. 45 is stronger than the superseded paragraphs of SAP No. 33 which required disclosure in the scope *or* opinion paragraphs of the principal auditor's report as to the division of responsibility.

In making reference in his report to the work performed by the other auditor, the principal auditor may name the other auditor,

but only with his express permission and provided that the report of the other auditor is presented together with that of the principal auditor.

Disclosure of Magnitude of External Service

When the principal auditor decides that he will make reference to the examination of another auditor, he is required to disclose, in his report, the magnitude of the portion of the financial statements examined by the other auditor by stating the dollar amounts or percentages of the appropriate criteria that most clearly reveal the extent of participation by the other auditor. This requirement was found nowhere in Chapter 10 of SAP No. 33.

An example of appropriate reporting by the principal auditor indicating the division of responsibility when he makes reference to the examination of the other auditor follows:

> We have examined the consolidated balance sheet of X Company and subsidiaries as of December 31, 197_ and the related consolidated statements of income and retained earnings and of changes in financial position for the year then ended. Our examination was made in accordance with generally accepted auditing standards and accordingly included such tests of the accounting records and such other auditing procedures as we considered necessary in the circumstances. We did not examine the financial statements of B Company, a consolidated subsidiary, which statements reflect total assets and revenues constituting 20% and 22%, respectively, of the related consolidated totals. These statements were examined by other auditors whose report thereon has been furnished to us and our opinion expressed herein, insofar as it relates to the amounts included for B Company, is based solely upon the report of the other auditors.

> In our opinion, based upon our examination and the report of other auditors, the accompanying consolidated balance sheet and consolidated statements of income and retained earnings and of changes in financial position present fairly. . . .

When two or more auditors in addition to the principal auditor participate in the examination, the percentages covered by the others may be stated in the aggregate.

The mention of work performed by other auditors in the report of the principal auditor, under the guidelines established in SAP No. 45, is only a factual explanation of the manner in which the examination was performed and an indication of the divided responsibility between the auditors and should not be considered a qualification of the opinion.

Inability to Utilize the Work or Report of the Other Auditor. A situation might arise in which the principal auditor concludes, based on the results of the inquiries and procedures outlined above, that he can neither assume responsibility for the work of the other auditor insofar as that work relates to the principal auditor's expression of an opinion on the financial statements taken as a whole, nor report in the manner set forth under "The Assumption of Limited Attestation Responsibility" above. In such situations, he should appropriately qualify or disclaim an opinion on the financial statements taken as a whole stating his reasons and the magnitude of the portion of the financial statements to which his qualification extends. Superseded paragraph 35 of Chapter 10 of SAP No. 33, which dealt with this situation, recommended the use of "except for" when the intention was to qualify the opinion. This recommendation is not repeated in SAP No. 45 as it was realized that situations of this kind could exist where a "subject to" qualification might also be appropriate.

Auditors' Responsibilities

Whether or not the principal auditor makes reference in his report to the examination made by the other auditors, the other auditors remain responsible for the performance of their examinations and for their own opinions.

In order to avoid confusion, this point warrants some discussion. One might wonder if it contradicts the idea expressed earlier that the principal auditor *can* assume responsibility for the report and work of other auditors. These two points, in my opinion, are not contradictory but are rather complementary, one really clarifying the other. Where the principal auditor assumes responsibility for the report and work of the other auditor, he does so only insofar as the other auditor's report and work affects the consolidated or combined financial statements taken as a whole. The other auditor remains responsible for the performance of his own examination and for his own opinion when the financial statements (or the part of the financial statements) upon which he is reporting are considered individually.

The principal auditor who utilizes the work and report of another auditor for the purpose of expressing his opinion on consolidated or combined statements, and assumes responsibility for the performance of the work and for the opinion of the other auditor to the same extent as though he had performed that work himself, is solely responsible to third parties who rely on the opinion of the principal auditor with respect to the consolidated or combined financial statements. The other auditors are solely responsible to third parties (including the principal auditor) who rely on the opinion expressed by them as to the individual financial statements (or part thereof) examined by them.

Other Aspects

Qualifications in the Report of the Other Auditor. If the report of the other auditor is qualified, an additional burden is placed on the principal auditor. He must decide whether the subject of the qualification is material in relation to the consolidated statements taken as a whole. If the subject of the qualification is material, a qualification in the report of the principal auditor would be required *whether or not* the report of the other auditor is presented.

It is interesting to note the terminology used in paragraph 14 of SAP No. 45 when stating the reporting requirements of the principal auditor with respect to referencing a qualification, contained in the report of the other auditor, which is not considered material in relation to the consolidated financial statements taken as a whole. There is an ever-so-slight difference in the terminology depending on whether or not the other auditor's report, containing such a qualification, is presented. The SAP states that if the subject of a qualification in the report of the other auditor is not considered material in relation to the consolidated financial statements taken as a whole "and the other auditor's report is not presented, the principal auditor *need not* (emphasis added) make reference in his report to the qualification; if the other auditor's report is presented, the principal auditor *may wish* (emphasis added) to make reference to such qualification. . . ." The terms "need not" and "may wish" both imply that it is not required that the principal auditor make reference to a qualification contained in the report of the other auditor which is not considered material in relation to the financial statements taken as a whole, but, the principal auditor can, if he so wishes, make reference to such qualification in his report in either case. Why, then, the difference in terminology? The slight difference implies that if the other auditor's report is presented it would be more appropriate for the principal auditor to make reference to such qualification than if the report of the other auditor was not presented; however, if reference is made in either case, the principal auditor should state that the subject and nature of the qualification in the report of the other auditor is not material in relation to the consolidated statements taken as a whole.

Reporting on Financial Statements of Prior Years Following a Pooling of Interests. The question as to what the principal auditor's function and responsibilities are when he is called upon to report on the related financial statements of one or more prior years following a pooling of interests transaction when other auditors have examined one or more of the entities included in such financial statements was not covered in Chapter 10 of SAP No. 33 but is discussed in SAP No. 45.

In these situations, the auditor may decide that, based on the guidelines discussed above, he cannot serve as principal auditor, in which case he would be unable to render an opinion as to the fairness of the financial statements taken as a whole. Also, in such cases, it is often impossible, inappropriate or unnecessary for the auditor to perform sufficient auditing procedures to enable him to express an opinion on the restated financial statements taken as a whole. However, his review may have been sufficient in scope (i.e.: checking the compilation for mathematical accuracy and for conformity of the compilation methods with generally accepted accounting principles) to enable him to express an opinion solely with respect to the compilation of such statements. SAP No. 45 indicates, however, that the auditor should not even issue an opinion as to compilation unless he "has examined the statement of at least one of the entities included in the restatement for at least the latest period presented." In reporting on the compilation of such restated financial statements the auditor does not assume responsibility for the work of other auditors nor the responsibility for expressing an opinion on the related financial statements taken as a whole.

Predecessor Auditor. When an auditor examines financial statements for the first time, he must either satisfy himself as to the account balances at the beginning of the period under examination and as to the consistency of the application of accounting principles in that period as compared with the preceding period, or he must appropriately qualify his opinion or disclaim an opinion and state his reasons for so doing. The auditor, in applying auditing procedures to the account balances at the beginning of the period under examination may consult with the predecessor auditor and may review the predecessor auditor's working papers, but the auditor cannot rely solely on the work performed by the predecessor auditor and relieve himself of responsibility for such work by making reference to the report or work of the predecessor auditor in his report.

Conclusion

As the concepts of accountants' legal liability are changing, there is a great deal of question and concern regarding the extent of the responsibility of both the principal and the secondary auditor when the principal auditor reports on financial statements where part of the examination has been made by other auditors. The new SAP should clarify the responsibility of both the principal and secondary auditor and should lead to better reporting practices and a clearer understanding as to the meaning of the disclosure of the use of the work of other auditors in an audit report. ∎

CASE 34

MACON COUNTY LINE CO.

You have just completed the annual examination of Macon County Line Co. (Macon) for the current year. Macon is a parent corporation with several subsidiary companies. One of its subsidiaries, Georgia Corporation (Georgia), is audited by another independent CPA. Georgia represents total assets and revenues constituting 16 percent and 14 percent, respectively, of the related consolidated totals for Macon and all of its subsidiaries.

Upon completion of your examination you issued the following auditor's report:

> We have examined the consolidated balance sheet of Macon County Line Co. and subsidiaries as of December 31, 19x0, and the related consolidated statements of income and retained earnings and changes in financial position for the year then ended. Our examination was made in accordance with generally accepted auditing standards and accordingly included such tests of the accounting records and such other auditing procedures as we considered necessary in the circumstances. We did not examine the financial statements of Georgia Corporation, a consolidated subsidiary, which statements reflect total assets and revenues constituting 16 percent and 14 percent, respectively, of the related consolidated totals. These statements were examined by other auditors whose report thereon has been furnished to us, and our opinion expressed herein, insofar as it relates to the amounts included for Georgia Corporation, is based solely upon the report of the other auditors.
>
> In our opinion, based upon our examination and the report of other auditors, the financial statements referred to above present fairly the consolidated financial position of Macon County Line Co. and its subsidiaries as of December 31, 19x0, and the consolidated results of its operations and the consolidated changes in its financial position for the year then ended, in conformity with generally accepted accounting principles applied on a basis consistent with that of the preceding year.
>
> (Signature and Date)

Assume that you completed your field work for the Macon County Line Co. engagement on February 15, 19x1, and that the other auditors completed their field work of the Georgia Corporation on the same day. On March 2, 19x1, you become aware that a major customer of the parent company, Macon, has filed for bankruptcy. The customer owed Macon $1,000,000 on December 31, 19x0, considered a material amount.

CASE DISCUSSION QUESTIONS

1. Assuming that you adjust the financial statements of Macon for the $1,000,000 bad debt expense, what date should you use for Macon's report? Explain, given the fact that no disclosure of the bad debt is made.

2. Suppose that you adjust Macon's financial statements and disclose the bad debt of $1,000,000 in a footnote. Discuss the methods available to you as the independent auditor regarding the dating of your report.

3. What factors regarding degree of involvement should you have considered before agreeing to serve as a principal auditor for Macon County Line Co.? Discuss.

4. Discuss situations that would cause you, as principal auditor of Macon, to refer to the work of the other auditor in your report.

5. In preparing your report on Macon's financial statements, reference was made to the work of another auditor.

    a. Discuss the significant points of such a report.

    b. Explain why your reference in the report to another auditor's work is not to be considered as a qualification of the opinion.

6. Explain how your report on Macon would be affected if the independent auditor's report on Georgia was qualified with respect to inventories. The qualification is due to the fact that the other auditor was unable to observe the taking of physical inventory.

7. On April 16, 19x1, the controller of Macon contacts you concerning the possibility of reissuing the company's 19x0 annual financial statements. She asks what your responsibility would entail with respect to the reissuing of your report on the 19x0 statements in an S-X filing with the SEC.

   The controller wants to know specifically if you will update your report and whether you will have to make further investigations. How would you respond to the controller's inquiries?

22

Special Reports

(Section 621, SAS No. 14, and Section 622, SAS No. 35)

A special report is a report for which wording which differs from that included in the auditor's standard report is required in order to identify the basis on which the information was prepared or to describe the special character of the engagement. Special reports are appropriate in circumstances when the CPA is requested to report on:

> Statements that are prepared in accordance with a comprehensive basis of accounting other than GAAP

> Specific elements, accounts, or items of a financial statement

> Compliance with contractual agreements or regulatory requirements related to audited financial statements

> Financial information presented in prescribed forms or schedules that require a uniform statement presentation or, in some cases, a prescribed form of report.

Reports meeting the above criteria are identified as special reports. SAS No. 14 does not apply to reports issued in connection with the following:

> Limited reviews of interim financial information

> Financial forecasts, projections, or feasibility studies

> Compliance with respect to contractual agreements or regulatory requirements unrelated to financial statements

Statements Prepared in Accordance with a Comprehensive Basis of Accounting Other than GAAP

The four standards of reporting apply when the CPA is reporting on statements prepared in accordance with a comprehensive basis of accounting other than GAAP.

The term, *financial statements*, refers to a presentation of financial data, including accompanying notes, obtained from accounting records and intended to communicate an enterprise's resources and obligations at a point in time or the changes over a period of time in compliance with a comprehensive basis of accounting.

GAAS are applicable when an auditor examines and reports on any financial statements of an entity. Balance sheets, statements of income and retained earnings, changes in financial position, and changes in owners' equity are traditional financial statements. For reporting purposes, the CPA should also consider the following types of financial presentations to be financial statements:

Statements of assets and liabilities that do not include owners' equity accounts

Statements of revenue and expenses

Summaries of operations

Statements of operations by product line

Statements of cash receipts and disbursements

Financial presentations prepared on a modified accrual basis or on the cash basis

In reporting on financial statements, the CPA's judgment as to overall fairness of financial presentation should be applied within the framework provided by GAAP. The meaning of present fairly in conformity with GAAP and the source of authoritative support for GAAP is discussed in SAS No. 5. In certain circumstances, however, a comprehensive basis of accounting other than GAAP may provide a suitable framework for determining overall fairness. Accordingly, financial statements may be prepared in accordance with GAAP or, alternatively, on one of the following bases:

A basis of accounting used by the enterprise in complying with requirements or financial reporting provisions of a government regulatory agency. Examples include the basis of accounting prescribed in a uniform system of accounts that the Interstate Commerce Commission requires railroad companies to follow and a basis of accounting used by insurance companies in complying with the rules of a state insurance commission

The same basis of accounting that the reporting enterprise uses to file its income tax return for the period covered by the financial statements

The cash basis modified to reflect the recording of such non-cash items as depreciation on fixed assets or accruing of income taxes

A basis of accounting having substantial support that is applied to all material items appearing in the financial statements, such as the price-level basis of accounting delineated in Accounting Principles Board Statement No. 3

When reporting on statements prepared in accordance with a comprehensive basis of accounting other than GAAP, the CPA should include in the audit report, in addition to a scope paragraph, the following information:

A separate paragraph that states or, preferably, refers to a note in the statements that states the basis of presentation

A separate paragraph that describes or, preferably, refers to a note that describes how the basis of presentation differs from GAAP or, if applicable, states that GAAP have not been established. The monetary effect of such differences need not be stated

A separate paragraph that states that the presentation is not intended to be in conformity with GAAP

A paragraph that indicates the auditor's opinion as to whether the statements present fairly the information on the basis indicated and discloses that the basis of accounting used is consistent with that used in the preceding period

When reporting on financial statements prepared on a comprehensive basis of accounting other than GAAP, the auditor should consider whether the statements (including the accompanying notes) include the necessary disclosures appropriate for the basis of accounting used.

When issuing a report on financial statements prepared in compliance with the requirements of financial reporting provisions of a government agency, the CPA may use a form of reporting specified by SAS No. 14 only if the financial statements are intended solely for filing with a regulatory agency, or if additional distribution is deemed appropriate by an AICPA accounting or audit guide or auditing interpretation.

Unless the financial statements are intended to be presented in compliance with a comprehensive basis of accounting other than GAAP, the CPA should use the standard report described in SAS No. 2 (509.07), *Reports on Audited Financial Statements*, modified as appropriate to reflect departures from GAAP.

The following is an illustration of an auditor's report on financial statements prepared on the cash basis which incorporates the above requirements:

> We have examined the statement of assets and liabilities arising from cash transactions of XYZ Company as of December 31, 19xx, and the related statement of revenue collected and expenses paid for the year then ended. Our examination was made in accordance with generally accepted auditing standards and, accordingly, included such tests of the accounting records and such other auditing procedures as we considered necessary in the circumstances.
>
> As more fully described in Note X, the Company's policy is to prepare its financial statements on the basis of cash receipts and disbursements; consequently, the financial statements do not include certain assets, liabilities, revenue, and expenses. Accordingly, the financial statements are not intended to present financial position and results of operations in conformity with generally accepted accounting principles.
>
> In our opinion, the financial statements referred to above present fairly the assets and liabilities arising from cash transactions of XYZ Company as of December 31, 19xx, and the revenue collected and expenses paid during the year then ended, on the basis indicated in the preceding paragraph, which basis is consistent with that used in the preceding year.

The CPA should consider whether the financial statements reported on are suitably titled. For example, a cash basis statement may properly be titled "Statement of Assets and Liabilities Arising from Cash Transactions." A financial statement prepared on a statutory or regulatory basis might be titled "Balance Sheet (Regulatory basis)." A CPA should avoid being associated with financial reports that contain titles that are misleading. For example, a statement of cash receipts and cash disbursements is not a balance sheet and should not be so titled.

Reporting on Specified Elements of Financial Statements

An auditor may be requested to report on one or more specified elements, accounts, or items of financial statements. In performing such an engagement, the CPA may present the specified element(s), account(s), or item(s) in the report or in a document accompanying the report in one of two ways.

1. A report expressing an opinion on one or more identified elements, accounts or items of a financial statement, such as rentals, royalties, or profit participation.

2. A report relating to the results of applying agreed-upon procedures to one or more identified elements, accounts or items of a financial statement.

Opinion on Identified Elements.   Since identified elements of a financial statement taken alone do not constitute a financial statement, the first standard of reporting (requiring a declarative statement regarding presentation in conformity with GAAP) does not apply. However, the other three standards of reporting are applicable (the presentation must be consistent, disclosure must be adequate, and the CPA must express an opinion or disclaim an opinion). Since each identified element of a statement must stand alone, the measurement of materiality must be compared to each individual element, account, or item examined rather than to the aggregate or the financial statements taken as a whole. Also, many statement elements are interrelated, for example, sales and receivables, inventory and payables, and fixed assets and depreciation. Consequently, an auditor should recognize, in planning this type of engagement, that it is usually necessary to perform a more extensive examination of each element. A CPA should not report on identified elements, accounts, or items included in financial statements on which an adverse opinion has been expressed or an opinion disclaimed based on an audit if such reporting would be tantamount to expressing a piecemeal opinion. When an auditor is engaged to express an opinion on one or more identified elements, accounts, or items of a financial statement, such as rentals, royalties, a profit participation, or provision for income taxes, the report should include the following:

> Identify the specified elements, accounts, or items examined

> State whether the examination was made in accordance with GAAS and, if applicable, that it was made as part of an examination of financial statements

> Identify the basis on which the identified elements are presented and when applicable, related agreements

> Describe and indicate the source of significant interpretations made by client during the examination that relate to the provisions of a relevant agreement

> Indicate whether in the opinion of the auditor the identified elements, accounts, or items are presented fairly on the basis indicated

> If appropriate, denote whether in the opinion of the auditor the disclosed basis has been applied consistently with that of the preceding period

When a CPA has made an examination in accordance with GAAS, it may be considered desirable to describe certain auditing procedures applied to provide more information as to the scope of his examination. Presented below is an illustration of a report relating to the amount of sales for purpose of computation of rental (with description of auditing procedures applied):

> Board of Directors
> ABC Company
>
> We have examined the statement of gross sales (as defined in the lease agreement dated March 4, 19xx, between ABC Company, as lessor, and XYZ Stores Corporation, as lessee), of XYZ Stores Corporation at its Main Street store, City, State, for the year ended December 31, 19xx. Our examination was made in accordance with generally accepted auditing standards and, accordingly, included such tests of the accounting records and such other auditing procedures as we considered necessary in the circumstances.
>
> Specifically, we examined weekly cash reports for the year submitted by the store manager. Those reports contained information as to gross sales, cash register readings, sales taxes imposed by governmental authorities, remittances made by the store manager, returns and allowances, discounts granted, and other information. We compared the monthly summary of those reports with the general ledger, and for selected days in each month we compared the daily net cash receipts shown in the weekly cash reports with the Corporation's bank statements.
>
> In our opinion, the statement of gross sales referred to above presents fairly the gross sales of XYZ Stores Corporation at its Main Street store for the year ended December 31, 19xx, on the basis defined in the agreement referred to above.

Reports on Agreed-Upon Procedures on Specified Accounts or Items   When the scope of examination is limited to agreed-upon procedures regarding one or more specified accounts or items not necessarily intended to be sufficient to enable the CPA to express an opinion on the specified accounts or items, this should be stated in the report. Moreover, a CPA should refrain from commenting on matters to which his or her competency has little relevance. Accepting an engagement to report on specified accounts or items is appropriate only when:

> The parties involved have a clear understanding of the specific procedures to be performed

Distribution of the report is to be made only to named parties

The CPA's report should (1) specify the identified elements, accounts, or items to which agreed-upon procedures were applied, (2) specify to whom the report will be distributed, (3) indicate procedures performed, (4) state the CPA's findings, (5) disclaim an opinion concerning the identified elements, accounts, or items, and (6) state that the report relates only to the elements specified and does not extend to the financial statements taken as a whole. In the event that the accountant proposes no adjustments to the identified elements, accounts, or items, a comment to that effect may be included in the report. For example, the report might contain the following comment:

> In connection with the procedures referred to above, no matters came to our attention that should be adjusted (specified elements, accounts, or items should be named)

Also, the CPA may decide to mention that additional procedures were performed concerning the identified elements, accounts, or items, or had the financial statements been examined in accordance with GAAS, other information might have been noted that would have been reported.

The second and third standards of field work and the standards of reporting are not applicable to an engagement limited by agreed-upon procedures to one or more specified elements, accounts, or items of a financial statement; however, the general standards and the first standard of field work do apply.

Presented below is an illustration of a report on agreed-upon procedures (report in connection with claims of creditors):

Trustee
XYZ Company

At your request, we have reviewed the claims of creditors against XYZ Company as of May 31, 19xx, as set forth in the accompanying schedules. Our review was made solely to assist you in evaluating the reasonableness of those claims, and our report is not to be used for any other purpose. The agreed-upon procedures we performed are summarized as follows:

> We compared the trial balance total of accounts payable at May 31, 19xx, prepared by the Company, to the Company's general ledger balance.

> We compared the claims received from creditors to the trial balance of accounts payable.

> We examined documentation submitted by the creditors in support of their claims and compared it to documentation maintained by the Company, including invoices, receiving records and other evidence of receipt of goods or services.

> Except as set forth in Schedule B, we reconciled differences between amounts claimed by creditors and amounts shown in the Company's records.

Our findings are presented in the accompanying schedules. Schedule A lists claims that are in agreement with or were reconciled to the Company's records. Schedule B lists claims that we were unable to reconcile and sets forth the differences in amounts.

Because those procedures do not constitute an examination made in accordance with generally accepted auditing standards, we express no opinion on the financial statements of XYZ Company as of May 31, 19xx, taken as a whole, or on any specific claims referred to in the accompanying schedules. Furthermore, had we performed additional procedures or had we made an examination of the financial statements in accordance with generally accepted auditing standards, matters might have come to our attention that would have been reported to you. The May 31, 19xx, financial statements of XYZ Company do not accompany or constitute a part of this report.

Compliance with Contractual Agreements or Regulatory Requirements

Compliance reports may be required by contractual agreements such as bond indentures and certain types of loan agreements, or by regulatory agencies. In certain instances, the borrower may be required to file financial information in addition to audited financial statements. The CPA normally satisfies this request by giving the lenders negative assurance relative to the applicable covenants. This kind of assurance may be expressed in a separate report or in one or more paragraphs of the CPA's standard report accompanying the financial statements. However, negative assurance should not be given unless the CPA has examined the financial statements related to the contractual agreements or regulatory requirements.

It should be made clear that the expression of negative assurance is being given in connection with an examination of the financial statements. The CPA may also wish to indicate that the examination was not conducted for the primary purpose of obtaining knowledge with respect to compliance. A separate report giving negative assurance should include a paragraph indicating that the financial statements have been examined, the date of the report indicated, and whether the examination was conducted in accordance with GAAS noted. An example of a report relating to assurance as to compliance with contractual agreements given in a separate report is presented below:

> We have examined the balance sheet of XYZ Company as of December 31, 19x1, and the related statements of income, retained earnings and changes in financial position for the year then ended and have issued our report thereon dated February 16, 19x2. Our examination was made in accordance with generally accepted auditing standards and, accordingly, included such tests of the accounting records and such other auditing procedures as we considered necessary in the circumstances.
>
> In connection with our examination, nothing came to our attention that indicated that the Company was in default with respect to the terms, covenants, provisions, or conditions of Section XX of the indenture dated July 21, 19x0. However, it should be noted that our examination was not directed primarily toward obtaining such knowledge.

Financial Information Presented in Prescribed Forms or Schedules

Preprinted forms or schedules often prescribe a uniform financial presentation and sometimes prescribe the wording of the auditor's report. This usually occurs with respect to reports for government regulatory agencies. When a printed form requires that an assertion be made that the auditor believes is not justified, the form should be reworded or a separate report attached. Regulatory authorities will usually accept reports with such modifications.

Reference

The following article entitled "Special Reports and the Local CPA" should be read in conjunction with the above summarization of SAS No. 14 as it discusses significant points covered in SAS No. 14 and recent auditing interpretations on special reports.

Special Reports
and the Local CPA

THOMAS D. HUBBARD
Professor of Accounting
University of Nebraska
Lincoln

JERRY B. BULLINGTON
Partner, Smith, Elliott & Company
Hagerstown, Maryland

(Portions of this article are based on information contained in **Statement on Auditing Standards No. 14,** "Special Reports," Auditing Standards Executive Committee (December 1976), and **Accounting and Auditing Updating Workshop,** (1978) Thomas D. Hubbard, both published by the American Institute of Certified Public Accountants, New York.)

Generally overlooked in the promulgation of accounting standards in particular, and in some degree auditing standards, is the information needs of the local business establishment operated by one or a few owners. In most localities it is the local CPA who serves the needs of the local business enterprise by providing a variety of services, including preparation of income tax reports, accounting services and the preparation of unaudited financial statements and, in many instances, engagements involving audited financial reports.

When the CPA is associated with his client's financial statements, audited or unaudited, such statements must be presented in conformity with generally accepted accounting principles (GAAP). If the statements are audited, the CPA must follow generally accepted auditing standards (GAAS). Promulgated accounting and auditing standards in many instances, emphasize the public accountability and reporting responsibility associated with the large national corporation and, accordingly, place a burden on the local business enterprise by requiring information or procedures in their financial statements that is unnecessary in many instances and not very useful in providing needed information for decision making.

Many CPAs have suggested for some time that there is a need for differentiating between GAAP necessary to meet the reporting responsibilities of the large public corporation and GAAP that will provide information that is useful in the smaller business enterprise. The controversy over "Big GAAP vs. little GAAP" will not be settled before meaningful service can be rendered.

Perhaps, with the issuance of **Statement on Auditing Standards (SAS) No. 14,** "Special Reports," a vehicle now exists for the local CPA to serve the needs of his clients in a meaningful fashion within the framework of promulgated accounting and auditing standards. For unaudited statements, the new **Statement on Standards for Accounting and Review Services** (SARS No. 1) now provides a meaningful reporting format for nonpublic clients.

Special Reports and SAS No. 14

In October 1957, the Committee on Auditing Procedure of the American Institute of Certified Public Accountants issued **Statement on Auditing Procedure (SAP) No. 28** on Special Reports.[1] SAP No. 28 provided a basis for differentiating between reports for which the wording of the usual auditor's short-form report was inappropriate and situations where special wording of the auditor's report was required. Topics covered by the Statement included cash basis reports or reports on another incomplete basis of accounting which was materially at variance with accounting practices customarily followed in preparing accrual basis statements. Reports for nonprofit organizations were also covered by the Statement. SAP No. 28 clearly indicated that most special reports including cash basis statements do not purport to present results of operations and financial position in conformity with GAAP and, accordingly, the first standard of reporting[2] was not applicable to such statements. The auditor was required to express an opinion on the fairness of the basis of presentation and avoid the implication that the basis of presentation was in conformity with GAAP.

SAP No. 28 was codified in SAP No. 33 and, subsequently, the auditing standards governing special reports were included in SAS No. 1, Section 620, which has now been superseded by SAS No. 14.

Statement No. 14 directs reporting on fairness of presentation of financial statements and financial

data based upon examinations in accordance with GAAS for engagements involving:

1. Financial statements that are prepared in accordance with a comprehensive basis of accounting other than GAAP.
2. Specified elements, accounts or items of a financial statement.
3. Compliance with aspects of contractual agreements or regulatory requirements related to audited statements.
4. Financial information presented in prescribed forms or schedules that require a prescribed form of auditor's report.

Reporting on Financial Statements Prepared in Accordance With a Comprehensive Basis of Accounting Other Than GAAP

GAAS are applicable when an auditor reports on financial statements. The term "financial statement" refers to a presentation of financial data, including accompanying notes that is intended to communicate an entity's economic resources and obligations at a point in time or the changes therein for a period of time in accordance with a comprehensive basis of accounting.

The auditor in expressing an opinion on fairness of presentation of financial statements must apply judgment concerning certain items. Judgment can be applied only within an identifiable framework, usually provided by GAAP.[3] With the adoption of SAS No. 14, however, the auditor now can make a judgment decision based on a comprehensive system of accounting other than GAAP. Other appropriate comprehensive basis of accounting, which may be applicable in selected circumstances, include the following:

1. Regulatory basis of accounting.
2. Income tax basis of accounting.
3. Cash basis of accounting
4. Other comprehensive basis of accounting.

A definite set of criteria having substantial support in the statements, such as the price-level basis of accounting described in APB Statement No. 3, "Financial Statements Restated for General Price-Level Changes."

Reporting in accordance with a comprehensive basis of accounting other than GAAP is restricted by Statement No. 14 to one of the

SPECIAL REPORTS [continued]

foregoing described basis of accounting. Fairness of presentation of financial statements or financial information on any basis of accounting other than those described above must be judged in accordance with GAAP, and the CPA must follow the reporting requirements in Section 509 (SAS No. 2).

When reporting on one of the identified comprehensive basis of accounting other than GAAP the auditor must include certain specific information in his report. In addition to identification of the statements examined and stating that the examination was made in accordance with GAAS the auditor must include a paragraph in his report (or refer to a note to the financial statements) that states the basis of presentation. In addition, a note should be included with the financial statements that describes how the basis of presentation differs from GAAP (Monetary amounts need not be stated) and the auditor should refer to this note in his report. The auditor must indicate in his report that the financial statements are not intended to be presented in conformity with GAAP. In expressing his opinion on fairness the auditor must say that the statements are presented fairly (or other appropriate opinion or disclaimer) in conformity with the basis of accounting described in the report. The second standard of reporting applies to financial statements presented on a comprehensive basis of accounting other than GAAP and the auditor must, accordingly, indicate whether the described basis of accounting used was applied in a manner consistent with that of the preceding period.

SAS No. 14 presents several illustrative reports based on an examination of financial statements presented on a comprehensive basis of accounting other than GAAP.

When the auditor is reporting on statements prepared according to the requirements of a government regulatory agency (regulatory basis), he may use the form of reporting described in SAS No. 14 only if the financial statements are intended solely for filing with the government agency or if additional distribution is recognized as appropriate by an AICPA Accounting or Audit Guide or an Auditing Interpretation.

The third standard of reporting on informative disclosure is applicable to special reports and may very well create problems in application. The financial statement disclosures required for reporting in conformity with GAAP are spelled out in promulgated accounting pronounce-ments, many in great detail; those required by accepted practice are generally identifiable. Disclosures required in financial statements prepared on a comprehensive basis of accounting other than GAAP are, on the other hand, not so clearly delineated. For example, what disclosures are required for cash basis statements? Is cash earnings per share information required? What disclosures are generally accepted when reporting on the income tax basis? Although a comprehensive basis of accounting does exist for the preparation of cash basis statements and statements based on the income tax rules and regulations disclosure standards necessary for fair presentation are not clearly defined and would seem to be a matter calling for the exercise of judgment. Perhaps the lack of guidance for disclosure in these areas is a blessing in disguise and CPAs will direct their attention to disclosing those matters that are of genuine interest to their clients in interpreting the information presented in the statements.

The Auditing Standards Board has recently issued an interpretation of SAS No. 14 titled **Adequacy of Disclosure in Financial Statements Prepared on a Comprehensive Basis of Accounting Other Than Generally Accepted Accounting Principles**, which clarifies somewhat the disclosure problems in such statements. The Interpretation states that when financial statements prepared on another comprehensive basis of accounting contain items that are the same as, or similar to, those in financial statements prepared in conformity with GAAP, the same degree of information disclosures is generally appropriate. The auditor must, of course, also consider disclosing other material matters.

The Auditing Standards Board, in SAS No. 26 **Association With Financial Statements**, has provided a standard disclaimer of opinion (for public companies) on unaudited financial statements prepared on a comprehensive basis of accounting other than GAAP. The Compilation or Review Report, as appropriate, in SARS No. 1, with revision for financial statement titles, would be used for reporting on a nonpublic company's statements presented on a comprehensive basis of accounting other than GAAP.

An auditor may be requested to report on special-purpose financial presentations that do not constitute a complete presentation of historical financial position or results of operations of an entity. For example, a governmental agency may require a schedule of gross income and certain expenses of an entity's real estate operations in which income and expenses are measured in conformity with GAAP, but expenses are defined to exclude certain items such as interest, depreciation, and income taxes. Such special-purpose financial presentations, as explained in an Auditing Standards Board Interpretation, **Reporting on Special-Purpose Financial Presentations**, constitute a comprehensive basis of reporting as specified in SAS No. 14. Accordingly, the auditor should express an opinion on the fairness of the presentation of the information taken as a whole in conformity with GAAP. The Interpretation presents examples of appropriate reporting format.

Reports on Specified Elements, Accounts or Items of a Financial Statement

Statement No. 14 permits reporting on one or more specified elements, accounts or items of a financial statement. These reports may include a report expressing an opinion on financial statement items, such as rentals, royalties, a profit participation agreement or a provision for income taxes. Also included would be a report relating to the results of applying agreed-upon procedures to one or more specified elements, accounts or items appearing on financial statements.

Audit engagements involving financial statement elements, accounts or items may be undertaken as a separate engagement or as part of an overall audit of the financial statements. An auditor should not, however, issue these types of special reports when he has expressed an adverse opinion or disclaimed an opinion based on an audit if such reporting would be regarded as the issuance of a piecemeal opinion. An auditor may, however, examine a client's financial statements, issue an adverse opinion or disclaimer and in a separate engagement, express an opinion on the fairness of presentation of specific elements, accounts or items appearing in the statements. This type of reporting is appropriate providing the content of the special report is not so extensive as to constitute a major portion of the financial statements.

An auditor's report covering specific elements, accounts, or items of a financial statement should identify the scope of his examination, state whether the examination was made in accordance with GAAS and, if applicable, that it was made in conjunction with an audit of the financial statements. Any modification of the report should also be indicated. The basis of presentation of the elements, accounts or items and the source of any significant interpretations made in the course of the engagement that may relate to the provisions of a relevant agreement should be described. The auditor will conclude his report by indicating whether the specified elements, accounts or items are presented fairly on the basis indicated and, if applicable, whether the disclosed basis has been applied in a manner consistent with that of the preceding period. The auditor may, if he wishes, describe certain auditing procedures that he has applied in the course of the engagement.

Reports Relating to the Results of Applying Agreed-Upon Procedures to Specified Elements, Accounts or Items

A CPA may be requested to perform selected procedures that he and his client agree upon concerning specific elements, accounts or items appearing on the client's financial statements or the financial statements of other companies involving amounts related to the client's operations. Statement No. 14, for example, indicates that such engagements would be appropriate in connection with a proposed acquisition or to assist in reconciling differences between amounts reported in a client's financial statement and claims of creditors. Such reports would involve issuance of negative assurance by the auditor, as for example "In connection with the procedures referred to above, no matters came to our attention that caused us to believe that the (specified elements, accounts or items) should be adjusted."

When the CPA and his client have reached a clear understanding regarding procedures to be performed relative to specified elements, accounts or items of a financial statement, the auditor may perform such engagements provided the report he issues is restricted to named parties and the financial statements of the entity do not accompany his report. In addition, the CPA should indicate the specific elements, accounts or items to which the agreed-upon procedures have been applied and state the intended distribution of the report. The procedures applied in the examination should be identified in the report and the CPA should state his findings, disclaim an opinion on the elements, accounts or items because of the limited scope of his review and state that the report should not be associated with the client's financial statements. If the auditor has no adjustments to propose, as a result of his review,

the report may include a comment to that effect. The auditor may also wish to indicate in his report that had he performed additional procedures or made an examination of the financial statements in accordance with GAAS, other matters might have come to his attention that would have been reported. An Auditing Standards Board Interpretation, **Understanding of Agreed-Upon Procedures,** describes the steps an accountant may take when he is not able to discuss the procedures directly with all of the parties who will receive a special report on the results of applying agreed-upon procedures.

Reports on Compliance with Aspects of Contractual Agreements or Regulatory Requirements Related to Financial Statements

Clients may be required by contractual agreements or regulatory agencies to furnish compliance reports by independent auditors. Such reports may, for example, be required under bond indentures or loan agreements. These reports may involve the preparation of audited financial statements. Contractual agreements or regulatory authorities may request assurance from the independent auditor that the borrower or regulated company has complied with covenants or regulatory requirements regarding accounting or auditing matters. The auditor will normally satisfy this requirement, according to Statement No. 14, by giving negative assurance. Negative assurance may be given in a separate report or in one or more paragraphs of the auditor's report accompanying the financial statements. Negative assurance, however, should not be given unless the auditor has examined the financial statements to which the contractual agreements or regulatory requirements relate.

An agreement may specify accounting practices to be used in the preparation of financial statements that depart from GAAP. A loan agreement, for example, may require the borrower to prepare consolidated financial statements in which investments in certain unconsolidated subsidiaries are presented on the equity method of accounting and investments in other unconsolidated subsidiaries are presented at cost (a basis that is not in conformity with GAAP in the borrower's circumstances). An Auditing Standards Board Interpretation, **Financial Statements Prepared in Accordance with Accounting Practices Specified in an Agreement,** states that a basis of accounting specified in an agreement is not a comprehensive basis of

accounting as specified by SAS No. 14. In these circumstances, the auditor should modify his report as to the conformity of the special purpose statements with GAAP. However, the auditor may also express an opinion on whether the statements are presented fairly on the basis of accounting specified in the agreement. The Interpretation presents illustrative examples of such reports.

Financial Information Presented in Prescribed Forms or Schedules

Printed forms or schedules designed by bodies with which they are to be filed often prescribe wording for an auditor's signature. When a printed report form calls upon a CPA to make an assertion that he believes he is not justified in making, he should reword the form or attach a separate report. When modifying preprinted forms, the CPA should type either an appropriate disclaimer or a reference such as, "see attached disclaimer of opinion," and submit his own disclaimer. Such a disclaimer might read:

This report has not been audited by us and accordingly we do not express an opinion on it. It has been prepared on a prescribed form for use by the State Corporation Commission [or other appropriate agency], and does not necessarily include all disclosures required for fair presentation of the financial position of the company in accordance with generally accepted accounting principles. [4]

Statement No. 14 implies that the existence of such a preprinted form may, in itself, indicate that a "Comprehensive Basis of Accounting" exists and, therefore, reporting on that basis may be accomplished by issuance of a special report.

Conclusion

Statement No. 14 has one characteristic that separates it from most authoritative pronouncements. That is, it provides guidelines which may be employed rather than those which must be employed. The local CPA and his clients may well benefit from its issuance if its guidelines are wisely utilized.

---

[1] **Statement on Auditing Procedure No. 28,** "Special Reports," **Journal of Accountancy,** December 1957, AICPA, New York, pp. 65-67.

[2] The first standard of reporting reads: "The report shall state whether the financial statements are presented in accordance with generally accepted accounting principles."

[3] For an explanation of the meaning of the phrase "present fairly in conformity with generally accepted accounting principles," see **Statement on Auditing Standards No. 5,** "The Meaning of 'Present Fairly in Conformity with Generally Accepted Accounting Principles' in the Independent Auditor's Report," Auditing Standards Executive Committee, American Institute of Certified Public Accountants, New York, July 1975.

[4] Source: **AICPA Technical Practice Aids,** Section 9110.01, AICPA, New York, 1977.

CASE 35

SPECIAL REPORTS

Your firm of Batsel, Barrett and Gunn (BB&G), CPAs, has examined the financial statements of Dean's Insurance Agency (Dean's), a sole proprietorship for the year ended December 31, 19x1. Dean's maintains its accounting records on an income tax basis. Upon completion of your examination you feel that you have been able to obtain sufficient evidence to support a fair presentation of assets and liabilities and revenue and expenses on the income tax basis. The working papers describe the accounting basis used in preparing the financial statements as the income tax basis. Included in the working papers is an explanation that certain revenue and related assets are recorded only when received as opposed to when earned on an accrual accounting basis and certain expenses are recognized when paid rather than at the time the liability is incurred. BB&G's examination was made in accordance with GAAS and, accordingly, included such tests of the accounting records and such other auditing procedures as was considered necessary in the circumstances. There were no scope restrictions.

The staff accountant who conducted the examination, Mr. B.B. Gunn, son of Mr. Robert B. Gunn, senior partner of the firm, has proposed the following special report to be issued in conjunction with your firm's examination of Dean's Insurance Agency.

> Mr. John Dean
> Dean's Insurance Agency
> 1300 R Street
> Lincoln, Nebraska 68588
>
> We have examined the balance sheet of Dean's Insurance Agency as of December 31, 19x1, and the related income statement for the year then ended. Our examination was made in accordance with generally accepted auditing standards.
>
> As more fully described in Note No. 1, the sole proprietorship's policy is to prepare its financial statements on the accounting basis used for income tax purposes; consequently, certain revenue and related assets are recognized when received rather than when earned, and certain expenses are recognized when paid rather than when the obligation is incurred.
>
> In our opinion, the financial statements referred to above present fairly the financial position and results of operations of Dean's Insurance Agency as of December 31, 19x1, and its revenue and expenses for the year then ended.
>
>   (Signature and date)

CASE DISCUSSION QUESTIONS

1. Dean's financial statements are prepared on the entity's income tax basis.

   a. What other types of engagements involve special reports?

   b. What other types of financial presentations could BB&G prepare for Dean's Insurance?

2. B.B. Gunn, in drafting his report for Dean's Insurance Agency, used the terms "balance sheet" and "income statement." Is it acceptable for the independent auditor to use such terms with a special report such as this? If not, explain.

3. Draft an acceptable report for Dean's Insurance Agency, including a paragraph to explain the basis of accounting used.

The basis of accounting used by Dean's differs from GAAP. Is BB&G required to provide information indicating the effect of the difference between GAAP and another comprehensive basis of accounting? Explain.

4. Does Batsel, Barrett, and Gunn's report on Dean's Insurance Agency satisfy the first standard of reporting? Explain your answer in detail.

5. Assume that BB&G has been asked to express an opinion concerning Dean's provision for income taxes contained in the financial statements.

 a. As independent auditor can they issue a separate report on an income tax provision? If so, your answer should state what BB&G should include in such a report.

 b. What if an adverse opinion or disclaimer of opinion was issued on the financial statements? Would that affect BB&G's decision to issue a separate report referred to in (a) above? Explain.

 c. With respect to BB&G's expressing an opinion on Dean's provision for income taxes, does the first standard of reporting apply? Discuss. Also, include in your answer the applicability of the general standards, standards of field work, and the third and fourth standards of reporting.

 d. Discuss the concept of materiality as it relates to BB&G's opinion on Dean's provision for income taxes.

6. Assume that Dean's Insurance Agency is contemplating the acquisition of another insurance agency, Checkly and Co., and that Mr. Dean has asked BB&G to conduct an engagement limited to applying agreed-upon procedures to the cash and accounts receivable balances of Checkly and Co. (the agreed-upon procedures are not considered sufficient to allow BB&G to express an opinion on cash or receivables).

 a. May BB&G accept such an engagement? Explain.

 b. Prepare the report for such an engagement. Assume the following information with respect to cash and accounts receivable balances of Checkly and Co. as of December 31, 19x1.

Bank	Balance per General Ledger
NBC	$15,000
Gateway Bank and Trust	29,650

Accounts receivable:

		Accounts Receivable Aging and Confirmation	
	Account Balance	Confirmation Results Requested	Received
Current	$200,000	$125,000	$ 75,000
Past due:			
Less than one month	80,000	40,000	28,000
One to three months	45,000	22,500	15,000
Over three months	70,000	70,000	25,000
	$395,000	$257,500	$143,000

 c. Does your report contain a form of negative assurance? If so, explain.

23

Letters for Underwriters and Filings Under Federal Securities Statutes

(Section 631, SAS No. 38 and Section 711, SAS No. 37)

LETTERS FOR UNDERWRITERS

Letters for underwriters or comfort letters, as they are sometimes referred to, are not required by the Securities Acts and copies are not required to be filed with the SEC. The comfort letter, which is normally prepared in connection with a registration of securities for sale to the public, is prepared solely for the benefit of underwriters. In registering securities with the SEC, the registration statement is filed on a given date but does not become effective until a later date, usually 20 or more days after filing. Under 1933 Act filings, financial statements included in the registration statement are required to be fair presentations as of the date the registration statement becomes effective. Underwriters usually request a comfort letter to provide them with assurance that no material events have occurred that would tend to make the financial statements materially false or misleading between the filing date of a registration statement and its effective date.

Comfort letters will generally refer to one or more of the following matters:

The independence of the accountants

Compliance as to form in all material respects of the audited financial statements and schedules with the applicable accounting requirements of the Act and the published rules and regulations thereunder

Unaudited financial statements and schedules in the registration statement

Changes in selected financial-statement items during a period subsequent to the date and period of the latest financial statements in the registration statement

Tables, statistics, and other financial information in the registration statement

The comfort letter ordinarily is dated at or shortly before the "closing date." The closing date is the date on which the issuer or selling security holder delivers the securities to the underwriter in exchange for the proceeds of the offering. The underwriting agreement (the contract between the principal underwriter and the seller of the securities) ordinarily specifies this date, often referred to as the "cutoff date," to which the letter itself relates. The cutoff date is generally a date five business days before the date of the letter. Letters may also be dated at or shortly before the effective date of the registration and, on rare occasions, letters have been requested to be dated at or shortly before the filing date.

Because the comfort letter is a result of the underwriter's request, many auditors address the letter only to the underwriter, with a copy furnished to the client. Some accountants, however, may address the letter to the client or to both the client and the underwriter. If the accountants are requested to address the comfort letter to any person other than the underwriter or the client, they should consult legal counsel.

Accountants customarily make a statement in the comfort letter concerning their independence. This is proper, and the accountant must be independent both within the meaning of the AICPA Code of Professional Ethics and requirements established by the SEC.

Underwriters may request accountants to express an opinion in the comfort letter concerning compliance as to the form of the statements covered by their auditor's report with the accounting requirements of the SEC. This is proper, however, because of the special significance of the date of the auditor's report and its implications regarding subsequent events, auditors should not repeat their opinion in the comfort letter. Underwriters may request negative assurance as to the auditor's report. Because auditors have a statutory responsibility with respect to their opinion as of the effective date of the registration statement, and due to the additional significance, if any, of a negative assurance regarding the auditor's opinion appearing in the registration statement is unclear, such assurance may give rise to misunderstanding and it is therefore inadvisable for the auditor to provide such negative assurance. However, with respect to unaudited financial statements and subsequent changes in the accounts, any statements made by the accountants should be limited to negative assurance.

The underwriter and the CPA should carefully discuss and agree upon the procedures to be performed in connection with the comfort letter. The agreed-upon procedures should be documented and the accountant's working papers relating to comfort letters should be prepared in a manner so as to constitute adequate evidence of exactly what has been done.

The comments included in the comfort letter concerning unaudited statements, summary of earnings, and schedules appearing in the registration statement, which should always be in the form of negative assurance, frequently relate to:

Conformity with GAAP

Consistency with the audited statements, summary of earnings, and schedules included in the registration statement

Compliance as to form with applicable accounting requirements

Comments as to subsequent changes should be in the form of negative assurance. In order that comments on subsequent changes be unambiguous and their determination be within the professional competency of the accountants, the comments should not relate to adverse changes, but should ordinarily relate to whether there has been any change in capital stock or long-term debt or decreases in other specified financial statement items during the change period (the change period would be the period covered by the comfort letter). In addition to making comparisons to determine material increases or decreases in various accounts specified by the underwriters, the accountants will ordinarily be requested to review minutes and make inquiries of company officials relating to the change period.

Comments in the comfort letter on the occurrence of changes in capital stock or long-term debt and decreases in other specified financial statement items are limited to changes or decreases not disclosed in the registration statement. Whenever it appears that a change or decrease has occurred during the change period, the accountants should refer to the registration statement to determine whether the change or decrease is disclosed therein.

As indicated at the beginning of this section, the SEC generally does not permit a registration statement to become effective until some time after the date of its filing. The SEC, except in extraordinary circumstances, will not permit a registration statement to become effective when the auditor's opinion is qualified. The SEC, however, will accept a "subject-to" type of qualification in the auditor's opinion when there is uncertainty as to:

The outcome of controversial matters such as litigation, the renegotiation of contracts, or disputes concerning income taxes

Recovery of research and development costs or other deferred charges

Other matters which are not susceptible of reasonable accounting determination, but which might have a material effect on the financial position or results of operations

The SEC will not allow a registration statement to become effective if the purpose of the sale of securities is a bailout. A bailout would be a sale of securities to obtain sufficient funds to avoid bankruptcy. A subject-to type opinion regarding going concern is, therefore, interpreted by the SEC to mean that the CPA is giving assurance that the company, if the securities are sold, will be a going concern for at least one year.

When the CPA's opinion on financial statements contained in a registration statement is qualified, the qualification should be referred to in the opening paragraph of the comfort letter by saying for example, " . . . Our reports (which contain a qualification as set forth therein) with respect thereto are also included in such Registration Statement."

Regarding tables, statistics, and other financial information appearing in the registration statement, accountants should refrain from commenting on matters to which their competency as independent public accountants has little relevancy. They should comment only with respect to information:

> Which is expressed in dollars (or percentages derived from such dollar amounts) and has been obtained from accounting records which are subject to the internal controls of the company's accounting system or

> Which has been derived directly from such accounting records by analysis or computation

> The accountants may also comment on quantitative information which has been obtained from an accounting record if the information is of a type that is subject to the same controls as the dollar amounts

SAS No. 43 (Section 1010.08) amends SAS No. 38 to delete the expression "presents fairly" from examples of letters expressing negative assurance. The language in those examples will now be consistent with Section 722, *Review of Interim Financial Information*.

FILINGS UNDER FEDERAL SECURITIES STATUTES

The Securities and Exchange Commission has stated:

> "The fundamental and primary responsibility for the accuracy of information filed with the Commission and disseminated among the investors rests upon management. Management does not discharge its obligations in this respect by the employment of independent public accountants, however reputable. Accountants' certificates are required not as a substitute for management's accounting of its stewardship, but as a check upon the accounting" [4 SEC 721(1939)].

The Securities Act of 1933, as amended, in Section 11(a) imposes responsibility for false or misleading statements, or for omissions which render misleading the statements made, in an effective registration statement on:

> . . . every accountant, engineer, or appraiser, or any person whose profession gives authority to a statement made by him or her, who has with his or her consent been named as having prepared or certified any part of the registration statement, or as having prepared or certified any report or valuation which is used in connection with the registration statement, with respect to the statement in such registration statement, report, or valuation which purports to have been prepared or certified by him or her. . .

Section 11 also makes specific mention of the independent auditor's responsibility as an expert when the audit report is included in a registration statement filed under the Act. Section 11(b) states, in part, that no person shall be liable as provided therein if such person shall sustain the burden of proof that:

> . . . as regards any part of the registration statement purporting to be made upon his or her authority as an expert or purporting to be a copy of or extract from a report or valuation of himself or herself as an expert (i) he or she had, after reasonable investigation, reasonable ground to believe and did believe, at the time such part of the registration statement became effective, that the statements therein were true and that there was no omission to state a material fact required to be stated therein or necessary to make the statements therein not misleading, or (ii) such part of the registration statement did not fairly represent his or her statement as an expert or was not a fair copy of or extract from his or her report or valuation as an expert . . .

In filings made under the Securities Act of 1933, frequently a statement is made in the prospectus that certain information is included in the registration statement in reliance upon the report of certain named experts. The name of the independent auditor should not be used in such a way as to indicate that the responsibility assumed is greater than intended.

To sustain the burden of proof that the auditor has made a "reasonable investigation," as required under the Securities Act of 1933, the auditor's procedures with respect to subsequent events from the date of his or her report up to the effective date or as close thereto as is reasonable and practicable in the circumstances should be extended. The auditor generally should:

> Read the entire prospectus and other pertinent portions of the registration statement

> Inquire of and obtain written confirmation from officers and other executives having responsibility for financial and accounting matters (limited where appropriate to major locations) as to whether there have occurred any events other than those reflected or disclosed in the registration statement which, in the officer's opinion, have a material effect on the audited financial statements included therein or which should be disclosed in order to keep those statements from being misleading

If the auditor concludes on the basis of known facts that the unaudited financial statements are not in conformity with generally accepted accounting principles, he or she should insist upon appropriate revision; failing that, a comment should be added to the report calling attention to the departure; further, the auditor should consider, probably with advice of legal counsel, withholding consent to the use of the audit report on the financial statements included in the registration statement.

CASE 36

THE PAMPLIN COMPANY

The Pamplin Company began its operations as a small furniture store in downtown Wilson, North Carolina in 1913, under the joint ownership of the J.A. Meyers and H.L. Heilig families. After about twenty years, the enterprise had expanded to twelve stores throughout the state. At this point, management disagreements arose between Heilig and Meyers, and the decision was made to split up the chain.

The stores retained by the Heilig faction have remained largely the same to this day while the Meyers group has produced a spectacular success story. By 1970 their original six stores had grown to thirteen, and during the year 1970 a merger was completed with the Derring Furniture Stores of Suffolk, Virginia, making a total of twenty retail stores in North Carolina and Virginia.

In 1972, the continuing expansion program was going so well that the company decided to "go public" under the provisions of the Securities Act of 1933 and make an initial offering of common stock to the investing public. The offering was priced at $15 per share and was made through an underwriting syndicate headed by investment bankers Barley Second Securities and Silverman Saks and Company.

Since that time, the company has continued to expand, though more slowly than in the initial years after the merger. As required, the annual and quarterly forms called for under the 1934 Securities Exchange Act have been filed with the Commission. The company has changed auditors once since the 1972 offering, due to a disagreement concerning audit fees and other administrative matters.

CASE DISCUSSION QUESTION

Under the Securities Act of 1933, underwriters connected with the registration statement are required to perform a "reasonable investigation" of financial and accounting data not covered by an accountant's report. In this connection, a usual condition stipulated in the underwriting agreement is that the independent auditor perform certain audit procedures and, based thereon, furnish a "comfort letter" for the underwriter. *Generally*, there are two time periods covered by such comfort letters, (1) the period from the date of the most recently audited financial statement to the effective date and (2) the period from the effective date to the closing date (the date on which underwriters and registrant exchange securities and funds).

a. Are comfort letters required by the SEC?

b. Appendix 1 presents a draft of a comfort letter to the underwriters concerning the Pamplin Company registration. This letter was prepared by a junior auditor. What changes, if any, would you recommend be made to the comfort letter?

c. Usually, underwriters request two comfort letters from the auditors. Why?

APPENDIX 1

Barney, Google & Company
New York, N.Y. 10005

This letter is furnished to you pursuant to Paragraph 6(d) of the Underwriting Agreement dated September 28, 1975, between Pamplin Company (the "Company"), certain shareholders of the Company, and Barney, Google & Co. as representatives of the several underwriters of shares of Pamplin Company.

1. We have examined the statements of Pamplin Company filed with the registration statement (No. 2-48000) filed with the Securities and Exchange Commission (the "Commission"). Such statement, and the related prospectus, are herein referred to respectively as the "Prospectus" and the "Registration Statement."

2. In our opinion, the statements examined by us, and included in the Prospectus and Registration Statement, were prepared in accordance with generally accepted accounting principles.

3. At the request of the Company, we carried out certain procedures and made certain inquiries with respect to the unaudited six-month period ending June 30, 1975. Though this examination was not in accordance with generally accepted accounting principles, it included such tests as we considered necessary in the circumstances. In addition, we extended our examination from July 1, 1975 to September 21, 1975 (we did not audit the period from September 22, 1974 to September 28, inclusive).

4. Based on the results of our examination, you have our assurance that:

    a. (i) The unaudited consolidated statements included in the Registration Statement are presented fairly in accordance with generally accepted accounting principles consistently applied, and (ii) all Commission requirements, rules, and regulations have been met.

    b. (i) There have been no changes in the capital stock account (other than normal exercises of stock options) or long-term debt (other than payments) of the Company, (ii) there are no material contingent or unrecorded liabilities.

5. We hope that this letter is satisfactory for your purposes. If we may be of further assistance, please do not hesitate to contact us, either personally or through your attorney.

Sincerely yours,

Certified Public Accountants

Reporting on
Internal Control*

(Section 642, SAS No. 30)

CPAs are sometimes asked to furnish reports on their review and evaluation of a client's internal controls for use by management, regulatory agencies, other CPAs, or the general public.

If the CPA learns of a material weakness in a client's internal accounting control during the examination of financial statements made in accordance with GAAS, the CPA is required to communicate such information to senior management and the board of directors or its audit committee. The CPA is required to disclose such information regardless of whether he is engaged by the client to review and report on the system of internal control.

Usefulness of Reports on Internal Control

Internal accounting control is technical by nature and complex. Understanding the nature of accounting control and the meaning and significance of reports based on a CPA's study and evaluation of a client's system of internal control requires some technical accounting background or, at a minimum, a familiarity with the business environment to which the controls apply. This understanding is necessary to comprehend the significance of the controls in effect and the impact of potential weaknesses in a system. The usefulness of a report on internal accounting control not only depends upon an understanding of the report, but also on an understanding of the action that can be taken by those to whom such reports are issued.

Management is responsible for establishing and maintaining the system of internal control. Regulatory agencies may be concerned with such controls because it is relevant to their primary regulatory purpose or to the scope of their examination functions. CPAs of one entity or organization may be concerned with the internal accounting control of another entity because it is relevant to the scope of their examination. It may be presumed that these groups include persons with an adequate understanding of the principles of internal control and the knowledge for understanding the CPA's evaluation of the system. It is evident, therefore, that reports on internal accounting control can serve a useful purpose to management, regulatory agencies, and other independent auditors and the issuance of reports on internal control to these groups is appropriate.

In contrast to the foregoing groups, the usefulness of reports on internal accounting control to the general public is somewhat questionable. Management, regulartory agencies, and other CPAs are directly concerned with internal accounting control and are in a position to take direct action as a result of reports thereon. On the other hand, any possiblle action that could be taken by the general public (stockholders and potential investors and others) as a result of such reports would be indirect since it ordinarily would be limited to making decisions concerning either a com-

---

*For additional guidance on reporting to another independent accountant on internal accounting control, see Section SAS No. 44, *Special-Purpose Reports on Internal Accounting Control at Service Organizations*.

pany's financial statements or its management. Accordingly, while the issuance of reports on internal accounting control to the general public is not prohibited, such action is questionable. Whether such reports or portions thereof would be useful to the general public is a decision that must be made by management and/or any regulatory agencies having jurisdiction. In no event, however, should a CPA authorize a report based on an evaluation of internal accounting control to be issued to the general public in a document that includes unaudited financial statements. Such reports would tend to lend the credibility of an audit examination to such statements when no such examination had been made.

Form of Reports on Internal Control

Presented below is an example of the reporting format CPAs should follow to avoid misunderstanding of the objectives and limitations of internal accounting control:

> We have made a study and evaluation of the system of internal accounting control of XYZ Company and subsidiaries in effect at (date). Our study and evaluation was conducted in accordance with standards established by the American Institute of Certified Public Accountants.
>
> The management of XYZ Company is responsible for establishing and maintaining a system of internal accounting control. In fulfilling this responsibility, estimates and judgments by management are required to assess the expected benefits and related costs of control procedures. The objectives of a system are to provide management with reasonable, but not absolute, assurance that assets are safeguarded against loss from unauthorized use or disposition, and that transactions are executed in accordance with management's authorization and recorded properly to permit the preparation of financial statements in accordance with generally accepted accounting principles.
>
> Because of inherent limitations in any system of internal accounting control, errors or irregularities may occur and not be detected. Also, projection of any evaluation of the system to future periods is subject to the risk that procedures may become inadequate because of changes in conditions, or that the degree of compliance with the procedures may deteriorate.
>
> In our opinion, the system of internal accounting control of XYZ Company and subsidiaries in effect at (date), taken as a whole, was sufficient to meet the objectives stated above insofar as those objectives pertain to the prevention or detection of errors or irregularities in amounts that would be material in relation to the consolidated financial statements.

In describing the material weaknesses the auditors should state whether the weaknesses relate to the prescribed procedures or to the lack of compliance with such procedures. The independent auditors may also include in their report recommendations for improvements, a discussion of corrective action taken or in process, or other comments they deem appropriate. The auditors should state the basis for any comments concerning subsequent corrective action, including the scope of any review and tests conducted by them. Although the first and last paragraphs of the report clearly indicate that weaknesses in the system are evaluated in ascertaining the nature, timing, and extent of auditing procedures necessary for expressing an opinion on the financial statements, the auditors may decide to make additional comments in this respect. If the auditors believe that certain weaknesses are an inherent part of the system and that correction action by management would be ineffective, they may so state in their report. However, if they learn of a material weakness, the auditors should communicate this information to management, regardless of whether or not corrective action is practicable. An example of such inherent weakness would be a situation where the organization is so small that proper segregation of duties is simply not possible.

During the course of the examination the auditors generally discuss weaknesses and needed improvements in the system of internal accounting control with the client as these matters arise. It is therefore appropriate for them to summarize these discussions in a letter to management rather than by using the form of report outlined above. Since other CPAs understand the nature of internal control, other formats may also be used in reporting to them.

Form for Reports on Internal Control Based on Special Studies

A special study of internal control would be a review, testing, and evaluation of internal control in which the scope is substantially more extensive than that required for an examination of financial statements in accordance with GAAS. Such special studies may relate to an existing system of internal control or to a proposed system. If reports on special studies are to be issued to regulatory agencies or to the general public the report form discussed above should be adapted to fit the special study scope and it should be used. Any limitations on the study should be reflected in the report. The form of reports based on special studies of internal accounting control systems for management or other CPAs is flexible.

REPORTS ON INTERNAL CONTROL BASED ON CRITERIA ESTABLISHED BY GOVERNMENTAL AGENCIES

When criteria established by a governmental agency are established in a questionnaire or other publication in reasonable detail and in terms susceptible to objective answers or application, the CPA's report may express a conclusion, based on the agency's criteria, concerning the adequacy of the procedures studied, with an exception as to any condition believed not to be in conformity with such criteria and is a material weakness. If requested, or at the discretion of the CPA, reference may be made to other conditions the CPA believes are not in conformity with the agency's criteria but is not a material weakness. The CPA, in issuing this form of report, does not assume any responsibility for the comprehensiveness of the reporting criteria established by the governmental agency. The CPA should, however, report all material weaknesses even though not covered by the agency's criteria.

When a CPA issues a report based on criteria established by a governmental agency, a statement that the report is intended for use in connection with the grant to which the report refers should be included and it should also be noted that the report should not be used for any other purpose.

CASE 37

REPORTS ON INTERNAL CONTROL

Farrier Construction Company is a small but successful construction company. It was founded in the late 1930s by Mr. J.B. Farrier. Mr. Farrier died in 1978 and the business is now owned by his son, J.D. Farrier. J.D. has other business interests and is not involved in the day-to-day management of the construction firm. Because of its success in the construction business and the managerial ability of J.B. Farrier, the firm has always been able to operate without borrowing working capital. Due to these circumstances, Farrier Construction has never had an occasion to have a CPA examine its accounting records.

Recently, however, Farrier's board of directors contacted your firm, Cook, Ross and Dixon, CPAs, and asked that the firm conduct a special study of Farrier's system of internal control. The study will not involve an examination of Farrier's financial statements at the present time. But management anticipates the need for audited financials sometime in the near future. When the study is completed, Cook, Ross and Dixon are to issue a report on Farrier's internal control to the board of directors with any material weaknesses in internal accounting control being reported.

CASE DISCUSSION QUESTIONS

1. Discuss the usefulness of the report on internal control to Farrier's board of directors and to other interested parties.

2. Assume that your firm, Cook, Ross and Dixon, are engaged six months from now to do an audit on Farrier Constructions' accounting records.

   a. Would the study of internal control that your firm has been asked to perform be useful for the audit engagement? Explain.

   b. Would such a study of internal control provide additional credibility to Farrier's audited financial statements? Discuss.

3.   Assume that Abel Concrete Company is considering the purchase of Farrier Construction Company and that they have asked a firm of independent auditors, Gateway and Anderson, CPAs, to examine Farrier's accounting records. Would the study of internal control made by Cook, Ross and Dixon be useful to other independent auditors?

4.   Assume that in your audit engagement (six months later) of Farrier's financial statements you become aware of internal control weaknesses in the areas of accounts receivable and inventories. For example, in the area of accounts receivable, there are no formal (written) procedures with respect to the granting of credit or the collection of receivables. Furthermore, it is noted that bad debts have increased by 20 percent during 1979. Also, it is noted that the firm has continued to do subcontracting work for a large contractor and that the contractor has an accounts receivable balance that is more than 270 days old.

   a.   Should Cook, Ross and Dixon inform Farrier's board of directors of the above weaknesses? If so, explain. For example, should the report state whether the weakness relates to prescribed procedures or to the lack of such procedures?

   b.   Prepare the appropriate paragraph(s) of the report that should be issued by your firm to Farrier's board members.

   c.   Should such a report disclose all weaknesses in Farrier's system of internal control?

5.   Discuss how a special study of Farrier's internal control would differ from a study that was conducted in an examination of financial statements in accordance with GAAS.

25

Review of Interim Financial Information

(Section 722, SAS No. 36)

SAS No. 36 provides guidance on procedures to be applied to a review of the interim financial statements of a public company and the appropriate form of report based on such review. Also, SAS No. 36 establishes standards regarding a note on interim financial information that may appear in the annual audited financial statements of a public or non-public company. SSARS No. 1 is applicable to a review of the interim or annual financial statements of a nonpublic company. SAS No. 36 does not apply to an accountant's involvement with interim information included in documents filed with the SEC pursuant to the 1933 Act unless the accountant has audited and reported on the statements which include such information in a note.

The objective of a review (as established in SSARS No. 1) is to provide the accountant with a limited assurance that there are no material modifications that should be made to the interim information or statements for it to be in conformity with GAAP. A limited review of interim information or statements does not provide a basis for expressing an audit opinion.

Since interim reports, to be useful, must be timely, information underlying interim reports is often based on estimates and related to expected annual amounts. For example, many costs and expenses (in accordance with APB Opinion No. 28, *Interim Financial Reporting*) are estimated to a greater extent than for annual financial statements. The role of the auditor, in connection with a limited review of interim information or statements, is to perform inquiry and analytical review procedures to gain limited assurance that the information was properly prepared in accordance with established standards (APB Opinion No. 28).

The procedures ordinarily applied in an interim review are outlined below:

1. Inquiry concerning:

   a. The accounting system and how transactions are recorded, classified, and summarized in preparing interim information.

   b. Any significant changes in internal accounting control and the potential effect of such changes on the preparation of interim information.

2. Analytical review procedures to provide information about the relationships of interim information and items that appear to be unusual:

   a. Comparison of financial information with comparable information for the immediately preceding interim period and corresponding previous periods.

    b.   Comparison of the financial information with anticipated results (such as budgets).

    c.   Study of the relationship of elements of financial information that would be expected to conform to a predictable pattern based on business experience and industry characteristics.

    d.   Consideration of the type of matters that have required adjustment in previous interim and annual periods.

3.   Reading the minutes to identify actions that may affect interim information (stockholders, board of directors, and committees of the board of directors).

4.   Reading interim information to determine, on the basis of information coming to the accountant's attention, whether it conforms with GAAP.

5.   Obtaining reports from other accountants who have reviewed interim information of significant components of the reporting entity (subsidiaries or investees).

6.   Inquiry of the client's financial and accounting officers regarding:

    a.   Whether the interim information has been prepared in conformity with GAAP and whether GAAP has been applied on a consistent basis.

    b.   Changes in business activities or accounting practices.

    c.   Exceptions that have arisen in applying the inquiry and analytical review procedures.

    d.   Subsequent events.

7.   Obtaining written representation from management concerning:

    a.   Management's responsibility for the financial information.

    b.   Completeness of minutes.

    c.   Subsequent events.

    d.   Other matters (see SAS No. 19 on client representation letters).

As indicated in the readings accompanying this section, an interim review may be a somewhat continuous process throughout the accounting year. Timing of some of the work before the end of the interim period does permit the work to be performed in a more efficient fashion and permits early consideration of significant accounting matters.

Understanding the client's internal accounting control system and knowledge of the client's accounting and reporting practices are important factors in the performance of a review of interim information. An understanding of the client's practices in preparing its most recent annual financial statements provides a sound basis for performing a limited review of interim information. An accountant who is the client's annual auditor would, of course, have this understanding. Being the annual auditor is not necessary to accept an engagement to perform a limited review of interim information. However, the necessity for a thorough understanding of the client's accounting system and controls is not diminished. The accountant performing a limited review of interim information who is not the annual auditor will, therefore, be involved in a more detailed study of his or her client's system and controls to provide a background for the limited review engagement.

Weaknesses in internal accounting control noted in the annual review and evaluation for audit purposes or in a study made as a basis for a limited review should be reported to management (see SAS No. 20, *Required Communication of Material Weaknesses in Internal Accounting Control*). Corrective action may also be communicated to management. The accountant should consider the effect of such weaknesses on the ability of an entity to develop reliable interim information. Such weaknesses may impose a restriction on the scope of a limited review engagement sufficient to preclude completion of such a review.

In performing a limited review the accountant should give due consideration to the impact of changed business conditions (such as a merger or acquisition, change in the nature of the client's business, extraordinary items, etc.) on the interim information. Also, new accounting pronouncements that may affect the presentation of the interim information must be considered.

An accountant engaged to review interim financial information at multiple locations should employ the same considerations as when examining financial information under GAAS. This will typically require the procedures to be performed at both the corporate headquarters and at selected outside offices.

An accountant would be required to extend his or her review procedures when information comes to the accountant's attention that leads him or her to question whether the interim information conforms with GAAP.

Limited review procedures may be modified (reduced) based on the results of auditing procedures that may have been applied during interim periods in connection with an annual examination of the client's financial statements.

An accountant may be associated with interim information or statements (consent to the use of his or her name in a report or document containing such information) provided he or she has made a review of the information as prescribed by SAS No. 36. If the review is restricted in any way and the accountant is unable to complete the review procedures, he or she should not be associated with such information.

The accountant's report on interim information or statements may be addressed to the company, its board of directors, or its stockholders. The report should be dated as of the completion of the review procedures. Each page of the interim information or statements should be clearly marked as "unaudited." There are no restrictions on the distribution of the report by the client. If an accountant considers it necessary to disclose information in an interim report subsequent to the completion of the review procedures, but before the information is released to the client, the report dating options in Section 530 of SAS No. 1 would apply. That is, the accountant may use dual-dating and avoid extending the review procedures or he or she may use a revised date for the review report, in which case the accountant would extend subsequent event review procedures to that date.

An example of an accountant's review report follows:

> We have made a review of (describe the information or statements reviewed) ABC Company and consolidated subsidiaries as of September 30, 19x1, and for the three-month and nine-month periods then ended, in accordance with standards established by the American Institute of Certified Public Accountants.
>
> A review of interim financial information consists principally of obtaining an understanding of the system for the preparation of interim financial information, applying analytical review procedures to financial data, and making inquiries of persons responsible for financial and accounting matters. It is substantially less in scope than an examination in accordance with generally accepted auditing standards, the objective of which is the expression of an opinion regarding the financial statements taken as a whole. Accordingly, we do not express such an opinion.
>
> Based on our review, we are not aware of any material modifications that should be made to the accompanying financial (information or statements) for them to be in conformity with generally accepted accounting principles.

If comparative interim information is presented and the accountant has reviewed the prior-period information, the report should cover both periods. For example, the above report would be modified to read as follows:

> We have made . . . of ABC Company and consolidated subsidiaries as of September 30, 19x1, and 19x2, and for the three-month and nine-month periods then ended . . .

An accountant who makes use and reference to the report of another accountant in reporting on a review of interim information or statements should modify his or her review report accordingly. For example, the above report would read as follows:

> We have made a review of . . . ABC Company and consolidated subsidiaries as of . . . in accordance with standards established by the American Institute of Certified Public Accountants. We were fur-

nished with the report of other accountants on their review of the interim financial information of the ADE subsidiary, whose total assets and revenues constitute 20 percent and 22 percent, respectively, of the related consolidated totals.

(Middle paragraph describing a review and disclaiming an audit opinion)

Based on our review and the report of other accountants, we are not aware of . . .

Normally neither an accounting change nor an uncertainty would result in modification of an accountant's review report. Providing, of course, that the accounting change or the uncertainty is appropriately accounted for and properly disclosed in the interim information of statements. Modification of a review report is required, however, if a change in accounting principle involves changing to a principle that is not generally accepted. Other departures from GAAP, if the effect is deemed material, would result in modification of a review report. For example, reporting assets at appraisal values. For such departures from GAAP, the accountant would indicate the departure in his or her report by stating what GAAP requires, what the client has done, and the effect of the departure, if known to the accountant. If information the accountant believes is necessary for adequate disclosure is omitted from interim information, the accountant should modify his or her report and, if practicable, include the necessary information. It should be recognized, of course, that APB Opinion No. 28 states that disclosure in interim statements or information is not required to be as extensive as for annual statements. There is a presumption in APB Opinion No. 28 that the reader of the interim information or statements is also the reader of the annual statements. The adequacy of interim disclosures should, accordingly, be viewed in this context.

Following are examples of the standard language of the accountant's review report for departures from GAAP, including inadequate disclosure:

Non-Conformity with GAAP

(Explanatory third paragraph)

Based on information furnished us by management, we believe that the company has excluded from property and debt in the accompanying balance sheet certain lease obligations that should be capitalized in order to conform with generally accepted accounting principles. This information indicates that if these lease obligations were capitalized at September 30, 19x1, property would be increased by $ . . . . . ., and long-term debt by $ . . . . . ., and net income and earnings per share would be increased (decreased) by $ . . . . . ., $ . . . . . ., $ . . . . . ., and $ . . . . . ., respectively, for the three-month and nine-month periods then ended.

(Concluding paragraph)

Based on our review, with the exception of the matter(s) described in the preceding paragraph(s), we are not aware of any material modifications that should be made to the accompanying (financial information or statements) for them to be in conformity with generally accepted accounting principles.

Inadequate Disclosure

(Explanatory third paragraph)

Management has informed us that the company is presently contesting deficiencies in federal income taxes proposed by the Internal Revenue Service for the years 19xx through 19xx in the aggregate amount of approximately $ . . . . . ., and that the extent of the company's liability, if any, and the effect on the accompanying (information or statements) are not determinable at this time. The (information or statements) fail to disclose these matters, which we believe are required to be disclosed in conformity with generally accepted accounting principles.

(Concluding paragraph)

Based on our review, with the exception of the matter(s) described in the preceding paragraph(s), we are not aware of any . . .

An accountant may be requested to make a review of interim information to permit the client to include such information in a report to stockholders or other third parties or the 10-Q form filed with the SEC. If the client represents that the accountant has reviewed the information, the accountant's report should be included or he or she should not consent to the use of his or her name and should not be associated with the information.

Certain companies are required by the SEC to include in audited statements a note containing selected interim information. Also, other companies (both public and nonpublic) may elect to include such information on a voluntary basis. The procedures in SAS No. 36 for a review are applicable to such information. The auditor ordinarily need not modify his or her audit report on the financial statements to make reference to the review of the interim information included in a note to the statements. The auditor's report should, however, be expanded if the scope of the review procedures regarding the information in the note was restricted or if the procedures reveal that the information is not in conformity with GAAP. The auditor should also expand the report if the information in the note was not reviewed, unless that fact is stated in the note. The information included in the note should be marked as "unaudited." If it is not, the auditor should expand his or her report to disclaim an opinion on the information.

In the case of events arising subsequent to the date of the issuance of an accountant's report on interim information or statements that may have a material effect on the accountant's report, SAS No. 36 refers the accountant to the provisions of Section 561 of SAS No. 1, *Subsequent Discovery of Facts Existing at the Date of the Auditor's Report* for guidance.

SAS No. 36 encourages the use of an engagement letter to document the understanding between the accountant and his or her client regarding the services to be performed in a review of interim information or statements. Also, adequate working papers are required to be developed by the accountant to support the review engagement.

SEPTEMBER 1979

Review of Interim Financial Information

Here is a timely analysis of the new auditing standard on
this important and growing professional service, together
with a flowchart for such a review engagement.

Joyce C. Lambert, CPA, Ph.D. and S. J. Lambert III, CPA, Ph.D.

THE Auditing Standards Board of the AICPA has issued *SAS No. 24: Review of Interim Financial Information*, which replaces SAS No. 10 "Limited Review of
Interim Financial Information" and SAS No. 13 "Reports
on a Limited Review of Interim Financial Information." The
purpose of this article is to discuss the Statement and
present a flowchart of its main features. The Statement is
effective for reports on financial statements or information
for interim periods ending on or after March 31, 1979.

Applicability

SAS No. 24 applies to reviews of interim financial
information presented alone including information that
purports to conform with APB Opinion No. 28, as
amended. Such information is issued by a publicly-held
entity to stockholders, boards of directors, or others for
filing with regulatory agencies. The new Statement applies
to reviews of financial statements or information for a
twelve-month period ending on a date other than the entity's normal year-end. In addition, the new Statement applies to the review of interim financial information included
in a note to audited financial statements. It does not apply
to a review of interim financial information in documents
filed with the SEC in accordance with the 1933 SEC Act
unless the accountant has examined and reported on the
financial statements which include the interim financial information in a note.

Objective of a Review

The objective of a review of interim financial information is different from the objective of an audit. In a review

*Joyce C. Lambert, CPA, Ph.D., Associate Professor of Account-
ing, University of Nebraska-Lincoln, is on the Board of Directors
of the Nebraska Society of CPAs. She is a member of AAA and
Academy of Accounting Historians and has been widely published. S. J. Lambert III, CPA, Ph.D., is Associate Professor of
Accounting, University of Nebraska-Lincoln. He is a member of
the AICPA, Louisiana and Nebraska State Societies, the AAA
among other organizations and has been widely published in
professional literature. Their article "Tentative Report on Internal
Accounting Control" appeared in our May 1979 issue.*

the objective is to provide the accountant with a basis for
reporting whether material modifications should be made
for the interim financial information to conform with generally accepted accounting principles (GAAP). The accountant objectively applies his knowledge of financial reporting practices to significant accounting matters of which
he becomes aware through inquiries and analytical review
procedures to arrive at a basis for the assurance expressed in his report. The objective of an audit is to provide a reasonable basis for expressing an opinion regarding the financial statements taken as a whole. Such an
opinion cannot be expressed in a review because in a
review there is no study and evaluation of internal accounting control, nor are there tests, inspection, observation, confirmation and other corroborative procedures as
there are on an audit.

Interim financial information has two important characteristics that distinguish it from annual information.
First, to provide the information on a timely basis, costs
and expenses are estimated to a greater extent than for
annual financial reporting. Second, APB Opinion No. 28
declared the basic accounting period to be the annual
period. The interim period is to be viewed as an integral
part of the annual period, with interim accruals, deferrals
and estimates made in light of anticipated annual results.
These characteristics affect the nature, timing and extent
of procedures the accountant may apply in reviewing interim financial information.

Nature of Interim Review Procedures

The nature of the procedures to be performed on a
review along with the timing and extent of the procedures
are essentially the same as stated in SAS No. 10. Ordinarily, the accountant's review of interim financial information will consist primarily of inquiries and analytical review procedures. (See Flowchart I.) First, inquiries will ordinarily be limited to determining:

• How are transactions recorded, classified and summarized for interim financial reporting; and

• Have there been any significant changes in the system of internal accounting control since the most recent
study and evaluation of the system that may affect the
preparation of interim financial information.

Analytical review procedures are defined in SAS No.

FLOWCHART I
SAS No. 24
REVIEW OF INTERIM FINANCIAL INFORMATION (IFI)

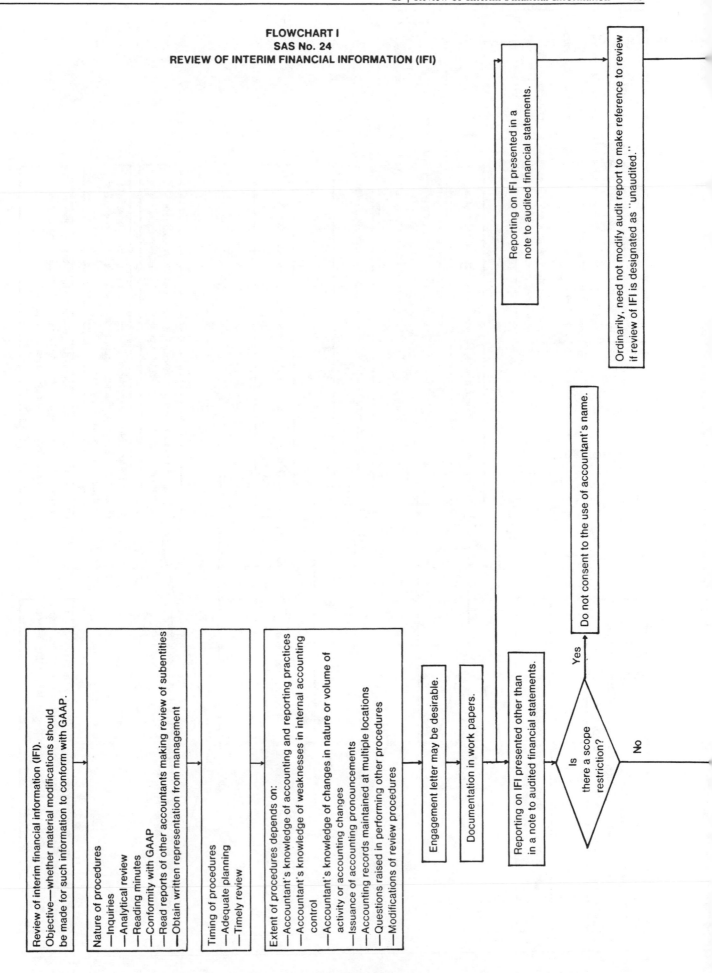

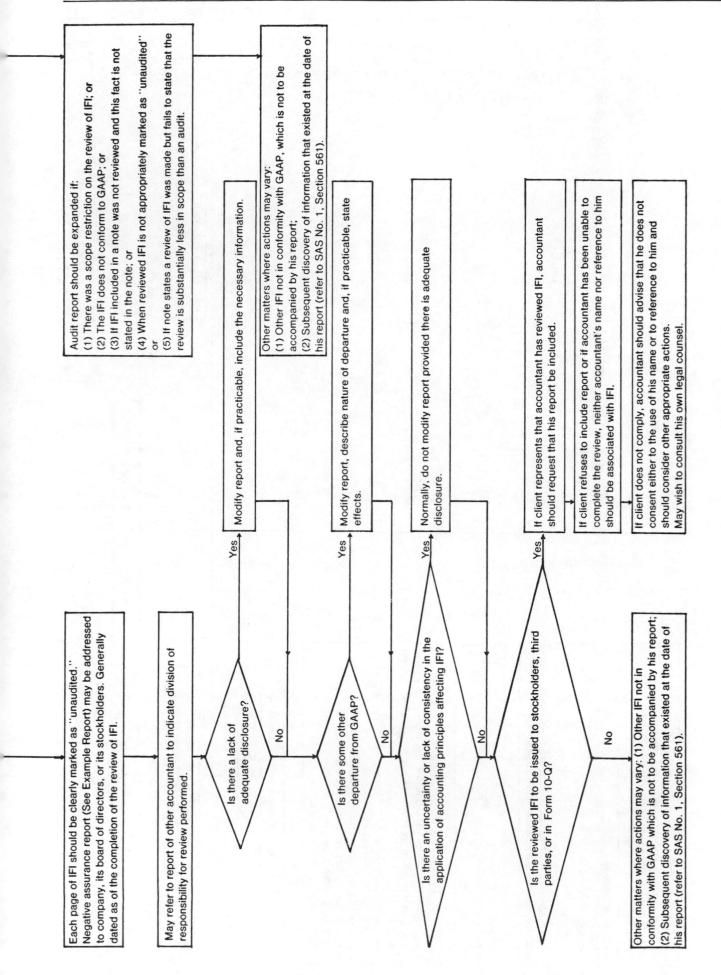

23 as " . . . substantive tests of financial information made by a study and comparison of relationships among data." In any given situation the specific analytical review procedures employed are matters of judgment based on the circumstances. Analytical review procedures provide

'In a review the objective is to provide the accountant with a basis for reporting whether material modifications should be made for the interim financial information to conform with . . . GAAP.'

evidential matter by demonstrating that expected relationships among data either exist or do not exist and serve to identify areas where inquiries should be made. When applied to a review of interim financial information, analytical review procedures are designed to identify and provide a basis for inquiry about relationships and individual items that appear to be unusual. These procedures consist of the following:

• Comparison of the financial information with comparable information for the immediately preceding interim period and for corresponding previous periods;

• Comparison of the financial information with anticipated results; and

• Study of the relationships of elements of financial information that would be expected to conform to a predictable pattern based on the entity's experience.

Other procedures designed to identify items that may

'Interim financial information has two important characteristics that distinguish it from annual information.'

affect the interim financial information and that the accountant ordinarily will follow include:

• Reading the minutes of meetings of stockholders, board of directors, and its committees;

• Reading the interim financial information for conformity with GAAP;

• Reading reports from other accountants who reviewed interim financial information of significant components, subsidiaries or other investees;

• Making inquiries of appropriate officers and other executives concerning (a) consistency and application of GAAP in the interim financial information, (b) important

changes in business activities or accounting practices, (c) any questions that may have arisen during the review, and (d) material subsequent events; and

• Obtaining a written management representation concerning its responsibility for the financial information, the completeness of the minutes, subsequent events and other relevant matters. This procedure appears for the first time in SAS No. 19 which was issued subsequent to the earlier standards on limited reviews.

Timing and Extent of Interim Review Procedures

In light of the need for interim financial information on a timely basis, interim review procedures should be adequately planned and performed as early during an interim period as feasible. The extent to which these inquiries and other review procedures are applied will depend on several considerations.

To perform the interim review the accountant must be knowledgeable of the client's accounting and reporting practices. If the accountant has previously audited the client's financial statements, then the accountant can be expected to have obtained an understanding of these practices. This understanding provides a basis for making inquiries and selecting other review procedures. If the accountant has not previously conducted an audit, then he must consider whether he can acquire the needed knowledge for the review.

The accountant must be knowledgeable of the client's system of internal accounting control. If he has previously audited the client's financial statements, he should have the requisite knowledge. His objectives for the interim review will be to study changes in the internal control system subsequent to his audit and to determine if the control procedures used in the interim period differ from those used in the audited period. If weaknesses exist which do not permit the preparation of interim financial statements in accordance with GAAP, he should consider if these weaknesses represent a scope restriction sufficient to preclude completion of the review. In addition, he should advise senior management and the board of directors or its audit committee of the weaknesses and he may suggest corrective action.

The accountant must be alert for changes in the nature or volume of a client's activity or any accounting changes that could affect the interim financial information. For example, business combinations, disposal of a segment, extraordinary, unusual or infrequent events, litigation and changes in application of accounting principles are among the events that could occur. Inquiring about these matters and their effects on the interim financial information would be appropriate. Also, the accountant should be aware of new accounting pronouncements as well as the applicability of existing pronouncements to new types of transactions or events.

Accounting records maintained at multiple locations usually involve application of interim review procedures at both corporate headquarters and other locations selected by the accountant. Additional inquiries or procedures would be performed if developments lead the accountant to question whether the interim financial information con-

> ## 'Analytical review procedures . . . serve to identify areas where inquiries should be made.'

forms to GAAP. Review procedures may be modified, as appropriate, to reflect the results of auditing procedures applied in performing an examination in accordance with generally accepted auditing standards.

Reporting Other Than in a Note to Audited Financial Statements

An accountant's report on interim information may accompany the interim financial information if a review has been performed in accordance with SAS 24. An example of such a report is shown. Each page of the interim financial information should be marked "unaudited." The principal difference between the reports on interim information in SAS No. 24 and in SAS No. 13 is that the latter report includes a disclaimer. The review report in SAS No. 24 expresses a form of negative assurance: " . . . we are not aware of any material modification that should be made . . . " to conform to GAAP.

When another accountant participates by reviewing the interim information of a subsidiary or division, the accountant may refer to the other accountant's review to

> ## 'In light of the need for interim financial information on a timely basis, interim review procedures should be . . . performed as early . . . as feasible.'

indicate a division of responsibility. A departure from GAAP or inadequate disclosure requires a modification in the review report. But uncertainties or lack of consistency normally would not require modification if there is adequate disclosure.

If the accountant has reviewed interim financial information which his client is presenting to stockholders, third parties or in Form 10-Q, the accountant should request that his report be included. If the client refuses to include the report or if the accountant has been unable to complete his review by reason of scope restriction, he should request that neither his name nor reference to him be associated with the information. If the client refuses to comply with this request, the accountant should consider other actions which may include consulting his legal counsel.

Example of Report on Review of Interim Financial Information*

We have made a review of (describe the information or statements reviewed) ABC Company and consolidated subsidiaries as of September 30, 19X1 and for the three-month and nine-month periods then ended, in accordance with standards established by the American Institute of Certified Public Accountants.

A review of interim financial information consists principally of obtaining an understanding of the system for the preparation of interim financial information, applying analytical review procedures to financial data, and making inquiries of persons responsible for financial and accounting matters. It is substantially less in scope than an examination in accordance with generally accepted auditing standards, the objective of which is the expression of an opinion regarding the financial statements taken as a whole. Accordingly, we do not express such an opinion.

Based on our review, we are not aware of any material modifications that should be made to the accompanying financial (information or statements) for them to be in conformity with generally accepted accounting principles.[1]

Reporting on Interim Financial Information Presented in a Note to Audited Financial Statements

If review procedures are performed prior to the issuance of quarterly data, they do not have to be repeated for an audit covering the period. When interim financial information is included in annual audited financial statements, there is no specific requirement to perform review procedures other than at the time of the audit.

When interim financial information is designated as "unaudited" in a note to audited financial statements, the auditor ordinarily need not change his audit report to refer to the review of the interim information. However, the audit report should be expanded (1) if the scope of the review of interim financial information was restricted; or (2) if the interim financial information is not in conformity

---

* Each page of the interim financial information should be clearly marked as "unaudited."

[1] Statement on Auditing Standards No. 24: Review of Interim Financial Information, American Institute of Certified Public Accountants, 1979, paragraph 18.

with GAAP; or (3) if the interim financial information included in the note was not reviewed, unless the note disclosed this fact; or (4) if the interim financial information included in the note is not appropriately marked as "unaudited" when only a review has been performed; or (5) if the note states a review has taken place but fails to state that the review is substantially less in scope than an audit.

Other Matters

There should be a clear understanding between the client and the accountant about the nature of the review services. A letter to the client describing the engagement may be desirable. The letter should cover a general description of the procedures and include an explanation that such procedures are substantially less in scope than an examination made in accordance with generally accepted auditing standards. A description of the form of the report should also be included. Working papers should document the review procedures and results. No specific comments on the form or content of working papers are given in SAS No. 24 other than a reference to SAS No. 1, Section 338.

The Statement also refers to reviewed interim financial information which departs from GAAP and which is not to be accompanied by the accountant's report. But no specific guidance for action is given other than to say that, because of a variety of conditions, actions may vary. Subsequent to the review, the accountant may become aware of facts existing at the date of his report that might have affected his review report. In these circumstances, the accountant is referred to SAS No. 1, Section 561, "Subsequent Discovery of Facts Existing at the Date of the Auditor's Report." Again, actions may vary with the circumstances.

Final Comments

The Accounting Review and Services Committee recently issued "Compilation and Review of Financial Statements" in which a report on review services of unaudited statements was recommended and that stated: " . . . (we are) not aware of any material modifications that should be made . . . to conform with generally accepted accounting principles." This limited assurance is a type of negative assurance similar to that appearing in SAS No. 24.

The accountant who performs a review of interim financial information is advised to avoid referring to his procedures as "audit procedures" or as an "audit." The report on a review of interim financial information does carry a type of assurance, that is, a negative assurance that the accountant is not aware of any material modification that should be made in order to achieve conformity with GAAP. The consequences of the assurance given are unknown; probably they can be determined only as a result of litigation. Offering any new type of service is subject to some risks. Let us hope that the new standard leads to an area of service beneficial to both clients and the public without significant liability to the profession. Ω

CASE 38

REVIEW OF INTERIM FINANCIAL INFORMATION*

Hindman, CPA, who has examined the financial statements of the Gateway Company, a publicly held company, for the year ended December 31, 19x1, was asked to perform a limited review of the financial statements of Gateway Company for the period ending March 31, 19x2. Hindman's engagement letter stated that a limited review does not provide a basis for the expression of an opinion. On receipt of the engagement letter, Gateway's controller raised several questions concerning Hindman's review of interim financial information. The questions asked included the following.

CASE DISCUSSION QUESTIONS

1. Explain why Hindman's limited review will *not* provide a basis for the expression of an opinion.

2. What are the review procedures which Hindman should perform and what is the purpose of each procedure? Set up the following captions in answering the question.

    | *Procedure* | *Purpose of Procedure* |

3. Hindman's report accompanying interim financial information he has reviewed should reveal specific facts concerning the review. List the points that should be made in his report.

4. Discuss the dating of the report and to whom Hindman should address the report.

5. Does SAS No. 24 preclude Hindman from referring to the report of another accountant on a review of interim financial information? Discuss.

6. Discuss in detail the circumstances that could require Hindman to modify his report with respect to his review of Gateway's interim financial information.

7. In connection with a limited review, the accountant may be requested to make a review of interim financial information to be included in documents issued to stockholders, third parties or the SEC. Under such circumstances, what are the CPA's reporting responsibilities? Include in your answer action the CPA should take if a scope restriction precludes the completion of the review.

8. SAS No. 24 permits interim information to be disclosed in an "unaudited" footnote to the financial statements. List and explain the circumstances that would cause the CPA to modify his *audit* report.

*(AICPA adapted)

Controls and Auditing
Procedures for Goods Held
in Public Warehouses

(Section 901, SAS No. 1)

Auditing procedures applicable to goods owned by a public warehouseman are similar to those applicable to owned inventories generally. This section applies, therefore, to those inventories in the possession of a public warehouseman that are owned by others. The procedures that should be applied to auditing such inventories by the CPA of the client using the warehouse as a depository for inventory are discussed. Internal controls of the warehouseman are also considered.

Procedures That Should be Followed by the Auditor of the Warehouseman

The independent auditor of the warehouseman should:

Make a study and evaluation of the effectiveness of both the accounting controls and the administrative controls, as defined in Section 320, SAS No. 1, relating to the accountability for and the custody of all goods placed in the warehouse

Test the warehouseman's records relating to accountability for all goods placed in his or her custody

Test the warehouseman's accountability under recorded outstanding warehouse receipts

Observe physical counts of the goods in custody, whenever practicable and reasonable, and reconcile his or her test of such counts with records of goods stored

Confirm accountability (to the extent considered necessary) by direct communication with the holders of warehouse receipts

The auditor of the warehouseman should apply such other procedures as considered necessary in the circumstances. Because both warehouse activities and the goods stored in warehouses are diverse, the auditor has the responsibility to exercise judgment in determining the procedures, including those listed above, which are necessary in the particular circumstances.

Warehouses may be classified functionally as either *terminal warehouses* or *field warehouses*. The principal economic function of a terminal warehouse is to furnish storage. It may, however, perform other functions, including packaging and billing. It may be used to store a wide variety of goods or only a particular type of commodity.

A field warehouse is established in space leased by the warehouseman on the premises of a customer of the owner. Field warehousing is essentially a financing arrangement, rather than a storage operation. The warehouse is established in order to permit the warehouseman to take and maintain custody of goods and issue warehouse receipts to be used as collateral for a loan or other form of credit.

A basic document used in warehousing is the *warehouse receipt*. Warehouse receipts may be negotiable or non-negotiable and may be used as evidence of collateral for loans or other forms of credit. Goods represented by a negotiable warehouse receipt may be released only upon surrender of the receipt to the warehouseman. Goods represented by a non-negotiable receipt may be released upon valid instructions without the need for surrendering the receipt. Since goods covered by non-negotiable receipts may be released without surrendering the receipt, the outstanding receipts are not necessarily an indication of accountability or evidence of ownership.

Goods held in public warehouses are not owned by the warehouseman and, therefore, do not appear as assets in his or her financial statements. The warehouseman is, however, exposed to the risk of loss or claims for damages and should maintain proper internal control over the goods placed in his or her custody. The controls should provide both for accountability and appropriate physical safeguards. The recommendation in this Section that the auditor include the study and evaluation of internal administrative control as a part of the examination of the warehouseman is based upon the important relationship of such controls to the custodial responsibilities of the warehouseman. Section 901 suggests internal controls that may be appropriate to a particular warehouse operation. The CPA's procedures relating to internal control might include, on a test basis, such procedures as the comparison of documentary evidence of goods received and delivered with warehouse receipts records, accounting for issued and unissued warehouse receipts by number, and comparison of the records of goods stored with billings for storage. In some circumstances, the CPA may consider it necessary to confirm from the printer the serial numbers of receipt forms supplied.

In the case of a field warehouse where goods are stored at many scattered locations, the CPA may wish to become satisfied that the warehouseman's physical count procedures are adequate by observing the procedures at certain selected locations. The amount of testing required will, of course, depend on the quality of internal control.

Since the confirmation of negotiable receipts with holders may not be possible, confirmation with the depositor to whom the outstanding receipt was originally issued would be evidence of accountability for certain designated goods.

The CPA should review the nature and extent of the warehouseman's insurance coverage and the adequacy of any reserves for losses under damage claims.

Controls and Auditing Procedures for Owner's Goods Stored in Public Warehouses

The internal control procedures of the owner of goods stored in a warehouse should be designed to provide reasonable safeguards over these goods. Ordinarily, the controls should include an investigation of the warehouseman before the goods are placed in custody, and a continuing evaluation of the warehouseman's performance in maintaining custody of the goods. The following procedures may be considered before placing goods in a warehouse:

Consideration of the business reputation and financial standing of the warehouseman

Inspection of the physical facilities to be used

Inquiries as to the warehouseman's control procedures and whether the warehouseman holds goods for his or her own account

Inquiries as to type and adequacy of the warehouseman's insurance

Inquiries as to government or other licensing and bonding requirements and the nature, extent, and results of any inspection by government or other agencies

Review of the warehouseman's financial statements and related reports of independent auditors

After goods are placed in the warehouse, suggested control procedures that may be applied periodically by the owner in evaluating the warehouseman's performance include the following:

Review and update the information developed from the initial investigation described above

Physical counts (or test counts) of the goods, wherever practicable and reasonable (may not be practicable in the case of fungible goods)

Reconcilement of quantities shown on statements received from the warehouseman with the owner's records

In addition to performing these checks, the client should review its own insurance, if any, on goods in the custody of the warehouseman.

SAS No. 43 (Section 1010.05) amends SAS No. 1 bringing those procedures considered necessary for inventories held in public warehouses into conformity with those delineated in Section 331.14.

CASE 39

WHAT HAPPENED TO ALL THAT K-8 AND K-10?

K-8 and K-10 are chemicals used extensively in the manufacture of a variety of pesticides. These pesticides are manufactured in large quantities for farming purposes by several different firms and are usually stored in terminal warehouses.

One large terminal warehouse used to store K-8 and K-10 is located in Texas and is operated by a Mr. Willie S. Best. Mr. Best is a major stockholder in Warehousing, Inc., the company owning the warehousing facilities. The company is planning to go public in the near future and desires an audit. Mr. Best has contacted your firm concerning the possibility of performing the examination.

You make a preliminary scope review of the operations of Warehousing, Inc., and perform tests of K-8 and K-10 storage facilities and related outstanding negotiable warehouse receipts. Since the goods in the custody of the warehouseman are supported by a material amount of outstanding warehouse receipts, you are particularly concerned that the warehouseman is maintaining adequate internal controls over the K-8 and K-10 chemicals in his possession.

As a result of your preliminary scope review and the tests performed, a junior staff accountant (she has only been with your firm for three months) seems to be concerned that there appears to be considerable warehouse receipts that have been issued for such a small amount of K-8 and K-10 in storage. She asked you where all that K-8 and K-10 could be stored. You raise the apparent incongruity with the partner in charge of the engagement and he says not to worry about it now, "we will find it later."

CASE DISCUSSION QUESTIONS

1. Distinguish between a *terminal warehouse* and a *field warehouse*. Which type of warehouse operation do you feel presents the most difficult problems with respect to gathering evidential matter for goods in storage? Explain.

2. Identify specific procedures that should be performed by the auditor of a warehouseman. How would these procedures vary with respect to the following:

   a. Terminal warehouse operation.

   b. Field warehouse operation.

   c. Negotiable warehouse receipts are issued.

   d. Non-negotiable warehouse receipts are issued.

3. Explain why the auditor of a warehouseman should include both the study and evaluation of internal accounting control and internal administrative control within the scope of his or her examination.

4. Why might the CPA auditing the records of a warehouseman consider it necessary to confirm from the partner the serial numbers of warehouse receipt forms supplied to his or her client? Explain.

5. Since negotiable warehouse receipts may change hands several times before the receipts are presented to claim the goods in storage, confirmation of outstanding negotiable warehouse receipts may be difficult or impossible. What other procedures may be employed to obtain sufficient evidence as to accountability for goods supporting the warehouse receipts? Explain.

6. Internal control procedures of the owner of goods stored in a warehouse should be designed to provide reasonable assurance that the goods are protected. What procedures should ordinarily be performed in investigating the warehouseman and testing his or her control procedures? Discuss.

7. What does the term "fungible goods" mean?

8. Consider the Warehousing, Inc., situation explained in the case. What are the potential audit problems? Does this case remind you of any "real-world" situation you may have heard discussed?